ACAD   2189   7500

THINKING AND LEARNING SKILLS

Volume 1:

Relating Instruction to Research

THINKING AND LEARNING SKILLS

Volume 1:

Relating Instruction to Research

Edited by

Judith W. Segal and **Susan F. Chipman**
National Institute of Education

Robert Glaser
University of Pittsburgh

LAWRENCE ERLBAUM ASSOCIATES, PUBLISHERS

1985   Hillsdale, New Jersey   London

Lawrence Erlbaum Associates, Inc., Publishers
365 Broadway
Hillsdale, New Jersey 07642

Library of Congress Cataloging in Publication Data

Main entry under title:

Thinking and learning skills.

  Bibliography: p.
  Includes index.
  Contents: v. 1. Relating instruction to research—
v. 2. Research and open questions.
  1. Learning. 2. Cognition in children. 3. Education
—Research. I. Segal, Judith W. II. Chipman, Susan F.
III. Glaser, Robert, 1921–
LB1060.T48 1985   370.15'23   84-25878
ISBN 0-89859-164-3 (set)
ISBN 0-89859-165-1 (v. 1)
ISBN 0-89859-166-X (v. 2)

Printed in the United States of America
10 9 8 7 6 5 4 3 2

Contents

Preface   ix
 Robert Glaser

Higher Cognitive Goals for Education: An Introduction
 Susan F. Chipman and Judith W. Segal 1

Introduction to Volume 1: Approaches to Instruction
 Judith W. Segal 21

Program Presentations and Analyses

Intelligence and Reasoning

1. Instrumental Enrichment, An Intervention Program
   for Structural Cognitive Modifiability:
   Theory and Practice
    Reuven Feuerstein, Mogens Jensen,
    Mildred B. Hoffman, and Yaacov Rand 43

2. Thinking Skills Fostered by Philosophy for Children
    Matthew Lipman 83

3. Teaching Analytic Reasoning Skills
   Through Pair Problem Solving
    Jack Lochhead 109

4. *Analysis*—Improving Thinking and Learning Skills:
An Analysis of Three Approaches
John D. Bransford, Ruth Arbitman-Smith,
Barry S. Stein, and Nancy J. Vye   133

Knowledge Acquisition

5. Learning Strategy Research
Donald F. Dansereau   209

6. Learning Strategies: The *How* of Learning
Claire E. Weinstein and Vicki L. Underwood   241

7. Teaching Cognitive Strategies and Text Structures
Within Language Arts Programs
Beau Fly Jones, MindaRae Amiran, and Michael Katims   259

8. Developing Reading and Thinking Skills in Content Areas
Harold Herber   297

9. *Analysis*—Acquiring Information from Texts:
An Analysis of Four Approaches
Joseph C. Campione and Bonnie B. Armbruster   317

Problem Solving

10. The CoRT Thinking Program
Edward de Bono   363

11. Strategic Thinking and the Fear of Failure
Martin V. Covington   389

12. *Analysis*—Instruction in General Problem-Solving Skills:
An Analysis of Four Approaches
Peter G. Polson and Robin Jeffries   417

Educators' Experience

13. A Practitioner's Perspective on The Chicago Mastery Learning
Reading Program with Learning Strategies
Walter E. Thompson   459

14. Making Choices: It Ought to be Carefully Taught
     Curtis Miles   473

15. Teaching Problem Solving to Developmental Adults:
    A Pilot Project
     Richard T. Hutchinson   499

16. Thinking Skills: The Effort of One Public School System
     Herbert W. Ware   515

17. The Development of Human Intelligence: The Venezuelan Case
     José Dominguez   529

Author Index   537
Subject Index   547

Preface

Robert Glaser
University of Pittsburgh

Currently, two streams of endeavor offer promise for improving school effectiveness in developing students' higher cognitive capacities. One of these is represented by the increased interest of school districts, colleges, and universities in identifying ways to help their students build the cognitive skills that enable them to learn and think effectively. What can be done, they ask, beyond teaching the fundamentals of reading, writing, arithmetic, and subject-matter knowledge, to enable students to use their skills and knowledge for effective problem solving, reasoning, and comprehension? The second stream is apparent in recent scientific advances in the study of intelligence, human development, problem solving, the structure of acquired knowledge, and the skills of learning.

This confluence of renewed educational interest and modern scientific investigation offers a challenging opportunity to attack the problem of "passive knowledge"—knowledge that students receive and express, but cannot use effectively for thinking and learning. Schools have not been well enough equipped for this task. Older theories of learning focused on simpler forms of learning and did not provide understanding of higher cognitive processes. Educational practices based on those theories resulted in improved instruction for fundamental skills; less emphasis was given to exercising thinking and problem-solving abilities in the course of schooling. Today, however, educators, educational researchers, developmental psychologists, and cognitive scientists are designing school programs and conducting investigations on understanding and problem solving in mathematics and science, comprehending and reasoning with text material, study skills and abilities to learn, and the role of memory organization in the acquisition of knowledge. These processes of human cognition and learning are being studied with particular attention to how conditions that foster them might be built into the materials, methodologies, and environments for learning and schooling.

In recognition of this potential, scientists at the National Institute of Education (NIE), Susan Chipman and Judith Segal, proposed the conference on which these volumes are based. Their goal was to examine educational practices and scientific investigation concerned with students' abilities to understand, reason, solve problems, and to learn. The plan for the conference was to bring together cognitive researchers, program developers, and teachers of cognitive skills to provide mutual advice and to discuss their theories, findings, and recommendations. In this way, a rich array of current work could be assembled that would be available for educators and researchers. In addition, the conference could provide information to NIE that would assist in identifying needs for future research.

The conference took place at the Learning Research and Development Center (LRDC) of the University of Pittsburgh, one of the major research and development centers funded by NIE, engaged in both basic and applied research on the relevant issues. Organizing the conference called for close collaboration between LRDC and NIE. Chipman and Segal at NIE and Michelene Chi and Robert Glaser of LRDC formed the initial planning committee. Conference contributions were carefully structured. Each chapter in these volumes was especially requested to fulfill a particular function. The aspirations and rationale for the conference are well described in Chipman and Segal's introductory chapter, "Higher Cognitive Goals for Education." They point out that whereas schools appropriately make the basic skills of reading, writing, and mathematics a high priority, skills in learning, reasoning, and general problem solving—including the more sophisticated aspects of reading and mathematics—are less emphasized or neglected. Thus, the burgeoning research on cognition fills an important need: to understand and describe these skills with the precision that would make it possible to teach them and assess their acquisition. The related practical requirement is to design instructional programs that successfully teach these higher cognitive skills.

These volumes, like the conference sessions, are organized by a classification of cognitive skills into three groups: intelligence and reasoning, knowledge acquisition, and problem solving. Although we recognize that there are features common to these areas, as well as important relations between them, these categories serve present purposes in reflecting attention to the three central themes of conference discussions.

While each of the editors has been concerned with both volumes, Volume 1 is particularly Judith Segal's contribution, and she introduces it. In Volume 1 she attempts to bring theory and practice into close perspective. Programs that have been implemented in schools are described by their developers. These programs encompass the range of approaches to cognitive skills instruction from which practitioners can currently choose. Their diversity offers readers a basis for exploring the advantages and limitations of different approaches to instruction. The developers describe the theories and assumptions underlying their programs, discuss the specific skills they are seeking to instill, offer examples of typical instructional methods and materials, and discuss the effectiveness of their programs.

In three invited essays, leading cognitive psychologists analyze the instructional programs presented. Their contributions look carefully at the ideas and practices recommended. They examine the assumptions built into the programs about the nature, development, and acquisition of thinking and learning skills; comment on the relationship of these assumptions to research findings and current theory; review evaluation data on these programs and discuss the problems of evaluation; and suggest additional ideas for research and further questions for exploration.

In the final section of Volume 1, we are fortunate to include chapters by educators who have implemented programs of instruction in cognitive skills in different settings. They comment on current efforts and describe impressions and results from their own experiences.

Volume 2 displays the guiding hand of Susan Chipman, who also has written an introduction to it. This volume contains a representative sample of contemporary research on cognitive skills and considers research issues and open questions that indicate future research directions. The papers she has brought together here exhibit the rich variety of theory and methodology currently being brought to the study of thinking and learning by cognitive scientists. Each major topical area—knowledge acquisition, problem solving, and intelligence and reasoning—includes perspectives from developmental psychology and from the study of cultural influences on human learning.

Reflected here is an issue prominent throughout the conference—the question of the generality or domain specificity of problem-solving and learning skills. Early seminal research emphasized the important common characteristics of problem solving in various task environments, but it is not obvious that these common characteristics can be treated as general, teachable skills. General skills may develop slowly and naturally out of much specific experience, and perhaps problem-solving skills can best be taught in the context of the acquisition of particular domains of knowledge. Many other fundamental research issues appear in Volume 2, including questions about the influences of learning, development, and social background on the acquisition of cognitive skills, and about the necessity for adapting instruction to the prior experience, knowledge, and skill level capabilities of students. Developmental differences also receive special attention in this volume.

The conference at LRDC was an exhilarating experience for those who attended, as we hope these volumes will be for those who peruse and study them. We have attempted to address a wide audience, and the conference and the resulting volumes should help to strengthen a community of interest that cuts across the boundaries separating basic researchers, program developers, and classroom teachers. These volumes should enlarge that community, helping to accelerate an integration of the efforts of all those concerned with guiding students in becoming more independent, effective learners and problem solvers throughout their lives.

Research on the training of cognitive skills is, as these volumes attest, a high priority in education—one supported by growing public interest and scientific advances. Few other educational possibilities beckon us to apply our energies and exploratory talents as much as this one does. Teaching thinking and the ability to learn have been long-term aspirations for schools, and now progress has occurred that brings these goals within reach. Our task is to produce educational environments where knowledge and skill become objects of interrogation, inquiry, and instruments for learning so that as individuals acquire knowledge, they also acquire cognitive abilities to think, reason, and continue learning.

There are many acknowledgments to be made in producing a work as extensive as this, and we would like to express our thanks to all who contributed to the success of the conference and to the production of these books. Karen Locitzer shouldered the responsibility for all the conference arrangements. Michelle von Koch handled the technical editing with Helen Craig's invaluable assistance. Emilee Luckett at NIE provided vital secretarial support for Chipman and Segal throughout the process of conference planning, writing, and editing. The conference was enriched by others who do not appear as authors, particularly Richard Anderson, Joseph Psotka, and Virginia Shipman, who made important contributions.

Robert Glaser

THINKING AND LEARNING SKILLS

Volume 1:

Relating Instruction to Research

Higher Cognitive Goals for Education: An Introduction

Susan F. Chipman
Judith W. Segal
National Institute of Education

In a rapidly changing technological environment, it is difficult to predict what knowledge students will need or what problems they will have to solve 20 years from now. What they really need to know, it seems, is how to learn the new information and skills that they will require throughout their lives. These general skills are prominent among the characteristics employers say they would like to see in the youth they hire (Chatham, 1982). Clearly, much of the value of education for students' later lives comes from whatever general thinking and learning skills have been acquired along with the specific knowledge that schools impart. Quite appropriately, schools place the highest priority on skills with very general applicability: reading, writing, and mathematics. However, skills in learning, reasoning, and general problem solving—including the more sophisticated aspects of reading and elementary mathematics—are neglected by the schools.

An Evident Need

Even in the earliest grades, teachers direct students to a lesson or reading assignment with instructions to learn information, concepts, or skills. Little is said to the child about how to go about learning. Recent research focused on reading has shown that explicit instruction in strategies for effective thinking and learning rarely occurs in classrooms (Beck, 1983; Durkin, 1984; MacGinitie, 1984). Similarly, it is assumed, or hoped, that repeated attempts to learn or to solve problems will automatically result in improvement of general ability to reason or solve problems; little is taught about ways of going about solving the problems.

1

The central research problem in this area is still to understand and to describe these skills with the precision that would make it possible to measure them. Nevertheless, Jencks (1978) has argued that it is the complex skills, not the basic skills, that are deteriorating. NAEP (National Assessment of Educational Progress, 1981) does report that the problem with student writing seems to rest in the quality of thinking and organization rather than in the mechanics. There is general agreement that reading comprehension, not decoding, is the most important problem area in reading instruction today. Repeated assessments have shown that students' mathematics problem-solving performance is much less satisfactory than their computational skill (NAEP, 1983). Instructors at the college level, especially in community and open admissions colleges, complain that students have great difficulty managing and evaluating their own learning efforts. Students agree: On the SAT questionnaire (College Entrance Examination Board [CEEB], 1981) students rate study skills as the skill area in which they feel the greatest need for assistance. Not surprisingly, the recent CEEB effort (1982) to define basic competencies for college entrance includes competencies in general reasoning, problem formulation and solution, studying, and general learning skills. Many of these competencies, of course, are not well defined. Current emphasis on measuring competencies and training for the competencies measured may be creating a still more unfavorable environment for the development of these more complex competencies that we do not yet know how to measure.

Research (Dansereau, Long, McDonald, & Actkinson, 1975) indicates that even good students know very little about techniques they might use to remember better the material they are studying. Nonetheless, one way successful students and more educated persons differ from the less successful and less educated is that they are likely to know and use learning techniques more sophisticated than rote repetition (Weinstein, 1978). For example, only good readers at the 12th-grade level are able to adjust their style of reading to the purposes for which they are reading (Smith, 1967). Although it would be difficult to set minimum competency standards for learning skills, it is clear that there is room for improvement: Even good students have a limited repertoire of such skills, and others have fewer still.

There is good reason to try to improve the characteristics of individual students as learners. Most commonly, educational research attempts to improve instructional techniques in general or in specific subject matter areas. Dansereau (1978) points out, however, that research at the college level indicates that truly different methods of instruction—lecture, discussion, reading, computers—have negligible effects on student performance, whereas there are large individual differences in student performance. Although carefully developed and researched instructional materials may enhance achievement of particular educational or training goals, such materials will never be available to meet all the needs of individuals. Only a few high priority subjects are likely to receive the necessary research and development investment, and learning about developing topics such as the frontiers of technology requires an independently active learner. It does make sense, therefore, to invest in the alternative strategy of improving learners, rather than simply improving instructional materials.

An Opportunity for Genuine Improvement

Because explicit instruction in thinking and learning skills has received little attention in the schools, it is likely that large improvements are possible. It is much easier to improve instructional outcomes in a new or neglected area than to achieve significant improvements in instructional methods that have undergone decades or centuries of evolutionary improvement by trial and error. Furthermore, there is reason to believe that increased efforts in this area hold promise for ameliorating the persistent problem of unequal school success for the diverse social and ethnic groups that make up our society. A recent investigation of the delivery of study skills instruction (USDE, 1982) indicated the rarity of serious school programs of study skills instruction and revealed that students, parents, and school staff all believe that these skills are learned primarily in the home. Unlike teachers and school administrators, however, most parents and students were unable to explain what is meant by study skills. Educational practice has evolved in relation to the surrounding culture, particularly the subcultures from which both educators and those participating most fully in schooling traditionally have come. Therefore, educational practice is grounded in tacit assumptions about the skills and knowledge students bring to school and about the supplementary assistance and training provided at home. Detailed observations are beginning to show that the forms of help with school work available at home vary dramatically in quality and quantity (Chall & Snow, 1982; Varenne, Hamid-Buglione, McDermott, & Morison, 1982). Obviously, students whose parents know what is meant by study skills are advantaged.

There is some evidence from cross-cultural psychological research that techniques for learning schoollike material are culturally influenced. For instance, Westerners and non-Westerners differ in the use of rote, associative forms of learning typical of less successful students here as opposed to the use of a more complex, organized, and strategic form of learning typical of more successful students (Scribner & Cole, 1976). Within our own society, parallel ethnic or socioeconomic differences in the use of such strategies may exist (Glasman, 1968; Jensen, 1969). In laboratory studies, parents' ways of directing children's behavior vary among social classes and ethnic groups (Wertsch, 1978). A plausible form of parental guidance—nonspecific encouragement to figure out reasons for events—has been shown to produce moderately lasting effects on the systematicity of problem solving in young children (Richards & Siegler,

1981). One suspects that such guidance would be differentially distributed across social groups and that its compounded effects over many years could be substantial.

Furthermore, parents cannot transmit skills that they themselves have not had the occasion to develop and practice in their own occupational and social situations (Ogbu, 1978). Consequently, there is reason to suggest that the omission of explicit training in thinking and learning skills from the school curriculum may be one reason why social class and cultural backgrounds are now so strongly predictive of school success. Among the research papers of Volume 2, some represent nascent efforts to examine the relation in our society between culture and cognitive function.

New Conceptions of Intellect

Cross-cultural cognitive research has been one influence contributing to a reconceptualization of human intelligence that is now in progress (Hunt, 1983; Sternberg, 1979, 1982). What in the past has been seen as innate cognitive ability or aptitude for learning may turn out to be largely a matter of opportunity to acquire skills critical for success in the school environment. Most people recognize that traditional measures of "intelligence" or IQ reflect experience and environmental opportunity as well as other factors. However, the fact that these measures were designed to classify individuals and to predict school performance has hindered progress in understanding either what was important in school performance itself or what really is important about differences in environmental experience. For example, many people would define intelligence as ability to learn. Most intelligence tests, in fact, measure how much people have learned from their general experience. Therefore, it has long been a puzzle in differential psychology why individuals with high IQs show little superiority in basic ability to learn (Tyler, 1965). It may be that the critical differences in intellectual functioning rest on the organization and management of our basic learning ability. Although it is likely that there are constitutional aspects to individual intellectual differences, Pellegrino and Glaser (1982) have found that both specific knowledge relevant to the test items and memory management strategies that might be learned or trained are important determinants of performance on intelligence test items.

We are not the first to suggest that there might be a need for systematic training to improve learning and thinking skills. Indeed, efforts to train and strengthen mental powers have a very long history (Mann, 1979). In 1706, John Locke said: "The business of education is not to make the young perfect in any one of the sciences, but so to open and dispose their minds as may best make them capable of any, when they shall apply themselves to it." Alfred Binet (1909), whose theoretical investigations of intellectual functioning initiated the technology of intelligence measurement, was himself convinced of the possible benefits of "mental orthopedics." In these volumes, we sample the curricular and theoretical research resources that are now available to work toward those long-standing educational goals.

At this descriptive level, it may sound as if we are talking about facts that have always been known. Because we are talking about the importance of self-knowledge and self-control of learning and problem-solving strategies, that is partially true. If an analysis is correct, skilled learners should recognize it as corresponding reasonably well to their own thinking. The critical difference is that modern research techniques take the descriptions to a level of precision and detail that is making it possible to communicate these strategies to those who do not already know them as well as to those who do know them. For example, there is little use in instructing students to identify the main ideas in material they are studying and to concentrate on them—a commonsense strategy—if students are unable to identify the main ideas. In fact, even many college students find it difficult to isolate the important points in texts (Brown & Smiley, 1978) and therefore cannot profit from study skill advice at that level. Training that is informed by current research, however, can overcome that obstacle (Brown & Day, 1983; Day, 1980). Rereading an earlier effort to summarize what was known about "learning about learning" (Bruner, 1966), one is struck both by the constancy of the general descriptions of intellectual skills and by the great progress in applicable specific knowledge of cognition.

A Renewed Challenge for Educators

In summary, the development of higher cognitive skills that enable students to be independent learners and independent, creative, problem-solving users of their knowledge has always been a very important goal for educators. There is evidence, however, that explicit instruction in these skills is rare and that students' mastery of them is frequently inadequate. Furthermore, there is reason to believe that improved instruction in such skills might help to overcome persistent socio-economic and cultural differences in the outcomes of education. Today, our long-standing aspirations for education can draw upon new resources provided by the recent, rapid growth of research into cognitive function, including developing reconceptualizations of intelligence or intellectual ability. Today, educators are being challenged to strive for excellence in their students' development—the higher goals of learning, thinking, and problem-solving skills as well as basic computational and decoding skills (National Commission on Excellence in Education, 1983). The cover article of the January, 1983, *New York Times Education Supplement,* "Teaching to Think: A New Emphasis," (Maeroff, 1983) illustrates the widespread concern and the growing educational response to this challenge.

RESOURCES TO MEET THE CHALLENGE

In these volumes, we have brought together a rich sample of the resources that educators may call upon to meet this renewed challenge. They are resources of two kinds. There are educational programs that have already been developed to teach learning, thinking, and problem-solving skills. The first of these volumes samples such programs, discussing both their relation to research understanding of cognitive functions and issues of practical implementation. A second kind of resource is the rich and growing body of modern cognitive research that will provide the foundation for new approaches to the teaching of cognitive skills. The remaining volume samples this research, touching upon both the analysis of the major skills and key open questions that surround the teaching of cognitive skills.

Research on cognitive skills and practical educational efforts to teach cognitive skills interlock in a complex way. Educators' goals are frequently more ambitious and broader in scope than the topics on which researchers have focused their analytic efforts. Yet, educators' conceptualizations of the skills they are attempting to teach are frequently derived from the efforts of previous generations of researchers. Both draw upon their own and others' introspective intuitions about the nature of learning, thinking, and problem-solving skills as one source of inspiration for their work. Thus, educational programs embody both the practical wisdom of gifted teachers and the theoretical understanding of intellectual functioning that prevailed at the time they were developed. New theoretical understanding of cognitive skills may suggest a reformulation of educational goals and provide considerable guidance for instruction, but the artful contributions of gifted teachers and curriculum developers also are needed to realize those goals. An important feature of Volume 1 is the set of analysis papers that were designed to foster the relationship between research and educational practice in cognitive skills training, drawing out the lessons that each enterprise has to offer the other. The authors were asked to analyze the presuppositions and educational activities of the programs in relation to research understanding of the skill domain in question, but they were also asked to identify important educational goals that seem to have been neglected as subjects of research.

Defining and Describing the Higher Cognitive Skills

For both research and practice, the issues of definition and description of complex learning, thinking, and problem-solving skills remain absolutely central. Past and present research focuses on these problems of definition—for example, on identifying the processes and strategies that good text comprehenders, good students, and effective problem solvers use. In educational practice, better understanding is needed so that we can measure the presence of these skills, set them as goals for instruction, devise reasonable methods of training, and evaluate the effectiveness of training. As our discussions of educational programs show, current understanding is generally insufficient to permit convincing evaluation of programs with respect to their claims to develop complex cognitive skills. Although the emphasis in Volume 1 is on the discussion of programs intended to develop general cognitive skills, the same problems in measuring efficacy exist for the more ambitious goals of traditional curricula. Today, striving to develop complex cognitive skills requires an element of faith from educators, but the price of excessive skepticism is likely to be the certainty of limited educational accomplishment.

As yet, there is no comprehensive and universally accepted theory capturing complex human intellectual functions in a single conceptual framework. For purposes of discussion, we have divided the general thinking and learning skills that are the subject of these volumes into three major areas: (1) knowledge acquisition, (2) problem solving, and (3) such very basic cognitive skills as approaching tasks in an organized, non-impulsive fashion, or drawing simple logical conclusions. Nevertheless, we recognize that there are common features to all these skills, and important relations among them. This can be seen in even the briefest of descriptions. In discussing knowledge acquisition, A. Brown (1980) characterized the key cognitive skills as: knowing when you know, knowing what you know, knowing what you need to know, and knowing the utility of taking active steps to change your state of knowledge. In problem solving, these skills include analyzing the problem, searching related knowledge, planning possible attempts at solution, keeping track of progress, and checking results against the overall goal or more immediate goals. The distinction between acquiring knowledge and making flexible use of that knowledge to confront new situations is helpful, but it cannot be sharply drawn. Especially when it comes to taking steps to improve one's state of knowledge, there is a problem-solving aspect to learning. And operational methods for problem solving are a kind of knowledge that one must acquire. In our third category, we have risked grouping together very disparate mental functions—elemental mental processes that form a part of many complex skills (cf. Sternberg's chapter) and very general self-control or self-management strategies that are also applicable in a wide range of situations (cf. Baron's chapter). Most of human experimental psychology contributes to our understanding of elemental mental processes. For the readers of these volumes, a relatively new research focus—metacognition, the study of individuals' knowledge of, awareness of, and control of their own cognitive processes—is most critical. Metacognitive sophistication—the deliberate and reasoned deployment of cognitive resources and strategies—is the goal of much cognitive skills training. Whether that is a reasonable goal and, if so, what instructional process is likely to achieve the goal is something we may learn from research on metacognition.

In the preceding paragraph, we provided first steps in the characterization of the elusive general cognitive skills that are the subject of these volumes. As a further introduction, we provide only brief summaries of the understanding of these skills that is emerging from research. These themes are elaborated throughout these volumes, first in the analysis chapters of Volume 1 and then in the research chapters of Volume 2, each of which gives a detailed view of some aspect of cognitive skill.

Knowledge Acquisition

How people acquire and add to complex bodies of knowledge is poorly understood, in spite of recent dramatic advances. Many years ago, Bartlett (1932) demonstrated that what a person remembers from a text or a drawing depends on previous general knowledge as much as on the material itself. More recent research in both cognitive psychology and artificial intelligence (Schank & Abelson, 1977; Winograd, 1972) has demonstrated that general knowledge is required to make sense of even simple sentences and texts; careful analysis shows that a great deal is left out, taken for granted. Anderson (1978) and others have been very active in showing the many ways that the reader's background knowledge or general expectations for a text affect its interpretation and what is remembered. Work towards explaining more precisely how such knowledge affects understanding and memory for information continues.

In addition, readers have knowledge about the general form of texts themselves—about, for example, the parts that can be expected in a story. Bartlett also demonstrated that such knowledge is part of our cultural heritage, that stories drawn from an unfamiliar culture are extremely difficult to recall. Although simple stories have received most attention from researchers, it is obvious the same point applies to literary genres in general. In addition, researchers are beginning to recognize and analyze the characteristic forms of other kinds of texts such as science textbooks or popular science articles.

Understanding the Skills of Comprehension.   The crucial question about the skill of comprehension is how the reader makes use of such knowledge in comprehending a text. One interesting conjecture (J. S. Brown, Collins, & Harris, 1978) is that comprehension of a story involves divining the plan and purpose behind the actions in the story. We understand the actions in a story because they fit plans that we ourselves might be able to generate. Brown and his colleagues suggested that a wide range of comprehension skills have this common characteristic—seeking to place the elements into a plan or purpose that makes sense for the whole. Another example they gave is comprehending a mathematical proof: To make sense of it you have to know that particular sequences of steps are intended to do something. That is, they form a larger conceptual unit that has a particular function in the proof.

These researchers are making progress in explaining what it is to "know what it is you know and what it is you need to know." You could know that you have to come up with a plan behind a text that makes it reasonable for everything that is there to be there. You could know that if certain things don't fit, then you still have a need to find some hypothesis that will make them fit. In the case of a simple story, it has been possible to observe skilled readers formulate a general plan for the entire story even before the main narrative begins (Olson, Duffy, & Mack, 1980). A surprising statement is recognized immediately as the introduction to the climactic event, and readers are able to predict that it will involve the character who has not been mentioned since the beginning of the story. (Otherwise, why would he have been there?)

Aids to Comprehension and Memory.   Much less is known about the process of acquiring complex knowledge, like that presented in school and college text-books, than is known about the comprehension of simple stories. As for stories, there may be characteristic expository patterns that good students can use to structure the information being presented, to identify the important points, and so on. Rather extensive attention (Mayer, 1979; Reder, 1980) has been given to the effect of such devices as advance organizers, interpolated questions, and elaborations of content upon memory for texts. The results of this research have been sometimes positive, sometimes negative, apparently because it was not founded on a theory that could describe the relation between particular questions, for example, and the content of the text. Techniques for characterizing the structure and content of texts in a reliable, consistent, and detailed manner are now available and may lead to more reliable techniques for assisting students' learning. On the other hand, the demonstrated important effects of the reader's prior knowledge on both comprehension and memory suggest limits to what can be achieved with an approach based on the text design alone.

· *Traditional Study Techniques.*   Traditional study skills techniques seem to have been informed by the same ideas that led to the instructional research on text design, with the important difference that the student is to supply the ques--tions and elaborations and to derive an advance organizer from a quick skimming of the text. In effect, the student is asked to act as his or her own instructional designer. It is not at all obvious that we should expect students to be able to do this, or that their efforts would be any more consistently effective than those of instructional researchers. Indeed, evidence for the effectiveness of traditional study techniques is limited (Anderson, 1980). Not surprisingly, extensive training in supporting skills such as the identification of main ideas seems to be required in order to achieve sucess with a study technique such as outlining (Barton, 1930). Brown (1980) has observed that underlining key points is an effective study technique for those who use it spontaneously, but not for others who are induced to use it. It seems likely that traditional analyses of study skills are too superficial and insufficiently detailed to be instructionally useful. Although research to date suggests that time-consuming study techniques like elaboration and imagery, self-questioning, and outlining are no more effective than simple reading and rereading (Anderson, 1980), more serious investigation of the relationship between these techniques and the rapid, seemingly automatic comprehension processes of skilled readers is needed. Obviously, the quality of what students are doing when they read and reread varies a great deal. Research should be done to determine whether overt study techniques can be used to improve the quality of covert processes in students' later reading to study.

Characterizing States of Knowledge.   A current trend in research on human knowledge is detailed description and contrasting of the knowledge of experts and novices in a particular field of endeavor. The scope of investigation in this research is much greater than that concerned with the mastery of and memory for brief passages of text. It has been facilitated by systems of notation in which concepts and their relations are represented as complex networks in a computer memory. The hope is that such systems may help us analyze students' states of knowledge, diagnose problems, direct instruction, and evaluate the effect of instruction upon the state of knowledge. Perhaps such work will lead to sensitively adapting computer-tutors. Characteristic patterns of information—of relations among concepts—can also become learning tools for the student (see chapters by Dansereau, Rissland, Jones).

Nevertheless, the formulation of a theory concerning the way in which knowledge develops from the novice to the expert form remains an important challenge for the future. Norman (1978) has provided an evocative, intuitively appealing description of the changes in knowledge as learning occurs: accretion, restructuring, tuning. By analogy to comprehension, one might speculate that the restructuring of knowledge involves an attempt to achieve an organization that conforms to some as yet unarticulated ideal.

The first stage of systematic analysis—introspective analyses of the process of learning new subject matter—is just now beginning. At this time, research on the learning of realistically complex bodies of knowledge demonstrates the incredible detail and complexity of relationships in the specific subject matter knowledge that experts have (cf. Rissland's chapter) and the importance of previous knowledge to the acquisition of new knowledge. But there are also tantalizing hints of more general tactics and strategies in learning that more effective students may use. The image of the student as instructional designer may have some value for suggesting the nature of learning and study skills that facilitate mastery of entire domains of knowledge, entire college courses.

Problem Solving

A Characterization of Problem-Solving Processes.   The scientific study of problem-solving behavior began early in this century when Gestalt psychologists undertook systematic descriptive and experimental studies. They found that sometimes a problem solution appears to be a sudden event, which Kohler (1927) called insight. By studying people trying to solve very difficult problems, however, these researchers were able to see and describe steps in the problem-solving process: First, the problem is recognized and defined; then there is a phase of exploration in which the elements of the situation and their relationships are examined; next the problem is analyzed, the information gathered is organized and structured, and a plan is formulated; and finally, the problem is attacked and an overall solution occurs. Obviously, much is unexplained in this account. What is meant by analysis? How does solution occur? The Gestalt psychologists thought of the information gathered as making up a perceptual field with built-in structural stresses and strains. As relations are considered or interpretations are varied, the perceptual field will suddenly restructure, they concluded, leading to a solution.

This is a rather vague theory. Nevertheless, these researchers were able to demonstrate that there were internal mechanisms of thought—even when problem solvers could report only sudden insight—that could be affected by various factors that the experimenter manipulated. Maier (1931), for example, influenced the likelihood of insight by delivering various verbal or visual hints. Other research showed that people could become stuck on the idea that a particular object had only a certain function—"functional fixedness." Similarly, a history of success with one method of solution tends to blind the problem solver to simpler approaches that would work in a particular case and would be seen by someone without that history (Luchins, 1942).

Instructional Implications.   The research did make major advances in the understanding of problem solving. Many of the findings could be translated into advice for problem solvers: for example, telling them to attempt redescriptions of situations, to break down fixed ideas about the form that must accomplish a given function, or about the function of particular objects or materials. Indeed, this research is the basis of most current attempts to teach problem solving. Research did not advance beyond those rather general descriptions, however, and consequently there was a lengthy fallow period in problem-solving research.

A New Theoretical Approach.   Research on problem solving revived with the pioneering work of Newell, Shaw, and Simon (1957), who began to work with computer simulations of problem-solving processes. When you can write a computer program that explores a problem, analyzes the relation between the goal and the present state, evaluates means of solution, and forms a plan, then your theory is no longer vague. The problem-solving performance of such programs can be impressive, and they are being developed to model human performance in an increasing number of subject matter domains like geometry (Greeno, 1982). Models of expert and novice problem solvers have been used to gain insight into the underlying difference in their skill (Simon & Simon,

1978). One interesting suggestion of this line of study is that novices in a field may show more evidence of control and general problem-solving skill than experts, for whom solutions seem to come automatically. Perhaps general problem-solving knowledge is most important during the acquisition of new skills and knowledge.

Efforts to simulate the performance of problem solvers at differing stages of learning resulted in a class of computer models called production systems (Simon & Newell, 1971). Productions consist of conditions of application, and of operations that occur if the appropriate conditions are met. The conditions of application are altered as a result of experience. Productions can be combined as a result of successful experience to yield more complex productions, and thus the appearance of automatic solution. One can easily see how fixation on a particular method of solution, as well as other observed features of problem-solving behavior, would develop in such a system.

New Instructional Implications. The influence of this theoretical approach to problem solving is now appearing in practical instructional efforts. In science and mathematics instruction, we are discovering that too little attention has been given to instruction in the conditions of application, to identifying when it is appropriate to apply a method of solution. Production system models tend to highlight the importance of specific knowledge and specific practice with particular kinds of problems, as opposed to general problem-solving skill. On the other hand, they also hint at the way experience might be designed to produce "general" problem-solving behavior, as a result of long experience. Research computer simulations have provided a set of concepts and a vocabulary that makes it possible to talk about problem solving in more concrete and better defined terms: control processes, memory capacity, conditions of application, etc. These concepts are beginning to influence the design and content of instruction.

Computer simulation studies of problem solving have concentrated on puzzle problems that can be described and worked out in symbols. Whereas, recent efforts to understand problem-solving in physics have begun to point out the importance of other representations of problems. Appropriate uses of schematic drawings or images—and skill in translating between verbal descriptions, drawings, and mathematical expressions—are critical to successful problem-solving performance. Perhaps this work is providing a more systematic version of the Gestalt theorists' exhortations to look at problems in new perspectives, a new explication of some instructional goals in problem solving.

Metacognition: Skills of Cognitive Control and Management

In both knowledge acquisition and problem solving, the vital importance of control of cognitive activities, of self-awareness, and self-management of cognitive activity is evident. The student must be alert to failure of comprehension in order to take corrective action. The problem solver must monitor progress toward a goal. Baron (1978) has suggested that there may be a number of very general "central" strategies that are desirable in the intellectual functioning of both children and adults. As possible examples of such strategies, he suggested: imposing limits, defining tasks into chunks that are appropriate to the person's capacity; subject organization, appropriate grouping, categorization, etc., of materials; checking, the use of multiple solution techniques to verify problem solutions. Although these strategies sound general, much specific knowledge may be required to display them. Considerable familiarity with a task may be required in order to judge its demands on capacity. Checking with multiple methods of solution requires knowing multiple methods of solution.

Indeed, Brown (1980) has suggested that metacognition—conscious awareness of and control of cognitive processes—emerges only as knowledge and skills in a particular domain become quite well developed. Perhaps it is not surprising, then, that developmental psychologists who study universal novices have given the most explicit research attention to people's awareness of thinking processes and to their knowledge about the workings of their own and others' minds. Some developmental theorists, working within the Piagetian tradition, postulate a fifth stage of intellectual development occurring in adulthood that would incorporate general, overarching comprehension of one's own intellectual functions (Arlin, 1975; Commons, Richards, & Kuhn, 1982; Fischer, 1980). Unfortunately, most research on metacognitive development is focused on rote-learning skills in quite young children (Brown, 1980; Flavell, 1977). It has not been common, for example, to query adults about their knowledge of problem-solving strategies in concert with investigations of their problem-solving performance. Gradually, the developmental research is broadening to examine the metacognitive aspects of a wider range of cognitive functions such as comprehension of instructions (Markman, 1979), selective attention (Miller & Weiss, 1982), or simple problem solving (Richards & Siegler, 1981).

Despite the limited scope of this research, it provides a number of observations that are important for cognitive skills training. Both children and adults may verbally display knowledge of effective learning techniques that they do not apply when confronted with a learning task (Brown & Barclay, 1976). It is equally true that they may not be able to articulate knowledge that they can readily put into action at appropriate times (Brainerd, 1973). Obviously, those who articulate insights about the way they go about solving problems or inventing mathematical proofs (Polya, 1945), or who describe the characteristic structure of literary genres, are exceptional individuals. This casts doubt on the prevalent approaches to cognitive skills instruction that rely heavily on verbal descriptions of strategies. Verbal instruction may be useful for older persons who already have the implicit knowledge to understand what is meant by the strategies, but not useful for those who need to learn them. On the other hand, children can learn to talk to themselves to pace their actions at critical points (Meichenbaum,

1978). Markman (1979) has found that first- to third-grade children's ability to evaluate inconsistencies in instructions was improved by asking them to demonstrate the instructions or by having them view others' partial demonstrations. This is another encouraging indication that it may be possible to teach these metacognitive skills.

OPEN ISSUES

The discussion of metacognition touched upon three unresolved issues that are of critical importance for anyone interested in education of the higher cognitive skills. These are the final 3 topics of Volume 2.

The Generality or Specificity of Cognitive Skills

The idea that there are very general learning or problem-solving skills is an attractive one. In essence, it is the idea that these volumes are meant to explore. It holds the promise of greater efficiency and longer lasting value for our educational efforts. It gives us an alternative view of what we might mean by general intelligence. But it is an unproven idea. General skills may not exist. That is, even though we might characterize an individual as using a particular strategy such as means–ends analysis in a variety of different problem domains, it might be that the individual must learn that strategy separately for each domain. There may be no deep psychological unity to the strategy across domains. A more likely hypothesis is that general skills must be built on the foundation of skills that have developed to an advanced state in at least one and probably more than one specific domain. The significance of this issue for the theory of human intellectual functions is obvious, but its practical importance is equally great. Some advocate teaching general cognitive skills and strategies as a separate school subject. Others believe that this is an emphasis that should be incorporated into the teaching of specific school subjects.

The Teachability of Cognitive Skills

Even if learning, thinking, and problem-solving strategies, whether general or specific, are shown to exist, it might not be possible to teach them directly. Perhaps they must spontaneously emerge as a consequence of substantial experience. At the very least, it should be possible to select and design experience to result in a more rapid and complete emergence of such skills. Probably more explicit instruction can be helpful as well. For example, we need to understand more about the value of verbal labels for cognitive activities and of conscious, deliberate control of cognitive activity. On the other hand, we need also to understand how verbal labels can be made meaningful to a wide range of students so that they evoke the desired cognitive activities. We need to understand how effortful, conscious, and deliberate patterns of cognitive activity can be taught in such a way that they will be transformed into efficient, automatic patterns. Volume 2 samples work that provides a promising beginning to the enterprise of teaching complex cognitive skills.

Developmental Differences

Whether young children and adults are fundamentally different learners remains an open theoretical question. Certainly, complex learning and problem-solving skills are found predominantly in older individuals. Some believe, however, that very sophisticated cognitive skills can be developed by quite young children in domains that they happen to know well or that are restricted in the content that must be mastered. Such domains might serve as a foundation for the development of widely applicable general cognitive skills.

It is more likely that older individuals will have developed the implicit concepts needed to understand abstract, verbal approaches to cognitive skills instruction. On the other hand, both older students most in need of help and younger children probably have similar needs for more concrete, intensive instruction. They may need training to develop the mental processes that make up strategies, not simply training to use processes that they have already mastered. They may need to learn to recognize and distinguish among their own mental processes as well as to learn the verbal descriptions that theorists and program developers use to talk about those processes. Cognitive skills training cannot be the same for all students and must adapt to the characteristics of the learner. Because of the practical importance of these issues for educators, a section of Volume 2 is devoted to them, and chapters on developmental studies appear in the major skill sections of Volume 2 as well.

A CLOSING AND OPENING WORD

These open questions beckon to researchers exploring the powers of the human mind. Theirs is an adventure we invite you to share in these volumes. It is an adventure shared and renewed in the life of each developing individual who experiences the unfolding of the intellect to encompass more and more of experience. The powers of the human mind are amplified, we hope, as the creative intellectual insights of one generation become the common self-knowledge of the next. Educators make that hope a reality by shaping the insights of exceptional thinkers or the hard won conclusions of analytic research into effective instructional experiences. In doing so, the teacher is privileged to share students' delight in their developing competence and to increase the number who experience it. Minds become capable of dealing with the future by mastering the insights and inventions of the past. The challenge to all who have contributed to these volumes, and to all who read them, is to bring about that translation from research into the thinking minds of our students.

ACKNOWLEDGMENTS

This introduction is partially based upon research area plans which were developed for the Basic Cognitive Skills program at the National Institute of Education, where Susan Chipman has been Assistant Director for Learning and Development and Judith Segal has been a senior staff member of that division. Just as it introduces this volume, a version of the research area plans was provided to the authors as an introduction to the purpose of the conference and of these volumes. Joseph Psotka and Rosalind Wu also contributed to versions of those plans and thus to this introduction. Although the National Institute of Education supported this work, the views expressed herein are the authors' own and do not necessarily reflect the official policy or position of the National Institute of Education. Chipman is now with the Office of Naval Research.

REFERENCES

Anderson, R. C. Schema-directed processes in language comprehension. In A. M. Lesgold, J. W. Pellegrino, S. D. Fokkema, R. Glaser (Eds.), *Cognitive psychology and instruction*. New York: Plenum, 1978.

Anderson, T. H. Study strategies and adjunct aids. In R. J. Spiro, B. C. Bruce, & W. F. Brewer (Eds.), *Theoretical issues in reading comprehension*. Hillsdale, N.J.: Lawrence Erlbaum, 1980.

Arlin, P. Cognitive development in adulthood: A fifth stage? *Developmental Psychology*, 1975, *11*, 602–606.

Baron, J. Intelligence and general strategies. In G. Underwood (Ed.), *Strategies of information processing*. New York: Academic Press, 1978.

Bartlett, F. C. *Remembering*. Cambridge: Cambridge University Press, 1932.

Barton, W. A., Jr. *Outlining as a study procedure*. New York: Columbia University Bureau of Publications, 1930.

Beck, I. L. Developing comprehension: The impact of the directed reading lesson. In R. Anderson, J. Osborn, & R. Tierney (Eds.), *Learning to read in American schools: Basal readers and content texts*. Hillsdale, N.J.: Lawrence Erlbaum Associates, 1983.

Binet, A. *Les idees modernes sur les enfants*. Paris: Ernest Flammarion, 1909.

Brainerd, C. J. Order of acquisition of transitivity, conservation, and class inclusion of length and weight. *Developmental Psychology*, 1973, *8*, 105–116.

Brown, A. L. Metacognitive development and reading. In R. J. Spiro, B. C. Bruce, W. F. Brewer (Eds.), *Theoretical issues in reading comprehension*. Hillsdale, N.J.: Lawrence Erlbaum Associates, 1980.

Brown, A. L., & Barclay, C. R. The effects of training specific mnemonics on the metamnemonic efficiency of retarded childen. *Child Development*, 1976, *47*, 70–80.

Brown, A. L., & Day, J. D. Macrorules for summarizing texts: The development of expertise. *Journal of Verbal Learning and Verbal Behavior*, 1983, *22*, 1–14.

Brown, A. L., & Smiley, S. S. Rating the importance of structural units of prose passages: A problem of metacognitive development. *Child Development*, 1978, *48*, 1–8.

Brown, J. S., Collins, A., & Harris, G. Artificial intelligence and learning strategies. In H. F. O'Neil (Ed.), *Learning strategies*. New York: Academic Press, 1978.

Bruner, J. (Ed.). *Learning about learning: A conference report*. Washington: U.S. Government Printing Office, 1966.

Chall, J., & Snow, C. *Families and literacy: The contribution of out-of-school experiences to children's acquisition of literacy*. Final Report on NIE–G–80–0086. Harvard Graduate School of Education, December 22, 1982.

Chatham, K. M. Employment practices with entry-level workers. *Research Brief*. Far West Laboratory, San Francisco, CA, December 1982.

College Entrance Examination Board. *National college-bound seniors*. Produced by the Educational Testing Service, Princeton, New Jersey, 1981.

College Entrance Examination Board. *Preparation for college in the 1980s: The basic academic competencies and the basic academic curriculum*. (1982, undated).

Commons, M. L., Richards, F. A., & Kuhn, D. Systematic and metasystematic reasoning: A case for levels of reasoning beyond Piaget's Stage of Formal Operations. *Child Development*, 1982, *53*, 1058–1069.

Dansereau, D. The development of a learning strategies curriculum. In H. F. O'Neil, Jr. (Ed.), *Learning strategies*. New York: Academic Press, 1978.

Dansereau, D. F., Long, G. L., McDonald, B., & Actkinson, T. R. Learning strategy inventory development and assessment (AFHRL–TR–FS–40, contract F41609–74–C–0013). Brooks Air Force Base, Texas, 1975.

Day, J. D. *Training summarization skills: A comparison of teaching methods*. Unpublished doctoral dissertation, University of Illinois, 1980.

Durkin, D. Do basal reader manuals provide for reading comprehension instruction? In R. Anderson, J. Osborn, & R. Tierney (Eds.), *Learning to read in American schools*. Hillsdale, N.J.: Lawrence Erlbaum Associates, 1984.

Fischer, K. W. A theory of cognitive development: The control and construction of hierarchies of skills. *Psychological Review*, 1980, *87*, 447–531.

Flavell, J. H. *Cognitive development*. Englewood Cliffs, N.J.: Prentice-Hall, 1977.

Glasman, L. D. *A social-class comparison of conceptual processes in children's free recall*. Unpublished doctoral dissertation, University of California, 1968.

Greeno, J. Forms of understanding in mathematical problem solving. In S. G. Paris, G. M. Olson, & H. W. Stevenson (Eds.), *Learning and motivation in the classroom*. Hillsdale, N.J.: Lawrence Erlbaum Associates, 1982.

Hunt, E. On the nature of intelligence. *Science*, 14 January 1983, *219*, 141–146.

Jencks, C. The *wrong* answer for schools is: (b) Back to basics. *Washington Post*, February 19, 1978.

Jensen, A. R. IQ and scholastic achievement. *Harvard Educational Review*, *39*, Winter 1969.

Kohler, W. *The mentality of apes*. New York: Harcourt, Brace, 1927.

Luchins, A. S. Mechanization in problem solving. *Psychological Monographs*. 1942, *54*(6), Whole No. 248.

MacGinitie, W. H. Readability as a solution adds to the problem. In R. Anderson, J. Osborn, & R. Tierney (Eds.), *Learning to read in American schools*. Hillsdale, N.J.: Lawrence Erlbaum Associates, 1984.

Maeroff, G. I. Teaching to think: A new emphasis. *The New York Times*, January 9, 1983, Education Winter Survey (Sec. 12), p. 1.

Maier, N. R. F. Reasoning in humans II: The solution of a problem and its appearance in consciousness. *Journal of Comparative Psychology*, 1931, *12*, 181–194.

Mann, L. *On the trail of process: A historical perspective on cognitive processes and their training*. New York: Grune & Stratton, 1979.

Markman, E. Realizing that you don't understand. *Child Development*, 1979, *50*, 643–655.

Mayer, R. E. Can advance organizers influence meaningful learning? *Review of Educational Research,* 1979, *49,* 371–383.

Meichenbaum, D. Teaching children self-control. In B. Kahey & A. Kazdin (Eds.), *Advances in child clinical psychology* (Vol. 2). New York: Plenum Press, 1978.

Miller, P. H., & Weiss, M. G. Children's and adults' knowledge about what variables affect selective attention. *Child Development,* 1982, *53,* 543–549.

National Assessment of Educational Progress. *Reading, thinking and writing: Results from the 1979–80 National Assessment of Reading and Literature.* Report No. 11–L–01, October 1981.

National Assessment of Educational Progress. *The third national mathematics assessment: Results, trends and issues.* Report No. 13–MA–01, Education Commission of the States, Denver, Colo. April 1983.

National Commission on Excellence in Education. *A nation at risk.* Washington: U.S. Government Printing Office, 1983.

Newell, A., Shaw, J. C., & Simon, H. A. Empirical explorations of the logical theory machine: A case study in heuristics. *Proceedings of the Joint Computer Conference,* 1957, 218–230.

Norman, D. A. Notes toward a theory of complex learning. In A. M. Lesgold, J. W. Pellegrino, S. D. Fokkema, & R. Glaser (Eds.), *Cognitive psychology and instruction.* New York: Plenum, 1978.

Ogbu, J. V. *Minority education and caste: The American system in cross-cultural perspective.* New York: Academic Press, 1978.

Olson, G. M., Duffy, S. A., & Mack, R. L. Knowledge of writing conventions in prose comprehension. In W. J. McKeachie (Ed.), *Learning, cognition, and college teaching.* San Francisco: Jossey-Bass, 1980.

Pellegrino, J. W., & Glaser, R. Analyzing aptitudes for learning: Inductive reasoning. In R. Glaser (Ed.), *Advances in instructional psychology* (Vol. 2). Hillsdale, N.J. Lawrence Erlbaum Associates, 1982.

Polya, G. *How to solve it.* Princeton, N.J.: University Press, 1945.

Reder, L. The role of elaborations in the comprehension and retention of prose: A critical review. *Review of Educational Research,* 1980, *50,* 5–53.

Richards, D. D., & Siegler, R. S. Very young children's acquisition of systematic problem-solving strategies. *Child Development,* 1981, *52,* 1318–1321.

Schank, R., & Abelson, R. P. *Scripts, plans, goals and understanding.* Hillsdale: N.J.: Lawrence Erlbaum Associates, 1977.

Scribner, S., & Cole, M. Etudes des variations sub-culturelles de la memoire semantique: Les implications de la recherche inter-culturelle. *Bulletin de Psychologie,* 1976, 380–390.

Simon, A., & Newell, A. *Human problem solving.* Englewood Cliffs, N.J.: Prentice-Hall, 1971.

Simon, D. P., & Simon, H. A. Individual differences in solving physics problems. In R. Siegler (Ed.), *Children's thinking: What develops?* Hillsdale, N.J.: Lawrence Erlbaum Associates, 1978.

Smith, H. K. The responses of good and poor readers when asked to read for different purposes. *Reading Research Quarterly,* 1967, *3,* 53–84.

Sternberg, R. J. The nature of mental abilities. *American Psychologist,* 1979, *34,* 214–230.

Sternberg, R. J. (Ed.), *Handbook of human intelligence.* Cambridge: Cambridge University Press, 1982.

Tyler, L. E. *The psychology of human differences* (3rd ed.). New York: Appleton-Century-Crofts, 1965.

U.S. Department of Education, Division of Management Systems Development, Organizational Performance Service, Office of Management. *Study skills instruction: A service delivery assessment.* December 1982.

Varenne, H., Hamid-Buglione, V., McDermott, R. P., & Morison, A. *The acquisition of literacy for learning in working class families.* Final Report on NIE–G–400–79–0046. Teachers College, Columbia University, 1982.

Weinstein, C. Elaboration skills as a learning strategy. In H. F. O'Neil (Ed.), *Learning strategies.* New York: Academic Press, 1978.

Wertsch, J. W. Adult–child interaction and the roots of metacognition. *Quarterly Newsletter of the Institute for Comparative Human Development,* 1978, *1,* 15–18.

Winograd, T. *Understanding natural language.* New York: Academic Press, 1972.

Introduction to Volume 1: Approaches to Instruction

Judith W. Segal
National Institute of Education

This volume represents an attempt to bring the theory and practice of instruction in thinking and learning skills into a closer relationship. In recent years, many new programs for teaching these critical skills have been proposed. The basic goal of the developers of such programs is an ambitious one—to enable students to adopt new ways of thinking and learning that will permit them to function more effectively in everyday learning and problem-solving situations, both within and outside the classroom.

We do not yet know whether these programs have been successful in accomplishing this ambitious goal. Many have not yet been evaluated systematically. In those instances where carefully controlled evaluations have been undertaken, one can often point to improvements in performance on tests of both intelligence and academic achievement. However, attempts to look more closely at the extent to which students have come to adopt more effective ways of thinking and learning have been hampered because we do not sufficiently understand many of the skills the developers are seeking to instill. As a result, we are unable to determine in unambiguous fashion whether students are actually using the skills taught in coping with novel learning and problem-solving tasks.

In building these instructional programs, developers have had to make assumptions about the kinds of skills and understandings involved in successful thinking and learning and about ways in which these can most effectively be acquired. In some instances developers have been quite explicit about the theories underlying their programs; in others, although they have been less explicit, we can infer their assumptions from the practices included in their programs. The developers have drawn from a wide spectrum of the research literature in psychology and related disciplines in selecting theoretical underpinnings for their programs. In addition, some of them have proposed new theoretical positions to guide their work.

While developers have been building assumptions into their programs, researchers have continued to add to the knowledge base from which program developers can draw. During the past several years, a substantial amount of work in cognitive psychology has focused on exploring the nature of competence on complex learning and problem-solving tasks typical of those that children encounter in school. As a result, we now have new insights concerning what successful thinkers and learners know and can do that distinguishes them from less successful individuals.

The chapters that follow attempt to bring the theory and practice of instruction in thinking and learning skills into closer relationship by examining the assumptions behind the various programs and by asking whether these assumptions are consistent with views emerging from basic research. More specifically, these chapters explore several programs of instruction in considerable detail, looking at the activities that students are encouraged to adopt, the instructional methods and materials used, and the evaluation data collected. A major theme in these explorations is to consider whether the programs are teaching skills that are consistent with our present knowledge of the processes involved in effective thinking and learning and whether they are using techniques consistent with our present knowledge of how these processes are acquired. Through this analysis, we hope to assist our readers to achieve a deeper understanding of the different approaches that program developers are recommending and of the strengths and limitations of these approaches.

Relating the programs to the research literature has the benefit of suggesting conclusions not only about the adequacy of the programs, but also about the adequacy of the research literature as a basis for supporting practical attempts at instruction. In building these instructional programs, the developers have encountered many issues about which the current theoretical literature is not able to offer any clear guidance. The chapters that follow call our attention to these issues and discuss additional research that might be undertaken to further extend theory in practically relevant directions. In short, we hope that the attempts made in this volume to relate the programs to the research literature will open a continuing dialogue between basic and more applied researchers that will serve to enrich the work of both groups.

CRITERIA FOR SELECTING PROGRAMS

A total of nine instructional programs have been selected for detailed discussion in this volume. We used four criteria in selecting these programs.

A first criterion was to focus on programs that had actually been tried in at least one site and that were sufficiently well documented to permit others to understand their nature through an examination of written materials. Secondly, we sought programs that, taken together, offered instruction in a wide range of thinking and learning skills and used many different instructional methods, so that an examination of the programs as a whole would familiarize readers with current debates concerning which skills to teach and what methods to use. To ensure that the programs covered a wide range of skills, we extrapolated ideas from current research in cognitive psychology about major domains of competence, and sought examples of programs within each domain. Our domains were: intelligence and reasoning, knowledge acquisition, and problem solving. Thirdly, we selected programs that we considered interesting either because they illustrated ways of applying new theoretical ideas or because they were receiving widespread usage.

Fourthly, we sought programs appropriate for use with older children and adolescents, rather than preschool and primary school children. Our interest in older children grew out of a practical concern with improving performance on the complex thinking and learning tasks that enter the school curriculum beginning in the upper elementary grades as students become involved in systematic attempts to acquire knowledge and solve problems in different academic content domains. Although this volume does not discuss programs for use with very young children, the programs discussed in the chapters that follow do cover a broad age range, including, at the lower end, some for use with upper elementary school children, and at the upper end, some for use with college students.

Our focus on older children and adolescents is consistent with recent suggestions that cognitive skills instruction be made available to individuals at many different points in their development. Many programs now exist for teaching fundamental cognitive skills such as perceptual analysis, classification and seriation, awareness of temporal and spatial relationships, and planning to young children (see Evans, 1975). For the most part, these programs have grown out of experimental efforts undertaken during the 1960s to help children from low-income families achieve greater success in school. Underlying these programs was the hypothesis that by teaching children from low-income families basic skills considered important to success in school, one might help them begin school on a par with children from middle-class families, thereby narrowing the academic achievement gap between these groups.

Long-term follow-up data on several of these programs are now available. Students participating in them appear to derive many benefits, some of which are more stable over time than others (Lazar & Darlington, 1982). On standardized tests of intelligence and academic achievement, experimental students typically attain substantially higher scores than controls immediately after training, but fail to maintain this advantage over time. On other measures, however, experimental students continue to look quite different from controls even ten to fifteen years later. For example, during the 10-year period following training, experimental students are less likely to be retained in grade or assigned to special classes for individuals failing to cope successfully with a normal school curriculum.

Although many educators and researchers have found it encouraging that instruction in thinking and learning skills administered during early childhood has had effects still evident 10 to 15 years later, others have begun to raise questions about timing issues (Rohwer, 1971). As children progress through the school curriculum, they confront increasingly complex thinking and learning tasks which demand use of more complex skills. Many of the skills needed to cope with these tasks are not typically displayed or mastered until late childhood or adolescence. These skills could be emphasized in programs of instruction for older children. By teaching thinking and learning skills at several appropriate points in a child's academic career, it should be possible to produce even more impressive and enduring improvements in academic performance. This volume should contribute to the exploration of this issue by offering to practitioners who are interested in working with older children and adolescents some ideas about the kinds of skills older students require and about appropriate instructional methods for developing them.

VARIATIONS IN THE PROGRAMS

Skills in Which Instruction Is Offered

Consistent with our program selection criteria, the programs presented here do provide instruction in a wide range of skills. The skills range from very fundamental ones, like learning to make simple perceptual comparisons, to more complex ones, like learning to trace the relationships among ideas in long and complicated passages of text. Many children have mastered certain of these skills by the time they reach the upper elementary grades; others pose a challenge even for sophisticated adults.

Underlying the variation in skills are variations in the kinds of students with whom the program developers work. Feuerstein, for example, working with adolescents from low socioeconomic backgrounds, prefers to begin instruction with simpler skills and gradually build up to more complex ones. Dansereau, in contrast, working with college undergraduates, prefers to begin instruction at a more advanced level, assuming that his students have already mastered many simpler skills.

Differences among the developers with respect to the kinds of skills they are seeking to instill center around three issues. One is whether to teach thinking processes or thinking strategies—that is, whether to teach basic processes that are considered essential to successful thinking or rules for using these processes in coping with different kinds of learning and problem-solving tasks. Although most of the program developers do not consider this to be an either-or question, there are differences in emphasis across these programs. Feuerstein, for example, devotes extensive instructional time to having students practice basic thinking operations like comparing and categorizing so that they will become more proficient in these areas. Covington, in contrast, argues that he is not attempting to help students acquire new cognitive abilities, but rather is teaching them strategies for using already acquired abilities in more effective ways. Dansereau shares Covington's preference for offering instruction in strategies. For example, he does not want his students to become more proficient comparers and categorizers, but he does want them to learn that making comparisons and noticing categorical relationships can be effective techniques for understanding and remembering information acquired from reading.

Another issue on which these developers differ is whether to teach general or specific skills. Herber, for example, seeking to have his students apply text-learning skills in different content domains, tends to work with skills that are deemed very general—for example, drawing inferences, noticing cause–effect relationships, and so on. Jones, in contrast, finds that her students frequently have difficulty modifying general skills for use in particular situations. She attempts to teach algorithms, or step-by-step procedures for applying specific skills to the different tasks for which they are appropriate.

Still a third issue dividing these program developers is whether to limit instruction in cognitive skills to cognitive processes or to attempt also to teach related affective dispositions. Lipman, for example, seeking to help his students become more effective thinkers, recommends not only teaching a wide range of skills that he considers essential to effective thinking, but also transforming the classroom into a community of inquiry that highly values use of these skills.

Instructional Methods

The program developers offer many different ideas on instructional methods. Some favor a more direct approach to instruction than do others. They are explicit in describing to students the exact nature and uses of the skills they want them to acquire. Whimbey and Lochhead, for example, attempt to help students understand the processes underlying effective thinking by providing protocols of experts thinking aloud as they work out solutions to problems, thereby revealing the different mental steps involved. Dansereau also favors a direct approach to instruction. He not only prescribes specific thinking processes, but also explains why he considers them effective and specifies the kinds of tasks to which they should be applied. Herber, in contrast, favors a more indirect approach to instruction. He argues that students can obtain deeper insights into the nature of effective learning strategies if they can be helped to invent these strategies, rather than learning about them from others. Thus, he devotes considerable attention to placing students in situations he considers conducive to facilitating such inventions.

A second difference of opinion with respect to teaching methods involves whether to offer separate courses of instruction in thinking and learning (a position recommended, for example, by de Bono), or whether to integrate instruction into already existing content area courses (a position recommended, for example, by Herber). The first approach has the advantage of calling students' attention to aspects of thinking and learning that may be general across different content areas, so that they have at their disposal a set of techniques that can be applied in many different domains. The second approach has the advantage of making instruction in thinking and learning more specific, so that students are not left to figure out how to adapt general techniques for use in various domains. A related issue involves the kinds of content to be used in instruction. Feuerstein, for example, works with exercises involving abstract content such as geometrical figures and symbols; de Bono, in contrast, works with content taken from everyday thinking and reasoning situations; Herber, exemplifying still a third position, works with more specialized content drawn from different academic disciplines.

Still another difference of opinion with respect to teaching methods centers around the issue of how to organize instruction. Jones, for example, argues that complex thinking and learning skills can best be taught by breaking them down into subskills and offering instruction in each. Dansereau, in contrast, argues that the gestalt of the more complex strategy should be conveyed from the very beginning so that students can have some sense of the kind of skill they are trying to learn.

A fourth issue involves the level of proficiency developers would like students to achieve in the skills they are attempting to instill. Feuerstein, for example, recommends extensive opportunities for practice so that students will come to execute the skills in a fluent and effortless manner. He argues that, if use of these skills requires a great deal of special effort, students will abandon them in favor of responses requiring less effort once the training intervention has ended. Although other developers also recommend opportunities for practice, there is less emphasis in their programs on repeated practice.

OVERALL PLAN FOR THE VOLUME

Having selected our nine programs, we asked their developers to prepare chapters for this volume describing their general approaches to instruction, the theories and evidence supporting these approaches, and some typical instructional materials and techniques. To obtain a deeper understanding of the possible benefits and practical difficulties associated with use of these programs, we also requested contributions from practitioners who have been deeply involved over the past several years in conducting cognitive skills instructional programs in schools and other settings. We asked the practitioners to discuss their reasons for wanting to provide instruction in thinking and learning skills and to discuss their practical experiences implementing programs of instruction in different settings. Our practitioners include classroom teachers who have implemented programs on an individual classroom basis, school administrators who have implemented programs on a schoolwide or districtwide basis, and a representative from Venezuela, a country now engaged in a massive attempt to improve the thinking and learning skills of its entire citizenry.

In addition to practitioners and program developers, we invited several leading cognitive psychologists to contribute to this volume. The psychologists were asked to analyze the instructional programs—that is, to look carefully at the ideas and practices recommended and to determine how these relate to ideas discussed in the relevant basic research literature. As noted previously, we grouped the programs into three sets on the basis of the kinds of skills emphasized: intelligence and reasoning, knowledge acquisition, and problem solving. We asked three leading cognitive psychologists specializing in these skill areas to serve as program analyzers. Each was asked to analyze one of the three sets of instructional programs.

More specifically, we asked these researchers (hereafter referred to as analyzers) to identify the assumptions built into these programs about the nature, development, and acquisition of thinking and learning skills, and to comment on whether these assumptions are consistent with views emerging from the relevant basic research literature in cognitive psychology and related disciplines. Secondly, we asked them to review the evaluation data on these programs, and to discuss the conclusions that can be drawn from the data and how one might go about conducting more adequate evaluations. Thirdly, we asked them to point out additional ideas in the research literature that might be worth exploring in future instructional programs and to suggest areas for future research, including new areas emerging from attempts to build programs of instruction.

In reading the analysis chapters, one should keep in mind that, with the exception of one of the nine programs, the analyzers have not had an opportunity to observe these programs in action. Their analyses are based on a review of documentation and on samples of typical instructional materials. In studying the different chapters in this volume, the reader will notice some redundancy between the developers' and analyzers' descriptions of the instructional programs. In the analyzers' chapters, however, these descriptions are quite brief; their purpose is to permit the analyzers to clarify their interpretations of basic program features before discussing them. These brief descriptions should be read in conjunction with the richer descriptive information about the programs and the kind of thinking that went into building them that is available in the developers' accounts.

ORGANIZATION OF THE VOLUME

The volume as a whole is organized into four sections. The first three, entitled respectively *Intelligence and Reasoning, Knowledge Acquisition,* and *Problem Solving,* contain contributions from the program developers and analyzers. Each of these focuses on a different domain of cognitive competence. Within each domain: (1) the developers discuss their instructional programs to help individuals become more proficient in the skills associated with that domain; and (2) an analyzer relates these programs to the relevant basic research literature in cognitive psychology. The fourth section of the volume, entitled *Educators' Experience,* offers contributions from practitioners. The practitioners discuss possible benefits and difficulties involved in teaching individuals how to become more effective thinkers and learners.

Intelligence and Reasoning

The first chapter in the *Intelligence and Reasoning* section, by Feuerstein, Jensen, Hoffman, and Rand, discusses the *Instrumental Enrichment Program,* a program developed by Reuven Feuerstein to help adolescents, immigrating to Israel from less technologically developed countries, acquire the thinking and learning skills required for successful participation in Israeli schools. The program is currently being used not only with immigrants to Israel seeking to adjust to life in a more technologically advanced country, but also with adolescents from low SES families in the United States and other countries seeking to function more effectively in school.

The *Instrumental Enrichment Program* has several interesting features that prompted us to include it in this volume. First and foremost, in contrast to other cognitive skills instructional programs, this one has been in existence for many years and is now widely used both in this country and abroad. The program's age and widespread usage have made possible continuing modification and refinement of program materials based on extensive feedback from teachers and students. Over the years, an important body of findings has accumulated on the effectiveness of the program, including findings from longitudinal studies assessing the performance of individuals long after participation.

In addition to age and widespread usage, a third interesting feature of this program is its scope. The *Instrumental Enrichment Program* is an ambitious one, offering instruction in a wide range of cognitive skills that its developers consider essential to successful thinking and learning in many different kinds of situations. Some of these skills are accessible to very young children—for example, making simple perceptual comparisons and noticing basic spatial and temporal relationships. Thus, at its initial levels, the program is reminiscent of some of the early intervention programs already mentioned. At more advanced levels, however, the program offers instruction in very sophisticated thinking operations. For example, as students progress through the program, they are taught to solve exercises in formal logic involving transitive relationships and syllogisms.

A fourth interesting feature of this program is its theoretical foundation. The program grows out of Feuerstein's theory of cognitive modifiability, a theory that calls our attention to the role that significant others play in helping children come to grasp fundamental ways in which objects and events can be related to one another. Still another intriguing feature is the program's use of what its developers describe as "relatively content free" instructional materials. That is, students are asked to work with concepts that can be readily grasped by all adolescents regardless of differences in background knowledge. This has the advantage of making the program accessible to adolescents from many different backgrounds.

Feuerstein et al. provide an overview of the theory underlying their program and describe the methods and materials used in instruction. They discuss the advantages of working with "relatively content free" instructional materials, and describe a bridging component designed to help students extend the skills they have learned in working with these materials to content more typical of the school curriculum. The authors also review the available evaluation data on their program and report that the program has been found to produce improvements in performance on measures of both intelligence and academic achievement.

The second chapter in the *Intelligence and Reasoning* section, by Matthew Lipman, discusses his *Philosophy for Children Program.* Lipman brings a perspective to the problem of improving thinking skills that is quite different from those of the other authors in this volume. Trained in philosophy, he derives many of his ideas about the nature of effective thinking and about instruction in thinking from the philosophical literature. For example, in contrast to Feuerstein, whose instructional exercises are often similar to items on intelligence tests, Lipman has written novels for children in which they are offered models of individuals engaging in philosophical inquiry. The characters in these novels explore concepts that are of interest to children—for example, friendship and fairness—and spend a substantial amount of time thinking about their own thinking and developing criteria for distinguishing better thinking from worse.

Lipman describes the broad range of thinking skills and logical insights that his program attempts to foster and summarizes the basic features of his instructional approach. As noted earlier, like several of the other developers who have contributed to this volume, Lipman is concerned not only with teaching children how to think more effectively, but also with having them come to value effective thinking, so they will put their newly learned skills to use. To this end, he discusses his concept of transforming the classroom into a community of inquiry and suggests how the different components of his program—the novels, the thinking exercises, and the classroom discussions—contribute to this goal.

Like the *Instrumental Enrichment Program,* the *Philosophy for Children Program* is in widespread use and has been the subject of several carefully designed evaluation studies. Lipman reviews the existing evaluation data and reports that participation in this program has resulted in improvements on measures of reasoning proficiency, reading and mathematics achievement, and creative thinking.

During the past several years, as a more diverse population of students has sought to enroll in colleges and other postsecondary institutions under open admissions and other special programs, many colleges have found it necessary to offer special courses to entering students to help them become better prepared for the college experience. Some of these courses have offered training in traditional areas like reading and writing, whereas others have focused on the development of thinking and reasoning skills. In the third chapter of the first section, Jack Lochhead discusses a course that he and Arthur Whimbey developed to help college students improve their *analytical reasoning skills*—a course now being used with both open admissions and more traditional students at a variety of postsecondary institutions. The course emphasizes the importance of systematic and precise thinking and teaches students to solve a variety of well-defined problems, including verbal reasoning problems, analogy problems, analysis of trend and pattern problems, and mathematical word problems. The course centers around a technique called pair problem solving, in which one student thinks aloud as he or she attempts to solve a problem, while a second student follows each step to check it for completeness and accuracy. Lochhead describes the basic features of this technique and explores its theoretical rationale by relating it to ideas in the research literature about the coordination of thought and language.

The final chapter in the section on intelligence and reasoning is Bransford, Stein, Arbitman-Smith and Vye's analysis of the three instructional programs. Many of the tasks in which students are offered instruction in these programs are tasks that psychologists have studied—for example, trend and pattern problems, syllogistic reasoning problems, and analogy problems. As part of their analysis, the authors compare the processes in which these programs are offering instruction with ones researchers describe as effective in coping with these tasks. They find that in some instances the literature can offer additional perspectives on what to teach that program developers might find helpful.

Of course, the goal of these instructional programs is not simply to teach students to solve well-defined, formal reasoning problems that appear on intelligence and aptitude tests, but rather to teach them how to become more effective thinkers and learners both inside and outside the classroom on tasks they have never before encountered. Thus, as a second part of their analysis, the authors ask whether the operations and strategies taught are ones that might be useful in a wide range of situations and whether they are taught in ways that can help students become aware of their generality. For example, they ask how people use analogies in everyday thinking situations and whether the skills involved are similar to those needed for solving the kinds of formal analogy programs included in these programs.

The authors look not only at what is taught in the programs, but also at the instructional methods, and ask whether the literature can help us to understand better how different methods may be achieving their results. For example, they look at techniques like pair problem solving and philosophical dialogue and find that these may be promoting the kinds of metacognitive assessments that researchers have described as characteristic of effective learners.

As a third part of their analysis, the authors review the existing evaluation data on these programs and ask what has been learned. They point out that, although evaluations of these programs indicate desirable gains in performance on measures like standardized achievement and aptitude tests, it is not clear whether these gains have occurred because students are thinking and learning in more effective ways, or whether they can be explained by other factors. To clarify this issue, the authors argue for "divergent effects" analyses in which differences between experimental and control groups are assessed both immediately after instruction, as well as later, when new opportunities for learning have occurred. They also call for "on-line" evaluations that look closely at the kinds of thinking and learning processes in which students engage as they confront problems not included in these programs.

Knowledge Acquisition

The second section, entitled *Knowledge Acquisition,* focuses on techniques for helping students learn complex bodies of knowledge, such as the interrelated sets of facts, theories, and methodologies that constitute typical academic content domains. In school settings, texts play an important role in communicating content-area knowledge to students. Thus, the programs discussed in this section devote considerable attention to teaching students ways to work with the information in texts to make it easier to understand and remember.

The first chapter, by Donald Dansereau, discusses his program of research on learning strategies instruction and describes a semester-long course that he developed for college undergraduates based on the findings from this research. A major reason for selecting Dansereau's course for inclusion in this volume is that it offers an interesting illustration of how one might go about applying some of the most recent theories in the cognitive psychology research literature to practical problems of instruction. Cognitive psychologists have described effective learners as having at their disposal a variety of techniques for transforming incoming information to make it more meaningful. Dansereau refers to these as comprehension and memory techniques. His course combines instruction in these techniques with instruction in support strategies for helping students achieve a suitable frame of mind for studying. More specifically, to help students grasp and remember the relationships among ideas in extended passages of text, Dansereau offers instruction in techniques like forming images, paraphrasing, analyzing key concepts, and networking. Networking, for example, involves translating textual information into a network map that explicitly labels the kinds of relationships obtaining among major ideas, and that displays these relationships in diagrammatic form.

Dansereau discusses his attempts to offer instruction in these techniques and reports that, following instruction, students demonstrate improvements in performance on several different kinds of text comprehension tasks. Some of the techniques with which Dansereau works, like paraphrasing and networking, are general ones in the sense that they can be applied to texts in many different content areas. As noted earlier, one problem developers have encountered in teaching general techniques is that students often find it difficult to adapt these for use in specific situations. Dansereau offers some new perspectives on this problem by discussing his efforts to combine instruction in general content-independent strategies with instruction in more specialized content-dependent ones.

A similar approach to instruction in learning strategies is presented in the chapter by Claire Weinstein and Vicki Underwood. Their approach centers around the *concept of elaboration*—that is, the idea that effective learners are active learners who have at their disposal a variety of strategies for making incoming information more meaningful by relating it to previously acquired knowledge. These include strategies like organizing information into categories, forming images, creating analogies, drawing inferences, seeking out implications, and so forth. Weinstein and Underwood discuss ways of incorporating ideas about elaboration strategies into instruments designed to diagnose students' learning difficulties, and explore how these ideas can form the basis for training interventions. They review research on the feasibility of training students in elaboration techniques and discuss their ongoing efforts to create a semester-long course in learning strategies for college undergraduates that combines instruction in elaboration techniques with instruction in more traditional study skills like note taking and test preparation. They also explore the feasibility of incorporating instruction in elaboration techniques into regular content-area courses. As one promising approach, they recommend creating a metacurriculum in learning strategies whereby content-area teachers make students aware of techniques used in the classroom to relate new ideas to previously acquired knowledge, so that students will come to adopt these techniques when studying on their own.

Like Dansereau and Weinstein, Beau Jones is also attempting to teach students different ways to work with the information contained in texts to make it easier to understand and remember. The chapter by Jones, Amiran, and Katims explores ways of incorporating instruction in learning strategies into the standard language arts curricula that are offered to students at the elementary and secondary school levels. The authors describe two programs of instruction in learning strategies within a language arts context: *Matrix Outlining and Analysis* (MOAN) and the *Chicago Mastery Learning Reading Program with Learning Stategies* (CMLR/LS). MOAN offers instruction in a novel system of outlining in which a body of information is translated into a matrix or two-dimensional table so that items can be easily compared along a variety of dimensions. Students receiving instruction in this system are taught how to use matrices as devices for remembering, analyzing, and reporting on comparative information. CMLR/LS is a set of reading instructional materials specially designed for use with low-achieving inner-city students in Grades 5 through 8. The materials offer systematic instruction in learning strategies and teach students how to apply these strategies to many different kinds of texts. Like Dansereau, in building their instructional program the authors of this chapter have struggled with the problem of whether to teach general strategies or more specific ones. They point out the difficulties low-achieving students encounter in applying general strategies to different text-learning tasks and indicate ways in which their instructional approach has evolved over the years into an increasingly specific one.

Harold Herber's program, *Teaching Reading in Content Areas,* has three features that distinguish it from other programs discussed in the knowledge acquisition section. One is that, instead of developing a separate course of instruction in thinking and learning skills, Herber integrates instruction into already existing content-area courses. His program consists of methods that elementary and secondary school content-area teachers can use both to help students derive meaning from regularly assigned classroom texts and to help them acquire some general comprehension skills useful in working with other texts.

Herber's preference for integrating instruction into content-area courses offers two advantages. First, because skills are taught in the contexts in which students are expected to use them, Herber avoids some of the generalization problems experienced by other program developers. Secondly, because skills are taught in conjunction with actual attempts by students to master complex bodies of knowledge, a broader range of comprehension skills can be taught. That is, instead of teaching students to comprehend isolated passages of text, Herber teaches them to extract from their reading a view of the structure of knowledge in the domain being studied that serves as background for interpreting additional texts in that domain.

A second distinctive feature of Herber's approach is that it is more indirect than those advocated by other program developers. Instead of providing explicit descriptions of the procedures involved in executing various skills, Herber seeks to help students discover these procedures on their own by involving them in special learning situations that he considers conducive to facilitating such dis-coveries. He describes these situations as "simulations" and discusses how this concept is implemented in the instructional exercises used in his program.

A third distinctive feature of Herber's approach is that, instead of offering teachers ready-made instructional materials for use in their classrooms, he seeks to help them develop their own materials. Thus, teacher training plays an impor-tant role in the implementation of his program. Herber describes the nature of his teacher-training workshops and points out the advantages and practical dif-ficulties associated with asking teachers to develop their own instructional materials.

The final chapter in the second section is an analysis by Campione and Armbruster of the four knowledge acquisition programs. As part of their analysis, the authors derive from the research literature views about the kinds of under-standings and skills possessed by expert learners and about ways in which these are acquired. They indicate areas in which researchers are in agreement on these issues and areas in which there are disagreements. They point out that many of the current controversies in the theoretical literature are on issues of concern to program developers and can inform decisions they face.

More specifically, they note that the program developers have taken different stands with respect to the issue of whether to offer instruction in general or specific skills, and ask what the research literature can tell us. They discuss analyses by researchers suggesting that these options have complementary advantages and limitations, and suggest ways of combining them to maximize their advantages and minimize their limitations. They also note that the program developers hold different views on the desirability of making learners consciously aware of the exact nature and uses of the strategies taught in their programs. Because it is commonly reported that lower ability students encounter difficulty in transferring learning strategies to new tasks, they argue that less competent learners must be offered more complete instruction. Students who are already competent learners may be able to acquire new strategies simply by being given brief descriptions of them. For other students, however, it is often necessary to spell out in explicit terms why, when, and how to use these strategies, so that they will become informed and thoughtful users. For still others, one must go even further. In addition to teaching strategies, one must teach executive skills like planning and monitoring, so that they will come to approach learning tasks in a more deliberate and systematic fashion.

In looking across the four knowledge acquisition programs, the authors note that the developers, as a group, seem to be aware of the need to modify instruction to accommodate differences in learner populations. They find that these programs differ not only with respect to the kinds of skills in which instruction is offered and the kinds of instructional methods used, but also with respect to the ages and ability levels of the students involved. The authors argue that such differences offer useful insights into ways in which one may want to modify instruction as one shifts from working with younger and less able students to working with older and more competent ones.

Problem Solving

Section III, entitled *Problem Solving,* focuses on techniques for helping students apply previously acquired knowledge in solving a wide range of problems involving many different kinds of content. The instructional programs discussed in this section vary considerably in the kinds of problems emphasized. The problems range from artificial puzzles (e.g., discovering which of several suspects is buried in an ancient tomb), to problems involving academic content (e.g., problems in the areas of social studies, mathematics, and science), to problems involving content taken from daily life experiences (e.g., the problem of making a consumer decision or selecting a career).

The first chapter, by Edward de Bono, describes the *CoRT Thinking Program,* a program based on de Bono's ideas about the importance of perception in thinking. De Bono conceives of effective thinking as involving two sets of processes: perceptual processes, whereby the thinker constructs a representation of the different elements involved in a thinking situation, and logical processes, whereby the thinker operates on that representation to reach some conclusions about the thinking situation. De Bono argues that the perceptual stage is essential to successful thinking. That is, he argues that, if an individual has constructed an adequate perceptual representation of the different elements involved in some thinking situation, drawing correct conclusions is often a trivial matter. However, if the individual has failed to construct an adequate perceptual representation, bringing sophisticated logical analysis skills to bear will often be of no avail because these skills will be applied to the wrong set of elements. In his emphasis on the importance of perception in thinking, and on the desirability of helping thinkers break away from preexisting perceptual patterns, de Bono reiterates many themes that were prominent in the research on problem solving conducted by Gestalt psychologists earlier in this century.

Consistent with de Bono's emphasis on the importance of perception in thinking, a major goal of the *CoRT Thinking Program* is to teach students to scan widely in thinking situations for purposes of developing an adequate representation of the many different factors that need to be considered. The *CoRT Program* combines instruction in techniques for scanning with instruction in techniques for thinking systematically and for offering appropriate evidence in support of one's conclusions. De Bono discusses the theory underlying his program, describes the different thinking tools in which he offers instruction, and discusses his instructional methods. Like many of the other program developers who have contributed to this volume, de Bono has struggled with the problem of structuring instruction so that students will transfer the thinking tools they have acquired from the exercises included in the program to a wide range of thinking situations for which these tools are appropriate. De Bono also discusses his approach to the transfer problem, which includes both employing special devices to focus students' attention on the thinking tools they are being encouraged to adopt, and having them practice using these tools on problems involving many different kinds of content.

The second chapter in this section is by Martin Covington, one of the developers of the *Productive Thinking Program.* This program is similar to the *CoRT Thinking Program* in its emphasis on problem formulation processes—that is, on teaching students how to define problems carefully, to explore all the different elements that may be important in solving them, and to explore different ways in which these elements may relate to one another. In contrast to some of the other programs discussed in this volume, the *Productive Thinking Program* has been available as a commercially published set of instructional materials for over a decade and has been the subject of many evaluation studies. Covington summarizes the evidence that has been collected, including data from several recent unpublished studies.

To help readers view the *Productive Thinking Program* in the context of recent research on problem solving, Covington describes the program as one approach to improving strategic self-management skills—that is, to improving the student's capacity to identify and analyze problems and to create and monitor plans for their solution. Covington reviews recent research on the nature of strategic self-management skills and offers ideas on ways to teach them. Like other contributors to this volume, Covington reminds us that cognitive functioning is influenced by both cognitive and affective factors, and argues that, if attempts to improve cognitive functioning are to be successful, they will have to take both kinds of factors into account. To that end, he explores the possibility of combining cognitive skills instruction with attempts to alter classroom reward systems so that students will become both more able and more willing to pursue academic achievement goals.

The third chapter in the *Problem Solving* section, by Polson and Jeffries, analyzes four programs of instruction, including the *Productive Thinking Program* and the *CoRT Thinking Program*. These two programs offer instruction in solving what are called in the research literature "ill-structured" problems, for example, problems like choosing a career or designing a building, where there is often more than one adequate solution and where the goals one is seeking to accomplish become clearer as one proceeds to work on the problem. The other two programs, Rubinstein's *Patterns of Problem Solving* and Wickelgren's *How to Solve Problems,* offer instruction in solving well-structured problems, such as, for example, formal problems in mathematics and science.

As part of their analysis, Polson and Jeffries derive from the current psychological research literature a theoretical framework for describing the nature of successful problem solving. They describe problem solving as involving a search through a problem space combined with a set of understanding processes that are used to generate the problem space. They use this framework as the basis for identifying criteria that successful programs of instruction in general problem-solving skills should meet, and consider to what extent and in what ways the four programs meet these criteria.

Like the authors of the other program analysis chapters, Polson and Jeffries suggest that the issue of whether to teach general skills or more specific ones deserves further attention from researchers. They note that many of the techniques taught in the problem-solving programs are general ones, which can be difficult to apply in specific situations. They argue that we do not know whether the problem-solving techniques theorists have described as general are actually experienced by problem solvers as general techniques or as methods that differ when applied to different kinds of problems. To further extend our knowledge in this area, the authors present several possible theoretical positions on the existence and learning of general problem-solving skills, and discuss how one might conduct research to compare these positions.

Lessons from Educators' Experience

The final section of Volume 1, entitled *Educators' Experience,* contains five chapters by practitioners who have implemented programs of instruction in cognitive skills in a variety of different educational settings. The first chapter, by Walter Thompson, discusses his experiences using the *Chicago Mastery Learning Reading Program with Learning Strategies (CMLR/LS)* in an inner-city elementary school. Thompson reports on difficulties inner-city students experience as they attempt to learn from content-area texts and more complex forms of literature typically introduced into the school curriculum beginning in the upper elementary grades. He describes many inner-city students as "word callers"—that is, as individuals who can pick up a textbook and read all the words aloud, yet completely fail to understand the meanings conveyed. He attributes their failure to the fact that they read word by word, making little effort to relate ideas to one another or to previously acquired knowledge. Thompson discusses how the CMLR/LS materials differ from more traditional basal reading materials in offering instruction in explicit strategies for interpreting and analyzing information. He discusses the procedures followed in implementing these materials in his school and documents a variety of impressive cognitive and affective changes that occurred in both students and teachers following use of these materials.

The next chapter, by Curtis Miles, discusses the need for instruction in choice-making skills. Miles documents a variety of difficulties that college students experience as they attempt to apply previously acquired knowledge in coping with typical academic and nonacademic problem-solving tasks. Miles reports both on his own observations of student performance, derived from his experience as a teacher in a 2-year technical college, and on observations by other practitioners working in other kinds of 2- and 4-year college settings. On the basis of such observations, he argues that many college students are not performing at a reasonable level of competence in applied thinking situations and describes several categories of skill in which they might benefit from instruction. For example, he indicates that even at the college level, many students approach problem-solving tasks in a mechanical fashion, blindly plugging in facts and formulas without thinking through their relationship to the problem at hand.

Miles finds that, although increasing numbers of teachers are now calling for instruction in choice-making skills, difficult barriers confront those who would like to introduce such instruction into their classrooms. For example, he mentions beliefs held by some teachers and administrators that thinking is an innately acquired ability rather than a learned skill. Similarly, he mentions lack of information on the part of many teachers concerning how to go about offering instruction in these skills. In concluding his chapter, Miles argues for the importance of expanding our knowledge with respect to instruction in choice-making skills. To that end, he lists several issues on which practitioners would appreciate further guidance from researchers and suggests ways practitioners and researchers can collaborate in exploring these issues.

In the third chapter, Richard Hutchinson reports on his experiences administering Whimbey and Lochhead's *Short Course in Analytical Reasoning* to adult students enrolled in a 2-year community college under an open admissions program. Hutchinson describes the difficulties open admissions students encounter in coping with routine college courses and discusses how training in analytical reasoning can help overcome such difficulties. He discusses his students' reactions to Whimbey and Lochhead's pair problem-solving method and materials and points out ways in which he found it necessary to modify these materials for use with this population. In particular, he mentions the feelings of defensiveness that many of these students bring to academic learning situations and discusses ways of combating these feelings.

Like Miles, Hutchinson also comments on the barriers involved in introducing systematic instruction in thinking skills into higher education settings. He suggests that offering instruction in thinking skills to academically underprepared students requires special competencies on the part of the instructor, and that institutions of higher education offer few incentives for acquiring such competencies. He also points out that it takes time for students to master new thinking and learning skills, and that incorporating instruction in these skills into semester-long courses covering extensive amounts of content-area information may create overwhelming demands for both teachers and students.

The fourth chapter in the final section, by Herbert Ware, describes the efforts of a suburban school system, Arlington, Virginia, to implement a program in thinking skills on a district-wide basis. Ware offers some interesting case study observations concerning the practical problems surrounding implementation of new instructional programs in the schools. He compares the difficulties Arlington encountered in introducing a program of instruction in thinking skills with its success in implementing a program of instruction in expository writing skills. He notes that in both cases there was a clear public mandate supporting new instructional programs. In addition, in the case of the expository writing program, there was widespread agreement among educators as to: (1) the exact nature of the skills that were to be enhanced; (2) the methods that could be used to assess student proficiency; and (3) the methods that were effective in improving proficiency. In short, there was a well-documented technology of instruction along with an underlying theory supporting use of these techniques. With respect to instruction in thinking skills, however, the situation was quite different. There were no clearcut objectives, there were no well-defined assessment procedures, and there was no agreement as to effective instructional techniques. As a result, although teachers were admonished to "do something" about helping their students become more competent thinkers, very few new instructional practices were actually introduced. Ware comments that we are still left with the need to help students become more competent thinkers and argues for additional basic research to create more adequate theoretical foundations for instruction.

The most dramatic attempt at cognitive skills instruction undertaken thus far is Venezuela's effort to improve the intelligence of its entire population. Under the direction of Luis Alberto Machado, Minister of State for the Development of Human Intelligence, Venezuela is now conducting and evaluating a vast array of projects to improve the thinking skills of individuals of all ages. Some of these projects are adaptations of programs that have been used in other settings, including both de Bono's *CoRT Thinking Program* and Feuerstein's *Instrumental Enrichment Program*. Other projects involve the development of new instructional materials and methods especially designed for use in Venezuela. For example, Venezuela is now exploring the feasibility of using the mass media to train vast numbers of parents and other adults in early childhood stimulation techniques. Venezuela's Minister of Intelligence has also contracted with Harvard University and Bolt, Beranek, and Newman, Inc., to develop a new program of instruction in thinking skills for use in the public schools and has projects underway to explore methods of enhancing the thinking skills and creativity of adults, both through training administered to individuals in their work settings and through other forms of adult education. In the final chapter of this volume, José Dominguez, General Advisor to Minister Machado, describes the general philosophy underlying Venezuela's attempts to improve human intelligence and provides a brief overview of projects currently underway.

AUDIENCES FOR THIS VOLUME

This volume was designed primarily for use by teachers, school administrators, and others seeking advice on whether to introduce instruction in thinking and learning skills into their classrooms and how to select appropriate programs. The approach adopted here to advising practitioners on these issues is to explore several instructional programs in considerable detail. These programs constitute a small sample of the expanding array of available programs. They were selected for detailed exploration because, as a set, they cover the range of approaches from which one can choose, rather than because they are the best available programs. Their diversity provides a focal point for examining the advantages and limitations of different approaches to instruction. As readers encounter new programs not reviewed in this volume, they will find that they share many features with those presented here. We hope that the information provided in this volume will help practitioners become more sophisticated consumers both of the programs discussed here, and of others, by alerting them to the advantages and limitations of such features.

Practitioners interested in adopting the specific programs reviewed in this volume should be reminded that several continue to undergo testing and revision. Thus, the reviewers' comments on them should not be accepted as final judgments. In some instances, developers have already informed us that we can look forward to new and improved versions of their programs that include attempts to cope with criticisms raised in this volume.

In addition to practitioners, the second audience for whom this volume was designed is researchers working to create a firm knowledge base to support instruction in thinking and learning skills. As noted earlier, in recent years, psychologists have become interested in studying performance on complex thinking and learning tasks typical of those encountered in school. They have begun to create a body of knowledge that can guide the development of practical attempts at instruction in these skills. To further this effort, the chapters that follow review current research on the nature and acquisition of thinking and learning skills and suggest promising directions for future research.

ACKNOWLEDGMENTS

The National Institute of Education supported preparation of this chapter by providing writing time to the author in conjunction with her responsibilities as a member of the Learning and Development Division. Although the National Institute of Education supported the chapter, the views expressed herein are the author's own and do not necessarily reflect the official policy or position of the National Institute of Education.

REFERENCES

Evans, E. D. *Contemporary influences in early childhood education.* New York: Holt, Rinehart, & Winston, 1975.

Lazar, I. & Darlington, R. Lasting effects of early education: A report from the consortium for longitudinal studies. *Monograph of the Society for Research in Child Development,* Serial Number 195, Volume 47, Nos. 2–3, 1982.

Rohwer, W. D., Jr. Prime time for education: Early childhood or adolescence. *Harvard Education Review,* 1971, *41,* 316–341.

Program Presentations and Analyses:
Intelligence and Reasoning

1 Instrumental Enrichment, An Intervention Program for Structural Cognitive Modifiability: Theory and Practice

Reuven Feuerstein
Bar Ilan University

Mildred B. Hoffman
Vanderbilt University

Mogens Reimer Jensen
Yale University

Yaacov Rand
Bar Ilan University

all of *Hadassah-WIZO-Canada Research Institute, Jerusalem*

In this chapter we describe Instrumental Enrichment (IE), an intervention program designed to help its recipients learn to learn and to reach higher levels of thinking. We begin by discussing the theory of structural cognitive modifiability from which IE derives. That is, we present our hypotheses regarding the nature of poor intellectual performance and the factors responsible for low levels of functioning. We then detail our approach to the problem of improving retarded performance. Finally, we indicate how our approach has been translated into a full-scale intervention program that does not content itself with merely helping individuals acquire cognitive skills, but attempts to change meaningfully their cognitive structure.

THEORY OF STRUCTURAL COGNITIVE MODIFIABILITY

Nature of Retarded Performance

IE is designed for a widely varied population of "retarded performers." In our use of the term, "retarded performers," we carefully distinguish between an individual's potential and his or her manifest or observed low level of functioning, and include a wide range of individuals who fail to learn from direct exposure to stimuli and thus are unable to benefit from formal and informal learning experiences. In defining retarded performers as individuals who have a reduced level of modifiability when they are directly confronted with new stimuli, we are classifying retarded performance on the basis of its structural characteristics, rather than on the basis of either extrinsic or psychometric criteria.

Extrinsic criteria, such as social index, socioeconomic status, parental education and occupation, family income and size, and so forth, have been used in the past to label individuals or groups of individuals as disadvantaged, marginal, deprived, or retarded. These extrinsic social criteria cannot, by any available information, be considered as direct determinants of outcomes that are predictable and unavoidable. Yet, the individuals who have been erroneously labeled by extrinsic criteria have been subjected to placement policies, educational programs, and remediation efforts that emerge from anchoring retarded performance in the outer environment. For example, remediation efforts based on the assumption that retardation stems from a poverty of stimuli will attempt to compensate for factors that may not even be present, except in a small proportion of the children labeled as retarded. There are also cases in which the educator can do little to alter the extrinsic social criteria to which retarded performance is attributed, so that the result is either a passive acceptance of the low-functioning child or a limited goal-bound attempt at remediation.

Other attempts at defining the population of retarded performers have drawn on tests constructed in accordance with current psychometric principles. The psychometric approach has its shortcomings as well. A norm-referenced classification of children, based on small samples of their observed levels of functioning, provides no instructive theoretical rationale for understanding why there is differential cognitive development. Moreover, the psychometric concerns of test-retest reliability and the ability of an item to discriminate are usually coupled with a belief in the immutability of intelligence. In practice, the search for those areas of behavior and those methods of test administration that yield stable and discriminating differences eliminates from tests those behaviors and skills that either large numbers of children have mastered, or that do not elicit a stable performance over time. Yet, these are the very items that could reflect the individual's potential for change. Psychometric theory thus causes the assessment and classification of children to be based on the more rigid, inflexible aspects of performance so that a child's correct response after a series of failures is considered a random meaningless occurrence. Test results are summarized in an overall score or average index that wipes out even that information on differential performance that may have been revealed in various subtests, and could reflect a potential for modifiability.

Neither definition by extrinsic criteria nor by psychometric measures has succeeded in gaining broad lasting support from the scientific community, although such definitions have continued to be influential in administrative decision making, resource allocation, and pupil placement. These definitions offer neither a theoretical explanation for differential cognitive development nor a prescription for remediation and intervention. However, if our proposed structural definition of retarded performance as a reduced level of modifiability is accepted and confirmed, it may serve as a theoretical guide for a concerted attack on the problems of the low-functioning child.

We feel that the most significant characteristic of low performers, one that permits their identification and inclusion in that population, is their reduced level of modifiability, which is the major evidence of a more pervasive condition of mediational deprivation; this we have elsewhere termed "cultural deprivation" (Feuerstein, 1979, 1980). Our use of the term "cultural deprivation" does not attribute differential value to diverse cultures, but refers instead to the fact that the child has been deprived of his or her own culture. An intra- and inter-generational transmission of culture reflects a profound need of both individuals and groups to insure the continuity of their existence. As such, the phenomenon of cultural transmission may be a powerful determinant of the nature of the interactions between parents and their children. We contend that the child who has not been the recipient of an intergenerational transmission of his or her culture is "mediationally deprived." Our use of this term places the descriptive and explanatory focus more closely within the realm of the psychological theory that we propose to account for the phenomenon of differential cognitive development.

The syndrome of mediational deprivation, primarily characterized by a reduced modifiability, manifests itself by a more or less pervasive lack of adaptability to situations, even after repeated exposure to them. This lack of adaptability is most easily observed when the individual must modify himself or herself in order to be able to cope with or adapt to a new situation. The more elementary the situation, the more isomorphic with the person's existing repertoire of cognitive functioning, the less the requirement for modifiability and, consequently, the less the need for adaptation. The individual who suffers from the condition of reduced modifiability may perform quite adequately, as long as the amount and nature of demands for adaptation do not require meaningful changes in his or her modality of functioning. However, when confronted with the need to acquire new information, new response modes, new content, or new thinking operations, the mediationally deprived individual will show rigidity, lack of flexibilty, and a lack of openness to the novel. It is in this sense that we refer to the condition of reduced modifiability as a structural condition. It represents a characteristic of the organism that manifests itself whenever the need to become modified is a primary requisite for adaptation. This need to become modified—and the lack of modifiability—may arise in a great variety of situations. It is not limited to academic, social, and vocational contexts, but extends to manifold areas of both the internal and external life-space of the individual.

The emphasis in our definition upon a lack of modifiability through direct exposure to stimuli should not be interpreted to mean that individuals who suffer from this condition are necessarily similar in other regards. However, the pervasiveness of the syndrome of mediational deprivation points to certain etiological characteristics of retarded performance that exert a more or less general influence that overrides the many differences in endowment, personality, and behavior that exist among retarded performers.

Direct Exposure Learning and Mediated Learning

In order to attempt a more complete explanation of the etiology of differential cognitive development, we would like to propose the fundamental assumption that cognitive processes are developed through two modalities by which the organism interacts with its environment: through direct exposure to stimuli and through Mediated Learning Experience (MLE). As shown later, this assumption is not intended to disregard the contribution of constitutional and maturational factors to differences in intellectual development, but rather serves to highlight the significance we believe should be attributed to more specific forms of interaction between organisms and their environment.

The first and most pervasive interactive modality through which the human organism becomes modified is by direct exposure to sources of stimulation. The changes that accompany the individual's direct exposure to his or her environment reflect the constitutional equipment and biological drives the organism brings to the interaction as well as the maturational processes that are part of its neurological substrata. Bringing about more or less lasting modifications in the individual's behavioral repertoire, such changes may be equated with learning. Learning by direct exposure is a continuous process throughout the individual's life-span, provided the stimuli to which he or she is exposed are sufficiently novel and unfamiliar to require adaptation.

In the direct exposure modality, individuals are exposed to stimuli impinging on their sensory apparatus and entering their systems in a largely randomized, accidental, unaltered, and unselected way. Reaching the organism in this way, the stimuli will produce such changes as may follow from stimulus familiarity. For example, the organism may learn new responses to stimuli and may even learn to tune out some stimuli following extensive exposure. Direct exposure learning will usually affect how the individual goes about perceiving and interacting with the environment to gratify already existing motives and need systems, such as, for example, biological needs.

The modality of learning by direct exposure, however, cannot by itself account for the development of human intelligence and what may be considered the ultimate characteristic of human beings—their modifiability. For this, we believe that a second modality of organism–environment interaction must be invoked. This modality, which we term Mediated Learning Experience, or MLE, is proposed as the proximal determinant of both the development of cognitive processes in humans, in general, and the phenomenon of differential cognitive development in particular.

By a mediated learning experience, we refer to the kind of interaction in which an experienced intentioned adult interposes himself or herself between a child and some external stimulus and alters the stimulus prior to its perception by the child. In this process of mediation, which typically operates from the beginning of the neonate's life, the adult mediator selects, frames, and filters the stimuli, interpreting them for the child. By scheduling, sequencing, and grouping, the adult organizes the stimuli, regulating their intensity and ordering their appearance. In other words, the stimuli impinging upon the child are no longer random and accidental. To the contrary, they now reflect the intentionality of the mediating adult who makes some stimuli more meaningful by repeating and reinforcing them, while ignoring or discontinuing others. By relating discrete stimuli in terms of their spatial and temporal aspects, and by producing anticipatory behavior in the child, the mediator imposes a spatiotemporal structure on the child's universe, thereby expanding it to areas inacessible to the child by the sheer activation of sensory processes.

In addition to building into the child the modalities of interaction with stimuli at the input phase, the mediator also interposes himself or herself between the organism and the response. The mediator thus affects the way the child responds to a stimulus by the regulation of his or her behavior. A direct result of the mediational process will be the control of impulsivity, the imposition of a tempo and rhythm to the response, and the choice of appropriate modalities for articulate responses. Mediational processes at the output phase are a combined function of the nature of the task and the level of the child's competency.

In the direct exposure modality, the randomized, fragmentary, and accidental nature of the stimuli impinging on the organism can become organized only by virtue of whatever transient biological need system is present in the child—a need system for which some stimuli are relevant and others are not. Those considered irrelevant are neglected or ignored. By contrast, in MLE, through a continuing process of transmission, need systems that are not a direct expression of the biological substrata of the individual become instilled and enlarged. As a result, the organism's perception of the world now differs from that resulting from direct exposure to the environment.

MLE typically starts at a very early stage in interactions between a mother figure and a child. Despite the young child's limited verbal communication skills, mediational interactions during this early period can have a very powerful effect. Later on, the mediational process is accomplished through growing reliance on verbal and symbolic representations. MLE is normally offered to the child throughout infancy and early childhood and may extend into later phases of childhood, revolving around areas novel to the child. The remarkable receptivity of early childhood, however, makes this an optimal period for the provision of MLE. Yet, as becomes clear in the pages that follow, we believe that a sharp distinction must be maintained between optimal versus critical periods.

Characteristics of the Mediated Learning Experience

Not all adult–child interactions have a mediational value. We have already mentioned some examples of mediation, such as filtering, framing, and ordering stimuli. However, above and beyond the specific operations undertaken by the mediator in a particular situation, there are three essential characteristics that describe and define all Mediated Learning Experience interactions. These are intentionality, transcendence, and meaning. In addition to these characteristics, specific MLE interactions may elicit mediation for regulation of behavior; mediation for feelings of competency; mediation of sharing behavior; mediation for individuation and psychological differentiation; mediation of goal seeking, goal setting, and goal achieving behavior; and mediation of challenge: the search for novelty and complexity.

Intentionality marks MLE mother–child interactions from the earliest stage of the child's development. The intention of the mediator, which is shared with the child, substantially alters the nature of the stimulus that is registered and produces an orientation that intensifies the stimulus involved, making both the child and adult more attentive. That is, intentionality produces a state of vigilance that is evidenced by an increased sharpness, focus, and acuity of perception. Intentionality can be observed at very early stages in the development of the child, and dyadic interactions between mother and child, even at the neonatal level, are marked with many signs of mutual intentionality. Intentionality is closely linked to the transcendent nature of the interaction and the meaning with which it is endowed.

The second essential characteristic of a MLE interaction is its *transcendence*. By transcendence, we refer partly to the character and partly to the goal of the interaction. The goal of MLE is always more than the production of a behavior in order to respond to an immediate need. That is, the interaction goes beyond the specific situation or need that elicited it and reaches out to goals that may be only slightly or even not at all related to the original eliciting situation. The particular eliciting event becomes a carrier or means leading to more distant goals.

Thus, for example, an interaction concerned with counting the number of objects in a specific set may transcend the particular situation and serve as an occasion for producing more general summative behavior. Playing with a typewriter becomes a vehicle for teaching cause-and-effect (pressing keys) and means–end (completing words and sentences) sequences. Building blocks may become a way for dealing with spatial orientation. A family outing becomes an opportunity for establishing planning behavior and temporal relations in the child.

Indeed, few are the situations that do not have a potential value for mediated learning; yet none of these situations are inherently of mediational value. The mediational value is lost, for example, if the child is just an extension of the adult, as when the adult asks the child to close the door without explaining the reason for the request. Reaching out to goals that in themselves may have little to do with an activity depends on the intentionality of the mediator. However, given such intentionality, transcendence becomes a powerful modality for the development and shaping of behavior. It is this transcendent nature of MLE that is responsible for the constant enlargement and widening of the human being's need system. With this we touch upon the third characterisic of a mediated interaction.

The third characteristic of MLE is the *meaning* the interaction lends to certain stimuli and events. In the interaction, the object or event presented to the child is not neutral, but has affective, motivational, and value-oriented significance. Meaning that is assigned cannot be grasped by the senses alone. Experiences are thus turned into the components of broader systems of needs whose establishment and perpetuation in the individual may be far removed and even devoid of connection with the needs systems determined by his or her biological substrata.

The first three characteristics, operating in conjunction with one another, are necessary conditions for all mediated learning interactions. Mediation for the regulation of behavior, mediation for feelings of competence, mediation of sharing behavior, the mediation for individuation and psychological differentiation, the mediation of goal seeking, goal setting, and goal achieving behavior, and the mediation of challenge: the search for novelty and complexity are functions of specific experiences and combine with these characteristics to make the adult–child interaction one of mediated learning. In mediation for the regulation of behavior, the adult, either explicitly or by modeling, introduces a differential rhythm of behavior and reduces the child's impulsivity in gathering, elaborating, and expressing information. The child's independence and willingness to take responsibility for his or her acts are fostered by the interaction. In mediating for feelings of competence, the mediator makes the child feel that he or she is capable of functioning independently. The mediator organizes opportunities for the child's success and interprets to the child the reasons he or she has succeeded. The affective and motivational elements that accompany the feeling of competence make the child willing to cope with new and strange experiences.

It is the mediation of sharing behavior that leads to all social behavior. Sharing behavior both determines and is determined by an affective bonding relationship between a child and his or her primary objects of love and attachment. To a very large extent, sharing behavior represents the energetic principle of MLE, which enables the mediator to impart to the child the stimulus that he intends to mediate. Mediation of sharing behavior starts at very early stages in the child's development with mediator–child eye contact, continues with the MLE partner's pointing and sharing the sight of an object, and follows with activities manifested in play in ideatory and affective interactions. Sharing behavior is thus the spearhead of the mediation which, by virtue of its affective, emotional quality ensures the effectiveness of the mediator in his or her mediational interactions with the child.

Almost opposite to sharing behavior is the mediation of the process of individuation and psychological differentiation through which the child's individuality is conveyed. Mediational processes address the child's capacity for and right to a psychological differentiation from both the mediator and from the rest of the world with which the child interacts. It is the mediation of psychological differentiation that creates the *ur* distance, the primal distance that removes the child from his adualistic condition and paves the way for a dualistic organism–world relationship.

In the mediation of goal seeking there is an interaction between the mediator and child which emphasizes the dissociation between means and goals, thereby creating the criteria for selecting certain behaviors. The individual's choice of a behavior is dictated by the degree to which it is helpful in attaining a specific goal. Goal seeking is often accompanied by an awareness, and contingent upon the individual's need system, attitudes, and values. Goal setting implies a choice among available objectives on the basis of the above-mentioned criteria. Goal achieving behavior is mediated by the endowment of a given goal with a positive valence and ensuring that indeed the meaning ascribed to the goal will become a source of power ensuring its attainment. The orientation toward goal-oriented and purposeful behavior is to a large extent the product of a mediational process, especially in areas that transcend the individual's immediate elementary and cyclic needs for which there is no biological support in the organism.

The mediation of challenge refers to an individual's behavior in seeking tasks which are challenging in terms of their novelty and complexity. It can be seen as a product of a process which reflects an orientation given by the mediator coupled with the individual's feeling of competence which has been mediated to him or her. The mediation of both the feeling of competence and the increased value of the new is necessary in order to enhance the individual's openness and readiness to engage in an interaction with the unfamiliar and to overcome the feelings of insecurity and anxiety that are generated by new and complex activities that demand more than what he or she has already achieved or mastered.

The Relationship Between Culture and Mediated Learning Experience

It is a truism to observe that cultures differ in their specific content, conventions, rules, beliefs, traditions, perspectives, outlooks, and values. However, a common denominator of all cultures is that characteristics, norms, and values of one generation become transmitted to another. The limits imposed by the biological substrata of life are overcome and continuity is ensured by this intergenerational transmission. As such, the phenomenon of culture may be a powerful determinant of the interaction between parents and their offspring, serving to animate parents with intentionality, orienting the interaction toward transcending goals, and providing the child's resulting experiences with meaning. In other words, the fulfillment of the three major criteria for MLE may be aided very substantially and powerfully by culture and the urge in humans to promulgate themselves and their kind by way of processes of cultural transmission. Culture, whether Eskimo, Yemenite, Bushman, Chinese, Israeli, Danish, Black American, White American, Mexican American, or any other of its many distinctive forms, can thus constitute a prime mover, so to speak, of the Mediated Learning Experience.

The phenomenon of culture, irrespective of the differences among its many distinctive forms, lends to MLE a character of universality. Regardless of the differences among cultures in their conventions, customs, beliefs, rules, perspectives, outlooks, mores, and traditions, the fact that all cultures possess some form of these implies that a complex set of motives, representations, and meanings exists within the bearers of each culture, animating their interaction with their progeny and increasing the likelihood that Mediated Learning Experience is offered to the young. Culture will point out ways in which the mediator should organize stimuli for the child, frame them, schedule their appearance, enhance or ignore their connections.

The Relationship Between Direct Exposure Learning, Mediated Learning Experience, and Cognitive Modifiability

We can formulate the relationship between learning by direct exposure, Mediated Learning Experience, and cognitive modifiability in the following way: The more MLE interactions an individual has received, the greater is his or her capacity to benefit from direct exposure to stimuli, to make efficient use of experiences, and to be cognitively modified. Conversely, the fewer MLE interactions, the less the child's cognitive modifiability and hence the smaller his or her capacity to benefit from and make efficient use of the modality of direct exposure to stimuli.

The effects of MLE upon its recipient can be described in terms of two categories. The first pertains to the acquisition of elements of experience that would not be accessible, were they not made available by a mediating agent through a mediational process. This category covers, among others, various universes of information and experiences, such as historical experience, knowledge of traditions and mores, perception and experience of ethnic–cultural identity and cultural aspirations.

The second category, albeit intimately meshed with the first, goes beyond the content of transmitted experiences and involves the formal aspects of cognition. Mediated Learning Experience enables organisms to establish in themselves modalities of interaction with stimuli that go beyond the limited field of sensorially perceived experience. In other words, the propensity to link, organize, relate, and transform relationships, and to employ representational, inferential, hypothetical, and interiorized modalities of thinking are all, to a large extent, the products of Mediated Learning Experience interactions.

Irrespective of the content triggering MLE, or the language in which this content is presented, by selecting and scheduling stimuli, MLE leads to focused, goal-oriented thought processes. These processes can be characterized as a

TABLE 1.1.   The Deficient Cognitive Functions

- Primary source of information: The Learning Potential Assessment Device
- Completeness of listing: No claims are made that the current list is either definitive or exhaustive
- Clinical appearance: Not necessarily in toto. Deficiencies need not be, but often are interrelated and overlapping with each other
- Clinical interpretation: The cognitive functions are weak and vulnerable, but rarely completely missing. Supercharged needs may elicit them
- Division into three phases of mental act: Basically artificial but important for diagnostic and prescriptive purposes
- Affective–motivational factors: May both influence and themselves be influenced by deficient cognitive functions

Input phase: Impairments concerning the quantity and quality of data gathered by the individual. Need not be related to deficiencies in other phases	Elaborational phase: Impairments concerning the efficient use of data available to the individual. Need not be related to deficiencies in other phases	Output phase: Impairments concerning the communication of the outcome of elaborative processes. Need not be related to deficiencies in other phases
Blurred and sweeping perception	Inadequacy in experiencing the existence of and subsequently defining an actual problem	Egocentric communicational modalities
Unplanned, impulsive, and unsystematic explorative behavior	Inability to select relevant, as opposed to irrelevant, cues in defining a problem	Blocking
Impaired receptive verbal tools and concepts that affect discrimination	Lack of spontaneous comparative behavior or limitation of its appearance to a restricted field of needs	Trial and error responses
Impaired spatial orientation, including the lack of stable systems of reference that impair the establishment of topological and Euclidian organization of space	Narrowness of the mental field	Lack of, or impaired verbal tools for communicating adequately elaborated responses
Impaired temporal orientation	Lack of, or impaired need for summative behavior	Deficiency of visual transport
Lack of, or impaired conservation of constancies (e.g., size, shape, quantity, orientation)		Lack of, or impaired need for precision and accuracy in communicating one's response
		Impulsive acting-out behavior

Lack of, or deficient need for precision and accuracy in data gathering	Difficulties in projecting virtual relationships
	Lack of orientation toward the need for logical evidence
Lack of, or impaired capacity for considering two sources of information at once, reflected in dealing with data in a piecemeal fashion rather than as a unit of organized facts	Lack of, or limited interiorization of one's behavior
	Lack of, or restricted inferential–hypothetical thinking
	Lack of, or impaired strategies for hypothesis testing
	Lack of, or impaired planning behavior
	Nonelaboration of certain cognitive categories because the necessary labels are either not part of the individual's verbal inventory on the receptive level, or they are not mobilized at the expressive level
	Episodic grasp of reality

Table 1.1

volitional imposition upon the stream of consciousness, resulting in a focus upon some specific subset of events. The scheduling of stimuli during mediated learning experiences helps the child impose a spatiotemporal framework on his or her world. The ordering, organizing, and grouping of stimuli during mediated learning interactions produce in the child a need and propensity for establishing relationships between objects and events and, subsequently, between relationships themselves, leading to propositional lattice types of thinking. Provoking anticipatory behavior during mediated learning experiences meaningfully affects the development of representational thinking, by which the child relates to the future as if it were present. The child, in other words, becomes able to experience time and space outside the immediate sensorially experienced field and to perceive the hypothetical through logical–inferential processes. Thus, the formal aspects of MLE, even more than its content, produce in individuals the prerequisites of higher mental processes. These, in turn, are the prerequisites for modifiability and hence, ultimately, of adaptation to the conditions of life requiring such levels of functioning.

The lack of Mediated Learning Experience produces in individuals a limited or reduced modifiability when they are confronted with direct exposure to stimuli. That is, the lack of MLE results in rigidity and, what is even more important, in a very limited orientation toward modifiability as a volitional, conscious, and goal-oriented act. This lack of modifiability is accompanied by a number of frequently observed attitudinal and motivational dimensions concerning the relationship between the individual and the surrounding world with which he or she interacts. Individuals who are culturally or mediationally deprived will relate to themselves at best as passive registrars of the experiences impinging upon them in a seemingly randomized, discrete, and unrelated fashion. Their self-image is often that of a passive recipient of information, rather than that of an active generator of information who is influential in determining the appearance, order, structure, and meaning of stimuli.

On a more molecular level, mediationally deprived individuals are characterized by a series of deficient cognitive functions that are the direct determinants of their low level of functioning and of their inefficient use of learning opportunities. We have listed these deficient cognitive functions in Table 1.1. For some mediationally deprived individuals, important cognitive functions may be missing from the behavioral repertoire. More commonly, however, such functions exist in these individuals as weak and vulnerable processes that depend on supercharged needs for their appropriate employment. Mediationally deprived individuals will typically possess a number of deficiencies involving many different areas of cognitive functioning. Deficiencies may be observed in perception, in the transformation and representation of problems, in the search for appropriate solutions, and in the evaluation and communication of results.

To provide but a few examples of the deficient cognitive functions resulting from mediational deprivation, one may note the characteristic blurred and sweeping perception of mediationally deprived individuals and their episodic grasp of reality. These two cognitive deficiencies, often appearing in conjunction with a number of others, may determine such features as the speed and rhythm of the perceptual process. Blurred and sweeping perception leads to a poverty of perceived details, lack of clarity and sharpness, imprecise borders, and, more generally, incomplete distinctions and discriminations. Such limitations in perception also affect the operation of other mental processes, elaborational and communicational processes, that may themselves be intact. Blurred and sweeping perception is not attributable to deficiencies in the perceptual apparatus itself, but rather to other cognitive and motivational factors associated with perception. Among these is the nature of the child's investment in the perceptual process, which becomes reflected in the speed and rhythm of perception and hence has an impact on such factors as the persistence, completeness, and accuracy with which information is gathered. These factors in turn depend on the goals that the elaborational process sets to guide the perceptual apparatus and will assume differential importance depending upon the familiarity and complexity of the stimuli involved. They are also sensitive to motivational conditions. Although the combination of these elements at times will reveal instances of focused and sharp perception (thereby indicating that peripheral limitations are not directly responsible), the absence of an intrinsic need for appropriate perceptual functioning restricts these instances to situations in which the basic physiological needs of the organism are involved. Conversely, the provision of Mediated Learning Experience to individuals will enable them to establish the habits, attitudes, and perceptual techniques necessary to ensure that appropriate perceptual functioning becomes pervasive, generalized, and to some degree independent of immediate, transient needs.

One of the most powerful and pervasive deficiencies characterizing mediationally deprived individuals is their episodic grasp of reality. This deficiency, although often related to and even responsible for numerous other deficiencies, refers specifically to the passive experiencing of the world as a series of events unrelated to each other. The mediationally deprived individual does not spontaneously and habitually link currently experienced events with preceding and subsequent ones. Rather, each event is perceived as being unique, isolated, transient, and discrete because the experiencer does not organize the stimuli and seek the relationships between them. This lack of summative behavior and a failure to compare and group discrete experiences prevent the individual from becoming detached from concrete stimuli perceived sensorially.

Overall, the result of mediational deprivation is a cognitive structure characterized by an array of deficient functions that often interact with each other in complex ways involving attitudinal, affective, and motivational dimensions. This constellation of factors, resulting from the absence or insufficient provision of MLE, is held to be responsible for the culturally deprived individual's limited amount of modifiability by *direct exposure to stimuli*. Our emphasis on direct experience at this point is meant to convey that only in this modality does the modifiability appear to be limited or meaningfully reduced.

Differential Cognitive Development, the Etiology of Retarded Performance, and the Question of Reversibility

Our attempt to explain the phenomenon of differential cognitive development derives fundamentally from the concept of Mediated Learning Experience. If the organism has been exposed to quantitatively and qualitatively adequate amounts of MLE, then the individual will manifest adequate cognitive modifiability and development. If, on the other hand, MLE has not been sufficient or appropriate, the individual will show the effects of mediational deprivation in an inadequate cognitive development and reduced modifiability.

This explanation does not presume that adequate cognitive development is always associated with equal amounts of MLE. In fact, the nature and amount of MLE necessary to produce adequate cognitive development may vary a great deal from individual to individual. Due to variations in constitution, natural endowment, and inherited or acquired conditions of the central nervous system, children may present varying obstacles to efforts to mediate to them. If ways are found to bypass these obstacles, the outcome may be adequate cognitive development despite the adverse conditions presented by the organism. However, if these barriers are not bypassed, the result will be mediational deprivation and inadequate cognitive development. In this way, the nature–nurture controversy is recast within our proposed theoretical framework as the ratio of differential investments to equivalent outcomes.

On the other hand, factors entirely unrelated to the organism may trigger a disruption or discontinuation of the mediational processes. Among such factors are parental apathy and emotional imbalance. Other factors that may threaten the provision of MLE are low levels of parental maturity, education, and socioeconomic status. In our clinical research each of these factors has been found to trigger a failure by parents to provide adequate mediated learning experiences. For example, poverty or a low socioeconomic level may orient parents toward the here and now. Such parents may concentrate on filling the immediate and basic needs of their children, while failing to enter into the types of interaction described as MLE.

On the basis of clinical experience and research with retarded performing children and children at risk, we would like to propose that there are two types of determinants of an individual's level of cognitive development. We have categorized the two types on the basis of whether or not they necessarily or unavoidably lead to predictable outcomes. The first type includes distal etiological factors, such as organicity, educational level, and socioeconomic status (see Fig. 1.1). The second set of factors, proximal etiological determinants, are represented in our theoretical framework as Mediated Learning Experiences. The relationship between the distal and proximal etiologies is believed to be the following: If the presence of a distal etiology triggers the absence of adequate MLE then the necessary outcome is inadequate cognitive development. If however, despite the presence of a distal etiology, MLE is provided to the organism, then the necessary outcome is adequate cognitive development. To give some specific examples, it is well known that a disproportionate number of low-functioning, retarded performing individuals are from low-income families. We believe this may be due to pressure to focus on immediate needs that poverty may exert. Such an orientation may result in a scarcity or even total absence of Mediated Learning Experiences for the child. On the other hand, there is no reason to believe nor is there evidence to support the notion that the presence of poverty *necessarily* will result in a scarcity or absence of MLE. In those cases where the presence of the distal etiology has not interfered with the provision of MLE, the necessary outcome is adequate cognitive development. To take another example, consider the existence of organic or neurological damage in the child, resulting in cerebral palsy, deafness, or blindness. Each of these conditions should be considered as a distal etiology that may pose a specific barrier to mediation. If these conditions trigger an absence of Mediated Learning Experience, the necessary outcome is retarded, low levels of functioning. If, on the other hand, ways are found to bypass these obstacles and MLE is provided to the organism, then the outcome is normal levels of cognitive functioning.

We have sought to capture the relationship between distal and proximal etiologies of cognitive development in diagrammatic form as shown in Fig. 1.1. The

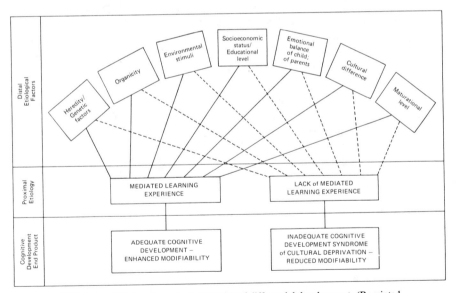

FIG. 1.1.   Distal and proximal etiologies of differential development. (Reprinted by permission from Feuerstein, R., Rand, Y., Hoffman, M. B., & Miller, R., *Instrumental Enrichment: An intervention program for cognitive modifiability.* Baltimore: University Park Press, 1980, p. 18.)

list of distal etiologies presented in Fig. 1.1 is not necessarily complete and only mentions some of the more important factors that may trigger insufficient provision of Mediated Learning Experience.

Now, as we have said, Mediated Learning Experience is considered the determinant of differential cognitive development, inasmuch as the capacity of an individual to become modified and benefit from learning experiences will be strongly affected by the amount, nature, and timing of the individual's exposure to MLE. Insufficient exposure to MLE will result in a series of inadequately developed cognitive functions that are seen to be directly responsible for retarded, low levels of functioning, and reduced modifiability. Yet, consistent with our view that MLE is the proximal determinant of cognitive development, we believe that it is possible to alter the reduced modifiability that characterizes the low functioning individual. Moreover, if a substitute can be found for early childhood MLE, we believe that meaningful returns may be expected on investments in low-functioning individuals, even at such late phases of development as adolescence and young adulthood.

Our belief in early childhood as an optimal period for MLE is explained by the fact that the earlier individuals have benefited from MLE types of intervention, the earlier they will be able to be directly exposed to the world of stimuli with the prerequisite equipment for active, productive, representational thinking that leads to higher mental processes. An individual who has received MLE at later periods has in the meantime forgone many opportunities for learning. This, however, does not imply that such an individual's condition is irreversible or not amenable to intervention. On the contrary, in our clinical work we have experienced the unexpected and paradoxical phenomenon of producing structural changes with greater facility in young adults than in adolescents.

At this point we are increasingly confident that structural cognitive modifiability is a phenomenon that can be relied on and produced at will. This optimistic prediction should not be understood to imply that this goal is accomplished with equal ease for all mediationally deprived children, adolescents, and young adults. Rather, to the contrary, we have found that Herculean efforts and considerable ingenuity are necessary to overcome the severe obstacles to mediational efforts presented by certain extremely low-functioning individuals. On the other hand, for the large groups of individuals who are usually classified as educable mentally retarded or trainable mentally retarded, there are many common and widely shared mediational deficits, thus permitting the construction of planned intervention programs.

NATURE OF THE INSTRUCTIONAL PROGRAM

The Instrumental Enrichment program attempts to provide low-functioning adolescents with the kinds of mediated learning experiences that adequately functioning children normally receive during their infancy and childhood preschool years. In other words, using materials that are appropriate for adolescents, the program attempts to offer a substitute MLE experience to individuals who failed to receive necessary and adequate MLE interactions. Thus, the three major characteristics of MLE, intentionality, transcendence, and meaning, have all contributed to shape the overall goals, materials, and didactics of the program. In the following pages, we present a description of Instrumental Enrichment and discuss this program's relationship with its underlying theory. We begin by discussing the goals of the program. We then offer the reader an overview of the program, including information about the scope of its materials and its implementation in the classroom. Next, we briefly describe several of the specific instruments used in the program and discuss how they relate to the kinds of cognitive functions, operations, attitudes, and broad understandings we want students to attain. Fourth, we discuss why we have chosen to work with relatively content-free instructional materials, and fifth, we discuss past and current attempts to evaluate the program.

Goals of Instruction

The major goal of Instrumental Enrichment is to enhance the capacity of the low-functioning adolescent to become modified as a result of exposure to new experiences. Within this broad goal are included six subgoals that have been important in guiding the construction of the instructional materials and in determining the didactics of the program.

The first subgoal is the correction of the deficient functions that are observed in the cognitive behavior of the retarded performer. As already noted, although the severity of impairment in mediationally deprived children will differ from one child to another as a function of its etiology and the child's degree of deprivation, the interdependence of cognitive functions typically results in many common deficiencies in the input, elaboration, and output phases of the mental act. These deficiencies were listed in Table 1.1. The Instrumental Enrichment program attempts to provide a generalized attack on a wide range of these deficiencies in order to change the cognitive structure, attitudes, and motivation of the retarded performer.

The second subgoal of Instrumental Enrichment focuses on the cognitive behavior required to complete the various instruments included in the program. Although the instruments themselves are said to be free of content (discussed later), the learner must acquire concepts, labels, operations, and an understanding of relationships, strategies, and skills in order to work with them. One of the IE teacher's major responsibilities is to determine which of these prerequisites of thinking are lacking in his or her students and to provide them with direct and suitable instruction. For example, teachers may need to define concepts like "constancy" and "conservation," and terms like "strategy," "relationship," "cues," "hypothesis," "characteristics," "dimensions," and so forth. Teachers may also need to provide students with a rationale for using both elementary operations, such as recognition and identification, and more complex ones, such as classification, seriation, and logical multiplication.

The third subgoal of Instrumental Enrichment is the production of intrinsic motivation through the formation of habits. That is, IE strives to help learners consolidate and internalize new operations, principles, and skills so fully that they are used as a result of an internal need and because of the economy that results from greater efficiency.

Habit formation, however, poses a number of problems for remediational efforts because it is often associated with overlearning, repetition, redundancy, and rote learning, which in turn may be accompanied by boredom and rigidity. However, in Instrumental Enrichment, learning is consolidated and habits are formed by shaping tasks so as to elicit numerous repetitions of functions and operations without using identical stimuli. This is done through continually asking the individual to rediscover redundant rules that are embedded in new content, or that require use of new modalities.

This effort to help students consolidate and internalize their newly acquired learning is an unusual feature of Instrumental Enrichment as contrasted with other instructional remediation programs. Most programs use a "hit-and-run" approach. They introduce children to new skills and concepts, but do not provide the repetition that is necessary for their establishment.

The hit-and-run approach entails two difficulties. The first is that one-shot acquisitions are extremely vulnerable and do not withstand the pressure of novelty or variation. As long as children are asked to apply what they have learned in situations similar to the original learning situation, they may be successful. However, when new content is introduced or different response modalities are required, the children fail to generalize and transfer their learning to the new situation. The second difficulty is that unless operations, principles, and skills become habits, their use depends on some external demand. Unfortunately, in their everyday experiences, retarded performers seldom, if ever, receive explicit demands to utilize higher mental processes. It is therefore of the greatest importance that these principles, operations, and skills become internalized, so that the learner will come to produce them spontaneously and fluently. Indeed, a higher mental act is elicited only when the need to perform it is not exceeded by the effort it requires. If the mental act is perceived as requiring too great an effort, it may be abandoned in favor of a lower type of response that requires a lesser investment of energy and is more readily available in the individual's repertoire. The production of intrinsic motivation through the enlargement of the need system through habit formation leading to greater efficiency is the only way to ensure routine application of higher mental functions.

The controlled repetition and organization of activities in Instrumental Enrichment may be considered as approximating the Mediated Learning Experience provided by caregivers as they organize and change the child's environment to render the novel familiar and to establish relevance and continuity across tasks. In Piagetian terms, we may refer to this process as establishing schemata that, following assimilation of new situations, are flexible enough to become accommodated to the new characteristics of the assimilated stimuli. Thus, in Instrumental Enrichment, repetition occurs within instruments in that some of the characteristics of the initial task are preserved in order to make rediscovery of principles and operations easier for the student. Repetition also occurs across instruments, in that previously learned concepts, functions, or operations can help the learner to adapt to new and quite different tasks.

A fourth subgoal of Instrumental Enrichment is the production of insight on the part of the student and teacher as to the nature and usefulness of different cognitive processes. Through insight, learners come to understand the relationship between a specific behavior and a particular outcome. They learn to understand the nature of their cognitive functioning, the reasons for failure and success, and the processes leading to specific results. Furthermore, insight into the strategies and operations leading to an outcome will endow them with significance so that they can be subsequently singled out and applied across a range of situations other than those encountered in the specific task provided in a given instrument.

The major burden for the production of insight lies on the teacher. It is the teacher who fosters the process of reflective thinking leading to insight by appropriate questioning and by exposing the students to models of behavior. The teacher also encourages the child to look for other situations in which the activities and functions elicited by the IE tasks become meaningful. Insight is probably the most important determinant of the transfer of training. However, the attempt to foster insight does not appear frequently in other remediational training programs.

The fifth subgoal of Instrumental Enrichment is the creation of task-intrinsic motivation. That is, we have attempted to create a set of instructional exercises that students will find intrinsically interesting. This goal is derived from the well-known influence of motivation upon learning. A commonly observed phenomenon in low-functioning adolescents is the premature shrinking of their fields of interest. As a result, the activity of the retarded performer becomes oriented toward the gratification of the most specific, elementary, and immediate needs. The necessity to overcome this phenomenon and to overcome the individual's negative attitude when confronted with instructional tasks greatly influences the shaping of the tasks, the choice of items, the levels of complexity, and the modalities of presentation. The instructional activity itself has been turned into a source of gratification. The aim has been to wire into the tasks an accessibility to higher levels of mastery by sequencing them with new challenges that the learner can easily perceive while working through the pages. This goal, we must admit, is not equally attained in all the instruments. There are clear differences among instruments in the amount of task-intrinsic motivation they elicit.

The complexity of the IE tasks, which makes them difficult for both teacher and student, is also a source of task-intrinsic motivation. All too often low-functioning children and adolescents feel singled out by the watered-down programs offered especially to them. Because their acceptance of these programs would be a tacit admission of their acceptance of a negative self-image, they often display an animosity and resistance toward such programs. However, the complexity of the tasks in Instrumental Enrichment, the meaning that the adult attributes to the tasks, and the confessed difficulty of the teacher in performing these tasks is socially reinforcing. The student thinks: "If it is difficult for the teacher, then it is worthwhile for me to do." Trained IE teachers do not shy away from admitting to students their own failures on one or more of the tasks in order to point out that the tasks are not something especially designed for retarded children. Rather, this work requires a considerable investment even from adults.

The fact is that even an experienced teacher who is called upon to help students or correct their work cannot do so simply by retrieving ready-made solutions. Instead, the teacher must actually perform the tasks to arrive at a solution. This factor is responsible for a change from the usual teacher–material–student relationship to one of greater equality. The student–teacher relationship assumes a character akin to a partnership.

The sixth and final subgoal of Instrumental Enrichment is to change the deeply ingrained self-perception of the retarded performer from that of a passive recipient of information to that of an active generator of new information. Even if and when the necessary components and operations for the construction of the required information are given or available in their repertoire and all they must do is organize, combine, and operate on what they have stored, the retarded performers' frequent response is "I don't know." "I have never learned that." or "Nobody told me."

The response, "I have never learned it," reflects the mediationally deprived individual's attitude toward himself or herself as incapable of doing anything but reproducing, in a ready-made way, the information that is offered. This attitude, based on a self-perception that one is limited to being a passive recipient and reproducer of information, is typical of mediationally deprived children and greatly lowers their functioning, obscuring the real status of their cognitive structure. In our assessments with the Learning Potential Assessment Device we have many examples of instances in which, after making children aware that they can construct their own responses, we are suddenly confronted with modalities of functioning and operations whose existence was not revealed at all by the child's typical level of functioning.

In Instrumental Enrichment, each of the tasks affirms to children that they are capable of discovering and rediscovering, through inferential processes, responses that they have not previously learned or heard, but that they produced independently. Teaching children to anticipate responses, to construct, invent, and solve hypothetical situations, and making them aware of how they produced these responses will penetrate the hard wall of their passive self-perception and low-self-esteem. The limitation of the individual's functioning to what Jensen (1969) has described as Level I behavior, is considered in our framework to reflect an attitudinal approach to oneself and to the world, rather than to constitute evidence of an immutable and irreversible condition of the individual's elaborative system.

Overview of Instructional Materials and Procedures

Consistent with our theoretical analysis of the nature of retarded performance, the overall goal of Instrumental Enrichment is to enhance the capacity of the low-functioning adolescent to become modified as a result of exposure to new experiences. As the reader can see, we are not simply concerned with helping students master the tasks included in the program. In addition to their intrinsic significance and value, the tasks can be considered the means to an end. Their function is to provide an efficient vehicle for mounting a direct attack on the deficient cognitive functions and operations responsible for the individual's reduced modifiability, as well as to create habits, encourage task-intrinsic motivation, and provide opportunities for the generation of new information.

Instrumental Enrichment combines an extensive series of exercises with a set of didactic techniques. The exercises remove a burden from teachers by providing them with materials that involve retarded performers in highly motivating activities that focus directly on their cognitive deficiencies. The material presents the teacher and student with systematically ordered and intentionally scheduled opportunities for mediational interaction. However, the teacher has an active role in Instrumental Enrichment, as the success of the program is contingent upon the mediation provided by the material and teacher conjointly. The teacher must help the learner acquire the concepts, vocabulary, and operations necessary for the mastery of the tasks. Through knowledge and creativity, the teacher must produce reflective, insightful processes in the learner and encourage divergent thinking from the content-free material to other situations and areas of interest. In addition, the teacher must provide a model for behavior.

Specifically, the Instrumental Enrichment program is composed of a series of pencil and paper exercises that are offered to low-functioning adolescents one page at a time. The tasks, which take from 200 to 300 hours to complete, are clustered into 20 instruments, 15 of which are used in a 2- or 3-year program. Each instrument focuses intensively on one or more cognitive functions, while simultaneously promoting others less intensively. Two or three instruments are taught alternately within the same time period, and are selected to meet the needs of the students, as well as to provide a balance both among the kinds of functions addressed and the modalities in which the tasks are expressed.

Several considerations are taken into account in sequencing the individual instruments. One is to follow a sequence that successfully develops and consolidates the cognitive functions and operations being taught. A second is to intersperse instruments that students find less intrinsically interesting with those that arouse greater interest. In this way, a high degree of task-intrinsic motivation generated by some instruments is generalized.

The program is typically implemented in classroom settings at a rate of 3 to 5 hours per week by a specially trained teacher who is also involved in regular subject-matter instruction. Although designed for group implementation, the program may also be used on an individual prescriptive basis. Class work follows a typical sequence. The teacher's first concern in the presentation of a page from an instrument is to define with the students the nature of the task with which they are confronted. Once the objective has been clearly defined, the teacher prepares the students to deal with the tasks by helping them acquire the necessary concepts, vocabulary, and operations, by elucidating the underlying relationships and rules, and by aiding in the identification of appropriate strategies. Next, students proceed to work on the task independently. While they are working, the teacher interacts with each student on a one-to-one basis, investigating cognitive processes, discussing strategies, and interpreting to the student the meaning of his or her way of approaching the task and its effects. Successes are reinforced, frustration prevented, and failure used as a source of learning. The interpretation of the child's behavior with an appropriate affective amplification constitutes an important role for the teacher in the mediation of feelings of competency and in the development and maintenance of the learner's motivation to seek greater autonomy and readiness to cope with tasks requiring higher mental operations. The group discussion that follows independent work focuses on developing insight into the functions and strategies that were useful in mastering the tasks and the applications of the principles emerging from the exercises to a variety of school and nonschool situations.

Both in the preparation and conduct of the IE lesson, the teacher must pay the same close attention to the parameters of the Cognitive Map as the authors did in developing the instructional materials for Instrumental Enrichment (see Feuerstein, 1980). The cognitive map is a system for classifying mental acts in terms of seven parameters. These parameters offer teachers a framework for analyzing the specific difficulties students encounter in coping with different kinds of thinking and learning situations. The seven parameters that constitute the cognitive map, and that serve as dimensions for analyzing mental acts, are briefly described as follows:

1. The universe of content around which the mental act is centered. The specific content may be so unfamiliar as to be a source of difficulty, or so familiar as to be boring.

2. The modality or language in which the mental act is expressed. The modality, which may be verbal, pictorial, numerical, figural, or symbolic, may seriously affect the individual's elaborative capacity. For example, a student may be able to complete a mathematics problem successfully when it is presented in numbers and signs, and fail when the same problem is translated into a verbal modality.

3. The phase of the cognitive functions that the performance of the mental act requires. A child's inappropriate response in a task may be the result of

deficiencies in input functions, elaborative functions, or output functions, as defined in Table 1.1. For example, a child may possess the appropriate elaborative and output operations required by a task, but may produce an incorrect answer because he or she has gathered incomplete information during the input phase of working on that task.

4. The individual cognitive operations involved in performing a mental act. These operations, which may be relatively simple or complex, refer to the processes by which information, from either internal or external sources, is organized, transformed, manipulated, and acted upon to generate new information.

5. The level of complexity of the mental act. Level of complexity is determined by the number of units of information that the learner must work with and their degree of familiarity. In IE, the difficulties that ensue from complexity are dealt with by processes of familiarization and by teaching children how to analyze complex wholes into their components.

6. The level of abstraction of the mental act. This refers to the distance between a given mental act and the objects or events it entails. For example, sorting objects and finding the relationship between them on a perceptual motor level has a lower level of abstraction than does finding the relationship between relationships.

7. The level of efficiency with which the mental act is performed. Efficiency is assessed through observing the rapidity, precision, and effort involved in performing some mental act. Efficiency can be significantly affected by any of the foregoing six parameters either singly or together. However it can also be affected by a host of permanent or transient physical, affective, and motivational factors such as fatigue, anxiety, or lack of motivation. Noise, temperature, and other environmental conditions can also affect the level of efficiency. Perhaps the most important determinant of efficiency is the degree to which the act is consolidated and crystallized.

The importance of the cognitive map in the construction and implementation of IE should be obvious. It is equally important to the teacher who, by its use, can anticipate difficulties and devise strategies to bypass or eliminate expected problems. The teacher can skillfully manipulate the parameters of the cognitive map to analyze and interpret a learner's performance and to plan the most effective and appropriate strategies for correcting deficiencies in performance when they are detected.

Description of Instruments

The various instruments that constitute the Instrumental Enrichment program are briefly described in the following sections. Except in a few instances, space limitations preclude illustrations of individual tasks taken from these instruments. A more comprehensive description of the instruments, along with examples of individual tasks, is available in Feuerstein, 1980. Additional task illustrations also appear in the Bransford, Arbitman-Smith, Stein, and Vye chapter in this volume.

Each instrument may be characterized by what we term its "molecular" and "molar" components. The molecular components of an instrument are the deficient cognitive functions being addressed by that instrument. These are intimately linked to the theory of cognitive modifiability. The molar components of an instruments are the kinds of tasks that are used as vehicles for strengthening these deficient functions. As noted earlier, each instrument focuses intensively on a small number of deficient functions while attacking others in a less intensive way. This means that functions that are established by one instrument are often further reinforced and consolidated by other instruments. In the discussion of instruments that follows, space limitations preclude mention of all the cognitive functions that each instrument attempts to strengthen. Thus we limit our description of individual instruments to a brief overview of the kinds of tasks that are involved and the functions that receive primary emphasis through use of those tasks.

Organization of Dots.   Organization of Dots is usually selected as the first instrument in the IE program for two reasons. The first is that its tasks are remote from those encountered in school subjects and, therefore, not accompanied by the negative affect of failure. The second is that a great number of the different components of the mental act can be remediated or established through its tasks. These components are parts of cognitive processes that appear in other instruments, and their treatment in Organization of Dots facilitates later work.

The molar aspect of the tasks is to organize an amorphous array of dots by projecting into them an order imposed by a given set of model figures. That is, the student must discover the relationships and rules of the structure underlying each model figure, project this structure onto an initially unorganized array of dots, and connect the dots one to another in accordance with the discovered rules and relationships.

Many cognitive functions are involved in the successful completion of the task. There must be a clear perception of the characteristics of the model figures and their labeling. Then a strategy for systematic search, other than trial and error, must be sought as part of a more general planning behavior. Relevant cues must either be recognized or constructed to aid in projecting the necessary relationships between the dots. A completed figure must be compared to the model to check its accuracy. Impulsivity must be restrained throughout the activity.

Among the thinking operations elicited by the tasks of Organization of Dots are the breaking down of a complex field into its parts, especially when the figures overlap; the representation of the figure, especially if it is asymmetrical, or if there is a change in its orientation; and thinking hypothetically and logically. Organization of Dots tasks become increasingly difficult and complex as students progress through the instrument in that the model figures become more irregular and unfamiliar, dots closer together, and figures more overlapping.

What transcends the molar task is the student's awareness that it is the individual who imposes order and structure on a universe whose objects and events are not organized. A person does so on the basis of internalized rules and relationships that he or she projects.

Instruments for Teaching Relational Thinking and Representation.   A major characteristic of retarded performers is their episodic grasp of reality. In other words, as mentioned earlier, they perceive objects and events as being discrete, isolated, and singular, rather than as being related to one another. The inability of the retarded performer to perceive and project relationships is a stumbling block to such forms of learning as trial and error, discovery, and induction. Instrumental Enrichment contains a number of instruments specifically designed to correct this deficiency. Prominent among them are Orientation in Space, Temporal Relations, Family Relations, and Numerical Progressions.

There are two Orientation in Space instruments, both of which attempt to develop in students a stable system of reference for describing spatial relationships. Orientation in Space I introduces the child to a personal, relative system of reference. Children learn that one's perception of an object or event depends on one's vantage point and that the relationship between pairs of objects and/or events shifts with the change in the position of one or both parties to the relationship. The necessity for "putting oneself into the shoes of the other" gains in meaning and transcendence with the understanding and even tolerance for the ideas and attitudes of another that stem from different perspectives. In this way, an effort is made to reduce the egocentricity of the retarded performer.

Orientation in Space II deals with an objective universal system of reference involving the use of compass points and coordinates. In both instruments, the emphasis is on representation, that is, on the ability to re-present stimuli that are not present in the perceptual field and to act upon them as if they were.

Both Organization of Dots and Orientation in Space illustrate the reinforced and creative repetition of Instrumental Enrichment. The same principle appears throughout the entire instrument, but each presentation is altered either in modality, content, or activity to supply the specific practice necessary for mastery and the automatization of the involved functions, while preventing the boredom that usually accompanies numerous repetitions of the same material. Motivation is also maintained through novelty, which requires the constant rediscovery and application of the learned principles and techniques.

It is impossible to define an object or event without reference to either its spatial or temporal attributes. The temporal field of the mediationally deprived adolescent in basically quite narrow and centered in the present, with a limited orientation toward the recent past and an anticipation that reaches only into the near future. The instrument, Temporal Relations, provides concepts and systems

The student must perceive the dots in an amorphous, irregular cloud so as to project figures identical in form and size to those in the given models. The task becomes more complicated by density of the dots, overlapping, increasing complexity of the figures and changes in their orientation. Successful completion demands segregation and articulation of the field:

Among the cognitive functions involved are:

Projection of virtual relationships

Discrimination of form and size

Constancy of form and size across changes in orientation

Use of relevant information

Discovery of strategies

Perspective

Restraint of impulsivity

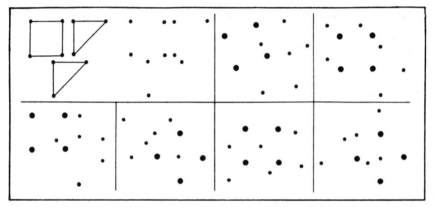

The thickened dots aid in projecting the square, but also serve as a distractor and prevent the perception of similarities between frames. In addition to the functions and operations already listed, the tasks involve labeling, precision and accuracy, planning, determination of starting point, systematic search and comparison to model. Successful completion aids in creation and maintenance of motivation.

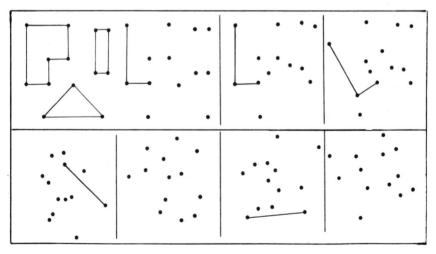

An asymmetric figure in the model necessitates representational re-orientation in space. The provided cues are reduced until extinction so that an alternate starting point must be found. Scientific thought: hypothesis, investigation and confirmation, as well as logical evidence, are necessary.

FIG. 1.2.   Examples from Organization of Dots (*to be continued*).

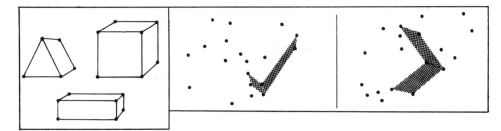

Addition of the third dimension complicates differentiation, internalization and spatial orientation. A dot, instead of connecting only two lines, serves as a nexus of three or more lines. The shaded cue is a synthesized whole, formed from parts separate in the model and each cue is relevant to a different form in the model.

FIG. 1.2.   Examples from Organization of Dots (*continued*).

of reference by which students can come to understand time both as a fixed interval and as a dimension. From the initial concept of time as a measurable, stable interval, the focus is expanded to include the relativity of future, past, and present, and the unidirectional, irreversible flow from one tense to another. The relative quality of time as a fixed interval is demonstrated in tasks that deal with the subjective perception and/or definition of objective time periods, as is evidenced in expressions like "the year I had the measles." Students are introduced to time as a dimension with such concepts as "early" and "late," "before" and "after," and "fast" and "slow." Finally, events that are asynchronous and synchronous are explored in order to determine cause and effect, means and ends, or purely accidental relationships.

In Temporal Relations, and throughout the IE program, the exploration of alternatives and divergent thinking is encouraged. The choice of a response is the product of reflection and is contingent upon external or specifiable criteria. The emphasis is upon the "why" and "how" of an answer. The learner is encouraged to evaluate the given data to decide whether they are sufficient to answer a question. Thereby, he or she learns that there are instances in which "I don't know" is not shameful but means "It is impossible to know" and is the most appropriate answer, and should lead to a quest for the additional information needed.

Family Relations is a good illustration of the relationship between the molecular and the molar aspects in Instrumental Enrichment. In this instrument kinship is used as the vehicle by which students are taught symmetrical, asymmetrical, and hierarchical relationships. The conservation of identity over transformations is presented through the multiplicity of roles family members can assume—for example, that an individual can simultaneously be a daughter, wife, mother, grandmother, aunt, niece, granddaughter, and sister-in-law. The ability to categorize and recategorize according to different principles is taught in the differentiation between status and role in the family. The union of two families through

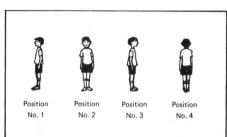

IV. Fill in what is missing

Position	Object	Direction in Relation to the Boy
1	The tree	
4		right
2		back
	The house	front
3	The bench	
2	The house	
	The tree	left
4		back
	The bench	
		left
3		back
4	The tree	
		right

FIG.1.3.   Orientation in Space I.

marriage and the addition of new generations illustrate the relative aspects of relationships in which a role is determined by its referent, and their temporal and spatial qualities.

In this instrument, there is a necessity to encode and decode, to use symbols and signs, to refer to several sources of information, to seek cues, and to define strategies and methods of evaluation. While reinforcing concepts and techniques learned in previous instruments, Family Relations also paves the way for more advanced logicoverbal instruments.

Numerical Progressions deals with the stable relationships that exist between seemingly unconnected events that can be discovered and then translated into rules for use in anticipating and predicting future events. Students are taught to search systematically for organizing rules and principles by comparing items in a series and recognizing the changes that occur from one item to the next. This instrument thus attacks the low performer's typical episodic grasp of reality, compelling him or her to seek laws and stable superordinate relationships even in instances that seem to have no connection. It also has been found helpful in reorienting the retarded performer's self-perception from a passive recipient to an active generator of information. Once retarded performers learn that they are able to predict future events and construct new situations through generating rules based on past observations, they experience a feeling of true mastery.

Analytic Perception is designed to correct the blurred, sweeping, global perception of the mediationally deprived individual that results in incomplete and imprecise information. Geometric figures were chosen as the molar content of this instrument because of the retarded performer's familiarity with them and their convenience in establishing the cognitive operations being emphasized. In Analytic Perception, the student learns that any whole may be divided into parts through structural or operational analysis, that every part is a whole, that there is a relationship between these parts and that there is the possibility of forming new wholes by a recombination of the parts. Finally, students learn that the analysis of a whole into parts is arbitrary and depends on external criteria, and that the entire process is reversible. A variety of cognitive operations are involved in the successful solution of these tasks, including: identification, differentiation, discrimination, categorization, representation, hypothetical thinking, and logical reasoning.

Mediationally deprived individuals are able to compare, but their comparative behavior is elicited only in response to a limited set of needs. Rarely do they compare spontaneously. In the absence of comparative behavior, many details, features, and attributes of an object may be neglected. Without comparison, each experienced stimulus remains isolated and discrete. The instrument, Comparisons, induces an awareness of the importance and meaning of comparative behavior, establishes the prerequisites for comparisons, and contains exercises that provide specific practice in the techniques of comparing. Comparative behavior requires a clear and stable perception of the items being compared, the conservation of constancies and invariants across transformations, thorough and systematic exploration, and a receptive and expressive repertoire of concepts and labels for use in making comparisons. The tasks teach the student to compare two objects or events along the same continuum, using the same dimensions. Similarities and differences are processed at the same time rather than sequentially. Students are taught to find the most relevant and meaningful dimensions for use in making comparisons, and to ignore others.

The instrument, Categorization, is based on the skills and processes learned in Comparisons and leads to more complex logicoverbal instruments. This instrument focuses on the mediationally deprived individual's difficulties in the elaboration and organization of data into superordinate categories. Successful completion of the tasks requires analytic perception, comparison, the simultaneous use of several sources of information, the projection of relationships, and the use of verbal labels on a receptive and expressive level. Among the required cognitive operations are the articulation of the field and flexible divergent thinking.

Exercises in the instrument progress from the concept of set membership to the concepts of subsets. Tasks require the identification of set members and the assignment of the same objects to different categories on the basis of different principles of classification. The student learns the difference between sorting and categorizing, between a relationship established by an association and one that is based on grouping according to underlying principles. The instrument provides the student with the insight that it is he or she who is the primary determinant in the organization of stimuli.

The instrument, Instructions, emphasizes the process of decoding verbal instructions and translating them into a motoric act, and encoding perceptions and acts into a verbal modality. The instrument's tasks require planning behavior and counteract impulsive responses, while reinforcing previously acquired functions, strategies, and skills. Using a verbal and figural modality, Instructions are given both directly and indirectly, explicitly and implicitly. The students must infer and rely on partial cues that must be combined in order to clarify ambiguities and make decisions. The reduction of egocentricity, the restraint of impulsivity, and a readiness to defer action until the relevant information has been gathered and elaborated are encouraged throughout the instrument.

Advanced Instruments.   Several other instruments constitute a more advanced level of Instrumental Enrichment. They include Transitive Relations, Syllogisms, and Representational Stencil Design.

Transitive Relations is a logicoverbal instrument that explores the differences existing between members of ordered sets that can be described in terms of larger than, equal to, and smaller than. It focuses on the inferences that can be made from known relationships between two or more elements and the conclusions that can be drawn from those with reference to relationships among other elements. Equally important, however, the rules governing transitive thinking are presented to permit the student to ascertain when transitive thinking is appropriate for the solution of a problem.

The instrument, Syllogisms, is based on the commonality between set members. Like Transitive Relations, this instrument is highly sophisticated and deals in formal logic. An effort has been made to make the logical operations as

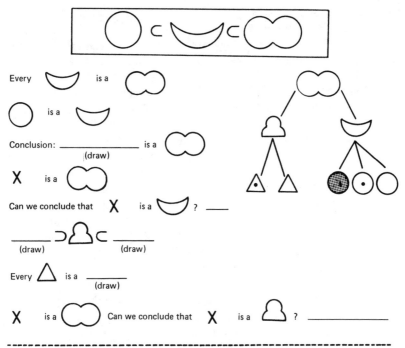

Conclusion: _____ is a (draw)

Can we conclude that **X** is a ◡ ? ___

Every △ is a _____ (draw)

X is a ◯◯ Can we conclude that **X** is a ⌂ ? _____

- -

Each one of the above shapes represents a set. Every set has a name.
The names of the sets are: salt, spices, food, ice-cream, dessert, cake.
Fill in the name of the set.

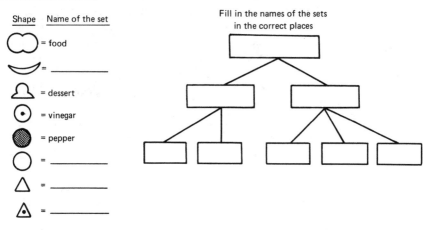

FIG. 1.4. Syllogisms. Logico-verbal reasoning becomes highly abstract. Meaning is based on the rules which have been acquired regarding members of sets and subsets. The task involves encoding and decoding, the use of signs, finding relationships, discovering the principles upon which categories have been formed, choosing and processing relevant data and thinking logically.

73

abstract as possible by using symbols and signs in place of words. Drawing on a host of cognitive functions and operations already addressed in previous instruments, Syllogisms seeks to produce in the learner an intrinsically oriented, compelling need for deductive and inductive reasoning, inferential thinking, and logical proof.

In Representational Stencil Design, which is adapted from Arthur's Stencil Design Test (1930), the student completes a complex sequence of steps involving a purely representational reconstruction of a model figure. Our instrument differs from Arthur's test both in its demand for solving the tasks representationally and in the complexity of the model designs that are offered. The model design in each task results from the superimposition of separate stencils, which vary in color and in the size and shape of the figures cut out of them. The task consists of a mental reconstruction of the design by choosing the appropriate stencils from among those printed on a poster, and specifying the order in which each must be superimposed on the other. To accomplish the task, the student must first analyze the complex design and identify its various components, the shapes of which are transformed in the course of superimposition. A cumulative representation of the transformations must be maintained while anticipating the changes that must still be produced in order to complete the design.

Although Representational Stencil Design calls upon all the cognitive processes, it places particular emphasis on the elaborational level due to the exceptionally high demand for such cognitive functions and operations as comparison, differentiation, segregation, transformation, and internal representation. The accessibility of this type of task to the retarded performer often comes as a total surprise to the teacher whose training in special education emphasizes the concrete. In particular, the demand upon the student for purely internal representation, without any motor manipulation, is often met with disbelief. Yet, it has long been our contention that motor manipulation and trial-and-error behavior may impede rather than assist a retarded performer because they interfere with the use of cognitive functions that, although in need of strengthening, frequently are available to such individuals.

Although the emphasis in Instrumental Enrichment is on cognitive development, there is a concern with the affective and nonintellective factors as well, especially insofar as these reinforce cognitive aspects of behavior. This concern is reflected in the construction of the instruments, the order in which they are implemented, and the didactics of the program. In addition, one instrument, Illustrations, deals with the interaction between the cognitive, affective, and motivational components of behavior.

The instrument consists of a number of situations presented pictorially that are designed to lead to a disruption of equilibrium and the student's subsequent search for an explanation and solution. Awareness of the existence of a problem, gained through a sharp perception of details, comparative behavior, and a search for the transformations that occur from one frame to another are among the functions and operations involved in this instrument. Pages depict absurd or humorous situations, as well as those in which there is a strong link between objective reality and its subjective perception. Through use of nonthreatening situations, it is possible for the teacher to address sensitive affective and motivational problems.

Instruments Currently Undergoing Development and Testing.   A number of additional instruments, such as Illusions, Organizer, and Divergent Thinking, have been completed and are being field tested with a variety of populations differing in their levels of functioning and the nature of their deficiencies. Still other instruments, such as Humor and Absurdities, and an instrument for language development and use are in various stages of development.

Illusions centers on the cognitive processes involved in perception—that is, how the configuration, the perceptual field, and our experiential background affect the way we perceive the world. This instrument is a powerful means for producing insight, reflective thinking, and hypothesis testing in a way that leads to an enhanced cognitive articulation of the inner self.

The Organizer is a very sophisticated instrument in which given information must be synthesized in order to extrapolate relationships. The tasks require that items or events be organized spatially and temporally in relation to one another on the basis of integration, inference, and hypothesis testing. The learner cannot rely on only one source of information, no matter how complex it may be, but must compare and join several propositions in order to reach a conclusion. The operations involved include inferential thinking, representation, and inductive and deductive reasoning. In its requirements for a given sequence and order of relationships, the Organizer is an example of an instrument that leads to convergent thinking.

Basis for the Content-Free Nature of Instrumental Enrichment

As we mentioned earlier, and as the reader can judge from our brief overview of instruments, the Instrumental Enrichment exercises are basically and relatively content free. That is, children are asked to work with concepts that can be understood without a great deal of specialized background knowledge characteristic of most school situations. The relatively content-free nature of the materials has given rise to numerous questions pertaining to the efficiency of such an approach for preparing the learner for real-life situations and, more specifically, for academic activities. The decision to produce a relatively content-free program, in which the content is primarily a carrier of the program's goals rather than a goal in itself, is derived from the theory of Mediated Learning Experience.

As noted earlier, our theoretical position holds that Mediated Learning Experience is the proximal determinant of differential cognitive development. Consistent with this position, we have modeled the Instrumental Enrichment program on the Mediated Learning Experience. Earlier, we described the nine major characteristics of Mediated Learning Experience as intentionality, transcendence, meaning, mediation of feelings of competency, mediation for the regulation of behavior, mediation of goal seeking, goal setting, and goal achieving behavior, and the mediation of challenge: the search for novelty and complexity. The use of relatively content-free materials helps us design learning experiences that possess these characteristics. That is, the choice of relatively content-free material forces the activity that emerges from interaction between learner, teacher, and material to transcend the specific content that initiates these interactions. The meaning of these learning experiences is engendered by the Instrumental Enrichment teacher who fosters insight and helps students generalize from the content-free exercises to academic, vocational, and other areas of experience. The involvement of increasingly more complex and remote areas of content and of higher mental processes is determined by the intentionality of the teacher–mediator and learner working together.

Our decision to produce a relatively content-free program, modeled upon the Mediated Learning Experience, is supported by noting the number of resistances associated with the use of academic content matter in teaching formal modalities of thinking. The first source of resistance, whenever there is an attempt to derive more generalizeable propositions from school subject-matter content, is the child. Children's resistance is even stronger whenever a specific content, such as a story, is used in order to equip the learner with some specific prerequisites of thinking. Children, especially retarded performers, are opposed to any interruption in the flow of a series of events. They resist efforts to make them stop and deal with specific content for purposes of elaborating, organizing, framing, or relating it to information previously acquired. Many children, especially those who are targets for our intervention, tend to be "materialistic." They measure learning by the quantity of material covered. Stopping to explore a sentence in depth every few minutes leaves them with little to show for what they have accomplished during a whole class period. The children's propensity to act may also frustrate attempts to make them reflect upon the content matter they have completed. For these reasons, the typical content of the school curriculum is an inadequate medium for encouraging elaborational activity unless the learner has been especially prepared by an intensive exposure to materials or experiences in which the formal aspects of thinking have been developed and shaped.

A second source of resistance associated with attempts to use the content of the school curriculum for teaching the prerequisites of thinking comes from the academic disciplines themselves. As indicated by the subgoals of Instrumental Enrichment, IE materials must be carefully shaped to meet a specific set of conditions necessary for attaining structural cognitive change. Academic knowledge domains, such as literature, mathematics, and social studies, to name but a few, cannot be meaningfully responsive to such needs as the correction of deficient functions, the production of intrinsic motivation through habit forma-tion, or the production of insight. Any attempt to reshape the content of the school curriculum to make it responsive to these needs will, of necessity, be harmful to the subject matter involved, which has its own pace, rhythm, structure, and internal consistency. We believe, therefore, that it is more advisable to develop the prerequisites of learning in a specially designed intervention program and "wire into" this program all the components necessary for bridging to other constantly expanding areas of interest and concern.

The third source of resistance associated with the use of school subject-matter content for the development of cognitive processes has to do with the teacher. Thirty years ago, one of the authors (Feuerstein & Richelle, 1957) naively believed that all that teachers needed to offer instruction in thinking and learning was a set of model exercises or ideas to serve as a paradigm that they could then superimpose upon their regular instructional materials. It was only after the author decided to offer teachers the highly structured materials of the IE program that he understood how erroneous his earlier belief had been. All too often teachers lack training in necessary and explicit modalities of reasoning; this may not impair their own thinking, but may doom their attempts to teach children, espe-cially the mediationally deprived, more appropriate modalities of cognitive func-tioning. Moreover, even when teachers are skilled in explicit modalities of cognitive functioning, they often encounter difficulties in using their knowledge to shape the content of the school curriculum to the specific needs of the child. However, when teachers are equipped with a set of structured materials that transcend any specific content and are organized and shaped to provide mediation, they can use all their creativity for producing divergent examples, or even addi-tional exercises. More important, equipped with these materials, they may be able to help children gain insight into the more general meaning and significance of their work.

A fourth and final resistance that is all too often produced when school subject-matter content is used in remediational programs derives from the familiar phe-nomenon of children's avoidance of content involving previous failure experi-ences. For retarded performers, many academic areas, such as reading and other basic skills, are associated with failure experiences. Any attempt to make the child use areas of previous failure as a point of departure for learning more elaborate, operational, and formal types of thinking will confront the overloaded negative meaning these subject matter areas have come to represent. On the other hand, if the subject matter is too familiar or too easy, it will quickly become boring and, again, not a source of motivation and meaningful activity. The use of relatively content-free materials avoids many of the pitfalls in the motivational structure of the low-functioning child and adolescent. Because there are no significant differences among students in their previous exposure to content-free materials, use of such materials may create a more equitable relationship between low-functioning students and their more advanced classmates, and perhaps even between the students and the teacher.

The reader will recall that the Mediated Learning Experience is not dependent on any specific content nor on any specific language or modality of presentation. However, Instrumental Enrichment attempts to avoid the use of any modalities that could make the program inaccessible to retarded performers. Specifically, the program avoids excessive use of the verbal modality due to the poor command of language of some retarded performers. When language is needed, it is used very carefully in order to make successful performance in Instrumental Enrichment independent of the individual's level of language competence. The instruments typically used at the outset of the program, Organization of Dots and Analytic Perception, are both accessible to illiterates. Several of the other instruments also require a minimum of verbal skills. However, in all the instruments and activities associated with them, there is an important underlying language system.

DIVERGENT EFFECTS OF INSTRUMENTAL ENRICHMENT

One of the major hypotheses underlying the Instrumental Enrichment program is that a direct attack on the deficient cognitive functions responsible for low performance will modify individuals by creating in them an increased capacity to use their life experiences for learning. If this theoretical framework is valid and IE proves to be an efficient substitute for missing or inadequate mediated learning experiences, then individuals who participate in IE should show an increased capacity over time to activate assimilation and accommodation processes, resulting in the widening of operational schemata. The expected changes after exposure to Instrumental Enrichment should be cumulative. That is, a divergent pattern of growth should be observed between the individuals who participate in IE and control subjects, with IE students continuing to become increasingly different from controls long after they have completed the program. Such cumulative changes would be expected if the program is able to provide individuals with the requisite cognitive tools that permit and encourage a continuous process of development. It is obvious that short-term effects can be more easily achieved with activities focusing more directly on narrowly restricted content domains, rather than with the more content-free Instrumental Enrichment tasks.

Consistent with this divergent effects hypothesis, we have attempted in our assessment of Instrumental Enrichment to determine whether observed changes would perpetuate themselves over time, or whether we would find the more static, stable, or even declining pattern of effects often observed with other intervention programs. In our initial evaluation of Instrumental Enrichment (Feuerstein, 1980), results obtained immediately following a 2-year period of intervention indicated that IE produces fairly substantial gains in performance on a variety of intellectual tasks. We briefly summarize these results in the following paragraphs and then discuss our attempts to follow the students involved in this research 2 years after their participation in Instrumental Enrichment.

In brief, this study was conducted in four settings, two of which were residential centers and two of which were day schools, geared mainly toward providing basic academic skills and vocational training. In each of the settings, one site was designated as an experimental site using Instrumental Enrichment, and one was designated as a control site using a program called General Enrichment (GE). Both Instrumental Enrichment and General Enrichment were integral parts of the regular school curriculum.

Pre–post comparisons indicated that the IE group was superior to the GE group on a great variety of measures assessing cognitive ability, academic ability, and interpersonal behavior.

1. Although there were no significant differences between the IE and GE groups on the preintervention administration of Thurstone's Primary Mental Abilities Test (PMA), significant differences were found at the end of the experiment in favor of the IE group in comparisons that used PMA pretest scores as covariates. Significant differences between groups were found both on composite PMA posttest scores and on scores on four of the PMA subtests.

2. Despite the fact that the GE group had approximately 300 more hours of instruction in academic subject matter areas than the IE group, in no case was the IE group inferior to the GE group on achievement performance. On the contrary, on some of the achievement tests, the IE group performed significantly better than the GE group.

3. As to interactional variables, as measured by the Classroom Participation Scale 2 (Tannenbaum–Levine), significant positive results in favor of the IE groups were found on three factors: interpersonal conduct, self-sufficiency, and adaptiveness to work demands.

In addition to these pre–post comparisons, several other tests were administered on a posttest-only basis to assess further differences between the two groups. On the D–48, the Kuhlmann–Finch Postures Test, and the Lahy Precision–Rapidity Test, and on a variety of measures pertaining to global versus analytic cognitive style, the IE group was significantly superior to the GE group.

To investigate our divergent effects hypothesis, we conducted a follow-up study on this same population approximately 2 years later. At this time, students in both the original experimental and control groups had been drafted into the army and subjected to army intelligence tests. We compared the two groups in terms of their scores on these tests, using earlier PMA pretest scores as covariates. This comparison yielded a highly significant difference between IE ($M = 52.52$) and GE ($M = 45.28$) groups ($F = 28.8$, $p < .001$), which indicated that the gains achieved by the IE groups on the posttests immediately following the intervention continued to be maintained even after a 2-year period without any additional intervention. When the population was divided into high and low performers on the basis of pretest and follow-up scores, four categories resulted: (1) low pretest performers, low follow-up performers; (2) low pretest performers, high follow-up performers; (3) high pretest performers, low follow-up performers; and (4) high pretest performers, high follow-up performers (see Fig. 1.5). Analysis of the differences yielded by partitioning procedures using chi-square analysis within and between IE and GE groups showed significant differences between IE and GE groups with respect to their overall performance on the army intelligence test ($X = 8.67$, $df = 1$, $p < .005$). Further analysis indicted that 87% of the GE group, as opposed to 54% of the IE group who were low on the pretest remained low on the follow-up test; whereas 88% of the IE, as opposed to 53% of the GE subjects who were initially high on the pretest remained high on the follow-up test. 46% of the IE, as opposed to 13% of the GE subjects who were low on the pretest, subsequently scored high on the follow-up test, whereas only 12% of the IE, as opposed to 47% of the GE subjects who scored high on the pretest were low scorers on the follow-up test.

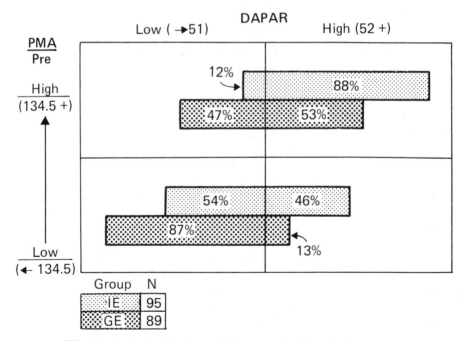

FIG. 1.5.   Instrumental Enrichment: Follow-up study. Percentages in categories of PMA-Pre and Dapar-Post (High vs. Low); ($N = 184$).

These results indicated that exposure to Instrumental Enrichment tends to produce proportionately nearly four times as much change from an initial low to a subsequent high level of performance, whereas in the absence of such intervention the long-term effect is a tendency for retarded performers who scored high on initial tests to regress. The findings rule out the possibility that gains achieved by the experimental students were due to the special residential care programs in which some of the students were participating. Despite their less optimal living environment, the day school students receiving IE performed as well as, and in some respects even better than students receiving IE as part of a total care residential program. When a trend analysis was performed on the differences between IE and GE groups, using Z standard scores, relating to measures taken on the PMA at the pre-, mid-, and posttesting, and on the Dapar Army intelligence test, we found that the actual results approximated a linear progressive curve, and were statistically different from the quadratic curve expected when gains fade away in time.

The follow-up study and its findings provide an initial, yet eloquent confirmation of the structural nature of the changes produced in low-functioning individuals through the mediated learning experience provided by Instrumental Enrichment. They offer preliminary but compelling evidence for the presence

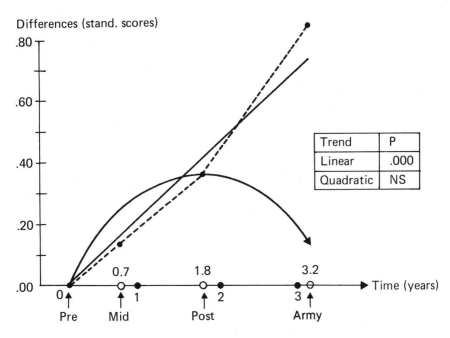

FIG. 1.6. Instrumental Enrichment: Follow-up study. Differences between IE and GE groups on PMA and Dapar mean standard scores at Pre, Post, and Follow-up stages, vs. linear and quadratic models; (N = 163).

of the three main characteristics of structural cognitive modifiability: the whole–part relationship in which, by help of MLE, students learn to integrate discrete experiences into a meaningful whole as their experiential field organizes itself; the occurrence of transformations in cognitive functioning as a result of variations in stimuli and experiences over space and time; and finally, the perpetuation of an initiated change that requires time to unfold.

ACKNOWLEDGMENTS

This chapter was written during Professor Feuerstein's sabbatical at Yale University, 1980–1981. The authors would like to acknowledge with gratitude the support of The Ford Foundation, The Bush Center, and the Psychology Department, Yale University. The authors would like to acknowledge also their gratitude to Marjorie Martus, Program Officer, The Ford Foundation, and to Miriel Small, President, Hadassah–WIZO Organization of Canada.

REFERENCES

Arthur, G. A. *A point scale of performance tests: Clinical manual* (Vol. I). New York: Commonwealth Fund, 1930.

Feuerstein, R. *The dynamic assessment of retarded performers. The Learning Potential Assessment Device, theory, instruments, and techniques.* Baltimore: University Park Press, 1979.

Feuerstein, R. *Instrumental Enrichment: An intervention program for cognitive modifiability.* Baltimore: University Park Press, 1980.

Feuerstein, R., & Richelle, M. *North African Jewish children.* Tel Aviv: Youth Aliyah, 1957.

Jensen, A. How much can we boost IQ and scholastic achievement? *Harvard Educational Review,* 1969, *39,* 1–123.

2 Thinking Skills Fostered by Philosophy for Children

Matthew Lipman
Montclair State College

"Thinking skills" is a catchall phrase. It ranges from very specific to very general abilities, from proficiency in logical reasoning to the witty perception of remote resemblances, from the capacity to decompose a whole into parts to the capacity to assemble random words or things to make them well-fitting parts of a whole, from the ability to explain how a situation may have come about to the ability to foretell how a process will likely eventuate, from a proficiency in discerning uniformities and similarities to a proficiency in noting dissimilarities and uniquenesses, from a facility in justifying beliefs through persuasive reasons to a facility in generating ideas and developing concepts, from the power of discovering alternative possibilities to the power of inventing systematic but imaginary universes, from the capacity to solve problems to the capacity to circumvent them or forestall their emergence, from the ability to evaluate to the ability to reenact—the list is endless, because it consists of nothing less than an inventory of the intellectual powers of mankind. Insofar as each intelligent human activity is different, it involves a different assemblage of thinking skills—differently sequenced, synchronized, and orchestrated.

To dream of constructing a curriculum that would nurture and sharpen such an array of skills must certainly be considered quixotic; to have an impact on no more than a token selection of such skills is something we may aspire to without realistically hoping ever to achieve. On the other hand, education is at an impasse, and only the improvement of thinking skills holds out the promise of lifting the whole of education, and not merely this or that aspect of it, to a new level of excellence. Should this contention be correct, then the problem would be to identify and utilize the most promising of the thinking-skill approaches. If we choose not to move in this direction, quixotic though it may appear to be, what promising educational alternatives beckon to us and invite us to apply our energies to their exploration?

Yet we may choose to foster thinking skills simply because we despair that we lack realistic alternatives, and there is thus the danger that we may rush impetuously to embrace something far more complex and mysterious than we had anticipated. Out of ignorance, we may resort to simplistic solutions. We might, for example, simply insist that all children now study formal logic. Or we might draw up a list of our favorite thinking skills (such as classification, generalization, and hypothesis formation) and insist that children perform various exercises to improve such skills. But there is an enormous difference between drilling children until they improve their performances on specific skills—such improvement being merely superficial and transient—and involving children in an educational process in which a wide spectrum of thinking skills is sharpened.

In the pages that follow, we describe the Philosophy for Children Program—a program that is attempting to sharpen a wide spectrum of thinking skills in a manner we think is producing educationally significant results. We begin this chapter with an overview of some of the basic ideas and assumptions that we think should characterize an effective program of instruction in thinking skills. Next, we describe the kinds of thinking skills in which we offer instruction. Our program presently consists of materials for students in grades K to 12. In this chapter, we describe the kinds of skills that are emphasized at the middle school level (Grades 4 to 8). We list several specific skills and describe some of the more general cognitive dispositions that we want students to learn. Having thus given the reader some insight into the skills and attitudes our program attempts to foster, we briefly describe some of its major pedagogical features. Finally, we review the evaluation data on the program.

BASIC IDEAS AND ASSUMPTIONS UNDERLYING EFFECTIVE INSTRUCTION IN THINKING SKILLS

As already noted, our broad goal is to help children discover their intellectual capabilities. But here we must be extremely careful, for when we isolate and test the individual child, we have by that very isolation introduced an arbitrary variable into the situation. What if, as Vygotsky (1962) and Cole, John-Steiner, Scribner, and Souberman (1978, pp. 68–70) have shown, children are capable of functioning intellectually at a higher level when in collaborative or cooperative situations than when they are compelled to work individually? What if the enlisting of children's social impulses were to result in improved cognitive performance—would we still try to measure cognitive abilities solely through tasks that required, for their performance, the dismemberment of the classroom community?

Thus, we could do worse than to begin our attempts at instruction in thinking skills with the objective of converting the classroom into a community, if communality does indeed have a wholesome and positive effect upon cognitive proficiency. But what kind of community? Obviously it would involve shared experience, but beyond that, it would necessarily involve a common commitment to a method of inquiry. But what is that method? Surely it must be the collection of rational procedures through which individuals can identify where they may have gone wrong in their thinking; in short, it is the method of systematic self-correction. And such a classroom—one that had been converted into a community of inquiry—would find disrespect for persons repugnant. For the community would draw on the experience of each and make the resultant meanings available to all.

Now, it would be totally futile to expound such an objective to children themselves. Even if they could understand it in outline, they would hardly grasp its relevance to themselves. Somehow, they would have to be encouraged to hope that the ideal they had glimpsed might be feasible for those who, like themselves, were still young and inexperienced. This is where we must call upon their imaginative powers and have recourse to the magic of fiction. For instead of wearying them with an explanation of the merits of inquiry in the classroom, we can *show* them, in fictional form, a classroom community of inquiry, composed of children much like ordinary, live children, but thinking about matters of grave importance to children: matters like truth and friendship, personal identity and fairness, goodness and freedom. These fictional youngsters also spend a considerable portion of their time thinking about thinking, and about the criteria for distinguishing sound from unsound reasoning.

As the novels unfold, the characters in them are shown using the very thinking skills that one would hope the live children in the classroom through a process of identification would likewise utilize. Perhaps "identification" does not suitably convey what occurs, for in fact, the students in the classroom tend to reenact the intellectual processes of their young heroes and heroines, much as, in reading romantic fiction, they go through, live again, reenact the emotional processes of their heroes and heroines. This occurs not merely in the private recollections of each reader, but, more importantly, in the classroom discussions that follow the role playing or script reading of each episode in the novel. Children are quick to note that the fictional persons have their own styles of thinking, just as they have their own temperaments and moral characters. Some are quick to take intellectual risks; others are less venturesome. Some are analytical, others are experimental. Some are empirical, some are speculative. The variety of thinking styles is not provided merely for dramatic purposes. Children must be encouraged to express themselves with style, as well as efficiently, and they must also be encouraged to think with style, as well as efficiently. Indeed, we can hardly expect children's thinking to be well expressed, unless it is well reasoned, nor sensitively and gracefully expressed, unless it is sensitively and gracefully reasoned. There is no precise way of separating the thinking that goes into writing—to take one form of expression—from the writing itself.

In the Philosophy for Children program, the sharpening of thinking skills does not take place exclusively in classroom discussions, but it is there that the exercise and strengthening of such skills is most evident. Some children like to read, some like to write, but almost all love to talk. The problem is to transform the energy of this impulse into cognitive skill, much as the transmission system of an automobile transforms the raw power of the engine into the disciplined and directed movement of the wheels. Mere talking must be converted into conversation, discussion, dialogue. This means learning to listen to others, as well as to respond effectively. It means learning to follow the various lines of reasoning taking place as the discussion proceeds: sizing up the assumptions that underlie each utterance, drawing inferences, testing for consistency and comprehensiveness, learning to think independently by freely choosing one's own premises. At any given moment in a conversation, each participant is engaging in countless mental acts, some in harmony with others, some quite independent of others, some convergent, others divergent. It is the task of the regimen of logic to discipline the dialogue. This is accomplished by enabling the participants to utilize the rules of logic as criteria of legitimate inference—in effect, as criteria for distinguishing between good and poor thinking.

But logic can do no more than impart a *formal* character to the dialogue. Unless children find something worthwhile to talk *about,* they will jabber about trivia, or lapse into silence and apathy. We need to show them how they can go beyond the mere exchanging of reports of their feelings and opinions to learning and discussing their ideas—ideas that many of them consider most precious because these are their most personal possessions, with which they most closely identify themselves.

That children should prefer primarily to discuss their own ideas—or what they take to be the ideas of children—should come as no surprise to us. We are all familiar with the experience of encountering in secondary sources ideas that in their original sources had seemed so thrilling, and that now, in their restated version, appear so flat and stale. To be told about other people's thoughts is no substitute for having and thinking one's own. Moreover, we have the distinct impression that our thoughts regarding truth or friendship or justice are our own, whereas our thoughts of the Pyramids or of the Counter-Reformation are paler versions of a reality independent of us and remote from us in time and space. In short, we prefer our own, immediately presented thoughts to those that are re-presentational. This is a major reason for the warm response that children give to philosophy and poetry, for philosophical and poetic ideas are directly available to us in their original form and are not copies of things in a world beyond our immediate knowledge or experience.

No program of instruction in thinking skills can be thoroughly sound unless it strikes a balance between its encouragement of discovery and its encouragement of invention. Children are eager to discover both what lies within and what lies outside their powers. They are not distressed at finding that the rules of a game are coercive, or that the laws of nature have a compulsory character that we flaunt only at our peril. But children also want to know what they are free to initiate and invent. They want to know the areas in which they can exercise creativity or, at the very least, discretion. "No fact in all the world is more wonderful than our understanding of that fact," one of Harry Stottlemeier's teachers tells him in one of our novels, and it gives Harry an insight into priorities that all children need to share.

THE PHILOSOPHY FOR CHILDREN PROGRAM

Skills and Dispositions Taught

The following list (pp. 88–96) is not intended to be exhaustive of the thinking skills that the Philosophy for Children Program aims at sharpening. It is a representative list, and for each skill, an example or exercise involving use of that skill is cited. The examples are taken from the novels we have created to introduce children to effective thinking skills; the exercises are taken from the instructional manuals that accompany these novels. The examples students are given are not meant to be models or paradigms. Usually, we have tried to choose typical examples, taken from everyday life experiences, rather than excellent examples. In this way, students are encouraged to find still other examples of situations in which they can use these skills and thereby create additional opportunities for practice.

No doubt there is considerable arbitrariness in any list of cognitive skills that an educational program is said to promote, and the present list is no exception. Some of the 30 skills listed are fairly closely related (for example, there are several varieties of deductive inference listed), and numerous others are not included because they are borderline cases, or because they represent higher order combinations of these skills. An instance of the latter variety would be reading. For the comprehension of written materials of some complexity, a student would have to be able to call upon most of these basic skills, especially the inferential ones. But if only the inferential skills were operative, the student would acquire meanings, but the more dynamic thinking processes would fail to ignite. It is when all the skills are operative and ready for deployment that the materials cause the student to raise questions about what is being said, consider alternatives, inquire as to underlying assumptions—in short, to be

List of Skills and Dispositions Taught

	Skill	Description	Example
1.	Formulating concepts precisely	In applying a concept to a specific set of cases, children should be able to identify those cases that are clearly within the boundaries of the concept, and those that fall clearly outside the boundaries. Children should be encouraged to cite counterinstances if they think the boundaries of the concept have been incorrectly drawn. Exercises and discussion plans concentrate on borderline cases.	Discussion plan for exploring the concept of friendship: 1. Do people have to be the same age in order to be friends? 2. Can two people be friends and still not like each other very much? 3. Is it ever possible for friends to lie to one another? —from *Philosophical Inquiry*, p. 354.
2.	Making appropriate generalizations	Given a set of facts, students should be able to note such uniformities or regularities as do exist and to construct a generalization that would apply to all of these and to similar instances. Students should also be aware of the hazards involved in such generalizations.	Exercise: What generalizations can be drawn? 1. I get sick when I eat raspberries. I get sick when I eat strawberries. I get sick when I eat blackberries. —*Philosophical Inquiry*, p. 112 2. The Rolling Stones are young men and rock stars; the BeeGees are young men and rock stars; thousands of young men are rock stars; the Mean Jeans are young men; are they rock stars? —*Philosophical Inquiry*, p. 113
3.	Formulating cause–effect relationships	Students should be able to identify and to construct formulations that suggest specific cause–effect relationships. They should also be able to discover instances of the "after this, therefore because of this" fallacy.	1. Because I always get hiccups when I see a mouse, and I only get hiccups when I see a mouse, must the cause of my hiccups be my seeing a mouse? —*Philosophical Inquiry*, p. 112 2. Which part of the sentence describes the cause and which the effect: "The rivers were flooded, due to the heavy rains." —*Philosophical Inquiry*, p. 396
4.	Making immediate inferences from a single premise	Students should be able to perform logical conversions, and know the rule governing valid and invalid conversions. They should also know and be able to construct exceptions to the rule, such as identity statements.	1. "If a true sentence begins with the word "no" then its reverse is also true. But if it begins with the word 'all,' then its reverse is false." —*Harry Stottlemeier's Discovery*, p. 4

5. Drawing syllogistic inferences from two premises

Students should be able to draw correct conclusions from valid syllogisms, and be able to identify by inspection at least some instances of invalid inference.

1. "All dogs are animals; all collies are dogs; therefore all collies are animals." "See," said Lisa, "if you're given the first two sentences you can figure out the third."
   —*Harry Stottlemeier's Discovery*, p. 75

2. "It must be that when you put the word 'fish,' the word that cancels out, *at the end* of each of the first two sentences, you made the conclusion turn out false!"
   —*Harry Stottlemeier's Discovery*, p. 77

6. Knowing elementary rules of standardization

Students should be familiar with and able to apply elementary rules of standardization.

1. Sentences that take "all" include: "Each American is patriotic," "Americans are patriotic," "Every American is patriotic."

2. Sentences that take "no" include: "Submarines are never airplanes," "Not one submarine is an airplane."

3. Sentences beginning with "Only" should have their subjects and predicates reversed, and then be treated as "All" statements.
   —*Philosophical Inquiry*, p. 31

7. Knowing the rules governing ordinal and relational logic

Students should be conversant with rules governing transitive and symmetical relationships. They should also learn the standardization rule to convert nontransitive into transitive relationships.

2. Fill in the blank with a word that will make this an identity statement: "All grown-ups are _____."
   —*Philosophical Inquiry*, p. 14

1. If Sue is sadder than Sally, then Sally can't be sadder than Sue. However, if Lola detests boys, it doesn't follow that boys detest Lola.
   —*Philosophical Inquiry*, p. 184

2. If grease is slimier than oil and oil is slimier than water, then grease is slimier than water.
   —*Philosophical Inquiry*, p. 208

3. Given: France is larger than England. France is smaller than Canada.
   Reverse the relationship of one of the sentences (e.g., Canada is larger than France) so as to make the "carryover" possible.
   —*Philosophical Inquiry*, p. 210

89

8.	Recognizing consistencies and contradiction	Students should be able to recognize the consistency or inconsistencies in a given set of data. They should also be able to formulate and apply the formal rules of contradiction.	1. "If I really cared about animals, I wouldn't eat them." —*Lisa*, p. 6 2. Two sentences are mutually contradictory when, if either one is true, the other must be false. Example: "Some wrestling matches are not crooked" is contradicted by "All wrestling matches are crooked." —*Philosophical Inquiry*, p. 306
9.	Drawing inferences from conditional syllogisms in propositional logic	Students should be able to distinguish between valid and invalid inferences when working with hypothetical ("If . . . then. . . .") syllogisms.	1. In hypothetical deduction, it is valid to affirm the antecedent or deny the consequent. It is invalid to deny the antecedent or deny the consequent. For example, it is valid to say, *assuming the truth of the premises*, "If I push this button, the world will blow up. It didn't blow up. So I must not have pushed the button." (denial of consequent) —*Philosophical Inquiry*, p. 414
10.	Formulating questions	Students should be familiar with some of the defects with which questions are frequently contaminated, and should be able to formulate their questions in ways that avoid these difficulties.	1. Questions may be based on incorrect assumptions, may be vague, loaded, or self-contradictory, or may make no sense. Example: "How many digits are there in the largest possible number?" —*Philosophical Inquiry*, p. 129
11.	Identifying underlying assumptions	Given a true statement, students should be able to specify an assumption that underlies the true statement, and upon which the truth of the statement in question is contingent.	1. "Lisa's arguing that whether it's true or false depends on what we're assuming. If it's the opposite of whatever we're assuming, and if our assumptions are true, then it's false." —*Mark*, Ch. 4, part 1, p. 39. 2. Find the underlying assumption: "I love your hair that way, Peg. What beauty parlor did you go to?" —*Philosophical Inquiry*, p. 347

12.	Grasping part–whole and whole–part connections	Students should know how to avoid part–whole mistakes—i.e., assuming that if a member of part of a group has a feature, the entire collection has that particular feature. Also to be avoided are the converse; whole–part mistakes in which a feature of the group or whole is attributed to the part. Students should become acquainted with the ambiguities of the expression "is a part of."	1. Part–whole fallacy: "If Mike's face has handsome features, he must have a handsome face."
			 2. Whole–part fallacy: "If Marie has a pretty face, her face must have pretty features."
			   —*Philosophical Inquiry*, p. 330
			 3. "If Hawaii is part of the United States, and the United States is part of North America, is Hawaii part of North America?"
			   —*Social Inquiry*, p. 222

13.	Knowing when to avoid, tolerate or utilize ambiguities	In logically analyzing information, ambiguities need to be identified, as they can be very mischievous. Certain ambiguities in social relationships may need to be tolerated because they cannot be or should not be eliminated. And in poetic writing, ambiguities are very valuable because they add to the richness and suggestiveness of the work. Students should be able to distinguish ambiguities due to particular words from ambiguities due to word-arrangements (i.e., semantical versus syntactical ambiguities).	1. Which word can have more than one meaning in the following sentence: "Good steaks are rare these days so don't order yours well done."
			   —*Philosophical Inquiry*, p. 87
			 2. Harry doesn't know whether or not Bill regrets having thrown a stone at Harry. Bill's conduct is ambiguous. But Harry invites him to a "sleepover" anyway.
			   —*Harry Stottlemeier's Discovery*, p. 63
			 3. "Almost touching?" "Oh, you mean physically touching and touching like in feelings." "It could have meanings on several levels."
			   —*Suki*, p. 90

14.	Recognizing vague words	Vague words lack clear cutoff points to their applicability. Students should be able to recognize such words and to distinguish contexts in which vague words are unsuitable from those in which they are acceptable.	1. "At precisely what temperature does water become warm?"
			   —*Philosophical Inquiry*, p. 89
			 2. "Can a society be democratic and yet lack representative government?"
			 3. "Can a society where there are many parties be undemocratic?"
			   —*Social Inquiry*, Ch. 1

15. Taking relevant considerations into account

Very often we jump to conclusions because we have neglected to take all relevant considerations into account. Students can develop skill in asking themselves—and one another—if they have overlooked anything in the course of their inquiry.

1. "Something may look wrong to do, but then when you take everything into account, it may look okay. Or just the other way 'round. . . ."
   —*Lisa*, p. 5

2. Would you say that the following is an instance of good reasoning, or of jumping to conclusions: "My father's been reading in the paper that smoking causes cancer, so he says he's going to give up reading."
   —*Philosophical Inquiry*, p. 61

16. Recognizing the interdependence of ends and means

Ordinarily, when a goal or objective is cited, the means of achieving it also needs to be cited. Likewise, nothing is a means unless it is cited as a means to some specified end.

Students should be able to supply consequences for the use of given means and means for the achievement of given ends.

1. "That doesn't prove his way is any better than mine," said Lisa. "He can show how he proceeds, and you can't," said Harry.
   —*Harry Stottlemeier's Discovery*, p. 93

2. Tony: "Lisa, you were right, but for the wrong reason." Mr. Spence: "If you'd been wrong, another innocent person would have suffered."
   —*Harry Stottlemeier's Discovery*, p. 90

17. Recognizing informal fallacies

Many of the nonformal fallacies are due to our reliance upon irrelevant considerations or our omission of relevant ones; hence they hinge upon judgments of relevance. They occur in written form and as violations of dialogical procedure. Students can be alerted to their presence and to the need for handling them with caution.

1. Skills for coping with some of these fallacies have already been identified:
   for *ambiguity*, see #13.
   for *vagueness*, see # 14.
   for *amphiboly*, see # 13, syntactical ambiguities.
   for *composition*, see part–whole, #12.
   for *division*, see whole–part, # 12.
   for *post hoc*, see # 3.

2. For *appeal to alarm*, and *illegitimate authority*, see *Harry Stottlemeier's Discovery*, p. 49.

18.	Operationalizing concepts	Concepts that are not operationalized in terms of specific effects often become empty abstractions. To say that a thing is *heavy* means (in terms of its effects) that it will fall; to say it is *hard* means that many things will not scratch it. Students should be able to cite observable effects for the concepts they employ.	1. "When you questioned the claim that there is no force of gravitation, and said that perhaps things just behave gravitationally, I answered that there may not be something called 'the imagination' that's the cause of our imaginings. Imagining is something we do. . . ." —*Suki*, p. 12
19.	Giving reasons	When students behave in questionable ways, we often ask them to *defend* their actions with reasons. We also ask them to cite reasons in defense of questionable opinions. Students should be able to distinguish between giving reasons and giving explanations—the latter are not defenses, but both employ the term "because."	1. "My mother decided to keep me home because I wasn't feeling well." (reason) 2. "My brother's moped stopped because it ran out of gas." (cause) —*Philosophical Inquiry*, pp. 404–405 3. "We're going to prove the sentences we've just written by arranging them so that they follow correctly from premises we can make up for them." —*Lisa*, p. 90

20.	Recognizing the contextual nature of truth and falsity	When we call statements "true" or "false," we generally fail to specify the context, because we assume that it is already understood. Students can be helped to see the importance of spelling out the contexts to which they refer when making assertions.	1. Under what circumstances could the following statements be *true?*
			  a. Water doesn't put out a fire.
			  b. A house floats away in the air.
			2. Under what circumstances could the following statements be *false?*
			  a. There is nothing living on the moon.
			  b. Washington is the U.S. capital.
			—*Philosophical Inquiry*, p. 19

21.	Making distinctions	Students should be skilled at distinguishing between closely allied concepts that in everyday conversation are frequently confused with one another. This skill is related to skill in developing concepts (#1), insofar as counterinstances are required to distinguish what lies within from what lies outside the boundaries of the concept.	1. Distinction between truth and possibility. "Is it possible that there is life on planets in other galaxies?" "Is it possible the universe was created, even though it might always have existed?" —*Philosophical Inquiry*, p. 338

22. Making connections

Students should be able to make connections and identify the grounds for making such connections. Among the frequently cited grounds are juxtaposition, cause–effect, resemblance, and similarity of effects. This skill is important for reasoning (finding middle terms) and for constructing similes and metaphors.

2. Distinguishing description from explanation. Would you say this tells *what* happened or *why* it happened: "In earlier paintings the sky was painted gold; later it was painted blue."
   —*Philosophical Inquiry*, p. 402

1. The sky was clear and dark blue, except for a huge white cloud that was moving slowly overhead. Suddenly Mark exclaimed, "Harry, it's North America!"
   —*Harry Stottlemeier's Discovery*, p. 25

2. To answer the question, "Are the Shetland Islands part of Great Britain?" Harry connects two bits of information: that the Shetland Islands are a part of Scotland and that Scotland is a part of Great Britain.
   —*Harry Stottlemeier's Discovery*, p. 41

23. Working with analogies

Analogies represent similarities not just of single traits, but of whole systems or structures of traits. Analogical reasoning is an important link between logical and creative thinking. One way of grouping analogies is in terms of the philosophical categories that they illustrate. Once students have learned to identify relationships, they are prepared to recognize that analogies involve a relationship of similarity between two relationships. Thus, "Puppies are to dogs as kittens are to cats" is an instance of the statement that one offspring–parent relationship resembles another.

1. Appearance and Reality: "Insanity is to sanity as irrationality is to: (a) courage; (b) faith; (c) rationality."

2. Process and Product: "Sawing is to furniture as chiseling is to: (a) sculpture; (b) painting; (c) graffiti."

3. Cause and Effect: "Germ is to disease as candle is to: (a) wax; (b) wick; (c) white; (d) light."
   —*Philosophical Inquiry*, pp. 117–121

24. Discovering alternatives

Careful thinkers do not rely solely on hunches or intuitions to identify what alternatives there might be to established views or procedures; they have recourse to the logical alternatives that exhaust the logical possibilities. And creative thinkers look for fresh approaches even when accepted views or methods are generally

1. "If you have got two sets, each with two possibilities, that makes four possibilities altogether. . . . First, ice cream and cake; second, cake but no ice cream; third, ice cream but no cake; and fourth, neither ice cream nor cake."
   —*Harry Stottlemeier's Discovery*, p. 67

25.	Constructing hypotheses	thought to be satisfactory, in the hope of finding still better solutions. Those individuals who work out various possible solutions to a given problem are in effect generating hypothetical alternatives. Hypotheses are ideas that represent possible ways of resolving problematic situations. When we encounter surprising or disturbing facts, we invent hypotheses to account for them. All laws of nature were once hypotheses that were gradually confirmed until they won acceptance. Skill in constructing hypotheses both entails and encompasses skill in making predictions.	1. Tony wrote: "If Sandy had taken the briefcase, it would still be here in the room at two forty-five. But it wasn't in the room at two forty-five. Therefore Sandy didn't take the briefcase." —*Harry Stottlemeier's Discovery*, p. 89 2. "The best guess we could make was that the stream led to the river. . . . We tried it out, and sure enough, we found our way back to the mansion." —*Lisa*, p. 143
26.	Analyzing values	Our values are our beliefs as to what is important. (Everything has some *value*; only people have *values*.) But we can reason about our values. We can ask if they are consistent with one another, if they are in accord with the facts, if we are capable of acting on them, and if they are defensible. Students who offer reasons for what they say and do are already engaged in analyzing their values.	1. "Can you think of any circumstances under which a *cruel* act would also be a *good* act?" —*Philosophical Inquiry*, p. 198 2. "When we deplore fraud, violence, evil, ugliness, and falsehood, what values do we imply that we believe in?" —*Philosophical Inquiry*, p. 202 3. In the following statement, "Looking just at natural resources, India is wealthier than Ireland," the *value* of "wealth" is measured by the *standard or criterion* of "natural resources." —*Philosophical Inquiry*, p. 203
27.	Instantiating	Many children who have difficulty generalizing and developing abstract concepts have facility in offering instances and examples—just the reverse of what is true of many adults. But ability to instantiate is important, not just as a counterweight to the ability to generalize, but as essential to the capacity to apply ideas to life situations.	1. Mr. Portos suggests that only man has a culture. Can you think of any other creatures that have cultures? —*Philosophical Inquiry*, p. 170 2. Name three features you would most like a friend of yours to have. —*Ethical Inquiry*, p. 381

28.	Constructing definitions for familiar words	When children encounter words they don't know, they may look up the definitions of those words in the dictionary. But they should be able to construct for themselves the definitions of words whose meanings they already know.	3. A widely accepted generalization is that "frustration often leads to aggression." Can you give an illustration of this? —*Social Inquiry*, p. 243 1. Tony wrote: "All gems are *stones*; only gems are *precious* stones. Therefore, the word 'gem' means 'a precious stone.' —*Suki*, p. 4 2. Six rules for constructing definitions. —*Writing: How and Why*, Ch. 1
29.	Identifying and using criteria	Whenever we make judgments of value (such as in ethical or aesthetic matters) or of practice (in estimating quantities or qualities), we employ standards or criteria. It is important that students know the criteria that they employ in making such judgments, and that they utilize the criteria that are most appropriate to the situations in which the judgments are to be made. Criteria are especially important in the construction of definitions.	1. "Standards are what we use to judge *how* important, or *how* valuable, something is." —*Lisa*, p. 103 2. "You have to choose a movie in which to give an Oscar. How would you rank *acting, photography, plot?*" —*Ethical Inquiry*, p. 323 3. "Shouldn't we know *in general* how we tell the difference between what's bad and what's good?" "Sure, there are standards you can judge by." —*Suki*, p. 95 4. "When we have a bunch of criteria, is it possible we need still *another* criterion to be able to decide which of the first bunch we should pick?" —*Mark*, Ch. 1, Episode 2, page 4.
30.	Taking differences of perspective into account	Insofar as people are different, they perceive the world differently—they have different perspectives. But insofar as they can take one another's points of view and thereby exchange perspectives, they obtain an objective rather than a merely subjective understanding.	1. "If she were to go up front, she would see only faces, and if Mr. Spence were to go to the back of the room, he would see only backs of heads." —*Harry Stottlemeier's Discovery*, p. 94 2. Achieving objectivity through broader frames of reference. —*Philosophical Inquiry*, p. 440

inquisitive, reflective, thoughtful. Common parlance, of course, has it that reading, writing, and mathematics are "basic skills," meaning thereby that reading, writing, and mathematics are important in any estimation of what it is to be an educated individual. The fact that we label these skills "basic," however, does not imply that they cannot be analyzed into scores of more elementary thinking skills. If students are taught how to perform and coordinate these more elementary thinking skills, improved performance should result, as indeed is reported in some of the Philosophy for Children evaluation studies discussed later.

The *coordination* of thinking skills is of the very first order of importance. Thus, it is possible to induce improved student performance in some individual skill, without such improvement being reflected in improved academic performance. For example, our search of *Psychological Abstracts* over the past 50 years revealed dozens of experiments in which children were given instruction in logic. In these experiments, test performances in logical reasoning often improved, but this failed to result in better performance in such subjects as mathematics and reading. Reinforcement of skills once learned is no less important than coordination. In the Rand School study discussed later, the gains of fifth-grade students were intact 2 years later with no reinforcement, but 4 years later, all differences between the experimental and control groups had disappeared. On the other hand, in the Newark–Pompton Lakes study, also discussed later, students participated in the program for an entire year rather than only 9 weeks, so that newly learned skills could receive reinforcement and become consolidated. In this study, the longer children were in the program, the greater the gains. Thus, without reinforcement, gains wash out; with reinforcement, gains can be cumulative.

If the learning of individual thinking skills does not assure that such skills will be employed in a coordinated fashion, what needs to be done to obtain such assurance? The answer would seem to lie in the acquisition by children of certain cognitive dispositions. These dispositions are not themselves skills, but they represent a readiness to employ such skills—and to employ them in a coordinated and cumulatively reinforcing fashion. There are, of course, many dispositions that have long been considered desirable in students, and that overlap with those under discussion. Examples would be trust, cooperativeness, readiness to listen, attentiveness, and respect for others. These are certainly familiar features of a congenial and smoothly functioning classroom. But to the extent that the classroom is converted into a community of inquiry, new dispositions also emerge that are more cognitive in nature. These include: trust that the method of inquiry will be self-correcting; care for the procedures of inquiry; a considerateness of others' points of view; and a readiness to apply the same critical spirit to oneself as one does to others, that is, to be self-appraising as well as appraising of one's peers. When students acquire cognitive propensities such as these, all of which could perhaps be summed up in the term "commitment to inquiry," they are motivated to mobilize their skills effectively. Those students who can be counted on to use their intellectual resources in a unified and consistent fashion are precisely those who have already developed habits of so doing. It is the job of a thinking skills program to develop these habitual dispositions, and not just the skills themselves.

It is sometimes said, in support of Philosophy for Children, that most adults distrust philosophy because of unfortunate experiences they have had with its formidable terminology or with the abstractness, remoteness, or the tedium of certain philosophical issues. Thus, Philosophy for Children is welcomed because of its efforts to make philosophical issues less remote. Another comment frequently made in support of Philosophy for Children is that the sort of inquiry presently taught in the schools is too narrowly restricted to scientific inquiry, with a resulting failure to recognize that philosophical investigation is another form of inquiry, which in some ways it overlaps and in others remains distinct from.

Supporting views such as these are of course most welcome, but they fail to mention the appeal that philosophy has for the motives and inclinations of the child. It is commonplace knowledge, certainly, that children have a powerful social impulse and are amazingly curious. But the interpretations we place on these needs and tendencies are rather one-sided. We often take the social impulse to require only affective gratification, without acknowledging the child's search for intellectual camaraderie with peers and with others of other ages. The classroom as a community of inquiry can offer such camaraderie. We may also misinterpret the child's persistent "Why?" as a request for explanation (specifically, for causal explanation), without acknowledging that the question might be aimed at acquiring reasons, purposes, or, in short, meanings. This is all the more odd in light of adult behavior toward children. When adults ask children why they did this or that, replies are expected in terms of reasons or justifications, and an explanatory response is often considered an evasion. Yet many of these same adults will presume that the child's "Why?" can be satisfied by an explanation, and will not respond to the need for inquiry into possible justifying reasons.

Adult views regarding the expenditure of intellectual effort are highly culture-conditioned; we expect such effort to be productive. Questions are useful because they lead to answers, games because they lead to winning, courses because they lead to grades. One reason for the frequent disparagement of philosophy is that it so manifestly lacks answers, and that philosophical discussion seems never to yield winners or losers. Philosophy seems to disallow decision procedures, keeping its dialogue open-ended, and indeed, were a decision procedure to be discovered for a particular issue, that issue would quickly be banished from philosophy and assigned to science. To the practical adult, love of intellectual inquiry for its own sake often appears the height of capriciousness. But to the child it is a breath of fresh air. It means there is nothing wrong with playing with ideas, speculating about possibilities, exploring mysterious concepts. It is precisely a philosophic absence of executive or managerial purposiveness, combined, of course, with a gamelike insistence upon rigorous observance of the rules and methods of inquiry, that makes this kind of thinking seem so delightful to children.

When we hear children searching for some elusive criterion, we should hear it in the context of our own fumbling efforts to do the same thing: "He's been in a coma for years; he's just a vegetable." "So what, a vegetable's something living." "Sure, but it's not a person." "What's a person?" and so on. We struggle over such questions; we agonize over them. No consensus is in sight, and we would be suspicious if one were. But what philosophers, thoughtful adults, and children can generally agree on is that the dialogue is worthwhile in and of itself, and that there is a moral urgency to its being continued.

If we want children to grow up to be reflective adults, we should encourage them to be reflective children. It is obvious that the continuity between means and ends implies for us a rule of procedure: Tomorrow's results, whatever they may be, will bear the stamp and character of today's procedure and practices. Thus, if thinking skills are to be taught, they should be taught in the context of ongoing communities of inquiry whose scrupulous attention to method can be internalized by each participant. And to the extent that this occurs, each participant becomes a reflective and reasonable individual.

Major Pedagogical Features

In this section, we summarize the major pedagogical features of the Philosophy for Children program, several of which have already been alluded to, and we discuss why we think each is important.

Modeling as a Teacher-Training Technique.   Teachers for our program should be taught in the same manner they are expected to teach. If teacher trainers lecture in training workshops, future teachers will simply turn around and lecture to the children in their classrooms. If, on the other hand, the training workshops are arenas for open and lively discussions, then the teachers will be likely to conduct their own classes in the same fashion. Similarly, trainers should be taught the methods and material in the same manner they are expected to convey it to teachers. The transition process should be seamless and its stages symmetrical.

Operationalizing Concepts Through Student Exercises and Activities.   Individuals who reason vapidly usually have some dim awareness of what they are struggling to put into words. But they are aware of no need to specify the evidence on which their ideas rest, the boundaries of their concepts, the consequences of holding certain views, or the way ideas might be put into effect. To counteract vapidity, an ideal curriculum would be one that is thoroughly operationalized: no concept would be broached without exercises, activities, discussion plans, and research assignments that would enable the children in the classroom to see ideas work.

Beginning with Children's Own Experiences.   A discussion approach can have little hope of success if geared to getting children to discuss other people's experience rather than their own. Yet, when other people's experience is made available to children in an engaging activity or a work of art to be appreciated, the children readily appropriate and are eager to explore the meanings it may contain. Beginning a class with artificial and contrived "problems," devoid of a general, experiential context for the child, is likely to appear alien and arid, however meaningful these problems may seem to an adult.

Encouraging Group Dialogue.   When teachers encourage children in class-room conversation, rather than constant one-to-one dialogue with the teacher, the purpose is not merely to promote sociality. Children need to learn to cooperate in the practice of inquiry and to share in its benefits. They need to listen to each other, determine one another's assumptions, appraise each other's consistency, and follow together the entire line of argument. The teacher must be able to delegate these functions to the children, while remaining a co-participant in the inquiry.

Responding to Children's Craving for Meaning.   As educational incentives, meaning and truth are very different. The more the community of inquiry concerns itself with the perfection of its method, the less likely it is to settle hastily on this or that as "true." There will always be room for new evidence, for further review of procedures, and for consideration of far-reaching new theories that demand reconsideration of knowledge hitherto considered firm and secure. Children are not as hot for certainty as many adults think they are; they can cope handily with the notion that truths that are not truths of definition carry with them no stamp of finality. Meaning, on the other hand, is what children want here and now—nor is there any good reason why they should not have it. Meanings, for children, are treasures to be sought, and to be found on every side. Children do not question the truth of much of what they are told, but they do contend that it is often meaningless to them. It is unlikely that an educational process can work if it fails to take this craving for meaning into account.

Teaching Thinking Skills Apart from Typical Academic Knowledge Acquisition and Problem-Solving Tasks.   When the primary aim of education is conceived to be the promotion of children's thinking, knowledge acquisition and subject-specific problem solving readily assume a subsidiary status; they remain valuable functions but are no longer the focus of learning. Philosophy must be taught as a subject in its own right, rather than ignored or taught only as a subcomponent of other academic knowledge acquisition and problem-solving activities. Reflective children will generally be able to inquire after and locate the knowledge they require, but the converse does not necessarily follow. Children with knowledge can very well be unreflective, uncritical, and lacking in a commitment to inquiry.

The question may be raised whether we are conceiving of education in a fashion that is diffuse, impractical and unrealistic, in that thinking skills are taught apart from the practical knowledge acquisition and problem-solving tasks that students encounter in other areas of the school curriculum. But if education is to produce individuals who are intellectually flexible, resourceful, and judicious, the cognitive processes of the young must be sharpened in an enormous variety of ways, not merely those that are memory or action oriented. All too often, those we entrust with the responsibility of resolving difficulties have been inadequately instructed in the skills of applying criteria, exploring alternatives, considering consequences, and other such indispensable preliminaries, with the result that problems remain unsolved and their adverse effects are aggravated.

Education has always been an amphitheater of illusions, and the illusions that surround instruction in thinking skills are particularly cruel because they represent further postponement of the kind of reconstruction which education desperately requires. There is the illusion that computer literacy represents a bundle of cognitive skills which will readily translate into enhanced academic proficiencies, the illusion that the skills needed to learn a subject matter can be taught at the same time as the subject matter is taught, and the illusion that a short course in logical fallacies and argument analysis will transform the average student into a crisply critical reasoner. The realistic alternative is to add a subject to the K–12 curriculum with the objective of developing and maintaining the cognitive dispositions and skills which, once acquired, will be applied by the students themselves to each and every subject they study. The newly introduced subject would concentrate on reasoning through dialogue about contestable issues, and would therefore constitute a sustained practicum in concept formation as well as in the methodology of inquiry. If such a subject were genuinely desired, room for it in the curriculum could readily be found by trimming the dead wood from other subjects. Of course, there is no need to invent such a discipline, since it already exists in the form of philosophy for children. In learning to think in the discipline of philosophy, children prepare themselves to think in the other disciplines as well.

Evaluation Data

Evaluation research on the Philosophy for Children program has been conducted both by the program developers and by others who have sought to replicate these studies. A summary of this research follows.

The Rand School Study.   The first evaluation of the Philosophy for Children program was carried out in 1970 by Lipman and Bierman in the Rand School, an economically and racially heterogeneous elementary school in Montclair, New Jersey (Lipman, 1976b). The aim of this study was to determine the feasibility of teaching reasoning to fifth-grade children. Forty students participated in the study, and were divided into two randomly assigned groups. The experimental group received 18 40-minute sessions of the Philosophy for Children program over a period of 9 weeks. The control group was assigned to a social studies experiment.

Both groups were initially tested on the long form of the California Test of Mental Maturity (CTMM), 1963 revision. On the initial testing, there was no significant difference between groups. At the end of 9 weeks, both groups were retested on the short form of the same instrument. On the second testing, the experimental group achieved mental age scores that were 27 months higher than those of the control group, a difference that was statistically significant. To determine if the experimental program produced long-term gains in reading comprehension, the children's reading scores on the Iowa Achievement Test taken prior to the experiment and 2 years afterward were examined. Although there were no significant differences between the experimental and control students on the first set of Iowa scores, significant differences were found on the second set.

The Newark Study.   A second evaluation of the Philosophy for Children program was conducted in 1975 in the Newark, New Jersey public schools. The study director was Hope Haas of the Institute for Cognitive Studies at Rutgers University (Haas, 1975). This evaluation employed Solomon's quasi-experimental four-group design—a design that controls for the effects of pretesting. Altogether, 400 fifth- and sixth-grade students participated in the study, half of whom constituted the experimental group. The students were enrolled in 16 different classrooms in two experimental and two control schools. The experimental students worked with the Philosophy for Children program for an entire academic semester. Several criterion measures were used to evaluate the effectiveness of the program. One was the reading subtest of the Metropolitan Achievement Test (MAT). This instrument was administered to the students by the Newark Public Schools as part of their annual testing program. The MAT assesses several aspects of reading comprehension, including: (1) ability to recognize the main idea of a reading passage, (2) ability to draw correct inferences from text, (3) ability to perceive and understand details in reading passages, and (4) ability to recognize the correct meanings of words in text. In addition to the MAT, the students were tested individually on several experimental instruments assessing skills and attitudes related to critical thinking.

Several findings were reported. At the sixth-grade level, experimental students made significantly greater gains than controls in the following areas: reading, critical thinking, and interpersonal relationship skills. At the fifth-grade level, experimental students in contrast to controls evidenced more positive attitudes toward intellectual freedom after having participated in the program. However, when the fifth- and sixth-grade data were combined, there was only one significant difference between the experimental and control groups. This was in the area of reading comprehension. Over the 10-month academic year, from one test administration to the next, the experimental students as a group gained 8 months on the MAT reading comprehension subtest in contrast to 5 months for the controls. This overall pattern of gains included some quite dramatic gains for a few of the experimental classrooms; one class jumped 2½ years; another 1 year and 4 months. In contrast to the differences in reading scores, there were no significant differences between the combined fifth- and sixth-grade experimental and control groups on the other variables assessed in the study, including: curiosity, logical thinking, and the use of analytical and creative questions. In short, in contrast to the Rand School study discussed previously, in the Newark study there were clear gains in reading comprehension but not in logical thinking. Inasmuch as the students in the Rand School study were taught by a college logic instructor, this pattern of results suggests that the effects of the Philosophy for Children program may be highly teacher related. That is, teachers who stress reading may be able to produce significant improvements in reading, whereas teachers who stress reasoning may be able to produce significant improvements in reasoning.

The Newark-Pompton Lakes Study. A still more extensive and carefully controlled evaluation of the Philosophy for Children program was conducted by Dr. Virginia Shipman of the Educational Testing Service (ETS) (Shipman, 1978). This study was initiated in September 1976 and was concluded in June 1978, under a grant from the New Jersey Department of Education. The first year of the study was devoted to the construction and pilot testing of a criterion-referenced instrument to assess children's reasoning. The second year involved an evaluation of the Philosophy for Children program in two New Jersey communities—Newark and Pompton Lakes. In each community, children were selected for participation in the study from both a large, inner-city area and a suburban, lower middle-class area. Altogether, there were 200 subjects in Newark and 160 in Pompton Lakes. The students were in grades 5 to 8. To the extent possible, control classes were matched to experimental ones in terms of socioeconomic variables. Experimental teachers received a year of special training, during which they met with a team of university professors once a week for 2 hours. During that same year, they also taught the experimental classes. Experimental students participated in the program for approximately 2½ hours per week for an entire academic year.

The study examined whether participation in the program resulted in improvements in the following areas: (1) reasoning, (2) ideational fluency, (3) academic readiness, and (4) reading and mathematics performance. The instruments listed in Table 2.1 were used.

The findings revealed significant improvements in several areas. In Newark, three of the four grade levels participating in the study achieved significant gains in formal reasoning skills as compared with controls. Length of exposure to the program appeared to be important in producing their gains. Secondly, in most of the grade levels in Newark and in some of the grade levels in Pompton Lakes, significant improvements were reported on measures of creative reasoning skills. That is, the experimental students achieved higher scores on instruments assessing ability to discover alternatives, perceive possibilities, and provide reasons. These results suggest that logical reasoning and intellectual creativity are not mutually inhibitive and that both can be improved by the same program. This is important, because the enhancement of critical thinking skills alone can be superficial and empty without concomitant improvements in creative thinking skills. Thirdly, in Newark, the program had a significant impact on reading and mathematics achievement.

In addition to test-score data, several more informal results were reported. Both in Newark and Pompton Lakes, teachers' appraisals of the impact of the program upon their pupils were extremely favorable. Students appeared to be significantly more curious, more attentive to learning tasks, more considerate of one another, and better able to reason. Students also appeared to have become more effective communicators. Students whom teachers had initially characterized as slow readers seemed especially to benefit from participation in the program.

In the test-score data already reported, students in Newark made many more significant gains than those in Pompton Lakes. The Educational Testing Service evaluation report, looking more closely at these data and also taking into consideration the anecdotal data discussed previously, suggests that the real effects of the intervention in Pompton Lakes may have been masked by the fact that

TABLE 2.1
Overview of Newark-Pompton Lakes Study

Skill Area	Instrument
1. Reasoning	
a. Drawing formal inferences	Criterion-referenced formal reasoning test designed by ETS (also known as Q–3)
	Inference Subtest from the California Test of Mental Maturity
b. Discovering alternatives and possibilities	"What Can It Be?" Test
	"What Can It Be Used For?" Test
c. Providing reasons	"How Many Reasons?" Test
2. Ideational productivity	Same instruments as in 1b and 1c above
3. Academic readiness	Child Description Checklist
4. Reading and mathematics achievement	Newark: Metropolitan Achievement Test
	Pompton Lakes: California Test of Basic Skills

both experimental and control students were enrolled in the same school. That is, in Pompton Lakes, both experimental and control students improved from pretest to posttest, thus suggesting that the experimental students may have benefited directly from the intervention, and the controls may have benefited indirectly through contact with the experimentals.

As a result of the ETS experiment, the Philosophy for Children program received Title IV-C validation in New Jersey. After a 2-day review of the data by a team of out-of-state educators, the program was given 124 of a possible 126 points for effectiveness and 45 of a possible 45 points for exportability.

Other Evaluations.   Several other evaluations of the Philosophy for Children materials have been completed or are now under way. One was an exploratory study by Charlann Simon (1979) examining the appropriateness of these materials for use with emotionally handicapped children enrolled in a special school. Again, evidence was reported indicating that the materials were effective. A second study (Karras, 1980) involved 600 elementary school children in Lexington, Massachusetts. As in the Newark–Pompton Lakes study, the instrument used to assess program outcomes was the ETS-developed Q–3 Instrument, and again significant differences were found between experimental and control students, with greatest improvements in reasoning occurring among average and below average students. A third study, this time involving a briefer intervention, was carried out by Nancy Cummings (1980) in Bedford, Texas. This study was a replication of the Rand School evaluation described earlier, and again, gains were reported on the CTMM. A fourth study, by William Higa (1980), involved 12 elementary school classes in Hilo, Hawaii. Again, gains were reported in ETS' Q–3 instrument, although this time, because of resource limitations, there was no control group. Other more recent studies have also reported significant gains on various measures of reading comprehension and/or logical thinking. These include: a control group study involving use of the Philosophy for Children materials with sixth graders (Yeazell, 1981), a control group study with fourth graders (Reed & Henderson, 1981), a study in which the Philosophy for Children materials were used with academically talented fifth graders (Cinquino, 1981), and a study involving continuous use of the Philosophy for Children materials with the same students over a 3-year period (Burnes, 1981; Weinstein & Martin, 1982).

The most extensive research to date on the Philosophy for Children program took place in 1980–81, in New Jersey and Pennsylvania, involving over 3000 middle school students. Both experiments were designed and evaluated by Dr. Virginia Shipman of the Educational Testing Service, Princeton, N.J. The findings reported here are based on one subset of a larger body of data that are still being analyzed.

The New Jersey research (V. Shipman, 1982a), which was principally funded by the Bureau of Research, Planning, and Evaluation of the New Jersey Department of Education, took place in Grades 5, 6, and 7 in the following urban, suburban, and rural communities: Hope, Totowa, Hillsboro, East Orange, Union City, Skillman, Princeton, Secaucus, Paterson, and Blairstown. All students, of whom approximately three-fifths were experimental and the remainder were control populations, were pretested and posttested, using an ETS-designed, criterion-referenced testing instrument, known as the Q–4. An analysis of covariants for the 33 grade-level comparisons that adjusted for any differences in children's pretest performances showed on the average greater improvement for children in the experimental groups than for the control population. When examining the mean gains across grade levels from pre- to posttest, it was found that the experimental group's gain of 5.23 was 80% greater than the control group's gain of 2.91.

The Pennsylvania experiment (Shipman, 1982b) was sponsored by the Bethlehem Area Board of School Directors, and was organized by Dr. Robert La Franke, Bethlehem's Superintendent of Schools. Thirty-two sixth-grade classrooms in Bethlehem received the Philosophy for Children program, and all showed improvement in reasoning on the Q–4 instrument. Twenty-nine classrooms showed significant improvement at the .05 level, and nineteen of these showed highly significant improvement at the .005 level. For the remainder of the classrooms, the gains ranged between .06 and .10.

Although these studies show the effectiveness of the Philosophy for Children materials, additional evaluation data on three facets of the program would be of great value. It would be desirable to look more closely at the kinds of attitudinal changes that may occur as a result of participation in the program. More attention also needs to be paid to obtaining an in-depth assessment of children's thinking processes, as opposed to merely assessing thinking outcomes. Finally, a great deal of attention needs to be devoted to determining which pedagogical techniques successfully elicit cognitively meaningful dialogue, as contrasted with mere verbalization.

SOME CONCLUSIONS

The evidence thus far suggests that students who have been exposed to the program are more reasonable and more thoughtful, and that their teachers are not merely better at teaching specific subjects, but also are more effective in developing general thinking skills. These are two significant contributions that teaching philosophy can make to education. A third is the potential of philosophy to modify our conception of education. Rather than conceiving of education as helping children acquire the knowledge that adults possess, we might begin to recognize that a central objective of education is to create communities of inquiry, through which children learn to value independent and autonomous thinking. This goal recognizes the child's rational capability and personhood. It also renders untenable the assumption that cognitive development is indifferent to the mode or content of pedagogical intervention.

The introduction of new and improved educational techniques will produce better education only insofar as certain underlying assumptions can be modified or replaced. Assumptions about education that are urgently in need of replacement are that thinking skills need not be taught, that they cannot be taught, and that the rigors of philosophical analysis are peripheral to sound thinking, and to programs to foster it. Such assumptions are consistent neither with one another nor with the larger objectives of education.

REFERENCES

Burnes, B. Harry Stottlemeier's discovery—the Minnesota experience. *Thinking,* 1981, *3*(1), 8–11.

Cinquino, D. An evaluation of a philosophy program with 5th- and 6th-grade academically talented students. *Thinking,* 1981, *2*(3 & 4), 79–83.

Cole, M., John-Steiner, V., Scribner, S., & Souberman, E. (Eds.). *Mind in society: The development of higher psychological processes.* Cambridge, Mass.: Harvard University Press, 1978.

Cummings, N. Improving the logical skill of fifth graders. *Thinking,* 1980, *1*, 90–92.

Haas, H. J. *Evaluation study: Philosophy for children.* Unpublished manuscript, 1975.

Higa, W. R. Evaluation of the Hawaii Philosophy for Children program. *Thinking,* 1980, *2*(1), 21–31.

Karras, R. W. Final evaluation of the pilot program in philosophical reasoning in Lexington Elementary Schools 1978–79. *Thinking,* 1980, *1*, 26–32.

Lipman, M. *Harry Stottlemeier's discovery.* Upper Montclair, N.J.: IAPC, 1974.

Lipman, M. *Lisa.* Upper Montclair, N.J.: IAPC, 1976. (a)

Lipman, M. Philosophy for children. *Metaphilosophy,* 1976, *7*, 17–39. (b)

Lipman, M. *Suki.* Upper Montclair, N.J.: IAPC, 1978.

Lipman, M. *Mark.* Upper Montclair, N.J.: IAPC, 1980.

Lipman, M., & Sharp, A. M. *Social inquiry: Instructional manual to accompany Mark.* Upper Montclair, N.J.: IAPC, 1980. (a)

Lipman, M., & Sharp, A. M. *Writing: How and why—Instructional manual to accompany Suki.* Upper Montclair, N.J.: IAPC, 1980. (b)

Lipman, M., Sharp, A. M., & Oscanyan, F. S. *Ethical inquiry: Instructional manual to accompany Lisa.* Upper Montclair, N.J.: IAPC, 1977.

Lipman, M., Sharp, A. M., & Oscanyan, F. S. *Philosophical inquiry: Instructional manual to accompany Harry Stottlemeier's discovery.* Upper Montclair, N.J.: IAPC, 1979.

Reed, R., & Henderson, A. Analytic thinking for children in Fort Worth elementary schools: Initial evaluation report, Summer 1981. *Analytic Teaching,* 2(1), 5–12.

Shipman, V. *An experiment with philosophy for children in Newark and Pompton Lakes, N.J.* Unpublished manuscript, 1978.

Shipman, V. Personal communication, June 11, 1982. (a)

Shipman, V. C. Evaluation of the Philosophy for Children program in Bethlehem, Pennsylvania. *Thinking,* 1982, *4*(1), 37–40. (b)

Simon, C. Philosophy for students with learning disabilities. *Thinking,* 1979, *1*, 21–33.

Vygotsky, L. S. *Thought and language.* (E. Hanfmann & F. Vakar, eds. and trans.). Cambridge, Mass.: MIT Press, 1962.

Weinstein, M. L., & Martin, J. F. Philosophy for children and the improvement of thinking skills in Queens, New York. *Thinking*, 1982, *4*(2), 36.

Yeazell, M. I. A report on the first year of the Upshur Country, West Virginia Philosophy for Children project. *Thinking*, 1981, *3*(1), 12–14.

3 Teaching Analytic Reasoning Skills Through Pair Problem Solving

Jack Lochhead
University of Massachusetts, Amherst

THE PROBLEM OF PASSIVE LEARNERS

Traditionally we have attributed academic success to innate intelligence and hard work. From this perspective teachers have two responsibilities: to motivate students to work, and to present material clearly so that it can be grasped by some of the less clever students. Although there can be little doubt that the foregoing factors influence student performance, careful studies of the differences between good and poor problem solvers suggest that a third factor may be critical: that of the students' learning strategy. This, in turn, depends on the students' own theory of knowledge (i.e., their epistemology). Their actions are guided by their views on how they learn, their ideas on what is involved in thinking, and finally their concepts of the nature of knowledge. When these views are at odds with the natural functioning of the mind, as they often are, students persist in ineffective strategies (Papert, 1971a, 1971b, 1980). Probably the most common example is the copy theory, according to which students believe they can understand a subject simply by memorizing (copying into memory) the definitions and rules as given in a textbook.

Students' stubborn adherence to ineffective learning strategies may be the single most important deterrent to effective education. If we could teach students to learn more efficiently we would, in effect, raise their intelligence. Unfortunately most instruction seems to produce precisely the opposite result. Students tend to view learning as a passive experience in which one absorbs knowledge or copies facts into memory. Little of what they do in school leads them to question that perspective. But research on clever thinkers shows that the smartest students have quite a different view.

In 1950, Bloom and Broder reported on an intensive study of the differences between good and poor problem solvers. They found differences in four areas:

1. Understanding the nature of the problem,
2. Understanding the ideas contained in the problem,
3. General approach to the solution of problems,
4. Attitude toward the solution of problems.

At first glance, these categories support the notion that performance differences are the product of innate intelligence and effort, but more careful scrutiny suggests otherwise. Good problem solvers *pulled* key ideas out of the problem, poor problem solvers did not. Good problem solvers *brought* relevant information to bear on the problem; poor problem solvers did not, even though they often knew the needed information. As suggested by Bloom and Broder (1950): "The major difference between the successful and the non-successful problem solvers in their extent of thought about the problem was in the degree to which their approach to the problem might be characterized as active or passive. [pp. 28–29]." In short, good problem solvers simply did more than poor problem solvers.

The inactivity of poor problem solvers could be attributed to laziness but there is an alternative explanation. Poor problem solvers are less active because they do not believe there is anything for them to do. Their view of both problem solving and learning places them in the passive role of absorbing information and repeating it. They think you either know the answer to a question or you do not. Although this attitude may seem naive, it is in fact the logical consequence of most schooling. Instruction, whether by textbook, lecture, or cookbook laboratory, places students in the role of copiers. Rarely are they asked to generate their own knowledge. Although teachers certainly know that learning is not just copying, they often act as though they don't. This may be because they are not quite sure of how to teach students whose level of competence is substantially below their own. The problem is summarized in the comment of a psychology professor at a British university. When his department's offerings were criticized as being too dependent on rote recall he replied, "but it is well known that undergraduates cannot think until their fifth year." Faced with this type of instruction it is not surprising that many students never learn how to learn.

The importance of changing student views on learning has of course been recognized by many educational innovators. Active learning paradigms such as those of Dewey, Montessori, and Piaget have had considerable impact on many aspects of the educational system. But they have had less of an effect on student learning than their proponents had originally hoped. It seems that changing student attitudes towards learning is a bit more difficult than the innovators expected. One reason for this failure may be that new curricula usually have little impact on the teacher's style of instruction. Teachers who have the well-developed habit of explaining everything as clearly as they can, find it hard to hold back and let the students learn/discover for themselves. Yet it is essential that they do this, if students are to take a more active role in their own learning (Finkel & Monk, 1978).

PAIR PROBLEM SOLVING: BASIC FEATURES

In order to make students more active and more intelligent learners, it is necessary to change the traditional roles of both student and teacher. One approach that has proved effective is pair problem solving. In it, students work together in pairs on sets of specially designed problems. Each member of the pair has a distinct and well-defined role. One partner reads and thinks aloud, while the other listens. On subsequent problems the partners change roles, taking turns as problem solver and listener.

The partner who listens plays a critical role in the learning process. He or she must not sit back inattentively but, instead, must concentrate on two functions: (1) continually checking for accuracy; and (2) demanding constant vocalization. The approach is described fully in *Problem Solving and Comprehension* (Whimbey & Lochhead, 1980), where the listener is given the following instructions:

Continually Check Accuracy
    Since accuracy is all-important, the listener should continually check the accuracy of the problem solver. This includes every computation he makes, every diagram he draws, every conclusion he reaches. In other words, the problem solver's accuracy should be checked at every step of the problem, not just when he gives his final answer. For example, if in working the problem shown earlier the problem solver concluded that the word *sentence* has nine letters, the listener should have immediately caught the error and pointed it out.
    Catching errors involves several activities. First, the listener must actively work along with the problem solver. He should follow every step the problem solver takes, and he should be sure he understands each step. If the listener takes a passive attitude—if he does not actively think through each step—he won't know for sure whether or not the problem solver's steps are totally correct.
    Second, the listener should never let the problem solver get ahead of him. This may often mean that the listener will have to ask the problem solver to wait a moment so that he can check a conclusion. In this program the emphasis is on accuracy. Both the problem solver and the listener should concentrate on accuracy. If the listener needs a moment to verify a conclusion, this will give the problem solver a chance to go over his work and check his own thinking. The problem solver should, in the back of his mind, constantly have the thought "Is that correct—should I check that?" as he works a problem. This will slow him down a little so that the listener will be able to keep pace. However, if the problem solver is working too hastily, at the expense of accuracy, the listener should ask him to slow down—so that he can follow accurately and analytically. Moreover, even if

the problem solver is not working too hastily to be accurate, the listener may still occasionally ask him to stop a moment while he checks a point he is unsure of.

Third, the listener should not work the problem separately from the problem solver. When some listeners first learn the procedure used in this program, they turn away from the problem solver and work the problem completely on their own. Occasionally they even finish the problem long before the problem solver. This is incorrect. The listener should listen. He should actively work along with the problem solver, not independently of him.

Finally, when the listener catches an error he should only point it out—he should never give the correct answer. By the same token, if the listener sees an answer or a conclusion before the problem solver sees it, he should not furnish it, but should wait for the problem solver to work it out. If the problem solver seems completely stuck, the listener may provide a suggestion on the first step to take. But he should not actually take the first step and obtain a partial answer. Instead, the problem solver should do all the work.

In summary, the listener should understand that he is not being picky or overly critical of his partner when he points out errors. He is helping him improve his scholastic problem solving skill—a skill which will be useful in all academic courses. The listener should check every step taken and every conclusion reached by the problem solver. He should never let the problem solver go on to a second step until he checks the first one. And when he detects an error he should point it out without actually correcting it.

Demand Constant Vocalization

The second function of the listener is to insure that the problem solver vocalizes all of the major steps he takes in solving a problem. Thinking aloud is a primary part of this program. It is the only way to communicate and to monitor thinking. It should not be neglected. Even the solution of simple problems should be vocalized entirely—so that vocalizing can be done easily when difficult problems are met. If the problem solver skips through one or more steps without thinking aloud, the listener should ask him to explain his thoughts at that point [pp. 30–31].

In the pair problem-solving approach, the teacher acts more like a coach than a lecturer. Initially, this involves watching the student pairs work and making sure they play by the rules outlined in the text. Later, as skills improve, the teacher provides feedback on how well individual students are performing in the role of listener or verbalizer, with advice on how to do better. Because the central goal of pair problem solving is to make students more active learners, the teacher must refrain from any actions that would place the student in a passive role. Questions should be answered with questions; statements with challenges such as "Are you sure?" or "How do you know that?" Thus, the teacher should act more like a listener than a problem solver. This innovative approach to teaching is sometimes referred to as Socratic dialogue or, alternatively, as teaching according to the Talmudic tradition.

In order to free the teacher from the roles of information provider and answer verifier, each problem is followed by a detailed solution. These solutions stress the importance of slow, meticulous work and of frequent checking. They differ from traditional solutions largely by their acknowledgement of human frailty. Instead of pretending that good problem solvers always perform flawlessly, they include blind alleys, memory lapses, and other inelegancies. These help to build student confidence and, at the same time, illustrate how good problem solvers deal with their own errors and weaknesses. They also encourage students to verbalize *every* step in their own reasoning. Figure 3.1 gives an example of the thinking of a good problem solver.

When problem solutions are prepared in such detail and with such a corresponding lack of formality, students recognize that there is no one best solution method. To further emphasize this point some problems are followed by several

---

Original Problem

Yes   No

If the word *sentence* contains less than 9 letters and more than 3 vowels, circle the first vowel. Otherwise circle the consonant which is farthest to the right in the word.

Problem-Solver's Response

The problem solver read the entire problem aloud.	"If the word *sentence* contains less than 9 letters and more than 3 vowels, circle the first vowel. Otherwise circle the consonant which is farthest to the right in the word.
	"I'll start from the beginning.
	"If the word *sentence* contains less than 9 letters.
The problem solver pointed to the letters with his pen as he counted.	"I'll count the letters in *sentence*. 1,2,3,4,5,6,7,8. Let me check it. 1,2,3,4,5,6,7,8. So it does have less than 9 letters. I'll write the word *yes* above the problem. That way I'll remember it.
The problem solver wrote yes over the sentence (see original problem).	
The problem solver resumed reading.	"And more than 3 vowels.
The problem solver pointed with his pen as he counted.	"1,2,3. Let me check that. 1,2,3. It contains exactly 3 vowels, not more than 3 vowels. I'll write *no* on the problem to remind me.
	"Circle the first vowel.
	"So I won't do that.
	"Otherwise circle the consonant which is farthest to the right in the word.
	"The consonant farthest to the right? Let me see. Which is my right hand? This is my right hand. OK, so the last letter is the one farthest to the right. But the last letter is E. The next letter over is C. So it is the consonant farthest to the right. I'll circle the C."

FIG. 3.1.   Verbalization of an expert problem solver. (Reprinted from Arthur Whimbey and Jack Lochhead, *Problem solving and comprehension*, 3rd edition, copyright 1982, by permission of The Franklin Institute Press.)

Problem

A train can travel 10 mi in 4 min. How far will it travel in 14 min?

There is more than one way to solve this problem. We will look at three ways, which we will call solutions 1, 2, and 3. Each solution can be viewed in terms of the underlying logic, and in terms of the mathematical computations. Looking at the solution in terms of the underlying logic is slower and less elegant. But in a sense it is more important. People who try to apply mathematical formulas without comprehending the underlying logic of a problem stand a good chance of using an incorrect formula and arriving at a wrong answer. Therefore we will begin with the logic and then look at the mathematical computations.

Solution 1

Logic of the Solution: Here is one way to look at the problem. If the train can travel 10 miles in 4 minutes, then it can travel 20 miles in 8 minutes, and 30 miles in 12 minutes. If it travels still another 2 minutes (to make a total of 14 minutes) it will go 5 more miles, for a total of 35 miles. This is shown below:

4 min	10 mi
4 min	10 mi
4 min	10 mi
2 min	5 mi
14 min	35 mi

This is also represented in the following diagram:

10 mi	10 mi	10 mi	5 mi
4 min	4 min	4 min	2 min

Mathematical Solution of the Problem: Notice that in constructing the table above we counted off how many times 4 minutes goes into 14 minutes. We found that it does three times, with 2 minutes left over. At the same time we counted off the same number of 10-mile sections, and concluded that the train travels 35 miles in 14 minutes. We do the same thing arithmetically when we divided 4 minutes into 14 minutes and then multiply this by 10 miles. Thus:

$$14/4 = 3\frac{1}{2} \qquad 3\frac{1}{2} \times 10 = 35$$

The important thing to understand is that this procedure of dividing and then multiplying is really a shortcut method of spelling out the entire situation, as was done in the table and the diagram above. The diagram shows that we are thinking in terms of 4-minute intervals. In other words, 12 minutes is exactly three 4-minute intervals; and 2 minutes is one-half of a 4-minute interval. Moreover, the train travels 10 miles in each 4-minute interval, and 5 miles in one-half of a 4-minute interval. So it goes 35 miles total.

10 miles	10 miles	10 miles	5 miles
4-minute interval	4-minute interval	4-minute interval	½ of a 4-minute interval

FIG. 3.2.   Example of alternative solutions (*to be continued*).

Solution 2

Logic of the Solution: Another way to solve the problem is to think in terms of ratios that are equal to each other. This approach requires more mathematical background and experience than the other two solutions. Don't use this method with any of the later problems in this chapter unless you are absolutely certain you understand exactly what you are doing.

The logic of the solution is shown in the following diagram:

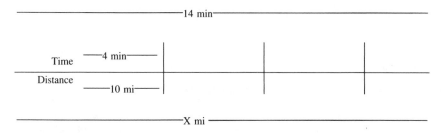

Note the X in the diagram. This is what the problem asks you to find, the distance traveled by the train in 14 minutes.

From the diagram you can see that since 14 minutes is 3½ times more than 4 minutes, the unknown distance X must be 3½ times larger than 10 miles. In other words, the ratio of 14 minutes to 4 minutes is equal to the ratio of X miles to 10 miles. With this idea in mind we can write the following equation:

$$\frac{14}{4} = \frac{X}{10}$$

On the left side of the equation we have the ratio of 14 minutes to 4 minutes. And on the right side we have the ratio of X miles to 10 miles. The equal sign means that these two ratios must be numerically equal.

Mathematical Solution: Once you have set up this equation of ratios, you find X by using simple arithmetic and algebra. Here are steps you could employ:

1. Initial equation: $\quad\quad\quad\quad\quad\quad\quad\quad\quad\quad\quad \dfrac{14}{4} \quad = \quad \dfrac{X}{10}$

2. Multiply both sides of the equation by 10 so that just X will remain on the right side. $\quad\quad\quad \dfrac{10(14)}{4} \quad = \quad \dfrac{X(10)}{10}$

3. Cancel on both sides of the equation. $\quad\quad\quad \dfrac{(5)\ (7)}{\cancel{10}\cancel{(14)}} \quad\quad\quad \dfrac{1}{\cancel{X}\ \cancel{(10)}}$

4. Multiply the numbers to get X. $\quad\quad\quad\quad\quad (5)(7) \quad = \quad 35 = X$

FIG. 3.2.   Example of alternative solutions (*to be continued*).

Solution 3

Logic of the Solution: A third approach begins by asking how many miles the train travels in 1 minute, and then multiplying this by 14 minutes to find the total distance traveled by the train. The following diagram shows that since the train travels 10 miles in 4 minutes, it must travel 2½ miles in 1 minute.

Once we know that the train travels 2½ miles in 1 minute, it is easy to find out how far it travels in 14 minutes. We just add up 14 of these intervals, as shown below.

Mathematical Solution: First you need to determine how many miles the train travels each minute:

$$\frac{10 \text{ mi}}{4 \text{ min}} = 2\frac{1}{2} \text{ mi per min}$$

Once you know that the train travels 2½ miles each minute, you can multiply this by 14 to find how far it travels in 14 minutes.

$$2\frac{1}{2} \text{ mi each min} \times 14 \text{ min} = 35 \text{ mi}$$

Summary

All three solutions are correct. They use different computationnal approaches and formulas, but they are based on basically the same picture of what happens as the train's traveling time increases from 4 minutes to 14 minutes.

FIG. 3.2.   Example of alternative solutions (*continued*). (Reprinted from Arthur Whimbey and Jack Lochhead, *Problem solving and comprehension*, 3rd edition, copyright 1982, by permission of The Franklin Institute Press.)

different solution strategies (See Fig. 3.2). The procedure of working in pairs also stimulates students to compare alternative approaches. One reason for the emphasis on multiple methods is that it helps free students from the tendency to copy the solution given in the book. For if there actually were one best method students might become discouraged about the likelihood of discovering it on their own. Teachers need to be especially sensitive to this point; their tendency to show off a more elegant, quicker, or more efficient strategy can be extremely stifling to the student who has just solved a difficult problem on his or her own.

To encourage students to derive their own solutions rather than imitate those in the book, the first problems in each section are so easy and straightforward that most people can solve them with no instruction. Problems then become gradually more difficult, leading the students, step by step, from a simple, familiar procedure to the complex strategy we are trying to teach. This approach also has the advantage of requiring little if any explanation from either the textbook or the teacher. Explanations tend to place students in a passive role; thus, they should be avoided whenever possible. When one is given, it should be as a summary of work that has already been done, and preferably it should be written by the students rather than by the teacher or textbook author. In our new text *Developing Mathematical Skills* (Whimbey & Lochhead, 1981), we managed to satisfy the reviewer's needs for explanations by placing them at the end of each chapter, where they do the least harm.

The notion of gradually increasing problem difficulty is not exactly new. I would like to distinguish our use of it from several other popular applications. One is the strategy of teaching for success, as advocated by Montessori and others. We believe that failure (and consequent disequilibrium) is critical to learning. An excellent way to illustrate a point is to lead students deliberately into a cognitive trap. The time when one has just failed to solve correctly a problem that appeared simple is the time one is best able to learn. Of course constant failure is no more instructive that constant success (and certainly less fun). The art of teaching revolves around finding the right balance, as Wertime (1979) points out in his interesting paper on this subject.

Our use of progressively more difficult problem tasks also bears some resemblance to the shaping strategies of behaviorism, as used, for example, in programmed learning. Our appoach differs mainly in style. When we break a complex task into smaller components, we make a special effort to prevent students from learning each subtask simply by rote. This can be done either by not providing a detailed solution algorithm, or when such an algorithm is appropriate (for example, in teaching long division), by providing an explanation that helps students see why the algorithm works. In either case, the students' understanding is tested in later problems specially designed to trip up rote learners who overgeneralize an algorithm's domain of application. Unfortunately we are not always successful in designing tests for each kind of misconception, and some students are able to slip by. Further research on problem solving of the type that has been supported by both the National Institute of Education and the National Science Foundation should be useful in identifying and testing for such misconceptions.

As already noted, we have used the pair problem-solving approach in two of our textbooks: *Problem Solving and Comprehension* and *Developing Mathematical Skills*. The latter book offers instruction in solving arithmetic, geometry, and simple algebra problems. *Problem Solving and Comprehension* offers instruction in solving problems in the following four areas: verbal reasoning and reading comprehension, analogical reasoning, analysis of trends and patterns, and mathematical word problems. Figures 3.3 and 3.4 contain examples of problems taken from this text. The four topic areas covered in the text were picked because they are representative of the types of problems used on scholastic

Original Problem

Cathy knows French and German, Sandra knows Swedish and Russian, Cindy knows Spanish and French, Paula knows German and Swedish. If French is easier than German, Russian is harder than Swedish, German is easier than Swedish, and Spanish is easier than French, which girl knows the most difficult languages?

Problem Solution

Step 1. Strategy For Beginning The Problem: The question asks which girl knows the most difficult languages. Therefore the first step is to order the languages by difficulty. This information is contained in the second sentence of the problem, so the solution starts with the second sentence.

Step 2. If French is easier than German . . .

This can be shown in a diagram. The easier language has been arbitrarily put below the harder language.

German┼
French┼

Step 3. . . . Russian is harder than Swedish.

This can be shown in a separate diagram.

Russian┼
Swedish┼

Step 4. . . . German is easier than Swedish . . .

This information shows how the two diagrams can be combined. German is placed below Swedish since it is easier.

Russian┼
Swedish┼
German┼
French┼

Step 5. . . . Spanish is easier than French.

This can be added to the diagram.

Russian┼
Swedish┼
German┼
French┼
Spanish┼

Step 6. The diagram shows that Russian and Swedish are the two most difficult languages. In order to answer the question it is necessary to find the girl who speaks these two languages. Scanning the first sentence shows that Sandra speaks them.

Sandra speaks Russian and Swedish, the most difficult languages.

Original Problem

horse is to *animal* as _____is to _____.

a. cow: milk, *b.* farm: pig, *c.* oak : wood, *d.* saddle: stallion

Problem Solver's Response

The Problem Solver read the relationship sentence aloud, then considered the four options in turn.

"*Horse* is to *animal* as blank is to blank." A horse is an animal. It is a type of animal.

"Cow: milk." A cow isn't a type of milk . . . it gives milk.

"Farm : pig." A farm isn't a type of pig.

"Oak : wood." Oak is a type of wood. So this forms an analogy.

"Saddle : stallion." A saddle isn't a type of stallion.

Answer *c* is best. A horse is a type of animal and oak is a type of wood.

FIG. 3.3.   Example word problem and analogy problem. (Reprinted from Arthur Whimbey and Jack Lochhead, *Problem solving and comprehension,* 3rd edition, copyright 1982, by permission of The Franklin Institute Press.)

Original Problem

2 7 4 9 6 11 8 13 ___ ___ ___

Problem Solution

The Problem Solver read and thought aloud, pointing to the numbers with his pen.

2 7 4 9 6. The numbers seem to be going up and down. Let's see the rest. *11 8 13*. Yes, they're going up and down.

I'll look at the differences between the numbers to see if there is a pattern.

2 to *7* is up 5. *7* to *4* is down 3. *4* to *9* is up 5. *9* to *6* is down 3. *6* to *11* is up 5.

The Problem Solver wrote each of these differences as he computed it.

+ 5 − 3 + 5 − 3 + 5 − 3 + 5
2 7 4 9 6 11 8 13 10 15 ___ ___ ___

It seems to be going up 5, down 3, up 5, down 3. I'll check the rest.

11 to *8* is down 3. *8* to *13* is up 5.

I'll fill in the blanks. The last pair of numbers were *8* to *13*, which is up 5. So the next should go down 3. *13* minus *3* is *10*. I'll write that in the first blank.

+5 − 3 +5 − 3 +5 − 3 +5
2 7 4 9 6 11 8 13 10 15 ___ ___

Next the numbers should go up 5. *10* plus *5* is *15*. I'll write that.

+5 − 3 +5 − 3 +5 − 3 +5
2 7 4 9 6 11 8 13 10 15 ___

Then they should go down 3. *15* minus *3* is *12*.

+5 − 3 +5 − 3 +5 − 3 +5
2 7 4 9 6 11 8 13 10 15

Pattern description: The pattern is add 5, subtract 3, add 5, subtract 3, etc.

Original Problem

The number of cows owned by farmer Smith is the number owned by farmer Thompson divided by the number owned by farmer Jones. Farmer Thompson, who owns 42 cows, would own 8 times as many cows as farmer Jones if he owned 14 more cows. How many cows does farmer Smith own?

Problem Solution

Step 1. The problem asks how many cows farmer Smith owns.

FIG. 3.4. Example pattern problem and mathematical word problem (*to be continued*).

Step 2. The number of cows owned by Smith is the number owned by Thompson divided by the number owned by Jones.

$$\text{Smith's cows} = \frac{\text{Thompson's cows}}{\text{Jones' cows}}$$

Step 3. Thompson has 42 cows.

Thompson—42 cows

Step 4. If Thompson owned 14 more cows he would own eight times as many cows as Jones.

Thompson's cows $+$ 14 $=$ 8 $\times$ Jones' cows

Step 5. If Thompson owned 14 more cows he would own:

$$42 + 14 = 56 \text{ cows}$$

Step 6. So 56 cows is eight times as many cows as Jones owns.

$$56 = 8 \times \text{Jones' cows}$$

Step 7. To find Jones' cows divide 56 by 8.

$$\text{Jones's cows} = \frac{56 \text{ cows}}{8} = 7 \text{ cows}$$

Step 8. To get the number of cows owned by Smith, the division shown in step 2 must be carried out.

$$\text{Smith's cows} = \frac{42}{7} = 6 \text{ cows}$$

Step 9. Smith owns 6 cows.

FIG. 3.4. Example pattern problem and mathematical word problem (*continued*). (Reprinted from Arthur Whimbey and Jack Lochhead, *Problem solving and comprehension*, 3rd edition, copyright 1982, by permission of The Franklin Institute Press.)

aptitude and intelligence tests. The experience of the test constructors suggests that the skills necessary to solve such problems are those most critical to academic success.

THEORETICAL ISSUES RELATED TO USE OF PAIR PROBLEM SOLVING

In this section I consider two sets of theoretical issues related to the use of pair problem solving. First, I examine the theoretical rationale for use of this technique. That is, I consider different lines of theory and research that can help us better understand why this technique may be effective in enabling students to become better thinkers and problem solvers. Secondly, I discuss some theory and research related to identifying constraints that may prevent students from adopting this technique.

Rationale for Use of Pair Problem Solving

I now consider some of the cognitive theory behind pair problem solving. First, I should stress that some of these theoretical underpinnings have been constructed post hoc. The original development of the program was based only on careful observation of student problem-solving behavior and on a long period of trial-and-error attempts to overcome some of the most glaring deficiencies. I feel it is especially important to stress these humble roots now, in this volume, with its emphasis on cognitive science. The chapters in this book mark a new direction in education in which cognitive science is having an increasing impact on curriculum development. This impact has already been delayed too long. But cognitive theory is far from complete and it is essential that we use what theory we have as an aid to curriculum development rather than as a barrier to experimentation. The best innovations will continue to come from teachers who know little theory; some innovations even may turn out to be inconsistent with the current theoretical positions. Education, like engineering, needs to remain an empirically based science in which the advice of theorists is treated with skepticism.

First let us consider the theory behind pair problem solving as it is presented in *Problem Solving and Comprehension* (Whimbey & Lochhead, 1980):

> The ability to analyze complex material and solve problems is a skill just like any other skill such as the ability to play golf or the ability to drive an automobile. However, there is a peculiar difficulty involved in teaching analytical skill. Generally there are two phases to teaching a skill. First the skill is demonstrated to the student. Then he is guided and corrected as he practices it. For example, golf is taught by showing the beginner how to grasp the club, how to place his feet, how to move his arms and his body as he swings. The beginner can watch a golf pro—he can even watch a slow motion form of the pro in action—and in this way can learn the pro's technique. Furthermore, the pro can observe the beginner as he practices, he can point out his flaws, and he can show him how to improve.
>
> In contrast to playing golf, analyzing complex material is an activity which is generally done inside your head. This makes it somewhat difficult for a teacher to teach and for a learner to learn. In other words, a beginner cannot observe how an expert thinks and solves problems. And the expert has trouble demonstrating his technique to a beginning student. There is one way to reduce this difficulty—to have people think aloud while they solve problems. If both students and experts vocalize their thoughts as they work through complex ideas and relationships, the

steps that they take are open to view and their activities can be observed and communicated.

In this book, the procedure of asking people to think aloud while they solve problems is applied in two ways. Experienced problem solvers (a group of graduate students and professors) were asked to think aloud as they solved the problems that are presented in the book. Their responses were tape-recorded, and then the steps they took in solving a problem were summarized and written out. These summaries are presented under the heading Problem Solution. In other words, the problem solution which follows each problem is a summary of steps taken by an experienced problem solver as he or she worked the problem aloud.

The second application of the procedure consists in asking you, the reader, to think aloud as you work each of the problems. In doing this, you make your thinking visible to other people so that they can observe your attack on a problem. Thus, they can learn the techniques you use; they can help point out any errors you make, and they can compare the steps you take with the steps listed in the problem solution. Furthermore, you will find that by thinking aloud you will be able to look at your own thinking activities more carefully. You will be able to see exactly what strategies you use, and what difficulties you have in solving a problem (pp. 23–24).

The eventual objective of pair problem solving is to get each student to be at all times both listener and problem solver. Thus when working a problem the student should be able to listen to himself or herself think, follow the chain of reasoning, catch, and critique errors. When listening to a lecture, on the other hand, the student should also *act* as problem solver, thinking along with the lecturer, puzzling out the issues, organizing and reorganizing the material. We can conceptualize this objective as the development of a self-correcting feedback loop in which students can observe and modify their own cognitive behavior. John Dewey in *How We Think* (1933) referred to this ability as "reflective thought" and considered its development to be the single most important objective of higher education.

Thus far, I have argued that the purpose of requiring verbalizations is to help students externalize ideas and strategies so that they can examine and improve on them. In the subsections that follow, I consider different lines of theory and research that further suggest how making ideas and strategies overt may shed light on errors and lead to improvements in thinking.

The Role of Verbalization in Permitting More Precise Observations.   We have all heard the maxim, "You don't know a subject until you have taught it." We have experienced the importance that discussion with colleagues has in furthering our own understanding. We acknowledge, often begrudgingly, the impact that writing a paper or proposal can have on clarifying our ideas. All these examples illustrate the positive effects of putting thoughts into words.

Unfortunately, very little theoretical work has dealt with this issue; we really do not understand why verbalization is as useful as it is.

Educational theory not only ignores the importance of verbalization, it often actively discourages it. We tell students to read faster by suppressing even subvocalization. We attempt to improve a child's grasp of arithmetic by telling him or her not to count on fingers. We discourage the use of scratch paper and stress the importance of "doing it in your head." Finally, there is our attitude about people who talk aloud to themselves—they are crazy, weird, and maybe, geniuses. Perhaps it is time we look at why so many geniuses talk to themselves.

Piaget has outlined the basis of a theory for the role that verbalization plays in careful thought. His argument begins with an example. We all know how to crawl and could do so automatically if we got down on all fours. But few people can describe the order in which they would move their limbs. Do the four move in sequence; if so what sequence? Do two limbs move together? It might be the left leg and the left arm but then it could be the left leg and the right arm. It turns out that few adults can answer these questions without some effort and those answers have interesting properties; for example, mathematicians tend to give one answer and physicists another (Piaget, 1976).

The point of the foregoing example is the following. We all possess a cognitive routine for crawling; it is stored as a sequence of muscle movements and is not available to conscious examination. When we verbalize that routine, perhaps by watching ourselves or others, we rerepresent it as a series of verbal instructions and probably also as a sequence of visual or kinesthetic images. The verbal instructions are available to conscious examination. They may be systematically studied, and individual components can be varied, deleted, or elaborated. Thus the act of verbalizing is directly associated with bringing the subconscious to consciousness.

Piaget (1974) has speculated that the connection between verbalization and consciousness is communication. A mental procedure enters consciousness when it is formulated in a communicable representation. Often this is verbal but it may also be visual as in diagrams, or kinesthetic as in body language. Communicable representations are in consciousness not because we can relay them to other people but because we can relay them to ourselves. We may run through the steps of a procedure and observe each one in sequence. This self-observation is awareness and thus the basis of all consciousness.

The primary advantage of bringing a thought to consciousness is that we may observe it. We can understand how the various parts are related to each other. We may systematically analyze and modify the components and this permits us to alter and improve faulty routines.

Austin (1974) has shown how this can work in the case of juggling. For the novice, three-ball juggling is a mysterious, awe-inspiring activity. Most people are unable to observe the exact path that the individual balls follow and they see only a blur of activity. By videotaping and carefully observing jugglers at work, Austin was able to write a verbal description for each component of the procedure. His description is so effective that most people can learn to juggle three balls with no more than 10 to 15 minutes of practice. One striking result of this training is that when observing another juggler it is possible to track each ball; thus what 10 minutes earlier had been a blur is now a smooth, even slow, easy-to-follow routine.

The advantage of representing the juggling routine as a series of verbal commands is in learning the initial skill. Refined juggling needs to be more automatic; it should be nonverbal and subconscious. Thus, although consciousness can be useful it is not always desirable. Its primary value is in learning and self-critical analysis (Fischer, Brown, & Burton, 1977). Once a routine has been perfected it works more efficiently when it is removed to the subconscious. However, if the routine has a communicable representation we can, whenever we choose, return it to consciousness for further examination and refinement. If the routine was never verbalized we may find it difficult or impossible to conceptualize, examine, or improve.

So far all the examples have involved motor skills. As pointed out earlier, the advantage of analyzing motor skills is that they can be seen or, more accurately, that the result of each subcomponent is observable. The routines themselves are not observable. A mental skill, such as solving equations, produces much less in the way of observable output. Although verbalizing helps to bring more of the process into view, it is a representation of the process and may involve significant alternations. The full extent to which verbalizing changes thought patterns is probably unknowable. Those of us who do research in the area feel that the changes are much less than the skeptics fear. Although subjects often report that verbalizing initially inhibits their thoughts, with practice most find verbalizing to be an aid. But for the present, little hard evidence exists to support the hypothesis that the relationship between motor skills and their verbalization is similar to that between mental skills and verbalization (Ericsson & Simon, 1980). This ought to be a productive area for future research.

Role of Verbalization in Symbolizing Variables: Research in Progress.   Research now being conducted on the topic of symbolization may eventually improve our understanding of the role verbalization plays in thinking. An example will illustrate the kinds of issues under current investigation. When students write or read algebraic equations they often have difficulty interpreting the meaning of variables. For example, the following sections of dialogue are taken from a half-hour interview with a student who was asked to interpret the following equation (Rosnick, 1982):

$$6R + 2B = 40$$

The given information is that records cost $6.00 each and books $2.00; a total of $40.00 was spent altogether. During the interview the student was frequently asked to explain the meaning of the letter *B*.

S: Well, *B* is the number of books, but it—; more importantly— in terms of figuring out how much they cost —B is—is a price, which is $2.00.

I: So you say *B* is the number of books and—

S: at $2.00.

I: at $2.00.

S: Well, no—; B—B is . . . B is the—is the um, the variable that equals the books at $2.00 . . .

At other times during the half hour the student said:

1.   . . . Well, *B* is one book because it—it; *B* has something to do with the price of the book . . .

2.   . . . *B* equals the books . . .

3.   . . . *B* equals 5 times the price of a book—of the books which is $2.00 . . .

4.   . . . Um . . . (11 sec) . . . No, I think *B* is equal to 1 . . . but, um . . . it—I think you're referring to it right here . . . where you could say *B* is equal to 5 . . . ?

These sections of dialogue indicate that the student has no consistent interpretation for the letter *B*. Instead of making a precisely articulated definition where *B* would represent the number of books (correct) or the cost of one book (incorrect), the student maintains an inarticulate, vague image of "books." Any and all booklike properties can be associated with the letter *B*. At the present time we do not know what cognitive factors distinguish such students from those who are more precise in their thinking. But it appears that one difference concerns the degree of verbalization. Precise thinking requires a carefully verbalized definition for each variable. The verbalization must include all the meaning of the variable and the variable must mean all the things included in its verbal definition. For the student described here the letter *B* seemed to represent at times more and at other times less than what had been put into words. Thus there appears to be a failure to effectively coordinate thought and language.

Role of Verbalization in Stimulating Conceptual Development.   Another source of post hoc theoretical support for pair problem solving is constructivist epistemology as espoused by Piaget (1969), Von Glasersfeld (1979), and others. Constructivism is concerned with the process by which we are able to learn new concepts and the effect these concepts have on our perception of the external world. Piaget uses the terms *assimilation* and *accommodation* to describe the flux between our perceptions and our conceptions. At any particular instant we can only perceive those things for which we have concepts. Thus a baby may assimilate the perception of a cup to the concept "object" because the more refined concept "cup" has not yet been formed. Through extended experience with this and other objects, say a block, the infant may begin to notice different properties. This realization is at first vague and ill defined. It creates a state of disequilibrium in which objects that had been all the same now seem different. Eventually the child differentiates its concept "object," perhaps in conjunction with the development of the concept "in" into two groups: those that can contain other objects and those that cannot. The concept "object" has now been accommodated to form a new concept "container."

It should be obvious that it does little good to lecture to infants on the properties that distinguish cups from blocks. Until the concept "container" exists in the child's head it cannot be perceived—no matter how clearly it is explained. What we can do is give the child opportunity to explore containers, blocks, and other objects. (Actually the term "explore" suggests too structured an activity; a more accurate description is "mess with." The importance of this activity is stressed in Kenneth Graham's *The Wind in the Willows* (1918) when Rat states, "There is *nothing*—absolutely nothing—half so much worth doing as simply messing about." We may also model the behavior of placing blocks into containers and then watch the child struggle to put the container into the block. But in spite of all we do to manipulate the child's activity, the concept "container" must be formed by the child; we cannot pipe ideas into its head.

A similar situation exists when 16 years later the child encounters a concept such as "potential energy." To most high school and college students potential energy, kinetic energy, and feeling good are all part of the undifferentiated, vaguely defined concept of "energy." Lecturing to such students may help them make distinctions, but it is just as likely that the speaker's contrasts will all be assimilated to a single concept. Once again the student must create the distinctions and accommodate old concepts to form new conceptions. Our most effective leverage is obtained not by telling students what we think, but by placing them in situations where they must confront the relevant differences themselves. It is only after they have formulated the essential concepts that our attempts to communicate with them can be effective.

Thus, according to the constructivist viewpoint, lectures and textbooks are inefficient mechanisms for stimulating conceptual change. The ideas presented in them will most likely be assimilated to the student's current concepts. On the other hand, Socratic dialogue and argument can be effective mechanisms for encouraging conceptual growth (Arons, 1973, 1974). The alteration between listening and explaining can force students to reformulate their ideas and to test them against those of other students. The simple fact that this situation forces students to play with ideas leads the constructivist to have faith in it.

Constraints that May Prevent Students from Adopting Active Learning Strategies

Whereas the constructivist doubts the effectiveness of lectures and favors discussion or debate, most students prefer authoritative presentations. As I have already stated, this student view seems to be based on a copy theory of learning. The roots of copy theory lie in everyday experience. Our normal perceptions seem to be direct, unaltered reflections of an external reality. We seem to learn about our environment by copying and remembering what we see. The active role we take in organizing and interpreting our own perceptions is hidden from us. By the time we are old enough to question how we learn, most of us have built a complete conceptual system founded on some form of copy theory.

William Perry (1970) has chronicled the enormous difficulties that confront students when they begin to change their view on learning. In an extensive longitudinal study of Harvard undergraduates he has shown how students gradually develop new epistemologies during their 4 years at college. The developmental pattern moves from a copy theory in which the source of truth is what the experts tell you, to a more relativistic system in which each individual must determine truth for himself. This developmental process is extremely complicated because it involves changing the students' entire conceptual system, including their sense of values and ethics. It cannot result from a few scattered courses but rather is the product of an intensive immersion in an intellectual community that permeates every aspect of the students' lives.

If the copy theory of learning is directly tied to the developmental stages described by Perry then we cannot expect students to change their views of learning rapidly. A single course on active learning strategies will have only a limited impact. Unless other courses that students take also stress active learning, the effect of any one course may be forgotten. This problem was perhaps most clearly explained to me by a student who said "I know what you are trying to do, you are trying to make me think. I don't need that—it won't help me get through this university."

A second implication of Perry's developmental scheme and of other work in developmental psychology concerns the age at which students can most easily learn the kinds of strategies that we are attempting to teach in our program. Most of the emphasis on active learning to date has been in the primary grades. Although constructivists would argue that all learning from infancy on is active learning, the kind of reflective thought described by Dewey and encouraged in our program (i.e., the notion of making students aware of themselves as thinkers) may be an aspect of active thought that emerges only at later developmental stages. For example, Perry's work suggests that students may not be ready to internalize the kinds of active learning strategies that we would like them to master until their second or third year in college. Thus, if students are to become fully competent as active learners, it would appear necessary to extend the emphasis on active learning from the primary grades into high school and college, with different aspects of active learning being encouraged at different ages.

EVALUATION OF PAIR PROBLEM-SOLVING INSTRUCTIONAL MATERIALS

Few formal evaluations have been conducted to assess the effectiveness of the pair problem-solving instructional materials. Teachers are usually satisfied to note the degree of student involvement in comparison to that of other modes of teaching. Furthermore, the students themselves often make very favorable comments and report how the procedure has helped them in other courses. They will say things such as "I feel smarter," and one teacher said recently, "I know it works because I know I am smarter than I used to be."

The most carefully designed evaluations have usually involved courses that used the pair problem-solving materials in conjunction with other approaches. One example is the 1979 summer Stress on Analytical Reasoning (SOAR) program. In this, 34 prefreshman students who had scored below grade 12 on the Nelson–Denny Reading Achievement Test were admitted to a special four-part summer program consisting of: participation in a Piagetian-based laboratory science program, instruction in analytical reasoning skills, instruction in vocabulary learning skills, and participation in quiz bowl competitions. The primary text for the analytical skills component was *Problem Solving and Comprehension*; 5 class hours per week were devoted to it.

A posttest was used that included both the Nelson–Denny Reading Achievement Test and the Preliminary Scholastic Achievement Test (PSAT). The average improvement on the Nelson–Denny was 1.4 grade levels. On the PSAT the average gain was 7.3 of a possible 160 points (equivalent to a 1600-point combined score on the Scholastic Aptitude Test). Among the 21 students whose pretest PSAT was below 70 the gain was 11.4 (Carmichael, 1979).

These results can be attacked in several ways, all of which help to illustrate the difficulties associated with conducting rigorous evaluations of this type of program. Because the students were preselected to have low test scores, their improvement should be due partially to regression toward the mean. This effect can only be factored out through the use of an appropriate control group. Such a control would have been politically difficult and in this case would also have reduced the experimental sample to 17 students. Comparisons to average student performance, or to similar populations in previous years or at other institutions are very difficult to interpret.

To run an experiment with an adequate sample size and proper controls one needs to be at a large, impersonal institution in which students can be randomly assigned to alternative modes of instruction without their being fully aware of what is being done to them. Furthermore, one needs to be working with a mainstream course with high enrollments. As present, I know of no university where the pair problem-solving approach is being used in such a course. Analytical skills development is simply not part of the standard curriculum.

If one were able to solve the problems of sample size and random assignment one would still face the question of preparing a valid and credible measuring instrument. Here one faces the age-old transfer problem. If the evaluation criterion is performance on a test similar to the Scholastic Aptitude Test, one can argue that the course was taught to the test. It then becomes necessary to show that the students are capable of using the skills they have learned not only on tasks similar to those used during instruction, but also in more typical academic learning situations. At this point, researchers often adopt grades as the criterion to use in determining effectiveness of instruction. Yet grades are a confounded criterion in that high grades do not always indicate that students have achieved a solid understanding of course material and low grades do not always indicate that they have failed to do so. (See McClelland, 1973). Our own experiments at the University of Massachusetts suggest that in the best of courses, less than 50% of the A students have a solid conceptual understanding of the material (Barowy & Lochhead, 1980; Gray & Lochhead, 1980). Thus, although pair problem solving should have a positive effect on subsequent grades, the effect may be masked by other factors, unless one uses rather large samples.

An alternative to using grades as a criterion would be some type of oral examination in which a faculty team would evaluate how well students had understood the material in a course they had taken following instruction in pair problem solving. To me, this is a more valid and credible measure, but it is expensive. Furthermore, it gives the students from the pair problem-solving course an advantage because they have had considerable experience with oral exams. Whether or not this advantage is unfair, or relevant, is itself an interesting question for future research.

Finally, there is the question of who should conduct the evaluation. In the past, curriculum evaluations have usually been run by the proponents of the new curriculum. These have not always been credible or complete. An example from my own experience will serve to illustrate the dangers. I once obtained 95 volunteers for a pair problem-solving course on mathematical modeling. After 30 volunteers were eliminated for scheduling reasons, 41 students were randomly selected for the experimental course and the remaining 24 took a parallel course on mathematical modeling. In a subsequent physics course the average grade of the experimental group was 2.5 (on a 4-point scale), whereas for the control group it was 1.8. This appears to be a clearly favorable result; yet for a variety of reasons I believe the difference between the groups may be more a function of inadequacies in the course offered to the control students then of the strengths of the one given to the experimental group. Follow-up measures may help to clarify this issue. In the meantime, I am left with statistical data that is clearly favorable, but subjective data that makes me skeptical of the result. This type of uncertainty is nearly always associated with evaluations, which is why I believe they should be conducted by impartial investigators.

The problems of evaluating a cognitive skills course—sample size, measurement validity, and evaluation impartiality—all argue for large-scale evaluations. Serious evaluations of significant new curricula should be conducted through either some sort of interuniversity cooperation and/or through large-scale government research support. Although such efforts are expensive, they are frequently cost effective when viewed in relationship to the amount of funding that has been devoted to curriculum development activities. Furthermore, if done properly they could provide the type of information curriculum developers need to improve their products. This is an area that I hope will become of increasing interest to those in cognitive science.

ACKNOWLEDGMENTS

I thank John Clement, Robert L. Gray, Judith W. Segal, and Arthur Whimbey for their comments on earlier drafts of this chapter. Research reported in this chapter was supported by NSF Award No. SED78–22043 in the Joint National Institute of Education/National Science Foundation Program of Research on Cognitive Processes and the Structure of Knowledge in Science and Mathematics.

REFERENCES

Arons, A. Toward wider public understanding of science. *American Journal of Physics,* 1973, *41*(6), 769–782.

Arons, A. Addendum to Toward wider public understanding of science. *American Journal of Physics,* 1974, *42*(2), 157–158.

Austin, H. *A computational view of the skill of juggling* (AI Memo 330). Cambridge, Mass.: MIT, 1974.

Barowy, W., & Lochhead, J. *Abstract reasoning in rotational physics.* Paper presented at the meeting of the American Association of Physics Teachers, Troy, New York, June 1980.

Bloom, B. S., & Broder, L. J. *Problem-solving processes of college students: An exploratory investigation.* Chicago: The University of Chicago Press, 1950.

Carmichael, J. W., Jr. *Project SOAR.* New Orleans: Xavier University, Summer 1979.

Dewey, J. *How we think.* New York: Heath Books, 1933.

Ericsson, K. A., & Simon, H. A. Verbal reports as data. *Psychological Review,* 1980, *87,* 215–251.

Finkel, D., & Monk, S. *Contexts for learning.* Seattle: University of Washington Press, 1978.

Fischer, G., Brown, J. S., & Burton, R. R. Aspects of a theory of simplification, debugging, and coaching. *Proceedings of the 2nd Annual Conference of Canadian Society for Computational Studies of Intelligence,* Toronto, July 1977.

Graham, K. *The wind in the willows.* New York: Charles Scribner's Sons, 1908.

Gray, R. L., & Lochhead, J. *Can cognitive theory help us teach physics?* Amherst: University of Massachusetts at Amherst, Cognitive Development Project, Department of Physics and Astronomy, 1980.

McClelland, D. C. Testing for competence rather than for intelligence. *American Psychologist,* 1973, *28,* 1–14.

Papert, S. *A computer laboratory for elementary schools* (LOGO Memo 1). Cambridge, Mass.: MIT, October 1971. (a)

Papert, S. *Teaching children to be mathematicians versus teaching about mathematics* (AI Memo 249). Cambridge, Mass.: MIT, 1971. (b)

Papert, S. *Mindstorms: Children, computers, and powerful ideas.* New York: Basic Books, Inc., 1980.

Perry, W. G., Jr. *Forms of intellectual and ethical development in the college years: A scheme.* New York: Holt, Rinehart, & Winston, 1970.

Piaget, J., & Inhelder, B. *The psychology of the child.* New York: Basic Books, Inc., 1969.

Piaget, J. *Origin of consciousness.* Paper presented at the University of New Hampshire, Spring 1974.

Piaget, J. *The grasp of consciousness.* Cambridge, Mass.: Harvard University Press, 1976.

Rosnick, P. *The use of letters in precalculus algebra.* Unpublished doctoral dissertation, University of Massachusetts at Amherst, 1982.

Von Glasersfeld, E. Radical constructivism and Piaget's concept of knowledge. In F. B. Murray (Ed.), *The impact of Piagetian theory on education, philosophy, psychiatry, and psychology.* Baltimore: University Park Press, 1979.

Wertime, R. Students, problems, and courage spans. In J. Lochhead & J. Clement (Eds.), *Cognitive process instruction.* Philadelphia: Franklin Institute Press, 1979.

Whimbey, A., & Lochhead, J. *Problem solving and comprehension: A short course in analytical reasoning* (2nd ed.). Philadelphia: Franklin Institute Press, 1980.

Whimbey, A., & Lochhead, J. *Developing mathematical skills: Computation, problem solving, and basics for algebra.* New York: McGraw-Hill, 1981.

4 Improving Thinking and Learning Skills: An Analysis of Three Approaches

John D. Bransford
Vanderbilt University

Barry S. Stein
Tennessee Technological University

Ruth Arbitman-Smith
*George Peabody College
at Vanderbilt University*

Nancy J. Vye
University of Western Ontario

The purpose of this chapter is to analyze three programs designed to help people develop the ability to think and learn more effectively. In alphabetical order they are: (1) Feuerstein's *Instrumental Enrichment*; (2) Lipman, Sharp, and Oscanyan's *Philosophy for Children*; and (3) Whimbey and Lochhead's short course in *Problem Solving and Comprehension*. Each was developed independently and each claims considerable success.

One of the goals of this chapter is to describe the three programs—to sketch the theoretical rationale for each approach as well as the instructional procedures that are used. A second goal is to compare the approaches with one another. Have the innovators of each program independently arrived at similar conceptualizations of the nature of thinking and learning? Do they agree on the methods for facilitating development that educators might use? The third goal of the chapter is to compare each of the programs with the experimental literature on cognition and cognitive development. Are these programs based on principles that are congruent with current theoretical thinking? If not, does the major problem lie with the program or with the current state of the theoretical art?

Before describing the three programs, it is instructive to note that the idea of designing curricula to help people improve their ability to think and learn represents an old and well-established tradition (Mann, 1979). If this were the early 1800s, for example, we might be discussing a program that makes promises such as the following:

> (If you come to us we) will teach with SCIENTIFIC CERTAINTY that most useful of all knowledge—YOURSELF; YOUR DEFECTS, and how to obviate them;

133

where you are liable to imperfections, errors and excesses; and direct you SPE-CIFICALLY on what mental faculties and functions you require especially to cultivate and restrain . . . All this you can obtain, at moderate cost, from those who have devoted their entire lives to this study and practice, and understand it perfectly, by calling at our Rooms [In Mann, 1979, p. 225].

Many aspects of this program sound useful and relatively up-to-date; for example, the program emphasizes the development of self-knowledge (metacognition?), plus the correction of imperfections and mental errors.

The preceding quotation is an excerpt from an ad signed by Fowler and Well, Phrenologists. Phrenologists believed that they could assess the development of particular mental faculties or abilities by measuring bumps on the skull. Different bumps were assumed to reveal cognitive abilities such as local or short-term memory, verbal memory, mechanical ability, judgment, cautiousness or care-fulness, and so forth (see Mann, 1979). The reasoning was that particular abilities were localized in particular parts of the brain. If someone had well-developed abilities, a well-developed verbal memory for example, this area of the brain would be enlarged and hence produce protrusions on the skull. Phrenologists' use of head measurements was therefore designed to serve a function similar to today's mental tests. Many phrenologists did not stop here, however; they used their assessment techniques to derive training programs that might improve cog-nitive functioning. Some dramatic successes were reported (one involved a 19th-century Helen Keller), and many educators were highly enthusiastic about the breakthroughs promised by this new approach (see Mann, 1979).

The phrenologists were by no means the first to stress training that "expanded the mind's powers" of thinking and reasoning (Mann, 1979). Plato emphasized the importance of process over mere content; some might characterize his position as emphasizing the importance of developing the mental *discipline* necessary to reason and think. For example, Plato sometimes argued that the study of arith-metic and geometry was especially conducive to the development of mental discipline:

Have you observed that those who have a natural talent for calculation are generally quick at every other kind of knowledge; and even the dull, if they have had an arithmetical training, *although they may derive no other advantage from it*, always become much quicker than they would otherwise have been?

Arithmetic stirs up him who is by nature sleepy and dull, and makes him quick to learn, retentive, and shrewd. He makes progress quite beyond his natural powers.

In all departments of knowledge, as experience proves, any one who has studied geometry is infinitely quicker of apprehension that one who has not. [In Mann, 1979, p. 125].

Mann (1979) notes that an emphasis on the importance of mental discipline appears again and again throughout history. In the late 1500s, for example, Francis Bacon advocated the study of mathematics to remediate basic problems such as lack of attention. Bacon wrote:

> If a boy has a light, inattentive inconstant spirit, so that he is easily diverted, and his attention cannot be readily fixed, he will find advantage in mathematics, in which a demonstration must be commenced anew whenever the thought wanders even for a moment [In Mann, 1979, p. 13].

Others began to recommend the learning of Latin as well as mathematics. Why? Because it provided training in how to learn.

In the 1690s and 1700s, we find John Locke espousing the benefits of mental discipline. As pointed out by Bennett and Bristol (1906):

> All pleasant methods of teaching children necessary knowledge are false and ridiculous. It is not a question of learning geography or geometry: it is a question of learning of work; of learning the weariness of concentrating one's attention on the matter at hand [p. 24, 26].

Similar ideas were picked up in America and practiced later at many levels of education. The following is a statement published in 1829, by Yale University, that explains the essential purpose of a college education:

> The two great points to be gained in intellectual culture are the *discipline* and the *furniture* of the mind; expanding its powers and storing it with knowledge. The former of these is perhaps, the more important of the two [In Woody, 1951, p. 202].

How did Yale faculty purport to expand the mind's powers? By subjecting students to daily and vigorous exercises that would develop the faculties necessary to master any content area one might eventually choose to learn (Mann, 1979).

We mention these selected excerpts from the history of what we now call "cognitive process training" (Mann, 1979) because they highlight issues that surface in the present chapter. None of the programs we discuss advocate that students be forced to learn Latin or arithmetic in order to develop "mental discipline." Nevertheless, we see an emphasis on "systematic analysis," "the need for precision," "criteria for valid reasoning," and so forth. Some sense of the concept of mental discipline seems to be operating here. We also encounter the issue of whether there are general skills and strategies that can transfer to a wide variety of content areas, or whether most transfer is based on specific elements that are common across situations (Thorndike, 1913). In short, we face many issues that have been discussed before.

It is also instructive to note that the preceding quotations from Plato, Locke, and others do not adequately reflect the approaches to learning and thinking that were proposed by these distinguished scholars. For example, Mann (1979) notes that Locke sometimes seems to be a faculty psychologist who stresses "mental discipline," yet at other times appears to hold a very different view of education. Similarly, theorists have emphasized ideas from Plato (Socratic dialogues, for example) that seem quite different from the ones expressed in the previous quotations about the discipline derived from studying arithmetic and geometry (see Lipman, Sharp & Oscanyan in this chapter). The approaches developed by Plato, Locke, and others are so rich and multifaceted that it is easy to mischaracterize their positions by focusing only on selected parts. A similar potential for mischaracterization arises in the present chapter. As authors, we face the problem of interpreting each of the programs reviewed. We try to do this in a manner consistent with the intentions of the program developers, of course, but only the broad outlines can be described here and it would be naive to assume that our personal experiences and biases play no role in this process. The mere fact that our review must be *selective* suggests that we may miss points the developers consider crucial to their approach. The problem of accurate interpretation is compounded by the fact that we have had the opportunity to see only one of these programs, Feuerstein's *Instrumental Enrichment,* in operation in the classroom. This experience has convinced us of the importance of direct observation; it is easy to miss the significance of many statements about the program when one's only exposure to it is through the medium of the printed word.

We use the following format when discussing the programs reviewed in this chapter. First, we present a *theoretical overview,* where we try to capture the program developers' basic assumptions about the general problem of thinking and learning. We then describe the basic *procedures of instruction* and attempt to relate these to the program developers' theoretical approach. The third section of each review involves an *overview of program content*; here we provide examples of some of the problems and skills that each program attempts to teach.

The fourth part of each program review is an analysis of the instructional approaches and procedures used in the program; this is divided into three parts. We first discuss the possible advantages and disadvantages of those instructional procedures that remain invariant across all aspects of the program. Next, we discuss the degree to which each program helps students learn to solve the types of problems presented as class exercises; there appear to be important differences between programs that simply present students with a series of practice problems and those that provide instruction that can help students learn to solve these problems. In the third subsection of part four, we ask whether each program's procedures appear to be useful in helping students develop more general thinking and learning skills. We also discuss existing evaluation data for each program.

The overall goal of the program analysis is to identify basic theoretical issues that warrant further analysis and research.

WHIMBEY & LOCHHEAD'S PROBLEM SOLVING AND COMPREHENSION

In the preface to their book *Problem Solving and Comprehension: A Short Course in Analytical Reasoning* (1980), Whimbey and Lochhead (hereafter W & L) argue that "the one element that has not been emphasized in modern education is careful thinking [p. iii]." The purpose of their short course is to help students improve their analytical reading and reasoning skills. In their words:

> It is fascinating to imagine what might happen to our national literacy and math competency if all teachers from elementary through college level saw one of their major roles as teaching students to think carefully in acquiring and using information from the academic disciplines [p. iii].

Theoretical Overview

W & L view thinking as a complex set of skills that can be acquired through practice. In an earlier book, Whimbey (1976) cites Bartlett's *Thinking* as support for this position. According to Bartlett (1958), as quoted by Whimbey:

> It seems reasonable to try to begin by treating thinking provisionally as a complex and high-level kind of skill. Thinking has its acknowledged experts, like every other known form of skill, and in both cases much of the expertness, though never, perhaps, all of it, has to be acquired by well-informed practice. Every kind of bodily skill is based upon evidence picked up directly or indirectly from the environment, and used for the attempted achievement of whatever issue may be required at the time of the performance. Every kind of thinking also claims that it is based upon information or evidence which, again, must be picked up directly or indirectly from the environment and which is used in an attempt to satisfy some requirement of the occasion upon which the thinking takes place.
>
> It would be easy enough to go on pointing out a number of other likenesses, or a similar general character, between bodily skill and thinking [p. 117].

Fitts and Posner's book *Human Performance* (1967) provides additional support for the thesis of similarities between symbolic and perceptual motor skills (cf. Whimbey, 1976). Whimbey also notes that Bloom and Broder (1950), two educators who created an early thinking-skills program for college students, suggested that it was helpful to trainees to emphasize the close connection between learning a physical skill, such as tennis, and learning the thinking skills necessary for academic reasoning. W & L follow this advice in their book.

W & L make four points about the relationship between physical skills and mental skills. As noted already, they propose that the ability to analyze complex materials and to solve problems is a skill similar to the ability to play golf or drive an automobile. They therefore stress that thinking is a learnable skill rather than some mysterious ability that is either present or absent at birth. Second, W & L suggest that there are two phases to learning (or teaching) any new skill. Students first need to see it demonstrated (a golf swing, for example), and then need practice plus feedback. The third point made is that thinking skills are harder to teach because they tend to be hidden; it is much easier to observe golf swings than thinking processes. Their program therefore makes thought processes quite explicit (both to the learner and the teacher), so that there is more opportunity for corrective feedback. The final point that W & L make about relationships between physical and mental skills is that both take time to develop. They note that from 10 to 40 hours are required to complete their book on analytic reasoning and then ask: "Suppose you took 25 hours of golf lessons, what would you accomplish? Would you expect to reach the ranks of a professional [p. 2]?" They proceed to note that 10 to 40 hours is sufficient to teach only the fundamentals of thinking, golf, and so forth. Furthermore, they emphasize that students need to accept the responsibility of practicing and evaluating on their own. Although W & L do not cite specific studies, there seems to be considerable agreement that the development of professional expertise requires a considerable amount of practice (Chase & Simon, 1973; Norman, 1978).

It is interesting to note that W & L use the analogy between physical skills and mental skills to help students understand the purpose and limitations of their short course in analytical thinking. They assume that physical skills are less mystifying to students than mental skills; the former are therefore used as a basis for understanding the latter, for making the strange familiar. (We say more about this general approach to teaching and learning later in this chapter.) When teaching physical skills, for example, instructors frequently organize training into basic components such as how to hold a tennis racket, how to swing the racket, how to serve to a particular spot, and so forth. A good instructor also teaches according to the level of development already reached by the student. One does not try to teach tennis to an infant who cannot walk and run, for example, because these skills are prerequisites for tennis (one might, however, teach eye–hand coordination at an early age). Similarly, if an adult does not have the strength to hold a tennis racket for more than a minute, one might begin with weight training rather than tennis training per se. A good instructor would not place an intermediate player in a class for beginners; it would be too boring. The point is obvious, but it should be noted that approaches to teaching new skills depend on the skills already developed. It is therefore important to identify the skills that W & L presuppose in their course and to differentiate these from the ones that are the focus of instruction. This issue is discussed next.

Some Components of Problem Solving

Consider the following problem from W & L (p. 7):

1. There are 3 separate, equal-size boxes, and inside each box there are 2 separate small boxes, and inside each of the small boxes there are 4 even smaller boxes. How many boxes are there altogether?

   a. 24   b. 13   c. 21   d. 33   e. some other number

Assume that someone misses this problem. What kinds of skills might one teach to help the person become able to solve problems such as this?

Decoding. It seems clear that people could miss the preceding problem because they lacked the ability to decode adequately. This problem might be circumvented by presenting the problem orally; however, the person would then confront additional difficulties because the problem contains a considerable amount of information that could easily exceed short-term memory constraints (Newell & Simon, 1972). Decoding can be viewed as a general skill that can also be analyzed into components (Huey, 1908; LaBerge & Samuels, 1974). We shall not attempt to analyze decoding skills because the W & L program is designed for high school and college students who are presumed to have developed them. We discuss decoding simply to make the obvious point that decoding can be viewed as an important component of many problem-solving skills (especially for problems that contain a good deal of information that could be overwhelming if presented in an oral form). W & L do not attempt to teach decoding skills.

Vocabulary. Students could have developed basic decoding skills yet still miss the problem presented here because they lack familiarity with some of the vocabulary used in the problems. One needs to know the meaning of "boxes," for example, and of "inside," "smaller," "altogether," and so forth. A lack of vocabulary knowledge can be an important reason for failure to solve many problems. W & L assume that most of their problems do not exceed the working vocabulary of the intended students. The primary goal of the W & L program is not to teach new vocabulary per se.

Basic Arithmetic Operations. A third reason for failing the previous problem about boxes is that students may be able to decode and may be familiar with all the vocabulary items in the problem yet may lack knowledge of basic arithmetical operations such as addition and subtraction. If a student could not add, for example, questions such as the one about boxes would be missed. Skills such as addition, subtraction, and multiplication can also be broken into subskills. As in the case of decoding, however, it is assumed that the high school and college students who take the W & L course have already developed these skills.

Imprecise Thinking.   A fourth reason for errors on the boxes problem, and the one emphasized by W & L, is "sloppy or inprecise thinking." Students may be able to decode the words in the boxes problem, may know the necessary vocabulary and be able to add adequately, yet they may still make errors because they lack the skill of "thinking precisely." W & L provide the following protocol from a student who attempted to solve the "boxes" problem.

> I pictured the three boxes and the two smaller boxes inside the three boxes. . . .
> I added three plus two (which gave five) and counted the four other boxes twice.
> Five plus eight gave me thirteen.

This student failed to specify the correct relationships among the boxes and hence added the wrong things. The present authors have asked several high school and college students to answer W & L's test questions and have found another reason why many frequently miss this problem: They represent the sequence of boxes correctly yet add only the smaller boxes, thereby arriving at the answer of 24. The problem asks, "How many boxes are there *altogether?*" It is easy to miss this feature of the problem, yet it is clearly necessary for successful solution.

The Concept of Precise Thinking

It seems clear that instances of "sloppy thinking" such as those just noted frequently result in errors in problem solving. Is it possible to define "sloppy thinking" (or its opposite, "precise thinking") in more detail? W & L make three different attempts to help their readers break the general concepts of "precise" and "sloppy" thinking into subcomponents. For example, they discuss four reasons for problem-solving failure:

1. Person fails to observe and use all the relevant facts of a problem.
2. Person fails to approach the problem in a systematic step-by-step manner. He makes leaps in logic, jumping to conclusions without checking them.
3. Person fails to spell out relationships fully.
4. Person is sloppy and inaccurate in collecting information and carrying out mental activities (p. 13).

W & L note that these sources of error tend to be interrelated, although different people may be prone to different ones.

W & L also provide students with a checklist of sources and types of errors in problem solving. These are:

1. Inaccuracy in reading (failure to concentrate on meaning, to reread different parts, etc.).
2. Inaccuracy in thinking (failure to place a high premium on accuracy, failure to perform operations like counting carefully, failure to check answers, etc.).
3. Weakness in problem analysis; inactiveness (failure to break problem into parts, failure to draw upon prior knowledge for interpretation, failure to construct a mental representation or draw one on paper, etc.).
4. Lack of perseverance (solving the problem mechanically without much thought, giving up too soon, etc.) [p. 20].

And W & L make a third attempt to analyze the concepts of sloppy versus precise thinking. This time they list positive attitudes of good thinkers:

1. Positive attitude (a strong belief that academic problems can be solved).
2. Concern for accuracy (an "almost compulsive" attempt to understand correctly and check).
3. Breaking the problem into parts (starting at a point where one can make sense of the problem and then working from there).
4. Avoiding guessing (working carefully and avoiding making jumps).
5. Activeness in problem solving (trying to understand, asking questions, creating diagrams and other helpful representations, etc.) (p. 28).

It seems clear that although these attempts to define "sloppy" and "precise" thinking contain some important components (e.g., using diagrams or mental representations, rereading difficult parts), the descriptions are still quite vague and general. For example, W & L suggest that problem-solving failures occur when people "fail to use the relevant facts," yet it is not clear what procedures one might use for assessing relevance or irrelevance. Similarly, they advise problem solvers to search for a sensible starting point. Again, one might ask on what basis to troubleshoot alternative starting points, or what to do in the event that a sensible starting point is not apparent. In general, W & L's suggestions provide descriptions of what good problem solvers do rather than hint about how to do things oneself. Furthermore, many of the components they emphasize seem to overlap considerably and to have lost some of the skills approach to "precise thinking." For example, it is not clear that a "positive attitude" or a "concern for accuracy" should be construed as a skill.

Note, however, that W & L do not rely heavily on their verbal descriptions of the components of precise thinking. They certainly do not assume that students who simply memorize their descriptions of good problem-solving skills will become good problem solvers. Instead, W & L attempt to enhance certain types of interactions with the problems encountered in the text. We need, therefore, to ask what kinds of activities and problems are emphasized and how these experiences might enhance problem solving. These questions are addressed next.

Basic Procedures of Instruction

Early in their book, W & L ask readers to take the 38-item Whimbey Analytical Skills Inventory (WASI). They note that the WASI is similar to the tests one takes when applying for a college program or for a job. They also make the following point about tests of this nature: The feedback is usually extremely limited. There are times, they argue, when people do not even receive information about their overall test scores. Even if they do, this provides no information about the particular items that were missed. Furthermore, information that a particular item was missed does not necessarily ensure that people are told the correct answer, and information about the correct answer does not necessarily enable students to understand why they made errors.

W & L emphasize the importance of learning from one's performance on the WASI. If students are reading the book as part of a course, they will spend several days going over the test item by item. If they are reading the book on their own, students are encouraged to have a friend take the WASI and then compare answers and strategies for each problem. The comparison of strategies is an extremely important aspect of the short course in analytical reasoning; W & L want to help people take stock of their own thinking habits and compare them with others. One of their goals is to demystify the process of taking mental tests.

What might it mean to "compare one's problem-solving strategies with others"? How do W & L help people learn to do this? W & L's instructional procedure can be divided into three phases.

During the first phase, students are encouraged to examine how experts might approach certain problems. Protocols from expert problem solvers are presented as models of precise thinking. These protocols also help familiarize students with the basic procedure of thinking aloud. For an example of such a protocol, see Lochhead, this volume. The protocols consist of a sample problem and an expert's response to that problem. W & L also provide a description of some general characteristics of each expert's approach.

During the second phase of instruction, students are asked to think aloud while working various types of problems. Ideally, students work in pairs. One thinks aloud while the other listens; later the individuals switch roles.

W & L stress that the person adopting the role of listener should perform two important functions. First, the listener should continually *check the accuracy* of each step used by the problem solver. The listener should not simply attempt to solve the problem on his or her own and then compare answers; instead, the listener should focus on each step taken by the problem solver. This may involve asking the problem solver to slow down so that the listener can check (emphasis is always placed on accuracy, not speed). The listener must also ensure that the thinker's remarks are comprehensible; otherwise accuracy cannot be checked.

In addition to monitoring accuracy and comprehensibility, the listener's second role is to *ensure that the problem solver vocalizes all the major steps* taken in reaching a problem solution. The problem solver should not be allowed to skip any steps. W & L stress that students who are adopting the role of listener should understand that they are not being unduly picky or critical when they demand explicitness and point out errors in the problem solver's step-by-step approach to problem solution. The role of the listener is one of a beneficent critic attempting to help someone develop important academic skills.

In addition to utilizing models (experts' protocols) and encouraging thinking aloud, W & L add a third phase to their instructional procedure. They ask students to devise problems similar to the ones they receive in the course. "Devising problems based on other problems allows you to see them from the inside out. You come to understand how the various parts of the problems operate and how they relate to each other [W & L, p. 32]. W & L's emphasis on the advantages of problem generation represents an interesting theoretical claim that is discussed later in more detail.

Overview of Course Content

The basic purposes of the short course in analytical reasoning and the description of the thinking-aloud procedure are introduced in the first part of the W & L book. The remaining pages are devoted to problems to be solved, suggestions for how to solve various types of problems, and solutions to each, explained in systematic steps. (In general, a problem occurs on one side of a page and a step-by-step solution to it appears on the other.) W & L note that their list of the steps toward solution may not be identical to the ones agreed upon by the problem solver and the listener; however, the final answer should be the same. If it is not, the two should rethink their work step by step.

The heart of the W & L short course involves practice solving a variety of well-defined problems. Because these are presumably practiced in the context of the thinking-aloud procedure, students receive feedback concerning the processes involved in solution rather than mere information about whether their final answer was correct. W & L divide their set of practice problems into four basic types: verbal reasoning problems, analogies, analysis of trends and patterns, and mathematical word problems. For examples see Lochhead, this volume. Further discussion of particular problems and of W & L's suggestions for solving them occurs in the analysis section that follows.

Analysis

It is well beyond the scope of this chapter to provide a detailed evaluation of every aspect of the W & L program (we encounter the same difficulty with the other programs). Our approach is therefore to focus on some general questions one might ask about the effectiveness of various program components, and to identify some important theoretical issues. We begin by discussing those aspects of instruction that remain invariant across topics (verbal problems, analogies, mathematical problems, etc.). We then consider more specific aspects of the program (e.g., W & L's treatment of analogy problems) in greater detail.

Analysis of Invariant Instructional Procedures

The most salient of the invariant features of the program involves thinking aloud about well-defined problems in the presence of a listener–critic who monitors the adequacy of one's thoughts (W & L also present models of experts thinking aloud). Thinking aloud protocols have proven very valuable for research purposes (e.g., Newell & Simon, 1972). Is thinking aloud a valuable instructional technique as well?

Thinking Aloud from the Perspective of the Teacher.   From a teacher's perspective, it seems clear that it is much more valuable to ask students to think aloud while solving a problem than to simply monitor the students' final answers. If students make errors one needs to know *why* they made them; furthermore, students can sometimes produce the right answer for the wrong reason. As an example, consider the following analogy: Bee is to honey as cow is to _____ (milk). This analogy was almost never missed by a group of academically less successful fifth and seventh graders (Arbitman–Smith & Bransford, 1980), but most were solving it on the basis of association (cow–milk) rather than analyzing the problem analogically. Students who are sometimes correct despite erroneous methods may remain confused because they don't understand why they miss some problems but not others. W & L's method of thinking aloud facilitates the assessment of processes rather than mere products. We doubt that anyone would argue against the importance of assessing the processes students use.

Assume, however, that the aforementioned fifth and seventh graders had been asked to think aloud while solving the bee–cow analogy; a listener or teacher might thereby discover that they were using an association strategy. What does one do now? At some point, it seems clear that the listener or teacher has to help the students develop a new, more appropriate way of thinking about the problem. The students may not understand the general nature of analogy tasks, for example, or may not understand how to compare items along multiple dimensions. Effective teachers do not only assess students' present states; they also know how to intervene appropriately (see Case, 1978; Siegler, 1981, for informative examples). However, the mere fact that someone is thinking aloud does not guarantee that a teacher will know how to intervene in effective ways.

W & L ask their students to adopt the role of teacher as well as thinker; they ask students to work in pairs in order to critique each other's steps toward solutions. This format of monitoring a fellow student who is thinking aloud sets the stage for effective assessment and intervention but by no means guarantees it. For example, W & L provide some general suggestions for what the listener should do (see Section on Basic Procedures of Instruction), but these are indeed general. It is also instructive to note that W & L provide models (protocols) of experts solving particular problems but include no models of thinker–listener interchanges. It is possible that W & L model these interchanges in their classroom settings; we simply note that the thinker–listener dyads appear to be an important component of the program that needs to be spelled out more fully. It is also possible that students may learn something by playing the role of critic that they don't learn in the role of "thinker." This is an issue that might be explored.

Thinking Aloud from the Perspective of the Thinker.   We argued that W & L's format of thinking aloud in the presence of a critic has the potential to be very valuable from the perspective of a teacher who is interested in assessment and intervention. Does it, however, have any special value for the student? In particular, note that an important function of W & L's course is to provide suggestions about how to solve various problem types (e.g., analogies). Assume that W & L provide these suggestions, yet omit the think-aloud procedure. Would anything be lost?

In our opinion, W & L's thinking-aloud procedure does add something important. Many students—even "good" high school and college students—are not particularly well aware of the steps involved in problem solving. For example, we asked several high school students to try some of W & L's analogy problems, including:

Thermometer is to temperature as _____ is to _____.

a. telescope : astronomy   c. scale : weight
b. clock : minutes   d. microscope : biologist

The students first solved each analogy on their own; their answers were correct, but they were not especially confident. We then prompted them to think aloud while solving the same problems and to be explicit about each step. After some persistence on our part, the students were eventually able to articulate the reasons for their previous choices. For example, one student had originally chosen answer

(c) over (b) because "it just felt right." After being prompted to unpack this intuition, the student eventually realized that (c) was better because "weight" and "temperature" were names of dimensions but "minutes" was part of the dimension of time. This increased his confidence in the correctness of his answer. One could, of course, simply tell students to do these kinds of things (e.g., "look for dimensions"); and indeed, W & L do so. (We discuss their suggestions in more detail later.) However, it is not at all clear that students would explicitly follow these suggestions and evaluate them "in action" unless they were prompted to think aloud.

In general, prompting students to think aloud seems to encourage various "metacognitive assessments" (Brown, 1977a, 1977b; Brown & DeLoache, 1978; Flavell & Wellman, 1977; Markman, 1977). They become likely to ask, "Did I systematically evaluate all alternatives? Did I recheck each step?" Students may also be encouraged to monitor the degree to which their statements are comprehensible and hence learn to state ideas more precisely.

The Role of Problems in Thinking Aloud.   It is important to note that W & L's choice of problems seems to play an important role in determining the effectiveness of the thinking-aloud procedure. The problems generally allow their intended audience—high school and college students—to discover something interesting about their thought processes while thinking aloud. Our assumption is that these discoveries occur most readily in thinking about domains where the content is not too unfamiliar, and where the skills required are within the repertoire of the problem solver. In essence, we are assuming that Vygotsky's (1978) concept of the "zone of maximal sensitivity to instruction" applies to one's ability to learn while thinking aloud, as well as to situations where one attempts to learn from direct instruction (see Bloom, Lightbown, & Hood, 1975; Case, 1978; Goldman, 1979; Siegler, 1981; for examples that can be interpreted as support for Vygotsky's principle). An obvious implication of this position is that the problem types used by W & L would have to be modified if one wanted to use the program with younger learners or with learners who were academically less mature.

We should also note that some of W & L's problems seem much more informative (in the sense of providing a context for discoveries about thinking) than others. There are also places in the program where we question whether problems are sequenced adequately; sometimes the initial problems in a series seem to be more difficult than later problems. This could cause difficulties for some students because they initially experience only confusion while thinking aloud. It should not be difficult to collect data on the types of problems students find interesting (from the perspective of learning something by thinking aloud). One could also assess how much thinking aloud is necessary in order to develop problem-solving efficiency and whether students become bored with the process of thinking aloud.

One final point about W & L's choice of problems is that it undoubtedly alleviates some of the difficulties with the thinker–listener dyads that we discussed earlier. In particular, listeners may not be prepared to perform the assessment and intervention necessary to help thinkers improve their abilities to solve various types of problems. Because most of W & L's problems require knowledge and skills that are within the repertoire of both the thinker and listener, these potential difficulties are reduced to a considerable degree.

Analysis of W & L's Suggestions for Solving the Types of Problems Included in Their Course

As noted earlier, W & L provide suggestions on how to think about the problem types included in their short course; our present question concerns the adequacy of these suggestions. Many of the problem types used by W & L are similar to ones that have been analyzed by other researchers. Examples include trend and pattern problems (Brown & Campione, 1979; Kotovsky & Simon, 1973), analogies (Goldman & Bisanz, 1980; Sternberg, 1977), verbal problems involving syllogistic reasoning (Johnson-Laird, 1980), and mathematical word problems (Hayes, 1978; Simon & Hayes, 1976; Wickelgren, 1974). Are W & L's suggestions to students congruent with the procedures that these other researchers would recommend?

As an illustration of the advice provided, consider helping students learn to solve formal analogy problems. The analogy problem cited earlier is reproduced here:

Thermometer is to temperature as _____ is to _____.

  a. telescope : astronomy   c. scale : weight
  b. clock : minutes   d. microscope : biologist

W & L's basic approach to helping students solve analogy problems is to emphasize the importance of creating "relationship sentences" that capture the essence of the analogy. In the problem cited here, for example, W & L ask students to look at the terms *thermometer* and *temperature* and to then create a relationship sentence such as "A thermometer measures temperature." The next step might involve asking whether each of the answers conforms to this relationship. Because a telescope does not measure astronomy and a microscope does not measure a biologist, the problem solver can narrow the alternatives to (b) and (c).

Proceeding further, the problem solver may be helped to notice that a clock can measure hours as well as minutes; it therefore measures time as a dimension. Because a thermometer measures temperature as a dimension and scale measures weight as a dimension, the best answer would be (c). At a general level, W & L attempt to help students grasp the importance of formulating explicit relationship sentences, and they encourage students to evaluate these relationships. They also emphasize that the relationships involved in *each* possible answer must be explicitly tested before deciding upon a final choice.

Overall, W & L's procedure of having students think aloud seems to emphasize many of the metacomponents of analogical problem solving that Sternberg (1977) identifies in his research. W & L's procedure should therefore help students learn to evaluate various components of their problem-solving process; to notice when they have encoded a word inadequately, for example, or when they have failed to evaluate a hypothesis about relationships due to a nonsystematic exploration of all the alternatives or foils. We suspect that W & L could help students improve their effectiveness as listeners (critics, teachers) by more systematically explaining some of the components to watch for while assessing the reasoning processes employed by a problem solver (Sternberg's analysis is very valuable here). Furthermore, if the program were used with younger or less mature learners one would expect different thinker–listener dynamics; much more time might be spent on the problem of grasping the nature of the task, for example, or on more basic components such as comparison of pairs of concepts (see Goldman & Bisanz, 1980). Nevertheless, W & L's procedure seems to emphasize the evaluation of one's thinking processes; this is quite different from simply providing a list of hints or rules that students memorize and then apply blindly.

How valuable are W & L's suggestions for solving the other types of problems included in their short course? In general, W & L seem to do a relatively good job. They emphasize the importance of generating explicit "pattern descriptions" when solving trend and pattern problems, for example; this seems to be consistent with the type of analysis suggested by Kotovsky and Simon (1973). W & L also encourage students to create representations (drawings, graphs, Venn diagrams) for many of the problems in their book. Their suggestions for solving mathematical word problems seem mildly confusing (see pp. 220–223) but are probably interpretable and helpful, given the types of math problems included in the short course (all are quite simple mathematically).

It is important to note, however, that a major reason why W & L's suggestions are helpful is that the problems are structured in a way that enables these suggestions to work. It can be helpful to recommend that students draw a visual representation if it is clear to them what to include in this representation; similarly, it is sufficient to say "break the problem into parts" if each of the parts is clearly defined. In the "boxes" problem cited in the Theoretical Overview section, for example, it is clear what the parts are and it is obvious what one should draw in order to represent the problem in visual form.

One of W & L's goals is to help students gain confidence in their ability to solve some basic problems (ones that often occur on mental tests) that the students presumably could not solve previously. From this perspective, W & L's short course seems very worthwhile. However, W & L also identify some goals that seem much broader than the goal of increasing students' confidence and abilities to solve the types of problems presented in the short course. In the next section we consider the degree to which they achieve these broader goals.

Analysis of W & L's Program Relative to Their General Goals

On the opening page of their book, W & L pose the question: "Would you like greater skill in solving math and logic problems? Would you like to sharpen your grasp of ideas you read in scientific publications, medical reports, textbooks and legal contracts?" W & L note that most people answer "yes" to these questions. So did we. The authors then begin a section entitled "The Payoff," where they tell students the following: "The techniques you learn in this book can help you in at least three ways—on tests, in school, and at work [p. 2]." Students should do better on tests such as the SAT, GRE, and Civil Service examinations, which frequently include the problem types taught in the short course (e.g., analogies, mathematical word problems requiring simple operations). Students should do better in school because they will be better thinkers, learners, and test takers. Students' increased ability to learn should also help them in their jobs, because almost all jobs require one to learn technical knowledge and skills.

We do not doubt that the W & L program can help some individuals in a way that extends to tests, school, and their jobs. It has been our experience that many people need to develop enough confidence in their problem-solving abilities to keep them from retreating at the first sign of uncertainty or failure (see also Holt, 1964; Tobias, 1978). W & L's program seems excellent for such people. Nevertheless, we believe that W & L's program could be improved by considering more explicitly the types of skills necessary to think and learn in school, or in one's job. Some illustrations are provided in the following section.

Relationships Between Relevant Parts and Problem Definition.   Consider first one of W & L's most frequent suggestions for problem solving: "Break the problem into parts." As noted earlier, this suggestion is sufficient for problems that have well-defined parts, but people are often unable to identify the parts. To what extent do W & L help people realize that relevant parts are a function of one's initial assumptions about what the problem is?

As an example, consider the classic 9-dot problem.

The task is to connect all nine dots with four straight lines without lifting the pencil and without retracing any line. Are the relevant parts in this pattern the dots, the rows or columns of dots, the steps one takes in reaching the solution? Most people assume that the lines must stay within the confines of the perimeter of dots; they never question this basic assumption. One might therefore argue that part of the task of "breaking the nine-dot problem into relevant parts" is to question one's assumptions about the definition of the problem and to search for alternative problem definitions. Problem definition is an extremely important component of problem solving (Adams, 1974; de Bono, 1970) that is not emphasized by W & L.

Analogical Thinking.   The general issue of creative approaches to problem definition is also relevant to other aspects of the W & L program—to their approach to analogies, for example. W & L introduce their section on analogies by noting how this type of thinking has resulted in many new discoveries and inventions. They provide the following explanation to students;

> This chapter asks you to work analogy problems. The primary role which analogous thinking plays in scientific invention, mathematical induction, and literary creation indicates that when a person systematically analyzes an analogy he uses the same mental skills that are important in comprehending and integrating all areas of advanced human knowledge [W & L, p. 134].

Many theorists argue that analogic thinking is an important and pervasive characteristic of intelligent functioning (Bransford & Nitsch, 1978; Brown, Campione, & Day, 1980; Newell, 1980; Sternberg, 1977). But, will practice solving formal analogy problems help students develop skills of "everyday analogical thinking" and improve their abilities to discover, invent, and create?

Formal analogy problems *do* seem to help one learn to evaluate the appropriateness of analogies, and one would surely want to emphasize evaluation in a program designed to facilitate "everyday analogic thinking." However, the basic criterion for evaluation in formal analogy tasks is simply to choose the best answer among the set of available foils. In everyday thinking, criteria vary tremendously. An analogy may be appropriate for some purposes but not for others; for example, a mental skill—physical skill analogy may be fruitful for many purposes (e.g., helping people demystify the concept of thinking) yet be insufficient for others (e.g., a precise theory of thinking). Formal analogy problems emphasize a search for the correct answer (actually, someone else's—the testmaker's—correct answer) rather than helping students understand how appropriateness must be defined relative to various assumptions and goals (see Bransford, 1979; Brown, Bransford, Ferrara, & Campione, in press, for other examples of this general issue).

Consider some everyday examples of analogical thinking. The book *Till Death Us Do Part* (Bugliosi, 1978) describes a famous murder trial held in California; it is an informative book for psychologists because it reveals some of the analogical thinking that lawyers allegedly employ. During the closing arguments of the California trial, the defense lawyer creates an analogy for the jury. He correctly notes that the trial was based on circumstantial evidence and then argues that a trial of this type is like a chain. A chain is only a strong as its weakest link, of course, and the jury needs a strong chain in order to convict the defendant.

The defense lawyer then proceeds to show that there is not only one weak link, but several weak links in the chain.

The prosecutor speaks to the jury next; he obviously wants to counter the previous argument. He has comprehended the analogy posed by the defense lawyer but would be in trouble if he merely stayed at the level of comprehending it; he has to create a new and more appropriate (from his perspective) analogy. The prosecutor therefore compares the trial to a rope rather than a chain. A rope is composed of a number of independent strands; several of these can break without having much effect on the overall strength of the rope. The prosecutor then acknowledges that there are indeed a few questionable strands; however, the rest of the evidence is more than strong enough to keep the rope intact. (For whatever it is worth, the prosecutor wins the case.)

We mention the preceding example because it is not clear that practice in solving the types of formal analogy problems used by W & L will develop the types of analogic thinking skills exhibited by the California prosecutor or by some of the scientists and inventors that W & L mention. For example, the authors note that Alexander Graham Bell was able to invent the telephone, in part, because he formed an analogy between the structure and function of the telephone and the human ear. This presumably occurred because Bell discovered his own basis for a new analogy. An emphasis on the search for 'someone else's correct answer' fails to help students realize the value of creating their own analogies.

However, W & L *do* include a "generate your own example" phase of instruction in each part of their course (see section on Basic Procedures of Instruction). Nevertheless, students may not develop an understanding of the purpose or function of analogy formation in everyday thinking. We suspect that students in the W & L course will generate their own examples of formal analogy problems because these are the only models of analogy that have been called to their attention. There appear to be important differences between the act of "creating an analogy problem for the sake of creating an analogy problem" and the act of "searching for analogies in order to understand something more adequately or to understand it in different ways."

It seems to us that one could create a program that emphasizes more directly the types of analogic thinking skills that may be useful in everyday situations. For example, one might begin by helping students understand the function of analogy formation. Analogies often help us make the strange familiar; people may understand new information more adequately by relating it to something already known. W & L provide an excellent example in the introduction to their program, where they attempt to help students understand the nature of mental skills by relating them to physical skills (see Theoretical Overview section). However, W & L never alert the reader to the fact that this is an example of analogic thinking. It would seem valuable to help students appreciate that the formation of analogic relationships can facilitate understanding. One might encourage them to think about "intelligence," for example, and then let them see how a consideration of physical skills might help them conceptualize mental skills.

Development of General Learning Skills.   The task of helping students develop skills of "everyday analogical thinking" is also relevant to the general topic of learning. W & L emphasize the importance of helping students become better learners so that they can acquire new information necessary for their schoolwork and their jobs. Note that W & L do not claim that their course teaches people to solve every kind of logical or mathematical problem possible; for example, we doubt that W & L would expect their students to be able to solve all the problems present in other problem-solving books such as those by Adams (1974), Rubinstein (1975), and Wickelgren (1974). However, W & L presumably assume that students who take their course will be better able to learn from books such as these because they have developed greater confidence in their abilities and have acquired critical comprehension skills. As noted earlier, W & L also assume that students will be better able to grasp the ideas they read in "scientific publications, medical reports, textbooks and legal contracts [p. 1]." To what extent do W & L help students develop critical comprehension skills?

The following problem from W & L is one that seems designed particularly to develop skills of critical comprehension (all their problems are designed to do this to some extent):

If deleting the letters B, R and A from the word *burglary* leaves a meaningful 3-letter word, circle the first R in this word burglary. Otherwise, circle the U in the word burglary where it appears for the third time in the exercise [p. 95].

It seems clear that the ability to solve this type of problem requires a considerable degree of systematic analysis and checking, and it also seems clear that many students can benefit from practice with these types of problems (see Whimbey, 1976). However, are problems that require people to focus on minute details and to recheck each step sufficient to develop "critical comprehension" skills?

Note first that people can learn to carry out instructions systematically without understanding what they are doing. Learning to follow instructions systematically can be helpful in certain situations. For example, such skills may help one fill out an IRS tax form or assemble a radio. However, there is an important difference between understanding how a radio works (i.e., its design and structural components) and merely following step-by-step directions that resemble a paint-by-numbers project. The skills necessary to following instructions carefully (as in the "burglary" problem, for example) are not necessarily equivalent to those that enable people to use what they know to understand reasons for instructions and to evaluate whether they are as coherent as they might be (Markman, 1977).

We should note that W & L do not always use problems that encourage people to follow instructional sequences without trying to evaluate their significance; for example, W & L clearly attempt to help people understand mathematical rate problems rather than simply providing a list of instructions or procedures to follow. Nevertheless, W & L do not consistently help students learn to use what they know to understand and evaluate information; their instructions for rate problems help students understand these problems, but do not necessarily help them develop the skills they will require to understand new domains on their own.

The act of utilizing available knowledge to evaluate information (the significance of particular sets of instructions, for example) is important for mastering new factual content in the context of schoolwork or job-related activities. As an example, imagine a biology novice who is reading a passage about veins and arteries. The passage might state that arteries are thick, elastic, and carry blood from the heart that is rich in oxygen; veins are thinner, less elastic, and carry blood rich in carbon dioxide back to the heart. To the biology novice, even this relatively simple set of facts can seem arbitrary and confusing. Is it veins or arteries that are thin? Was the thin one or the thick one elastic? Which one carries carbon dioxide from the heart (or was it to the heart)?

The novice must do more than simply identify each feature of veins and arteries; the novice must also master this information. One possible approach to mastery is to use mnemomic techniques (see Weinstein, 1978). However, as has been argued elsewhere (Bransford, Stein, Shelton, & Owings, 1981; Campione & Ambruster, this volume; Stein & Bransford, 1979), the use of these procedures can help one memorize facts while failing to help one understand the significance or relevance of these facts. For example, assume that people remember "Arteries are elastic" by imagining a rubber band holding a tube (artery) or by creating a verbal cue such as "Art(ery) wore pants that had an elastic waistband." What if these people are confronted with the task of designing an artificial artery? Would it have to be elastic? What are the potential implications of hardening of the arteries? Would this have a serious impact on people's health? Learners who used the previously mentioned mnemomics would have little basis for answering these questions. Indeed, the rubber band and waistband mnemomics could easily lead to misinterpretations: Perhaps hardening of the arteries affects people's ability to stretch their arms and legs.

Mnemonic techniques are useful for many purposes, but one must take a very different approach to learning in order to develop an understanding of veins and arteries—to develop an understanding that will facilitate transfer. An important component of this learning process involves the activities needed to evaluate whether or not one has comprehended and mastered new information (Baker & Brown, in press; Flavell & Wellman, 1977; Markman, 1977). We emphasize the activities necessary for evaluation because it seems clear that "metacognitive evaluation" is usually not a passive or automatic process. Effective learners attend to factual content, but they also seem to know when to seek additional information that clarifies the significance or relevance of facts. For example, the passage about veins and arteries stated that arteries are elastic. What's the significance of elasticity? How does this property relate to the functions that arteries perform? An effective learner knows when to seek information that can clarify this relationship. Some of the steps involved in this process have been discussed elsewhere (Bransford et al., 1981); we shall not elaborate on them here.

W & L provide few suggestions on how to approach the problem of learning new information. One might argue that the idea of thinking aloud in the presence of a colleague will enable students who take the W & L course to think more effectively about new information, but we noted earlier that the think-aloud paradigm provides no guarantee that people will learn to think about problems more effectively. A student may think aloud about mnemonic techniques for mastering facts about veins and arteries; a fellow student may monitor this thinking in order to ensure that each fact is considered and that a mnemonic is used for each one. These students may never realize that there are alternate ways to approach new information and that these alternatives can help one understand the significance of facts rather than simply memorize them. The students may also fail to realize how different approaches to learning affect the types of questions they can answer later on (e.g., comprehension versus memory questions).

There are undoubtedly other aspects of learning that need to be emphasized by a program designed to help students improve their ability to learn new information more readily. The goal of a program such as this is not to help students master a particular content area—nor simply for a teacher to present appropriate analogies or provide critical tasks that enable students to assess their current states of comprehension and mastery. Instead, the goal is to help students learn to perform these types of activities on their own. In our opinion, activities such as those just discussed are important components of the more general skill of critical comprehension. W & L's exercises appear to help people become more careful and analytical; this is undoubtedly important, and we suspect that many people benefit from their instruction (especially in terms of their confidence in themselves). However, these same individuals may discover that the approach to critical comprehension that seemed to work so well given W & L's problems leaves a great deal to be desired when they confront the task of understanding and mastering new information. W & L provide a good beginning to the problem of developing critical comprehension skills, but it seems that more could be done.

THE PHILOSOPHY FOR CHILDREN PROGRAM

The Philosophy for Children program is very broad in scope; Lipman and colleagues (Lipman, 1980; Lipman & Sharp, 1978; Lipman, Sharp, & Oscanyan, 1980) envision a curriculum that will eventually extend from kindergarten through the 12th grade (at present the curriculum focuses on Grade 5–10). The specific content of the curriculum varies from grade to grade, of course. Nevertheless, there are some general principles that remain invariant across grades.

Theoretical Overview

Lipman et al. (1980) reject the assumption that "the learning process [consists] in nothing more than the transmission of the contents of human knowledge from the old to the young [p. 41]." They adopt an alternate position that emphasizes the importance of "generating thinking activities [p. 4.]" Lipman et al. argue that just as there are differences between learning historical facts and learning to think historically, or between learning scientific facts and learning to think scientifically, there are important differences between learning philosophical facts and learning to think philosophically. The Philosophy for Children program is not designed to teach children *about* philosophy in the traditional sense; for example, children do not learn about famous philosophers and their particular theories or positions. Instead, Lipman and colleagues attempt to help children learn to think philosophically. We consider three aspects of their position:

1. What does it mean to "think philosophically"?
2. Why is this relevant for children?
3. If it is relevant, how would one teach this sort of activity?

The Concept of Philosophical Thinking

It should come as no surprise that it is extremely difficult to provide a precise definition of philosophical thinking. Despite these difficulties, it seems possible to delineate some general characteristics of philosophical thinking; we focus here on the relationship between philosophical thinking and thinking per se.

Lipman et al. (1980) emphasize that philosophical thinking does not simply involve thinking and reasoning; it involves thinking about thinking. In their words:

It is well to remember that when philosophy emerged in Greece in the sixth century, B.C., it did not burst suddenly out of the Mediterranean blue. The development of societies of reasoning creatures—what we call civilization—had been a process to be measured not in thousands but in millions of years. Human beings became civilized as they became reasonable, and for an animal to begin to reason and to learn how to improve its reasoning is a long, slow process. So thinking had been going on for ages before Greece—slowly improving itself, uncovering the pitfalls to be avoided by forethought, endeavoring to weigh alternative sets of consequences intellectually. What happened in the sixth century, B.C., is that thinking turned round on itself; people began to think about thinking, and the momentous event, the culmination of the long process to that point, was in fact the birth of philosophy [Preface].

What might it mean to say that the early philosophers began to "think about thinking?" In general, they began to emphasize that it was important to think explicitly about basic values and beliefs (e.g., to evaluate the "truth," and "fairness" of ideas and actions), and that there may be criteria for distinguishing better thinking from worse. For example, Socrates emphasized that thinking must be rigorous. Each belief must be subjected to the tests of logic and experience. According to Lipman et al. (1980):

> It does not matter whose opinions they are, or whose ideas they are—they must submit to the requirement that they be internally consistent, and their proponents must divulge the evidence that supports them. Intellectual inquiry is thus a discipline that has its own integrity, and is not to be dissolved into scientific inquiry, nor permitted to masquerade as a political or religious ideology. Socrates does not deceive himself into thinking that, because he converses with a general, he is discussing strategy, or that, because he converses with a statesman, he is discussing statecraft. He knows he is dealing with the *assumptions* of these disciplines, and these assumptions must be treated philosophically. Thinking must be rigorous, and philosophical thinking is a unique discipline that must be carried on independently of other intellectual pursuits [Preface].

Note that Socrates emphasized the existence of criteria for the evaluation of thinking. It is not *who* says something that makes arguments true or valid or reasonable; instead, these properties depend on people's initial assumptions and on the internal consistency of their arguments. This is an extremely important insight: It applies to one's own reasoning as well as to everyone else's and is relevant irrespective of the particular topic one explores. Philosophical thinking therefore involves a concern for *coherence* (internal consistency), for the *correspondence* between ideas and available data, and for the *assumptions* that underlie one's arguments. Philosophical thinking is also *imaginative*; for example, one must often search for alternative sets of assumptions. Socrates encourages people to imagine possibilities and to separate what is possible from what is momentarily true. Socrates also emphasizes the *relevance* of philosophical inquiry for the management of everyday activities; he argues that people's lives can be improved by thinking things through.

The Importance of Teaching Philosophy to Children

Lipman and colleagues do not subscribe to the view that philosophical thinking is beneficial only for adults; they maintain that it is beneficial for children. One of their arguments is based on the assumption that philosophical thinking is relevant to everyday life; children's spontaneous questions often indicate a concern for many of the issues explored by philosophers. (This does not necessarily mean that children realize they are asking philosophical questions, of course.)

For example, children are interested in concepts such as friendship and fairness; these ideas are relevant to their everyday lives. Lipman et al. also argue that children are interested in understanding reasons, and in the exploration of alternatives. It is natural for children to ask about purposes and causes, and children are eager to examine assumptions and to explore alternative points of view. These interests are compatible with the principles of philosophical inquiry discussed previously.

However, Lipman and colleagues (1980) warn that children's natural sense of wonder about philosophical issues tends to become more adultlike by *decreasing* rather than increasing with development; this sense of wonder can be maintained and developed only through interactions with knowledgeable parents, teachers, or peers. In their words:

> Many adults have ceased to wonder because they feel that there is no time for wondering, or because they have come to the conclusion that it is simply unprofitable and unproductive to engage in reflection about things that cannot be changed anyhow. Many adults have never had the experience of engaging in wondering and reflecting that somehow made a difference in their lives. The result is that such adults, having ceased to question and to reach for the meanings of their experience, eventually become examples of passive acceptance that children take to be models for their own conduct.
>
> Thus, the prohibition against wonder is transmitted from generation to generation. Before long, children now in school will themselves be parents. If we can somehow preserve their natural sense of wonder, their readiness to look for meaning, and their hunger to understand why things are the way they are, there might be some hope that at least this upcoming generation will not serve as models of unquestioning acceptance to their own children [p. 31].

Lipman and colleagues' emphasis on preserving children's natural sense of wonder involves more than a concern for the fact that they may become less interested in philosophical issues; Lipman et al. also assume that the act of engaging in philosophical inquiry about various issues develops thinking skills. The goals of their Philosophy for Children program include improvements in children's abilities to make connections and draw distinctions, to define and classify, to assess factual information objectively and critically, to separate what is true from what is logically possible, and so forth. Lipman et al. discuss 30 more specific thinking skills that children should develop as a function of the Philosophy for Children program (See Lipman, this volume). They warn that the list is not exhaustive and that there is considerable overlap among many of the categories. And they emphasize that the acquisition of cognitive dispositions representing a readiness to employ such skills is as important as the development of the skills per se. Perhaps the most important aspect of Lipman and colleagues' program involves their assumptions about how these skills can be developed—

their assumptions about the nature of teaching and learning. We discuss this issue next.

Ways of Developing Critical Thinking Skills

We have already noted that Lipman et al.'s view of philosophical thinking emphasizes rigor, relevance, and imagination; and we argued that it certainly seems valuable to introduce children to these concepts. However, how does one do this? As discussed earlier, one approach that Lipman et al. do *not* adopt is to attempt to teach children *about* philosophy. Some individuals have tried to do this and have concluded that the enterprise is not feasible.

> Having observed few children eager to browse through Kant or even to pursue the livelier passages of Aristotle, having met with little success in our efforts to convey directly the impact and urgency of the greatest happiness principle, we have been led to draw the irresistible inference that there is an unbridgeable chasm between the disciplined reflection that is philosophy, and the unbridled wondering characteristic of childhood. It is clear that the plausibility of this inference is now under attack [p. 42].

An alternative to introducing children to philosophical content is to attempt to develop specific thinking skills that are exemplified by philosophers. Lipman and colleagues (1980) endorse this approach at a general level, but they warn against simplistic approaches to skill development:

> We might, for example, simply insist that all children now study formal logic. Or we might draw up a list of our favorite thinking skills (such as classification, generalization, and hypothesis formation), and insist that children perform various exercises we construct to improve such skills. But there is an enormous difference between drilling children until they improve their performance on specific skills— such improvement being merely superficial and transient—and involving children in an educational process in which a wide spectrum of thinking skills is sharpened in an educationally significant fashion [p. 2].

How might one develop educationally significant skills? Lipman and colleagues emphasize the method of engaging people in dialogue and encouraging them to reflect on their discussions. Dialogue generates reflection and enables children to view thinking as something other than a private and mysterious activity that takes place in individual minds.

> The common assumption is that reflection generates dialogue, when, in fact, it is dialogue that generates reflection. Very often when people engage in dialogue with one another, they are compelled to reflect, to concentrate, to consider alternatives, to listen closely, to give careful attention to definitions and meanings, to recognize

previously unthought of options, and in general, to perform a vast number of mental activities that they might not have engaged in had the conversation never occurred [p. 22].

An important assumption underlying this view of the value of dialogue is that people engage in it in "a spirit of reasonableness." Lipman et al. therefore emphasize the importance of developing a "community of inquiry" where people value the process of evaluation rather than simply attempt to express opinions and beliefs. Ideally, dialogue represents a collaborative effort; Lipman and colleagues cite Vygotsky's (1978) claim that children are capable of functioning at a higher intellectual level when working in cooperative or collaborative situations than when compelled to work individually.

How does one develop a community of inquiry where people engage in dialogue in a spirit of reasonableness and collaboration? Lipman and colleagues argue that the Socratic dialogues provide a model for the development of inquiry skills. First, Socrates does not *tell* people about effective inquiry, he *shows* them by providing a model of how inquiry might proceed. As stated by Lipman et al. (1980):

Socrates does not say, "Make all necessary connections and draw all necessary distinctions!"; for he knows the worthlessness of such a command. Instead, he operationalizes whatever he recommends; if there is a concept to be discovered— of friendship, of courage, of love, of beauty–then there are specific and sequential steps that can be taken to flush that concept out of its concealment [Preface].

Lipman et al. argue that Socrates emphasizes procedures of inquiry rather than the products of his own thinking, and he makes clear his assumption that everyone is capable of thinking like this. Socrates also appears to acknowledge that the potential relevance of philosophical inquiry may not be readily apparent to many people; he therefore emphasizes the importance of beginning with topics that are of vital interest to individuals (e.g., the management of their everyday activities).

Lipman and colleagues make extensive use of the Socratic technique of providing models of philosophical inquiry. Through the use of fiction they provide models of children and adults engaging in dialogue about significant issues of life. During these dialogues, these people begin to think about criteria for distinguishing better thinking from worse. The idea of providing models of dialogue seems valuable; indeed, Lipman et al. note that the general idea of embedding philosophy with the media of literature or drama has been lost for much too long a time. Lipman and colleagues make extensive use of models, but they also encourage children to engage in dialogue of their own in order to learn to think for themselves.

Basic Procedures of Instruction

Providing Models of Philosophical Inquiry

The models provided by Lipman and colleagues are somewhat different from those in W & L's program. Students are provided with stories about groups of children and adults who engage in dialogue concerning issues that arise in the course of everyday activities. These models of dialogue and reflection are presented in novels. As explained by Lipman et al. (1980):

> The books are works of fiction in which the characters eke out for themselves the laws of reasoning and the discovery of alternative philosophical views that have been presented through the centuries. The method of discovery for each of the children in the novels is dialogue coupled with reflection. This dialogue with peers, with teachers, with parents, grandparents, and relatives, alternating with reflections upon what has been said, is the basic vehicle by which the characters in the stories learn—by talking and thinking things out [p. 82].

As an illustration of the novels, consider some excerpts from *Harry Stottlemeier's Discovery* (hereafter *Harry*): The major purpose of this 96-page novel is to help fifth and sixth graders discover information about the structure and function of formal and informal logic. The excerpts that follow occur in the context of a science class. Harry, who has been daydreaming during a lecture on the solar system, suddenly realizes that the teacher, Mr. Bradley, is calling on him: "What is it that has a long tail, and revolves about the sun every 77 years? [p. 1]." Harry realizes that he doesn't know the answer because he wasn't listening; however, he does remember that earlier Mr. Bradley had said: "All planets revolve around the sun." Because planets revolve around the sun and the thing with the long tail revolves around the sun, Harry decides that the answer to the teacher's question is "a planet."

> He wasn't prepared for the laughter from the class. If he'd been paying attention, he would have heard Mr. Bradley say that the object he was referring to was Halley's comet, and that comets go around the sun just as planets do, but they are definitely not planets.
>
> Fortunately the bell rang just then, signaling the end of school for the day. But as Harry walked home, he still felt badly about not having been able to answer when Mr. Bradley called on him.
>
> Also, he was puzzled. How had he gone wrong? He went back over the way he had tried to figure out the answer. "All planets revolve about the sun," Mr. Bradley had said, very distinctly. And this thing with the tail also revolved about the sun, only it wasn't a planet.
>
> "So there are things that revolve about the sun that aren't planets," Harry said to himself. "All planets revolve about the sun, but not everything that revolves about the sun is a planet."

And then Harry had an idea. "A sentence can't be reversed. If you put the last part of a sentence first, it'll no longer be true. For example, take the sentence "All oaks are trees." If you turn it around, it becomes "All trees are oaks." But that's false. Now, it's true that "All planets revolve around the sun." But if you turn the sentence around and say that "All things that revolve around the sun are planets," then it's no longer true—it's false!"

The story continues by describing Harry's fascination with his discovery. He tries it out on a few more examples (e.g., "All cucumbers are vegetables.") and decides that it works.

Note that the preceding descriptions provide a model of Harry thinking to himself (and being intrigued by the process). As the chapter progresses we find models of dialogue involving Harry and his friends. Some remark "Who cares?" when he mentions his discovery. Another friend, Lisa, produces a counterexample to the rule Harry has fashioned. She notes that one can reverse "No eagles are lions," yet the statement is still true.

For the second time that day, Harry felt that he had somewhat failed. His only comfort was that Lisa wasn't laughing at him.

"I really thought I had it," he said to her. "I really thought I had it."

"You tried it out?" she asked. Her grey eyes set wide apart, were clear and serious.

"Of course. I took sentences like "All planets revolve about the sun," and "All model airplanes are toys," and "All cucumbers are vegetables," and I found that when the last part was put first, the sentences were no longer true."

"But the sentence I gave you wasn't like yours," replied Lisa quickly. "Every one of your sentences began with the word 'all'. But my sentence began with the word 'no'.

"If it's true that no submarines are kangaroos," began Harry, "then what about no kangaroos are submarines?"

"Also true," replied Lisa. "And if no mosquitos are lollipops, then it's true that no lollipops are mosquitos."

"That's it!" said Harry excitedly. "That's it! If a true sentence begins with the word 'no', then its reverse is also true. But if it begins with the word 'all', then its reverse is false."

Still later in the first chapter we find Harry returning home and finding his mother talking with a neighbor, Mrs. Olson.

Mrs. Olson was saying, "Let me tell you something, Mrs. Stottlemeier. That Mrs. Bates who just joined the PTA, all she ever talks about is helping the poor. Well, I believe in that too, of course, but then I keep thinking how all those radicals keep saying that we ought to help the poor, and that makes me wonder whether Mrs. Bates is well, you know . . ."

"Whether Mrs. Bates is a radical?" Harry's mother asked politely.

Mrs. Olson nodded.

Suddenly something in Harry's mind went "CLICK!" "Mrs. Olson," he said, "just because, according to you, all radicals are people who say they want to help the poor, that doesn't mean that all people who say they want to help the poor are radicals."

"Harry," said his mother, "This is none of your business, and besides, you're interrupting."

But Harry could tell by the expression on his mother's face that she was pleased with what he'd said. So he quietly got his glass of milk and sat down to drink it, feeling happier than he had felt in days.

Note that this episode provides a model of inappropriate reasoning that is eventually corrected (and corrected by a child).

It is important to note that *Harry Stottlemeier's Discovery* covers much more than the issue of rules of basic logic. Even the brief excerpts presented here provide a rich source of additional information; they mention daydreaming and attention, for example, and they highlight some connections between reasoning processes, school performance, and everyday life. Personal reactions to being laughed at by the class are also emphasized; so is the excitement of discovery, the urge for experimentation, and the confrontation with counterexamples. Additional examples of issues and discoveries that occur throughout the novel are discussed later. For present purposes the important point is that the novels are designed to serve as models for intra- and interpersonal dialogue about a wide range of thinking activities. The novels also provide models of a variety of personal thinking styles; children in the novels reveal predispositions for individual styles of thinking. According to Lipman et al. (1980):

These predispositions to think in certain ways make up the different styles of thinking; one such style tends to be formally deductive, others include variants of the good reasons approach. Those that predominate are wondering (Harry Stottlemeier), thinking in formal logical patterns (Tony Melillo), intuitive or hunch-like thinking (Lisa Terry), seeking and enjoying explanations (Fran Wood), being sensitive to the feelings of others (Anne Torgerson), and thinking creatively (Mickey Minkowski). While this is only a partial list of types of mental acts and associated styles of thinking illustrated in *Harry,* one can already see that they constitute a very broad network. [p. 147].

Encouraging Philosophical Discussion

A second component of the Philosophy for Children program involves philosophical discussion among students in the classroom. The idea of holding class discussions is hardly new, of course, but Lipman and colleagues emphasize the importance of *philosophical discussions* and attempt to differentiate these from other types of dialogue. Teachers in the Philosophy for Children program have to learn the characteristics of philosophical discussions because teachers act as models and play an important role in facilitating class discussions. Lipman and colleagues note that the program is by no means "teacher proof" and that good discussions do not merely happen by accident. They devote an entire chapter (Chapter 7) to the issue of "Guiding a Philosophical Discussion," yet they note that even this is insufficient for teacher training. (See Lipman et al., 1980, for a description of teacher training). Because we have not had the opportunity to participate in any of Lipman and colleagues' training sessions, our comments are restricted to 'best guesses' about the types of discussions emphasized by the program developers. These best guesses are based on descriptions provided in teacher's manuals and in Lipman et al. (1980).

The teacher's manual (*Philosophical Inquiry*) that accompanies *Harry* suggests that teachers begin discussion by asking students to identify points from the novel that they found interesting. (Students read the novel in parts; not all at once). The purpose of this first phase of discussion is to uncover issues that are interesting to the students (following the Socratic emphasis on beginning with matters that people feel are important). The types of discussion encouraged after the initial phase of "interest identification" seem to have three different functions, which often occur simultaneously. Each of these is discussed in the following section.

First, students are encouraged to reflect on their own contributions to the discussion. Have they barged in and hence violated rules of social etiquette? Are they contributing ideas that are relevant and that do not merely repeat what others said (students therefore have to learn to listen)? Are students expressing their ideas in a comprehensible manner, and have they presented good reasons for their beliefs and opinions? Are their current arguments consistent with previous ones they have given? Can they articulate some additional implications of their present positions? Teachers in the Philosophy for Children program attempt to increase awareness of the importance of these endeavors and to improve use of each one. They also attempt to help children appreciate the cooperative nature of the enterprise and to realize the value of hearing other opinions and views.

A second function of discussions in the program is to help children identify particular events as illustrations of more general principles or issues. In the first chapter of *Harry*, for example, Harry discovers that the statement "All planets revolve about the sun" does not imply that "All things that revolve about the sun are planets." Lipman et al. want children to learn more than the information conveyed in particular episodes such as this one; these episodes are designed to set the stage for discussing general principles or "leading ideas."

The teacher's manual suggests various leading ideas that teachers can select for purposes of discussion (ideally, these are congruent with the direction of the class discussion). The episode about Harry's attempts to reverse the "planet" sentence, for example, can lead to a discussion of the general issue of "The

Process of Inquiry." Are there general stages through which all kinds of inquiry proceed? A second leading idea is "Discovery and Invention." What are the differences between these? Why are they exciting? A third is "The Structure of Logical Statements." What do we mean by rules of logic? When do they apply and when don't they apply?

Other leading ideas are more appropriate for other aspects of the first chapter of *Harry*. For example, at one point in the chapter Harry feels resentment toward Lisa because she shows him his rule does not work. The teacher's manual includes a leading idea on "Resentment": How does it differ from anger? Are there times when such feelings are justified? One could imagine another leading idea on "Consistency," relating to the episode where Harry's mother tells him he is interrupting the conversation yet seems pleased at his contribution. The important point is that the introduction of leading ideas is designed to help students view particular episodes as instances of more general issues. Lipman and colleagues make use of the philosophical literature in order to formulate general issues to be explored.

A third function of the discussions held in the Philosophy for Children program is to facilitate mastery of particular concepts and principles. The first chapter of *Harry* mentions some rules for reversing sentences; students need to learn these rules. Lipman et al. also encourage children to generate examples that conform to various rules; this enables teachers to assess understanding, plus allows the children to see the relevance of these rules for their own experiences.

Providing Exercises to Strengthen Thinking Skills

In addition to the use of models and the emphasis on effective discussions, Lipman and colleagues use exercises as part of their instructional procedure. The exercises assigned for a particular lesson depend on the leading ideas emphasized during class discussion. If discussion is focused on "Discovery and Invention," for example, students may receive a list of items such as "electricity," "electric light bulb," and so forth; the task is to decide which are examples of discoveries and which of inventions, and to explain why. A class that is exploring "The Structure of Logical Statements" may receive exercises that allow individuals to practice reversing sentences and to assess the effects on the truth value of each sentence. The teacher's manuals include exercises for most of the leading ideas.

There are several reasons for assuming that the exercises constitute an important component of the instruction. First, they help students assess the degree to which they have understood concepts and principles mentioned during the discussion. Second, they allow teachers to assess the progress of each individual student. Finally, the exercises provide a basis for additional interaction because students discuss their reasons for choosing particular answers.

Overview of Program Content

The Philosophy for Children program originated in 1969 and has been steadily expanded since 1974. Lipman and colleagues envision a program that will eventually span grades K–12. At present, the curriculum for Grades 5–6 centers around the novel *Harry Stottlemeier's Discovery* and the teacher's manual *Philosophical Inquiry*. The primary emphasis is on the acquisition of formal and informal logic. Another novel, *Tony*, is designed for sixth graders and explores the presuppositions underlying scientific inquiry. It includes a teacher's manual, *Scientific Inquiry*, as well.

For Grades 7–9 the program explores ethical inquiry, language arts, and social studies. The novel *Lisa* and the teacher's manual *Ethical Inquiry* are a sequel to *Harry* and focus on ethical and social issues such as fairness, naturalness, lying and truth-telling, sex discrimination, and so forth. The interrelationships of logic and morality are stressed. *Suki* is a novel about Harry and his friends who are now freshmen in high school and face assignments in writing prose and poetry. Harry has difficulty writing, so this process is explored. The teacher's manual, *Writing: How and Why,* concentrates on the writing of poetry.

In Grades 8–10 students encounter the novel *Mark*, in which the fictional characters are high school sophomores. Mark is accused of vandalism; the class tries to determine who is guilty. In the process they explore a number of social issues such as the function of the law and bureaucracy, the concepts of individual freedom, justice, and so forth. A teacher's manual, *Social Inquiry,* is included as well.

Lipman and colleagues plan five additional novels and manuals for Grades 11 and 12 that would explore more advanced areas of philosophical specialization. Examples include ethics, epistemology, metaphysics, aesthetics, and logic. Each would reinforce and develop the skills stressed in earlier grades.

Each of the novels introduces a wide variety of information. In *Harry,* for example, the characters in the novel discover principles of formal reasoning and informal reasoning (e.g., the importance of giving reasons), and they discuss metaphysical and ethical aspects of thinking. There is also a strong emphasis on different styles of thought, presumably both to demonstrate that their use can be adjusted to their goals and to foster appreciation of varied styles of instruction. It seems worthwhile to provide some examples of the types of issues that are portrayed in this novel.

Consider some excerpts from the third chapter of *Harry*. The chapter opens with three of the characters—Lisa, Jill, and Fran—eating lunch. Their conversation turns to ideas: Where they come from (e.g., "I guess they're just like bubbles in my soda—they just bubble up out of nowhere."); the reality of thought (e.g., "They're not real like things in your room.", "I'll bet there are lots of other things like numbers that are real only in your mind."); the personal importance of thoughts (e.g., "My thoughts make me happy. . . . Like, I think of my dog, Sandy."); and the importance of thoughts in leading to understanding (e.g., "When you already know something, and you want to go beyond what you already know, you have to think. You have to figure things out.").

In addition to the metaphysical aspects of thinking, the chapter also describes a discussion between Tony and his father. Tony has been ruminating over the value of an earlier discovery (that the subject and predicate of sentences beginning with the qualifier, all, can't be reversed and still be true). He unearths its value by applying it to a situation of personal importance. Tony's father wants him to be an engineer because he is good in math. Tony points out that it is erroneous to infer that all people who are good in math are engineers. The chapter concludes with Tony's father explaining the reason for the nonreversal rule. He introduces Venn diagrams as a means of illustrating part–whole relationships, sets, subsets.

The remaining chapters of *Harry* are structured in a similar manner. Students are seen thinking about the relevance of feelings and thoughts, discovering aspects of formal inference making, and instantiating their discoveries in discussion. Over the course of the novel, the students make discoveries about reasoning such as the following: (1) generalization of the nonreversal rule of sentences beginning with the qualifiers "each" and "every." (2) identification of the three types of qualifiers (all, none, some); (3) distinction between statements about degree versus kind (e.g., taller than versus "to be" predicates); (4) contradiction of sentences beginning with the three types of qualifiers (all classes are interesting versus some classes are not interesting); (5) "carry-over" relationships (e.g., if Lee is taller than Mary, and Mary is taller than Jane, then . . .). These discoveries accumulate so that, by the end of the novel, students are solving formal and hypothetical syllogisms (e.g., "if he's vaccinated, he won't get smallpox. He got smallpox, therefore . . .").

In addition to the formal aspects of inference making, *Harry,* as we've seen, introduces students to the metaphysical aspects of thinking. The novel also provides models of informal reasoning; the characters engage in discussions about stereotyping, ethics, values, aesthetics, etc. They are seen applying some of the rules of inference previously discussed, as well as learning more general principles (e.g., the need for providing reasons for opinions, avoiding scare tactics and appeals to unrecognized authority, and distinguishing between cause and effect as well as description and explanation).

Analysis

We begin our evaluation of the Philosophy for Children program by considering those aspects of the program that remain invariant across grades and topics; we then consider Lipman et al.'s approach to particular topics in more detail.

Analysis of Invariant Instructional Procedures

Three aspects of Lipman et al.'s instructional procedures remain invariant across their program: The use of novels, the emphasis on discussion, and the completion of exercises. We consider some potential advantages and disadvantages of procedures such as these:

The Structure of the Novels. One unusual feature of the Philosophy for Children program is its use of fiction rather than textbooks. The novels include elements such as uncertainty, surprise, momentary failure, and so forth (see Brewer & Lichtenstein, 1980, for a discussion of the importance of these often neglected elements). Embedded within the overall story are models of the types of activities one would like students to emulate. In general, the stories emphasize the process of discovering, developing, and revising ideas; this is quite different from texts, which simply present the products of someone else's thoughts. The novels also emphasize the social nature of learning and thinking (Vygotsky, 1978); most of the discoveries in the novels derive from interactions with others rather than from thinking alone. The children in the novels also react to their successes and failures. For example, the excerpts from *Harry* cited earlier (see section on Basic Procedures of Instruction) include descriptions of Harry's feelings about making an error in class, his resentment toward Lisa when she provides a counterexample to his rule, and so forth. These episodes set the stage for discussing general issues concerning emotions and emotional reactions—issues that are certainly relevant to children's social and academic lives (see Norman, 1980, for a discussion of cognition and emotion).

The novels used by Lipman and colleagues would also seem to be more interesting to students than would typical didactic textbooks. Nevertheless, the stories still take place within an academically oriented context (e.g., many of the dialogues center around classroom discussions). One could imagine other settings that might more effectively capture the initial interest and attention of many students (the importance of thinking about thinking could be developed in the context of surviving on a deserted island, for example, or in the context of space travel, camping, and so forth). It would be useful to gather information about the range of students who are attracted to the materials used by Lipman et al., and to explore the degree to which different interests affect the development of thinking skills.

In our opinion, theorists might devote more attention to the potential advantages (and disadvantages) of presenting information in the form of novels rather than didactic textbooks. Novels and narratives may provide excellent media for modeling some of the processes involved in discovery and revision (including people's personal reactions to these events); didactic texts may be more valuable as reference guides because they are organized around concepts and topics rather than around temporo-spatial episodes (Tulving's 1972 distinction between episodic and semantic memory may be relevant here; see also Nelson & Brown,

1978). Some theorists argue that narratives provide a more basic structure for comprehension and retention than do didactic text structures (e.g., Olson, 1977); on the other hand, one can often understand a novel yet fail to develop a systematic network of general concepts that provides an organized basis for analyzing new situations. Note that Lipman et al. do not simply ask children to read the novels; children are also prompted to analyze episodes from the novel and to conceptualize them more broadly (e.g., in terms of more general principles or leading ideas). We discuss this aspect of their instruction later on.

The Emphasis on Reading.   The novels used in the Philosophy for Children program are written (rather than portrayed in the form of cartoons, for example); children in the program should therefore receive a great deal of practice reading. The degree to which they also receive practice evaluating and analyzing what they read will depend on the way that teachers structure discussion in the class (we discuss this later). This heavy emphasis on reading has both advantages and disadvantages. The advantages are obvious: Children receive extra practice reading. A potential disadvantage is that the program may presuppose such a high level of reading proficiency that many children—perhaps those that most need to develop thinking skills—are discouraged from completing the course.

The Role of Discussion.   As noted earlier, Lipman et al. do not simply ask children to read the stories; they also encourage discussion. The striking feature of these discussions is their flexibility. Teachers can choose to emphasize one of many possible leading ideas for each chapter that, ideally, are selected according to the interests expressed by members of the class. There are many advantages to flexibility, of course, but one would also like to know how an approach influences the types of skills developed. For example, Lipman (1980) notes that students seem to make gains in various areas (e.g., reading, reasoning) depending on the approach adopted by various teachers. Ideally, one would like to know what teachers do that facilitates reading and what they do that facilitates reasoning; this would permit an individual teacher to adopt various approaches depending on particular goals.

As an illustration of how different approaches might influence the development of different skills, consider two different approaches to the initial phase of Lipman et al.'s discussion. One approach might be to ask students to describe episodes from the story that they found interesting. Given that a few suggestions emerge and that the class agrees they are worth exploring, discussion might proceed. This procedure seems fine for many purposes, but it may also fail to facilitate the development of various comprehension skills.

An alternate approach might begin by encouraging students to summarize the main points of the chapter. This differs from the previous procedure because the focus is on understanding the structure of the story rather than on reading until some point of interest catches one's eye. Once the class has agreed on the main points of the story, students might then explore the question of which points are interesting. (One could also consider interest from the perspective of different people in the story, or ask for a summary of the general principles of the story rather than a summary of the episodes, and discuss the interest value of these principles.)

There are obviously many other ways that one could approach the initial phase of discussion. Those just mentioned are simply illustrations of ways that different procedures might facilitate the development of different skills. It seems clear that people read differently depending on their goals or purposes; the goal of "being able to state something that was interesting" may lead to very different comprehension activities than the goal of "being able to summarize the main points of a story." Ideally, one would like to help students understand these relationships between acquisition activities and subsequent goals (e.g., see our discussion of W & L's program relative to their general goals).

We should also note that, despite the flexibility built into the Philosophy for Children program, Lipman and colleagues (1980) prescribe some characteristics of useful discussion. For example, they argue that the discussions led by teachers in the Philosophy for Children program are quite different from the types of discussions frequently conducted in other classrooms. One of the differences is presumably that the philosophy teachers emphasize the importance of giving reasons for one's arguments and the importance of evaluating arguments in terms of their redundancy with previous statements, their relevance to immediate discussion, and the significance of their contribution to the general discussion. In addition, students are encouraged to explore the assumptions underlying each other's remarks. In general, these activities would appear to develop important metacognitive skills. However, Lipman et al. provide little information about how these procedures are implemented. It is possible that more details are provided during teacher training.

The Role of the Exercises.   In addition to discussion, students in the Philosophy for Children program usually receive exercises that are related to the leading idea that has been the focus of discussion. The exercises come in about every conceivable form (e.g., true–false, multiple choice, open-ended questions, etc.). How important are these exercises for skill development? One might ask, for example, whether students would develop important thinking skills if classes involved discussion but no exercises. It is possible that the exercises are the most important part of the program. Many of the tasks that Lipman et al. use for evaluation include syllogisms and other reasoning tasks that seem quite similar to the exercises performed in the classroom; it is possible that students would perform even better on these evaluation tasks if more class time were devoted to working on problems (plus discussions of steps toward solution), rather than to reading or to general discussion (note that the course would therefore have a format more similar to that used by W & L; see our review of their program in an earlier section of this chapter).

Analysis of Instructions for Solving Class Exercises

The purpose of this section is to evaluate the degree to which Lipman et al,'s instruction is sufficient to help students learn to solve the problems that are presented as class exercises, to solve various types of reasoning problems, for example. Of course, the Philosophy for Children Program is designed to do more than provide students with the skills necessary to solve particular types of problems. Indeed, as noted in our theoretical overview section Lipman et al. (1980) warn against "simplistic" approaches to skill development; they criticize programs that simply ask students to study formal logic or to perform particular exercises that require skills such as classification, generalization, hypothesis formation, and so forth. According to Lipman, exercises such as these result in improvement that is merely superficial and transient. Nevertheless, students in the Philosophy for Children Program are presented with a wide variety of exercises; Lipman et al. must assume that these exercises play some role in skill development. By focusing first on Lipman et al.'s approach to helping students develop the ability to solve various types of poblems, we hope to clarify, in the sections that follow, what the role of the novels and the discussions might be. The problems cited are from the teacher's manual that accompanies *Harry*.

Syllogistic Reasoning Problems.   Consider first Lipman et al.'s approach to helping students learn to solve syllogistic reasoning problems. One possible approach to syllogistic reasoning is to teach students some procedures to follow; to teach them to use Venn diagrams, for example. This is the approach adopted by W & L (see review of program above). Lipman et al. also introduce students to Venn diagrams; however, they do not simply present students with syllogisms and then teach them to use Venn diagrams. Instead, they gradually develop the concept of syllogistic reasoning. This development occurs in the novel *Harry* and is paralleled in the class exercises as well.

As noted earlier, children in the Philosophy for Children program are first exposed to the simple idea that the truth value of many types of sentences is changed when the sentence is reversed ("All dogs are animals" is true, yet "all animals are dogs" is false). Students then learn that the reversal rule is appropriate for logical statements that conform to a particular structure and they learn what constitutes a permissible structure (e.g., what types of qualifiers, subjects, verbs, and predicates are allowable). Students receive exercises that ask them to construct statements out of sentence fragments (e.g., are, horses, all, animals) and to reverse statements that are written in logical form (e.g., all chickens are birds). Once students have practiced these exercises, they are asked to assess the truth value of sentences that don't begin with the qualifier "all" (e.g., no lemons are snowballs). This last exercise leads to exercises on standardization, which are illustrated in Table 4.1. Table 4.1 also illustrates subsequent exercises that gradually develop the skills necessary for hypothetical syllogistic reasoning.

In general, Lipman et al. seem to do a good job of helping students develop the ability to solve syllogistic reasoning problems. They help students develop various component skills (e.g., to recognize the structure of logical statements, to learn rules of standardization, to use Venn diagrams) before asking them to solve complex problems of hypothetical syllogistic reasoning. We assume that they also help children overcome the 'empirical bias' (e.g., Scribner, 1977), which drives people to answer a hypothetical reasoning problem on the basis of assumptions about the truth of a conclusion relative to the 'real world,' rather than on the basis of whether it follows from hypothetical premises. It is also instructive to note that the novels provide information about ways to solve syllogistic reasoning problems (although it seems clear that teachers supplement this instruction). For example, one of the dialogues in *Harry* involves a discussion between Tony and Tony's father. The latter introduces Venn diagrams in order to help Tony understand why Harry's rule for reversing sentences frequently works.

We should note, however, that it is unclear what Lipman and colleagues do if students have difficulty solving some of the problems in the exercises. It is one thing to create a series of exercises that increase in complexity; it is another matter to help children become aware of the types of thinking processes necessary to solve each of the exercises. Some children might benefit from the types of "think aloud plus feedback" exercises emphasized by W & L (see first section of this chapter).

Formal Analogy Problems.   In *Harry*, formal analogy problems receive much less emphasis than syllogistic reasoning problems. Nevertheless, it is instructive to consider how Lipman et al. attempt to help students learn to solve problems such as these. In the teacher's manual, formal analogy problems are introduced in conjunction with the leading idea "Flexible and Inflexible Thinking"; the ability to think analogically is viewed as one example of flexible thinking.

The analogy exercises presented in the teacher's manual are grouped into various subcategories of relationship (e.g., means and ends, instance and type, part to whole, permanence and chance). Illustrations of three different subcategories are as follows:

1. Means and Ends   "turning a key" is to "opening a door," as "flicking a switch" is to . . . (a) putting out the cat; (b) lighting the room; (c) changing partners; (d) slowing the horse.

2. Appearance and Reality   "dream" is to "waking," as "fantasy" is to . . . (a) understanding;   (b) hoping;   (c) loving; (d) remembering.

TABLE 4.1
Exercises on Syllogistic Reasoning Skills
(From the Philosophy for Children Program)

I. Standardization of sentences using "All," "No," and "Some" as qualifiers

Standardize the following:

1. Only the elms are diseased.
2. Not a television set is working.
3. Quite a few paints aren't poisonous. . . .

II. Venn diagrams

Draw and label circle diagrams for the following sentences:

1. All windows are things made of glass.

III. Reversal of sentences expressing asymmetrical, symmetrical, and nonsymmetrical types of relationships

Assume that the following statements are true. Indicate whether the sentence that results when the terms are reversed will be true, false, or undetermined, and identify the type of relationship.

1. The Amazon is longer than the St. Lawrence.
2. Kentucky is far from New Jersey.
3. Richard is in love with America.

IV. "Carry-over" of sentences expressing symmetrical, asymmetrical, and nonsymmetrical types of relationships

Assume that the first two sentences are true.

a. Write in the third sentence that results from combining the first two.
b. Indicate whether the third sentence is true, false, or undetermined.
c. Identify the type of carry-over relationship.

1. A lake is larger than a pond.
2. A pond is larger than a puddle.

V. Syllogisms

In the spaces below, fill in the blanks so that the syllogisms are valid.

All dogs are mammals.
All _____are animals.

All dogs are animals.

VI. Contradictions

What are the contradictions of the following statements?

1. Some drugstores are open all night.
2. Some glinks are not scoobles.
3. All sleighs are drawn by reindeer.

VII. Hypothetical syllogisms

When the compound sentence in a hypothetical reasoning pattern begins with "only if," be sure to reverse the antecedent and consequent before proceeding to draw your conclusion. When trustworthy, draw conclusions from the following:

Only if spring has arrived will the trees begin to bud. Spring has arrived. . . .

3. Cause and Effect   "germ" is to "disease," as "candle" is to . . .
(a) wax; (b) wick; (c) white; (d) light.

It is unclear whether Lipman et al. provide much instruction about how to solve analogies. Some of W & L's suggestions for forming explicit relationship sentences and systematically evaluating each of the foils may be valuable here.

Informal Reasoning Problems.   The teacher's manual that accompanies *Harry* also includes a variety of informal reasoning problems that deal with evaluating reasons, making inferences, uncovering assumptions, and drawing distinctions. Lipman et al. carefully define important concepts necessary for completing the exercises (e.g., what is meant by a good reason). They also attempt to help children understand why some answers are better than others by having students discuss their answers as a group.

Creativity and Verbal Fluency Exercises.   The teacher's manual for *Harry* also includes a number of exercises designed to promote "creativity and verbal fluency." To enhance verbal fluency, students receive exercises on generating synonyms, identifying and improving ambiguous statements, and using context to determine word meanings. The exercises on creativity involve the use of metaphor and the invention of rules. Once again, we are unclear about any procedures that may be suggested in order to help students who have difficulty with exercises such as these. Some of the procedures suggested by de Bono (1970) may be relevant here.

Overall, it seems clear that students are encouraged to do a wide variety of exercises in the context of their work on the novel *Harry*. Some of these exercises, especially the ones involving syllogistic reasoning, seem to develop nicely so that component skills are introduced before students are expected to tackle more complex problems. Other exercises seem to develop much less systematically. They tend to pop up as a function of the leading ideas discussed by the students in the class. It is difficult to say whether students master the skills necessary to solve many of the problem types (to solve formal analogy problems, for example), especially as there is such a wide variety. However, the teacher's manual emphasizes the importance of helping students master the exercises presented in class.

Note that our discussion of Lipman et al.'s approach to helping students learn to solve the problems in the exercises has also uncovered one function of the novels and the discussion. One function of the novels is to provide information about how to solve various problems; for example, Venn diagrams are introduced in *Harry*. Similarly, one function of discussion is undoubtedly to help students learn to solve various problems more effectively. Nevertheless, it seems clear that these are not the only functions of the novels or the discussion; for example, a discussion of how to solve a particular type of problem is not equivalent to Lipman et al.'s concept of a philosophical discussion. The major purpose of the novels and the philosophical discussion is presumably to help students develop general thinking skills that will enable them to do much more than merely solve particular types of formal problems. The degree to which the Lipman et al. program seems to develop more general thinking skills is discussed next.

Analysis Relative to General Goals

Lipman and colleagues list the following as their basic goals:

1. Improvement in reasoning ability.
2. Development of creativity.
3. Personal and interpersonal growth.
4. Development of ethical understanding.

To what extent might the Philosophy for Children program facilitate the achievement of these goals?

Reasoning. Consider first the goal of helping students reason more effectively. We noted earlier that Lipman et al. provide students with a wide variety of reasoning exercises. However, we also acknowledged their criticism of programs that concentrate exclusively on formal exercises; they argue that this approach results in improvements that are superficial and transient. What is it about the Philosophy for Children program that might help students develop socially and educationally relevant thinking skills?

It seems to us that the novels play an important role in helping students develop reasoning skills applicable to a wide variety of situations. In particular, they help students understand the relevance of various principles of reasoning for their everyday lives. Consider the excerpts from the first chapter of *Harry* presented earlier. One involved Harry's realization that his mother's friend had violated a basic principle of logic. The simple principle that Harry had discovered earlier therefore had relevance for his everyday activities. Similar examples occur in *Harry* again and again.

In essence, Lipman et al.'s novels develop the idea of thinking about thinking by introducing basic principles (e.g., rules for reversing sentences) and then providing examples of the applicability of these principles. Once students have been introduced to a basic principle, this information provides a background for interpreting the significance of examples that relate to the principle, which in turn should clarify the student's previous knowledge of the principle. Through this reciprocal interplay between principles and examples, one would expect students gradually to access this information in everyday reasoning situations (Bransford, 1979; Bransford et al., 1979; Bransford & Nitsch, 1978; Brown, in press; Brown & Campione, 1979). Students who receive only formal reasoning exercises may have a very limited idea of the purpose of those exercises; they might therefore learn to activate appropriate skills and knowledge when confronted with recognizable problem formats yet fail to do so in other contexts (e.g., Brown et al., in press; Maratsos, 1977). Lipman et al.'s use of novels that illustrate the significance of concepts and procedures for a wide variety of everyday activities may therefore play an important role in developing educationally significant thinking skills. Their emphasis on a wide variety of reasoning activities (i.e., on the general importance of giving reasons, analyzing assumptions, noticing various rules of standardization, etc.) greatly increases the potential relevance of the program as well.

We assume that the philosophical discussions play an equal if not more important role in helping students develop the ability to monitor and evaluate the types of reasoning activities that occur in everyday situations. Recall that one function of the discussions is to help students monitor their own contributions (for relevance, consistency, etc). Another function of the discussion is to discuss "leading ideas" that are relevant to a wide range of endeavors. Both seem to facilitate the development of skills that might not be acquired if students only received practice solving formal reasoning tasks.

There may, nevertheless, be a number of ways to structure the reasoning portion of this program so that it is both more efficient and more general. In *Harry,* for example, Lipman et al. place very little emphasis on analogical reasoning, although they do provide students with some formal analogy exercises. We noted earlier (see analysis of W & L program) that practice in solving formal analogy problems may not be the best way to develop everyday skills of analogic thinking. Lipman et al. also do not emphasize how the search for reasons can facilitate mastery of new information, and mastery skills seem to be very important for most academic endeavors. Also, the flexibility in the program (i.e., teachers presumably select different leading ideas for discussion depending on the students' interests) may affect students' mastery of various aspects of the reasoning process. Perhaps the teacher training emphasizes that some leading ideas and exercises are mandatory whereas others are optional. If it doesn't, it is not clear that students will receive the instructional sequencing that they might need.

Creativity.   The second goal of the Philosophy for Children program is to enhance creativity. To what extent might the program be expected to achieve this goal? Clearly, the answer depends on what one means by creativity. Aspects of the program seem to encourage creative activities; for example students are prompted to analyze assumptions and to imagine alternative possibilities. Students also receive various exercises such as "Invent an imaginary island and draw a map on it." Nevertheless, there are important differences between suggesting exercises that could provide an opportunity for people to be creative and providing suggestions for how to increase creativity (e.g., see de Bono, 1970). Lipman et al. do encourage each student to discuss his or her approaches to particular creativity exercises; perhaps exposure to alternative perpsectives plus the permission to be creative are the most important ingredients for helping students learn to create or invent on their own.

Personal and Interpersonal Growth.   According to the authors, personal and interpersonal growth take place primarily in the course of discussion and reflection about discussion. The idea is that discussion promotes the child's awareness of personalities, interests, values, and biases, and that this interpersonal awareness is necessary for social development. Although Lipman et al. concede that it is too early to tell whether the program actually fosters this development, it seems clear that the program is designed with social development in mind. The students in *Harry* are presented as a diverse group; the novel contains many examples of their different thinking styles, different values, and so forth. Furthermore, the dialogue in the novel models the interpersonal awareness that Lipman et al. wish students to emulate. Teachers presumably stress the value of different styles of thinking as well.

Development of Ethical Understanding. It is *not* the stated goal of the program to teach students particular moral rules; rather, the goal is to help students learn to identify moral issues as they occur and to sensitize students to methods for moral judgment.

Lipman et al. identify three aspects of the program that are assumed to contribute to an understanding of methods for making moral judgments: the development of logical reasoning skills (e.g., impartiality, consistency); the development of imagination (e.g., the consideration of alternative points of view); and the development of an awareness of personal feelings and the feelings of others. It seems important that students should learn to reason impartially and consistently when making value judgments. It also seems important that they should be able to consider the consequences of their actions from the perspective of others who could be affected. Finally, it seems important that issues are discussed in an atmosphere in which students feel comfortable about expressing their feelings and ideas, which, in turn, implies that each student values the contributions of other students.

Analysis of the Existing Evaluation Data

The purpose of this section is to analyze the existing evaluation data on the effectiveness of the Philosophy for Children program. The major evaluation studies and their results are summarized in Lipman's discussion in the section of his article called "Evaluation Data." Many of the results seem impressive (e.g., improvement in reasoning, math, and reading for some students in some classes). Not surprisingly, however, one could raise a number of questions about data such as these. One always faces the question of whether teachers who choose to receive training in a new program are more motivated and skilled than control teachers. (We suspect, however, that Lipman et al.'s teacher training develops important skills.) One would also like more precise information about the ways students improve in reading, mathematics, reasoning, creativity, and verbal fluency. We discuss each of these issues in turn.

Reading.   Consider first the improvements in reading. We noted earlier that the Philosophy for Children program involves a considerable amount of reading. Furthermore, it includes exercises such as selecting vocabulary words, making inferences from texts, and so forth. Are students in the Philosophy for Children program simply receiving extra practice at decoding, vocabulary drills, and inference tests? Might they improve even more if their time was spent in extra reading classes? It is quite possible that the program does indeed develop general thinking skills that transfer to a wide variety of reading tasks. The existing data are unclear on this point.

We should also note that there is a hidden variable in at least one of the evaluation studies (the ETS study) that, in our opinion, could have important effects on outcome measures. In particular, it is our understanding that some schools (e.g., Pompton Lakes) are compartmentalized (students go to different teachers for different subject areas) whereas others are not (e.g., Newark). Note that in the ETS study, it was the students from Newark who showed the most gains in reading and math. One reason for this may be that in Newark (but not in Pompton Lakes), the same teacher who taught the philosophy program to the children usually taught them reading as well. Lipman et al. (1980) argue that there were fewer differences between experimentals and controls in Pompton Lakes because of a possible spillover effect of the program that enhanced the performance of the controls. It does not seem unreasonable to assume that spillover effects can occur (i.e., experimentals and controls in Pompton Lakes were from the same schools and everyone in the system was presumably especially excited about the program; in contrast, experimentals and controls in Newark were from different schools). However, in our opinion the issue of whether schools are compartmentalized or not is equally if not more important. There are differences between assessing the effects of a thinking skills *program* on achievement in areas such as reading, and assessing the impact of teachers specially selected and trained in thinking skills, who teach the children other subject matters in addition to the special program. From a practical standpoint, it seems highly likely that the implementation of thinking-skills programs will result in more improvement if these teachers teach the children other topics (e.g., reading) as well.

Mathematics.   The preceding arguments about reading are relevant to data indicating that children in the Philosophy for Children program sometimes show improvement on mathematics achievement tests. We see no exercises in the Philosophy for Children program that deal explicitly with mathematics; gains in this area therefore seem particularly impressive. However, what are students who received the Philosophy for Children program doing in mathematics that they were not doing before the program? Are they better at computation? At solving word problems? Are they more motivated during testing? Ideally, students who take the Philosophy for Children program will be more likely to learn in their mathematics classes, perhaps because they try to understand what they are doing rather than simply attempt to memorize formulas. It might be illuminating to compare data on the approaches to learning new aspects of math that are adopted by children who are and are not in the program. It would be very impressive to find that children in the Philosophy for Children program take an active approach to learning that focuses on understanding mathematics rather than on simply memorizing formulas that may be supplied by a teacher or a text.

We should note once again, however, that gains in mathematical achievement may depend strongly on whether the same teacher (or a similarly trained teacher) teaches mathematics. As we understand it, the Philosophy for Children teachers in the Newark system (see the ETS study) taught the experimental children their math as well as their reading; this could have had strong effects on the results obtained.

Reasoning.   The evaluation data for the Philosophy for Children program also suggest that students in the program often show gains in reasoning ability. Many of the problems on the evaluation tests (e.g., the CTMM) seem quite similar to exercises performed during class (syllogisms, standardization exercises, etc). There is nothing wrong with this, of course. The test items are not exact duplicates of the class exercises. Nevertheless, we argued earlier (and so do Lipman et al.) that the ability to solve various types of formal reasoning problems is no guarantee that students reason more effectively in everyday settings. One of the strong points of the Philosophy for Children program is that children are helped to understand the importance of thinking about thinking for their everyday lives.

One could imagine several possible ways of exploring whether students in this program do indeed become sensitive to the importance of evaluating the types of reasoning that occur in everyday settings. For example, assume that groups of students from experimental and control classes were asked to discuss a topic as a group. Would students in the Philosophy for Children program be more likely to keep the discussion on track by monitoring their own contributions as well as others? Would they identify general issues (leading ideas) that are relevant to the particular topic? It would be quite impressive to find evidence for activities such as these.

An alternate approach to evaluation might be to present students with dialogues that do or do not develop appropriately (two people may be interpreting some key words totally differently and hence miss each other's point, each person may be internally inconsistent, etc.). Would students be able to evaluate dialogues such as these and identify where things went astray? One could also ask students to evaluate passages such as those used by Markman (1979). Would students in the Philosophy for Children program be more likely to detect the inconsistencies (see Baker & Brown, in press, for further examples)?

Creativity and Fluency.   The evaluation data for the Philosophy for Children program also suggest that children frequently improve in creativity and verbal fluency. Many of the tests used to measure these abilities present children with a stimulus (e.g., a visual pattern) and ask them to generate as many uses or interpretations as they can. Johnson (1972) argues that fluency tests of the sort used by Lipman et al. often encourage students to produce a greater number of ideas that are of lower than average quality. There seem to be important differences between procedures that emphasize the quality of ideas and those that emphasize the quantity of ideas. (One could draw an analogy to the greater quality, but not quantity, of moves considered by chess masters versus nonmasters; see Chase & Simon, 1973.) It is important to note, however, that Lipman et al. appear not to measure the mere quantity of each child's output; instead, they measure the appropriateness of each response. We have no details about the criteria for appropriateness that they use.

Summary.   Overall, the evaluation data reported by Lipman et al. (1980 and this volume) certainly warrant optimism. Nevertheless, it seems clear that the evaluation procedures could be improved. It might be particularly important to evaluate the program on line, to devise ways to evaluate progress through the course (see Tyler & White, 1979, for discussions of testing for assessment). The evaluation data indicate that different groups of students appear to make gains in different areas. One would like to know why this happens so that instructional procedures can be selected depending on particular goals. At a more general level, on-line evaluation can help developers define particular subgoals more precisely and provide a feedback mechanism for improving the instructional procedures. We would prefer to see more of an emphasis on *improving* programs (this holds for all programs, not just Lipman et al's.) than on attempts to prove that the program works.

FEUERSTEIN'S INSTRUMENTAL ENRICHMENT PROGRAM

Feuerstein's Instrumental Enrichment program (Feuerstein, Rand, Hoffman, & Miller, 1980; Feuerstein, Rand, & Hoffman, 1979) represents a specific application of his more general approach to cognition and development. The program grew out of Feuerstein's efforts to develop new methods for assessing learning potential, which in turn emerged from his efforts to help hundreds of displaced adolescents who were immigrating to Israel.

Conventional test scores revealed that unusually high numbers of these adolescents were functioning 3 to 6 years below their age norms; many received IQ scores between 50 and 70, and even lower. Feuerstein believed that these scores reflected the adolescents' deficiencies in problem-solving skills, which were the result of lack of sufficient exposure to mediators (i.e., parents, teachers), and that their potential to learn was much greater than the conventional test scores indicated. In order to overcome the negative expectations generated by past performance, and to develop ideas about the types of intervention needed, Feuerstein created a dynamic method for assessing students' potential to learn new information. This method includes a set of tests known as the Learning Potential Assessment Device (LPAD). The purpose of LPAD assessment is to provide children with focused learning experiences in order to assess strong and weak aspects of their cognitive functioning and to evaluate the amount of intervention required to produce change (see Feuerstein et al., 1979).

On the basis of his work with the LPAD, Feuerstein was able to demonstrate that numerous individuals had far greater potential than previously believed, and he was able to identify a number of "deficient cognitive functions" that frequently accompanied poor cognitive performance. This led to the development of the Instrumental Enrichment program, which is designed to help children develop their potential to learn on their own.

In this chapter, we focus primarily on Feuerstein's Instrumental Enrichment (IE) program rather than on LPAD. However, the basic constructs explored underlie both the IE program and the LPAD.

Theoretical Overview

Feuerstein's approach centers around the concept of mediated learning experiences (MLE). This concept emphasizes the role of human agents (parents, teachers, peers) in the cognitive development of the child. Few would deny that human agents play an important role in normal cognitive development. As an illustration, consider the atypical development characteristic of feral children such as the "Wild boy of Averon." Human agents provide information that would not be available in a nonhuman environment. Information about the names of objects represents a simple case in point.

Feuerstein's theory of MLE emphasizes that effective mediators are not simply sources of information, analogous to physical stimuli, that "enrich the child's perceptual environment." Instead, effective mediators perform activities that help the child interpret various experiences. Children who lack parents or "significant others" are not the only ones who are deprived of MLE.

We discuss three aspects of MLE to set the stage for our discussion of Feuerstein's Instrumental Enrichment program: (1) what does it mean to mediate a child's learning? (2) why might children be deprived of sufficient MLE, and what are the consequencies if they are? and (3) what can be done to make up for a lack of MLE?

Mediating Children's Learning

Consider first the issue of what it means to "mediate a child's learning." In general, it means that an agent intentionally influences the interaction between a child and his or her environment in a way that facilitates the child's ability to interpret and organize events. The agent need not be aware that he or she is mediating, of course; effective mediation occurs in the course of interactions between adults and children in everyday activities.

Imagine a parent helping a child complete a puzzle. One parent may simply tell the child which piece to pick next, or may encourage the child to proceed as quickly as possible by using trial and error. In such an instance, the primary emphasis is on the *product* or end result. Another parent may provide the type of support that enables the child to learn something about the processes involved in reaching a solution. The parent may encourage the child to decide which piece to start with, for example; this sensitizes the child to the importance of planning, as well as to the value of searching for relevant cues (see Wertsch, 1979, for protocols of parent–child interactions). An effective mediator may also help the child see how the processes involved in completing puzzles are related to other aspects of life.

A related example of mediation involves instances where parents may ask children to do something: "Please buy three bottles of milk." A request such as this may get the job done but it also misses an opportunity for mediated learning; it does not help the child appreciate the reasoning underlying the request. Feuerstein contrasts the preceding request with the following: "Please buy three bottles of milk so that we will have enough left over for tomorrow when the shops are closed" (Feuerstein et al., 1980, p. 21). This simple elaboration of the earlier statement involves the child in the reasoning underlying the request. It may help the child notice some important ways to organize temporal experience (e.g., weeks, weekends), and it emphasizes the importance of planning. One can imagine hundreds of similar examples where an interchange between a mediator and a child may or may not encourage the types of activities that help the child organize his or her experiences and understand reasons for actions and events. In short, effective mediators are not those that simply provide exposure to a wide variety of content; instead, they perform activities that sensitize the child to dimensions and procedures that transcend the particular events that provide the focus on instruction. As pointed out by Feuerstein et al. (1980):

Whether a child is taught to build a canoe or to complete a puzzle, the underlying cognitive structure will not necessarily differ in a fundamental way. In learning to master a given situation, the child must learn to cope with a sequence of events situated in space and time, to dissociate the means from the goal, and to indulge in anticipatory representational thought [p. 22].

The basic function of MLE is to prepare the child to take an active role in problem solving and to learn on his or her own.

Causes and Consequences of Insufficient MLE

Why might some children be deprived of sufficient MLE and what are the consequences? We consider the initial part of this question first. Lack of MLE does not necessarily imply a lack of parents or significant others. Feuerstein emphasizes that the quality of MLE depends on characteristics of both the child and the mediating agent. A lack of MLE can occur when the agent fails to mediate to the child (e.g., apathy of the parent, diminished expectations of the parent), or when the child poses barriers to mediation (e.g., emotional disturbance). Of particular significance is Feuerstein's claim that organic conditions of the child (e.g., "brain damage") should, in many cases, be viewed as barriers to effective mediation rather than as direct causes of "thinking deficits." The case histories described in Feuerstein et al. (1979, 1980) underscore the importance of this perspective; many seemingly hopeless cases have improved dramatically when the barriers to effective mediation have been identified and alternate modes employed (see especially the case histories on pp. 44, 45, 51, 107, in Feuerstein et al., 1980). Note that the more barriers the child poses to mediation, the greater the likelihood that the "everyday" and "intuitive" aspects of parenting and teaching may be insufficient, or inappropriate, for effective mediation.

What are the consequences for children who lack sufficient MLE? In general, these children manifest a diminished level of cognitive functioning. In many cases their scores on conventional tests will fall within the mildly retarded or moderately retarded range. It is commonplace to refer to these individuals as retarded; the invited inference is that they are retarded *individuals*. Feuerstein uses the term retarded *performers*. Their poor performance does not necessarily mean that they lack the capacity to think and learn. A common reaction to children with low test scores is to create simplified learning environments that do not require the representational and symbolic forms of thought believed to be beyond the reach of these children (see Feuerstein et al., 1980, p. 60). Feuerstein argues that this approach is self-defeating. In essence, it simply perpetuates the child's lack of exposure to MLE by depriving the child of the learning experiences needed most.

Feuerstein maintains that a child who lacks sufficient MLE can exhibit various cognitive deficiencies. He also distinguishes deficient cognitive functions from deficient cognitive operations; cognitive functions are assumed to be prerequisites to internalized, representational, and operational thought. Consider a child who is unable to classify a series of objects or events. As stated by Feuerstein et al. (1980):

> Underlying the operation of classification are a number of functions such as systematic and precise data gathering, the ability to deal with two or more sources of information simultaneously, and the necessity to compare the objects or events to be classified. Failure to correctly classify objects or events may either be caused by inability to apply the logical operations governing classification, or may result from deficiencies in the underlying functions that are presupposed in the operation [p. 71].

Feuerstein also argues that basic cognitive functions may be relatively intact, yet an individual may often fail to utilize them spontaneously. For example, a person may consistently fail to consider two sources of information unless explicitly prompted, or a person may fail a comparison problem that requires simple counting because there is no tendency to count spontaneously or because counting is still a laborious, nonautomatized activity. In other domains—in a situation involving choices among groups of cookies, for example—the same person may spontaneously compare and count (although these activities may still be laborious and inefficient). (See Feuerstein, Jensen, Hoffman, & Rand, this volume, Table 1.1, for a list of the deficient cognitive functions.)

Feuerstein warns that his list of deficient cognitive functions is neither definitive nor exhaustive and that there is considerable overlap among categories. It is not our goal to discuss them fully here. (One can develop a better understanding by focusing on the instructional procedures used in the Instrumental Enrichment program.) However, there are two points about the deficient functions that seem to be especially important for understanding Feuerstein's approach.

First, Feuerstein's concept of deficient cognitive functions is designed to provide an alternative to the commonplace assumption of deficient thinking *abilities*. The latter leads to negative expectations that affect the type of intervention or mediation that is tried. It is easy to underestimate the importance of negative expectation unless one has worked with retarded performers; the natural tendency is to present few or no challenges because the child might get upset (see Brown, et al., in press, for further discussion of this point). When one sees Feuerstein working with these children on the LPAD, a very different view of their potential emerges. Parents are often amazed at the performance of their child in these sessions and, in some cases, they change their approach to interacting with (i.e., mediating to) their child. The children are often amazed at their performance as well.

The second point about Feuerstein's list of deficient cognitive functions is that one could analyze each one in isolation yet miss the significance of his basic message. One must consider the relationships among various functions in order to understand an individual's general approach to interacting with the world. According to Feuerstein et al. (1980):

> A common thread running through virtually all of the . . . deficient functions is the phenomenon that we refer to as an episodic grasp of reality.
>
> . . . In essence, grasping the world episodically means that each object or event is experienced in isolation without any attempt to relate or link it to previous or anticipated experiences in space and time. An episodic grasp of reality reflects a passive attitude toward one's experiences because no attempt is made by the individual to actively contribute to his experience by organizing, ordering, summating, or comparing events and thereby placing them within a broader and more meaningful context.
>
> . . . An episodic grasp of reality is also responsible for the limited readiness of the individual to respond to incompatibilities in the field that provide the basis for the recognition of the existence of a problem.
>
> . . . Very often, the behavior attributed to the retarded performer is an expression of his episodic grasp of reality, which is manifested in his failure to act on and go beyond the mere registration of incoming stimuli and information. In terms of our approach, any attempt to modify a child must involve a fundamental reorientation of his encounter with reality [p. 102–3].

Feuerstein argues that general patterns of deficient cognitive functions must be corrected for a "reorientation of one's encounter with reality" to occur.

Compensating for Insufficient MLE

Feuerstein makes some important assumptions about the possibility of overcoming problems resulting from insufficient MLE. First, he denies that the basics of development are "over by the age of three"; he argues that significant changes in cognitive functioning can occur much later in life. Feuerstein does not deny the importance of early childhood experiences, but he emphasizes the need to differentiate the concept of optimal periods of development from the concept of critical periods of development. Clarke and Clarke (1976) provide an excellent discussion of many assumptions about the irreversibility of early experiences that become highly questionable when explored in detail.

In essence, Feuerstein argues that one can make up for a child's insufficient MLE in early years by supplying systematic and organized MLE later in life. The purpose of the later MLE is to provide the child with the tools, confidence, and motivation necessary to learn and solve problems independently. Feuerstein notes that his Instrumental Enrichment (IE) program is one of many possible ways to provide the kinds of mediation he envisions. We should also note that the program is designed to develop a wide variety of skills; it is therefore assumed that even people who are relatively high-functioning individuals can benefit from the program.

Basic Procedures of Instruction

The instructional procedures employed in Instrumental Enrichment (IE) center around a series of exercises or "instruments" (15 are currently in use) that provide a context for mediated learning. Beginning students usually receive the "Organization of Dots I" (ODI) instrument and the "Orientation in Space I" (OSI) instrument; students work on one or the other on alternate days. Figure 4.1 illustrates problems from two different pages of the ODI instrument. (There are a total of 20 pages in this instrument.) The problems within each instrument are ordered in increasing difficulty. For example, the problems in Fig. 4.1b are more difficult than those in Fig. 4.1a.

The basic task of ODI is to connect the dots so that they conform to the model. Each dot must be used once and only once; the figures drawn in each frame (e.g., square, triangle) must be identical to those in the model in size and number, but each figure may differ in orientation from the model. Students usually find the task interesting and are highly motivated to complete the problems. However, the IE teacher does not simply hand out a page from the instrument and collect students' work when they are finished. The teacher's task is to

Connect the dots. The figures at the left appear in new arrangements in each panel.

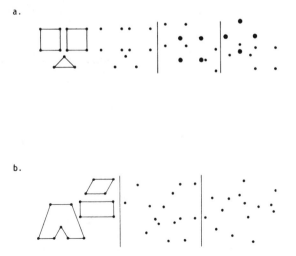

FIG. 4.1.   Sample exercises from the Organization of Dots (from Feuerstein et al., 1980).

mediate, by encouraging cognitive activities relevant to the materials. A typical IE lesson can be divided into four phases: (1) introduction; (b) individual work on the problems; (3) class discussion; and (4) summary. Within these phases, various aspects of mediated learning occur. Our interpretation of important instructional components that occur within various phases is provided in the following section. (These interpretations are based on direct observation of teacher-training workshops in Nashville as well as on Feuerstein et al.'s books.)

Problem Definition and Use of Stategies

An important component of each IE lesson involves problem definition. Imagine that students have received a page from ODI. They will be asked to define what they think the task is and to explain why. Beginning students may be helped to use models and examples to infer various rules (e.g., each dot is to be used once and only once). Students are also prompted to consider how the present dot problems are similar to and different from previous problems. For example, students are prompted to notice changes in the models (new forms, more complex forms, etc.), in the number and type of cues provided, in the density of dots, and so forth.

An additional step involves the anticipation of difficulties that may arise from changes in the problem format. For example, students may be helped to notice that, for some problems, the answer seems "readily apparent." At other times one confronts difficulty and must resort to a more systematic, analytic approach. Students are therefore prompted to select and evaluate different strategies for solving problems. For example, in ODI, students are prompted to consider which figure should be searched for first, and why. When more complex figures are presented, they are prompted to consider strategies for making the problem more manageable. For example, the concepts of "finding a starting point" and "systematic search from one's starting point" are introduced. Systematic search may involve starting the search from an outside dot and then projecting imaginary horizontal and vertical lines (students therefore learn the concepts "horizontal" and "vertical," but these are introduced only when they are relevant for a particular task). It is important to note that plans and strategies are not simply discussed by teachers. During the introductory discussions, students explain strategies they plan to use. Later, they all discuss the ones each used while working a particular page. The merits of each approach are then weighed.

Informed Practice

Nearly every IE lesson devotes a considerable amount of time to practice. Students are prompted to evaluate strategies while applying them to the problems. They are also encouraged to devise strategies for checking. In Orientation in Space I, for example, they are introduced to the strategy of working backwards to check their work.

The instruments are designed to provide a great deal of practice, but each problem encountered is novel. One advantage of this is the virtual impossibility of memorizing the answers to each problem. Even teachers who have taught for several years have to work most problems anew. This helps the teacher serve as a model for the students and is quite different from simply having the teacher provide answers. Students who finish the problems quickly also act as 'teacher'; they are encouraged to help other students who are experiencing difficulty. Once again, it is impossible simply to provide the correct answers. The student–student dyads discuss strategies for solving the problem at hand.

The instruments are also designed to correct the deficient cognitive functions noted earlier. Some students begin IE unable to recognize a square or triangle when it is rotated; others seem to have no notion of the advantage of "projecting virtual relationships" (i.e., filling in lines with one's imagination), or of "visual transport" (keeping the image of a figure in mind while 'moving' it, to compare it with something else). Still other students impulsively begin to connect dots without evaluating the adequacy of their approach. The ODI instrument is designed to improve a wide variety of cognitive functions. Other instruments concentrate on more limited subsets of cognitive functions.

Introduction of Basic Concepts

A third component of most IE lessons involves introduction of relevant basic concepts. Concepts such as "model" and "rules" may be introduced in the context of defining the problem; concepts such as "planning," 'strategy," and "checking" may be introduced in the context of attempts to work the problems. Students may also be helped to notice the importance of labeling various aspects of each page in order to facilitate group discussion. At times, standard labels (e.g., square, rectangle, triangle) are most appropriate; at other times students must confer about the label ("Let's call this one a tepee").

Training for Transfer

Our discussion so far has concentrated on the instruments as the focus of instruction. Two aspects of IE instruction are designed to help students understand how their experiences with the instruments are relevant to other aspects of their lives.

First, each IE lesson focuses on one or two principles that have broad generality. For example, the cover page of ODI does not include any dot problems such as those in Fig. 4.1; instead, it provides a view of stars connected into familiar constellations such as the Big Dipper. Students are encouraged to discuss whether these stars are really connected or whether we simply imagine them to be, and, if the latter, why? Students can thereby be introduced to a general principle such as "organization is imposed on the environment for certain purposes" before ever beginning to solve problems involving dots.

Each of the subsequent lessons involving dots (and all the other instruments, for that matter) are organized around at least one major principle. Sometimes one or two additional principles are introduced, although they may not be developed to the same extent. Examples of principles are: "When cues diminish, we frequently have to change strategies"; "A good strategy for self-checking is to reverse an operation"; "When stimuli are very similar, more careful analysis is needed to distinguish the differences"; "There are differences between universal and particular labels"; and so forth. A major function of a principle is to organize the lesson so that it has a focal theme. Clearly, some principles can be used as themes in more than one lesson.

The examples of principles cited in the preceding paragraph are still relatively abstract, of course, and hence need to be instantiated. The second aspect of relating IE to other experiences involves the concept of 'bridging' to provide examples of situations where a principle is applicable. Students are encouraged to generate their own examples and to evaluate the adequacy of examples suggested by others. Bridging is extremely important and serves four functions. First, it prompts the students to draw on their own experiences. Second, because there are an indefinite number of examples of the application for each principle, the teacher learns about the students' life experiences and knowledge and the students learn from one another. Third, the generation of examples shows whether a student has understood a principle precisely. Finally, instantiation in a variety of contexts encourages transfer.

The act of summarizing various segments of each lesson also seems important for transfer. It provides practice in extracting main ideas, plus practice in relating strategies and principles to social and academic life. Teachers often provide the summary, although most attempt to help students develop the skills to provide summaries themselves. Having each lesson focus on one or two principles taught in the context of an instrument (e.g., Organization of Dots) seems to make this task more manageable.

Overview of Program Content

The IE program is designed for students from 10 to 18 years of age and usually consists of 15 instruments (units) that, as a group, add up to approximately 500 pages of problems. The program can be taught in intact classrooms or in small groups in clinical settings. Usually one lesson a day is taught three to five times a week, for 2–3 years. For remedial programs, particular instruments for an individual student's specific deficiencies can be selected. The program has been taught to students identified as educable mentally retarded (EMR), learning disabled (LD), and behavior disordered (BD), as well as to students in resource rooms (VE), low-functioning students in regular classes, deaf and hearing-impaired students, children of migrant Mexican-American farm workers, and students for whom English is a second language. Unorganized, unmotivated students who exhibit a potential for higher performance, and gifted students have also used the program. One of the reasons for IE's wide range of applicability is that it focuses on metacognitive awareness; even gifted students are frequently unaware of the processes they use while solving various problems. Furthermore, a wide variety of principles and bridging exercises can be introduced, depending on the needs and characteristics of particular groups.

Figure 4.2 illustrates some sample problems from the most commonly used instruments. Some of the instruments are discussed in more detail in the analysis section that follows (see also Feuerstein et al., 1980, Chapter 7, and Feuerstein et al.'s chapter in this volume).

Analysis

We begin our evaluation of the IE program by considering those aspects of instruction that remain invariant across all the instruments; we then focus on more specific aspects of the program. General theoretical issues are considered as the discussion proceeds.

Analysis of Invariant Aspects of Instruction

There appear to be three important aspects of IE instruction that remain invariant throughout the program. These involve: (1) the use of instruments that include a variety of problems to be solved; (2) the emphasis on generation and evaluation of problem definitions and strategies; and (3) the identification of general principles and of specific illustrations of these principles. To what extent are these general aspects of instruction congruent with the goal of helping students learn to think and learn on their own?

Difficulty of the Materials.   It seems clear that any program designed to teach thinking and learning skills must choose materials that do not presuppose skills and content knowledge that are far beyond the reach of the learners. On the other hand, the materials must be challenging enough to enhance the development of various skills. In general, the IE Instruments do not presuppose sophisticated content knowledge (especially the instruments used early in the program), yet they include problems that require considerable attention to problem definition and to the use of strategies. Those concepts necessary for successfully completing the instruments are introduced when they are relevant. Most of the problems in the instruments are also difficult enough to warrant a sense of satisfaction and mastery when they are completed successfully. Note further that most of the instruments—especially those used early in the program—do not require sophisticated reading abilities or vocabulary.

Interest Value of the Problems.   The IE instruments are designed to be intriguing and to differ from the types of exercises children usually confront in the classroom. Feuerstein argues that many children have had negative experiences with school-related materials and that their resistance to these materials

Analytic Perception

Choose the square which contains all the parts that make up the design on the left and write its number in the circle provided.

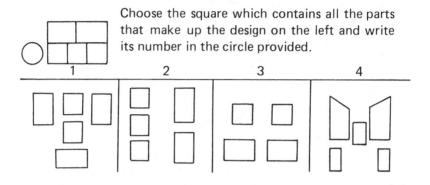

Categorization and Family Relations

Here is another family:

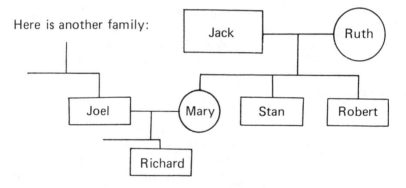

Jack is the father of Robert _____, and _____, and the _____ of Ruth. He is also the grandfather of _____ .

Mary is Joel's _____ . She is Jack's _____ and _____ mother.

Richard is the _____ of Joel and _____ . He is also __ the grandson of _____ and _____ .

Use one word in place of each phrase:

The father's father or the mother's father = _____ .

The son of the son or the son of the daughter = _____ .

FIG. 4.2. Sample Problems from IE Instruments (*to be continued*). (From Feuerstein et al., 1980.)

Instructions

On the line draw a triangle, two squares and a circle, not according to size order. The squares are to be equal in size, the triangle is to be larger than the squares and smaller than the circle, and the largest figure is to be on the left side.

Temporal Relations

Bill and John rode home from school on their bikes. They traveled at the same speed yet Bill got home about half an hour later than John (without any problems or accidents en route).

Explain: _____

_____

_____

_____

a. ___ to reap   ___ to plow   ___ to sow

b. ___ it is raining   ___ the man is   ___ the sky is clouding
                         getting wet

c. ___ past   ___ future   ___ present

Numerical Progressions

Look at the formula and at the first number of the progression. Can the last number be 9, 12, 19 or 7? Circle the correct answer.

Now construct the progression.

Transitive Relations

Every day Joan bought a tuna sandwich and a cup of coffee for lunch. She usually ate at Joe's Cafe, but one day she decided to eat at Tip's Tea Room, a place that had just opened. The total bill for her egg sandwich and cup of tea was exactly the same as it usually was at Joe's for her regular lunch; however, she noticed that the price of the sandwich at Tip's was higher than at Joe's. She immediately concluded that:

The coffee at Joe's [ ]   The tea at Tip's Tea Room

When $A + B$ $\boxed{=}$ $C + D$
And A $\boxed{\leq}$ C
Then B $\boxed{\geq}$ D

FIG. 4.2. Sample Problems from IE Instruments (*continued*).

can be difficult to overcome. Teachers of IE commonly report a problem that is quite different from those often experienced in regular classrooms: They frequently have difficulty getting the children to stop working on the instruments rather than getting them to start.

It is instructive to note that the problem of designing materials that maintain students' interest throughout a long-term program may be quite different from the problem of designing subunits that are then tested in short-term experiments. Students may express interest in exercises that are completed while participating in an experiment or while having a "guest teacher" (experimenter) for several days because the situation is novel. The same exercises may become quite tedious when taught every day. Feuerstein's instruments seem to interest students over long periods of time.

Generation and Evaluation of Problem Definitions and Strategies. One of the goals of IE is to promote "insight" into one's problem-solving and thinking processes. Students in IE are prompted to define problems, to compare current problems to previous problems, to predict the difficulty of problems, to evaluate alternative strategies, to devise and evaluate procedures for checking their work, and so forth. At a general level, this aspect of the IE program seems quite consistent with the instructional procedures that would be recommended by researchers in the area of metacognition (Brown, 1977a, 1977b; Brown & DeLoache, 1978; Flavell & Wellman, 1977; Markman, 1977). For example, Brown and DeLoache (1978) state the following:

> The basic skills of metacognition . . . include predicting the consequences of an action or event, checking the results of one's own actions (did it work), monitoring one's ongoing activity (how am I doing), reality testing (does this make sense) and a variety of other behaviors for coordinating and controlling deliberate attempts to learn and solve problems [p. 14–15].

Of course, no one assumes that metacognitive skills such as those just mentioned are developed simply by telling people about them. In IE, students are prompted to generate and evaluate various problem definitions and strategies in the context of solving the problems in the instruments. The problems are designed to provide a great deal of practice, but, as noted earlier, each problem is also novel. It is instructive to consider the issue of novelty in more detail, because different ways of introducing novelty into a set of practice exercises may facilitate the development of different types of skills.

One way to introduce novelty into a set of practice exercises is simply to change the content of each problem. In statistics, for example, one could construct a set of independent probability problems differing only in content (the particular numbers used, whether the problem involves marbles or oranges, etc.). In dots (Fig. 4.1) one could keep the model constant (e.g., a square and triangle), keep the rules constant (use each dot once and only once), and vary whether the square is to the right of the triangle (when it is drawn in the dots), to the left of the triangle, and so forth. These examples of novelty provide the opportunity for practice and hence seem important; nevertheless, they may fail to help people develop certain types of skills.

As an illustration of this point, consider the statistics exercises described previously. Students who work these problems know that the same formula applies to each problem; they may therefore fail to learn about the conditions under which this formula is applicable. (Students may fail to learn when they should use independent versus dependent probability formulas, for example.) In the previous Organization of Dots example, students may search mechanically for squares and triangles without giving much thought to the importance of looking at the model, and they may use the same basic strategy over and over again without asking themselves how strategies may need to be revised depending on the problem at hand (e.g., the nature of the figures in the models). It seems clear that the sequencing and degree of novelty of practice problems can have important effects on skill development (Bransford, 1979; Bransford et al., 1979; Nitsch, 1977). Some sequences prompt activities such as problem definition and the creation and evaluation of strategies; others prompt students to mechanically apply a set of procedures in a particular way.

In general, Feuerstein's instruments prompt students to evaluate problems and strategies. In Organization of Dots, for example, the models change frequently, the cues provided for various problems change and often disappear, and dot patterns are frequently rearranged so that one's strategies must be revised. On the other hand, the rules for connecting the dots (e.g., use each once and only once) never change, the problems always involve the use of all the figures in the model rather than only some of them, and so forth. One might therefore argue that the instrument could be redesigned in order to prompt even more evaluation and more strategy changes. However, other IE instruments do prompt an even greater degree of problem analysis and strategy change than one finds in ODI (dots); for example, in many instruments the rules change from problem to problem. Since ODI is usually the first instrument to be taught, some consistency in the problems is necessary in order to prevent the tasks from becoming overwhelming.

The instruments also provide a context for the acquisition of important concepts ("strategy," "model," "rules," etc.). As noted earlier, concepts are taught in contexts where they are relevant; for example, the concepts of horizontal and vertical are taught in the context of devising strategies for completing some of the problems of ODI. This approach to teaching new concepts seems quite different from ones that merely supply students with definitions of new concepts, or even from ones that supply definitions plus a few isolated examples. The idea of creating contexts that enable students to understand how various concepts are relevant to their current activities appears to be very important (see Dewey, 1933/

1961/1963, on the tool function of concepts). This is an issue that warrants further research.

Discussion of General Principles and of Examples.   The instruments are designed to facilitate the development of general concepts, skills, and attitudes that will enable students to learn more efficiently on their own. Aspects of each IE lesson are designed to help students grasp its relationship to other social and academic endeavors, and to help them see various relationships on their own. These aspects of instruction include (1) discussion of general principles, and (2) bridging exercises.

Consider first the discussion of general principles embedded in a particular lesson. A student could understand a concept such as organization in the context of ODI yet fail to understand it elsewhere. Thus, a student may not make the connection between organizing dots and organizing the stars into constellations unless explicitly helped to make this connection. Similarly, students may need help understanding how the general principle of organization applies to tasks related to school or the home (e.g., IE students are helped to understand the importance of organizing folders for the lessons. Each student maintains his or her own file).

A second component of IE instruction—bridging—helps children generate their own examples of general principles; it helps them learn to relate concepts and ideas to their daily lives. One advantage of bridging is that students are encouraged to take an active role in learning, and not simply to memorize. A related advantage is that these activities may help students learn to monitor the degree to which they understand basic concepts and principles. The attempt to generate examples of concepts or principles uncovers uncertainty about their applications (see our analysis of the W & L program).

We should note that there is considerable flexibility within the IE program with respect to the types of principles that are introduced and the types of bridging exercises that are encouraged (e.g., a teacher may encourage students to generate examples from particular areas such as mathematics or from any area they choose). It is, of course, important to permit flexibility on the part of the teacher. Nevertheless, it seems to us that the introduction of principles and the bridging exercises are especially important components of the program and hence might be analyzed and explained more precisely. For example, Feuerstein et al. (1980, p. 399) note that bridging—especially to academic content areas—has not been developed as systematically as it might be.

Analysis of Suggestions for Solving the Problems in the Instruments

The purpose of this section is to evaluate IE instruction on the problems in the instruments, an essential subgoal of IE. Feuerstein assumes that the exercises can help correct deficient cognitive functions and can develop confidence and motivation.

The IE format generally seems excellent for helping students learn to solve the problems in the instruments. The instruments and the instruction are coordinated well. For example, the IE instruction explicitly focuses on activities such as problem definition and strategy evaluation. The exercises provide the type of experience needed to develop these activities. If the work sheets seldom required students to define new problems or to generate and evaluate new strategies, it is doubtful that discussions of the importance of these endeavors would have much effect.

There is an additional sense of compatibility that seems to play an important role in helping IE students develop the ability to solve the problems in the instruments. The activities emphasized by the instruction and the instruments seem to be compatible with the current level of knowledge and skills available to the intended learners. For example, imagine that one attempted to help students develop comparison skills by asking them to solve formal analogy problems. The comparisons required in these types of problems are often quite complex; thus, a student may be asked to compare the relationship between thermometer and temperature to the relationship between scales and pounds. Many of the students in IE have difficulty comparing items that are much simpler than those found in formal analogy problems (e.g., most students initially have difficulty with items on the "Comparison" instrument; see Fig. 4.2). Furthermore, many of these students would undoubtedly have difficulty understanding the nature of formal analogy tasks.

Much of the early instruction in IE is designed to help students develop basic skills and cognitive functions that provide a basis for solving some of the more complex problems included in later instruments (Transitive Relations, Syllogistic Reasoning, Categorization, Instructions, etc.). In general, IE seems to progress by beginning with a basic set of metacognitive activities (the need to define problems, to generate and evaluate strategies, etc.) that are applied to increasingly more complex domains. Problems within each instrument proceed from simple to more complex, and, in general, each instrument deals with more complex problems. Does work on the early instruments provide a basis for helping students solve the problems contained in the later instruments? We do not know the answer to this question, but it seems clear that it could be answered.

Analysis Relative to General Goals

Feuerstein et al. (1980) list the following as subgoals of IE:

1. The correction of deficient cognitive functions.
2. The teaching of specific concepts, operations, and vocabulary required by the Instrumental Enrichment exercises.
3. The development of an intrinsic need for adequate cognitive functioning and the spontaneous use of operational thinking by the production of crystallized schema and habit formation.

4. The production of insight and understanding of one's own thought processes, in particular those processes that produce success and are responsible for failure.

5. The creation of task-intrinsic motivation.

6. A change in orientation toward oneself from a passive recipient and reproducer to that of an active generator of information.

We shall not attempt to analyze each of these subgoals separately; instead we discuss the general goal of helping students develop the confidence, motivation and skills necessary to learn on their own.

Many of the instruments used in IE (coupled with the metacognitive focus of the instruction) seem to provide a context for developing skills that are applicable to a wide variety of endeavors. The "Instructions" instrument provides a nice example of exercises that, when accompanied by appropriate classroom instruction, would appear to develop comprehension and communication skills that have considerable generality. For example, some of the exercises ask students to write descriptions of visual patterns. (The patterns include squares, triangles, and so forth arranged in various positions.) After writing their descriptions, students are to recreate the original patterns, which are no longer visible. This appears to be an excellent way of helping students to understand the importance of verbal precision and to develop communication skills.

Other exercises in "Instructions" also seem valuable. For example, in one set of exercises, students receive a verbal description of patterns and are then asked to draw the patterns (e.g., the square must be larger than the triangle and to its left; the circle must be above the square). A nice feature of many of these exercises is that students must learn to read the entire description before beginning to draw. Students therefore learn to conceptualize before attempting to carry out any particular step. In addition, they are helped to question whether only one drawing or several alternatives are correct.

Many of the other instruments in IE have valuable features. In "Illustrations" for example, students are helped to develop the skills necessary to view particular episodes (cartoons) as illustrations of more general principles (e.g., a particular cartoon may provide an illustration of the importance of cooperation). In "Categorization," students learn principles for organizing domains of knowledge into various subcategories and into alternative sets of hierarchies. The instrument "Temporal Relations" includes exercises designed to help students understand basic relationships between distance, speed, and time, and to separate causal sequences of events from mere co-occurrences. There are many additional instruments (e.g., Syllogisms and Transitive Relations) that deal with important concepts and skills that should be applicable to a wide variety of domains.

The degree of transfer exhibited by IE students may be influenced by the types of principles and bridging exercises introduced by teachers. As a simple example, assume that IE students finish the "Categorization" instrument where they learn, among other things, to categorize domains into alternative sets of hierarchies. If students are now provided with a list of potentially categorizable pictures and asked to study them for a recall test, would one expect IE students to be more likely to categorize than a matched set of non-IE controls? The exercises in "Categorization" do not deal explicitly with remembering, so IE students could develop categorization skills yet have little idea about their effects on memory. This type of information could be presented easily as general principles to be discussed that then become a focal point for bridging. Using categorization strategies when confronted with intentional memory tasks could thus be encouraged (see Brown, Campione, & Day, 1980).

As an additional example of the ways that principles and bridging exercises might affect transfer, consider once again the second exercise from the "Instructions" instrument discussed earlier. Ideally, students learn to evaluate the adequacy of verbal descriptions for reaching a particular goal (i.e., students should learn to evaluate whether the descriptions are precise enough to permit one to reproduce the pattern). It seems clear, however, that there are a variety of precise communication goals besides the goal of describing visual patterns. One may need to evaluate the adequacy of instructions for playing a new card game (Markman, 1977), or the adequacy of one's information for testing understanding of a new topic, and so forth (e.g., see Baker & Brown, in press; Bransford et al., 1981). The exercises in "Instructions" seem excellent because they set the stage for discussing general problems of evaluation and precision. Nevertheless, if teachers fail to help students explore a wide variety of additional examples in detail, their students may fail to utilize their skills and knowledge in these other areas. In short, the degree to which IE students develop skills and knowledge that permit transfer may be strongly influenced by the types of principles and bridging exercises introduced in class.

Overview of Existing Evaluation Data.   The purpose of this section is to review existing evaluation data on the IE program. The results of studies conducted in Israel and the United States are summarized in the following paragraphs. In general, these studies use conventional methods of assessing intellectual functioning (e.g., Thurstones' Primary Mental Abilities [PMA] Test; Lorge–Thorndike Nonverbal Intelligence Test; Porteus IQ Test).

One study reported by Feuerstein, Rand, Hoffman, Hoffman, and Miller (1979) used a sample of 218 adolescents, aged 12 to 15, who ranged between borderline and EMR as indexed by the PMA test. Half of the subjects participated in the IE program (at either residential or day-care centers) for 2 years. The other half spent an equal amount of time (5 hours per week) in a general enrichment program (GE) that provided supplementary instructional experiences in areas related to the school curriculum. Both kinds of training were administered in conjunction with the formal school curriculum. Several measures were taken before and after completion of the 2-year training program. These measures included the PMA test, a Project Achievement Battery (assessing achievement in a variety of academic content areas), the Classroom Participation Scale, and the Levidal Self-Concept Scale. Because pretest findings indicated significant differences between the IE group and the GE group, a sample of 57 matched pairs was selected (one member from IE, one member from GE) for subsequent analysis. The subjects were matched on the basis of age, sex, ethnicity, and total score on the PMA.

An analysis of overall performance on the PMA posttest indicated that the IE group performed significantly better than the GE group on four of the eight subtests of the PMA (number, addition, spatial relations, and figure grouping). The results obtained on the Project Achievement Battery indicated that the IE group also performed significantly better on two of the twelve subtests (Bible and Geometry). The results obtained with Classroom Participation measures indicated the IE group's similar success on two of the six scales (self-sufficiency and adaptiveness to work demands). No effects were found on measures of self-concept. In addition to these measures, several tests were used to assess specific cognitive functions. The results indicate greater gains from IE training on the Embedded Figures Test, the Human Drawing Test, the Postures Test of Spatial Orientations, and the Lahy Test (number correct).

Haywood and Smith (1979) report two studies that assess the effectiveness of the IE program. These studies involve adolescents ranging from 11 to 18 years of age who were classified as EMR, LD, BD, VE, slow learners, or culturally and linguistically different (CD). In the first study, students in the experimental group received 3 to 4 hours of IE training per week while students in the control group spent the same amount of time learning the regular academic curriculum. Both kinds of training were administered in conjunction with the formal school curriculum. The data collected in this pilot study at Nashville and Louisville were based on an average of 59 hours of training. (Students therefore never received any of the second-year instruments.) Pre- and posttreatment scores on the Lorge–Thorndike Intelligence Tests (nonverbal) were calculated for four categories of students (EMR, LD, BD, VE). The results indicated significant improvements in IQ for all IE students. The average gains were significantly larger than those for students in the control group. Pre- and posttreatment scores were also obtained for the Letter Series subtest of the PMA Test. The mean gain for students in IE was significant. Performance improvements were observed across all categories of students except EMR. In comparison, the control group showed a slight decline in performance from pretest to posttest.

The second study reported by Haywood and Smith utilized a similar design and sampled similar students from Nashville, Louisville, and Phoenix. The duration of training averaged 93 hours. (Again, however, students never received any of the second-year instruments.)

The results of this study did not indicate significantly greater improvements in the IQ for the whole sample. Nevertheless, there were significant improvements for various categories. Students classified as varying exceptionality (VE) in the IE group showed significantly greater gains on the Lorge–Thorndike (Nonverbal) Intelligence Test than students in the control group. This IE group also showed significantly greater gains on the Spatial Relations Subtest of the PMA. Increases on the General Information subtest of the Peabody Individual Achievement test were significantly greater for all students in the IE group than for students in the control group. IE students classified as culturally different (Mexican–American classes) also showed appreciably greater gains on Raven's Standard Progressive Matrices than the control group. The IE students in the behavioral disorder (BD) category showed gains of at least 1 academic year on the Woodcock–Johnson Psychoeducational Battery (full scale) and on the Reasoning, Memory, and Reading Aptitude clusters. However, data from a comparison group were not available.

Analysis of the Evaluation Data.   Overall, the results discussed in the preceding section suggest that IE may facilitate improvement on certain measures of intellectual performance and on achievement. Some of these data seem less than satisfying, however; especially if one asks whether the gains stem from the fact that some of the problems on the instruments are similar to those found on the IQ tests. The gains on achievement tests seem much more impressive than those on the IQ tests.

It is important to note, however, that Feuerstein, Haywood, and others are not interested in simply teaching students particular skills that will enable them to solve certain test problems more adequately. The goal of the IE program is to help students learn to learn; thus, the preceding studies represent only an initial phase of the evaluation research.

One way to conceptualize the learning to learn issue is to consider the type of data necessary to show that the IE program works in the way it is intended to. Imagine that the IE and the non-IE students receive achievement or IQ tests not only after the IE program terminates but again 2 years later, and perhaps 2 years after that. To show that IE worked, one would want to find a difference between IE and non-IE students immediately following IE instruction, a still bigger difference after 2 years, and a further one in the final testing session. Feuerstein refers to this as the "divergent effect." Feuerstein et al. (1980) have collected long-term evaluation data to assess the possibility of a divergent effect as a function of IE, but they explain that their data are not conclusive (e.g., the same tests were not used both before and after). Haywood and Smith (1979) also plan to collect data on the divergent effect as their research project proceeds. For present purposes, the important point is that the idea of a divergent effect is central to Feuerstein's approach.

Why would one expect a divergent effect? Because, ideally, students who have received IE have not just acquired specific knowledge and skills that the non-IE students have not; instead, the IE students have learned to learn on their own. For example, consider once again Feuerstein's arguments that many individuals exhibit an episodic grasp of reality. They fail to actively relate present experiences to previous ones, and hence fail to learn as much from each particular experience. (In Feuerstein's terms, they exhibit less of a propensity to be modified by particular interactions with their environment.) The primary goal of IE is to help students learn to learn on their own.

There seem to be important differences between assessments of what people know and can do at a particular point in time and assessments of their potential to benefit from experiences. Indeed, it is this difference that is central to Feuerstein's emphasis on the advantages of Learning Potential Assessment (Feuerstein et al., 1979) over more traditional forms of assessment (i.e., static tests). It seems clear that this concept of assessing learning potential could be applied to evaluations of the IE program (or any program). Students' abilities to learn could be assessed before and after participation in the IE program. Each assessment would include: a test to determine what students know already; an opportunity to learn new material; and finally, a test to determine how much students were able to learn either on their own or with instruction. In order to explore the issue of cognitive modifiability, it seems important for researchers to focus their attention on changes in people's ability to learn new information rather than on static assessments that provide information about what people know at particular points in time.

TENTATIVE CONCLUSIONS

Each of the programs reviewed in this chapter has some excellent features, and each deserves more detailed examination than we have been able to provide. For example, the theoretical bases of the programs are much richer than is evident from our discussion, and there are numerous details of each program that we were unable to mention. Furthermore, we discussed only the formal evaluation data (e.g., scores on standardized tests) that were available for each of the programs; we said little about more informal data such as enthusiasm of students, parents, and teachers. There are undoubtedly many cases where teachers and parents are sure they see marked improvements in students despite the fact that these may not be measured by the formal evaluation tests.

Despite our enthusiasm for each of the programs, it seems clear that there are issues about enhancing thinking and learning skills that require further classification. A basic issue involves the question of teaching general versus specific skills.

In the introduction to this chapter, we noted that attempts to improve students' abilities to think and learn represent an old and well-established tradition. We also noted that many "formal disciplinarians" advocated the study of difficult subjects such as Latin in order to develop basic "cognitive faculties" that would enable students to learn in a wide variety of contexts. Near the turn of the present century, E. L. Thorndike (1913) proposed his "identical elements theory of transfer," which emphasized that transfer was specific rather than general. This theory represented a reaction to the formal disciplinarians: Rather than study Latin in order to develop general skills that may enable one to learn to spell, to solve math problems, etc., Thorndike argued that it was better to practice the latter tasks directly. How might the programs discussed in this chapter be characterized with respect to their assumptions about general versus specific skills?

Many aspects of W & L's program seem quite consistent with Thorndike's emphasis on task-specific transfer. W & L encourage students to practice solving formal analogy problems in order to learn to solve formal analogy problems, and to practice solving mathematical word problems in order to learn to solve mathematical word problems. W & L also claim that their course can help students learn new information more effectively. We questioned this claim (see our analysis of the W & L program). What was our suggestion for helping students improve their abilities to learn new information? In essence, we argued that they needed practice on knowledge acquisition tasks.

Lipman et al.'s program also seems to acknowledge the task specific nature of transfer. For example, students in the Philosophy for Children Program are encouraged to complete a wide variety of exercises. One of our basic concerns was that due to the flexibility of the program, students may not receive as much practice as they need. We also noted that, in conjunction with ETS, Lipman et al. were attempting to develop a criterion-referenced test to assess the reasoning portion of their program. It seems clear that the way to achieve success in such an endeavor is to ensure that students receive sufficient practice on the types of problems to be included on the test; or conversely, to construct test problems that are congruent with those practiced during class. Similarly, if one wants students to improve their performance on reading tests, it seems wise to emphasize the types of exercises included on reading tests.

To what extent does the Feuerstein program use task-specific training to promote transfer to similar tasks? Clearly, there is an emphasis on training students to solve certain types of problems so that they will be able to solve similar problems on their own within each instrument. For example, Feuerstein does not assume that practice on "Organization of Dots" is sufficient to enable students to solve the problems in the "Syllogisms" instrument.

In general, Thorndike's (1913) basic message seems extremely important: Have students practice on tasks that are similar to those one wants them to perform later on. Many school systems have begun to pay more attention to this advice; for example, educators have become increasingly aware of the importance of "time on task" (Berliner & Rosenshine, 1977). Furthermore, many school systems (e.g., the Metroplitan Nashville System) have begun to analyze the types of tasks found on National Achievement Tests (e.g., spelling, word problems) and are emphasizing the need to have students practice these types of activities. There is also an effort to make parents aware of various critical tasks so that they can help their children develop the necessary skills. Inasmuch as the criterial tasks on achievement tests are deemed important, it is difficult to argue with the wisdom of this approach.

How does the goal of developing "general thinking skills" differ from the idea of providing students with practice on the types of problems one wants them to solve later? It seems clear that each of the program developers wants to help students develop skills that permit transfer to tasks that may be quite different from those practiced in the course. When discussing Feuerstein's program, for example, we noted that some of the tasks on the IE instruments are similar to those found on intelligence tests. However, Feuerstein could undoubtedly do a much better job of teaching to these tests if that were his intention. Feuerstein, like the other program developers reviewed in this chapter, wants to help students develop general skills that enable them to do more than merely increase their ability to solve the problem types that they practiced previously. The idea of developing general skills that permit transfer to a wide variety of domains seems similar to the idea of teaching formal discipline. To what extent have the programs reviewed developed general thinking skills? As far as we can tell, there is no strong evidence that students in any of the three thinking-skills programs improved in tasks that were dissimilar to those already explicitly practiced.

Despite the lack of hard data, we feel that there are general skills that may be applicable to a wide variety of contexts (see Brown, Collins, & Harris, 1978; Simon, 1980) and that each of the programs reviewed provides some ingredients necessary for general transfer. In particular, each program emphasizes various "metacognitive" aspects of instruction. Students are not simply asked to solve a variety of problems; instead, they are helped to become aware of the processes involved in problem solving. W & L emphasize thinking aloud in the presence of a critic; Lipman et al. stress the importance of dialogue plus reflection; and Feuerstein emphasizes processes such as problem definition, strategy evaluation, and so forth. There are differences among the programs with respect to the types of processes emphasized; for example, W & L seem not to emphasize how assumptions about relevant parts are influenced by one's definition of the problem, and it is not clear that Lipman et al. encourage students to articulate the processes involved while solving various problems (e.g., formal analogies). On the other hand, Lipman et al. *do* seem to encourage students to reflect on their own contributions to class discussion (relevance, consistency, etc). Furthermore, both Lipman et al. and Feuerstein attempt to help students understand the relevance of particular exercises for other aspects of their social and academic lives. Lipman et al. present applications of principles in their novels and encourage philosophical discussions of leading ideas. Feuerstein emphasizes the introduction of general principles and bridging exercises. In contrast, W & L focus more explicitly on the processes necessary to solve various problem types that frequently occur on mental tests.

The aforementioned differences are important. Each of the program developers might learn something by exploring these differences. Nevertheless, at a general level, each of the program developers appears to view practice problems as *means* to developing an understanding of the problem-solving process rather than as *ends* in and of themselves. For example, one could imagine creating a program that centers around the problem of teaching Latin in order to help students learn something about the general processes of learning and problem solving. This would be quite different from presenting students with Latin exercises and doing nothing to help them become aware of the processes involved.

Even an excellent program that used Latin (or any other content, for that matter) as a medium for helping students learn about various processes of learning and problem solving would, however, still look quite weak when evaluated from Thorndike's (1913) perspective. It seems obvious that students who participated in the Latin program would not perform any better if suddenly presented with a German language test than would students who did not participate in the program. However, this is not the appropriate way to evaluate such a program. If the Latin program really helped students develop general learning skills, one would expect students who participated in this program to be more proficient at *learning* German than would those who did not participate. One therefore has to give these students a chance to learn the new information (e.g., German). Students who have developed general thinking and learning skills are not suddenly immune to the need to be exposed to new knowledge domains, or to the need to practice using this knowledge in a variety of contexts. Ideally, however, these students have learned to structure and evaluate their own practice more efficiently; they have learned to learn.

The primary goal of "thinking skills" programs should be to help students use thinking skills to learn more efficiently. Do the programs reviewed in the present chapter help students achieve this goal? Each probably does to some extent, but as suggested, this might be accomplished more effectively (see also Bransford et al., 1981; Brown et al., in press; Brown et al., 1980). Evaluation of programs whose goal is to increase students' ability to learn can also be improved through methods including "divergent effect" analyses and learning potential analyses (Feuerstein, et al. 1980). The utilization of these types of evaluation techniques may help clarify the extent to which educators can help students learn to learn.

ACKNOWLEDGMENTS

This chapter was commissioned for the NIE–LRDC Conference on Thinking and Learning Skills, through the National Institute of Education grant #OE–NIE–G–78–0215 and was also supported in part by grants NIE–G–79–0117 and NIE–G–80–0028.

REFERENCES

Adams, J. L. *Conceptual blockbusting: A guide to better ideas.* New York: W. W. Norton & Company, 1974.

Arbitman–Smith, R., & Bransford, J. D. *Investigations of analogical reasoning.* Manuscript in preparation, Vanderbilt University, 1980.

Baker, L., & Brown, A. L. Metacognitive skills of reading. In D. Pearson (Ed.), *Handbook of reading research.* New York: Longmans, Green & Co., in press.

Bartlett, F. C. *Thinking: An experimental and social study.* New York: Basic Books, 1958.

Bennett, C. E., & Bristol, G. P. *The teaching of Latin and Greek in the secondary school.* New York: Longmans, Green, Co., 1906.

Berliner, D. C., & Rosenshine, B. The acquisition of knowledge in the classroom. In R. C. Anderson, R. J. Spiro & W. E. Montague (Eds.), *Schooling and the acquisition of knowledge.* Hillsdale, N.J.: Lawrence Erlbaum Associates, 1977.

Bloom, B. S., & Broder, L. *Problem-solving processes of college students.* Chicago: University of Chicago Press, 1950.

Bloom, L., Lightbown, P., & Hood, L. Structure and variation in child language. *Monographs of the Society for Research in Child Development,* 1975, *40* (2, Whole no. 160).

Bransford, J. D. *Human cognition: Learning, understanding and remembering.* Belmont, Calif.: Wadsworth Publishing Company, 1979.

Bransford, J. D., Franks, J. J., Morris, C. D., & Stein, B. S. Some general constraints on learning and memory research. In L. S. Cermak & F. I. M. Craik (Eds.), *Levels of processing and human memory.* Hillsdale, N.J.: Lawrence Erlbaum Associates, 1979.

Bransford, J. D., & Nitsch, K. E. Coming to understand things we could not previously understand. In J. F. Kavanagh & W. Strange (Eds.), *Speech and language in the laboratory, school and clinic.* Cambridge, Mass.: MIT Press, 1978.

Bransford, J. D., Stein, B. S., Shelton, T. S., & Owings, R. Cognition and adaptation: The importance of learning to learn. In J. Harvey (Ed.), *Cognition, social behavior and the environment.* Hillsdale, N.J.: Lawrence Erlbaum Associates, 1981.

Brewer, W. F., & Lichtenstein, E. H. *Event schemas, story schemas and story grammars.* Unpublished manuscript, University of Illinois, 1980.

Brown, A. L. Development, schooling and the acquisition of knowledge about knowledge. In R. C. Anderson, R. J. Spiro, & W. E. Montague (Eds.), *Schooling and the acquisition of knowledge.* Hillsdale, N.J.: Lawrence Erlbaum Associates, 1977. (a)

Brown, A. L. Knowing when, where, and how to remember: A problem of metacognition. In R. Glaser (Ed.), *Advances in instructional psychology.* Hillsdale, N.J.: Lawrence Erlbaum Associates, 1977. (b)

Brown, A. L. Learning and development: The problems of compatibility, assess and induction. *Human Development,* in press.

Brown, A. L., Bransford, J. D., Ferrara, R., & Campione, J. Learning, understanding and remembering. In J. H. Flavell & E. Markman (Eds.), *Mussen handbook of child psychology* (Vol. 1, *Cognitive development,* 4th ed.). New York: John Wiley & Sons, in press.

Brown, A. L., & Campione, J. C. *Inducing flexible thinking: The problem of access.* Paper presented at the NATO International Conference on Intelligence and Learning, York, England, July 1979.

Brown, A. L., Campione, J. C., & Day, J. D. *Learning to learn: On training students to learn from texts.* Paper presented at the meeting of the American Educational Research Association, Boston, April 1980.

Brown, A. L., & DeLoache, J. S. Skills, plans, and self-regulation. In R. Siegler (Ed.), *Children's thinking: What develops.* Hillsdale, N.J.: Lawrence Erlbaum Associates, 1978.

Brown, J. S., Collins, A., & Harris, G. Artificial intelligence and learning strategies. In H. F. O'Neil (Ed.), *Learning strategies.* New York: Academic Press, 1978.

Bugliosi, V. *Till death us do part.* New York: Bantam Books, 1978.

Case, R. Implications of developmental psychology for the design of effective instruction. In A. M. Lesgold, J. W. Pellegrino, S. D. Fokkema, & R. Glaser (Eds.), *Cognitive psychology and instruction.* New York: Plenum Press, 1978.

Chase, W. G., & Simon, H. A. The mind's eye in chess. In W. Chase (Ed.), *Visual information processing.* New York: Academic Press, 1973.

Clarke, A. M., & Clarke, A. D. B. *Early experience: Myth and evidence.* London: Open Books Publishing Ltd; New York: Free Press, 1976.

de Bono, E. *Lateral thinking: Creativity step by step.* New York: Harper & Row, 1970.

Dewey, J. How we think. Portions published in R. M. Hutchins & M. J. Adler (Eds.), *Gateway to great books* (Vol. 10). Chicago: Encyclopedia Britannica, Inc., 1963. (Originally published by Heath, 1933, 1961.)

Feuerstein, R., Rand, Y., & Hoffman, M. B. *The dyanmic assessment of retarded performers.* Baltimore: University Park Press, 1979.

Feuerstein, R., Rand, Y., Hoffman, M. B., Hoffman, M., & Miller, R. Cognitive modifiability in retarded adolescents: Effects of Instrumental Enrichment. *American Journal of Mental Deficiency,* 1979, *6,* 539–550.

Feuerstein, R., Rand, Y., Hoffman, M. B., & Miller, R. *Instrumental Enrichment.* Baltimore: University Park Press, 1980.

Fitts, P. M., & Posner, M. I. *Human performance.* Belmont, Calif.: Brooks/Cole, 1967.

Flavell, J. H., & Wellman, H. M. Metamemory. In R. V. Kail, Jr., & J. W. Hagen (Eds.), *Perspectives on the development of memory and cognition.* Hillsdale, N.J.: Lawrence Erlbaum Associates, 1977.

Goldman, S. R. *Knowledge children use in producing stories about problem solving.* Paper presented at the meeting of the American Psychological Association, New York, September 1979.

Goldman, S. R., & Bisanz, J. *Understanding the development of analogical reasoning ability.* Paper presented at the meeting of the American Educational Research Association, Boston, April 1980.

Haywood, H. C., & Smith, R. A. *Modification of cognitive functions in slow learning adolescents.* Paper presented at the meeting of the International Association of Mental Deficiency, Jerusalem, August 1979.

Hayes, J. R. *Cognitive psychology: Thinking and creating.* Homewood, Ill.: Dorsey Press, 1978.

Holt, J. *How children fail.* New York: Dell, 1964.

Huey, E. B. *The psychology and pedagogy of reading.* Cambridge, Mass.: MIT Press, 1908.

Johnson, D. M. *A systematic introduction to the psychology of thinking.* New York: Harper & Row, 1972.

Johnson-Laird, P. N. Mental models in cognitive science. *Cognitive Science,* 1980, *4,* 71–115.

Kotovsky, K., & Simon, H. A. Empirical tests of a theory of human acquisition of concepts for sequential patterns. *Cognitive Psychology,* 1973, *4,* 399–424.

LaBerge, D., & Samuels, S. J. Toward a theory of automatic information processing in reading. *Cognitive Psychology,* 1974, *6,* 293–323.

Lipman, M. *Thinking skills fostered by the middle-school philosophy for children program.* Unpublished manuscript, Montclair State College, 1980.

Lipman, M., & Sharp, A. M. *Growing up with philosophy.* Philadelphia: Temple University Press, 1978.

Lipman, M., Sharp, A. M., & Oscanyan, F. S. *Philosophy in the classroom.* Philadelphia: Temple University Press, 1980.

Mann, L. *On the trail of process: A historical perspective on cognitive processes and their training.* New York: Grune & Stratton, 1979.

Maratsos, M. P. Disorganization in thought and word. In R. Shaw & J. Bransford (Eds.), *Perceiving, acting and knowing.* Hillsdale, N.J.: Lawrence Erlbaum Associates, 1977.

Markman, E. M. Realizing that you don't understand. *Child Development,* 1977, *48,* 986–992.

Markman, E. M. Realizing that you don't understand: Elementary school children's awareness of inconsistencies. *Child Development*, 1979, *59*, 643–655.

Nelson, K., & Brown, A. L. The semantic–episodic distinction in memory development. In D. A. Ornstein (Ed.), *Memory development in children*. New York: John Wiley & Sons, 1978.

Newell, A. One final word. In D. T. Tuma & F. Reif (Eds.), *Problem solving and education: Issues in teaching and research*. Hillsdale, N.J.: Lawrence Erlbaum Associates, 1980.

Newell, A., & Simon, H. A. *Human problem solving*. Englewood Cliffs, N.J.: Prentice-Hall, 1972.

Nitsch, K. E. *Structuring decontextualized forms of knowledge*. Unpublished doctoral dissertation, Vanderbilt University, 1977.

Norman, D. A. Notes toward a theory of complex learning. In A. M. Lesgold, J. W. Pellegrino, S. D. Fokkema, & R. Glaser (Eds.), *Cognitive psychology and instruction*. New York: Plenum Press, 1978.

Norman, D. Twelve issues for cognitive science. *Cognitive Science*, 1980, *4*, 1–32.

Olson, D. R. The languages of instruction: The literate bias of schooling. In R. C. Anderson, R. J. Spiro, & W. E. Montague (Eds.), *Schooling and the acquisition of knowledge*. Hillsdale, N.J.: Lawrence Erlbaum Associates, 1977.

Rubinstein, M. F. *Patterns of problem solving*. Englewood Cliffs, N.J.: Prentice–Hall, Inc., 1975.

Scribner, S. Modes of thinking and ways of speaking: Culture and logic reconsidered. In P. N. Johnson-Laird & P. C. Wason (Eds.), *Thinking*. Cambridge, Eng.: Cambridge University Press, 1977.

Siegler, R. S. *Monographs of the Society for Research in Child Development*, 1981, *46*, whole no. 189.

Simon, H. A. Problem solving and education. In D. T. Tuma & F. Reif (Eds.), *Problem solving and education: Issues in teaching and research*. Hillsdale, N.J.: Lawrence Erlbaum Associates, 1980.

Simon, H. A., & Hayes, J. R. The understanding process: Problem isomorphs. *Cognitive Psychology*, 1976, *8*, 165–190.

Stein, B. S., & Bransford, J. D. Constraints on effective elaboration: Effects of precision and subject generation. *Journal of Verbal Learning and Verbal Behavior*, 1979, *18*, 769–777.

Sternberg, R. J. *Intelligence, information processing, and analogical reasoning: The componential analysis of human abilities*. Hillsdale, N.J.: Lawrence Erlbaum Associates, 1977.

Thorndike, E. L. *Educational psychology* (Vols. 1 & 2). New York: Columbia University Press, 1913.

Tobias, S. *Overcoming math anxiety*. New York: W. W. Norton & Co., 1978.

Tulving, E. Episodic and semantic memory. In E. Tulving & W. Donaldson (Eds.), *Organization of memory*. New York: Academic Press, 1972.

Tyler, R. W., & White, S. H. (Eds.). *Testing, teaching and learning: Report of a conference on testing*. Washington, D.C.: National Institute of Education, 1979.

Vygotsky, L. S. *Mind in society: The development of higher psychological processes*. (M. Cole, V. John-Steiner, S. Scribner, & E. Souberman, Eds. and trans.) Cambridge, Mass.: Harvard University Press, 1978.

Weinstein, C. E. Elaboration skills as a learning strategy. In H. F. O'Neill, Jr. (Ed.), *Learning strategies*. New York: Academic Press, 1978.

Wertsch, J. V. From social interaction to higher psychological presses: A clarification and application of Vygotsky's theory. *Human Development*, 1979, *22*, 1–22.

Whimbey, A. *Intelligence can be taught*. New York: Bantam, 1976.

Whimbey, A., & Lochhead, J. *Problem solving and comprehension: A short course in analytical reasoning*. Philadelphia: The Franklin Institute Press, 1980.

Wickelgren, W. A. *How to solve problems: Elements of a theory of problems and problem solving*. San Francisco: W. H. Freeman, 1974.

Woody, T. *Liberal education for free men*. Philadelphia: University of Pennsylvania Press, 1951.

Program Presentations and Analyses: Knowledge Acquisition

5 Learning Strategy Research

Donald F. Dansereau
Texas Christian University

The research and development efforts reported in this chapter are based on the premise that an individual's capacity for acquiring and using information can be enhanced by training in appropriate information-processing strategies. More specifically, the focus of this chapter is on strategy training designed to assist students in learning and applying information presented in college-level science textbooks. Over the past 4 years the author and his colleagues have developed, evaluated, and modified components of an interactive learning strategy system. This system is composed of both *primary* strategies, which are used to operate on the text material directly (e.g., comprehension and memory strategies) and *support* strategies, which are used to maintain a suitable state of mind for learning (e.g., concentration strategies). Assessments of the overall strategy system and system components indicate that strategy training significantly improves performance on selected text-processing tasks (Collins, Dansereau, Garland, Holley, & McDonald, 1981; Dansereau, 1978; Dansereau, Collins, McDonald, Holley, Garland, Diekhoff, & Evans, 1979; Dansereau, McDonald, Collins, Garland, Holley, Diekhoff, & Evans, 1979; Holley, Dansereau, McDonald, Garland, & Collins, 1979). Before describing this system and the associated research, an attempt is made here to delineate a set of important issues and concepts underlying learning strategy research in general, in order to sensitize the reader to problems associated with this research and to provide a potential framework for planning and conducting future work.

AN OVERVIEW OF CRITICAL ISSUES

Because issues germane to both theory and application of cognitive psychology are involved in work on learning strategies, the research poses a unique complex of problems. In this section the issues and concerns associated with three aspects of learning strategies research are discussed: identifying strategies in which to offer instruction, determining how to teach these strategies, and assessing the effectiveness of instruction.

Identifying Strategies in Which to Offer Instruction

Before we discuss how one might go about selecting and/or creating instructable strategies, we need to give the reader a better sense of what we mean by learning strategies. In the subsection that follows, we describe some of the major characteristics of learning strategies.

Strategy Characteristics.   An effective learning strategy can be defined as a set of processes or steps that can facilitate the acquisition, storage, and/or utilization of information. Learning strategies may vary along a number of important dimensions. For example:

1. A strategy may have direct impact on the target information (i.e., a *primary* strategy), or it may have an indirect impact by generally improving the level of the learner's cognitive functioning (i.e., a *support* strategy).
2. A strategy may be algorithmic (i.e., sequences of processes that remain fixed over tasks) or it may be heuristic (i.e., a sequence of processes that may be modified, depending on task conditions and the needs and skills of the individual learner).
3. Strategies may differ with respect to the scope of the task they are designed to accomplish. The *S*urvey, *Q*uestion, *R*ead, *R*ecite, *R*eview (SQ3R) strategy (Robinson, 1946) is typically employed with large bodies of material (textbook chapters), whereas the first letter mnemonic technique (forming an acronym from the first letters of a set of to-be-learned materials) is typically used with very limited amounts of material (e.g., a relatively short list of words).
4. Strategies may differ in the degree to which they are specialized for particular tasks. For example, SQ3R is a high-level, general-purpose strategy for learning from textbooks. It can be generalized to a wide range of textbook learning tasks, regardless of the text's content. In contrast, Brooks and Dansereau (1981) have created and assessed a very specific knowledge schema strategy for learning about scientific theories.

Although there are a number of other potentially important strategy dimensions (e.g., potency, amount of cognitive effort required, degree of approximation to the learner's present techniques), the foregoing list is sufficient to give the reader an overview of learning strategy characteristics. Perhaps the most important strategy dimension is the last one mentioned, the degree of specificity, in that a decision concerning specificity can have a strong impact on all subsequent decisions.

There appears to be a trade-off between the specificity of a strategy and the likelihood of being able to train students to use that strategy effectively. Unfortunately, attempts to provide general (relatively content-independent) strategy training have been at best only moderately successful (e.g., Dansereau, 1978; Gagné & White, 1978; Mansfield, Busse, & Krepelka, 1978). The typical finding is that positive transfer is observed only when the training tasks and the test (or transfer) tasks are highly similar. It appears that the participants in strategy training programs have a great amount of difficulty adapting strategies to new contexts. On the other hand, training individuals on specialized strategies that are applicable to only a specific class of tasks produces built-in restrictions on generality. Obviously, one approach to solving this problem is to choose strategies within some midrange on the generality–specificity continuum, strategies that are specialized enough to be employed effectively and yet general enough to have a relatively wide range of applicability. A second related approach is to train people on a hierarchy of strategies, beginning with more general content-dependent ones, and then breaking these down into more specialized content-dependent ones. This latter approach is the one that the author and his colleagues have taken in their development of a learning strategy system. Further discussion of this approach is presented in later sections of the chapter.

Selection and/or Creation of Particular Strategies for Training.   After the class of tasks and level of strategy specificity have been decided upon, one needs to select and/or create a set of strategies in which to offer instruction. In identifying these strategies, one needs to keep two sets of criteria in mind. First, one must evaluate possible strategies in terms of practical criteria. That is, one must ask about the potency of the strategy and the amount of training effort required to instill the strategy. Secondly, one must evaluate possible strategies in terms of theoretical criteria oriented around the question: "If the strategy is successful, can we determine why it worked?" Unfortunately, most strategies that would appear to satisfy practical criteria have numerous impacts on the learner's cognitive processing, thus making it difficult to determine specific theoretical implications. For example, networking or mapping strategies (Holley et al., 1979) that require the learner to produce two-dimensional maps of the concepts and interrelationships appearing in a segment of text, may be effective because they force the learner to increase depth of processing (Craik & Lockhart, 1972), reorganize the material (Shimmerlik, 1978), generate a content schema (Rumelhart & Ortony, 1977), and/or make use of mental imagery (Paivio, 1969). When an omnibus strategy like networking is successful, one does not know which alteration in cognitive activity is responsible. Consequently, one does not necessarily know what changes to make to improve the strategy. The approach favored by the author is to work with strategies that potentially meet practical criteria and that are supported by a number of existing cognitive theories. After determining the overall success of such strategies, one can remove or enhance facets related to presumed alterations in cognitive processing to determine the contribution of each facet to overall performance. It appears that this may be a reasonable way to create a "strategy science" without losing sight of the importance of practical application.

There are three main sources of information to guide the selection and creation of strategies that potentially satisfy both applied and theoretical criteria: protocols and questionnaires identifying the strategies that effective learners actually employ; task analyses illustrating the processes necessary for successful completion of different text comprehension tasks; and strategy kernels that have been investigated in the basic research literature. In the author's experience, it has been clear that utilizing a combination of these sources is beneficial. Unfortunately, at this stage in cognitive skills instruction, the selection and creation of strategies is far more an artistic endeavor than a scientific one. Consequently, the success of a strategy training program may be as dependent on the imagination of the creators of the program as on their scientific capabilities. As research in this area progresses, and effective strategy dimensions are identified, the shift from art to science should occur.

Determining How to Go About Offering Instruction in Learning Strategies

In this subsection, we discuss four issues that have arisen in connection with our attempts to develop a practical program of instruction in learning strategies. These are: determining the overall scope and philosophy of instruction, determining the sequence in which individual skills should be taught, identifying instructional techniques, and determining how to vary instruction to accommodate individual differences.

Scope and Philosophy of the Training Approaches.   One of the first considerations in the development of a program concerns the breadth and depth of training. Within the domain of text processing, a student could be given strategy training on any or all of the following task categories: comprehension, memory, recall, test taking, and concentration. Naturally, exclusively focusing on a specific subtask leads to less overall training time, reduces the possibility of overloading the learner with diverse techniques, and allows for a more precise assessment of the effectiveness of the strategy and training. On the other hand, a focused approach to strategy training may mask potential interactions between strategy components. At one level, this would be analogous to fixing an engine in a car that also has transmission trouble, or putting in new pistons that are incompatible with the rest of the engine. In both cases, the effects of the manipulations would be obscured by problems occurring in other parts of the system. As has been argued elsewhere (Dansereau, Collins, McDonald, Holley, Garland, Diekhoff, & Evans, 1979), the complexities of academic learning require that the learner have available a mutually supportive set of interactive strategies in order to maximize learning potential. Consequently, to examine and capitalize on these interactions, students must be taught large portions of the strategy system. Unfortunately, if such broad scale strategy training is successful, it is difficult, if not impossible, to determine why and to appraise the differential contributions of the component strategies. In order to cope with this set of problems, we have used the focused and broad level approaches to strategy training in combination. Large segments of a strategy system are presented and assessed in college-level learning skills courses. During this training, the students are asked to rate subjectively the impact of the specific components of the system. Based on these ratings, individual components are then selected for focused training and assessment. As seen in later sections, this has proved useful in clarifying the learning strategy domain.

In addition to the scope of training, another important, broadlevel consideration involves training philosophy (i.e., the general framework or climate for training). Although the overall philosophy of training can potentially influence many aspects of a learning strategy program, it appears that its most critical influence is on the motivational level of the participants. One of the main decisions in this regard is whether to attempt to cultivate intrinsic or extrinsic motivation. Intrinsic motivation appears to be maximized when the learners bring to the program a need to improve their skills, when substantial rationale for the strategies is provided, and when the learners are encouraged to practice the strategies on material of their own choosing. The possibility of extrinsic motivation becomes available when the trainers can provide incentives such as grades, money, or partial course credit for successful strategy acquisition. Our prior experiences suggest that in the university setting, at least, it is generally necessary first to provide extrinsic motivators in order to maintain a sufficient level of commitment to the training. However, once the students have had some experience with the program, their intrinsic motivation appears to increase and, as a consequence, the emphasis on extrinsic motivation can be reduced.

Training Sequences.   At least two levels of decisions concerning the sequencing of training need to be considered. These involve decisions about the order in which strategies should be trained when broad level training is the goal, and decisions about the presentation sequence of aspects within a particular strategy. Little information is available on the training of a collection of strategies to guide the program developer. In general, research on instructional sequencing has produced equivocal results. In an extensive review of the literature, Dansereau,

Long, Evans and Actkinson (1980) were unable to identify valid and reliable principles. However, in a recent study on sequencing *primary* and *support* strategy training, Dansereau, Holley, Collins, Brooks, and Larson (1980) found an advantage to requiring the students to learn primary (text manipulation) strategies prior to learning support (cognitive climate) strategies over the reverse. This result is discussed further.

In sequencing the training within a particular strategy we have explored two possibilities. One is a building block approach where subcomponents of the strategy are learned first, using simplified training materials, and then later combined to form the overall strategy. In teaching concept-link networks, for example (that is, teaching students to produce two-dimensional maps of the concepts and their interrelationships appearing in a segment of text), the learners apply parts of this strategy to single sentences, then to paragraphs, and finally, to larger bodies of material. This approach is the most prevalent in the training literature and has been advocated by a number of educational theorists (e.g., Gagné, 1977). Disadvantages to the building block approach include the following:

1. Processes that are effective with the simplified materials used at the beginning of training may not be effective with the actual texts students are expected to be able to read as a result of instruction. Consequently, the learner may have to break habits developed during the early stages of training.

2. The learner's motivation may suffer if the training materials and exercises are seen as too distant from the target task.

3. The learner may have a very difficult time acquiring the gestalt of the strategy through the building block approach, simply not seeing the forest for the trees.

In general, our experience with the building block approach to strategy training has not been very satisfactory. Many of the students never adequately acquire the terminal strategy.

An alternative approach is one that first communicates the gestalt of the strategy and then later adds detail and precision. Using this approach in training students to create networks would involve first letting them identify and lay out important concepts spatially, without worrying about the precise relationships between concepts. As the students become more comfortable using this informal spatial strategy, further training can be given to assist them in producing maps that more precisely represent the relationships between concepts. This approach has the advantage of allowing the students to practice on the target material almost from the beginning of training. We have found this gestalt approach to be far more appealing to the students and, therefore, encourage its use whenever possible.

Training Methods.   No attempt is made in this chapter to review exhaustively alternative skills and strategy training methods; rather, the focus is on those methods we have implemented in our previous research on a specific learning strategy system. Before presenting a brief description of the training techniques we have employed, it is important to note that most of the studies designed to assess the effectiveness of training and teaching methods have produced equivocal results. Dubin and Taveggia (1968), in an extensive review of the educational literature, concluded that there appears to be no difference among truly distinctive methods of college instruction. More specific instances of this equivocality have been pointed out by Carroll (1971) and Dansereau (1978). In spite of these discouraging findings, our informal observations lead us to believe that different training methods have differential impacts on the students' attitudes and behaviors.

Our subjective experiences have indicated that one of the most potent methods of communicating learning strategies is modeling (i.e., demonstrations of correct strategy usage). However, due to the covert nature of learning, modeling demonstrations present a number of unique challenges. To date, we have had substantial success with the following modeling approaches:

1. Presentation of the products of correct strategy usage (e.g., a completed network) with annotations indicating how they were created. Typically, the learner is given a body of material with which to practice a particular strategy. Following the learner's attempt at processing the material, a model product with annotations is provided as feedback.

2. Real-time modeling by an expert. The expert provides a verbal protocol evidencing correct application of the strategy.

3. Interactive peer modeling. Typically, pairs of learners interact over a body of text material. One member of the pair attempts to process the material orally while the other serves as a commentator or critic. The roles of the pair members are periodically reversed. McDonald, Dansereau, Garland, Holley, and Collins (1979) have shown that this pair learning procedure facilitates subsequent strategy usage in an individual study situation.

In conjunction with modeling, we have found it very useful to provide specific feedback on the products representing the learner's attempts at strategy usage. The purpose is to assist the learner in identifying and remediating specific "bugs" that may inhibit effective application of the strategy.

Training and Individual Differences.   Most of the studies assessing training methods have not looked at the interaction of training with individual differences. Although we also typically have not focused on assessing interactions between strategy training methods and individual differences, we have observed that learners scoring in the midranges of standard verbal ability measures (e.g., SAT–Verbal) benefit more from our strategy training than those scoring at either extreme. Also, a study by Holley et al.(1979) suggests that students with low grade-point averages benefit more from networking training than students with high grade-point averages. In order to ameliorate potential negative impacts of mismatches between instructional methods and individual differences, we typically use multiple methods of strategy instruction. We also attempt to assist the learners in tailoring the strategies to their own strengths, needs, and cognitive styles.

Assessing the Effectiveness of Instruction

Within the following separate subsections, statistical, design, and measurement problems associated with the assessment of learning strategy training are discussed.

Statistical and Design Considerations.   In our experiments, the students typically study a text excerpt for a fixed period of approximately an hour, and then, after a 5-day delay, they take a series of tests. We have found consistently high within-cell variance (i.e., individual differences variance) in experiments that have used this paradigm. Naturally, this high error variance reduces the power of the statistical test to detect significant differences between experimental groups. We have attempted to ameliorate this situation by employing a reasonably large number of subjects in each cell (typically 20 to 30) and by using analyses of covariance with multiple covariables. With regard to covariates, we have had the most success with measures of verbal ability, in particular, the Delta Reading Vocabulary Test, a 10-minute measure developed by Deignan (1973), and pretest scores that are obtained by putting all subjects through the study–test paradigm (with a passage that is different from the postassessment passage) prior to any training manipulations.

Although there has been some controversy over its validity in this domain (e.g., Cronbach & Furby, 1970), we have also used this multiple covariate approach to compensate for initial differences between treatment and control groups in our broad level strategy training studies. In these studies, which are usually conducted in conjunction with a regular college course on learning techniques, it is usually impossible to assign students to groups randomly. Rather, the control group for the course is usually drawn from the general psychology subject pool. Although attempts are made to attract control subjects who are interested in learning strategy training and who exhibit the same profile of characteristics as the treatment groups, there is no guarantee that initial text-processing differences between groups do not exist. Consequently, we typically use a pre–post assessment design with measures of verbal ability and pretest performance serving as covariates for analysis of posttraining performance. Overall and Woodward (1977a, and 1977b) have provided mathematical and conceptual justifications for the validity of this approach. Although this quasi-experimental design is frequently necessary in assessing broad level strategy training, in our in-depth studies of components of the strategy system we typically draw from a homogeneous pool of subjects and randomly assign individuals to groups.

Another important issue with respect to control groups revolves around the decision to use a placebo versus a no-treatment control procedure. In our experience, attempts at equating training time by having students practice their own or less effective competing methods on the training material have led to suppression of mean performance in comparison with untrained students using their own techniques (Collins, 1978; Garland, 1977; Long, Dansereau, McDonald, Collins & Evans, 1976). Subjective reports from participants in these placebo groups indicate that they do not view the training as meaningful and consequently become frustrated and bored with the task. These reactions apparently carry over to the assessment phase, leading to a reduction in mean performance. It should also be emphasized that the college-age students participating in these experiments have had 12 to 14 years of experience and practice with their own study methods (particularly with naturally occurring prose) and can therefore be considered no-treatment controls in name only. As a result we have not employed placebo treatment procedures. The issues of placebo control and covariance analysis have been described and analyzed in much greater detail in a recent paper by Holley and Dansereau (1980).

Measurement Issues. Earlier work on study skills training (Briggs, Tosi, & Morley, 1971; Whitehall, 1972) primarily used global indices of academic performance, such as grade-point average, as dependent measures. These types of measures are contaminated by other variables such as the student's academic major and extracurricular activities. Therefore, they are at best imprecise indices of the impact of strategy training and, further, due to their global nature, provide very little diagnostic evidence on which to base modifications. At the other extreme, more basic studies in educational and cognitive psychology have typically used single tests over short text passages (usually 500 words or less, and often narrative or artifically constructed prose) to assess the results of training on processing strategies. The set of cognitive activities required to succeed under these task conditions may be quite different from those required to process larger bodies of text such as chapters or entire books. For example, organizational strategies may become more important as the amount of text increases. If this is so, the generalizability of the findings from these basic studies to more applied situations is in question.

To help reduce these measurement problems we have chosen a middle ground. Typically, we require students to study 2500 word excerpts from naturally occurring science text for 50 minutes. Five days later they are given a series of tests (e.g., essay, short-answer, multiple-choice, and cloze). The study time is controlled so that the potential confounding of the results by differential study time is reduced. A delay period between study and test has been found necessary to magnify treatment–control differences. (This appears to be due to a functional "ceiling" effect that occurs with immediate testing.) Multiple measures are used to assist in determining the locus of the strategy effect. For example, in many of our studies (Dansereau, Collins, et al., 1979; Holley et al., 1979) we find positive effects on the uncued tests (e.g., essay) due to treatment, and no significant differences on the cued tests (e.g., multiple-choice). This pattern of findings has led us to conclude that the major impact of strategy training is on recall rather than on recognition.

In addition to the text-processing paradigm already described, we also use self-report measures (administered pre and post) to assess the students' perceptions of their own abilities, problems, etc. These types of measures are primarily used in our broad scale strategy studies. Standard measures such as the Test Anxiety Scale (Sarason, 1956) and the Survey of Study Habits and Attitudes, Form C (Brown & Holtzman, 1965) are supplemented by more specialized measures developed to assess "consumer satisfaction" and perceived strategy training weaknesses. Although one must certainly be cautious in interpreting self-report data of this type, it can be argued that the student is in the best position to evaluate the present level of his or her skills. Consequently, self-reports should be considered valuable supplements to more objective measures of text-processing performance. Synthesizing the results from objective and self-report measures provides convergence on the effectiveness of the strategy treatments.

Learning Strategy Research Issues: Summary

In this section, an attempt has been made to describe briefly some of the critical issues in conducting learning strategy research. These issues can be clustered under three general catagories: selection and development of strategies, approaches to strategy training, and assessment of training outcomes. Under each of these topics some of the problems and potential solutions that have evolved from our work with a particular learning strategy system have been delineated. In the next two sections, these research and development efforts are discussed in greater detail. It should be noted that at this point systematic learning strategy research is still in its infancy. Consequently, it is impossible to derive a solid set of principles that can be used to plan and conduct future studies. However, it is hoped that some of the information presented in this section will serve to focus attention on the more critical aspects of research in this domain.

RESEARCH ON CONTENT-INDEPENDENT LEARNING STRATEGIES

In this section, we describe our attempts to offer instruction in relatively content-independent strategies, strategies that can be applied to a wide range of text-processing tasks having quite diverse content. In the next section, we describe our attempts to offer instruction in more content-dependent strategies.

Description of the Content-Independent Strategy System

Our general approach to identifying strategies in which to offer instruction has been strongly influenced by the fact that effective learning requires that the student actively engage in a complex system of interrelated activities. To assist the student in this endeavor, a set of mutually supportive strategies has been created. As described earlier, this set can be divided into primary strategies, used to operate directly on text, and support strategies, used to help the learner maintain a suitable mood for studying. Further subdivisions of these sets of strategies are presented in Fig.5.1. The primary set includes strategies for acquiring and storing information (comprehension/retention strategies), and strategies for subsequently retrieving and using this stored information (retrieval/utilization strategies). In some of our implementations of this system we have communicated the substrategies that fall under these two categories and their associated support strategies by using the acronyms first-degree MURDER for comprehension/ retention and second-degree MURDER for retrieval/utilization. The letters in each of the two MURDERs represent the names of the substrategies and the order of the letters represents the sequence that the student is instructed to follow in implementing them.

Support strategies have been divided into three categories: planning and sceduling; concentration management; and monitoring and diagnosing. Concentration management has been further subdivided into mood setting and mood maintenance. These support strategies are designed to assist the student in developing and maintaining an internal state conducive to effective implementation of the primary strategies.

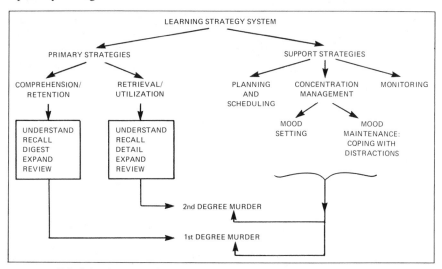

FIG. 5.1. Overview of the learning strategy system.

In the following subsection, we provide an overview of the various primary and support strategies that make up the two MURDER executive strategies and offer detailed descriptions of some of the individual substrategies. The reader should note, however, that a detailed description of the entire system is beyond the scope of this chapter. Various portions of the system have been presented in a number of other technical reports and publications (Dansereau, Actkinson, Long, & McDonald, 1974; Dansereau, Collins, McDonald, Garland, Holley, Evans, & Diekhoff, 1978; Dansereau, Long, McDonald, & Actkinson, 1975; Dansereau, Long, McDonald, Actkinson, Ellis, Collins, Williams, & Evans, 1975; Dansereau, Long, McDonald, Actkinson, Collins, Evans, Ellis, & Williams, 1975a; Dansereau, et al., 1975b; Dansereau, et al., 1975c).

Primary Strategies.   As already mentioned, we have divided the primary strategies into two groups: comprehension/retention strategies and retrieval/utilization strategies. The comprehension/retention strategies teach students how to process incoming information to make it easier to understand and remember. The first-degree MURDER acronym has been used to communicate these strategies to students. The steps in MURDER include setting the *mood* to study (which is discussed under support strategies); reading for *understanding* (marking important and difficult ideas); *recalling* the material without referring to the text; correcting recall, amplifying and storing the material so as to *digest* it; *expanding* knowledge by self-inquiry; and finally, *reviewing* mistakes (learning from tests).

The four basic comprehension/retention steps (understand, recall, digest, and expand) are similar to the processes suggested by the SQ3R technique (Robinson, 1946) and some of its derivatives. Although varying slightly in surface structure, the main differences between the core of first-degree MURDER and the SQ3R approaches occur in the details of the steps. Typically, training on SQ3R is nonspecific. The steps are described and students are expected to translate these descriptions into operative substrategies; they determine on their own what kinds of activities are involved, for example, in recalling or reviewing a passage of text. It appears that a large number of students have a great deal of difficulty in making this translation. To alleviate this problem, we have designed detailed instructions and practice exercises to communicate the substrategies. As an example of this approach, the *recall/transformation* substrategies (represented by the R in MURDER) are described here briefly.

After an initial reading, the student is instructed to recall the material he or she has read. This is considered the most important phase of the comprehension/retention strategy. To help students recall, three substrategies have been developed:

1. *Paraphrase/imagery.* This substrategy involves having students summarize the material in their own words and then form mental pictures of the concepts underlying this material. The student is trained in both techniques and is instructed to vary their use, depending on the nature of the material being studied. In an

earlier study, it was found that both techniques led to improved performance on a delayed essay test in comparison to a no-treatment control group (Dansereau, 1978). Further, a study by Spurlin, Dansereau, and Brooks (1980) has provided information on how frequently students should create text summaries to maximize performance. (This study is discussed in greater detail in a later section.)

2. *Networking.* Unlike the paraphrase/imagery technique, which requires the student to transform text material into natural language or pictures, the networking strategy requires material to be transformed into node–link maps or networks. During acquisition, the student identifies important concepts or ideas (nodes) and represents their interrelationships (links) in the form of a network map. As an aid in this endeavor, students are taught a set of named links that can be used to code the relationships between ideas. The networking process emphasizes the identification and representation of hierarchies (type/part), chains (lines of reasoning/temporal orderings/causal sequences), and clusters (characteristics/definitions/analogies). (See Fig. 5.2 for a schematic representation of these three types of structures and their associated links and Fig. 5.3 for an example of a summary network of a nursing textbook chapter.) The two-dimensional maps that result from an application of this technique provide the student with a spatial organization of the information contained in the passage.

Assessments of networking (Dansereau, McDonald, Collins, Garland, Holley, Diekhoff, & Evans, 1979; Holley et al., 1979) have shown that students using this strategy perform significantly better on text-processing tasks than do students using their own methods. Further support for this type of mapping strategy has also been obtained by Armbruster (1979).

3. *Analysis of key concepts.* Like networking, the analysis of key concepts strategy is also derived from network models of memory (Diekhoff, Brown, & Dansereau, 1982). Using this strategy, students identify key concepts in a body of text, define these concepts, and determine how they relate to one another. They are aided in these activities by worksheets that specify categories of relationship. These categories are isomorphic to those used in networking. For example, in defining operant conditioning, one might say that it is a *type* of learning paradigm for a *part* of many behavior modification programs, or that it *leads to* increases in the target behavior.

The major difference between analysis of key ideas and networking is that the key ideas approach is structured and linear and provides for only local interrelationships between concepts, whereas the networking technique is relatively unstructured and spatial and provides for global interrelationships.

In summary, the comprehension/retention techniques include an executive strategy that guides students in a variety of more specific techniques for expanding and transforming incoming information to make it easier to understand and remember. After comprehending and storing a body of information, the student must be able to recall and use the information under appropriate circumstances

Structure	Link	Description	Key Words
Hierarchy	Part (of) — hand → p → finger	The content in a lower node is part of the object, idea, process or concept contained in a higher node.	part of segment of portion of
	Type (of)/ Example (of) — school → t → public	The content in a lower node is a member or example of the class or category or processes, ideas, concepts, or objects contained in a higher node.	type of category example of kind of Three "x" are
Chain	Leads to — practice → l → perfection	The object, process, concept, or idea in one node leads to or results in the object, process, idea, or concept in another node.	leads to results in causes is a tool of produces
Cluster	Analogy — T.C.U. → a → factory	The object, idea, process, or concept in one node is analogous to, similar to, corresponds to, or is like the object, idea, process, or concept in another node.	similar to analogous to like corresponds to
	Characteristic — sky → c → blue	The object, idea, process, or concept in one node is a trait, aspect, quality, feature, attribute, detail or characteristic of the object, process, concept, or idea in another node.	has characterized feature property trait aspect attribute
	Evidence — broken arm → e → x-ray	The object, idea, process, or concept in one node provides evidence, facts, data, support, proof, documentation, or confirmation for the object, idea, process, or concept in another node.	indicates illustrates demonstrates supports documents proof of confirms evidence of

FIG. 5.2. Hierarchy, chain, and cluster structures.

(e.g., in taking tests or on the job). To aid the student in this task a second strategy with alternative substrategies has been developed. This strategy consists of six steps: setting the *mood; understanding* the requirements of the task; *recalling* the main ideas relevant to the task requirements (using means–ends analysis and planning); *detailing* the main ideas with specific information; *expanding* the information into an outline; and *reviewing* the adequacy of the final response. These six steps were given the acronym "second-degree MURDER" in order to facilitate recall of the technique.

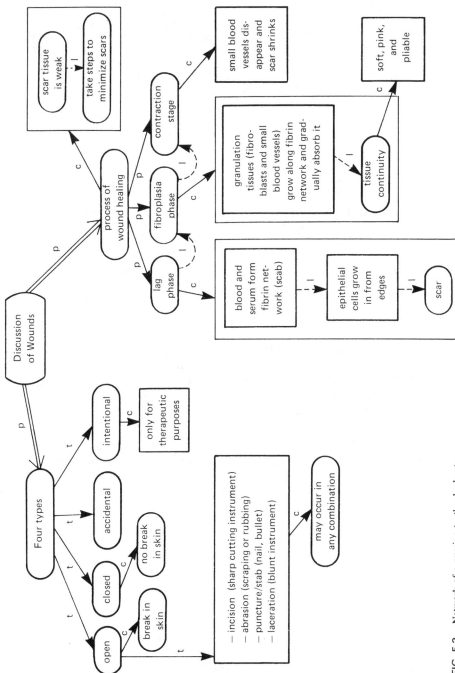

FIG. 5.3.   Network of a nursing textbook chapter.

Support Strategies.   Regardless of the effectiveness of the primary strategies, their impact on learning and performance will be less than optimal if the psychological state of the student is not optimal. Consequently, support strategies were designed to assist the student in developing and maintaining a good internal state. These support strategies include planning and scheduling, concentration management, and monitoring and diagnosing the dynamics of the learning system.

1. *Planning and scheduling.* Students employ a workbook to specify their long- and short-term goals and to schedule their time. Students are instructed to monitor their progress in achieving their goals and alter their schedules when appropriate.

2. *Concentration management.* Students employ a concentration management technique designed to address attitude problems and problems in coping with distractions. This technique combines elements of systematic desensitization (Jacobsen, 1938; Wolpe, 1969), rational behavior therapy (Ellis, 1963; Maultsby, 1971), and therapies based on positive self-talk (Meichenbaum & Goodman, 1971; Meichenbaum & Turk, 1975).

The students are first given experiences and strategies designed to assist them in becoming aware of tension, negative and positive emotions, self-talk, and images they generate in facing a learning task. They are then encouraged to evaluate the constructiveness of their internal dialogue and are given heuristics for making appropriate modifications. Worksheets and experimenter-generated sample statements are used to assist the students in this task. They are then taught relaxation and constructive self-talk techniques and are instructed to use these techniques to establish an appropriate mood for studying and test-taking, and to cope with any distractions that may arise during these activities. These mood-setting and mood-maintenance strategies comprise the M in MURDER. This particular combination of concentration management strategies has been shown to lead to significantly better performance on text-processing tasks in comparison to students using their own methods (Collins et al.,1981).

3. *Monitoring.* To be effective, students must be able to detect when their behavior is not sufficient to meet task demands so that they can make appropriate adjustments. We have not treated monitoring as a separate component, but have embedded monitoring principles in the concentration management component and the two MURDER strategies. The students are trained to evaluate their progress intermittently and take corrective actions if necessary.

Overview of the Research Approach

In order to meet the applied and theoretical criteria discussed in the first section of this chapter, our approach to conducting research on content-independent learning strategies has been to evaluate loosely the overall effectiveness of the strategy system in the context of a college-level learning techniques course.

Using these data, we then modify the individual components and evaluate their effectiveness under more carefully controlled conditions. The modified components are then recombined and the overall system is subjected to further examination.

The major intent of the overall system evaluation studies is to use objective and subjective data to determine which individual components are most valuable and compatible. That is, in the overall system evaluation studies, the emphasis is on gathering information for purposes of further improving the system rather than for pruposes of assessing its effectiveness under carefully controlled conditions. For example, every effort is made to communicate clearly individual strategies to students, even when this interferes with the experimenter's ability to specify and control the kind of information students receive about the strategies. In contrast, in studies of individual system components, the goal is to conduct a more formal evaluation. Consequently, greater emphasis is placed on experimental design issues like specifying and controlling the communication to participants and randomly assigning individuals to experimental groups. In the next section we describe two system assessments and in a subsequent section we discuss a series of component studies.

General Assessments of the Strategy System

As mentioned previously, we believe that a mutually supportive set of interactive strategies is required to maximize learning potential. In order to examine and capitalize on these interactions, students must be taught large portions of the strategy system. Unfortunately, the time and student motivation required for training precludes exploring this system in typical short-term experiments. Consequently, the strategy system has been examined in the context of two administrations of a college-level learning strategies course. In the first assessment, (see Dansereau, Collins, McDonald, Holley, Garland, Diekhoff, & Evans, 1979, for further information) a two-credit hour, one-semester (15 week) course was offered, on a pass/no credit basis, to Texas Christian University undergraduates during the 1977 spring semester.

In order to evaluate the effectiveness of the strategy system, two interlocking experiments were created. In one (the comprehension/retention experiment), a class of 38 undergraduates heterogeneous with respect to grade level and majors was compared with a no-treatment control group composed of 28 students recruited from general psychology classes. Comparisons were made of student performance on short-answer and multiple-choice tests developed for three 3000-word passages from college-level textbooks. The students were given an hour to study each of these passages and then a week later were given 45 minutes to take the corresponding tests. The dependent measures were administered to the class members and controls before the course began (precourse test), approximately halfway through the course (midcourse test), and after the course was completed (postcourse test). For the final testing, the 36 participating class members were subdivided into three groups of 12 each. Each group received training in one of three different comprehension and retention substrategies: paraphrase/imagery, networking, or key ideas.

For the second experiment (the self-report experiment), the performance of the class members on a set of self-report measures was compared with a no-treatment control group composed of 21 volunteers from general psychology classes. Data were collected from the experimental students both before and after participating in the learning strategies course. The self-report measure included: a 37-item Test Anxiety Scale (a slightly modified version of the one used by Sarason, 1956), the Survey of Study Habits and Attitudes, Form C (Brown & Holtzman, 1965), a 46-item questionnaire designed to tap concentration difficulties and coping skills, and a 12-item learning attitude inventory designed to assess students' perceptions of their own academic abilities.

Class members were given 2 hours of training each week for 12 weeks. The two control groups were not given any training during this time period. The strategy components described earlier formed the basis of the strategy class training. In general, training on primary and support strategies was intermixed to illuminate the interactions between the components. Training methods included short lectures, practice exercises, and small group or pair discussions.

Specific training for the class members, following the precourse test, consisted of 12 hours of training in goal setting and scheduling, learning from a test, comprehension, problem solving, and introduction to MURDER. The class then took the midcourse comprehension/retention test ($n = 25$). Following this, they were divided into subgroups for a final 12 hours of training. As noted earlier, each subgroup received training in one of three strategies: paraphrase/imagery, networking, and key ideas. Each subgroup also received training in concentration management techniques. Finally, the experimental students were asked to complete the self-report forms.

The results of the comprehension/retention experiment revealed that the learning strategy class members showed significantly greater positive precourse–postcourse changes on the comprehension/retention tests and on the self-report measures than did the no-treatment controls. Further, the training appeared to have a greater impact on the short-answer portions of the tests than on the multiple-choice portions. Comparisons of the three subgroups receiving training in different comprehension/retention strategies indicated that the networking strategy produced somewhat greater positive changes from the midcourse test to the postcourse test than did the other two strategies. One possible explanation is that the organizational aspects of networking (i.e., the production of two-dimensional maps) were responsible for the mean differences in performance.

In short, the formal evaluation data provided evidence that the strategy system improved the students' learning behaviors and attitudes. In addition to the formal assessments, participants rated the perceived value of each strategy component included in the program. Although all components were rated positively, networking, concentration management, and the MURDER executive routine received the highest ratings. In subsequent studies these components were evaluated independently, modified, and then recombined to form the basis for the second general assessment.

The purposes of the second assessment (see Dansereau, Holley, Collins, Brooks, McDonald & Larson, 1980, for further information) were to replicate and extend the first assessment and to determine the effects of training sequence on dependent measure performances. Fifty-seven participants were given the training in one of two sequences: primary strategies followed by support strategies or support strategies followed by primary. A no-treatment group served as a control. In general, the results revealed that strategy training significantly improved performance in both text processing and self-report measures. The group trained in primary strategies typically scored higher than the other group on the text processing measures.

The results of these two system assessments provide support for the effectiveness of the overall strategy program. Further, they also provided the basis for more detailed examination of promising system components. The results of a selected set of these component studies are described in the next subsection.

Studies Assessing Component Strategies

In this section we describe briefly the results from a series of studies that were designed to assess some of the promising component strategies emerging from our overall system evaluations. These include: summarization (paraphrase/imagery), networking, concentration management, and cooperative (pair) learning (pairs of students interactively processing text material).

Summarization. A number of prior studies (Anderson & Biddle, 1975; Dansereau, 1978; Ross & DiVesta,1976) have shown that individuals taught or instructed to summarize explicitly what they have read exhibit significantly better performance on text recall measures than either individuals using their own study methods or those using a read/reread strategy. Unfortunately, this phenomenon has not been related to existing theoretical perspectives. Further, the lack of detailed information on this phenomenon has inhibited the application of summarization strategies in real-world educational settings. The present study (see Spurlin et al., 1980, for further information) was designed to be a first step in rectifying this state of affairs.

Of particular interest was the effect of the frequency of noncumulative summarizing on different performance indices. It was expected that frequent summarizing would focus the learner's attention on the microstructure or details of the text (Kintsch & Van Dijk, 1978) perhaps at the expense of the macrostructure including main ideas, organizing framework, gist. Conversely, infrequent summarization was expected to lead to an increase in focus on the macrostructure, perhaps at the expense of the details. Given the aforementioned conditions, explanations based on the notion of depth of semantic processing (Andre & Womack,1978; Craik & Lockhart, 1972) would predict that frequent summarizing would lead to better recall performance than infrequent summarizing, whereas explanations based on the importance of higher order organizational schemes for memory (Shimmerlik, 1978) would predict the opposite.

Forty-eight general psychology students were randomly assigned to one of three experimental groups: Frequent Summarization ($n = 16$, who created four equally spaced, noncumulative summaries while studying a 2400-word excerpt from a college-level geology textbook); Infrequent Summarization ($n = 16$, who created two equally spaced summaries); and Control ($n = 16$, who used their normal study methods). Five days after studying, all groups took essay, short-answer, multiple-choice, and cloze tests on the geology excerpt. Analysis of covariance (the Delta Vocabulary Test, Deignan, 1973, was used as the covariate) and subsequent post hoc analyses revealed that the Infrequent Summarization group outperformed the Control group on essay organization and essay content. All other differences were nonsignificant. This pattern of findings suggests that infrequent summarization, which presumably focuses the learner's attention on macrostructure, is more effective than frequent summarization, which presumably leads the learner to focus on microstructure. Unexpectedly, the Frequent group produced higher quality notes during studying than did the Infrequent group. This negative relationship between note quality and essay performance should have important implications for training designed to improve notetaking.

Networking. A study by Holley et al., (1979) directly compared the text-processing performance of students ($n = 17$) who were given 6 hours of networking training (see previous subsection on the description of the content-independent strategies) with that of students ($n = 21$) using their normal study methods. The bases of comparison were essay, short-answer, multiple-choice, and cloze tests over a 3000-word excerpt from a geology textbook studied 5 days earlier. A Hotelling T^2 test indicated that the Networking group significantly outperformed the Control group on the dependent measures. Further analyses showed that the major differences between groups were attributable to the cloze and essay tests, both of which were designed to assess performance on main ideas. This pattern of results suggests that networking is valuable in assisting the student in the extraction and retention of main ideas but does not appear to affect the extraction and retention of details. Finally, 2×2 factorial analyses of high and low grade-point average (GPA) subgroups indicated that the networking strategy may be more beneficial for low GPA students.

Concentration Management.   A study by Collins et al. (1981) was designed to provide an independent assessment of the concentration management component of the learning strategy system.

Three strategies for controlling affective responses during academic tasks were evaluated. One strategy, Self-Initiated Relaxation (SIR), required participants ($n = 17$) to employ a combination of relaxation techniques to set and maintain constructive study and test-taking states. The second strategy, Self-Coaching (SC), was an extension of the positive self-talk techniques developed by Meichenbaum (1972). Students ($n = 19$) were taught to coach (talk) themselves into constructive states and to maintain these states during studying and test taking. Finally, a third strategy, which combined SIR and SC, was created ($n = 17$). Results of a series of analyses of covariance (GPA serving as the covariate) indicated that in comparison with a no-treatment control group ($n = 20$) the third strategy, SIR plus SC, significantly ($p < .05$) facilitated performance on multiple choice and cloze tests over a 3000-word excerpt from a geology textbook studied 5 days earlier. This result corroborates Meichenbaum's (1972) findings and Deffenbacher's (1978) suggestion that a combination of self-talk and relaxation techniques is more effective than the individual components alone.

Cooperative (Pair) Learning.   The term cooperative learning has generally been applied to situations where the interactions among students are not based on fixed teacher/learner roles. Usually the participants are viewed as equal partners. Although often indicating positive effects on academic achievement (Sharan, 1980; Slavin, 1980), prior studies on cooperative learning have not systematically examined the dimensions of the experience (e.g., processing strategies, individual differences). A more precise understanding of cooperative learning is necessary before its potential as a tool for learning content and skills can be maximized.

As a first step in this direction, McDonald et al. (1979) developed a strategy that required student pairs to read approximately 500 words of a 2500-word passage. One student then served as a recaller and attempted to summarize orally from memory what had been learned. The other member of the pair served as the listener/facilitator and attempted to correct errors in the recall and to facilitate the organization and storage of the material. This process was repeated over each 500-word segment, with pair partners alternating roles. Students trained to use this strategy were compared on the initial acquisition of 2500-word college-level textbook excerpts, with students who developed their own pair learning method and students studying individually. A subsequent test (for which all students studied individually) was conducted to determine transfer from dyad to individual study. Results indicated that pairs of students outperformed the individual study group in initial acquisition, whether or not they were given the experimenter-provided strategy. Students given the experimenter strategy significantly outperformed the other two groups on the transfer test, suggesting they acquired skills that transferred from dyad to individual learning.

A study by Spurlin, Dansereau, Larson, and Brooks (1982) extended the McDonald et al. (1979) study by examining the roles and activities of the experimenter-provided strategy group. In learning scientific text passages, one member of the cooperating pair served as a recaller/oral summarizer and the other as either an *active* or *passive* listener/facilitator. Members of some treatment conditions alternated recaller/listener roles, while those in other conditions had fixed roles. The results indicated that both types of role and listener activity are important variables in cooperative learning. On free recall of text main ideas, fixed recallers outperformed fixed listeners, and pairs incorporating an active listener outperformed those that did not. Certain combinations of role type and listener activity resulted in better performance than that achieved by individuals using their own study methods.

General Discussion and Future Directions of the Research on Content-Independent Strategies

In the previous subsections I have described a content-independent learning strategy system, reported on two overall evaluations of this system, and presented the results of studies designed to provide independent assessments of the more promising component strategies. The results have indicated that the overall strategy program is effective in improving performance on selected text-processing tasks administered immediately after training. This program is sufficiently content independent to be potentially applicable in a wide variety of instructional environments. The evaluations of the component strategies have indicated that these components can be profitably used in isolation to remedy specific learning deficiencies. More specifically, these primary and support strategies have typically led to a 30–40% improvement in performance in comparison to students using their own learning methods. It should be noted that the lack of differences across the board on the comprehension/retention tests administered indicates that the positive findings are not due to placebo factors.

Even though the results obtained to date are generally positive, there are a large number of important issues that require resolution. First, we have focused almost exclusively on immediate assessment of the effects of training. The only long-term follow-ups have been done via questionnaires administered 3 months after the completion of training. Although these questionnaire assessments indicate that the students continue to be postively influenced by the strategies, we do not have evidence as to whether the objective text-processing results would still pertain. We plan to address this issue in future studies.

In addition to our lack of knowledge about the long-term benefits, we also know very little about the relationships between individual difference variables and training effectiveness. In some of the studies we have attempted to relate variables such as verbal ability, field independence, and internal–external locus of control to changes from pre- to posttraining, but to date have been unable to observe reliable interrelationships (although, as mentioned previously, there is a tendency for students in the midranges of verbal ability to benefit most from strategy training). If we could establish such interrelationships we would have a basis for selecting participants and for tailoring the subsequent training to the needs and skills of the individuals involved. This is an area of inquiry that should be emphasized in future experimentation.

Although we have conducted component studies to determine the critical aspects of the overall system, we still know very little about why the strategies work. We don't know what alterations in the participant's cognitive processing are responsible for the improved test performance. More finegrained basic research is needed before we can begin to answer these questions.

During training, the most frequently occurring problem students report is in adapting the primary strategies to specific types of text material. In essence, they have difficulty in generalizing the primary strategies. This state of affairs has led us to explore the effectiveness of strategies that are tailored to the processing of text with specific characteristics. In the next section of this chapter two examples of this type of research are presented.

EXAMPLES OF RESEARCH ON CONTENT-DEPENDENT LEARNING STRATEGIES

This section contains brief descriptions of research on two types of strategies: one designed to assist students in learning about scientific theories; and one designed to assist learning from texts that contain embedded headings. Both of these sets of strategies are targeted toward text with specific characteristics and, as a consequence, are more specialized than those discussed in previous sections.

A Knowledge Schema Strategy for Learning About Scientific Theories

A strategy based on schema-theoretic notions has been developed to assist students in learning about scientific theories. Before discussing the specific technique, we present a brief overview of the concept of schema.

The central propostion of schema theory, as it applies to text processing, is that prior knowledge and the text's characteristics (titles, headings, and other immediately preceding material) interact to influence the interpretation and subsequent recall of new information. By this conceptualization, the prior knowledge of the reader is seen to be organized as a set of schemata, and the characteristics of the material are thought to activate or inhibit particular sets of schemata.

A schema can be described as the abstract prototype of a class of objects, events, or situations. Schemata are usually viewed as being hierarchically arranged into various subsets of placeholders within more general or higher order schemata.

The processing of academic material should be facilitated by form schemata that specify hierarchical sets of categories of information that a well-informed learner should know about a particular topic. (These types of schemata are labeled here *knowledge schemata*.) Although this aspect of schema theory has not been investigated previously, it is an important one, if schema theory is to have practical implications for academic learning. Focusing on the use of knowledge schemata as facilitators of descriptive prose learning, the present experiment was an initial step in expanding schema theory to the field of applied educational psychology.

Knowledge schemata, as defined here, are analogous to Kintsch's (1977) schemata for stories. These story schemata contain the general frames or categories typically important in understanding narrative prose. The results of an experiment by Thorndyke (1977) support the importance of these types of narrative schemata. He found that subjects who initially received a narrative passage, identical in structure, but unrelated in content to a target passage, recalled 22% more information in the target passage than did subjects who initially received a narrative passage unrelated in both structure and content to the target passage.

The knowledge schema employed in the present study specified the categories of knowledge representing an individual's understanding of a scientific theory. This schema was created on the basis of a survey given to 30 individuals at various levels of education (e.g., from freshman college students to upper level graduate students). The survey required each person to list what he or she considered the important categories of information relevant to understanding a scientific theory. Informal analysis revealed that these responses could be subsumed under six basic headings. Each of these six categories could be further divided into sets of subcategories. This information was then combined to form the following knowledge schema (given the acronym DICEOX to facilitate retention):

1. *Description* A short summary of the theory which should include:
   a. Phenomena
   b. Predictions
   c. Observations
   d. Definitions
2. *Inventor/History* A brief account of the theory's history, which should include:
   a. Name(s)
   b. Date
   c. Historical background
3. *Consequences* A concise summary of how the theory has influenced man. This should include:
   a. Applications
   b. Beliefs

4. *Evidence*   A short summary of facts that support or refute the theory. This should include:
   a. Experiments
   b. Observations
5. *Other Theories*   A concise summary of theories dealing with the same phenomena. These are usually of two types:
   a. Competing theories
   b. Similar theories
6. *X-tra Information*   An open category, which should include any important information not in one of the other five DICEOX categories.

Thirty-two students enrolled in a Techniques of College Learning class participated in the experiment on knowledge schema training as part of their course requirement. These students were randomly assigned to two groups: the DICEOX group ($n = 15$), which received training in the use of the knowledge schema just described; and the Control group ($n = 17$), which received instruction and participated in group discussions of concentration management during studying and test taking.

Following 6 hours of training, all participants studied for 55 minutes a 2500-word passage (excerpted from a geology textbook) on the theory of plate tectonics. Five days later, they took essay, short-answer, multiple-choice, and cloze tests over the passage. Results of a series of analyses of covariance (the Delta Vocabulary Test, Deignan, 1973, was used as the covariate) indicated that the DICEOX group performed significantly better than the Control group on the essay exams [$F(1, 23) = 6.59, p < .02$]. No other differences reached significance. This pattern of findings is not unexpected, if it is assumed that in the present case the DICEOX schema was functioning primarily as a recall aid. That is, at the time of recall, the knowledge schema may have facilitated performance by providing the student with additional retrieval cues on the essay test that were not available to students in the Control group. This interpretation of the results is partially supported by Anderson and Pichert's (1978) finding that participants will recall different aspects of a narrative story, depending on which of two schemata they are using at the time of recall. In other words, information that is relevant to the categories subsumed under a particular schema is more likely to be recalled than information not important to that schema.

Although the lack of significance on the cloze, multiple-choice, and the short-answer tests may be due to the fact that the knowledge schema is not useful when retrieval cues are present within the test questions, as is the case with the three tests already mentioned, at least two other possible explanations for these findings should be considered. First, the cloze, multiple-choice, and short-answer measures may not be sufficiently sensitive to reflect treatment differences. This possibility can be substantially discounted, however, based on the fact that previous experiments have found significant differences between treatment groups on these measures (Dansereau, Collins, McDonald, Holley, Garland, Diekhoff, & Evans, 1979; Dansereau, McDonald, Collins, Garland, Holley, Diekhoff, & Evans, 1979). A second possibility arises from the fact that the Control group was given training that may have attenuated the differences between the two experimental groups. This possibility is supported by prior research, which has shown that support strategies of the type communicated to the Control Group can increase performance on dependent measures similar to those used in the present study (Collins, 1978). Therefore, it appears that the current test of knowledge schema training is very conservative, and that it is not surprising that some of the dependent measures failed to show significant differences between the two groups. Under these conditions, the significant differences on the essay exam provide strong support for the efficacy of knowledge schema training.

Embedded Headings as Text Processing Aids

Although embedded headings and intact outlines are commonly included in textbooks, the research supporting their utility as text-processing aids is sparse. Studies in this domain have typically examined headings and outlines separately and have generally produced mixed results. A study reported by Dansereau (1982) was designed to correct some of the methodological shortcomings of the previous research to determine the impact of headings and outlines on the processing of science texts. In this study, randomly assigned college students studied 2500-word basic science passages containing the following supplementary materials: both intact outlines and embedded headings, intact outlines only, embedded headings only, and no outlines or headings. It was expected that intact outlines would provide the student with information concerning the superordinate topics and their relationships, while headings would provide information on the relationships between superordinate and subordinate ideas. The results from immediate and delayed testing paradigms indicated the supplementary materials had only a slight impact on immediate testing, but that headings significantly ($p<.05$) improved performance on the dependent measures during delayed testing.

Although this study indicated that the mere presence of headings could facilitate prose processing, the question remained as to whether instruction in the use of headings could further improve learning from text. To resolve this issue an experiment by Brooks, Dansereau, Spurlin, & Holley (1981) was designed. One hundred and six students were recruited from general psychology classes at Texas Christian University. All participants were randomly assigned to the following groups: Instruction-plus-Headings ($n = 31$) were given instructions on using headings to facilitate the input and output processing of text; Headings-Only ($n = 44$) studied text material containing headings but did not receive instructions; Control ($n = 31$) studied text material that did not contain headings.

After instructions and practice, all participants studied a 2500-word excerpt from an ecology textbook for 55 minutes. The Instruction-plus-Headings and Headings-Only groups studied identical passages containing headings. Five days later, the participants were sequentially administered the four dependent measures (essay, outline, short-answer, and multiple-choice) over the passage studied earlier. A series of analyses of covariance (the Delta Vocabulary Test used as the covariate) and subsequent post hoc analysis indicated that on essay content the Instructions-plus-Headings group significantly outperformed the Control group ($p < .05$); on outline content (participants were to create a well-organized outline of the passage), the Instructions-plus-Headings group performed significantly better than the Headings-Only group ($p < .01$) and the Control group ($ps<.01$). No other comparisons were significant.

The pattern of results obtained in this study suggests that headings may have their greatest effects as retrieval aids. Specifically, this contention is supported by the fact that the Instruction-plus-Headings group significantly outperformed the Control group on the uncued tests (essay and outline), but not on the cued exams (short-answer and multiple-choice). Further support is also dervived from the Dansereau (1982) study in which delayed testing proved more sensitive to headings effects than immediate testing. Presumably, retrieval becomes a more critical process as the time between studying and testing increases. In any case, the results do suggest that a learning strategy targeted specifically toward heading usage can facilitate text processing.

Discussion and Future Direction of the Research on Content-Dependent Strategies

The knowledge schema (DICEOX) and headings strategies both appear to be effective facilitators of text processing. However, at this point, we have barely scratched the surface of the domain of content-dependent strategies. For example, using the same basic approach, the knowledge schema strategy can be modified and extended to include the processing of information about systems (e.g., nervous system), events (e.g., World War II), techniques (e.g., operant conditioning), etc. Extensions of the headings strategy can also be developed to facilitate the use of other supplementary materials that typically appear in textbooks (e.g., overviews, summaries, pictures). Given the results to date, both of these directions appear to warrant further attention.

Although it will be useful, in the future, to compare the effectiveness of content-dependent and content-independent strategies, a more pragmatically important direction may be the evaluation of a system that integrates both types of strategies. Such a system would be hierarchically structured, with content-independent strategies containing more specialized, content-dependent ones.

GENERAL SUMMARY AND CONCLUSIONS

The key problems associated with learning strategy research fall into three categories: selection and development of the strategies, strategy training, and assessment of strategy effectiveness. In our work with a particular learning strategy system we have evolved potential solutions to problems in each of these categories. Although it is obvious that a great deal of further exploration is needed, our approaches to this research should provide a preliminary basis for the development of a learning strategy science.

The research program reported in this chapter has focused on the development and assessment of a content-independent learning strategy system and an exploration of potentially effective content-dependent strategies. The results of a number of assessments of the overall strategy system and component strategies indicate that strategy training can significantly improve performance on selected text-processing tasks administered immediately after training.

Although these results are promising, application-oriented studies are needed to assess the long-term effects of strategy training, the effects of training on more global measures such as grade-point average, the possibility of integrating learning strategy training with regular courses, and the possibility of providing training to younger students. In addition, basic theoretical studies are needed to determine why the strategies are effective, by relating the strategy manipulations to existing theoretical perspectives.

ACKNOWLEDGMENTS

Research reported in this chapter was partially supported by a contract with the Defense Advanced Research Projects Agency, MDA–903–76–C0218, ARPA Order 3204, and a grant from the National Institute of Education, NIE–G–79–0157. The views and conclusions contained are those of the author and should not be interpreted as necessarily representing the official policies, either expressed or implied, of the National Institute of Education or the Defense Advanced Research Projects Agency.

REFERENCES

Anderson, R. C., & Biddle, W. B. On asking people questions about what they are reading. In G. Bower (Ed.), *Psychology of learning and motivation* (Vol. 9). New York: Academic Press, 1975.

Anderson, R. C., & Pichert, J. W. Recall of previously unrecallable information following a shift in perspective. *Journal of Verbal Learning and Verbal Behavior*, 1978, *17*, 1–12.

Andre, T., & Womack, S. Verbatim and paraphrased adjunct questions and learning from prose. *Journal of Educational Psychology*, 1978, 79(5), 796–802.

Armbruster, B. B. An investigation of the effectiveness of *"mapping" text as a studying strategy for middle school students*. Unpublished doctoral dissertation, University of Illinois, 1979

Briggs, R. D., Tosi, D. J., & Morley, R. M., Study habit modification and its effect on academic performances: A behavioral approach. *Journal of Educational Research*, 1971, *64(8)*, 347–350.

Brooks, L. W., & Dansereau, D. F. *Knowledge schema training and descriptive prose processing*. Paper presented at the meeting of the American Educational Research Association, Los Angeles, April 1981 (ERIC Document Reproduction Service No. ED 199 288).

Brooks, L. W., Dansereau, D.F., Spurlin, J. E., & Holley, C. D. *Instructing students on the use of headings as aids in processing scientific text*. Paper presented at the meeting of the American Educational Research Association, Los Angeles, April 1981.

Brown, W. F., & Holtzman, W. H. *Survey of study habits and attitudes* (Form C). New York: The Psychological Corporation, 1965.

Carroll, J. B. *Learning from verbal discourse in educational media: A review of the literature* (ETS RB-71-61). Princeton, N. J.: Educational Testing Service, October 1971.

Collins, K. W. *Control of affective responses during academic tasks*. Unpublished master's thesis, Texas Christian University, 1978.

Collins, K. W., Dansereau, D. F., Garland, J. C., Holley, C. D., & McDonald, B. A. Control of concentration during academic tasks. *Journal of Educational Psychology*, 1981, *73*, 122–128.

Craik, F. I. M., & Lockhart, R. S. Levels of processing: A framework for memory research. *Journal of Verbal Learning and Verbal Behavior*, 1972, *11*, 671–684.

Cronbach, L. J., & Furby, L. How we should measure "changes" or should we? *Psychological Bulletin*, 1970, *74(1)*, 68–80.

Dansereau, D. F. The development of a learning strategy curriculum. In H. F. O'Neil, Jr. (Ed.), *Learning strategies*. New York: Academic Press, 1978.

Dansereau, D. F., Actkinson, T. R., Long, G. L., & McDonald, B. A. *Learning strategies: A review and synthesis of the current literature* (AFHRL–TR–74–70, Contract F41609–74–C–0013). Brooks AFB, Texas: Air Force Systems Command 1974. (AD–A007–722).

Dansereau, D. F. *Effects of individual differences, processing instructions, and outline and heading characteristics on learning from introductory science text*. (Final report, Grant No. NIE–G–79–0157, Project No. 9–0548). January, 1982. Section I: *Utilizing intact and embedded headings as processing aids with non-narrative text* (ERIC Document Reproduction Service No. ED 218 150).

Dansereau, D. F., Collins, K. W., McDonald, B. A., Garland, J. C., Holley, C. D., Evans, S. H., & Diekhoff, G. M. *Learning strategy training material: A selected subset* (AFHRL–TR–78–64, AD062739). Lowry AFB, Colo.: Technical Training Division, Air Force Human Resources Laboratory, September 1978.

Dansereau, D. F., Collins, K. W., McDonald, B. A., Holley, C. D., Garland, J. C., Diekhoff, G., & Evans, S. H. Development and evaluation of an effective learning strategy program. *Journal of Educational Psychology*, 1979, *71(1)*, 64–73.

Dansereau, D. F., Holley, C. D., Collins, K. W., Brooks, L. W., & Larson, D. *Effects of learning strategy training on text processing*. Paper presented at the meeting of the American Educational Research Association, Boston, April 1980.

Dansereau, D. F., Holley, C. D., Collins, K. W., Brooks, L. W., McDonald, B. A., & Larson, D. *Validity of learning strategies/skills training* (AFHRL–TR–79–84, Final Report, Contract MDA–903–76–C–0218). Brooks AFB, Texas: Air Force Systems Command, April 1980. (ADA 085–659)

Dansereau, D. F., Long, G. L., Evans, S. H., & Actkinson, T. R. Objective ordering of instructional material using multidimensional scaling. *Journal of Structural Learning*, 1980, *6*, 299–314.

Dansereau, D. F., Long, G. L., McDonald, B. A., & Actkinson, T. R. *Learning strategy inventory development and assessment* (AFHRL–TR–75–40, Contract F41609–74–C–0013). Brooks AFB, Texas: Air Force Systems Command, June 1975. (AD–A014721)

Dansereau, D. F., Long, G. L., McDonald, B. A., Actkinson,T. R., Collins K. W., Evans, S. H., Ellis, A. M., & Williams, S. *Learning strategy training program: Paraphrasing strategy for effective learning* (AFHRL–TR–75–46, Final Report, Contract F41609–74–C–0013). Brooks AFB, Texas: Air Force Systems Command, June 1975. (AD–A014–723) (a)

Dansereau, D. F., Long, G. L., McDonald, B. A., Actkinson, T. R., Collins, K. W., Evans, S. H., Ellis, A. M., & Williams, S. *Learning strategy training program: Visual imagery for effective learning* (AFHRL–TR–75–47, Final Report, Contract F41609–74–C–0013). Brooks AFB, Texas: Air Force Systems Command, June 1975. (AD–A014–724) (b)

Dansereau, D. F., Long, G. L., McDonald, B. A., Actkinson, T. R., Collins, K. W., Evans, S. H., Ellis, A. M., & Williams, S. *Learning strategy training program: Questions and answers for effective learning* (AFHRL–TR–75–48, Final Report, Contract F41609–74–C–0013). Brooks AFB, Texas: Air Force Systems Command, June 1975. (AD–A014–725) (c)

Dansereau, D. F., Long, G. L., McDonald, B. A., Actkinson, T. R., Ellis, A. M., Collins, K. W., Williams, S., & Evans, S. H. *Effective learning strategy training program: Development and assessment* (AFHRL–TR–75–41, AD014–722). Lowry AFB, Colo.: Technical Training Division, Air Force Human Resources Laboratory, June 1975.

Dansereau, D. F., McDonald, B. A., Collins, K. W., Garland, J. C., Holley, C. D., Diekhoff, G., & Evans S. H. Development and evaluation of a learning strategy system. In H. F. O'Neil, Jr. & C. D. Spielberger (Eds.), *Cognitive and affective learning strategies*. New York: Academic Press, 1979.

Deffenbacher, J. L. Worry, emotionality, and task-generated interference in test anxiety: An empirical test of attentional theory. *Journal of Educational Psychology*, 1978, *70(2)*, 248–254.

Deignan, G. M. *The Delta reading vocabulary test*. Lowry AFB, Colo.: Technical Training Division, Air Force Human Resources Laboratory, 1973.

Diekhoff, G. M., Brown, P. J. & Dansereau, D. F., A prose learning strategy training program based on network and depth-of-processing models. *Journal of Experimental Education*, 1982, *50(4)*, 180–184.

Dubin, R., & Taveggia, T. C. *The teaching–learning paradox*. Eugene: University of Oregon Press, 1968.

Ellis, A. *Reason and emotion in psychotherapy*. New York: Lyle Stuart, 1963.

Gagné, R. M., *The conditions of learning* (3rd ed.) New York: Holt, Rinehart, & Winston, 1977.

Gagné, R. M., & White, R. T., Memory structures and learning outcomes. *Review of Educational Research*, 1978, *48*(2), 187–222.

Garland, J. C. *The development and assessment of an imagery-based learning strategy program to improve the retention of prose material*. Unpublished master's thesis, Texas Christian University, 1977.

Holley, C. D., & Dansereau, D. F. Controlling for transient motivation in cognitive manipulation studies. *Journal of Experimental Education*, 1980/81, *49(2)*, 84–91.

Holley, C. D., Dansereau, D. F., McDonald, B. A., Garland, J. C., & Collins, K. W. Evaluation of a hierarchical mapping technique as an aid to prose processing. *Contemporary Educational Psychology*, 1979, *4*, 227–237.

Jacobsen, E. *Progressive relaxation*. Chicago: University of Chicago Press, 1938.

Kintsch, W., On comprehending stories. In M. A. Just & P. A. Carpenter (Eds.), *Cognitive processes in comprehension*. Hillsdale, N.J.: Lawrence Erlbaum Associates, 1977.

Kintsch, W., & Van Dijk, T. A. Toward a model of text comprehension and production. *Psychological Review*, 1978, *85*(5), 363–394.

Long, G. L., Dansereau, D. F., McDonald, B. A., Collins K. W., & Evans, S. H. *The development, assessment, and modification of an effective learning strategy training program*. Paper presented at the meeting of the American Educational Research Association, San Francisco, April 1976.

Mansfield, R. S., Busse, T. V., & Krepelka, E. J. The effectiveness of creativity training. *Review of Educational Research*, 1978, *48*(4), 517–536.

Maultsby, M. *Handbook of rational self-counseling*. Madison, Wisc.: Association for Rational Thinking, 1971.

McDonald, B. A., Dansereau, D. F., Garland, J. C., Holley, C. D., & Collins, K. W. *Pair learning and transfer of text processing skills*. Paper presented at the meeting of the American Educational Research Association, San Francisco, April 1979.

Meichenbaum, D. Cognitive modification of test anxious college students. *Journal of Consulting and Clinical Psychology*, 1972, *39*, 370–380.

Meichenbaum, D. H., & Goodman, J. Training impulsive children to talk to themselves: A means of self-control. *Journal of Abnormal Psychology*, 1971, *77*, 115–126.

Meichenbaum, D. H., & Turk, D. *The cognitive–behavioral management of anxiety, anger, and pain*. Paper presented at the Seventh Banff International Conference on Behavioral Modification, Canada, 1975.

Overall, J. E., & Woodward, J. W. Common misconceptions concerning the analysis of covariance. *Journal of Multivariate Behavioral Research*, 1977, *12*, 171–185. (a)

Overall, J. E., & Woodward, J. A. Nonrandom assignment and the analysis of covariance. *Psychological Bulletin*, 1977, *84*, 588–594. (b)

Paivio, A. Mental imagery in associative learning and memory. *Psychological Review*, 1969, *76*, 241–263.

Robinson, F. P. *Effective study*. New York: Harper, 1946.

Ross, S. M., & DiVesta, F. J. Oral summary as a review strategy for enhancing recall of textual material. *Journal of Educational Psychology*, 1976, *68*(6), 689–695.

Rumelhart, D. E., & Ortony, A. The representation of knowledge in memory. In R. C. Anderson, R. J. Spiro, & W. E. Montague (Eds.), *Schooling and the acquisition of knowledge*. Hillsdale, N.J.: Lawrence Erlbaum Associates, 1977.

Sarason, I. G. Effect of anxiety, motivational instructions and failure on serial learning. *Journal of Experimental Psychology*, 1956, *51*, 253–260.

Sharan, S. Cooperative learning in small groups: Recent methods and effects on achievement, attitudes, and ethnic relations. *Review of Educational Research*, 1980, *50*(2), 241–271.

Shimmerlik, S. M. Organization theory and memory for prose: A review of the literature. *Review of Educational Research*, 1978, *48*(1), 103–120.

Slavin, R. E. Cooperative learning. *Review of Educational Research*, 1980, *50*(2), 315–342.

Spurlin, J. E., Dansereau, D. F., & Brooks, L. W. *Text processing: Effects of summarization frequency on performance*. Paper presented at the meeting of the Southwestern Psychological Association, Oklahoma City, April 1980.

Spurlin, J. E., Dansereau, D. F., Larson, C., & Brooks, L. W. *Cooperative learning as an active and passive process*. Paper presented at the meeting of the American Educational Research Association, New York, April 1982.

Thorndyke, P. W. Cognitive structures in comprehension and memory of narrative discourse. *Cognitive Psychology*, 1977, *9*, 77–110.

Whitehall, R. P. The development of effective learning skills programs. *Journal of Educational Research*, 1972, *65*(6), 281–285.

Wolpe, J. *The practice of behavioral therapy*. New York: Pergamon, 1969.

6 Learning Strategies: The How of Learning

Claire E. Weinstein
Vicki L. Underwood
University of Texas at Austin

The term *learning strategies* is used in a very broad sense to identify a number of different competencies that researchers and practitioners have postulated as necessary, or helpful, for effective learning and retention of information for later use. These competencies include cognitive information-processing strategies, such as techniques for organizing and elaborating on incoming information to make it more meaningful; active study strategies, such as systems for note-taking and test preparation; and support strategies, such as techniques for organizing study time, coping with performance anxiety, and directing attention to the learning task at hand. In addition, there is a range of metacognitive strategies that learners can use to detect discrepancies between what they know and what they do not know and to monitor and direct their acquisition of the new information. It should be noted that the term "learner" is being used here to refer to any person trying to acquire new knowledge, attitudes, or skills, regardless of whether this occurs in a formal school setting, an on-the-job placement, or an informal interaction.

This chapter describes some of the work that has been conducted as part of the Cognitive Learning Strategies Project at The University of Texas, a project that is concerned both with increasing our basic understanding of human learning and with the development of programs and teaching practices to help students become more effective learners. Here we focus on the more applied aspects of our work. We begin by briefly reviewing some recent research on the nature of effective learning strategies that provides a conceptual framework for much of our instructional work. Next, we discuss our progress on the development of an instrument that can provide diagnostic information about students' strengths and weaknesses as learners. Finally, we describe the kinds of instruction in learning strategies that we offer students, and briefly discuss some of the research we have undertaken on various aspects of our instructional program.

FOUNDATIONS OF LEARNING STRATEGIES RESEARCH

Recent research and development efforts in psychology, education, and training have resulted in changed perceptions of the roles assumed by learners and instructors. In these new conceptions of the teaching/learning act (Wittrock, 1974, 1978), effective learners are seen as active information processors, interpreters and synthesizers, who use a variety of different strategies to store and retrieve information. Such individuals assume much of the responsibility for their own learning, as evidenced by their efforts to adapt the learning environment to fit their needs and goals.

In the past, learning was viewed as an almost mechanical response to incoming stimuli; it was believed that the learner was greatly limited in what he or she could do to improve comprehension and memory. Gradually, the growth of cognitive psychology shifted the attention of many researchers to studying the ways learners process incoming stimuli. George Miller (1956) was one of the first researchers to investigate the methods by which individuals transform, or code, incoming information to make it easier to learn and remember.

Miller was interested in the operations by which stimulus inputs could be coded to form higher order units called chunks. He hypothesized that people tend to organize incoming information into these chunks, or groups, as a way of reducing limitations imposed on learning and memory by our limited capacity information-processing capabilities. Another type of coding operation that enables one to reduce the amount of information to be processed involves selecting a specific portion of the to-be-learned information as the critical element to code and then using this portion as a cue for reconstructing the entire stimulus. Coding by stimulus selection can occur whenever a stimulus can be analyzed into component parts (Navon, 1977).

Not all coding operations reduce the amount of information to be processed. Some operations may require that the learner expand incoming information to make it easier to learn and remember. Examples of this type of process include the use of imaginal or verbal elaboration (Paivio, 1971; Reder, 1980; Rohwer, 1970; Weinstein, 1978). The use of these strategies requires a learner to create some type of symbolic construction, such as an image, an analogy, or an inference, to help make the new information more meaningful. Creating imaginal and verbal elaborators to learn new information can be done any number of ways. One could relate the new information to previously acquired knowledge or experience, or one could examine the new material and identify logical relationships among the component parts or attempt to draw inferences from its content. For example, learning about arbitration and how courts try to settle disputes may be made easier if this unfamiliar process is compared to students' knowledge about how friends settle disputes. The goal of each of these processes is to relate the new, unfamiliar material to the old, already learned store of knowledge and experiences possessed by the learner.

When learners try to relate new knowledge to what they already know, we call this active, or generative, learning (Wittrock, 1974, 1978). It is generative because the learner must generate the relationships between what he or she already knows and the new information to be learned. For example, if students were studying a unit about the circulatory system, generating comparisons to an analogous system, such as the operation of a sink and its plumbing, could help them to learn this new information. Creating inferences about the role of the circulatory system and its relations to other parts of the body could also help in understanding the functions and operations of the circulatory system. Each of these strategies involves taking active steps to manage one's own learning processes to facilitate knowledge acquisition and comprehension.

Research on learning strategies received even more attention after the national trend in the 1960s to establish open admission or special admission policies. Colleges and universities began to accept students who previously would not have been admitted. Gradually, learning theorists began to recognize that "the new students" were not only lacking in reading skills, motivation, and stress management skills (Cross, 1969) but also in active coding and information-processing strategies (Rohwer & Ammon, 1971; Rohwer, 1973). More recent studies of the learning strategies used by Army recruits, community college students, and university students indicate learning strategy deficits that are inversely related to the level of education attained (Weinstein, Wicker, Cubberly, Roney, & Underwood, 1980).

Still other researchers, such as Golinkoff (1976) and Ryan (1980), have noted that active information-processing strategies play an important role in successful reading comprehension—good readers differ from poor ones in their use of a variety of strategies for transforming the information contained in texts so that it becomes easier to understand and remember. A large body of research on reading comprehension has documented the effects of the learner's schemata (knowledge structures) on comprehension and recall (see Anderson, Spiro, & Montague, 1977). Schema theorists argue that comprehension depends on an interaction between two factors: (1) the learner's knowledge of the characteristics of the message and the context in which it is given; and (2) his or her efforts to relate the incoming idea units to each other and to previously acquired information. Additional evidence of this interaction is found in a number of structure-of-text studies showing that experienced readers are able to infer the author's textual schemas with explicit cues, whereas inexperienced readers are not (e.g., Meyer, 1980).

Given these and similar findings, some researchers have turned their attention to the investigation of methods and programs for instructing students to use effective learning strategies. However, in contrast to classic experimental designs, the paradigms used in learning strategies training research are often quasi-experimental, the instruction is typically long in duration, and students are taught a range of different strategies that are considered to be effective for different kinds of learning situations (Anderson, 1979; Dansereau, Collins, McDonald, Holley, Garland, Diekhoff, & Evans, 1979; Jones, Amiran, & Katims, this volume; McCombs, 1981; Sticht, 1979; Weinstein, 1978; Weinstein, Underwood, Wicker, & Cubberly, 1979; Weinstein & Underwood, 1982). The work by Jones and Sticht has focused on embedding learning strategies instruction into regular reading curriculum materials, whereas the work of Anderson, Dansereau, McCombs, and Weinstein has focused on the development of special training programs that are used as an adjunct to regular classroom instruction. In addition, a paradigm that involves training subject matter teachers to incorporate instruction in learning strategies into their regular classroom presentations has also been proposed (Monroe, Fegan, & Scott, 1980; Weinstein, 1982).

Regardless of which paradigm is used, successful implementation and evaluation of a learning strategies training program requires a reliable and valid means for measuring students' deficits. An accurate diagnosis of students' entry-level learning strategies deficits could be used to create individualized prescriptions for training, and subsequent assessments could be used to evaluate the effectiveness of that training.

ASSESSING LEARNING STRATEGIES

Currently, the majority of instruments available for assessing learning strategies focus on the individual's study practices. These instruments are generally used in high school or college settings for a number of purposes, including: (1) prediction of academic performance; (2) counseling students concerning their study practices; and (3) screening or criterion measures for study skills courses.

Several study skills instruments are available commercially. A review of these instruments (Schulte & Weinstein, 1981) revealed that most of them covered traditional areas of study skills, such as note-taking, time management, work habits, and student attitudes toward school and study. Generally, these instruments use a self-report format and sample a broad range of topics within the area of study skills. For those instruments that provide such data, reliability was generally found to be in the acceptable range of .80 and above (Anastasi, 1976). However, subscales, partially due to their shorter length, often were found to have somewhat lower reliability (.46 to .93).

Most of these inventories have used what Svensson (1977) terms a "correlational" approach. That is, they seek to find behaviors or activities that are correlated with successful studying, but may not be the direct cause of successful learning. Such a correlational approach is reflected by the manner in which study skills inventories are typically constructed and validated. For example, Carter (1958) constructed his California Study Methods Survey by weighting items on the basis of how well they distinguished between students with high and low grade-point averages who had similar IQ and achievement test scores. A similar procedure was used in selecting items for the Survey of Study Habits and Attitudes (Brown & Holtzman, 1967), the Effective Study Test (Brown, 1964), and the College Adjustment and Study Skills Inventory (Christensen, 1968).

Although all of these inventories predict grade-point average to a moderate degree (.19 to .60), they do not yield information about *how* the student learns, only the conditions under which he or she does it best. Svensson (1977) distinguishes this correlational approach from a functional approach that seeks to find qualitative differences in how students study that may affect learning outcomes. For instance, Svensson found that students learned reading passages by attending to either specific details of the text or by searching for overall meaning. He found that a student's strategy for reading influenced both the amount and the type of information recalled from the text.

Goldman and Warren (1973) constructed a study strategies questionnaire to determine if different types of learning strategies were used by successful versus poor students across various college majors. Using discriminant analysis, the authors found that the items that highly discriminated between students with high and low grade-point averages across all majors seemed to tap two dimensions of effective study. These were diligence in study habits and an active learning style. They defined an active learning style as one that involved building on previous understanding of subject matter or relating new information to material learned in other classes.

Another instrument, the Inventory of Learning Processes (Schmeck, Ribich, & Ramanaiah, 1977), is one of the few instruments developed expressly to measure the kinds of information-processing activities students use while trying to learn academic material. This instrument consists of four scales obtained by factor analyzing students' responses to the inventory items. Three of the scales assess information-processing strategies students use while learning. The Elaborative Processing Scale contains items concerning the use of an active learning approach whereby the to-be-learned information is related to the learner's previous knowledge in the same field, as well as in other topic areas. The Synthesis–Analysis Scale contains items measuring the learner's use of organizational strategies. The third scale, Fact Retention, examines the learner's techniques for remembering specific facts and details. The last scale, Study Methods, consists primarily of items assessing learners' use of traditional study techniques on a regular basis.

Schmeck et al. (1977), as well as Schmeck and Grove (1979), and Schmeck and Ribich (1978), provide extensive reliability and validity information for the Inventory of Learning Processes. Test–retest reliability for the scales ranges from

.79 to .88. Scale scores were found to correlate with performance on several types of learning measures, such as a test over the material covered in a classroom lecture, and both recall and recognition scores on verbal learning tasks.

Dansereau (Dansereau, Long, McDonald, & Actkinson, 1975) has also developed a questionnaire designed to measure individual differences in college students' learning strategies. The Learning Strategy Inventory consists of 201 multiple-choice items based both on previous study skills inventories and on descriptions of learning techniques derived from the current psychological and educational literature. Based, in part, on research with their questionnaire, Dansereau and his associates have identified four areas where students may use strategies to help themselves complete academic tasks: selection of material that needs special attention because it is unfamiliar or important, comprehending and retaining important information, retrieving information from memory, and coping with internal and external distractions that can occur while studying (see Dansereau, this volume).

Weinstein has also developed an assessment instrument to measure learning strategies; however, she has used a slightly different format from the ones used for the instruments previously discussed. The Learning Activities Questionnaire (Weinstein et al., 1980) asks respondents to describe the methods they would use to learn various types of stimulus materials including paired-associate and free-recall lists, and reading passages. In one section, learners respond to open-ended questions that require them to provide descriptions of how they would learn the information contained in the various learning tasks. In a second section, the same questions are presented, but are followed by a checklist that describes several different strategies. In this section, learners need only recognize the strategies they would use. Descriptions of learners' strategies are then classified into one of six strategy categories: (1) verbal elaboration; (2) imagery; (3) grouping; (4) physical similarities; (5) rote responses; and (6) unscorable responses. Test–retest reliability for the instrument is .88. Interrater reliability is .90.

Although a number of these experimental instruments have proved to be highly useful research tools, they have limited utility as diagnostic measures. In fact, after an extensive review of both commercially available and experimental instruments conducted as part of our current work on the Cognitive Learning Strategies Project, the following conclusions were reached:

1. Across study skills inventories, there seems to be no consistent definition of study skills. The term includes a broad range of topics, and inventories vary in their coverage of these topics. In addition, the specific topics covered by a particular inventory often are not specified.

2. Although several inventories have subscales that measure specific topics within study skills (e.g., note-taking, scheduling), the reliability of the subscales is often so low that the subscales cannot be used separately.

3. Most of the recommended or "good" study practices in study skills inventories have not been empirically validated. Therefore, a high score on a study skills inventory does not necessarily mean that a student's study practices are effective.

4. No instrument has been validated for use as a diagnostic instrument. The majority of validity studies have demonstrated the usefulness of a given instrument as a predictor of academic achievement.

5. Most of the instruments can be easily faked. That is, students who want to give the impression that they use effective learning strategies could respond to the instrument in ways that would not provide accurate information about their actual strategy use.

6. Although recent research has suggested that there are two components to effective study—consistent and regular study, and an "active" learning style—most items in published inventories deal primarily with the first component.

Given these problems, a major goal of our current work on the Cognitive Learning Strategies Project has been to develop an instrument to help educators and trainers diagnose strengths and weaknesses in students' learning and study strategies in order to provide individualized remedial training. To accomplish this goal an instrument is needed that: (1) assesses a broad range of topics within the area of learning strategies in a reliable and valid manner; (2) assesses covert and overt behaviors that are related to learning and that could be altered through training; (3) reflects the current state of the art in learning strategy research *and* cognitive psychology; and (4) is validated for use as a diagnostic instrument. For the past 2 years we have been developing an instrument to meet these criteria. This measure, the Learning and Study Strategies Inventory (LASSI), a 90-item self-report measure, has undergone extensive pilot testing and a small-scale field test. In addition, several concurrent validity studies have been conducted using both self-report (e.g., test anxiety) and performance measures (e.g., reading comprehension and note-taking). Several larger scale field tests are also underway.

The results thus far are highly encouraging. The LASSI is being used in high school, community college, and university settings as a diagnostic tool and as a basis for designing individualized interventions. Information gathered from these programs will be used to refine the instrument and finalize its content. The current form emphasizes both active cognitive strategies and more traditional study skills and support strategies. Potential subscales include information processing, anxiety management, elaboration, motivation, attitudes and attributions, selecting main ideas and themes, test preparation, review and practice, and memory.

Items selected for inclusion in the LASSI assess both overt and covert strategies and skills that can be modified through training. This is an important consideration for a diagnostic instrument. An item such as "My mother read to me when I was a child," may be highly predictive of performance, but would be useless as a basis for designing remedial training.

In addition to providing a tool for individual assessment and prescription, the data obtained from administering the LASSI have helped to focus the curriculum designs for our experimental training programs. In particular, studying the patterns that differentiate between more and less successful students helps us to identify training priorities. Given the realities of limited time and resources for learning strategies programs in either the public schools or higher education settings, this data base is helping us identify the skills and strategies most critical for inclusion in learning strategies instructional programs, such as elaboration, selecting the main idea, and self-testing and monitoring activities.

DEVELOPING LEARNING STRATEGIES TRAINING PROGRAMS

For the past several years, we have been involved in a program of applied research to determine how to help students acquire more effective learning strategies. We have used several approaches in conducting this research. In the sections that follow, we first describe one of our brief training studies and indicate how the findings that have emerged from this approach have provided an empirical basis for our more extended attempts at instruction. Next, we describe our semester-long course in learning strategies and our attempts to evaluate it. Finally, we discuss other approaches to incorporating learning strategies instruction into the school curriculum.

Our brief training studies have attempted to build on the cognitive psychology research literature discussed earlier in this chapter documenting that effective learners attempt to relate incoming information to their previously acquired store of knowledge to make the new information easier to understand and remember. We have referred to the methods effective learners use to relate incoming information to previous knowledge as elaboration skills. In our brief training studies, we have asked whether it is possible to teach these skills to students, whether doing so would produce improvements in their ability to learn and remember academic material, and what instructional techniques should be used.

To make the nature of our instruction in elaboration skills clearer to the reader, we discuss some learning tasks that students frequently encounter in school and indicate how the use of elaboration skills can help them more effectively cope with these tasks. One set of academic tasks is to memorize arbitrary associations between symbols and their referents. For example, in a driver education class, students might be asked to learn the following arbitrary association: Round signs on a highway warn a driver that railroad tracks are ahead. Effective learners approach the task of remembering arbitrary associations by using their background knowledge to impose meaning on these associations. That is, as an aid in remembering that "round" and "railroad" go together, they might imagine these two terms interacting in some meaningful way, such as through the formation of an image of the *round* wheels of a *railroad* train. In short, the effective learner's strategy for remembering isolated bits of information is to think up some meaningful way in which they can be seen as related to one another.

Another task that students frequently encounter in school is to learn complex bodies of information in which the individual facts already bear a meaningful relationship to one another. The effective learner's approach in situations like these is to attempt to discover these meaningful relationships—that is, to use their previously acquired background knowledge or experiences to draw inferences, seek out implications, look for underlying themes, and so on. All these different methods for coping with learning and memory tasks may be described under the general label of elaboration skills in that they involve expanding on the material to be learned in ways that make it more meaningful to the learner.

Initial Feasibility Study

In the initial research study, Weinstein (1975) explored whether students could be taught to use elaboration strategies as an aid in coping with school learning assignments, and whether their use of these strategies would result in improvements in their ability to understand and remember academic materials. Toward this end, she created a diversified elaboration skills training program for use with ninth graders. Instruction centered around the following five strategies: using sentences as elaborators, using images as elaborators, forming analogies, drawing implications, creating relationships, and paraphrasing. Instruction involved teaching students how to apply these strategies to a variety of learning tasks typically encountered in school, including paired-associate learning tasks, free-recall learning tasks, and reading comprehension tasks. The stimulus materials used during instruction were drawn from the ninth-grade curriculum in science, history, English, foreign language, and vocational education. More specifically, one of the reading comprehension tasks involved a passage from a science textbook describing the features that distinguish arteries from veins. Students were asked to read this passage and to learn and remember the information it contained. They were taught that an effective strategy for learning and remembering information from text about concepts and their attributes was to use sentences and images as elaborators. That is, they were told to try to think up meaningful associations between the concepts discussed in the text and the information that was provided about their defining attributes. For example, to remember that veins are thinner than arteries, students were told to try to form a picture in their minds of veins as being thin tubes, or to make up sentences associating veins with thin tubes such as "the vein woman is thin as a rubber tube."

For this study, 75 ninth-grade students were randomly assigned to one of three groups: training, control, or posttest-only. The training group participated in a series of five 1-hour elaboration skill training sessions, administered at approximately 1-week intervals. Students were exposed to a set of 19 learning tasks. They were required to create a series of elaborations for each of these tasks. Experimenter-provided directions for the early tasks emphasized the properties of an effective elaboration strategy. The later training sessions provided opportunities for additional practice in using these skills with little or no experimenter-provided instructions. The control group was exposed to the same stimulus materials, but their task was simply to learn the information without any type of strategy prompts or directions. A posttest-only group was not exposed to the stimulus materials but did participate in the posttesting sessions. The immediate posttest was administered a week after the conclusion of the training, and the delayed posttest was administered approximately a month later. Both immediate and delayed posttests consisted of two reading comprehension tasks, two trials of paired-associate learning and serial recall, and a one-trial free-recall task.

The results of the data analyses for the immediate posttest revealed significant differences between group means on the free-recall task and Trial 2 of the paired-associate learning task. In each instance, the training group's performance surpassed the performance of the control and posttest-only groups, which did not differ significantly from each other. On the delayed posttest, a significant difference was obtained for the reading comprehesion tasks and Trial 1 of the serial learning task. Again, these differences favored the training group. It seemed that students could learn to use these elaboration strategies, but further research was required to determine the optimal conditions for their learning and use. Much of our later research has focused on this issue.

Developing an Experimental Learning Strategies Curriculum

Studies such as the one just described helped to provide the foundation for more extensive training programs developed as part of the Cognitive Learning Strategies Project. In addition, a variety of other sources was used to help refine both the content of these programs and the instructional methodologies used. For example, student interviews during learning sessions and analyses of individual talk-aloud protocols provided additional information about the learning strategies used by good and poor students. A more extensive data base was also created by administering the Learning Activities Questionnaire and the Learning and Study Strategies Inventory to students at a variety of educational levels.

This work also led to the creation of an experimental, integrated learning strategies curriculum. This curriculum has been implemented in a three-credit lower division course established in the Department of Educational Psychology at the University of Texas at Austin. The preliminary research design and development of this course is described by Underwood (1982). While providing a needed service for students attending The University of Texas, the course, entitled Individual Learning Skills, also provides a real-world laboratory for our project. Both the successes and the problems identified in this course often form the basis for further research.

Course Overview.   Although the students who enroll in this course range from freshmen to seniors, the majority are lower division students. Many students are advised to take the course because they are doing poorly in their studies or have been placed on academic probation. However, a number of the students who take Individual Learning Skills do so because they want to improve their learning ability in preparation for advanced study or graduate programs.

Specific goals for the course are developed individually with each student after a battery of entry measures is administered. These include the Learning and Study Strategies Inventory, the Survey of Study Habits and Attitudes (SSHA) (Brown & Holtzman, 1967), the Trait Anxiety Inventory portion of the State–Trait Anxiety Inventory (STAI) (Spielberger, Gorsuch, & Luschene, 1970), and the Test Attitude Inventory (TAI) (Spielberger, Gonzalez, Taylor, Algaze, & Anton, 1978). In addition to these self-report measures, the Nelson–Denny Reading Test, either Form C or D (Brown, Nelson, & Denny, 1973), is also administered. The information obtained from these measures, from individual interviews, and from group discussions is used in designing the curriculum, individual focus projects, and laboratory exercises.

One of the many problems in designing a course of this nature is that of individualization. This is difficult to achieve with one teacher and 30 students per section. Therefore, given these and other logistical constraints, both group and individual goals are established.

General course goals are that, upon finishing the course, students will: (1) be able to monitor and modify their use of learning strategies; (2) increase their ability to use effective learning strategies; and (3) be able to reduce the stress and negative affect often associated with academic tasks. To help operationalize these goals, a variety of specific content areas is discussed.

Course Content.   Although the specific content varies, general topics include: background information about motivation and cognition, for example, information documenting the importance of being an active learner or discussions of basic cognitive principles and concepts that form the foundation for the course; methods students can use to monitor their understanding and help direct their learning activities, such as stopping periodically while reading and using self-testing to determine if comprehension has occurred; instruction in a variety of information-processing strategies that students can use to help themselves acquire and remember new knowledge, for example, using imaginal or verbal elaboration to create a link between the new, unfamiliar information and already learned information; instruction in more traditional study skills techniques such as note-taking, selecting main ideas and themes, and test taking; and a variety of support skills such as techniques for managing stress, improving negative self-images, improving concentration, and organizing one's study time.

The majority of principles, strategies, and skills discussed in the course can be generalized to a variety of academic content areas. However, much of the training research literature documents the problems of transfer without specific training. We have found that effective methods for dealing with this problem include: (1) referring to a variety of academic content areas when presenting material about learning principles and strategies; (2) directly addressing the issue of transfer when providing examples; (3) providing practice exercises in a variety of content areas; (4) conducting group discussions of strategy or skill use, using a "brainstorming" format; and (5) requiring that students document their use of learning strategies in a journal reviewed by the instructor.

Instructional Methods.   In spite of limited resources and a traditional format of three 1-hour classes per week, the instructional methods used in this course are quite eclectic. Mini-lectures, group discussions, role playing, peer tutoring, and practice-feedback exercises are among the in-class activities. Special sessions are devoted to individual consultation or small-group consultation on a shared problem. Instructional feedback sessions are also conducted for analyzing and evaluating instructional procedures, which are continually being modified as a function of these sessions, other research conducted by our project, and other projects described in the literature.

A critical component in the instructional plan focuses on student activities. In a series of studies we conducted that were designed to identify the key variables involved in learning strategy acquisition, two variables were found to be important: opportunities to *practice* as well as to *receive feedback* about both the new strategies and the kinds of self-monitoring activities necessary for selecting, modifying, and evaluating strategy use. In fact, we discovered that the provision of numerous examples by the instructor prior to student practice and feedback sessions can inhibit strategy acquisition and use, particularly for those strategies that can be characterized as heuristics. For example, the use of elaboration as a knowledge acquisition strategy centers around the general principle of relating to-be-learned information to knowledge already present in the student's semantic network. Unlike an algorithm that specifies the precise steps necessary to achieve a specified goal, such as the directions for building a model, the use of elaboration involves applying a set of general guidelines that must be operationalized, tested, and perhaps modified to meet a specific need. When the instructor provides more than a few examples prior to the students having an opportunity to try out the strategy and practice using it, students may attempt to mimic what they perceive to be the "right" way to use the strategy. That is, novices or individuals attempting to improve their ability to use a learning strategy will often try to copy what they perceive to be a correct method used by an expert. Although this can be capitalized on by the instructor when presenting highly routinized processes or procedures, it is a problem when teaching heuristics.

To help overcome this problem most learning strategies discussed in the course are presented in a cyclic manner. First, the instructor will discuss how the strategy can help address one or more problems described by the students or identified in the entry-level assessments. These discussions are also related to the initial class sessions that cover student motivation, the concept of the active learner, and the need for students to take more responsibility for managing their own learning. Following this, the instructor will identify the key elements of the strategy and provide two or three examples.

Given the state-of-the-art in the learning strategies literature, this is not always an easy task. Much of our research has been directed to identifying the important attributes of a variety of learning strategies. The older literature is replete with folklore and common-sense notions about study skills that only recently are being subjected to more systematic empirical study, and much of the literature on cognitive strategies is too new to offer well-documented procedures. When these problems occur, we must create instructional guidelines based on the data available. These new instructional sequences are then field tested in supplementary studies and in the course itself. This is a challenging and laborious task, but a necessary step toward the development of effective training programs.

In the course, practice exercises are presented after the rationale for a type of strategy is established and the characteristics of the strategy have been discussed. As the issues of transfer and generalization are important, exercises are selected from a variety of content areas, including other courses in which the students are enrolled. During each set of exercises (a set includes a maximum of three tasks), the instructor provides individual feedback and assistance. Following each set of exercises, there is a group feedback and discussion session that also incorporates an expanded discussion of the strategy. For certain topics, such as setting up a weekly time schedule, this amount of in-class practice and discussion might be sufficient, whereas for other topics, such as comprehension monitoring during reading, it is not. For the more complex or difficult strategies, additional practice and feedback discussions are provided.

Out-of-class assignments are also used. These assignments take a variety of forms. A journal describing progress on individual problems is updated on a weekly basis. Short papers describing particular strategy applications and problems encountered are also completed on a weekly basis. Practice exercises and guidelines for practicing in other classes are provided at each class meeting.

As the student's repertoire of strategies develops, attention is also given to integrating the use of various strategies into more comprehensive learning and study systems, in which individual strategies can be used in a coordinated fashion. Students are taught how individual strategies relate to one another and the holistic properties of systematic approaches to learning and study are discussed. These discussions occur frequently throughout the semester. There are also periodic review sessions and special problem sessions where individuals or small groups can be helped to improve their use of one or more specific strategies.

Evaluation Data.   In addition to the various problem papers, homework assignments, and quiz grades, performance changes are also assessed by a battery of postcourse measures. These include a readministration of the entry-level measures as well as responses to simulated student learning problems. The results have been very exciting. Significant increases in performance on a variety of tasks have been demonstrated. For example, students have made substantial gains in reading comprehension as measured by the Nelson–Denny Reading Test. At the beginning of the course, the average score for the entire group was at the 44th percentile; at the end of the course, the average score was at the 65th percentile—a gain of 21 points. For students whose scores on the Nelson–Denny upon entering the course were in the bottom one-third, there were even larger gains; these students demonstrated average gains of 45 points. In addition, self-reported levels of anxiety have been reduced and the use of effective learning and study strategies has increased. Follow-up studies of student grade-point averages also demonstrate significant gains.

Indirect evidence is also provided by the increasing number of students registering for the course and the feedback from academic advisors about students who have participated. Despite the relatively heavy work load in this class, students suggest it to their friends and listed it as a top priority for students on academic probation.

However, these findings are difficult to interpret due to the lack of control data. We have encountered a number of obstacles to obtaining an appropriate control group, for example: Although the enrollment has increased each semester, we are still able to accommodate all students wishing to enroll, which precludes the use of a waiting-list control group. Few courses have as diverse a student enrollment as this course, but even for those that do, (1) the students are not comparable, for example, in terms of motivational levels; and (2) even the most cooperative instructors feel imposed upon when asked to donate from three to six class periods for research purposes. The use of volunteers would present its own unique set of problems with respect to comparability. Thus, appropriate comparison data are not available at this time, but we are able to demonstrate significant improvements during the semester for students enrolled in the course.

The Metacurriculum—An Alternative Training Method

Providing an adjunct course or program for teaching learning strategies is just one method of imparting this knowledge to students. Part of our research has focused on the role of content-area teachers in high schools and community colleges in developing students' learning strategies. Teaching students how to learn and process knowledge more effectively is a metacurriculum that can be included in any content-area course. By using teaching and instructional methods that cue, demonstrate, and reinforce the use of learning strategies, instructors can enhance their students' ability to be independent and effective learners while also teaching the content-specific material in a course. Incorporating this meta-curriculum into content-based curricula enhances student learning in both areas.

As teachers, we have many opportunities to teach learning competencies while we are teaching the knowledge, skills, and attitudes that comprise our content areas. In fact, it is almost impossible to separate effective teaching strategies from effective learning strategies in a didactic interaction. Many effective teaching strategies are just the flipside of effective learning strategies. The teacher who gives a variety of examples of a principle is trying to make contact with the individual experiential backgrounds of his or her students. The instructor who creates an analogy that relates the topic under study to an everyday phenomenon is trying to help the students use knowledge they already possess to elaborate on the new information and make it more meaningful. Converting these teaching strategies to a learning strategies metacurriculum involves making these effective teaching processes more explicit and incorporating discussions and examples of learning competencies that may not have been included before.

For example, in introducing the court system used in the United States, teachers often try to relate legal forms of settling disputes to their students' experience with arguments and disagreements. They compare the judge to the teacher, parent, or police officer who tries to settle the differences, or to decide who is to blame for the damage. The jury may be compared to a group of friends who try to help two members of a group settle a dispute, and so on. Clearly, the instructor is trying to help his or her students understand the court system by relating the components to their own experiences and previous knowledge by creating analogies. With very little effort, this excellent teaching device could also be used as part of the metacurriculum for teaching learning strategies simply by making the technique explicit. Instead of just presenting these analogies and then continuing with the class, the teacher could take a few moments and draw attention to the method being used, why he or she thought it would help the students learn the new information, and how they could use this technique on their own when studying. Clearly, this one experience would not be sufficient for most students to learn to use analogies as an information-processing strategy, but repeated exposures to this technique in a variety of contexts over time, along with prompting and corrective feedback, can contribute to students' development of effective learning strategies.

Thus far, we have only produced pilot programs to train teachers to implement a learning strategies metacurriculum. Results in both high school and community college settings have been very encouraging. Teacher interest and motivation have been high, even though the training sessions are usually conducted after normal working hours. Follow-up data indicate student performance gains after a 6-month interval. In a time of budget cuts and limited resources, this cost-effective training method is worthy of further investigation. Part of our future focus will concentrate in this area.

CONCLUDING COMMENTS

This chapter has presented a brief survey of learning strategies research and an overview of some training studies being conducted by the Cognitive Learning Strategies Project. If, as educators, we expect individuals to take greater responsibility for their learning and to have the skills necessary to adapt the learning environment to fit their needs and goals, then we should be able systematically to teach students to use effective learning strategies. Research is still needed to address a number of basic issues in this area: (1) identifying the types of strategies used by successful learners; (2) investigating the nature and critical attributes of those strategies; (3) selecting the most important strategies to teach; (4) developing assessment methods for identifying individual learner deficits; (5) developing instructional methodologies and curriculum materials to teach learning strategies; (6) creating appropriate assessment instruments for training programs; and (7) fostering generalization of the use of these strategies across different content areas. A number of efforts to address these issues are discussed in this book, but reaching the goal of teaching students to be active learners who use effective information-processing strategies will require the combined efforts of cognitive psychologists, educational psychologists, instructional psychologists, curriculum developers, and classroom teachers.

ACKNOWLEDGMENTS

The research reported in this chapter was supported in part by Contract No. DAHC19–76–0026 with the Defense Advanced Research Projects Agency (monitored by the Army Research Institute for the Behavioral and Social Sciences), Contract No. B505 with the Spencer Foundation, and Contract No. MDA903–79–C–0391 with the Army Research Institute for Behavioral and Social Sciences. Views and conclusions contained in this chapter are those of the authors and should not be interpreted as necessarily representing the official policies, either expressed or implied, of the Defense Advanced Research Projects Agency, the Spencer Foundation, the Army Research Institute, or of the United States government.

We would like to thank the following staff members of the Cognitive Learning Strategies Project for their assistance in conducting the research for this chapter: Marianne Poythress, Ann Schulte, Eduardo Cascallar, Cassie Schmidt, Pat Butterfield, Magdalena Rood, Celeste Conlon, Thomas Kennedy, Mary Morrow, and Cathy Comstock. We would also like to thank Diane Schallert and Ann Schulte for reviewing an earlier draft.

REFERENCES

Anastasi, A. *Psychological testing*. New York: Macmillan, 1976.

Anderson, R. C., Spiro, R. J., & Montague, W. E. (Eds.) *Schooling and the acquistion of knowledge*. Hillsdale, N. J.: Lawrence Erlbaum Associates, 1977.

Anderson, T. H. Study skills and learning strategies. In H. F. O'Neil, Jr., & C. D. Spielberger (Eds.), *Cognitive and affective learning strategies*. New York: Academic Press, 1979.

Brown, J. I., Nelson, M. J., & Denny, E. C. *The Nelson-Denny Reading Test*. Boston: Houghton Mifflin, 1973.

Brown, W. F. *Effective study test*. San Marcos, Tex.: Effective Study Materials, 1964.

Brown, W. F., & Holtzman, W. H. *Survey of study habits and attitudes*. New York: The Psychological Corporation, 1967.

Carter, H. D. *California study methods survey*. Monterey, Calif.: California Test Bureau, 1958.

Christensen, F. A. *College adjustment and study skills inventory*. Berea, Ohio: Personal Growth Press, Inc., 1968.

Cross, K. P. *The junior college: A research description*. Princeton: Educational Testing Service, 1969.

Dansereau, D. F., Collins, K. W., McDonald, B.A., Holley, C. C. D., Garland, J., Diekhoff, G., & Evans, S. H. Development and evaluation of a learning strategy training program. *Journal of Educational Psychology*, 1979, *71*, 64–73.

Dansereau, D. F., Long, G. L., McDonald, B. A., & Actkinson, T.R. *Learning strategy inventory development and assessment* (AFHRL–TR–75–40). Lowry AFB, Colo.: Air Force Human Resources Laboratory, 1975.

Goldman, R., & Warren, R. Discriminant analysis of study strategies connected with college grade success in different major fields. *Journal of Educational Measurement*, 1973, *10*, 39–47.

Golinkoff, R. A. A comparison of reading comprehension processes in good and poor comprehenders. *Reading Research Quarterly*, 1976, *11*, 623–659.

McCombs, B. L. *Transitioning learning strategies research into practice: Focus on the student in technical training*. Paper presented at the meeting of the American Educational Research Association, Los Angeles, April 1981.

Meyer, B. J. F. *Signaling in text*. Paper presented at the meeting of the American Educational Research Association, Boston, April 1980.

Miller, G. A. Magical number seven, plus or minus two: Some limits on our capacity for processing information. *Psychological Review*, 1956, *63*, 81–97.

Monroe, A., Fegan, M., & Scott, R. *Matching instruction with district goals and assessment: A strategy for school improvement*. Paper presented to the American Association of School Administrators, Boston, February 1980.

Navon, D. Forest before trees: The precedence of global features in visual perception. *Cognitive Psychology*, 1977, *9*, 353–383.

Paivio, A. *Imagery and verbal processes*. New York: Holt, Rinehart, & Winston, 1971.

Reder, L. M. The role of elaboration in the comprehension and retention of prose: A critical review. *Review of Educational Research*, 1980, *50*, 5–53.

Rohwer, W. D., Jr. Images and pictures in children's learning. *Psychological Bulletin*, 1970, *73*, 393–403.

Rohwer, W. D., Jr. Elaboration and learning in childhood and adolescence. In H. W. Reese (Ed.), *Advances in child development* (Vol. 8). New York: Academic Press, 1973.

Rohwer, W. D., Jr., & Ammon, M. S. Elaboration training and paired-associate learning efficiency in children. *Journal of Educational Psychology*, 1971, *62*, 373–386.

Ryan, E. B. Identifying and remediating failures in reading comprehension: Toward an instructional approach for poor comprehenders. In T. G. Waller & G. E. MacKinnon (Eds.), *Advances in reading research* (Vol. 2). New York: Academic Press, 1980.

Schmeck, R. R., & Grove, E. Academic achievement and individual differences in learning processes. *Applied Psychological Measurement*, 1979, *3*, 43–49.

Schmeck, R. R., & Ribich, F. D. Construct validation of the Inventory of Learning Processes. *Applied Psychological Measurement*, 1978, *2*, 551–562.

Schmeck, R. R., Ribich, F. D., & Ramanaiah, N. Development of a self-report inventory for assessing individual differences in learning processes. *Applied Psychological Measurement*, 1977, *1*, 413–431.

Schulte, A. C., & Weinstein, C. E. *Inventories to assess cognitive learning strategies.* Paper presented at the meeting of the American Educational Research Association, Los Angeles, April 1981.

Spielberger, C. D., Gonzalez, H. P, Taylor, C. J., Algaze, B., & Anton, W. D. Examination stress and test anxiety. In C. D. Spielberger & I. G. Sarason (Eds.), *Anxiety and stress* (Vol. 5). New York: Hemisphere/Wiley, 1978.

Spielberger, C.D., Gorsuch, R. L., & Luschene, R. E. *Manual for the State–Trait Anxiety Inventory.* Palo Alto, Calif.: Consulting Psychologists Press, 1970.

Sticht, T. G. Developing literacy and learning strategies in organizational settings. In H. F. O'Neil, Jr., & C. D. Spielberger (Eds.), *Cognitive and affective learning strategies*. New York: Academic Press, 1979.

Svensson, L. On qualitative differences in learning: III—Study skill and learning. *British Journal of Educational Psychology*, 1977, *47*, 233–243.

Underwood, V. L. *Self-management skills for college students: A program in how to learn.* Unpublished doctoral dissertation, University of Texas, 1982.

Weinstein, C. E. *Learning of elaboration strategies.* Unpublished doctoral dissertation, University of Texas, 1975.

Weinstein, C. E. Teaching cognitive elaboration learning strategies. In H. F. O' Neil, Jr. (Ed.), *Learning strategies*. New York: Academic Press, 1978.

Weinstein, C. E. A metacurriculum for remediating learning strategies deficits in academically underprepared students. In L. Noel & R. Levitz (Eds.), *How to succeed with academically underprepared students*. Iowa City: American College Testing Service National Center for Advancing Educational Practice, 1982.

Weinstein, C. E., & Underwood, V. L. Teaching cognitive learning strategies. In R. Glaser & J. Lompscher (Eds.), *Cognitive and motivational aspects of instruction*. New York: North–Holland Publishing Company, 1982.

Weinstein, C. E., Underwood, V. L., Wicker, F. W., & Cubberly, W. E. Cognitive learning strategies: Verbal and imaginal elaboration. In H. F. O'Neil, Jr., & C. D. Spielberger (Eds.), *Cognitive and affective learning strategies*. New York: Academic Press, 1979.

Weinstein, C. E., Wicker, F. W., Cubberly, W. E., Roney, L. K., & Underwood, V. L. *Design and development of the Learning Activities Questionnaire* (Tech. Rep. No. 459). Alexandria, Va.: U.S. Army Research Institute for the Behavioral and Social Sciences, August, 1980.

Wittrock, M. C. Learning as a generative process. *Educational Psychologist*, 1974, *11*, 87–95.

Wittrock, M. C. The cognitive movement in instruction. *Educational Psychologist*, 1978, *13*, 15–29.

7 Teaching Cognitive Strategies and Text Structures Within Language Arts Programs

Beau Fly Jones
Chicago Public Schools

MindaRae Amiran
State University of New York at Fredonia

Michael Katims
University of Texas at Austin

As even a casual glance at these volumes will indicate, in recent years psychologists have acquired many new insights concerning the nature of effective learning strategies. As new knowledge has accumulated, some of it has begun to work its way into the school curriculum in the form of systematic instruction in learning strategies. In this chapter, we describe two sets of curriculum materials that offer students instruction in strategies for acquiring, analyzing, and reporting on information from texts. These materials are: Matrix Outlining and Analysis (MOAN) and the Chicago Mastery Learning Reading Program with Learning Strategies (CMLR/LS).

MOAN (Amiran, Jones, & Fridell, 1980) offers instruction in a novel system of outlining in which a body of information is translated into a matrix or two-dimensional scale so that items can be easily compared along a variety of dimensions. Students receiving instruction in this system are taught how to use matrices as devices for remembering, analyzing, and reporting on comparative information. They are also taught how to use matrices as aids in systematically producing effective compare-and-contrast type essays. MOAN may be used as one component of an English composition course in high school or college, or as a core developmental course for low achieving junior college students.

CMLR/LS is a set of instructional materials in reading for grades K–8 developed by the Chicago Public Schools (Chicago Board of Education, 1980). These materials were field tested in various Chicago public schools in 1978–81, and

259

are now being implemented on a citywide basis. As the title indicates, each unit of instruction is organized according to principles of mastery learning. However, unlike other mastery learning curricula, these materials also offer systematic instruction in learning strategies and teach students how to apply a range of learning strategies to the different kinds of texts they are likely to encounter in school. In the sections that follow, we first describe MOAN, then CMLR/LS, and then offer some concluding remarks about instruction in learning strategies.

MATRIX OUTLINING AND ANALYSIS

Because matrix outlining is applicable only to information that can be simultaneously classified along two dimensions, we begin our presentation of MOAN with some examples of this kind of information, and with a discussion of the frequency with which students are likely to encounter information of this kind in school situations. We then describe the knowledge base that underlies MOAN. That is, we discuss what we have learned from basic research about the techniques individuals use to learn two-dimensional information and ways to improve their learning. Next, we describe current MOAN instructional materials, giving the reader a sense of how they have evolved from basic research understanding. Finally, we discuss some issues associated with the evaluation of these materials.

Types of Information that Can Be Analyzed Through Use of Matrix Outlining

As already indicated, matrix outlining is a technique that can help one organize a body of facts for purposes of making systematic comparisons. When using matrix outlining, one forms a two-dimensional table or matrix, with the names of the things being compared serving as column headings and their attributes serving as row headings. For example, when trying to compare two complex historical events like World War I and World War II, one might try to organize one's facts about these events into a matrix with the names "World War I" and "World War II" serving as column headings and the categories along which they can be compared (causes of war, outcomes of war, etc.) serving as row headings. Organizing the facts into a matrix helps to simplify the data by making it possible to combine items into categories. This makes the data easier to grasp, describe, and remember. Organizing the facts into a matrix also helps to analyze the data by permitting one to look across categories so that patterns and underlying relationships become easier to notice. Matrices can be applied to any set of data where the goal is to make comparisons. For example, a matrix could include data about objects, events, people, places, ideas, theories, etc. More generally, matrices can be useful for making comparisons across any set of categories to which one can assign names. Because matrices help one look across sets of "name" categories in terms of their attributes, they can be described in an abstract way as name–attribute classifications.

Because so many formal educational experiences involve making systematic comparisons, matrix outlining can be a useful technique in helping students cope with the school curriculum. From elementary school on, students are frequently confronted with assignments to write compare-and-contrast essays. Even when they are not explicitly told to make systematic comparisons, doing so may help them more readily assimilate a body of knowledge. Musgrave and Cohen (1971) go so far as to describe all the information in school content-area textbooks as having an underlying name–attribute structure that students need to grasp if they are to understand the content covered in the text. Some school texts in fact follow a fairly overt name–attribute organizational framework in presenting information to students. Consider, for example, a social studies text that defines selected institutions such as government or religion by giving examples from difference societies, or a biology text that defines different processes or systems by describing them in various plants and animals. Other texts follow other organizational principles, but often contain facts that can be more easily grasped if students spontaneously make systematic name–attribute comparisons while reading.

Improving Students' Ability to Learn and Remember Comparative Information: Experiments Leading to the Development of MOAN

The MOAN instructional materials grow out of a body of research investigating how students learn comparative information and how their learning can be improved. We now turn to this research.

Over the past decade, a series of studies has investigated the problem of learning about persons, places, and things and their attributes. These studies have asked whether such information is easier to learn when it is organized by name or by attribute, or when it is presented in a random fashion. This work has employed a task originally developed by Frase (1969). In this task students are given sets of sentences describing names of objects (chess pieces) and their attributes. Some sets are ordered by name, some are ordered by attribute, and some are randomly ordered. One major finding from this research is that ordered information is easier to remember than unordered information (Frase, 1969; see also Myers, Pezdek, & Coulson, 1973). A related finding is that instructing students to use the name or attribute organization underlying a passage enhances the recall (Di Vesta, Schultz, & Dangel, 1973; Perlmutter & Royer, 1973). Because ordered information is easier to remember, one might expect that telling students to impose a name or attribute organization on random sentences might also enhance recall. Surprisingly, however, this type of intervention did not yield improvements in recall (Di Vesta et al., 1973; Perlmutter & Royer, 1973).

The finding that ordererd information is easier to learn and remember than unordered information has important implications for schools because, although many textbooks are organized by name or attribute categories, some are poorly organized. Moreover, much of the material that students need to learn comes to them in an unorganized fashion. That is, from junior high to college, students are required to search through diverse sources of information such as texts, lectures, and discussions to find some way of organizing and integrating their content. Because information is easier to recall when it is organized, what is needed, it would seem, is some method of translating the unorganized information into a structured, ordered form. Jones (1976) hypothesized that a more extensive training intervention than previous researchers had used might be necessary to teach students how to impose name or attribute organization on unordered information. Whereas previous researchers had simply told students to group sentences by name or attribute categories, Jones created a step-by-step instructional program for teaching college students how to do this.

Study I. In this study college students were randomly assigned to a cross-classification training group or to a control group involving unrelated training. The cross-classification training consisted of two phases. First, step-by-step instructions showed students how to place information from a set of randomly ordered sentences into a name–attribute matrix. More specifically, the students were told to: (1) scan the sentences to establish what name and attribute categories are involved; (2) make a two-dimensional table such that the column headings correspond to the name categories and the row headings correspond to the attribute categories; (3) fill in the appropriate information in the cells working sentence by sentence. Second, the students were instructed to memorize the information in the table in a serial order. That is, they were told to rehearse the attribute values listed under each name in the same fixed order in which they appeared in the table, as items in a list.

Cross-classification was found to be effective both on an immediate and on a delayed recall test. The mean number of sentences recalled by the trained and control groups were 25.47 and 17.37 respectively ($p_1 < .001$), of a total of 36 sentences. Trained students not only recalled more sentences, but also gave evidence that they were using the serial memory strategy in which they were trained—that is, for each name category, they systematically produced attribute values in a fixed order. On a surprise posttest administered a week after training, the experimental students again manifested greater recall and followed the same serial order strategy they had produced earlier, despite the fact that this posttest involved different content-related cues than were available in the original learning situation. Thus, four important findings emerged from this research: (1) that students could be taught to cross-classify unorganized, comparative information; (2) that this strategy enhanced their ability to remember the information; (3) that students were able to produce this strategy successfully on the delayed posttest without strategy prompts; and (4) that in cross-classifying the information, the students appeared to be learning an underlying structure for it, even when they were given different content-related cues to access the information.

Study II.   Study I demonstrated that college students could improve their performance in free-recall situations by learning to cross-classify comparative information. However, field observations in junior high schools indicated that students are seldom required to provide information on a free-recall basis. Most often, they are requirerd to provide information for a multiply-choice test or for a compare-and-contrast essay. This observation raised the question: To what extent could cross-classification training be adapted to facilitate performance on either of these test situations? Pilot analysis of the two test situations indicated that whereas cross-classification training seemed to be largely irrelevant to multiple-choice tests, it was highly appropriate for answering compare-and-contrast essay questions. For example, to compare and contrast day-care education in the United States and Israel, it is necessary to specify the attribute categories for day-care education and then systematically compare this type of education in two name categories: the United States and Israel. Moreover, research conducted by Davis (1976) indicates that listing and rearranging attributes relative to name categories greatly stimulates the production of analytical statements.

Accordingly, Jones and Hall (1979) reasoned that, because MOAN forces the learner to list and rearrange attributes, it could be a useful tool in helping students analyze comparative information for purposes of writing compare-and-contrast essays. More specifically, they reasoned that forming a matrix would make it easier for students to notice similarities and differences among name categories because, within the matrix, information for the different name categories would be immediately adjacent. To illustrate, for the attribute "number of hours spent in a day-care facility," one could notice immediately from examining a matrix whether the number was the same or different for the countries being compared. Jones and Hall further reasoned that matrices could serve as systematic guides in helping students organize compare-and-contrast essays. That is, the analytical statements produced by looking across each attribute row in the matrix could serve as topic sentences for paragraphs in the essay. Thus, one could produce an effective essay simply by drawing conclusions from each attribute row of the matrix, using these as topic sentences for paragraphs, and supporting them with details taken from appropriate cells in the matrix. For example, in an essay on day-care education in Israel and the United States, one topic sentence drawn from the matrix might be that American children spend more hours in day-care centers than do Israeli children. This sentence could be supported in a paragraph using numbers and details from appropriate cells in the matrix.

Study II compared the performance of students who were randomly assigned to a cross-classification training group with that of a control group receiving unrelated training. This time, cross-classification training included not only the step-by-step instruction given in Study I for putting information into a matrix, but also training in using a matrix as an aid in organizing a compare-and-contrast essay. This training consisted of teaching seventh graders: (1) to make analytical statements based on information in the rows of the matrix; and (2) to use these statements as topic sentences in determining the paragraph structure for their essays. During the course of instruction, the students were asked to write four essays. Three involved content they had covered in school that year. The fourth involved content that was independent of specific course materials.

It was evident from analysis of the recall posttests that cross-classification training facilitated recall of unordered information for younger students in much the same way that it had facilitated recall for college students. The trained seventh graders remembered many more items and remembered them in a more systematic order than did the untrained students. More important, however, the trained students also produced more effective essays. The essays were scorerd by external reviewers for: (1) the presence of a topic sentence for each paragraph, (2) the quality of the topic sentence, and (3) the amount of information presented in support of the topic sentence. On all these measures, regardless of the content of the essay, the trained students scored significantly higher than the untrained students.

Although Study II further documented the usefulness of matrix outlining as a learning strategy, it also identified some limitations in the instructional materials used in the study. One limitation was that the materials did not devote sufficient attention to the problem of helping students discover on their own which attribute categories to use in making comparisons. The four essay posttests used in Study II varied in the amount of help students were given in identifying specific attributes to include in their matrices. On the three posttests where students were given direct instruction as to which attribute categories to use, either during training or as part of the posttest question itself, they wrote excellent essays. However, on the fourth posttest where the students had to discover appropriate attribute categories on their own, their essays were of a markedly inferior quality. This suggests that a critical problem for essay instruction at the junior high school level is that students lack world knowledge concerning the dimensions that are important in comparing different kinds of content.

A second limitation of the Study II training materials was that although the matrices were useful in helping students organize their essays into topic sentences and supporting details, they did not go very far in helping them analyze the body of facts contained in the matrix. In other words, the training materials helped students describe a set of name categories in terms of several attribute dimensions, but did not help them understand the rich diversity of underlying relationships among variables in the matrix—relations that, if analyzed, would add greatly to their understanding of the subject matter at hand. Thus, using the findings from Studies I and II as encouraging evidence supporting the potential usefulness of matrix outlining, we proceeded to develop a more comprehensive set of instructional materials to address the limitations just noted.

Description of Current MOAN Materials

An entirely new set of materials was developed by Amiran, Jones, and Fridell (1980) to address the limitations of the Jones and Hall study. The new materials seek to train college and high school students to select attribute categories as well as to produce a broad range of analytical statements and inferences systematically. The problem of training students to select appropriate attribute categories was solved in part by instructing them to utilize headings, subheadings, and other emphasis devices in prose passages, and in part by instructing them to make marginal notes. The problem of expanding the number of analytical statements was solved by expanding the matrix structure to include space for main ideas, details, and inferences as well as inductive and deductive generalizations (See Table 1).

Altogether, the students are instructed to make 15 different types of analytical statements, several of which are illustrated in the following paragraphs. Students are taught to make four different types of generalizations within individual rows and columns: identification of patterns and trends in a row or column, analysis of factors underlying these patterns and trends, predictions based on the observed patterns and trends, and causal analysis or interpretation of the observed patterns and trends. Students are also taught to analyze the meaning of information within each cell, to make comparisons and notice covariances between rows or columns, to specify the relationships between specific examples and the generalizations they support, and to analyze the meaning of titles. For each of these 15 types of analytical statements, students are given definitions, examples, guided practice, and independent practice using exercises that provide extensive feedback as to errors. Thus, the new materials provide instruction not only in organizing information into a matrix, but also in using a variety of strategies to analyze this information—strategies that would presumably be labeled "structural schemata" in schema theory terminology (Rumelhart & Ortony, 1977).

In the example in Table 1, for instance, an appropriate row generalization (topic sentence) for Row 2 (enjoyment) would be as follows: In the mid-19th century, it was believed that childhood was essentially a happy time for most children, whereas in the mid-20th century the predominant view was that childhood was a time of psychological crisis. This topic sentence could then be supported by reference to the details given in Cells 2a and 2b. The paragraph could be elaborated or extended to include inferences as to (1) why it was believed that childhood was a happy time in the mid-19th century, and (2) why mid-20th century ideas were different (e.g., some reference to Freud), as well as row causal inferences as to why the change of ideas came about. Here the writer could refer to societal conditions that fostered the growth of psychoanalytical views of childhood. Column generalizations could include summary statements to the effect that mid-19th century ideas presented children as basically innocent with regard to morality, enjoyment, and knowledge. Additional statements that could be made in the concluding paragraph might include (1) a probability statement suggesting that perhaps children were seen as innocent in other ways, (2) reasons for this proposition, and (3) parallel probability statement about mid-20th century ideas about children.

These analytical and organizing strategies are reinforced by a scoring system that is used by both teacher *and* students. The scoring card lists each type of

TABLE 7.1.
Sample Expanded Matrix Outline Structure: Historical Comparison of Ideas about Children

	Mid-Nineteenth Century Ideas	Mid-Twentieth Century Ideas	Row Generalizations
Morality #1	1a	1b	
main ideas propositions	Children are entirely good and innocent, but society may corrupt them.	Children have strong impulses that have to be modified (socialized) so they can live with other people.	summary conclusions causal inference and reasons
		Children need love and care; otherwise they will grow up poorly adjusted.	
details examples reasons	Children are trusting and friendly with all. Children of robbers may be taught to steal.	Children are naturally jealous of their siblings. Most delinquents are unwanted.	probability statement and reasons
Inference			
Enjoyment #2	2a	2b	
main ideas propositions	Childhood is the happiest time of life, unless the child is orphaned, handicapped, or very poor.	Childhood is a time for inner conflict and confusion. For lucky children, it may be a happy time.	summary conclusions causal inference and reasons
details examples reasons	Children laugh and play a lot. Children don't have to worry about things.	Most children have a hard time finding out who they are. Children are afraid of things.	probability statement and reasons
Inference			

Knowledge #3	3a	3b	
main ideas propositions	Children suspect nothing about the motives of others and have a very limited understanding of everything.	Children are aware of much of what goes on around them and are deeply interested in adult motives.	summary conclusions causal inference supporting information probability statement and reasons
details examples reasons	Children don't suspect anyone has bad motives. Children believe in the tooth fairy.	Children love to eavesdrop.	
Inference			
Column Generalizations	summary/conclusions causal inference and reasons probability statement and reasons	summary/conclusions causal inference and reasons probability statement and reasons	

sentence that is needed for an A grade for writing a compare-and-contrast essay. The card also provides scoring criteria for each kind of sentence that receives more than one point. Students use the card as a checklist during the process of writing to identify precisely the type and order of each kind of sentence that is needed; the score card is therefore an additional prompt. The teacher then uses the same card to score each sentence in the essay. This method of scoring is highly analytical as compared to the more holistic methods that teachers typically use. However, it is far less cumbersome than existing analytical scoring methods. This method of scoring also allows teachers and researchers to separate entirely the scoring of organization from the scoring of content. A modified version of this method was developed and field tested by Amiran (1980) as part of the Chicago Criterion-Referenced Testing Program for high school.

These newly developed materials are contained in a large student workbook of several hundred pages. The book is divided into three main parts plus two appendices. Part I, *Text Matrices*, guides the student to construct matrices and essays using expository and/or narrative texts. Part II, *Fiction Matrices,* guides the student to construct matrices and essays using excerpts from actual pieces of fiction. Part III, *Research Matrices*, guides the student to construct matrices that integrate information from multiple sources, as is necessary in writing research papers. In each section the student must write two or more complete essays. The instructional materials are sequenced so that the student works first with activities that are simple and concrete and later with activities that are increasingly complex and abstract. The final test for this section requires integrating information from 11 different sources, each of which simulates a different reference source and genre such as a news article, a documented text, a propaganda statement, or a survey.

Appendices in MOAN provide model test questions and schemata (matrix structures) for understanding literary and social science texts. Each type of text, such as a novel or research paper, is described as having an underlying structure that can be analyzed in terms of two dimensions. A "disaster novel," for example, can be viewed as the description of different characters' responses (one dimension) at various periods of time with regard to the disaster (the other dimension). The macrostructure of such a novel can be analyzed into a matrix with character names as the name categories and with time periods (before, during, and after) as attribute categories. The category headings can be either simple or complex. Complex categories are ones that can be further subdivided (e.g., there may be several phases during the disaster or its aftermath).

Issues Related to the Evaluation of MOAN

Initially, it was planned to evaluate one or more of the parts of MOAN in a series of closely monitored studies, using randomly selected low achieving students in high school or junior college. This investigation was not carried out because field tests using junior college students admitted under an open admissions policy indicated that the materials were too difficult. Recently Jones and Katims along with Anderson and Armbruster reconceptualized MOAN to take on some of the capabilities of mapping. This was part of a school/university collaboration with the Chicago Public Schools and the Center for the Study of Reading, University of Illinois at Champaign. The collaboration involves staff from both institutions working together to develop materials to improve social studies instruction.

In the absence of empirical data, we can begin to consider the practical usefulness of MOAN by asking the question: What does MOAN do that is not done by such systems as: *network outlining* (see Dansereau, McDonald, Collins, Garland, Holley, Diekhoff, & Evans, 1979), the *Socratic tutorial method* (Collins, 1977 and Volume 2 of this series; see also Resnick, 1977, modification), *semantic analysis* (Bereiter & Scardamalia, 1982), and *mapping* (T. H. Anderson, 1979; Armbruster, & T. H. Anderson, 1980)? All of these methods, including MOAN, seek to help students cope with typical school knowledge acquisition and analytical tasks by giving them insight into the organizational framework underlying various forms of discourse. Each method provides rules for: (1) identifying the ideas and relationships among ideas underlying segments of text; (2) elaborating these ideas; and (3) with the exception of Collins, using these as the basis for generating different kinds of essays and other products.

However, each method focuses on a different task and therefore a different thinking/writing paradigm. Although MOAN addresses both descriptive and expository tasks, clearly it focuses heavily on the cross-classification paradigm in which thinking and writing proceed through steps involving simultaneous encoding and analysis of information along two dimensions. Network outlining involves outlining information on a hierarchical network that represents relations within and between sets of ideas. In contrast to matrix outlining, the thinking and writing process underlying network outlining is basically a series of linear paths whose branches are followed sequentially through each level of information. Like MOAN, network outlining can be used to address many different tasks but is most appropriate for representing and analyzing expository, narrative, and persuasive texts and is not well suited for compare-and-contrast analysis. Collins' Socratic method helps students represent complex causal chains in which large numbers of factors interact with one another. These factors can have both linear and nonlinear relations. In contrast to network outlining, the Socratic method requires integrating information from diverse sources. Semantic analysis also involves integrating information from more than one source, but the outline structure that is developed and the kinds of compositions that can be written from this method involve persuasive and other superordinate/subordinate genres rather than compare-and-contrast or causal analysis. Mapping is a method of processing information in which the learner classifies relationships within and among sentences according to meaning *and* type of information (temporal, name/ attribute, etc.) and arranges them in a visual display. It is most useful for situations when one needs to learn many different types and levels of information.

Thus, it would seem that each method of outlining is best suited to a particular type of analysis and writing assignment.

Another way to assess the practical usefulness of MOAN is to consider how well it provides instruction for each phase of organization and writing. According to criteria developed by Hayes and Flower (1980); Flower & Hayes, in press), there are four phases of developing a composition: generating ideas, organizing levels and topics in terms of the writing goal and the audience, translating the organizational structure into writing, and reviewing/editing—each of which has numerous levels and specific procedures. Generally speaking, MOAN provides instructions for each phase, level, and procedure, including those for selecting topics as well as those for constructing overall organization, paragraphs, and clauses. However, MOAN does not provide instruction regarding audience, author's purpose, cohesiveness (cf. Bracewell, Fine, & Ezergaile, 1980), or reformulation of previous points of view to account for conflicting information (Bereiter & Scardamalia, 1982). At the same time, MOAN does generate famil-iarity with the compare-and-contrast test and text grammars (Bereiter & Scar-damalia, 1982; Hidi & Hilyard, 1980), inferences from texts involving large distances between reference points (Whiting, 1980), and, most important of all, a closure in outline and composition structure that forces the individual: (1) to analyze systematically all possible relations once the matrix is constructed; and (2) to be aware of missing information in empty cells.

To summarize, MOAN emerged from two strands of research. First, a series of passage organization studies indicated that college students spontaneously used name or attribute category clustering and serial order strategies to learn organized information but did not use the same cross-classification strategies to learn unorganized information. Explicit instruction to organize the unorganized information into a two-dimensional matrix and then learn it as lists in serial order generated the same pattern of organization and high recall in randomly organized passages as that obtained in previous studies for passages organized by name and attribute. Secondly, work with seventh graders indicated that matrix outlining and analysis training could be useful not only in improving memory for com-parative information, but also in facilitating writing performance on compare-and-contrast essays. Both lines of research led to the development of current MOAN materials that teach students how to use matrices as memory aids, as tools for analyzing comparative information in sophisticated ways, and as aids in organizing effective compare-and-contrast essays.

THE CHICAGO MASTERY LEARNING READING PROGRAM WITH LEARNING STRATEGIES

The Chicago Mastery Learning Reading Program with Learning Strategies is a structured, K–8 instructional program in reading developed by the Chicago public schools to be used in conjunction with the stories of a basal reader. Like MOAN,

CMLR/LS is an attempt to offer students systematic instruction in learning strategies, building on current ideas in the research literature as to the nature of effective strategies. We begin our discussion of CMLR/LS with a brief review of the practical problems the Chicago public schools were trying to address in developing this program. We then describe the instructional material used in the program, giving the reader a sense of the learning strategies that are taught, the teaching methods that are used, and the mastery learning context in which instruction occurs. Next, we discuss the theoretical ideas underlying the program, indicating how our theories about learning strategies instruction evolved as we confronted the task of engaging in a large scale curriculum development effort. Finally, we discuss the effectiveness of the program.

Practical Problems Addressed Through Development of CMLR/LS Materials

CMLR/LS was addressed to two sets of problems: the problem of low student achievement in reading and the problem of creating an instructional program that could be successfully used in hundreds of different classrooms—a factor that is almost never considered in developing experimental materials. Chicago has about a half-million students, most of whom are 1-to-3 years behind in reading. These students are housed in about 440 schools with 18,000 teachers. Before the current promotion policy, Chicago schools were organized in an ungraded continuous progress structure involving 1,500 objectives that spanned 13 reading levels. Of these, 273 were selected as key objectives for assessment by a criterion-referenced test. In order to be promoted from one level to the next, students were required to pass 80% of the key objectives at each reading level. Under this system, there were several problems of instruction, including: an unwieldy number of objectives and tests; a lack of standardized, effective instructional materials directly addressed to key objectives; a lack of effective mechanisms to accelerate the pace of instruction for the low achieving students; high rates of mobility among students and teachers due to absenteeism and transfer; and, finally, highly heterogeneous classrooms. It was against this background that the Chicago Board of Education decided to undertake the development and testing of CMLR/LS.

In May 1981, the Chicago Board of Education mandated a new promotion policy involving both a return to a graded organizational structure and the use of CMLR/LS materials throughout the city. The promotion policy was a bold move in several ways. To begin with, it is the first time that a large city has provided standardized instruction and standards of performance at each grade level for all its students in order to stop social promotion. Second, promotion is now based on mastery of instructional units. That is, in order to be promoted from one grade level to the next, students must master 79–83% of the instructional units of each grade level. Third, instructional goals were built into the program by requiring students to work through a specified number of units before receiving a mark for each of the four report card marking periods. In essence, therefore, promotion is now based on content covered (Katims, Jones, & Adelman, 1981). Additionally, there are record forms for the principal to monitor the progress of all classrooms in a school and for the district superintendent to monitor the progress of schools in a district. Thus, efforts to increase and regulate the quality and pace of instruction are built into the management system at three different levels: the classroom, the school, and the district.

Description of CMLR/LS Materials

CMLR/LS consists of nine sets of books: one set for each grade from K–8. At each grade there are both *Student Books* and *Teacher Manuals*, which include teaching activities, exercises from *Student Books*, and answer keys. The instructional materials at each grade level except kindergarten have two strands: Comprehension and Word Attack/Study Skills, totaling 17 volumes of instructional materials in all. Each set of materials is bound into a volume of about 250–400 pages. Thus, about 7,000 pages of instructional materials have been generated and field tested between 1976 and 1982, using a staff of 3–15 writers each year. Initially, the idea of applying research on learning and reading strategies to reading instruction was only for grades 5–8. Consequently, all writings prior to 1981 describe CMLR/LS as the grades 5–8 sections of CMLR. However, in the fall of 1980, it was decided to extend this idea to instruction for grades K–4 by embedding reading/learning strategy instructions in the *Teacher Manuals* for grades K–2 and/or in the *Student Books* for grades 3–4. Thus, CMLR and CMLR/LS are now interchangeable terms. Nevertheless, all the description and data here refer to the development and testing of materials for grades 5–8 only.

The Mastery Learning Component: The Concept of the Learning Unit. Mastery learning refers to Bloom's (1976) philosophy, which assumes that most students can learn as well as the best students if they are given appropriate learning conditions. Mastery learning programs attempt to organize instruction so that students have these conditions. Particularly, Bloom emphasized that mastery learning instruction differs from traditional instruction mainly by the use of a four-phase cycle of instruction for each learning unit: teach, test, reteach, retest. The heart of this cycle is the systematic correction of errors that are diagnosed in the first test and then corrected in the reteach phase, which uses alternative teaching/learning strategies to address variations in students' learning patterns and styles.

CMLR/LS materials are organized into learning units that embody this philosophy. Each unit is addressed to one or more objectives. Generally, at grades 5–6 there are from 18-to-24 pages of teacher and student activities addressed to the objectives for the teach phase. This phase is conducted using whole-group instruction (i.e., all 26–32 students in the class). Following the teach phase, there is a formative test that differentiates mastery and nonmastery students according to previously specified levels of mastery (80–100%). This constitutes the test phase. Next, nonmastery students are required to do a corrective activity (four to eight pages) and take a second criterion-referenced test. These activities constitute the reteach and retest phases. During these latter phases, mastery students have three options: (1) two to three pages of enrichment activities that extend instruction for the unit objective(s); (2) peer tutoring; or (3) inferential, silent reading.

The Learning Strategies Component.   A learning strategy may be broadly defined as the mental operations or thinking steps that are used to encode, analyze, and retrieve information. What differentiates learning strategies from incidental learning is that learning strategies are essentially goal oriented; either consciously or unconsciously the mental operations that are used in a learning strategy are directly addressed to a specific purpose or learning objective. The mental operations that occur during incidental learning are not goal oriented.

Altogether, in using the CMLR/LS materials, students are instructed in five broad types of strategies for acquiring information from text: (1) *organizational strategies*—noticing how a text is organized and how the ideas it contains are related to one another (examples: recognizing different types of paragraph structures, using headings and subheadings as organizational clues, categorizing information into matrices, etc.); (2) *imagery strategies*—forming mental pictures and making drawings for purposes of more adequately encoding the meanings of words and ideas (examples: visualizing objects and events while reading, drawing pictures to illustrate newly learned vocabulary words, etc.); (3) *contextual strategies*—using context clues to define unfamiliar words and make inferences from text (examples: inferring topic sentences, using signal words as clues in categorizing information, etc.); and (5) *reflective thinking strategies*—approaching reading comprehension tasks in a systematic way (examples: carefully checking to make sure one has understood the question to which one is responding; carefully checking to make sure one has systematically analyzed all the multiple choice response options offered before making a selection, etc.). Examples of several of these strategies may be found in the sample CLMR/LS curriculum materials included in the Appendix. It is important to note that the CMLR/LS curriculum is spiraled so that each of these five basic strategies is taught at different grade levels using different types of content, different task formats, and different levels of difficulty.

The Structure of Text Component.   In CMLR/LS, the concept of text structure is not limited to fictional and nonfictional prose. Also included are the structures typically found in a range of discourse types such as poetry, analogies, dictionary terms, etc. Because of this diversity of "text structures," it is not possible to list each type. However, over the course of years from grade 4 to grade 8, the students learn to recognize and analyze many different types of paragraph structures, including: proposition plus reasons, topic plus details, compare and contrast, and cause and effect. Additionally, there are several units for grades 5–8 that require the students to analyze prose text structures in terms of two to three levels of organization: main idea and details, major and minor ideas, controlling ideas that span several paragraphs, and so on. In terms of fictional text structures, there are also numerous units that deal with the recognition and analysis of various components of story grammars, including the five W's (who, what, where, when, and why), mood, character traits, conflict, and plot.

Instructional Strategies.   These may be explained in three dimensions. First, each unit has the same *instructional structure* (Jones, 1980). Each unit begins with an explanation of the unit objective, which involves a concept, a skill, or a set of information (L. W. Anderson & Jones, 1981). Each concept, skill, or set of information to be learned is defined and illustrated in a series of examples. These examples are accompanied by a set of thinking steps that constitute a thinking-aloud model of how to process the concept, skill, or information. If the model is complex, involving many steps or parts (see Appendix examples), usually there is a second model using a fill-in-the-blank procedure to guide students to engage in the appropriate processing activities.

The examples and thinking-aloud models are followed by prompted practice exercises. The exercises contain content-specific prompts that guide the student to apply the definition and thinking-aloud model to the exercise problems. Prompts are given by means of adjunct questions, usually in the form of "Step 1," "Think" statements, or "Ask yourself" questions (e.g. "Ask yourself: Is this a similar-meaning word pair or an opposite-meaning word pair?" Prompted practice exercises are followed by unprompted exercises. If the concept, skill, or information is complex, these procedures are repeated for each part. After the formative test, there is a corrective activity using a different mode of presentation (e.g., visual, if the initial instruction was verbal) and/or a different mode of information processing (e.g., inductive, if the initial mode of presentation was deductive), plus an enrichment activity devised to extend the level of learning for that objective.

Second, each unit follows a *sequencing model* in that: (1) each unit provides instruction in prerequisite skills; and (2) each unit begins with information that is simple, concrete, familiar, explicit, and short in length and progresses to information that is increasingly complex, abstract, unfamiliar, inexplicit (requiring inferences), and long (see Stoll, 1980). Thus, the unit on Main Ideas and Details begins with categorizing words and progresses to paragraphs that are only three sentences long in the beginning of the unit but become increasingly longer. Moreover, this unit, like all others, does not assume that all the students know what a main idea is, even though there is a unit on finding the main idea at virtually every grade level.

Third, each unit has a prescribed mastery learning *instructional process* (Katims, et al., 1981). As indicated previously, there are four phases: teach, test, reteach, retest. In the teach phase, the first activity is a teacher-directed activity in which the teacher elicits from the students paraphrases and summaries of the instructional text as well as new examples, explanations of examples, and so on. He or she may also prompt the students, to help them with the correct answer. The next activity involves guided practice, i.e., the teacher circulates around the room monitoring the students to make certain that they understand the instructions, vocabulary, text, and strategy. Guided practice is followed by independent practice.

Formative Evaluation Procedures.   Materials for Grades 5 and 6 were tested in three classrooms in each of two schools, selected to represent typical socio-economic and ethnic school characteristics, learner characteristics (in terms of number of years below national norms for age), and classroom conditions. Both schools were very high in the percentage of students classified as being minority students and as being below the poverty level. Academically, the students were 1–3 years below national norms in reading. Classrooms in both schools contained one to four reading levels and a range of up to three-year age differences. Materials for Grades 7 and 8 were tested in two classrooms in a different school. In one, the students were reading near grade level; in the other they were 1–2 years below level.

Formative evaluation procedures followed guidelines established by Katims, who developed the procedures for *criterion-referenced field testing*. Each classroom is visited daily by a CMLR staff member for observations and interviews with both students and teacher. The comments are then used as the basis for revisions. Additionally, formative test scores are analyzed for total number of mastery and nonmastery scores as well as error patterns. If less than 50–60% of the students in most classes master the objectives, the initial instruction and/ or poor test items are revised and field tested again. If less than 80–90% of the remaining students master the second test after the remediation, the remediation is revised and field tested again. Thus, the very definition of the field test procedures is mastery based in that it is based on student mastery in attaining prespecified criteria. (See Jones, 1981 for further description of field test procedures.)

Comparison to Other Programs

In terms of the mastery learning component, CMLR units and procedures are similar to other good mastery learning programs (Bailey, 1983; Barber, 1979; see also L. W. Anderson & Jones, 1981) in the provision of teach, test, reteach, retest cycles. However, whereas most other mastery learning programs ask teachers to make their own materials as the primary mode of delivery, CMLR provides all of the materials needed for instruction and assessment (Jones, 1981). CMLR involves whole group instruction whereas, with some notable exceptions such as Red Bank, New Jersey (Abrams, 1979), most other mastery learning programs involve individualized or small-group instruction. Additionally, CMLR is unique in its criterion-referenced field-testing concept.

CMLR is unusual (though not unique) in the extent to which it provides learning strategy instructions, sequencing and prerequisite skills instruction, instruction regarding text structures, and instruction in the process of applying the learning strategies and text structure information to the exercise problems. None of the commercial basals provide this type of instruction. In fact, the only other programs known to the authors that do are those described in these volumes and in this conference, Sticht (1979), and T. H. Anderson (1979). And, except for Sticht's military curriculum materials, the other programs that involve learning strategies instruction and structure of text analysis are adjunct programs, which apply to, but are separate from specific subject-related courses. Moreover, none of these programs involve the development of instructional material for K–8 in reading.

The Evolution of CMLR/LS: From Theory to Practice

Mastery Learning Research.   Mastery learning, as conceived by Bloom (1976), and as operationalized by Block and L. W. Anderson (1975; see also L. W. Anderson & Block, 1976), holds that all or at least most students can learn to a desired criterion if they are taught at an appropriate level of instruction, taught to publicly stated objectives, diagnosed for errors, retaught by different methods if they do not show mastery on the diagnostic test, and retested. Numerous studies (e.g., Block & Burns, 1977) have shown that these procedures effectively help all or most students master units of instruction in the content areas, mathematics, and reading, while improving their self-concepts and attitudes toward school. What, then, might be gained by applying learning strategies theory and research to mastery learning?

Reading/Learning Strategies Research: Initial Conceptualization.   It was evident from the outset (Jones, 1980) that two strands of research related to the development of the CMLR/LS curriculum materials: reading research and learning strategies research. In essence, both strands of research indicated that the major difference between low- and high-achieving students is that high-achieving students appear to develop spontaneously a repertoire of effective reading/learning strategies so that by the end of high school they are functioning approximately at the level of college students. This developmental shift for high-achieving students begins to take place at about Grades 4–5 and continues throughout adolescence. Low-achieving students fail to develop effective reading/learning strategies during adolescence and show little improvement in reading comprehension as they progress through junior and senior high school. The data that support this developmental shift hypothesis are extensive (see Allington, 1980; Auchenbach, 1975; Brophy & Good, 1970; Brown & Campione, 1978, 1980; Brown, Campione, & Day, 1982; Brown, & Smiley, 1978; Brown, Smiley, & Lawton, 1978; Cromer & Wiener, 1966; Deffenbacher, Miscik, & Jarombek, 1974; Jenkins, 1974; Jones, 1976; Levin, 1973; Marshall & Glock, 1978; Mason, 1977; Mason & Kendall, 1979; Meyer, Brandt, & Bluth, 1980; Rohwer, 1971, 1973; Stein, 1978; Tierney, Bridge, & Cera, 1979; Tighe, Tighe, & Schechler, 1975; Tulving, 1962, 1968; Wagner & Rohwer, 1981; Weinstein & Rabinovitch, 1971, Weinstein, Underwood, Wicker, & Cubberly, 1979; Wittrock, 1979).

These data raise the question: To what extent is it possible to facilitate the learning performance of low-achieving students? Recent research suggests that there are several ways to enhance the performance levels of these students. First, low-achieving students may be trained to use many of the *specific reading/ learning strategies* that high-achieving students come to acquire partially through their own efforts and partially through school instructional experiences. That is, there is some evidence that low-achieving students can be trained to use some of these strategies at least under limited experimental conditions. However, it is not clear to what extent they can then generalize these strategies to the range of learning situations and materials that students normally encounter in school (see R. C. Anderson & Hiddle, 1971; T. H. Anderson, 1979; Andre & T. H. Anderson, 1978; Armbruster & T. H. Anderson, 1980; Brown, Campione, & Day, 1982; Brown et al., 1978; Dansereau, 1979; Dean & Kulhavy, 1979; DiVesta et al., 1973; Doctorow, Wittrock, & Marks, 1978; Hall & Madsen, 1978; Jones, 1976; Jones & Hall, 1979; Kurth & Moseley, 1978; Levin, 1976; Peper & Mayer, 1978; Pressley, 1977; Raugh & Atkinson, 1975; Rickards & August, 1975; Rohwer, 1971; Salomon & Auchenbach, 1974; Steingart & Glock, 1979; Sticht, 1979; Weinstein et al., 1979). Second, there is some evidence that *mode of presentation* is important to learning and that for some students some modes of presentation are more effective in producing good learning than are others. For example, for some students pictures can be more effective than print (Lesgold, DeGood, & Levin, 1978; Levin, 1976; Pressley, 1977). Third, the data from *structure of text* research suggest that certain types of emphasis devices such as headings and italicized words facilitate learning (Frase, 1969, 1973; Frase & Schwartz, 1979; Furukawa, 1977; Kintsch, Mandel, & Kozminski, 1977; Marshall & Glock, 1978; Mason & Kendall, 1979; Meyer, 1977, 1982; Nezworski, Stein & Trabasso, 1979; Pearson, Hansen, & Gordon, 1979; Sindell & Restaino, 1978; Stein & Nezworski, 1978; Weaver, 1979; Weinstein & Rabinovitch, 1971; Whiting, 1980). Fourth, Jones and Hall (1982) discovered that it was difficult, if not impossible, to begin instruction for low-achieving students using complex tasks. It was necessary *to sequence instruction* so that initial tasks were simple and then build up to tasks that were complex (see Case, 1978;

Rosenshine, 1979; Stoll, 1980). Thus, sequencing skills instruction is critical to solve problems of instruction in heterogeneous classrooms in which some students may lack the prerequisite skills.

Armed with these data, we thought it essential to provide low-achieving students with reading/learning strategy instructions, diverse modes of presentation, diverse text structures, and a sequencing model that built in prerequisite skills instruction prior to instruction in complex tasks. Accordingly, each initial unit for Grades 5–8 provided: (1) instruction in using specific reading/learning strategies (e.g., instructions to find the main ideas, use context clues, summarize, etc.); (2) diverse modes of presentation (visual/verbal and/or inductive/deductive); (3) definitions of different text structures; and (4) prerequisite skills instruction.

Reading/Learning Strategy Instruction: Reconceptualization and Revision.   During our first field test year, we had the opportunity to observe that some of our instructional materials were more effective than others, and to reflect further on the conditions required for successful learning strategies instruction. First, we observed that it simply was not possible to ask low-achieving students either to use learning strategies, such as finding the main idea, or to do complex reading-related tasks, such as solving an analogy problem, without providing explicit instruction as to *how* to do it. Instructing these students to find the main idea without guiding them through the thought processes that are necessary (even in an easy-to-learn text) is just another form of comprehension assessment (assessing the student's understanding of what is read), rather than comprehension instruction (assisting students to understand the meaning of what they read), to borrow Durkin's (1978–79) terminology. Assessment without instruction provides limited opportunities to learn. Our initial instructional materials had included some specific *how to* guidance, and we learned from our first field test year that more of this was needed.

Secondly, we found that it was important to build this *how to* instruction into the instructional materials due to problems created by the size of the school system: namely, the high rates of teacher and student mobility, and the unwieldiness of teaching-training programs, when the number of teachers is many thousands. In other words, we realized that for our population a large part of the burden of instruction needed to be carried by the materials, so that the program could continue to be properly implemented despite changes in teacher and student populations. To build processing instructions into the materials, we had included some adjunct questions and processing models in our first set of materials. We observed during our field test that these adjunct aids were crucial to the success of the program and that more were needed.

Thirdly, we observed that, for our population of low-achieving elementary and junior high school students, it was important to teach specific learning strategies as well as general ones. For example, in teaching students a widely applicable strategy such as summarizing passages of text, we found that it was not effective to limit instruction to one general procedure for different kinds of texts. Rather, we needed to help students come to understand how different kinds of text passages are organized, and to provide them with different formulas for summarizing each kind of passage. For example, we found it necessary to provide one formula for summarizing a compare-and-contrast paragraph, another for summarizing a simple story, etc. That is, our students could not work out these modifications on their own, but rather needed different formulas for applying a given strategy to each of the different kinds of texts.

Fourth, we observed that our students lacked a great deal of world knowledge that is important to successful reading and that this also needed to be built into the curriculum. We have already discussed their lack of knowledge of how different forms of text are structured. This is one kind of world knowledge that we attempted to build into our revised materials. A second kind of world knowledge that we built into our revised materials was vocabulary knowledge.

Having developed additional insights into the nature of effective learning strategy instruction from our field test experiences, we proceeded to reexamine the basic research literature to see if our insights were consistent with other investigators' experiences. In our own work, we had found that providing explicit processing instructions and explicit structure of text information were crucial to achieving successful training outcomes. We now asked whether these factors were also reported in the basic research literature. Our investigation yielded an interesting finding. We noticed that some studies with college student populations involved only LS—learning strategy instructions—without instruction in defining the structure of the text or the process of using the strategy (Schultz & DiVesta, 1972). However, most studies, both at the college level and with younger students, involved either: (1) a combination of LS and DS (definition of the strategy); (2) LS and DS and/or STI (structure of text information); or (3) LS and DS and STI and IPA (instruction in the process of applying strategy). Examples of each of the aforementioned combinations are from: (1) Peper and Mayer (1978), who defined generative underlining in terms of finding the sentence that gives the most information; for (2) almost any study training students to categorize, because any explanation beyond the word "categorize" must necessarily involve identification of the component parts of the text or list to be categorized; and (3) Day and Brown (1980), who provided summarizing rules, structure of text information, and extended instruction in applications. What was interesting was the discovery that training involving only LS was often unsuccessful, whereas training using DS, STI, or IPA was usually successful.

This reanalysis of the literature led to the development of a taxonomy of learning strategies (Jones, 1981) and a typology of text structures (Amiran & Jones, 1982; Jones, 1980) that we found useful in revising our curriculum materials. More specifically, in reexamining the basic research literature, we found that we could group the strategies in which we wanted to offer instruction into two categories based on their complexity. We characterized the simpler strategies as linking strategies—where the learner's task was to link new information to be learned directly with information already stored in memory (for example, labeling items to make them easier to remember). We characterized the more complex strategies as constructive ones—where the learner's task was to construct the meaning of new information by integrating it with relevant background knowledge (for example, making inferences from text). We also found that we could group text structures into categories based on their complexity. We distinguished three categories: (1) subordinate structures, which consist of one type of main idea plus details (for example, name plus attribute structures); (2) coordinate structures, which consist of two main ideas plus details (for example, compare-and-contrast statements plus details); and (3) sequential structures, which consist of a series of events plus details.

Additionally, our reanalysis of the literature led to a redefinition of the readability of text structures. Although we had never used traditional readability formulas, due to what we felt were obvious limitations, we had focused heavily on controlling or at least examining vocabulary. The reanalysis of the literature led to a new (holistic) definition of readability in terms of the degree of complexity of the text (its levels and its component parts), the density of the text (i.e., the memory load it placed on the student), the text texture or the degree of inferences required, the complexity of the learning/reading strategies required, and the degree of world knowledge it required (Amiran & Jones, 1982).

These changes in conceptualization required extensive revisions in the guidelines used by the writing staff. The revised guidelines for developing a unit included the following activities: (1) defining the text and test structures; (2) analyzing the text content for each of the dimensions that define content complexity; (3) analyzing the content for assumed world knowledge; (4) defining the skills required (matching, inference, etc.); (5) determining general strategy instructions; (6) defining instruction for the process of analyzing the text structure to perform the required skills; (7) defining the adjunct question levels and models for processing strategy constructions, and for analyzing text structure; (8) working up examples, nonexamples, explanations, and practice exercises; (9) creating parallel formative tests using locally developed guidelines; and (10) providing fun activities and enrichment activities related to the objectives. As a result of the comments by Campione and Armbruster in this volume, two other guidelines have been added: (1) stating the objective and/or purpose for learning directly to the students at the outset of each unit; and (2) whenever possible, teaching students to use their strategies in a flexible way—that is, teaching them how to access the strategy that is appropriate for the thinking/learning situation with which they are confronted.

Before moving on to the evaluation section, it may be useful to indicate the relevance of research to the development of specific units. Although there are numerous objectives for which there was no directly relevant research, several strands of research were quite useful. The research on prose text structures, especially the research of Meyer (1977, 1982) and Marshall and Glock (1978) was most useful, though we would alter some of Meyer's classifications of text structures (Amiran & Jones, 1982). Much of the research on inferences was far too abstract and overly focused on classification to be useful for instructional purposes, though the research of Pearson et al. (1979), Wagner and Rohwer (1981), and Goetz (1977), provided criteria for defining inference and for understanding the process of making an inference. For defining and teaching study skills such as outlining, finding the main idea, and summarizing, the research of T. H. Anderson (1979) and Brown (Brown & Campione, 1980) has been quite helpful. Vocabulary learning strategies were based largely on the research of Jones and Hall (1982) and R. C. Anderson and Shifrin (1980). The unit on analogies is a direct application of Sternberg's research (1977) and a series of studies by Auchenbach (1975). Regarding fiction, Stein's (1978) research on story grammars was useful in understanding fiction generally (even though most of her stories are at primary levels) and in developing a Grade 5 unit on listening comprehension.

Evaluation of CMLR/LS

Perhaps the most difficult problem of all in developing a large-scale program is evaluation of the program. Two problems are outstanding and possibly insoluble. First, it is difficult to assess the effects of specific instructional procedures. Second, CMLR/LS, like most mastery learning instructional programs, has been implemented as only one component of an evolving system in which many major parts may be implemented simultaneously; and all parts may be affected by changes of policy. There are also serious problems of data collection. The 1979 summer school data were unobtainable, due to the disorganization during the school system's financial crisis. This made comparisons for the 1978/1979 summer session impossible, and there was no mandatory summer school session in 1980. Another problem is out-of-level testing (testing children by age and previous reading level rather than testing by grade level), which creates a considerable variability from school to school in the assignment of students to test levels. Still another problem is inability to monitor the instructional program. It is not possible to regulate the amount of time given to the instructional program, the other materials, such as basal readers that are used in conjunction with an experimental program, or even, in some cases, to assure the correct use of the materials—unless there is some interested person in the school or district to monitor the implementation (e.g., a reading coordinator). In at least two attempts to obtain data, the permutations of materials in conjunction with assignment of reading levels and variations in time made the data uninterpretable.

Finally, there is the problem of inappropriate assignment of students to the materials. Many students who are above or below level are assigned to materials according to their age rather than their reading level, because they are in age-graded classrooms. These procedures obviously cause problems of design as well as interpretation. Because of these problems, the available data are very limited in terms of the opportunities for evaluation and are very preliminary in nature (see Jones, 1981).

Altogether, there are five sets of data available. First, there are the 1977–1978 field test data assessing the effectiveness of the overall set of curriculum materials used in the fifth and sixth grade formative evaluation classrooms for one academic year. In this study, six experimental classrooms were compared with six control classrooms matched for student reading level, student age, classroom heterogeneity, and student socioeconomic status. Comparisons were made for two tests: a locally developed criterion-referenced test and the Iowa Test of Basic Skills (ITBS). The latter was critical because it measures transfer and ability to access spontaneously the strategies taught in the CMLR/LS materials. Although only a small percentage of the items on the criterion-referenced test contain explicit strategy prompts, it may be argued that the item formats used on this test constitute implicit strategy prompts. That is, the very essence of mastery learning involves teaching to the objective. This involves, among other things, teaching the students in very specific terms about the structure and format of the test as well as teaching for each component part of the instruction. These procedures may function as cues to use specific strategies for specific test formats. The ITBS structure and format are quite different from any of the mastery learning units. Most important, the ITBS tests for comprehension of a variety of text structures and types of questions and is therefore a good measure of transfer and multiple access.

The results indicated that there were significant differences between the control and experimental groups' scores on both the criterion-referenced test ($p < .001$) and the ITBS ($p < .001$ for t-scores between groups and $p < .05$ for gain scores). In terms of grade levels, the average gains for experimental and control students were 10.5 and 8.9 months respectively over 10 months of school. The citywide gain for students the same age that year was 7.0 months. Because the students and teachers knew they were participating in an experimental program, the data may be interpreted in terms of a halo effect. However, given the marked variation in test performance of the experimental group on the various versions of the material being formatively evaluated, this seems unlikely.

Secondly, there is the case study of the 1978 summer school. In the spring of 1978, the Board decided to implement a mandatory summer school for all eighth graders who failed to meet the requirements of the promotion policy (mastery of 80% of the objectives for Grades 7 and 8). This involved about 11,000 students at nine high school sites. They were to attend summer school for 1½ hours a day for 7 weeks. The instructional program consisted entirely of selected CMLR/LS units from Grades 5–8. Additionally, the students were encouraged to read paperback books provided by the Board whenever they had completed an assignment. ITBS tests were administered to a random sample of three classrooms in each of the nine high school sites during the last week of the session. Using the April (1978) ITBS scores as pretests, the average gains in the 4 month period (April–August) for the 13- and 14-year-olds were 3.5 and 4.6 months respectively. These gains compared favorably with citywide gain of 7.0 months for 1977–1978 for students of the same age. However, the lack of comparative data renders the findings uninterpretable in terms of making causal inferences about instruction and reading achievement (Jones & Katims, 1980).

The third opportunity for evaluation was the 1979–1980 and 1980–1981 implementation of CMLR materials at May Elementary School. The 1979–1980 data evaluating use of CMLR/LS materials in eighth-grade classrooms show strong gains from the previous year. In 1978–1979, prior to implementation of CMLR/LS materials, the median reading scores for these two classrooms were 5.8 and 5.9 respectively; after using CMLR/LS materials in 1979–1980, the median reading scores were 7.3 and 7.1 respectively. Analysis of the schoolwide data the following year (1980–1981), in which CMLR/LS materials were used schoolwide at all of the upper grade levels, shows similar gains. These data are difficult to interpret, however. Examination of citywide scores for students in Grades 7 and 8 indicates substantial gains of 7.0 months to 10.0 months for that period — a fact that is inconsistent both with previous annual gain information for Chicago junior high school students and with the May School teachers' perception that an unusual degree of learning was taking place in their school. One explanation is that these data are a function of out-of-level testing and/or the differential effects of the new promotion policy on Grades 7 and 8. That is, in the spring of 1978 it was announced that Grade 8 students would not be promoted to high school without passing 80% of the criterion-referenced tests for Grades 7 and 8. This could make students in those grades work harder.

Additional data from May School involve several measures developed by Katims (Katims & Jones, 1981) assessing classroom and school effects. First, we compared the percentage of classrooms ($N = 32$) with gains of 7.0 months or more for 1978–1979, when only two classrooms had CMLR/LS materials, with 1979–1980, when all classrooms used these materials. For 1978–1979, only 37% of the classrooms attained an average of 1.00 year or more; for 1979–1980, 47% of the classrooms showed an average gain of 1.00 year or more. In addition, the standard deviation of classroom gains decreased from 1979 to 1980 and the correlation of pretest and posttest gains decreased from $r = .34$ ($p < .05$) to .03 ($p < .001$). Both results are predicted by mastery learning theory. The 1979–1980 gains are noteworthy not only because they were higher than those for 1978–1979 but also because they were attained in spite of the fact that the bottom eight of the 32 teachers did not fully implement the program for idiosyncratic reasons.

We then looked at school-level effects and found that the data reflected *both* phenomena predicted by mastery learning theory: increased achievement coupled with decreased variation. In 1978 May School had a mean gain of .55 years with a standard deviation of .60. In 1979, with the introduction of mastery learning, the gains equaled .73 and the standard deviation decreased to .44. In 1980, the gain was 1.03, and the variance declined to .29. This is in sharp contrast to similar statistics from other schools where the low variance is attained only when the gains are also low, or, in other words, when high gains are attained largely by the high-achieving students only and are therefore associated with high variance.

Fourth, though reading scores are unquestionably the most critical measures of the effects of a program, there is also evidence of other effects such as the reduction of student and teacher absenteeism as well as the lessening of student transfer and discipline problems reported by Thompson (this volume). But from a humanistic point of view, the most important effects of the program, thus far, appear to be the marked contrast between the 1979 and the 1980 acceptance of May Elementary School students at limited-enrollment magnet vocational schools that require successful performance on their own reading achievement tests as a criterion for admission. In 1979 the number of acceptances was seven; in 1980 it was 45—over one-third of the graduating class; and in 1981, all but 10 students were admitted to such high schools.

Fifth, there are data relating to the question of implementability posed at the outset of this section. The 1978 summer school involved only two 2½ hour inservice training sessions for district reading coordinators and one 1½ hour inservice session for the 1000 teachers and administrators who conducted the summer school. Although there was some disorganization in assigning materials to children and in obtaining materials for reassigned students, the summer program was essentially implemented by different staff almost entirely unaided by CMLR staff (Jones & Katims, 1980). Additional data are cited in a recent study by Levine (1982), who studied the organizational processes and arrangements in four Chicago schools and schools in District #19 in New York City, where CMLR is implemented districtwide. Levine argues that a major feature that distinquishes CMLR from other innovative programs is its obvious implementability, due to the existence of the standardized materials; the enthusiasm and commitment that teachers, principals, and students feel for the program; and the consistently positive data in schools that had previously shown negative results. Moveover, although staff development is clearly needed to monitor instruction and student progress, having standardized materials greatly reduces the problems of student and teacher mobility mentioned earlier.

Having said this, the final and ultimate test of implementability and reading achievement is the recent citywide implementation of CMLR. It is probably the largest scale implementation ever conducted in the United States, and it will be most interesting to analyze the data in years to come. Thus far, the results are highly encouraging.

CONCLUSION

Both CMLR/LS and the present version of MOAN have only limited data concerning effectiveness, although all available data are positive. As MOAN has developed over the years, it has become increasingly practice based, while CMLR/LS research has most recently focused on finding and applying appropriate research methods to use both for the evaluation of instructional materials and for the assessment of implementation procedures (Katims et al, 1981). However, schools have very limited resources for this type of research and development, and it is hoped that the movement to apply theory to practice will encourage university/school interaction to conduct program research, development, and evaluation in the schools.

ACKNOWLEDGMENTS

Funds for the development of the Chicago Mastery Learning Reading Program were provided by the Chicago Board of Education, the Spencer Foundation, and the publisher, Mastery Education Corporation. We wish to thank all three institutions for their financial aid and support.

REFERENCES

Abrams, J. D. Mastery learning in a smaller school system. *Educational Leadership*, 1979, *37*, 136–129.

Allington, R. L. Teacher interruptions during primary grade oral reading. *Journal of Educational Psychology*, 1980, *72*, 371–375.

Amiran, M. R. *Defining and testing high school reading objectives*. Paper presented at the meeting of the International Reading Association, St. Louis, May 1980.

Amiran, M. R., & Jones, B. F. Toward a new definition of readability. *Educational Psychologist*, 1982, *17*, 13–30.

Amiran, M. R., Jones, B. F., & Fridell, R. *Matrix outlining and analysis*. Unpublished instructional materials, 1980. (Available from Beau Jones, Department of Curriculum, Chicago Public Schools, 1819 W. Pershing Rd., Chicago, Il. 60609.)

Anderson, L. W., & Block, J. H. Mastery learning. In D. Treffinger, J. Davis, & R. Ripple (Eds.), *Handbook on teaching educational psychology*. New York: Academic Press, 1976.

Anderson, L. W., & Jones, B. F. Designing instructional strategies which facilitate learning for mastery. *Educational Psychologist*, 1981, *16*, 121–138.

Anderson, R. C., & Hidde, J. L. Imagery and sentence learning. *Journal of Educational Psychology*, 1971, *62*, 526–530.

Anderson, R. C., & Shifrin, Z. The meaning of words in context. In R. J. Spiro, B. C. Bruce, & W. F. Brewer (Eds.), *Theoretical issues in reading comprehension*. Hillsdale, N. J.: Lawrence Erlbaum Associates, 1980.

Anderson, T. H. Study skills and learning strategies. In H. F. O'Neil, Jr. & C. D. Spielberger (Eds.), *Cognitive and affective learning strategies*. New York: Academic Press, 1979.

Andre, M. D. A., & Anderson, T. H. The development and evaluation of a self-questioning study technique. *Reading Research Quarterly*, 1978–79, *14*, 605–623.

Armbruster, B. B., & Anderson, T. H. *Idea mapping: The technique and its use in the classroom, or, simulating the "ups" and "downs" of reading comprehension* (Tech. Rep. No. 36). Urbana: University of Illinois, Center for the Study of Reading, 1982.

Auchenbach, T. M. The children's associative responding test: A two-year follow-up. *Developmental Psychology*, 1975, *67*, 653–654.

Bailey, G. W. Focusing resources on school improvement goals. In A. Oddens & L. D. Webb (Eds.), *School finance and school improvement: Linkages in the 1980s*. Washington, D. C.: Education Commission of the States, 1983.

Barber, C. Mastery Learning through involved educational leadership. *Application for state validation*. Denver Public Schools, August 1979.

Bereiter, C., & Scardamalia, M. From conversation to composition: The role of instruction in a developmental process. In R. Glaser (Ed.), *Advances in instructional psychology* (Vol.2). Hillsdale, N. J.: Lawrence Erlbaum Associates, 1982.

Block, J. H., & Anderson, L. W. *Mastery learning in classroom instruction*. New York: Macmillan, 1975.

Block, J. H., & Burns, R. Mastery learning. *Review of Research in Education*, 1977, *4*, 3–49.

Bloom, B. S. *Human characteristics and school learning*. New York: McGraw–Hill, 1976.

Bracewell, R., Fine, J., & Ezergaile, L. *Cohesion as a guide to writing processes*. Paper presented at the meeting of the American Educational Research Association, Boston, April 1980.

Brophy, J. E., & Good, T. L. Teachers' communications of differential expectations for children's classroom performance: Some behavioral data. *Journal of Educational Psychology*, 1970, *61*, 365–374.

Brown, A. L., & Campione, J. C. The effects of knowledge and experience on the formation of retrieval plans for studying from texts. In M. M. Gruneberg, P. E. Morris, & R. N. Sykes (Eds.), *Practical aspects of memory*. New York: Academic Press, 1978.

Brown, A. L., & Campione, J. C. Training studies in developmental research: Inducing flexible thinking in the laboratory and in the classroom. I. M. Friedman, J. P. Das, & N. O. O'Connor (Eds.), *Intelligence and learning*. New York: Plenum Press, 1980.

Brown, A. L., Campione, J. C., & Day, J. D. Learning to learn: On training students to learn from texts. *Educational Researcher*, 1982, *10*, 14–23.

Brown, A. L., & Smiley, S. S. The development of strategies for studying texts. *Child Development*, 1978, *49* 1076–1088.

Brown, A. L., & Smiley, S. S., & Lawton, S. C. The effects of experience on the selection of suitable retrieval cues for studying texts. *Child Development*, 1978, *49*, 829–835.

Case, R. A developmentally based theory and technology of instruction. *Review of Educational Research*, 1978, *48*, 439–463.

Chicago Board of Education. *Chicago Mastery Learning Reading Program*. Chicago: 1980. Also, Watertown, Mass.: Mastery Education, 1980.

Collins, A. M. Processes in acquiring knowledge. In R. C. Anderson, R. J. Spiro, & W. E. Montague (Eds.), *Schooling and the acquisition of knowledge*. Hillsdale, N. J.: Lawrence Erlbaum Associates, 1977.

Cromer, W., & Wiener, M. Idiosyncratic response patterns among good and poor readers. *Journal of Consulting Psychology*, 1966, *30*, 1–10.

Dansereau, D. F., McDonald, B. A., Collins, K. W., Garland, J., Holley, C. D., Diekhoff, G. M., & Evans, S. H. Evaluation of a learning strategy system. In H. F. O'Neil, Jr., & C. D. Spielberger (Eds.), *Cognitive and affective learning strategies*. New York: Academic Press, 1979.

Davis, G. E. Research and development in training creative thinking. In J. R. Levin & V. E. Allen (Eds.), *Cognitive learning in children: Theories and strategies*. New York: Academic Press, 1976.

Dean, R. S., & Kulhavy, R. W. *The influence of spatial organization in prose learning.* Paper presented at the meeting of the American Educational Research Association, San Francisco, April 1979.

Deffenbacher, K. A., Miscik, J. G., & Jarombek, J. Acquistion and forgetting of information in long-term memory as a function of certain hierarchically structured variables. *Bulletin of Psychonomic Science*, 1974, *4*, 590–592.

DiVesta, F. J., Schultz, C. B., & Dangel, T. R. Passage organization and imposed learning strategies in comprehension and recall of connected discourse. *Memory and Cognition*, 1973, *1*, 471–476.

Doctorow, M., Wittrock, M. C., & Marks, C. Generative processes in reading comprehension. *Journal of Educational Psychology*, 1978, *70*, 109–118.

Durkin, D. What classroom observations reveal about reading comprehension instruction. *Reading Research Quarterly*, 1978–79, *15*, 481–533.

Flower, L. S., & Hayes, J. R. Uncovering cognitive processes in writing: A guide to protocol analysis. In P. Mosenthal, S. Walmsey, & L. Tamor (Eds.), *Research in writing practice and methods.* London: Longman, in press.

Frase, L. T. Paragraph organization of written materials: The influence of conceptual clustering upon the level and organization of recall. *Journal of Educational Psychology*, 1969, *60*, 394–401.

Frase, L. T. Integration of written text. *Journal of Educational Psychology*, 1973, *65*, 252–261.

Frase, L. T., & Schwartz, B. J. Typographical cues that facilitate comprehension. *Journal of Educational Psychology*, 1979, *71*, 197–206.

Furukawa, J. W. Cognitive processing capacity and learning mode effects in prose learning. *Journal of Educational Psychology*, 1977, *69*, 736–743.

Goetz, E. T. *Inferences in the comprehension of and memory for text* (Tech. Rep. No. 49). Urbana: University of Illinois, Center for the Study of Reading, 1977.

Hall, J. W., & Madsen, S. C. Modifying children's processing of categorizable information for memory. *Bulletin of the Psychonomic Society*, 1978, *11*, 291–294.

Hayes, J. R., & Flower, L. S. Identifying the organization of writing processes. In L. W. Gregg, & E. R. Steinberg (Eds.), *Cognitive processes in writing.* Hillsdale, N. J.: Lawrence Erlbaum Associates, 1980.

Hidi, S., & Hilyard, A. *The comparison of oral and written production of two discourse types.* Paper presented at the meeting of the American Educational Research Association, Boston, April 1980.

Jenkins, J. Remember that old theory of memory? Well, forget it! *American Psychologist*, 1974, *29*, 785–795.

Jones, B. F. *Individual differences in strategy use on diverse learning tasks and achievement in high school.* Unpublished doctoral dissertation, Northwestern University, 1976.

Jones, B. F. *Embedding structural information and strategy instructions within mastery learning units.* Paper presented at the meeting of the International Reading Association, St. Louis, May 1980.

Jones, B. F. *Research, instructional development, and implementation: The three faces of Ed.* Paper presented at the meeting of the American Educational Research Association, Los Angeles, April 1981.

Jones, B. F., & Hall, J. W. *Effects of cross-classification strategies for recalling prose and writing compare-and-contrast essays.* Paper presented at the meeting of the American Educational Research Association, San Francisco, April 1979.

Jones, B. F., & Hall, J. W. School applications of the mnemonic keyword method as a study strategy by eighth graders. *Journal of Educational Psychology*, 1982, *74*, 230–237.

Jones, B. F., & Katims, M. *Chicago's mandatory summer schools: The bottom line of a strict mastery-based promotion policy.* Paper presented at the meeting of the American Educational Research Association, Boston, April 1980.

Katims, M., & Jones, B. F. *Mastery learning reading in an inner-city school.* Paper presented at the meeting of the American Educational Research Association, Los Angeles, April 1981.

Katims, M., Jones, B. F., & Adelman, L. *Implementation manual: Chicago Mastery Learning Reading Program.* Chicago: Chicago Board of Education, 1981.

Kintsch, W., Mandel, T. S., & Kozminski, E. Summarizing scrambled stories. *Memory & Cognition,* 1977, *5,* 547–552.

Kurth, R. J., & Moseley, P. A. *The effects of copying or paraphrasing structurally cued topic sentences on passage comprehension.* Paper presented at the meeting of the American Educational Research Association, Toronto, March 1978.

Lesgold, A. M., DeGood, H., & Levin, J. R. Pictures and young children's prose learning. *Journal of Reading Behavior,* 1978, *9,* 353–360.

Levin, J. R. Inducing reading comprehension in poor readers: A test of a recent model. *Journal of Educational Psychology,* 1973, *65,* 19–24.

Levin, J. R. What have we learned about maximizing what children learn? In J. R. Levin & V. L. Allen (Eds.), *Cognitive learning in children: Theories and strategies.* New York: Academic Press, 1976.

Levine, D. U. Successful approaches for improving academic achievement in inner-city elementary schools. *Phi Delta Kappan,* 1982, *63,* 523–526.

Marshall, N., & Glock, M. D. Comprehension of connected discourse: A study into the relationship between the structure of text and information recalled. *Reading Research Quarterly,* 1978-79, *16,* 10–56.

Mason, J. M. *The role of strategy information in reading by the mentally retarded* (Tech. Rep. No. 58). Urbana: University of Illinois, Center for the Study of Reading, 1977. (ERIC Document Reproduction Service No. ED 145 406)

Mason, J. M., & Kendall, J. R. Facilitating reading comprehension through text structure manipulation. *Alberta Journal of Educational Psychology,* 1979, *24,* 68–76.

Meyer, B. J. F. The structure of prose: Effects on learning and memory implications for educational practice. In R. C. Anderson, R. J. Spiro, & W. E. Montague (Eds.), *Schooling and the acquisition of knowledge.* Hillsdale, N. J.: Lawrence Erlbaum Associates, 1977.

Meyer, B. J. F. Reading research and the composition teacher: The importance of plans. *College Composition and Communication,* 1982, *33,* 37–49.

Meyer, B. J. F., Brandt, D. M., & Bluth, G. S. Use of top level structure in text: Key for reading comprehension of ninth-grade students. *Reading Research Quarterly,* 1980, *16,* 72–103.

Musgrave, B. S., & Cohen, J. The relationship between prose and list learning. In E. Z. Rothkopf & P. E. Johnson (Eds.), *Verbal learning and the technology of written instruction.* New York: Teachers College Press, 1971.

Myers, J. L., Pezdek, K., & Coulson, D. Effect of prose organization upon free recall. *Journal of Educational Psychology,* 1973, *65,* 313–320.

Nezworski, T., Stein, N. L., & Trabasso, T. R. *Story structure versus content effects in children's recall and evaluative inference* (Tech. Rep. No. 129). Urbana: University of Illinois, Center for the Study of Reading, 1979. (ERIC Document Reproduction Service No. ED 172 187)

Pearson, P. D., Hansen, J., & Gordon, C. The effect of background knowledge on young children's comprehension of explicit and implicit information. *Journal of Reading Behavior,* 1979, *11,* 201–210.

Peper, R. J., & Mayer, R. E. Note-taking as a generative activity. *Journal of Educational Psychology,* 1978, *70,* 514–522.

Perlmutter, J., & Royer, J. M. Organization of prose materials: Stimulus storage and retrieval. *Canadian Journal of Psychology,* 1973, *27,* 200–209.

Pressley, M. Imagery in children's learning: Putting the picture in developmental prespective. *Review of Educational Research,* 1977, *47,* 585–623.

Raugh, M. R., & Atkinson, R. C. A mnemonic for learning a second-language vocabulary. *Journal of Educational Psychology*, 1975, *67*, 1–16.

Resnick, L. B. Holding an instructional conversation. In R. C. Anderson, R. J. Spiro, & W. E. Montague (Eds.), *Schooling and the acquisition of knowledge*. Hillsdale, N. J.: Lawrence Erlbaum Associates, 1977.

Rickards, J. P., & August, G. J. Generative underlining strategies in prose recall. *Journal of Educational Psychology*, 1975, *67*, 860–865.

Rohwer, W. D., Jr. Prime time for education: Early childhood or adolescence? *Harvard Educational Review*, 1971, *41*, 316–341.

Rohwer, W. D., Jr. Elaboration and learning in childhood and adolescence. In H. W. Reese (Ed.), *Advances in child development* (Vol.8). New York: Academic Press, 1973.

Rosenshine, B. V. Content, time and direct instruction. In P. Peterson & H. Walberg (Eds.), *Research on teaching*. Berkeley: McCutchan, 1979.

Rumelhart, D. E., & Ortony, A. The representation of knowledge in memory. In R. C. Anderson, R. J. Spiro, & W. E. Montague (Eds.), *Schooling and the acquisition of knowledge*. Hillsdale, N. J.: Lawrence Erlbaum Associates, 1977.

Salomon, M., & Auchenbach, T. M. Effects of four kinds of tutoring on associative responding in children. *American Educational Research Journal*, 1974, *11*, 395.

Schultz, C. B., & DiVesta, F. J. Effects of passage organization and note-taking on the selection of clustering strategies and on recall of textual materials. *Journal of Educational Research*, 1972, *63*, 244–252.

Sindell, L., & Restaino, L. C. R. *The effect of varying imagery level and propositional complexity in the comprehension of sentences*. Paper presented at the meeting of the American Educational Research Association, Toronto, March 1978.

Stein, N. L. *How children understand stories: A developmental analysis* (Tech. Rep. No. 69). Urbana: University of Illinois, Center for the Study of Reading, 1978. (ERIC Document Reproduction Service No. ED 153 205)

Stein, N. L., & Nezworski, T. *The effects of organization and instructional set on story memory* (Tech. Rep. No. 68). Urbana: University of Illinois, Center for the Study of Reading, 1978. (ERIC Document Reproduction Service No. ED 149 327)

Steingart, S. K., & Glock, M. D. Imagery and the recall of connected discourse. *Reading Research Quarterly*, 1979, *15*, 66–83.

Sternberg, R. J. *Intelligence, information processing, and analogical reasoning: A componential analysis of human abilities*. Hillsdale, N. J.: Lawrence Erlbaum Associates, 1977.

Sticht, T. G. Developing literacy and learning strategies in organizational settings. In H. F. O'Neil, Jr., and C. D. Spielberger (Eds.), *Cognitive and affective learning strategies*. New York: Academic Press, 1979.

Stoll, L. J. *A model for sequencing skills instruction*. Paper presented at the meeting of the International Reading Association, St. Louis, May 1980.

Tierney, R. J., Bridge, C., & Cera, D. J. The discourse operations of children. *Reading Research Quarterly*, 1979, *14*, 548–573.

Tighe, T. J., Tighe, L. S., & Schechler, J. Memory for instances and categories in children and adults. *Journal of Experimental Child Psychology*, 1975, *20*, 22–37.

Tulving, E. Subjective organization in free recall of "unrelated" words. *Psychological Review*, 1962, *69*, 344–354.

Tulving, E. Theoretical issues in free recall. In T. R. Dixon & D. L. Horton (Eds.), *Verbal behavior and general behavior theory*. Englewood Cliffs, N.J.: Prentice-Hall, 1968.

Wagner, M., & Rohwer, W. D., Jr. Age differences in the elaboration of inferences from text. *Journal of Educational Psychology*, 1981, *73*, 728–735.

Weaver, P. A. Improving reading comprehension: Effects of sentence organization instruction. *Reading Research Quarterly*, 1979, *15*, 129–146.

Weinstein, C. E., Underwood, V. L., Wicker, F. W., & Cubberly, W. E. Cognitive learning strategies: Verbal and imaginal elaboration. In H. F. O'Neil, Jr., & C. D. Spielberger (Eds), *Cognitive and affective learning strategies.* New York: Academic Press, 1979.

Weinstein, P., & Rabinovitch, M. S. Sentence structure retention in good and poor readers. *Journal of Educational Psychology,* 1971, *62,* 25–30.

Whiting, L. *Poor reader's comprehension of elliptical and nonelliptical text.* Paper presented at the meeting of the American Educational Research Association, Boston, April 1980.

Wittrock, M. C. Applications of cognitive psychology to education and training. In H. F. O'Neil, Jr., & C. D. Spielberger (Eds.), *Cognitive and affective learning strategies.* New York: Academic Press, 1979.

APPENDIX:
Sample CMLR/LS Materials

Name _____ Teacher _____

ANALOGIES
Student Activity #2

A. Review
   You should remember, from the exercises about word pairs, that words can be
   related to each other in many ways. Three of these ways are:

World Knowledge

	Word-Pair Examples	
Similar-Meaning Pair		smile – grin
Opposite-Meaning Pair		happy – sad
Part-to-Whole Pair		toe – foot

WHY ARE YOU SNEEZING SO MUCH?   I'VE GOT AN ANALOGY.

EXERCISE A INSTRUCTIONS   Identifying Word Pairs
---1. MAKE A MENTAL PITURE as you read each word pair in columns 1 and 3.
---2. DECIDE which type of pair it is. (How are they related?)   ---3. WRITE
Similar, Opposite, or Part-to-Whole in columns 2 and 4. The first comparison is
made for you.   *content specific prompt*

EXERCISE A CHART

Column 1 – Word Pair	Column 2	Column 3 – Word Pair	Column 4
A-1. frown – grin	Opposite	A- 6. asleep – awake	
A-2. beak – bird	_____	A- 7. house – building	
A-3. leaf – tree	_____	A- 8. guitar – band	
A-4. jeans – pants	_____	A- 9. room – house	
A-5. thin – skinny	_____	A-10. shirt –blouse	

B. What Is an Analogy?
   A word analogy means that the relationship between one pair of words is similar to
   the relationship between a second pair of words.

World Knowledge

Analogy Example

| Grandfather is to Grandmother as uncle is to aunt. |
| (Word 1)   (Word 2)   (Word 3)   (Word 4) |

Explanation: The example above is really a short code for saying the following:
Word 1 is related to Word 2 in the same way as Word 3 is related to Word 4.
REMEMBER THIS CODE!
When you apply this code to the example above, it looks like this: (Fill in the
blanks.)

Grandfather is related to _____ in the same way as uncle is related to _____ .
(Word 1)   (Word 2)   (Word 3)   (Word 4)

ANALOGIES
Student Activity #2

C.   The Word Analogy Strategy
     Doing word analogies is like breaking a code. It is a thinking process with
     specific steps and decisions. Once you understand the steps and decisions,
     solving word analogies becomes much easier and fun to do. To break this code, you
     must follow six thinking steps.

Thinking model to analyze structure of text

Example C-1

| Player is to team as student is to _____ |
| (Word 1)   (Word 2) (Word 3)   Word 4) |

Step 1.   Make a mental picture of Word 1 (PLAYER).
Step 2.   Make a mental picture of Word 2 (TEAM).
Step 3.   Compare the two mental pictures (PLAYER and TEAM).
Step 4.   Decide how Word 1 (PLAYER) is related to Word 2 (TEAM).
          This is Decision 1. Ask yourself if Word 1 and 2 form:
          a.   a Similar-Meaning Pair? _____
          b.   an Opposite-Meaning Pair?_____
          c.   a Part-to-Whole-Pair   ?_____
          PUT A CHECK ____ next to the type of pair you think Example B is.
Step 5.   Make a mental picture of Word 3 (STUDENT).
Step 6.   Think up a word that relates to Word 3 (STUDENT) in the same way that
          Words 1 and 2 (PLAYER - TEAM) are related. This is Decision 2.
          WRITE your answer here:_____
          Your answer have been the word CLASS because Word 3 (STUDENT) is related
          to Word 4 (CLASS) in the same way that Word 1 (PLAYER) is related to Word
          2 (TEAM). They are both part-to-whole word pairs.
          Now we have completed the analogy.

Player is to team as student is to class.

step-by-step prompts

Example C-2

| Toe is to foot as finger is to _____ . |
| (Word 1)   (Word 2) (Word 3)   (Word 4) |

visualizing strategy

It's your turn to fill in the correct word for each
step. The first word is filled in for you.

Box 1

Step 1.   Make a mental picture of Word 1 (TOE).
           Draw it in Box 1.

Box 2

Step 2.   Make a mental picture of Word 2 (_____).
           Draw it in Box 2.

Step 3.   Compare the two pictures (_____) and (_____).
           Think: Word 1 is physically attached to Word 2.

From *Chicago Mastery Learning Reading, Study Skills, Gold Book* (Grade 6), copyright 1982, Board
of Education of the City of Chicago, Chicago, Illinois. Reprinted by permission.

UNDERLINING AND OUTLINING
Student Activity #2

Outline Notes List
✓ Breathing difficulties   Outline #2
✓ Symptoms
   Avoid open fields   I. _____
   Swelling in the throat   Think: Headings I and II must be equally
   Stay indoors   general. Look at II. Find another major
   Treatment   idea on the list.
   Hay fever
   Watering eyes   A. *Symptoms*
✓ Take antihistamine tablets   1. *Breathing difficulties*
                                  2. _____
                                     Think: Details 1, 2, and 3 must be
                                     equal. What is another detail that
                                     is a symptom?

                                  3. _____
                                     Think: Details 1, 2, and 3 must be
                                     equal. What is another detail that
                                     is a symptom?

                               B. _____
                                  Think: Subheadings A and B must be
                                  equally general. Look at A. Find
                                  another minor idea that is related to
                                  the heading.
                                  1. _____
                                     Think: Details 1, 2, and 3 must be
                                     equal. What is another detail
                                     related to subheading B?

                                  2. *Take antihistamine tablets*
                                  3. _____
                                     Think: Details 1, 2, and 3 must be
                                     equal. What is another detail
                                     related to subheading B?

step-by-step prompts to analyze levels of information

Middle ear   II. Ear infection _____
Nausea
Symptoms   A. _____
✓ Ear infection   1. _____
   Hearing loss
   Dizziness   2. Dizziness _____
   Inner ear   3. _____
✓ Locations
   Fever   4. _____
✓ Outer ear
                                B. Locations _____
                                   1. _____
                                   2. _____
                                   3. Outer ear _____

From *Chicago Mastery Learning Reading, Comprehension, Gold Book* (Grade 6), copyright 1982, Board of Education of the City of Chicago, Chicago, Illinois. Reprinted by permission.

ANALYZING PARAGRAPHS
Student Activity #7

Example B: Identifying the Inferred Main Idea

As the race began, Marti took an outstanding lead in the bike race. His greatest
ambition in life was to win this bike rally. He had to prove to himself and his
family that all that time he had spent tuning his bike and improving his racing
skills was worthwhile. Proving that he was the best biker in town was his last
goal to reach, mountain to climb, before going to college. Down the stretch he
raced, sure he was going to win, when, out of the clear blue sky, Phil pulled
ahead and won by an eyelash. It was the biggest disappointment of Marti's life.
He was crushed. He knew he would never race again. But when he saw the gleam in
Phil's eye as he held the first-place trophy, Marti knew he had to try again next
year.

Explanation: To identify the inferred main idea in this paragraph, you can use
the three-step process.

Step 1: Ask yourself: Is there a topic sentence?
         Think: There is no clearly stated sentence to which all of the
         other sentences can relate; therefore, it is necessary to infer
         the main idea.

Step 2: Ask yourself: What is the purpose of the details?
         Think: All of the sentences describe the bike race and Marti's
         feelings about winning the race.

Step 3   Ask yourself: How can I best summarize how the details are related?
         Think: You can best describe how the details are related by saying,
         "Marti was greatly disappointed by not winning the bike rally, but
         he knew he had to try again next year." This statement then becomes
         the inferred main idea.

Content-specific prompts

EXERCISE B INSTRUCTIONS   Inferring the Main Idea

---1. READ the following paragraphs. ---2. FOLLOW the three-step process for
identifying the inferred main idea. ---3. WRITE the inferred main idea. The
first one is partially done for you.

EXERCISE B PARAGRAPHS   Paragraph B-1

The speech contest was going to be held Friday afternoon, and Sally wanted to be
ready. Each morning, she read over her speech as she ate breakfast. She
repeated the speech from memory as she walked to school. On the playground after
lunch, she made her girl friends listen to her practice it some more. Each eve-
ning she went to her bedroom and, using her tape recorder, she practiced some
more. When Friday afternoon arrived, Sally was ready. She won first place and
received a tall, silver trophy.

Step 1: Ask yourself: Is there a topic sentence already?
         Think *There is no clearly stated sentence to which all of the other
         sentences relate; therefore, it is necessary to infer the main idea.*

Step 2: Ask yourself: What is the purpose of the details?
         Think: _____

         _____

Step 3: Ask yourself: How can I best summarize how the details are related?
         Think: _____

         _____

The inferred main idea is: _____

_____

Content-specific prompts

From *Chicago Mastery Learning Reading, Comprehension, Gold Book* (Grade 6), copyright 1982,
Board of Education of the City of Chicago, Chicago, Illinois. Reprinted by permission.

8 Developing Reading and Thinking Skills in Content Areas

Harold L. Herber
Syracuse University

This chapter presents an instructional program for teaching reading and thinking skills as an integrated part of the various academic subjects taught in our schools. The program is fully explicated in two editions of the text *Teaching Reading in Content Areas* (Herber, 1970, 1978). This paper describes the instruction provided in the program, its theoretical base, and its implementation in school settings—including populations worked with, assessment measures used, data collected, and evaluation problems.

GENERAL INSTRUCTIONAL APPROACH

Time and Place

Traditionally, reading instruction is an identifiable entity in the school curriculum, offered to specific students at a specific time and in a specific place. Reading classes or laboratories are organized to facilitate instruction. Special materials are designed to serve as vehicles for the development and practice of reading skills. Special personnel are hired to provide instruction. In contrast, the instructional program described in this chapter is based on the belief that reading and thinking skills should be taught in the context in which they are required: the various academic content areas taught in schools. Instruction is provided by content-area teachers in their regular classrooms during their regular class time. No special personnel, facilities, or time are needed to make the program work. Similarly, the texts used for reading instruction are those that can best help students acquire content-area knowledge. Thus, specially constructed texts are not needed to provide students with opportunities to practice reading skills.

As students read their regularly assigned texts, they receive instruction in the reading and thinking skills involved in acquiring meaning from these texts. More specifically, the starting point for instruction in this program is the set of ideas that content-area teachers want students to acquire as a result of having studied some academic discipline. Once the teacher has identified these ideas, he or she selects a set of reading materials and teaches students how to read them, in the process both helping them understand the ideas and helping them acquire some general reading and thinking skills useful in working with other texts.

Curriculum Analysis

As suggested previously, the starting point for instruction in this program is an analysis of the content of the academic discipline being studied. From this analysis, the teacher can identify the instructional materials to be used and the reading and thinking skills to be taught. Following Gagné's (1970) notions regarding the structure of knowledge, teachers are encouraged to determine the essential principles, concepts, and details that comprise their curricula. For example, a literature unit might be organized around the general principle that "Literature, in part, is a record of man's attempt to gain a perspective on his fate, sometimes through an examination of reality, other times through an exercise of imagination." Different literary pieces would comprise the unit, each used to develop a concept supportive of the general principle: e.g., William Fryer Harvey's short story "August Heat" might be used to develop the concept that "An inability to distinguish between real and imagined events can lead to stressful speculation about one's fate"; similarly, Robert Frost's poem "The Road Not Taken" might be used to develop the concept that "Speculation on significant decisions leaves one with the consequences of the choice and the question of what might have been." Each work would provide detail in support of its concept, either through the actions and commentary of its character(s) or through the commentary of the author(s). As students read each work they would relate these details to form the more general concept in what Gagné calls a "chaining" process. They would then relate (or chain) the concepts from the various works to form the more general principle.

Curriculum analysis provides teachers with a basis for selecting instructional materials. For example, having identified the concepts to be taught, they can then examine different texts to determine whether sufficient detail is presented for readers to develop these concepts. Similarly, having identified the principles to be taught, they can examine different texts to determine whether the presentation of concepts is sufficiently comprehensive to allow the reader to perceive the overriding principles.

Curriculum analysis also facilitates instruction in the structure of the discipline. If teachers consciously perceive how the ideas in their discipline are organized, they will be more likely to utilize that structure to teach the content of the discipline. If students learn how the details, concepts, and principles of a discipline are formulated and interrelated, their understanding of that discipline is likely to be deeper and more long lasting.

Finally, curriculum analysis often leads to curriculum change: from a curriculum that is informationally based to one that is conceptually based. As one studies the formulation of principles from concepts and concepts from details, it does not take long to discover which are the more enduring and universally applicable. In our era of rapidly expanding and changing knowledge, our students are better served by focusing on the principles and concepts than on the details. The details they do study are momentary examples of the principles and concepts. Another generation may use a different set of details but deal with many of the same concepts and principles nonetheless.

Shifting the emphasis from detail to concept and principle creates a conceptually based curriculum. Having identified the concepts and principles in which they want to offer instruction, teachers then identify the "organizing idea" for each lesson. For a full unit, the "organizing idea" may be a broad-ranging principle. For shorter term lessons, the "organizing idea" may be a concept. In the latter case, students will develop that concept by a study of specific, illustrative details. In the former case, students will develop that principle by a study of several concepts and their related details.

Skills Identification

The general principle that "content determines process" governs the identification and selection of the skills to be taught in this program. After having analyzed possible instructional materials to determine how well they develop the concepts and principles students are to learn, one can analyze them to determine the skills involved in extracting meaning from these materials. These then become the reading and thinking skills taught in the program. Thus, there is considerable variation from one classroom to another in the specific skills that are emphasized. However, despite this variation, there are some very general reading and thinking skills that are developed with all students who participate in the program, regardless of the content areas they are studying.

The program centers around four general categories of reading and thinking skills and asks content-area teachers to adapt instruction in these skills to the material to be read in their content areas. The four categories are: (1) vocabulary acquisition; (2) comprehension; (3) reasoning; and (4) interpersonal communication. "Subskills" within these categories are very limited. In teaching vocabulary skills, the program emphasizes a distinction between the definitions and meanings of words. Students are taught how to use reference materials to determine word definitions and how to analyze words into component parts. Through a variety of different instructional activities, they are also helped to understand that words acquire meanings only as they are used in some context. In teaching comprehension skills, the program emphasizes three aspects of comprehension: literal, reading for significant detail; interpretive, for text-based inference; and applied, for a synthesis of prior knowledge with text-based concepts. Also stressed are the organizational patterns characteristic of expository text: cause–effect, comparison–contrast, chronological order, and enumeration. In teaching critical and creative reasoning skills, the program emphasizes both convergent thinking skills such as analysis and deduction, and divergent thinking skills such as synthesis and induction. In its emphasis on a small number of very general skills, the model of reading reflected in this instructional program is more aligned with Rumelhart's (1976) interactive model than LaBerge and Samuels' (1976) specific skills model. The program subscibes to a wholistic view of reading, emphasizing the commonality of reading processes across disciplines and grade levels.

Teaching Methods

This instructional program makes frequent use of highly structured student interaction in small-group settings to facilitate the acquisition of course content and related reading and thinking skills. Student interaction is structured through use of teacher-prepared reading guides that detail specific activities prior to and during reading. These guides are typically used in small-group settings so that students can have an opportunity to discuss both the ideas they are acquiring through reading and the methods they are using to acquire these ideas.

The teacher-prepared guides consist of activities designed to help students learn how to perform the various reading comprehension skills emphasized in each lesson. In helping students acquire new reading comprehension skills, we put more stress on learning by doing than on learning by telling. That is, instead of describing these skills to students, we attempt to create special situations in which students will be able to apply them successfully. Through the exercises contained in the teacher-prepared reading guides, we attempt to simulate the application of the skills, helping students experience what it feels like to apply them to specific textual materials.

For example, to simulate the experience of making inferences while reading, we give students a passage and a set of related declarative statements. These statements are inferences that one might draw from the passage. As the students read the passage, they determine whether sufficient information is available to warrant these inferences. Where they find evidence, they accept the statements as appropriate inferences and discuss their reasons with their fellow students. Where they fail to find evidence, they reject the statements and share their reasons. This act of marshaling evidence to determine whether sufficient information is available for some specific inference helps students experience, under simplified conditions, the processes involved in making inferences. That is, the teacher-prepared exercises create a simulated situation where students can come to understand the nature of inferencing so that they can subsequently use this skill in a more independent fashion.

After students have had a series of exposures to the simulation of inferencing, they are guided in the development of their own inferential statements. That is, they are given a new passage of text and are asked both to identify appropriate inferences and to offer evidence that these inferences are warranted. Similarly, with the other reading and thinking skills emphasized in the program, after students have had an opportunity to experience using them under simplified conditions, they are encouraged to practice using them in a more independent fashion.

The entire process of simulation is enhanced by having students work together in small groups. In the example already given on inferencing, students share the evidence they perceive to be relevant to the acceptance or rejection of each statement. As a result of this sharing, two things occur: (1) the students gain a fuller understanding of the content discussed in the passage; and (2) they come to understand more clearly how inferences are drawn from pieces of interrelated information. That is, both ideas and reasoning processes become clearer as the students talk them out with one another, so that students end up simultaneously acquiring both domain-specific content knowledge and insight into more general reading and thinking skills. An extended example of a simulation appears later in this chapter as part of the discussion of a literature lesson.

Return to Teaching

During the two decades from 1960 to 1980 there was a virtual explosion in the production of instructional programs and materials. The creative energies of the educational profession were focused on the design of "self-paced, self-managed, teacher-proof systems" to improve students' competence in designated skills and understandings. No area of education received a larger share of such materials than did the field of reading.

Leaving aside the question of the value of these materials, one result of their development was to change the teacher's role from teacher to manager. Rather than providing instruction, teachers facilitated the distribution and collection of materials, kept records of students' progress through prescribed sequences of materials, and approved their progression to new levels. Students often were asked to practice on skills that had not been taught. Thus, without understanding what they were doing, students were practicing error. It is difficult to reinforce a skill that has not been acquired.

This instructional program has returned to teachers their proper teaching role: *preparing*, rather than merely assigning; *showing how*, rather than merely telling; *developing*, rather than merely providing practice. As such, the program provides for flexibility within a structure: A structure is given lessons and materials, but flexibility within these is provided to accommodate different teaching and learning styles.

Staff Development

Because teaching, rather than managing, plays such a central role in this instructional program, considerable emphasis is given to inservice education of participating teachers. They engage in a formal study of the rationale for and application of the techniques emphasized in this program. That is, they receive instruction in techniques for teaching vocabulary skills, comprehension skills, reasoning skills, and student interaction skills. They also learn how to assess these skills, how to organize lessons, and how to develop instructional units (Herber & Nelson, 1976). Initial instruction requires 60–75 clock hours. Follow-up sessions are organized for review, refinement, and additional information. Participants exchange materials, observe and critique one another's classes, and conduct research studies to refine their skills and to further develop and evaluate various aspects of the program.

The staff development program is structured so participating teachers experience the same kind of instruction they are being taught to provide to their students. They are guided in their analysis of their curricula, in their use of various reading materials, and in their creation of materials for guiding students' reading and interaction, and in their small-group discussions. They are supported in their application of the instructional model by personnel with a grounding in the instructional program.

Summary

The instructional program described in this chapter avoids a dichotomy between the teaching of content and the teaching of reading and thinking skills. Content-area teachers, in their own classrooms, using instructional materials selected to improve student content-area knowledge, teach students how to read these materials. There are no separate lessons on reading, thinking, and study skills because students learn the requisite skills for an assignment as they read that assignment. Thus, there is a simultaneous development of content knowledge and reading and thinking skills. The efficiency of this approach to reading instruction is obvious to content-area teachers who study it. They need not be converted into "reading teachers" but, rather, they become more effective content-area teachers.

TYPICAL INSTRUCTIONAL TECHNIQUES

Many different instructional techniques can be used in conjunction with this program and each can be adapted to suit a teacher's own style of teaching. Thus, the variations are infinite. However, there is a common organization to the lessons regardless of the specific instructional techniques that individual teachers use (Herber, 1970). Each lesson is organized into three parts: *preparation* for reading; *guidance* during reading; and *independence* in the utilization of ideas and skills acquired.

The goal of the *preparation* phase of the lesson is to help students activate background knowledge and experience that is relevant to the concepts and principles to be learned. It also provides students with information and objectives that will allow them to participate fully in the activities of the lesson. The goal of the *guidance* phase is to show students how to perform the reading and thinking tasks that are essential in the lesson. It is in this phase that the simulation of reading and thinking skills takes place. The goal of the *independence* phase of the lesson is to provide an opportunity for students to apply the skills and concepts they have acquired through the first two phases. This application will be to concepts and materials that are relevant to what has been studied in each lesson. Because "independence" is a relative state, the levels of sophistication and abstraction required by this application will vary according to just how independently a given set of students can function.

To illustrate how individual lessons are organized and how students are guided in the skills needed to acquire new concepts and principles from reading materials, there follows an abbreviated description of a teacher-prepared lesson from an eighth-grade poetry unit. Where appropriate, materials used by students are reproduced.

Preparation (Teacher)

The poetry unit was introduced by the study of a collection of poems around the common topic of *time*. I established the organizing idea for the introductory lesson as follows: "Time has both quantitative and qualitative dimensions and every person experiences both dimensions differently". Although I did not share this statement with the students, it was the governing principle around which instruction was organized and the ultimate understanding to be derived from the lesson. I created the guides for students to use as they prepared to read the poems and as they actually read them. I located a recording that addressed the theme of *time* to use for purposes of interesting students in the lesson.

Preparation (Students)

After some introductory discussion, I played the recording entitled "Who Knows Where the Time Goes", as students followed the printed lyrics. I asked students for words that came to mind as they reflected on the song. They suggested several, related in one way or another to the concept of *time*, including the word "time" itself.

I placed students in groups and asked them to participate in a contest. They were to write a list of words related to a topic I would give them within a time limit of 2 minutes. The group with the longest list would win. The topic I gave them, just before I said "Go," was *time*. My purpose was to have students tap their experiences relative to *time* and share with and learn from their groups.

The winning group's spokesperson read their list to the whole class. Other groups then shared words from their lists that were different. We discussed possible subcategories under which their words could be organized. I then asked them to see if they could classify their words under two categories, which I wrote on the board under the word *time*, as follows:

TIME

Quantitative   Qualitative

We discussed briefly the difference between the two ideas and gave illustrations of each. Then each group classified their words.

In the process of classification, the students discovered that they had more "quantitative" words than "qualitative.". They also discovered that they had several words that could be classified either way, depending on the experiences they related to those words ("life," for example). My purpose in this classification was to prompt these discoveries and to stimulate both the convergent and divergent thinking that became evident.

With the discussion of their word lists and classifications as background, I then gave them the following list of statements to discuss.

1. Nothing is slower than time wished away; nothing is faster than time held dear.
2. People work for today and dream for tomorrow.
3. Time is a fence to be climbed, a chain to be broken.
4. What you do with your life is more important than how long you live.
5. Different people experience the same thing differently.

I read through the statements as students followed along. I asked them to make an immediate judgment as to whether or not each statement was acceptable or reasonable. They then discussed their responses with one another in their groups. Their directions were to discuss the reasons for their responses; that is, what they knew, experienced, felt, or believed that prompted their response. My purpose was twofold: (1) to help them get in touch with their own experience relative to these concepts and principles; and (2) to stimulate the critical and creative thinking that became evident in their small-group and full-class discussions of these statements.

Guidance

With all the prior discussions as background, I then randomly assigned to each group a different poem and related guide. The potential existed for differentiating materials with respect to concept load and other indicators of difficulty. However, this class did not require such differentiations. My purpose in having different poems was to provide an opportunity for each group to teach its poem to the rest of the class, sharing its message and soliciting from other groups their judgments concerning the meanings and applications of ideas from the poem (see the next section, "Independence").

Four poems (and guides) were distributed. To illustrate, the guide for the poem "The Day," by Theodore Spencer, follows:

Does time remain the same? Read this poem and see what the poet seems to think.

1. Before you read this poem, note the definitions of words below:
   shrank: past tense of shrink; to become smaller
   limped: past tense of limp; to walk favoring one leg

2. One person in the group should read the poem aloud to the rest of the group. They may listen and follow along or just listen.

3. After the poem has been read, show the comparisons the author made by drawing connecting lines among the three columns of words listed below:

day	minute	children
day	week	young men
day	hour	old men
day	year	dead men
day	month	lovers
day	forever	boys

4. Now check the following ideas you think this poem supports. Be ready to give reasons for your answers.
   _____a. Young time is short.
   _____b. Old time is fast.
   _____c. No time is endless.
   _____d. What people actually experience is the opposite of what you might think they should.
   _____e. The longer life is, the shorter time seems to be.
   _____f. Time affects how people move.

5. Look again at the set of statements about time that you discussed before reading

this poem. Place an x on the second line before each statement if you think the author of your poem would agree with it.

My purposes for each successive part of the guide were: first, to present key words to aid meaning acquisition and add understanding to the reading of the poem; second, to make certain students gained a sense of the total impact of the poem before studying it more closely; third, to help students perceive the essential information in the poem and the relationships that exist within it; fourth, to help students analyze the poem for explicit and implicit ideas and to guide them in doing this (*Note* that students were asked to cite evidence to support their acceptance or rejection of each statement to help them understand why some interpretations are more appropriate than others); and fifth, to teach students how to evaluate new ideas acquired from reading and to guide them in this process. The students were to determine if the author would agree or disagree with the ideas discussed at the very beginning of the lesson, ideas that students had accepted or rejected as valid for themselves. Determining the author's probable agreement with ideas one has already evaluated simulates the process of evaluating new ideas against previously acquired knowledge. Requiring students to discuss the reasons for their decisions helps them come to understand what is involved in determining whether a newly acquired idea is consistent with previous knowledge.

Independence

After each group completed the study of its poem, it shared the poem with the rest of the class by summarizing the poet's ideas or by reading the poem aloud. On the basis of this experience, the other groups were to determine whether or not that poet would agree with any of the five statements about time that the students had discussed at the beginning of the lesson. Again, students were asked to give reasons for their decisions.

My purpose in asking students to engage in these activities was to have them continue to use the skills they had been learning, but under conditions of calling for greater independence. Students had to apply the same skills to the new poems that they had applied earlier, except that they were not being guided so specifically. They had to identify the essential information and relationships, to perceive explicit and implicit ideas, and to evaluate these against prior understandings. Asking for evidence throughout heightened their consciousness of the processes they were applying.

EVOLUTION OF THE PROGRAM

This poetry unit, as noted, reflects several of the instructional techniques that can be used as part of the program, as well as the overall instructional framework into which these techniques fit. The instructional techniques, the framework, the materials, and the related staff development activities are based on a rationale that evolved through several overlapping stages.

Theoretical Background

The origins of this instructional program are similar to those of any other: a study of the theory and research of other professionals in the field. One finds productive avenues of inquiry, trends in the research, compatibility of ideas with one's own predilections. Gradually there is a synthesis of ideas and one builds the base for one's own work. And on this base questions arise that need to be tested.

Space permits the mention of only a few of the theorists and researchers who contributed to the program in its initial stages. Durrell's (1966) work in word analysis, recognition, and reinforcement led ultimately to activities for presenting, teaching, and reinforcing technical vocabulary in the various disciplines. His work with paired practice and structured small-group activities for promoting vocabulary acquisition and study skills highlighted the value of having students work in small-group settings and found its way into the practices of this program.

Bruner's (1960) thinking on the structure to be found in various disciplines was synthesized with that of Ford and Pugano (1964) on the structure of knowledge and the curriculum and later with that of Gagné (1970). These ideas made us sensitive to the need for teachers to be aware of the structure of their discipline so they can more easily communicate this knowledge to their students.

Ausubel's (1960) work with advance organizers stimulated an interest in cognitive processing and the organization of memory. This led to efforts to utilize technical vocabulary from various academic disciplines to organize students' knowledge of concepts in the form of structured overviews (Barron, 1971; Earle, 1970).

Complex models of intellect (Guilford, 1956; Holmes, 1965) were examined in light of theoretical taxonomies of cognition (Bloom, 1956) and compared to simple (Smith, 1963) and easily manageable (Gray, 1960) descriptions of the processes involved in comprehension. This led to a definition of comprehension as involving a small number of very general skills rather than a larger number of more specific ones (a conceptualization that was designed to make instuction in comprehension skills manageable for content-area teachers). Niles' (1965) definition of the organizational patterns found in exposition was similarly useful.

The theory and research of Russell (1956), Ennis (1962), Sochor (1958), and Bruner (1966) highlighted the need for an emphasis on critical thinking. This work, and a realization that there are levels of sophistication within the higher cognitive processes involved in critical thinking (Bruner, 1960), led to an emphasis on reasoning for students at all ability levels in the program.

Betts' (1946) Directed Reading Activity provided an initial organization for lessons and the related instructional strategies. However, the assumption in the Directed Reading Activity that students can read the text independently seems unfounded. It seems that they need to be guided *during* reading as well as before. Though Guzak (1967) found an excessive frequency of low-level questions asked by teachers, questioning continued to be the most widely accepted strategy for guiding students' reading comprehension. This, too, seemed to involve some assumptions about students' skills that may have been unwarranted. That is, in order to answer the questions their teachers were asking, students would have to already possess the skills that these questions were designed to develop. Bruner's (1960) idea that any concept can be taught to anyone at any level if broken down into manageable pieces triggered ideas that eventually led to pre-questioning strategies that are much less assumptive with respect to students' prior possession of the target skill(s) (Herber & Nelson, 1975).

Intuitive Pragmatism

Long-term work with content-area teaches was required to develop these ideas into a practical instructional program. Virtually nothing was available in the literature that showed content teachers how to reach their subject matter and related reading and thinking skills simultaneously. Drawing on the theory and research, but responding to the need for practicality, developers of this instructional program began to create materials and strategies to improve vocabulary, comprehension, reasoning, and interpersonal communication.

Criteria were established for teachers to select from passages of text the words to emphasize in helping students comprehend these passages (Herber, 1970, 1978). Strategies were devised for helping students distinguish between definitions and meanings of words and to be able to deal with technical vocabulary at both surface and deeper-meaning levels (Herber,1964, 1978). Teachers drew on students' general vocabulary background and, as appropriate, supplied technical vocabulary relevant to the concept being studied. This vocabulary was used to construct a visual display of the relationships that exist among the words used to develop and express the concept. This display, or "structured overview" (Barron, 1971), served as a framework into which students could fit the information and ideas they acquired from their reading and study about the concept.

Comprehension was defined as a three-level contruct: literal, interpretive, and applied (akin to Gray's "reading the lines, reading between the lines, and reading beyond the lines"). The levels were first thought to be hierarchical (Herber, 1970), but experience proved otherwise. Now they are seen as interactive, potentially operating either bottom up or top down (Herber, 1978). This construct is easily manageable by teachers and students and applicable to nearly all reading materials and other informational resources assigned in content classes.

Materials were designed to guide students' reading at these three levels of comprehension. At first, questions were used (Herber, 1970). Later, after speculation about prequestioning strategies (Herber & Nelson, 1975), guides were prepared using declarative statements (Herber, 1978). Similar materials were designed to guide students' utilization of organizational patterns found in expository materials (cause–effect, comparison–contrast, time order, simple listing). Materials were also designed to guide students' use of various reasoning strategies; those that focus more closely on an analysis of the material being studied, as well as those that spin off the material and elaborate on the ideas being expressed (Herber, 1978).

We played with *prediction* as a motivational device for reading and as an enhancement of students' natural curiosity for learning new ideas. Word association activities, pre-reading "reasoning guides," and other strategies were designed to help students tap into prior knowledge and experience with respect to the organizing idea for a lesson. Such activities seemed to provide an experiential context for students' study of organizing ideas. Their attitudes seemed better, their interest greater, and their motivations higher. It seemed to make the content more relevant even though the curriculum remained essentially the same.

In all cases, guide materials were coupled with small-group discussions among students in the class. We developed procedures and criteria for strengthening the group interaction and making it more productive.

EVALUATION OF THE PROGRAM

This program evolved over several years through a combination of research and practice. Much of what was developed intuitively in association with classroom teachers has been supported in research studies both by persons associated with this instructional program and by others. Instructional strategies were conceptualized and tried in schools to determine their practicality. Subsequently, they were examined more closely in research studies. The findings from those studies were then fed back into the school programs to determine if the practicality remained. Thus, there was an evaluation of the individual components of the program, mainly through dissertation research, and of the program as a whole, mainly through school-sponsored evaluations.

Evaluation of Program Components

Over the past 11 years, more than 20 interrelated dissertation studies have examined various materials and strategies related to this program. Although no single study has produced highly significant or singularly definitive results, there is much to be learned by an examination of the entire series of studies. Interestingly, basic research carried out at the Center for the Study of Reading has provided insights into the nature of skilled reading that are consistent with many of the instructional techniques used in this program.

Program components were examined by the dissertation studies in order to maximize their effectiveness singly and in combination. The eventual product hoped for was a well-tested program comprised of highly refined components. Because these studies were conducted in school settings, the researchers could not control for variables as tightly as they might had they been in a clinic or laboratory setting. Experimental and control groups were formed from intact classes. No special sample populations were identified. In most of the studies, the capacity and achievement of students within the classes reflected a normal distribution on the criteria employed (usually intelligence, reading, and content-area standardized tests) for determining comparability of groups. Frequently there were pretreatment differences between the intact classes on the criterion measures, and analysis of covariance had to be used with the data.

In the dissertation studies, a variety of dependent measures was used: standardized achievement tests to assess reading skills and content-area knowledge; experimenter-prepared tests of the concepts and principles taught; and experimenter-prepared, Likert-type attitude scales. The standardized tests usually were those normally used by the school districts in which the studies were being conducted. The experimenter-prepared tests were developed in concert with the participating classroom teachers, following a table of specifications, utilizing judges for face validity as appropriate, and piloting the tests to determine reliability.

The experimenters were able to monitor in four ways the work of the teachers who provided the instruction. Typically, the experimenters worked with the teachers in the design of the experimental materials to be certain that the appropriate concepts were being emphasized. The experimenters also instructed the teachers in the teaching procedures to use in implementing the program. Thirdly, the experimenters were able to monitor instruction on a regular basis in most of the studies. Finally, many of the experimenters requested that their participating teachers keep a log of their activities both as a reminder of essential tasks and procedures and as a source of confirmation that the experimental procedures and materials were being followed and used.

Data from the dissertation studies generally were reported at the .05 significance level. As frequently happens in field-based experiments, results from the studies were sometimes equivocal on two grounds: (1) where statistical differences occurred on the dependent measures, real score differences were sometimes not large enough to be educationally significant; and (2) where no statistical differences were found between treatment and control groups on dependent measures, teachers sometimes reported a contrary, subjective evaluation in favor of the treatment. Even though some studies produced equivocal findings, other studies yielded important information relative to the components of the program. In the following paragraphs, we summarize major findings from the dissertation studies, limiting our report of empirical findings to those that were both statistically significant and involved sufficiently large differences between experimental and control groups to seem educationally significant.

The structured overview was found useful in developing students' understanding of relationships that exist among words that comprise more complex concepts

(Earle, 1970). A variation of the structured overview, called graphic organizers, was found productive in aiding students' recall and interpretation of the ideas studied in a lesson (Barron, 1979). Alvermann (1980) found that the prereading use of a graphic organizer significantly affected the number of propositions readers recalled from attributive (simple listing) text when the organizer prepared students to anticipate comparisons that were implied in the text. Walker (1975) also found graphic organizers productive in developing students' recall of social studies material. Sanders (1970) found that when students used a modified levels guide, the frequency of their interpretive (rather than literal) responses to literature increased, with their interpretations being qualitatively better than those of the control group. These differences were retained during the subsequent independent reading of short stories. Vacca (1973) developed strategies for improving the interaction of students in small-group discussions and criteria for judging its effectiveness.

The three-level construct of comprehension does have construct validity (Honeycutt, 1971). It is also consistent with notions in schema theory that comprehension is both a top-down and bottom-up process. Pearson and Johnson's (1978) taxonomy of questions and answers for comprehension have a direct correspondence to the three levels of comprehension defined in this program: literal or textually explicit; interpretive or textually implicit; applied or scriptally implicit.

Using declarative statements rather than questions to guide students' reading of text material seems to be effective in improving comprehension, both on those passages of text for which guides are provided as well as on subsequent passages that students are asked to read independently (Herber & Nelson, 1975). As a prequestioning strategy, the use of declarative statements creates a "simulation" of comprehension as students respond to text. There is a need for transitional materials to move students from statements to questions as the guiding medium (Maxon, 1978). These results, coupled with trends that emerged as we looked across the series of studies, gave us a sense of validity in the instructional program. This sense of validity was strengthened as we studied the program in operation in schools.

Application of Program in Schools

The true tests of an instructional program are its acceptance by teachers and its positive effect on students' achievement. By these standards, the program has enjoyed success. Teachers find the strategies a valuable addition to their teaching. They are positive in their estimate of its impact on their students. However, much of the data are subjective rather than objective, leaving the value open to question to those who are not persuaded by subjective data.

The field-based evaluations of the program were motivated mainly by a need to obtain student and teacher reaction to extended usage of the instructional materials and strategies. Each district had its own agenda to meet with respect to evaluation; hence, each district collected data on instruments that were of particular importance to them. The length of time that the program was in operation in schools varied from 1 to 12 years. The evaluation reports were filed with local boards of education; few were reproduced for general distribution.

Students in the participating school districts were recipients of the instruction by virtue of their teachers' involvement in this program. Some teachers worked with low achievers, some with gifted, some with the full range. Thus, the program has been field tested with the entire range of student ability and achievement levels to be found in school settings.

The teachers who took part in these evaluations differed widely in years of teaching experience, academic preparation, subject-matter specialization, and time of involvement in the staff-development program. In most districts, teachers volunteered to be participants in the program. Thus, in terms of professional motivation and interest in change, they did not represent a normalized sample of the teaching profession. To determine the effects of the program on teachers themselves, districts have developed questionnaires, structured interviews, introspective–retrospective check lists, attitude scales, tests of knowledge acquisition, and procedures for demonstration teaching by videotape or live. In addition, teachers have developed anecdotal records of their experience and of the perceived effect of the program on their own students.

The data derived from the field-based evaluations of the instructional program suggest several benefits. Students benefit by a better attitude toward school and their studies, by greater self-confidence in their ability to meet academic requirements, by improved comprehension of their texts, by better performance on tests, by more communication with the teacher and fellow students in large- and small-group instruction, and by more time spent on concept development and less time on mere memorization of information. Teachers benefit by a lesson structure that enables them to simultaneously emphasize course content and reading and thinking skills, by instructional strategies that help them manage this combined emphasis on content and skills, and by materials that serve both as a support for the strategies and as a focus for their own study and refinement of their curriculum. In particular, teachers benefit from engaging in curriculum analysis, reporting new insights into what they teach as they lay out the structure of their curriculum and identify the "organizing ideas" for lessons and units of instruction. While reporting positive results in the use of the guide materials, teachers include two negative impressions, each with ameliorating conditions. Preparation of the materials takes a great deal of time, almost more than they are able to give. However, as more colleagues become involved in the program, they can work together and share what they produce. The added value of talking with colleagues about curriculum and teaching (plus the benefit to students) makes this cooperative work worthwhile. Teachers report that constant use of these materials tends to bore students and diminish the value of the materials. This occurs in the early stages of teachers' involvement in the program, when they are creating materials and testing their usefulness. However, as teachers internalize the instructional options and adapt them to their own teaching styles, the guide materials become a natural part of instruction and are used only as they fit naturally into the total lesson or unit. Even more important was the report that, as teachers gain experience in the program, they apply the principle of *guiding students's learning* whether they are using formalized written guides or not.

In the following paragraphs, we have attempted to summarize conclusions that can be drawn from a careful study of the results of the dissertation studies and the field-based evaluations considered together:

1. Teachers whose districts provide time for them to study the teaching of reading and thinking skills in content areas and who are given the opportunity to discuss this teaching and the related curricular issues with their colleagues, experience a positive change in their teaching and believe that their teaching has a positive impact on their students.

2. The reading and thinking skills that have been identified for emphasis in this instructional program seem to have equal applicability across grade levels and subject areas.

3. The materials designed to guide students' application of appropriate reading and thinking skills while reading required texts seem to meet that purpose effectively.

4. Students who have been guided in the development of the reading and thinking skills advocated in this program are able to apply these skills independently to similar tasks.

5. Students' attitudes and achievement are positively affected by opportunities to discuss concepts and to learn from one another in purposeful, well-structured group work.

6. A few students are not helped by this instructional program because their specialized learning needs fall outside its focus and purpose. Undoubtedly, there are other reasons for the program's lack of impact on some students, but none can be identified at present.

7. There are teachers who do not find this instructional program workable with their classes. This finding occurs more frequently in districts where teacher's participation is voluntary. There are, as yet, no hard data either to support a possible inference from this observation, or to draw profiles of teachers who like and teachers who do not like the program.

Evaluation Problems

Not all problems are negative. One can find many that are positive, especially in the further development of an instructional program.

Positive Problems. Conducting research and evaluation on instructional programs requires a "symbiotic relationship among (research) paradigms" (Pearson

& Samuels, 1980). These researchers suggest that the two paradigms involved are "naturalistic inquiry" occurring in "real environments," and "experimental research" occurring in "decontextualized environments." This instructional program has profited from such a symbiotic relationship. Specific materials and strategies were developed in response to instructional needs. Experimental research was conducted on the materials and strategies. Findings were applied in the naturalistic settings of content-area classrooms. Refinements were made, based on evaluations in that environment, and they, in turn, were subjected to experimental research. Through this cycle, the strategies and materials were refined to their present point of effectiveness.

The most recent application of this refining process is the creation of a Network of Secondary School Demonstration Centers for Teaching Reading in Content Areas, funded through the Basic Skills Program in the U.S. Department of Education (Herber & Nelson, 1980). Four school districts, each having been involved with this instructional program for several years, have joined two universities to create this network. In four different educational settings (megalopolis, urban–suburban, small city, regionalized district), the following are being demonstrated: staff development for content-area teachers; teaching reading and thinking skills in content areas; and field-based, "naturalistic" research. Under the supervision of the writer, as Director, and Dr. Joan Nelson of SUNY Binghamton, as Associate Director, the network will serve as a logical context for a continuation of this symbiotic relationship between the two worlds of research. Thus, the positive problem will continue: how to keep the information and ideas from the two worlds of research flowing smoothly between one another, to the benefit of students' learning and their teachers' instruction.

Negative Problems. The major problem of a negative nature is lack of instrumentation sensitive enough to measure the changes that seem to be taking place, but moderate in their demands on teacher and student time. Objective data are needed to confirm teachers' observations and subjective evaluations. Also needed are more research designs for use in "real world settings" that will combine rigor with realism and produce data in which researchers from both worlds will have confidence. These volumes are a grand step in this direction. Let us hope this step is the first of many.

REFERENCES

Alvermann, D. E. *Effects of graphic organizers, textual organization, and reading comprehension level on recall of expository prose.* Unpublished doctoral dissertation, Syracuse University, 1980
Ausubel, D. P. The use of advance organizers in the learning and retention of meaningful verbal material. *Journal of Educational Psychology*, 1960, 51, 267–272.
Barron, R. F. *The use of iterative research process to improve a method of vocabulary instruction in tenth grade biology.* Unpublished doctoral dissertation, Syracuse University, 1971.

Barron, R. F. Research for the classroom teacher: Recent developments on the structured overview as an advance organizer. In H. L. Herber & J. D. Riley (Eds.), *Research in reading in the content areas: The fourth report.* Syracuse: Syracuse University Reading and Language Arts Center, 1979.

Betts, E. A. *Foundations for reading instruction.* New York: American Book Co., 1946.

Bloom, B. S. *Taxonomy of educational objectives (cognitive domain).* New York: McKay, 1956.

Bruner, J. S. *The process of education.* New York: Vintage Books, 1960.

Bruner, J. S. *The act of discovery. On knowing.* Cambridge, Mass.: Belknap Press, 1966.

Durrell, D. D. *Improving reading instruction.* New York: Harcourt Brace Jovanovich, 1966.

Earle, R. *The use of vocabulary as a structured overview in seventh grade mathematics.* Unpublished doctoral dissertation, Syracuse University, 1970.

Ennis, R. H. A concept of critical thinking. *Harvard Educational Review*, 1962, *32*, 81–111.

Ford, G. W., & Pugano, L. *The structure of knowledge and the curriculum.* Chicago: Rand McNally, 1964.

Gagné, R. M. *The conditions of learning.* New York: Holt, Rinehart, & Winston, 1970.

Gray, W. S. The major aspects of reading. In H. Robinson (Ed.), *Supplementary educational monographs*, No. 90. Chicago: University of Chicago Press, 1960.

Guilford, J. P. The structure of intellect. *Psychology Bulletin*, 1956, *53*, 267–293.

Guzak, F. J. Teaching questioning and reading. *The Reading Teacher*, December 1967, *21*, 227–234.

Herber, H. L. *Success with words.* New York: Scholastic Book Services, 1964.

Herber, H. L, *Teaching reading in content areas.* Englewood Cliffs, N. J.: Prentice–Hall, 1970, 1978.

Herber, H. L, & Nelson, J. Questioning is not the answer. *Journal of Reading*, 1975, *18*, 512–517.

Herber, H. L., & Nelson, J. *Reading across the curriculum.* Homer, N. Y.: TRICA Consultants, Inc., 1976.

Herber, H. L., & Nelson, J. *A network of secondary school demonstration centers for teaching reading in content areas* (Grant #G008001963). Basic skills Improvement Program, Title II, 1980.

Holmes, J. A. Basic assumptions underlying the substrata-factor theory. *Reading Research Quarterly*, 1965, *1*, 5–27.

Honeycutt, C. D. *An investigation of the theoretical constructs of three levels of comprehension.* Unpublished doctoral dissertation, Syracuse University, 1971.

LaBerge, D., & Samuels, S. J. Toward a theory of automatic information processing in reading. In H. Singer & R. Ruddell (Eds.), *Theoretical models and processes of reading.* Newark, Del.: International Reading Association, 1976.

Maxon, G. *The effects of guiding reading using questions and declarative statements separately and in particular order.* Unpublished doctoral dissertation, Syracuse University, 1978.

Niles, O. S. Organization perceived. In H. L. Herber (Ed.), *Developing study skills in secondary schools.* Newark, Del.: International Reading Association, 1965.

Pearson, P. D., Johnson, D. D. *Teaching reading comprehension.* New York: Holt, Rinehart, & Winston, 1978.

Pearson, P. D., & Samuels, S. J. Editorial. *Reading Research Quarterly*, 1980, *15*, 429–430.

Rumelhart, D. E. *Toward an interactive model of reading* (Tech. Rep. No. 56). La Jolla: University of California, Center for Human Information Processing, 1976.

Russell, D. H. *Children's thinking.* New York: McKay, 1956.

Sanders, P. L. *An investigation of the effects of instruction in the interpretation of literature on the responses of adolescents to selected short stories.* Unpublished doctoral dissertation, Syracuse University, 1970.

Smith, N. B. *Reading for today's children.* Englewood Cliffs, N. J.: Prentice–Hall, 1963.

Sochor, E. E. Literal and critical reading in social studies. *Journal of Experimental Education*, September 1958, *27*, 49–56.

Vacca, R. *An investigation of a functional reading strategy in seventh-grade social studies*. Unpublished doctoral dissertation, Syracuse University, 1973.

Walker, N. *An investigation into the effects of graphic organizers on the learning of social studies readers in the middle grades*. Unpublished doctoral dissertation, Syracuse University, 1975.

9 Acquiring Information from Texts: An Analysis of Four Approaches

Joseph C. Campione
Bonnie B. Armbruster
University of Illinois at Urbana–Champaign

Our assignment as analyzers of the knowledge acquisition programs discussed in these volumes was to review a set of four programs aimed at facilitating learning from texts. We interpreted the task as one of comparing the programs with one another to determine the extent to which they seemed to agree on any general approaches to the instruction of critical reading skills, and commenting on their differences. We also intended to evaluate the relative merits of the programs by considering whether their emphases were consistent with recent theoretical and empirical advances in cognitive and developmental theory.

The first thing we learned was that although the programs shared the same global aim, they were strikingly different in so many basic ways that it makes no sense to try to determine which program or programs are most effective. For example, they differ in the developmental level of the subjects who are the target of instruction, the skills and activities that are to be taught, the form of instruction preferred, and the criterion task(s) against which success or failure of the programs might be evaluated. Given this state of affairs, we have opted for a different strategy. Rather than attempting to determine which program or programs are best, we have emphasized some of the dimensions of difference distinguishing these approaches, as well as pointing out where there is some agreement. If the differences can be regarded as indicating areas of controversy about how we might set up an instructional package, we might then evaluate the extent to which basic research and theory can help reconcile debates. If no answer emerges, we can at least ask if the controversies inferred from our review here are similar to those appearing in the theoretical literature, i.e., even if there are no answers, is there some agreement concerning the important questions?

In the first section, we provide a brief description of each of the programs to give its flavor. As each of the developers has a chance to describe his or her

317

own programs and assumptions elsewhere in this volume, our descriptions are brief and somewhat selective. In the next section, we highlight what we see as the major differences among the programs in terms of their views regarding comprehension and instruction. As what one feels is important is influenced considerably by his or her biases or theoretical preferences, we preface the discussion with a description of a general framework we have been using to guide some research on studying from texts, along with some views about the nature of the relation between learning and individual differences. Having thus raised a series of issues, we ask whether we can resolve any of them on the basis of available data, or whether there are fairly clear theoretical grounds for anticipating the probable final answers. The main aim is to indicate the kind of research necessary to move closer to a resolution of the issues. In the final section, we briefly describe what we see as some critical areas for future research.

DESCRIPTION OF THE PROGRAMS

The programs are described in the following order: Instruction in Learning Strategies (Jones, Amiran, & Katims—hereafter JAK); Instruction in Learning Strategies (Dansereau); Improving Reading in the Content Areas (Herber); and Cognitive Learning Strategies (Weinstein). For each program, the descriptions include the following topics: (1) background information; (2) general goals of instruction (as stated by the author or inferred), including the target population(s) with whom the author is working and the kinds of criterion tasks students should be able to perform upon completion of the program; (3) the nature of the comprehension skills in which instruction is offered; and (4) assumptions about pedagogy and the instructional method chosen.

Instruction in Learning Strategies (Jones, Amiran, & Katims)

The Instruction in Learning Strategies materials consist of two main parts: Matrix Outlining and Analysis, and the Chicago Mastery Learning Reading Program with Learning Strategies. The two parts are described separately.

Matrix Outlining and Analysis (MOAN)

Background and Goals.   Matrix Outlining and Analysis materials have been under development and revision since 1976. Although the results of research studies have suggested the potential usefulness of this technique, the materials had not yet undergone systematic field testing at the time of writing.

The goal of these materials is to teach students to use matrices as an aid in organizing and analyzing information from reading and prior knowledge and as an aid in reporting on this information in the form of compare-and-contrast type essays and research papers. Students are taught to translate information from school texts and other reading materials into two-dimensional tables, with the names of the objects or events being compared serving as one dimension of the table, and the categories along which they are being compared serving as the other. They are then taught how to look across these matrices for patterns and generalizations and how to use these generalizations as the basis for writing essays. The Matrix Outlining and Analysis materials are intended to be used as one component in an English composition course in high school or college or as a core developmental course for low-achieving junior college students.

Skills in Which Instruction is Offered.   The Matrix Outlining and Analysis materials are based on research showing that individuals can more readily acquire new information from prose when the information is presented in an organized rather than a disorganized form (Frase, 1969). Subsequent research by Jones (1976) and Jones and Hall (1979) demonstrated that college and junior high school students could be trained to use a two-dimensional matrix to cross-classify disorganized information and that this kind of training led to improvements in recall. The Matrix Outlining and Analysis materials are an extension of this research in an attempt to teach students how to impose an organization on information acquired through reading. However, in these materials, the goal of instruction has changed from organizing information to more adequately remember it, to organizing information to more adequately analyze and report on it.

The Matrix Outlining and Analysis materials aspire to provide instruction for each of the phases of developing a composition identified by Hayes and Flower (1978) and Flower and Hayes (1980): generating ideas, organizing levels and topics in terms of the writing goal and audience, translating the organizational structure into writing, and reviewing/editing. The materials are divided into three parts. The first unit, *Text Matrices,* teaches students to write, in expository prose, compare-and-contrast essays based on historical narrative materials. The second unit, *Fiction Matrices,* teaches students to write compare-and-contrast essays using fictional material. The third unit, *Research Matrices,* teaches students to write compare-and-contrast essays integrating information from multiple sources, as is necessary in writing a research paper. The units contain appendices describing the underlying structure of different kinds of literary and social science texts so that students can come to understand what dimensions to use in analyzing different text forms.

Pedagogical Assumptions and Instructional Methods.   In Matrix Outlining and Analysis, instruction proceeds in small steps, beginning with materials that are simple and familiar. Unlike CMLR/LS, however, these materials are missing the element of mastery learning. The materials are also more self-instructional and less teacher directed than CMLR/LS.

To convey a sense of the kinds of procedures that students are encouraged to follow and of the kind of step-by-step guidance that is offered, we briefly describe the unit on text matrices. At the beginning of the unit, students are assigned a compare-and-contrast type essay and a set of readings from which to draw information relevant to the essay. They are taught how to take notes on these readings and how to sort their notes into categories to determine appropriate dimensions for use in making comparisons. They are then taught how to transpose the information from their notes into a matrix and how to analyze the matrix, looking across the data in the rows and columns for patterns and generalizations. For example, they are taught to look across each row to determine whether the objects or events being compared are similar or different along each dimension, to try to understand what factors might account for these observed similarities and differences, and to make predictions about other likely similarities and differences, based on an understanding of these patterns. Having completed their analysis of the data, they are then taught to use their conclusions for organizing an essay. Each of the conclusions becomes a topic sentence and the information within the cells offers supporting details. Further descriptions and examples of instructional materials from the Matrix Outlining and Analysis program can be found in the chapter by Jones, Amiran, and Katims in this volume.

Chicago Mastery Learning Reading Program with Learning Strategies

Background and Goals.   Chicago has traditionally been well below the national norms in reading. In 1974, the Chicago Board of Education published the Curriculum Guide in Reading for the Elementary School, which identifies 273 key objectives in reading comprehension, literature, word attack, and study skills. According to Board policy, students must master 80% of these objectives, as determined by performance on a criterion-referenced test, in order to be promoted to the next level. To help teachers and students meet this goal, the Board has sponsored, since 1976, the development of the Chicago Mastery Learning Reading Program, an instructional program tied directly to the key objectives. The program spans reading levels K–8. The upper level of the program (Grades 5– 8) contains an additional learning strategies component and is designated the Chicago Mastery Learning Reading Program with Learning Strategies (CMLR/ LS). The materials for CMLR/LS are still being developed, tested, and revised. This chapter reviews the 1980 versions of the Reading Comprehension and Study Skills strands for Grades 5 and 6 only.

Although CMLR/LS as a whole has not yet been formally evaluated, several pieces of evidence point to its effectiveness: the program has been mandated citywide in Chicago; classrooms using CMLR/LS show increased gains on standardized reading tests over previous years when CMLR/LS was not used; there is a reported decline in absenteeism, student transfer, and discipline problems;

and acceptance rates have increased for CMLR/LS students at magnet vocational schools requiring successful performance on their own entrance reading test.

In general, the CMLR/LS materials are intended to improve the abillity of students in Grades 5–8 to comprehend text through the mastery of specific reading/learning strategies that research in cognitive psychology has indicated are fundamental to reading comprehension. The immediate objective of the program is to improve scores on criterion-referenced tests based on 131 key objectives defined by the Chicago school system.

Skills in Which Instruction is Offered.   Each CMLR/LS unit is addressed to one or more of the 131 key objectives for Grades 5–8 as defined by the Chicago school district. At each grade level, the objectives are divided into two groups: reading comprehension objectives and study skills objectives. The reading comprehension objectives focus on mastery of skills involved in comprehending different kinds of texts. Some examples of specific skills include: learning the different ways in which paragraphs can be organized (for example, distinguishing descriptive from explanatory paragraphs); understanding how different genres of text are organized (for example, learning the major elements that are typically included in a simple story); learning how to make inferences from text; learning how to summarize; learning how to outline and underline; etc. The study skills objectives include mastery of skills involved in locating information and in analyzing information presented in nontextual formats. Some examples are: learning to use dictionaries and card catalogues; learning to read maps, graphs, charts, and tables; understanding different ways that words and concepts can be related (finding opposites, completing analogies, identifying prefixes and suffixes, etc.).

Pedagogical Assumptions and Instructional Methods.   As indicated by the title of the program, the mastery learning model developed by Bloom (1968, 1976) and elaborated by Block (1971) and Block and Burns (1977) forms the pedagogical foundation of CMLR/LS. The developers of CMLR/LS assume that the mastery learning model can work in reading by: (1) providing instructional experiences to students that take into account individual differences in learning needs; and (2) allowing teachers as well as students to benefit effectively from regular success. A third key pedagogical assumption of CMLR/LS is that students can best learn new strategies by initially following step-by-step models that explain the sequence of mental operations involved in executing these strategies. These step-by-step models are followed by prompted exercises requiring use of the same steps. Transfer capability is encouraged by gradually withdrawing strategy instructions and prompts. A fourth pedagogical assumption underlying CMLR/LS is that instruction is more effective and promotes greater transfer if the sequence of examples and exercises proceeds from short, simple, concrete, and familiar to longer, more complex, more abstract, and less familiar.

The program is organized into units of approximately 20–40 pages. Each unit centers around a different reading comprehension skill and offers instruction in the concepts and procedures involved executing that skill. For example, the unit on summarizing familiarizes students with the concept of a summary and teaches them strategies for summarizing different kinds of paragraphs.

The first activity in each unit is teacher directed and explains the concepts and strategies to be learned. This is followed by one or more self-instructional activities that further develop these concepts and strategies and offer practice in their use. To explain new concepts and strategies, the program contains many step-by-step models of thinking processes. For example, the unit on analogies provides students with a six-step model of the thinking processes in solving analogy problems (e.g., problems of the variety A is to B as C is to D). The model encourages students to: (1) form a mental picture of the first word in the analogy problem; (2) form a mental picture of the second word; (3) compare the two mental pictures; (4) decide how the words are related, choosing from one of several different categories of relationship; (5) form a mental picture of the third word; and (6) think up a fourth word that extends the relationship to the second pair of terms.

As new concepts and strategies are introduced, there are many opportunities for practice with longer, more complex, and more abstract exercises. The exercises are usually prompted to remind students of the strategies. Prompts are gradually faded as students become more proficient. Prompts take the form of instructions to "think" something or "ask yourself" something. Students are given feedback in the form of a recommended response. Each unit contains a formative test that is keyed to the district's criterion-referenced tests, with 80% as the appropriate level of mastery. Students who pass the formative test have three options: peer tutoring, silent reading, or an enrichment activity designed to promote attainment of higher level objectives. Students who do not pass the formative test receive an additional activity consisting of a review of terms, a different teaching method, and more practice.

Although a major concern of the program is to guide students in the thinking steps involved in applying new concepts and executing new strategies, in practice there is some variation across the units in the extent of detailed instruction in thinking processes. That is, some of the units teach more by offering examples of concepts and strategies than by describing the steps students should follow in executing these strategies on their own. For example, the unit on finding main ideas gives students some examples of paragraphs in which main ideas and supporting details have been labeled, and then leaves them on their own to find main ideas and supporting details in additional paragraphs. Even when the materials offer detailed strategy instructions, students generally are not informed of the range of situations in which these new strategies are useful, nor are they taught what it is about these strategies that makes them effective. That is, strategies are often introduced as specific techniques to follow in responding to a particular kind of test item, rather than as more general approaches that can be useful in coping with a broad range of reading situations.

The appendix to the Jones, Amiran, and Katims chapter in this volume contains several examples of lesson segments from the CMLR/LS instructional materials. The material from the unit on analogies is especially helpful in illustrating the step-by-step models of thinking strategies. The material from the unit on underlining and outlining illustrates clearly how prompted exercises are used to give students guided practice in executing new strategies, and how prompts are gradually removed as students gain proficiency.

Instruction in Learning Strategies (Dansereau)

Background and Goals.   Dansereau's instructional program in learning strategies for college-age students has been under continuous expansion and revision since 1975. The program is currently being implemented as a semester-length college-level course and has been extensively evaluated. In two studies, students enrolled in the semester-length course performed better on comprehension measures and reported more positive postcourse learning behaviors and attitudes than did students in control groups. In addition, various components of the course (summarization, networking, concentration management, and pair learning) have been evaluated in empirical studies and have shown promising results on a range of reading comprehension measures (see Dansereau, this volume, for a discussion of these assessment studies).

Like JAK, Dansereau tries to teach students who do not typically use them the skills identified by cognitive psychologists as important in comprehending and learning from text. Whereas JAK's CMLR/LS materials are aimed at younger children, the target population for Dansereau's program is college-age students. The specific program objective is to "assist students in learning and applying information presented in college-level textbooks."

Skills in Which Instruction is Offered.   The semester-long college-level course teaches both *primary strategies* and *support strategies*. Primary strategies are actual comprehension and memory strategies for dealing with the text, whereas support strategies are techniques for achieving and maintaining an appropriate frame of mind for studying.

Primary strategies vary in their degree of specialization for particular texts and tasks. Among the more general primary strategies are the following comprehension techniques: (1) paraphrase/imagery, in which students intermittently rephrase the material and form mental images of the underlying concepts; (2) networking, in which students transform text into a "semantic map," or a diagrammatic representation of the important ideas and the specific relationships (e.g., temporal, causal, type/part) that connect these ideas (see Dansereau, this volume, Fig. 5.2 and 5.3); and (3) analysis of key concepts, in which students use structured guides to identify, define, expand, and compare key concepts. Other general primary strategies are designed to help the student remember and think through information. These include understanding the requirements of the type of task that will follow studying, recalling main ideas and details, expanding the information into an outline, and determining the adequacy of the outcome with respect to the task demands.

Other primary strategies are useful with only a limited range of materials. Specifically, students are taught organizational frameworks to use in learning information from particular types of text. For example, when reading about a scientific theory, students are taught to look for and learn information in the following categories: description, inventor, history, consequences, evidence, other similar or competing theories, and miscellaneous information.

Instruction in the support strategies for establishing conditions conducive to studying include the following: planning and scheduling, concentration management (setting the proper mood and coping with distractions), and monitoring studying behavior. Concentration management is the most heavily emphasized component.

Pedagogical Assumptions and Instructional Methods.   A key pedagogical assumption of Dansereau's program is that *modeling* is one of the most effective teaching strategies. One form of modeling is showing students the desired outcome of successful strategy use and describing how the outcome was achieved. Another form of modeling is having expert strategy users demonstrate the strategy while commenting on what they are doing. A third form of modeling is interactive modeling, in which students discuss and criticize one another's strategies. A second major pedagogical assumption is that students need to understand the relevance and usefulness of the strategies they are learning. Therefore, students are given a rationale for each strategy and told how it can be used to advantage. In addition, students practice the strategy on materials similar to "real-world" texts as well as on their own texts. A third pedagogical assumption is that college students can learn largely from self-instructional materials and do not require a great deal of teacher-directed instruction.

Dansereau has concluded from his own research that the instruction is most effective if students learn primary strategies prior to support strategies. Within the primary strategies, students usually learn the gestalt of the strategy before learning to apply it precisely. For example, students learn the networking technique by first creating networks without distinguishing the exact relationships; later they learn to identify and label individual relationships. With support strategies, students are first made aware of problems related to studying and are encouraged to generate their own solutions. Program materials then introduce recommended strategies for coping with the problem.

Because there are many versions and many parts to the materials, it is difficult to generalize about the organization within units. However, the following description seems to capture the flow of instruction. Units begin with an introduction informing students of the significance of learning the strategy—why it is helpful and how it can be used. For example, in early versions of a unit on networking, students are first given an incentive for learning the technique—they are told that networking can be used for note-taking, paper writing, and test taking and can lead to higher grades and a deeper understanding of course material. Then students are given a rationale for networking in the form of a brief simplified discussion of how the mind works according to network models of memory (which form the theoretical foundation for the technique). Students are told that networking is a good system to learn because it helps them organize information in the form of node-link maps "that are similar to the ones that appear to be stored in the brains of good learners."

Cognitive Learning Strategies Project (Weinstein)

Background and Goals.   The purposes of the Cognitive Learning Strategies Project at the University of Texas at Austin are to further understanding of learning processing, to identify the learning strategies used by effective learners, and to design and evaluate interventions that can lead to the development of effective instruction in learning strategies. As part of the project, an integrated, semester-long learning strategies training program has been established as a course in the University's Department of Educational Psychology. This course is the core of the project and should be the focus of review. Unfortunately, at the time this review was conducted, the descriptive material available on the course was not developed in sufficient detail for us to analyze it. Thus, our review of the project is limited to the materials used in some of the early training studies. A more complete description of the course and the initial evaluations of it are now available and are presented in Weinstein's chapter in this volume.

The overall goal of the Cognitive Learning Strategies Project is "to modify learners information-processing strategies." The intent is to teach unskilled learners some of the comprehension and memory strategies used by skilled and effective learners. In the materials available for review, the main objective appeared to be to improve memory for text as well as nontext (listlike) materials (for example, to remember the states of the United States or a quotation from Rousseau). The intended audiences for the reviewed instruction were armed services technical trainees, high school students, and college students. The goals of the semester-length college-level course are described by Weinstein in this volume.

Skills in Which Instruction is Offered.   Decisions about the kinds of skills to be taught were derived from two sources: (1) research and cognitive processes involved in learning and memory; and (2) data from interviews and question-naires administered to individuals at different educational levels (administered as part of the Cognitive Learning Strategies Project). Strategies that seemed most promising on the basis of research and that were favored by individuals at higher achievement levels became target strategies for the project.

In the materials available for review, training includes the strategies of mental imagery, meaningful elaboration, and grouping. *Mental imagery* refers to form-ing a mental picture of the concept. *Meaningful elaboration* involves relating new, unfamiliar information to prior knowledge, including creating logical rela-tionships and drawing inferences. In *grouping*, the learner first categorizes infor-mation and then learns the categories by means of imagery or elaboration.

As indicated in her chapter in this volume, Weinstein is providing instruction in a broader repertoire of skills in her semester-length college course, including traditional study skills as well as imagery, elaboration, and grouping.

Pedagogical Assumptions and Instructional Methods.   The Cognitive Learn-ing Strategies Project believes that an optimal training program should incor-porate varied learning tasks, materials, and strategies. In a series of experimental studies, Weinstein identified four major components of successful training pro-grams: first, student packets containing explanations of the strategies, examples of their use, and opportunities to apply them to a sample passage; second, basic processes instructions, or descriptions of characteristics of effective strategies and practice exercises; third, practice, or opportunities to use the strategies with additional reading passages; and fourth, discussion of student-generated examples and experimenter's feedback. Another conclusion from research was that training should *not* include guided discussion, perhaps because students tend to model examples provided rather than generate their own strategies. (See Weinstein [this volume] for a description of the instructional method used in the college-level learning skills course.)

Teaching Reading in Content Areas (Herber)

Background and Goals.   The program reviewed in this chapter is the second edition of Harold Herber's book entitled *Teaching Reading in Content Areas*. The term "program" is somewhat misleading, for the book does not constitute instruction for students, but guidelines for content-area teachers to help their students learn from instructional materials used in the classroom. Thus, it is somewhat difficult to deal with Herber's work in the same way that the other instructional programs are handled in this chapter. Nonetheless, the following description parallels as closely as possible the descriptions of the other three programs.

Herber's program, or components of it, has been evaluated both by formal (dissertation) studies and by more informal field-based evaluations. Although the formal studies have not demonstrated a clear advantage of the program over other approaches, the field-based evaluations are quite positive. Evaluation of the program is discussed in more detail in Herber's chapter in this volume.

Herber's ultimate objective is to improve students' ability to comprehend independently the kinds of reading materials teachers in Grades 4–12 assign in their classrooms. His more immediate objective is to facilitate students' understanding of specific reading assignments through the use of special teacher-prepared reading guides.

Skills in Which Instruction is Offered.   Because the skills taught by individual teachers are those needed to cope with reading materials assigned in their courses, there is considerable variation from one teacher to another in the kinds of skills emphasized. However, in addition to offering instruction in skills unique to specific courses and academic content areas, Herber recommends that all teachers working with his program offer instruction in a small number of general reading comprehension skills.

One important general skill is the ability to comprehend text at three levels: literal, interpretive, and applied. At the literal level, the reader's goal is to identify the various facts that are explicitly stated in a passage of text. At the interpretative level, the reader's goal is to interpret these facts—that is, to grasp ideas that are implicit rather than explicit in the text and to notice how the different ideas contained in a passage of text fit together to convey some overall message. At the applied level, the reader's goal is to relate the information conveyed by that passage to information obtained from other sources—that is, to determine whether the new information is consistent with other previously acquired information. Herber is also concerned with teaching other reading-related skills such as vocabulary acquisition skills (how to acquire word definitions and meanings from context, how to use a dictionary, how to recognize word prefixes and suffixes), and skill in identifying the kinds of patterns authors use to organize ideas presented in text (cause–effect organizational patterns, compare–contrast organizational patterns, etc.).

Pedagogical Assumptions and Instructional Methods.   Critical of the direct approach to reading instruction in which instruction in reading skills is offered separately from other school subject matter areas, Herber is a staunch advocate of a functional approach. That is, he believes that reading skills should be taught by regular classroom teachers rather than by special reading teachers, that the texts used for reading instruction should be the same as those typically used to help students acquire content-area knowledge, and that the skills taught during reading instruction should be those needed to comprehend these texts. In other

words, instead of making reading instruction a separate activity, Herber recommends teaching reading skills in each academic content area, as they are
needed, to cope with the reading assignments made in that area. Herber argues
that this approach has several advantages: (1) no special personnel are needed
for reading instruction; (2) no additional instructional time is needed; and
(3) students are not left with the problem of trying to determine how their reading
skills can be useful in coping with school reading assignments.

A second pedagogical assumption of Herber's program is that students should
not be taught *about* reading, but rather should be taught *how* to read. Students
should be led to execute reading skills properly in a way that helps them understand the process involved in using the skill effectively. For example, in teaching
students how to make inferences from text, Herber recommends presenting them
with a passage of text and a set of declarative statements, and asking them to
determine which statements can be legitimately inferred from that passage and
which ones cannot. That is, instead of telling them how to go about making
inferences, he puts them into a simplified inference-making situation—one where
the task is to recognize correct inferences rather than to produce them on one's
own. Herber assumes that as students go through the process of determining
whether each declarative statement is a legitimate inference from the passage in
question, and as they are helped by their teacher and fellow students to identify
criteria for recognizing legitimate inferences, they will come to know what is
involved in inference making and will eventually able to engage in this process
on their own.

A third pedagogical assumption of Herber's program is that students can
benefit both cognitively and affectively from working in small, randomly assigned
discussion groups.

Herber's main instructional methods are teacher-prepared lessons that guide
students in reading specific passages of text, and small-group discussions in
which students jointly carry out the exercises contained in the teacher-prepared
lessons. Although the overall sequence of skills is determined by each individual
teacher, Herber recommends that each lesson include three major stages:
(1) preparation of students for reading; (2) guidance of students during reading;
and (3) development of independence appropriate to the student's needs and
progress. The preparation stage involves establishing motivation for reading an
assigned passage of text, providing students with appropriate background information, helping them grasp the meaning of new vocabulary words, and giving
them directions for using the teacher-prepared reading guide for that passage.
During the guided reading stage, students attempt to comprehend the passage in
question by working either independently or in small groups on the exercises
contained in the teacher-prepared guide. As discussed previously, these exercises
are designed to help students get a sense of what is involved in executing various
reading comprehension skills by simplifying the conditions under which they

must work with these skills—for example, asking them to recognize legitimate inferences and helping them establish criteria for doing so as a way of teaching them how to produce such inferences on their own. The guided reading stage is followed by an independent reading stage in which students receive further practice in using the same skills but with less teacher guidance. The lesson segment on the topic of time described in the Herber chapter in this volume offers several examples of activities and exercises typical of each of the three stages of instruction.

COMPARISON OF THE PROGRAMS

We begin this section with a comment and a statement of our objectives in the remainder of the chapter. The comment is a fairly optimistic one, perhaps unnecessary given the existence of this volume and others like it attempting to relate findings from basic research on cognition to practical problems of instruction. As a result of studying these curricula and others, it seems clear both that some practitioners are aware of the current developments in cognitive and developmental theory and that some of the data and theories of the more basic disciplines are becoming of greater interest to those intimately involved in education. Although there are still many problems associated with the dissemination of basic knowledge and its implementation into practical programs, avenues for communication do seem to be emerging. This we see as a true advance; there remains only the minor problem of refining and filling out our theories and having them rigorously tested in the classroom setting.

Our major goals in this section are to build upon the descriptions of the programs presented in the second section and draw some conclusions about the similarities and differences among them. We want to use those conclusions as a springboard for pointing to convergences between practice and theory, noting areas where practice can inform theory and vice versa, and, more frequently, identifying questions basic to the development of both practice and theory. We do not attempt to determine which program or programs are the best. Rather we proceed by identifying crucial dimensions of difference. This will map the more general options available to someone building a curriculum, or, stated alternatively, indicate some of the choices that must be faced when deciding how to intervene. We believe this kind of analysis will be useful in at least two ways.

First, it will enable us to understand better what the program developers as a group believe concerning the emergence of text learning skills; after we have identified some of the ways in which the programs differ, we can ask whether these dimensions of difference are independent or correlated. Because the programs differ in terms of target populations, skills in which instruction is offered, and criterion tasks, we can examine the relationship between a developer's choices along one of these dimensions and influences on his or her choices along the others. For example, programs for older students may emphasize different kinds of skills and use different kinds of criterion measures than programs for younger students. In this way, we will come to see that underlying these differences, there is some consistency in the developers' views regarding the emergence of text learning skills.

Second, identifying dimensions of difference will enable us to consider whether and how these differences map onto controversies in the theoretical literature. Our conclusion is that there is considerable correspondence to be found. The dimensions we have chosen to emphasize and the different points along them, typified by different developers, match closely some traditional and enduring problems within scientific psychology, problems that are receiving considerable attention today. When we believe the evidence is sufficiently compelling, we will take a stand on points of controversy. At least as often, we will content ourselves with emphasizing the centrality of the problems to both theoretical and practical concerns. Convergence on a set of problems and issues from different approaches confirms their significance. The situation would be much more confusing if the questions occupying curriculum developers and researchers were mutually exclusive. Also, given the overlap, there is reason to believe that theory and practice should be able to inform each other; at least they are attending to the same issues.

Theoretical Background

The dimensions of the programs we have chosen to emphasize are determined at least in part by our own theoretical preferences and biases. A reviewer's theoretical preferences influence his or her judgment on the content of an instructional program and thus play a role in determining which aspects receive attention in a review. We begin by making our views and biases explicit. We can give them here only a severely abbreviated treatment. (See more detailed accounts in Anderson & Armbruster, 1982; Brown, 1982a, 1982b; Brown, Bransford, Ferrara, & Campione, 1983; Brown & Campione, 1980; Brown, Campione, & Day, 1981; Campione, Brown, & Ferrara, in press).

Any program that aims at improving comprehension skills in a variety of learners must rely on a number of at least implicit and ideally explicit theories. It would seem necessary to have a guiding theory of comprehension, covering the skills, knowledge, and activities that it entails. Having decided on some target skills to teach, it would be important to have a general view of learning to determine an appropriate method of instruction. Finally, within these theories, there must be a serious attempt to deal with the problem of individual differences—that is, to determine whether and how the context and form of instruction need to be modified to accommodate learners of different ages and ability levels.

Before considering the positions adopted by the four program developers, we reveal our own position.

Factors Involved in Learning from Texts

In several recent papers, we have made use of a very general, and hence somewhat vague, model of the factors that might influence the process of learning from texts. These factors are represented in the form of a tetrahedron comprising four main points: (1) the *nature of the material* to be learned; (2) the *special characteristics of the learner* that are the sum of his or her prior experience and individual talents, including, of course, his or her knowledge about the specific topic to be learned; (3) the *strategies*, or the activities engaged in by the learner, either spontaneously or under the guidance of a more knowledgeable other; and (4) the *criterial tasks*, or end result in the service of which the strategies are introduced. This tetrahedral model of the learning situation, which has been borrowed from Jenkins (1979) and Bransford (1979), is applicable with some modifications to most learning situations. Here we describe briefly how it can be applied to the task of learning from texts. The model is illustrated in Fig. 9.1.

Imagine expert learners designing a plan for learning from texts. First, they might consider the nature of the material to be learned. They would examine the text itself—is it a story? an expository text? an instruction book? Major forms of texts have quite standard structures that can be identified by astute learners to help them set up expectations that will guide the reading process. For example, stories, in general, have a characteristic structure (Brewer & Lichtenstein, 1981; Mandler & Johnson, 1977). A simple form would be that a main character reaches some desired goal after overcoming some obstacle. More complex forms include competition, conflict, or sharing between major characters (Bruce & Newman, 1978). Expository texts also take on predictable forms, such as compare and contrast, cause and effect, or form and function. Authors tend to flag important statements by such devices as headings, subsections, topic sentences, summaries, standard syntactic markers, and just plain "and now for something really important" statements. Expert learners, knowing about these patterns and devices, can use them as clues to help them concentrate on essential information.

Next the expert might consider the criterial task. An important factor in studying is knowing the goal of that activity, i.e., knowing what will be required of you as a test of the knowledge you are acquiring. As Bransford, Nitsch, and Franks (1977) point out:

> No self-respecting memory expert would put up with the way psychologists run most memory experiments. Experts would ask questions like, "What must I remember?," "How many items?," "How much time will there be?," "What's the nature of the tests?," etc. They would know what they needed to know in order to perform optimally—and would settle for nothing less [p. 38].

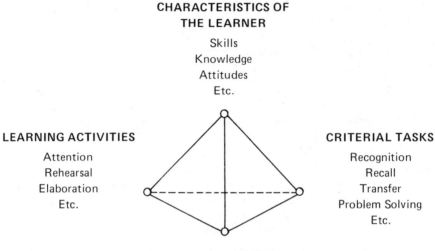

CHARACTERISTICS OF
THE LEARNER

Skills
Knowledge
Attitudes
Etc.

LEARNING ACTIVITIES

Attention
Rehearsal
Elaboration
Etc.

CRITERIAL TASKS

Recognition
Recall
Transfer
Problem Solving
Etc.

NATURE OF THE
MATERIALS

Modality
(visual, linguistic, etc.)
Physical structure
Psychological structure
Conceptual difficulty
Sequencing of materials
Etc.

FIG. 9.1.   An Organizational Framework for Exploring Questions About Learning. (Adapted from Jenkins, 1979 and Bransford, 1979.)

Expert learners would also take into consideration their own particular strengths and weaknesses. For example, everyone has a limited capacity for remembering large amounts of arbitrary material. Effective readers neither overburden their memories by attempting to retain large segments of texts, nor entertain too many pending questions or too many unresolved ambiguities (Collins, Brown, Morgan, & Brewer, 1977). They take remedial action to rectify the problem, such as looking back, rereading, consulting a dictionary or a knowledgeable other (Baker & Brown, in press-a, in press-b). Similarly, as arbitrary material is difficult to comprehend and retain, experts try to make the text more meaningful by trying to understand the significance of what they are reading, or by trying to fit the new material into their personal experience (Bransford, Stein, Shelton, & Owings, 1980; Campione, et al., 1983). The trick is to make the unfamiliar more familiar and hence more memorable.

Based on the evaluation of their own learning capacity and the task at hand, experts employ appropriate strategies to facilitate their learning. There is a considerable literature on the common study strategies used by students. Some of the traditional ones are note-taking, summary writing, underlining, and self-questioning, to which can be added more elaborate systems such as mapping and networking (Armbruster & Anderson, 1980). Deliberate attempts to monitor comprehension are also part of the strategic repertoire of the expert.

In short, expert learners are planful, active, and deliberate. They design their own effective routines for learning by considering the four points of the tetrahedron shown in Fig. 9.1. In teaching students how to be expert learners, we assume that we also need to consider these factors. For example, the specific strategies we choose to instruct depend on the learner's starting level, the kinds of materials to be learned, and the nature of the competencies we hope to achieve. Thus, the model serves to remind us of some of the questions we need to consider in designing instruction.

In reminding us of these questions, the model introduces two sources of complexity into the instructional process. First, it emphasizes the interactive nature of the components involved in learning from text. That is, it suggests that dealing with one component in isolation is likely to prove misleading both for the teacher and the student. Secondly, it emphasizes the role of awareness in learning from text. That is, it suggests that if individuals are to become independent learners, capable of selecting and designing their own learning activities, they need to do exactly what the expert learner is assumed to do. They need to be aware of the different factors highlighted in the model so that they can take them into account in selecting learning activities. This implies that cognitive skills instruction should not be limited to providing students with appropriate routines to follow in different learning situations. In addition, students may need to be made aware of what these routines are, of how they differ from one another, of the conditions under which they are effective, and of the reasons for their effectiveness, before they can be expected to apply them intelligently to new passages of text and to new kinds of text learning tasks.

In the sections that follow, we consider in further detail some of the issues raised by the model. We begin by looking at the strategies component. This leads us to raise a perennial issue in cognitive skills instruction—should students be taught general or specific strategies? Following our discussion of strategies, we give some attention to the role of awareness in instruction. We ask whether awareness is simply a desirable outcome of instruction or whether it is absolutely necessary to successful instruction.

Strategies.   By far, the lion's share of attention in both the psychological and educational literatures has been expended on strategies, although other knowledge factors have also been implicated as culprits in inadequate text processing (witness the current popularity of schema theoretic approaches). However, even given what some believe to be an undue emphasis on strategies, we think it is interesting to note that exactly what processes would qualify for inclusion or exclusion under that rubric is far from clear. In this tradition, the programs reviewed here, although agreeing that strategies are the animals to be trained, are in some disagreement concerning the nature of the beasts. Although of necessity somewhat vague in the definition of strategies, all would agree that experts do, and novices do not, engage in proper processing activities while learning from texts. But definitions of the activities differ in many important ways across programs.

An important underlying theme and perennial question is whether we should train specific or general strategies. This question appears not only when instruction in text processing is at issue, but also when any other kind of cognitive skills instruction is at issue (Brown & Campione, 1982; Campione et al., in press). If the goal is to elevate the performance of less capable students, we need to ask what is causing their low level of performance. Is their performance a reflection of breakdowns in the specific skills needed to work within some domain, or is it due to failure in the operation of more general skills that are useful across a variety of domains? For example, is a student's failure to solve some arithmetic problem due to an inability to perform some specific arithmetic operation or due to a failure to use some more general problem-solving strategy such as making sure one has understood the problem, considering the relationship between the problem to be solved and the operations one has learned, checking to make sure one is applying these operations appropriately, etc.? It is only after answering such questions that we can identify the kinds of skills in which instruction is necessary.

The specific-general controversy was a central question guiding the development of early theories of intelligence. Binet, for example, fluctuated from pole to pole, adopting as his concluding stance a compromise between specific and general factors. Although attributing great powers to specific knowledge and strategies, he identified four general factors as common to all intellective activities. "Comprehension, invention, direction and criticism—intelligence is constrained in these four words [Binet, 1909]." Three of Binet's four general factors, "direction and persistence of thought, autocriticism, and invention," are very similar to metacognitive factors emphasized in recent approaches to the topic of intelligence (Brown, 1974, 1978; Campione & Brown, 1978; Campione et al., in press), particularly the concepts of direction and autocriticism.

Binet believed not only in the existence of general factors, but also in their potential for modifiability. Following his description of inadequate functioning in retarded children, Binet goes on to describe his prescription for "mental orthopedics" for the retarded, which he also considered "useful for normal children [Binet, 1909, pp. 150–161]." His training procedures, which stress self-awareness and autocritical skills, are fascinating reading for contemporary psychologists interested in cognitive skills training. Similar suggestions come from Spearman (1904, 1923, 1927), who not only emphasized the importance of general factors (which he called g), but also described what he thought they were. Interestingly, Spearman's general factors are not unlike Binet's, and even more like contemporary theories of metacognition. The three principle components of g were educing relations, educing correlates, and self-recognition, or the "apprehension of one's own experience."

The specific–general distinction, together with questions of whether development proceeds from the general to the specific (e.g., Garrett, 1946), or whether specific abilities are primary and general factors derived from them via positive transfer effects (Ferguson, 1954, 1956), are alive and flourishing today. In his role as concluding speaker at the Carnegie–Mellon conference on Problem Solving and Education, Allan Newell (1980) stated that: "if there is one dichotomy that permeated this conference, it concerned the basic nature of problem solving. Specifically, the poles are the Domain independence of problem solving *vs.* the Domain specificity of problem solving. The dichotomy is an old one [p. 184]."

Newell's thesis is that although the basic question remains unresolved, considerable advances have taken place in our understanding. His taxonomy of existing positions on this issue is particularly illuminating. One of them, the 'big switch' position, emphasizes specific skills. Here the knowledge base consists of a large number of specific procedures with a discrimination net (the 'big switch') for gaining access to them. According to Newell (1980): "Tens of thousands of such procedures form a mosaic that covers the world of all tasks. Each procedure has a *small penumbra of generality,* so that in total a large area of novel tasks can be accomplished [p. 185]." One problem with the big switch position is that it leaves learners with the nontrivial task of having to sort through thousands of expert procedures to find the appropriate one to use in any specific problem-solving situation.

The 'weak methods' position attempts to avoid this access problem by conceptualizing learners as having smaller sets of more general strategies rather than larger sets of more specific ones. These general strategies are termed weak in that they trade generality for power. That is, although strategies are useful in giving individuals ideas as to how to approach problems, they do not actually permit the individual to solve the problem at hand unless they are used in conjunction with other more specific procedures. Some examples of general strategies that are useful in a wide range of thinking and learning situations are the kinds of self-regulatory skills that developmental psychologists have recently been investigating (Brown, 1978; Brown & DeLoache, 1978; Campione et al., in press; Flavell, 1981; Markman, volume 2). These include: planning the original approach to a problem, monitoring the success of the chosen approach, checking to see that the activities are being carried out correctly, etc. Still other examples of general strategies have emerged from the artificial intelligence literature. Several of these are described in the Polson and Jeffries chapter in this volume. These include: means–ends analysis, generate-and-test strategies, heuristic search strategies, and subgoal decomposition strategies.

A compromise incorporating the strengths of both approaches is Newell's 'weak-to-strong methods' position, which includes both specific and general procedures. Newell's metaphor is an expanding cone of methods of ever greater specificity and power. At the base of the cone are the multitudes of specific expert procedures with their penumbra of generality. In addition, at the apex of the cone are the general (but weak) ways of responding to tasks quite different from any for which the problem solver could have developed expert procedures.

This last position seems to us the most attractive. We assume that the knowledge base consists of a large number of specific rules with their own small penumbra of generality. Generality is extended via the mapping procedures of analogy and metaphor, which to some extent relieve the learner of the severe constraint of having to have a different procedure for each different situation (Brown, 1974, 1978; Campione et al., in press). This accomplishment results in the genesis of general strategies suitable for wider domains (problem solving, academic tasks, test taking, etc.), but there are still strong limits to this generality. We would add that the extent of generality an individual achieves is diagnostic of intelligent behavior (Campione & Brown, in press). Also, whether general skills simply emerge via transfer from specific skills may depend on the ability of the learner. For example, although there is considerable support for the notion that general factors simply emerge from the perfection of specific strategies, this position is not likely to play well in Peoria, where we do our work with slow-learning adolescents and college students. It is painfully obvious to those working with academically less gifted learners that something more than practice on the specifics is going to be required, and that the penumbras of generality for specific skills form very faint traces indeed.

Awareness.   This brings us to our second perennial controversy, learning with or without awareness. Our position is simply that one important aspect of instruction is to accompany specific skills training with a clear explanation of their rationale and information about the range of situations in which they are useful (Brown et al., 1981). This should *not* be taken as evidence that we accept a simplistic position that all learning must be accompanied by deliberate conscious awareness. Many of the "automatized" activities of experts are rarely brought to consciousness. For example, although mature readers typically engage in comprehension monitoring, it is not often or even usually a conscious experience (Brown, 1981). When comprehension is proceeding smoothly, good readers proceed as if on automatic pilot, until a problem is detected. Some triggering event (Collins et al., 1977) alerts them to a comprehension failure. Then and only then does the understanding process slow down and become planful, demanding conscious effort. Comprehension monitoring for the expert involves many automatic, overlearned components. However, the expert's knowledge can usually be brought to the level of conscious awareness.

In addition to the fact that many well-learned activities can become automatized and proceed below the level of consciousness, it is no doubt true that in proficient learners, a good deal of new learning goes on without accompanying awareness. That is, proficient learners acquire new ways of solving problems without ever stopping to bring those activities to consciousness. In contrast, in the case of poorer learners, who have frequently failed to internalize new approaches even when given comparable environmental input, we presume that making those approaches explicit, thus making the learners aware of exactly what they need to do and why, may be necessary. Even with effective learners, leading them to become aware of some rule they have been using implicitly improves subsequent use of that rule (see Ericsson & Simon, 1980; Gagné & Smith, 1962). A brief summary of our position is that making students aware of the resources they are being taught is necessary for poor learners, and potentially helpful for higher ability performers.

We emphasize the need for "cognitive training with awareness" because the whole history of attempts to instill study and learning strategies in ineffectual learners attests to the futility of having students execute some strategy in the absence of a concomitant understanding of why or how that activity works. To borrow an example from the reading area, consider the literature on underlining and notetaking. Successful students commonly report using one or both of these activities, but attempts to teach the strategies to less successful students have produced equivocal results. Until recently, by far the majority of studies on underlining or notetaking show these activities to be no more effective than passive studying techniques such as rereading (see Anderson & Armbruster, 1982). In all those studies, however, subjects were randomly assigned to treatment conditions. In a more recent study, Brown and Smiley (1978) compared high school students who were spontaneous users of these strategies with others who were told to use them. The spontaneous users underlined or took notes that favored the important information. Those induced to use the strategies did not show a similar sensitivity to importance. They took notes or underlined more randomly, with the result that their performance failed to improve. Such data indicate that taking notes or underlining are not desirable activities in themselves. Understanding the purpose of these activities (for example, that one should use underlining as an aid in focusing attention) and knowing how to execute them in ways that are consistent with these purposes are the desired end products of training, outcomes that do not necessarily result from simple instructions to engage the target activities.

When adequately learned, strategies such as note-taking and underlining can be regarded as relatively general ones. In addition to attempts to teach such general skills, there are of necessity instances where more specific skills must be the target of instruction. Here the need for informed training (Brown et al., 1981), or training with awareness is, if anything, clearer. As already noted, with an increasing number of routines, there is a corresponding increase in the problems of locating those appropriate to the task at hand and then effectively overseeing them. It is by now abundantly clear that failure to find transfer of trained skills is the norm rather than the exception, when the trainees are the kinds of students who typically experience difficulty in school. When a task appears in a slightly disguised form, these students often fail to recognize that strategies they have just learned may be useful. However, transfer can be enhanced to some extent when such students are taught general self-regulatory skills such as the ones indicated earlier—planning, checking, monitoring, etc. These self-regulatory skills may be described as "awareness" skills in that they require students to be constantly aware of their goals, strategies, and progress in coping with learning situations. Problem learners in particular appear to need deliberate instruction in these self-regulatory skills if they are to use specific strategies in coping with new learning materials and tasks.

In summary, we assume that the tetrahedral model provides an account of some of the factors that need to be considered in teaching people how to derive meaning from text. It indicates the types of activities and knowledge individuals need to use in processing text, and thus offers guidance to the instructor in determining what types of knowledge to teach. The emphasis on interactions among various types of knowledge highlights the complexity of the text learning process and indicates some of the difficulties associated with the development of instructional programs. Learners armed with much of the required knowledge and strategies still face the considerable problem of managing these resources, a problem for which lower ability learners in particular may need to receive special instruction. We now consider briefly the question of how the necessary resources may be acquired. In our discussion, we are especially concerned with approaches that foster both the acquisition of cognitive skills and their control.

The Nature of the Learning Process

Any cognitive skills training program must rely on a view of learning, and there are many to choose from. Again, perhaps because of our own theoretical biases, we find that some form of an internalization model underlies many of the programs examined in this volume, for example Whimbey and Lochhead, Dansereau, and most explicitly, Feuerstein. Internalization is also a hallmark of the classic Bloom and Broder (1950) training methods and of a number of more recent suggestions concerning cognitive skills training (Collins & Smith, 1982; Collins & Stevens, 1982).

An early and general form of this approach was outlined by Vygotsky (1978), in his emphasis on the role of social interaction in mediating knowledge acquisition. His argument is that all psychological processes are, in genesis, social processes, initially shared between people, particularly between children and adults. The process of internalization occurs gradually. First, the adult controls and guides the child's activity. Then, little by little, the adult and the child come to share control over problem-solving functions, with the child taking initiative and the adult correcting and guiding when the child makes mistakes. Finally, the adult cedes control to the child and functions primarily as a supportive and sympathetic audience. This developmental progression from other-regulation to self-regulation is the essence of mother–child learning dyads (Brown & French, 1979; Wertsch, 1979), but the age and relationship of the social agent are to some extent irrelevant. Teachers, tutors, and the master craftsmen in traditional apprenticeship situations all ideally function as promoters of self-regulation by nurturing the emergence of self-control as they gradually cede external control. In short, in a variety of learning situations, experts model many forms of control over their thinking and problem-solving activities, the controls that others must internalize if they are to become successful independent thinkers and problem solvers.

To say that Vygotsky (or anyone else) has a complete account of learning would of course be to overstate the situation considerably. The most glaring problem is that we do not understand well the central mechanism or how we can promote it—internalization is just assumed to occur. When, how, or why a particular learner should come to internalize some routine remains a bit mysterious. Nonetheless, this perspective does highlight a number of factors. First, learning is conceived as a social, rather than entirely individual, accomplishment. Second, the process of internalization is seen as a gradual one, proceeding as the expert is able to turn control over to the student. Third, implicit in this gradual transfer view is the notion that instruction should be constantly tailored to the student's current level. And finally, it is clear that what is likely to be internalized is influenced to a great extent by the nature of the social interaction. Specifically, processes not modeled by the expert/teacher are less likely to be acquired than would be the case if those processes had formed an important part of the interaction.

Adapting Instruction to Individual Differences

In addition to his interest in general developmental issues, Vygotsky (1978) was also concerned with the topic of individual differences, as illustrated most clearly in his concept of a zone of proximal development. When discussing individual students, Vygotsky emphasized both the student's current state of development, indexed by individual problem solving, and the level of potential development, as determined through problem solving in collaboration with more capable peers. The difference between these two levels (potential versus current) he called the child's zone of proximal development. As one example, Vygotsky examined children's performance on intelligence test type items under conditions where the children were given varying amounts of adult guidance in solving problems they could not solve independently. He found that some students needed less aid than others and that those students were also more proficient at transferring the result of their learning experience to new variants of the problems.

More recently, a number of researchers have similarly described less capable performers as needing more complete instruction, both to reach an original learning criterion and to transfer the fruits of that learning (e.g., Campione et al., in press; Resnick & Glaser, 1976). It is important to note that academically less capable students require more detailed instruction to reach an original learning criterion, and then, having reached the same criterion, still differ in the extent to which they can make use of what they have learned (Campione & Brown, 1984). A straightforward interpretation of those effects is that more efficient learners provide some of the instruction for themselves (see Brown et al., in press; Feuerstein, 1980). Based on the research we have already reviewed, we assume that some of what they provide includes the regulatory mechanisms implicated in flexible use of information. For example, high ability students may not need to be told to form some plan, to consider the possibility that the present problem may represent an instance of a more general class, etc., because they generate those thoughts spontaneously. As these regulatory mechanisms are crucial to both learning and transfer, they learn with less complete instruction and apply the learned activities more broadly.

If it is true that high and low ability students differ in their tendency to use such activities, it becomes necessary to teach them explicitly to poorer learners. This is in fact what seems to happen in the modal learning environment described by Vygotsky. The adult does not simply describe in detail the skill to be learned. Rather, the instructor begins each problem by modeling the kinds of self-regulatory processes that appear to be lacking in slow-learning children. The children then proceed to solve each problem on their own with the instructor offering general prompts at first and switching to more specific ones only when the general ones are not effective. This type of interaction is very similar to that characterizing Socratic dialogues engaged in by effective teachers and their students and analyzed in detail by Collins and his associates (see Collins & Stevens, 1982; see also Collins' paper in Volume 2 of this series). The advantage of these approaches theoretically is that they simulate and make more explicit to the student the processes underlying internalization and flexible access to stored knowledge.

Summary

Our theoretical views about the factors involved in learning from texts, the learning process itself, and the nature of individual differences in overall academic ability lead us to emphasize five points in our treatment of the four programs: (1) the four factors specified in the tetrahedron and their interaction; (2) the special place of general versus specific factors in training programs; (3) the necessity of having students be active participants in the learning experience, eventually aware of and in control of their learning activities; (4) the implications of internalization theories for the form of instruction required to maximize learning; and (5) the importance of individual differences in access to, and use of, knowledge.

Many of these views are controversial, and there are those who would disagree with some, if not all, of them. Accordingly, they would reach different conclusions about the programs being reviewed and make different suggestions for the kinds of research that should be conducted in the future. We hope that making our views explicit will make the grounds of any such conflicts readily apparent.

The Programs and Their Differences

In this section, we review some of the dimensions along which the programs differ, and for each indicate some of the specific choices that have been made by the various authors. We have classified some differences among the programs as superficial and others as central. Superficial differences include differences in subject populations, maturity of the program, and the amount of instruction required. Central differences are subdivided into three types. One concerns variations in the types of skills the developers are trying to instill. A description of these skills should provide some estimate of the implicit or explicit theory of comprehension underlying the program. A second is differences in teaching methods. Once the skills have been identified, one has to decide how to teach them. Ideally, instruction should be based on a theory of learning, and it seems possible to infer a developer's theory from his or her pedagogical decisions. A third central difference among the programs is the degree of attention given to individualizing instruction.

Some of our characterizations go well beyond the developers' statements, and our interpretations of their positions may not mesh very well with theirs. Fortunately, the reader of this volume can readily refer to their descriptions of their respective programs.

Superficial Differences

The most obvious variation across the programs is in the target populations. JAK work with children ranging from kindergarten through eighth grade, although we looked most closely at the portion of their program aimed at the fifth- and sixth-grade levels. Herber's program is designed for use with children from grade 4 through high school. Weinstein's target populations include high school students, college students, and armed services recruits. Dansereau works with college students.

The programs also differ in the time and effort expended on them to date and in the degree of further refinement planned. Herber's program is essentially complete and a published version is currently available, although he continues further testing and refinement of his ideas and methods. The other programs continue to undergo revision, and Weinstein's is the newest entry. Thus, although Weinstein and Dansereau deal with similar populations, they cannot be readily compared, given differences in their current state of development. Although

JAK's and Dansereau's programs are of approximately equal age, it is difficult to compare them directly because of the student differences.

Another dimension along which the programs differ is the amount of time spent in instruction. The Chicago Mastery Learning Program involves daily instruction over several years; Dansereau's program is scheduled like a one-semester college course; and Weinstein has worked with training interventions of differing lengths, ranging from experiments involving less than 2 hours to a semester-long course. (As the materials for the year-long course were not available to us, our statements here are based on the shorter interventions.)

Herber's program is more difficult to place along a time dimension for several reasons, one of which introduces yet another difference among the programs. Whereas JAK, Weinstein, and Dansereau devote primary attention to materials and lessons for the students, Herber centers his attention on the teacher. As noted previously, his book consists in large part of a set of recommendations to teachers concerning ways to facilitate students' comprehension of school subject matter texts. This approach, together with Herber's insistence that reading should be taught by regular classroom teachers rather than by special reading teachers, results in more teacher preparation time than do the other programs. The teachers need time to develop their own instructional materials, but the program presumably requires less student time, as there is no separate reading instruction.

Central Differences

Goals and Content of the Instruction.   On a very general level, the programs as outlined by their proponents would seem to have the same beginning point and the same goals. The authors begin by noting that a large number of students, particularly the younger and less able, do not employ the kinds of strategies and activities necessary for optimal text processing. They then specify what some of the missing activities are and attempt to instruct students in their use. The goal is to enable the students subsequently to study texts and other materials more effectively without additional prompting. That is, the stated goal is for students to apply spontaneously the various learning and/or retrieval strategies they have been taught, with the result that they are better able to acquire information from new texts and in new areas. Given this common orientation, it would appear that the programs are aimed at the same goals.

We would assert, however, that in our view, as inferred from the materials and instructional routines we reviewed, the programs have goals that are quite different from one another. This view is reinforced by consideration of the criteria against which the programs have been evaluated and/or have met with success. Such variation across programs is not surprising, given our somewhat limited understanding of the nature of text comprehension processes. One consequence of this lack of understanding is that it constrains our ability to assess how well students are going about comprehending. This leads researchers to rely on some-what gross measures of comprehension, such as standardized test scores, course grades, recall of text, ability to paraphrase, etc. In turn, these variations in the criteria for assessing comprehension influence the form and content of the instructional program.

To be more specific, the Chicago Mastery Learning Program was initiated in good part because of the fairly typical finding that a large number of the students attending urban schools were scoring poorly on standardized reading tests such as the Iowa Test of Basic Skills. Although other measures are employed in the Chicago program, the main criterion of effectiveness appears to be improvement in standardized test scores, and the skills taught are those necessary for efficient performance on those tests. Herber, and to a lesser extent Dansereau, aim at maximizing learning in academic subjects, and their criteria for success would ultimately be amount of content knowledge acquired in specific courses. Many of Weinstein's studies have been concerned with teaching a variety of subject populations to employ a number of mnemonic strategies to facilitate their recall of ideas or detail contained in prose passages. In this case, memory performance would seem to provide the most appropriate measure of the value of the instruction.

Given this argument, it is not surprising that JAK's instruction is, to a greater extent than any of the others, aimed at instilling specific skills. One problem we see with JAK's approach is that there is no real attempt to deal with the weaker but more general regulatory skills that we described in the section on theoretical background. Nor does this program appear to include any systematic attempts to teach students to combine sets of specific skills into larger, more powerful packages that are somewhat general. Thus, we would anticipate that many of the skills would remain relatively inaccessible, particularly for problem learners, and would appear only in situations where they were cued in some fashion. It may be worthwhile to speculate that the similarities between standardized test formats and the instructional formats involved in the program may be sufficient to enhance transfer to and thus increase performance on these tests, even while the routines are, to a great extent, inaccessible in everyday learning situations.

The contrasting approach is to teach more general, content-independent skills. The clearest problem with this approach is that these general approaches may require the use of more specific and powerful routines before they can be implemented successfully. Recall the examples of note-taking and underlining described earlier. Students instructed to underline did so randomly and did not benefit from the activity. In this context, we offer two comments, one concerned with individual/developmental differences and the second with within-individual variability.

The first comment is an obvious one. Students who are younger or less able are less likely to have acquired a repertoire of the specific skills necessary for the more general approaches to succeed. For example, holding materials constant, younger children are less able to identify the important ideas in a story than are older ones (Brown & Smiley, 1977); similarly, poor readers are less adept at identifying the main ideas in different kinds of texts than are readers of average ability (Smiley, Oakley, Worthen, Campione, & Brown, 1977). The second comment is that these skills are not stable within individuals, but vary considerably with tasks and materials (Brown et al., in press). That is, they do not appear full-blown at some particular developmental level. Work in our laboratory has shown that retarded children who cannot identify main ideas in narrative texts are quite able to do so with simple picture sequences, or with well-formed stories. Analogously, with regard to selectively studying difficult or missed items, grade school children are quite adept at this task in a free-recall situation (Masur, McIntyre, & Flavell, 1973), but not in text learning (Brown & Campione, 1979).

Given the latter point, the possibility exists that some types of subskills may not always be available even to proficient learners. This seems to be the conclusion to which Dansereau has been forced, given his most recent emphasis on content-dependent schemata. When the task is complex, even highly selected readers/studiers are not adept at discovering the main points, and the provision of additional content-dependent schemata is necessary. These schemata tell students what a body of experts has decided are the main points to attend to and absorb. This is obviously easier than teaching students how to find the main points themselves, or teaching them how to develop their own more specific schemata as needed to deal with unfamiliar genres of writing. This forced choice makes it clear that we do not know very much about how people manage to locate main ideas in new areas—our theories of comprehension are sorely lacking in this regard. In any event, even when college students serve as the targets of instruction, content-specific routines need to be provided. Evidence from a recent series of studies on summarization (Brown & Day, in press) also suggests that detailed teaching of highly specific factors should be included in training regimens aimed at junior college students.

In some cases, it may be misleading to conclude that different programs involve the same skills, even if the same labels are used. A good case in point is that of finding the main idea. This skill is certainly included in JAK's system and figures prominently in the work of Herber and Dansereau. However, the skill is a specific one in JAK's hands, but a more general one for the others. As reviewed in the second section, JAK have students locate the main ideas of descriptive and explanatory paragraphs; Herber and Dansereau, working on a more general level, want their students to find the main ideas of large segments of text. These activities may not be at all similar, a conclusion we believe Dansereau would support. In fact, given current restrictions, the former may be instructable and the latter not, a point to which we return later.

Why do some of the programs try to teach more content-free general skills while others try to teach more content-dependent specific ones? We have already suggested two factors that may influence this decision: the kinds of criteria the developers use as indices of improved comprehension and the cognitive maturity of their trainees. Concerning cognitive maturity, the developers appear to share the assumption that the younger the students, the more specific the instruction required. They assume that young children lack many of the more specific skills involved in deriving meaning from text and need to receive explicit instruction before they can learn other more general skills. This is certainly a reasonable assumption. It is difficult to see how to provide training aimed at selecting among, sequencing, accessing, and generally controlling skills that are not themselves available to the performer. As students mature and/or are more highly selected for academic learning ability, the developers assume that many of the subskills are intact, thus allowing instruction to proceed at a higher level. Once JAK are finished with their students, Weinstein and Dansereau can take over.

There is still a third factor that can influence the degree of specificity of the instructed activities, and this concerns the kinds of supports the program offers students as they attempt to learn new skills. For example, Herber, aiming in part at children of comparable level to some of JAK's, emphasizes a much smaller number of more general skills in his program. However, the fact that the teacher prepares reading guides is the reason he can proceed in that fashion. Students may not know how to find a main idea or be capable of activating the relevant prior knowledge necessary to deal with some text, but if the guide indicates what the main ideas are, or forces the students to attend to them, and if the guide provides information about what text-extrinsic material should be considered, those deficits may not be of importance. If the goal is to facilitate learning of course content, this division of labor could be seen to be a sensible one. The problem, of course, and one to which we return later, concerns the extent to which comprehension skills can be acquired through this kind of instruction. That is, one needs to ask whether poor readers in particular become capable of using these skills independently when special reading guides are no longer available to them.

As we suggested earlier, our preferred approach is to teach general and specific skills *explicitly,* a stance adopted only by Dansereau. Herber aims at general skills and pays little attention to more specific ones. Further, even with the general approaches, he does not advocate teaching any of them explicitly. His argument is that teaching reading skills directly takes up valuable time that could otherwise be spent on imparting content. The assumption is that leading students through the requisite activities via the use of adjunct aids will facilitate acquiring the content-area material and result in skill learning. JAK does not spend much time on general skills. Dansereau represents a middle ground. He teaches some general strategies explicitly, and offers instruction in a number of content-specific schemata. Our only concern, a minor one, is that he may overestimate the specific skills abilities of his subjects and that it may be profitable to spend more time on "basics."

Before leaving this topic, we find it necessary to complicate it further. In an important sense, the generality of a routine depends on the overall purpose for which that routine is being employed. For example, Weinstein treats imagery and elaboration as general routines that can be applied to lists of words or to segments of texts. An important component of her program is to teach students to elaborate on text material to render it more learnable and memorable. Elaboration in her system refers to the enhancement of the meaningfulness of text material by relating it to other (often arbitrarily chosen) aspects of the learner's knowledge. Although Weinstein would regard this as a general learning strategy, in our own view, it is a much more specific and limited technique.

We can illustrate the difference by comparing Weinstein's teaching method to that of Bransford et al. (1980). Both Weinstein and Bransford et al. have instructed students how to learn a passage about the properties of veins and arteries. The passage states that arteries are thick, are elastic, and carry blood that is rich in oxygen from the heart; veins are thinner, are less elastic, and carry blood rich in carbon dioxide back to the heart. Weinstein's (1978) directions for learning the passage are:

> I want you to learn the information contained in this paragraph and, most important, I want you to develop learning aids to study this information. You must learn to distinguish between the veins and the arteries. For example, the veins are thinner than the arteries. To help you remember this fact you might try to form a picture in your mind of a thin hollow tube when you think of a vein. Or you might make up a sentence or story which would associate a vein with a thin tube such as the vain woman was thin as a rubber tube. Although the word vain in this sentence is not the same as the word vein meaning a structure in the body it could still help you to learn this property of veins.
>
> Concentrating on pictures or images we form in our minds can be a powerful aid to our memory; so can forming sentences or little stories which help us to remember information we must learn. These are both different ways of trying to make new or unfamiliar material more meaningful to us so it will be easier to learn.
>
> You can also try to relate the information contained in the reading to something else you already know. Then try to figure out as many ways as you can that the two are related or similar. For example, a vein is like a thin rubber waterpipe. Both are thin tubes, relatively rigid and have fluid going through them.
>
> I would like each of you to read this passage carefully and try to create some learning aids that you think will help you to learn the different properties of arteries and veins [p. 45].

As Bransford et al. (1980) point out, this approach converts the text understanding task into one of free recall. The students are encouraged to undertake attempts to elaborate the material by *adding* context, context that is in fact unrelated to the passage. The alternative that Bransford et al. suggest is to encourage the students to search for the logical and meaningful relations that already exist in the text and are integral to understanding the passage. In this case, there are clear form and function relations that, if uncovered, facilitate memory of the properties *and* understanding of the circulatory system. For example, the passage includes the information that the arteries are more elastic than the veins; it goes on to point out that the arteries need to expand and contract to facilitate pushing the blood forward. As is not atypical, the passage already includes a meaningful form–function "elaboration" that is nonarbitrary. Instructions to the students do not tell them to look for and exploit such elaborations, but rather to search for personally invented, more arbitrary elaborations, which must be less effective. Given these instructions, the task does seem to be converted from one of attempting to understand the material to one of remembering the facts. We would argue that such elaboration strategies may be useful on some occasions—when the material is arbitrary, either because it has no structure or because the learner does not have the resources to discover the structure—but that it represents a fallback strategy.

Teaching Methods.   Approaches to instruction vary in many ways across the programs. For example, the programs differ with respect to the following issues: (1) determining the sequence in which individual skills should be taught; (2) deciding how much learners should be informed about the nature and uses of the skills they are acquiring; (3) determining whether instruction in text comprehension should constitute a separate course or should be combined with instruction in other school subject matter areas; and (4) determining how individual differences should be accommodated.

In some sense, there could be said to be almost no agreement across these programs on how instruction should be structured. This may reflect genuinely different views concerning how text learning skills are acquired or may be the result of other factors. An implication of the tetrahedral model (Fig. 9.1) is that the activities engaged in during some learning task should vary as a function of the nature of the material, special characteristics of the learner, and the criterion task on which the effects of the learning are to be assessed. Thus, some of the variations in instruction observed across these programs may reflect the fact that the developers are teaching different kinds of skills to different subjects with different criterial tasks in mind. We doubt that all the variations can be accounted for in this way, however. Rather, we believe the authors differ not only in their choice of subject populations and tasks, but also in their views concerning how text learning skills are acquired.

We cannot hope to provide any answers here, as the problems are exceedingly complex. Our goal is simply to·raise some issues for further research and occasionally to make some guesses about the form the answers might take. Consider first the individual skills that form the basis of any instructional program. One view is that the sequence of instruction in these skills should be from easy and concrete to hard and abstract (JAK), so that learning errors will be minimized. An alternative view is to expose the learner to the target situation initially and gradually add information and instruction as the subject requires it, the option favored by Dansereau. This latter procedure is also similar to a Socratic dialogue approach (Collins & Stevens, 1982). These methods feature the provision of general, regulatory cues first (How do you think you should start?), followed by more specific prompts and provisions of information (Put that piece there). From our perspective, the major difference is that the Socratic approaches include explicit modeling of the self-regulatory mechanisms involved in learning, whereas errorless learning can occur without this kind of modeling.

The JAK approach is built on the assumption that instruction of each skill should begin at zero level, that is, initial examples within each unit should require no specialized prior ability. The advantage of a zero-level starting point is that it becomes easier for poor learners to respond correctly even at the very beginning of instruction. They can then be led to master more complex forms by gradually fading in a series of variations. If each variation is small enough, errors should be rare, and the final target should be reached by all students. Dansereau's view, in contrast, is that the use of such simplified starting points may actually distort the skill being developed and thus serve as a possible source of negative transfer when the more typical and more complex situation is introduced.

Decisions about the order in which to teach the various skills involved in a program are more difficult the larger the number of these skills. There are some simple rules, of course, such as teach A before B if the execution of B requires A, but there are many cases where such analyses are impossible. The problem is most acute for JAK. Their decision is to work within an easy-to-hard sequence, although their ordering of skills is frequently highly subjective. Dansereau has a slightly different problem, as he deals with qualitatively different kinds of strategies, cognitive and affective. His suggestion is to teach the cognitive strategies first, followed by the affective, the rationale being that the cognitive set is more complex and hence should receive more attention and practice.

There is a more interesting question here, however, and this concerns the way in which instruction should proceed as various skills are added to the learner's repertoire. That is, as learners begin to have a large repertoire of skills to work with, how can they be taught how to access the appropriate skill in the appropriate situation? As already mentioned, in our review of the theoretical background of these programs, learning to execute a skill under some specific set of conditions does not in any way guarantee that the students will readily identify the next occurrence of those conditions, particularly when they are somewhat disguised. Thus, lessons should include situations where identification of problem type is a key issue, including both clear examples of different conditions and fuzzy cases. The instructional method that works best in teaching students how to execute a set of skills may be quite different from the method that works best in teaching them when to use these skills. For example, it may be possible that an easy-to-hard sequence works best to instill specific skills, whereas a Socratic format is most effective in teaching students when to use these skills.

Another major difference in approach concerns the degree of explicitness of instruction the developers feel is necessary to bring about learning. There are two aspects to this problem. One is the extent to which the developers clearly describe to students the various strategies in which instruction is being offered. The second is the extent to which the developers help students come to understand when and why these skills are useful. There are sizeable disagreements in the programs about the necessity for explicitness in either area. On one end, Dansereau and Weinstein like to provide their subjects with a lot of information about the strategies being taught. They provide explicit instruction regarding the execution of these strategies, including modeling procedures, explaining separate components, and giving feedback on subject-produced exemplars. Along the understanding dimension, they attempt to provide a justification for the approaches they champion by presenting the theoretical rationale underlying the strategies and illustrating some of their various uses. For example, Dansereau tells students that constructing a network representation can help them come to understand the organization and relationships inherent in a body of material, and can serve as a retrieval aid when taking a test or writing a paper.

JAK also opt for direct instruction, in that the details of the target procedures are made explicit, and subjects are carefully told how to carry out the requisite steps. They differ from Dansereau and Weinstein because they describe the components of the skills in detail, but they do not attempt to tell the subject much about the reasons those skills were chosen, or their range of applicability. The stronger contrast with the explicit teaching position, however, is that of Herber, who does not believe it necessary for the teacher to tell the students much if anything about the activities that are the targets of instruction. Herber is quite explicit in stating that students need not be taught about reading or reasoning, but rather should be induced to simulate the actual target activities by performing the exercises contained in teacher-prepared reading guides. Thus, Herber comes out strongly for what we have elsewhere (Brown et al., 1981) termed blind training and to some extent is joined there by JAK, whereas Weinstein and Dansereau argue for what we have called self-control training.

The final dimension mentioned here concerns the setting in which reading instruction should take place, with JAK and Herber representing the extremes along that dimension. JAK attempt to teach reading skills directly, using specially constructed and structured materials. (This approach is also the one selected by Feuerstein, this volume.) Herber insists that reading instruction should be done only when necessary to facilitate learning in a content area, should be offered as part of instruction in that content area, and should focus on teaching students how to comprehend the regularly assigned materials in that content area. The two main issues separating the JAK and Herber positions are time involvement and transfer. The time dimension has already been discussed. As important, in our view, is the transfer problem. Choosing or constructing special materials to illustrate specific reading skills should facilitate the learning of these skills, but to the extent that these special materials are different from regular classroom materials, transfer may not result. Thus, individuals working with specially constructed instructional materials may also have to include some form of bridging instructions to show students how the skills they are learning are useful with more typical classroom reading materials. (Again see Feuerstein, this volume.)

Concern with Individual Differences.   Concentration on individual differences varies appreciably across the programs, with JAK giving the matter the most explicit attention. A concern with individual differences is of course central to their mastery learning approach, which is based on the view that almost everyone can learn, given optimal conditions and sufficient time and instruction. In their program, poorer students tend to spend more time working on individual skills than do more capable students and also have the instruction complemented with an alternative method of imparting the same skill. Thus, instruction is supplemented both quantitatively and qualitatively to bring recalcitrant students to the preset criterion of mastery.

Such a position seems reasonable enough and has much to recommend it. It is worth noting, however, that from an alternative perspective, this program avoids another extremely important source of individual differences. Specifically, it is not necessarily the case that bringing individuals to the same state of mastery in some skill eliminates individual differences with regard to the use of that skill. For example, in a series of experiments, Campione and Brown (in press) have reported significant ability-related differences in the flexibility with which rules are used, even after all subjects have learned them to the same criterion. Similarly, students who learn more quickly (with less complete instruction) also tend to be more facile in the subsequent use of what they have learned. In this context, the mastery learning view of individual differences contrasts sharply with the views of those who emphasize access differences. The implications of these contrasting views for instructional programs have already been described.

The others have little to say about individual differences except to acknowledge their importance and the fact that they need to be considered in designing instruction. One concrete and interesting suggestion is offered by Herber. He argues that small-group formats, involving heterogenous learners, can be used to address some of the problems occasioned by the presence of individual differences. In his view, the use of small groups allows poorer students a greater chance to participate and become active contributors to the learning process. They recite more, answer more questions, and have their ideas responded to and evaluated more. The idea is reasonable, but the data, as Herber points out, are less than impressive. In fact, all the programs we have outlined, and many of those reviewed elsewhere in this volume, emphasize the potential role of small-group discussions and peer interaction in teaching and learning. We believe that many of the issues we see as important for future research can be illustrated through a consideration of small-group dynamics involved in instructional programs, and their effects on individual learners. We return to a discussion of some of these issues in our closing remarks.

Summary of the Comparison of the Programs

The programs differ from each other in terms of the target populations, types and number of skills taught, method of instruction, and treatment of individual differences. For the developers working with younger children and those working with children with potential reading problems, most notably JAK, large numbers of specific skills are taught, and instruction is designed to follow an easy-to-hard, errorless learning format. The emphasis is on instilling skills, without worrying about their control. Younger children are also afforded blind training in the sense that they are not treated as collaborators in the learning process (Brown et al., 1981). In both JAK and Herber, students are led to perform desired learning activities, but they are not told why and in what situations these activities are useful.

In contrast, Dansereau and Weinstein, generally working with college students, teach more general skills and provide much more context for those activities. They apparently and reasonably assume the availability of more specific subcomponents and concentrate their efforts on larger, more general constellations of skills. Instruction also proceeds differently in these programs. There is somewhat more self-instruction and the teacher–student interactions include much more explanation of the benefits of the skills being taught.

If we were to construct a composite program or view, it would be that younger students, particularly those with problems, need to be taught sets of specific skills in programmed situations, often using blind and repetitive training interventions. As students mature and the specific skills become acquired, broader and more general skills become the target of instruction, and students begin to receive more detailed information about the conditions under which these skills are useful and how they achieve their effects.

Although we do not know whether such a composite view would be subscribed to by the developers, nor how popular such a view would be elsewhere, it is consistent with some arguments regarding the treatment of inefficient learners. For example, Rosner (1979) has described the adaptation of instruction to individual differences. He distinguished between hard to teach (HTT) and easy to teach (ETT) children. In terms of the program to be employed, he emphasizes the need for more drill and practice, the more severe the learning problem. When he describes the characteristics of teachers who can accommodate students' unique characteristics, he includes the extent to which the teacher is willing (and able) to be pedantic and to be precise and repetitive—this in contrast to being the kind of teacher who thrives only where "discovery learning" is the desired outcome. HTT children are not good discoverers. If they were, they would not need compensatory education (Rosner, 1979, p. 144).

Although Rosner emphasizes this distinction explicitly, the same suggestion appears, at least implicitly, in a number of instructional situations. Although we do not have space here to review this literature (see Brown, Palincsar, & Purcell, in press, for a recent review), a few examples can be presented. Allington (1980) has noted that when reading errors are made, poor readers are more likely to interrupt their reading than good readers; and these interruptions occur immediately following errors for poor readers, whereas for good readers, the interruptions are delayed until the end of some meaning segment. Poor readers receive a large amount of practice in pronunciation and decoding, whereas good readers spend more time evaluating and criticizing what they have read (Au, 1980; Collins, 1980; McDermott, 1976). Collins (1980) also reports that teachers' corrections following reading errors tend to be local and frequently involve only the word on which the error was made for poor readers. In contrast, when good readers' errors are corrected, the corrected item is then reviewed in its appropriate context. Although many more examples could be given, the general conclusion that emerges clearly is that poor readers are consistently given less practice and instruction than good readers in the use of a variety of comprehension-fostering activities.

CONCLUDING COMMENTS

Problems of Evaluation

Once a program has been developed, there arise several immediate questions or sets of questions: Does it work? If so, how and why? If not, why not? Our primary suggestion is that any evaluation attempts be as specific as possible. The developers should be clear about what the program is designed to achieve. A general statement that comprehension should be increased is typically not very helpful, but even on this level some clear-cut statement would be a step in the right direction. For example, JAK might claim that the goal of their program is to improve performance on standardized tests such as the Iowa Test of Basic Skills. This at least makes clear how they would expect the program to be evaluated.

Others might want to quibble with their choice and argue that such a goal is not a reasonable one, as elevating test performance does not guarantee that the actual skills or abilities necessary for independent comprehension would be developed; the old question of whether teaching people to score well on ability tests makes them more intelligent pops up. It would then be incumbent upon those who object to develop a more adequate assessment plan. Whatever criteria are selected, they should be based on a specified theory of comprehension; that theory could then be used to design tests of the presumed important components of text processing. Armed with such tests, an evaluation of the program *in terms of that theory* could be conducted. Such evaluation clearly cannot be done in a vacuum. Reviewers will be content with the evaluation only to the extent that they buy the underlying theory.

We would also advocate the use of evaluation plans that are as thorough as is practically feasible. Programs can have indirect effects not anticipated by the developers. The broader the evaluation effort, the more likely these effects are to be detected. The ideal battery would involve multiple dependent measures, subsets of which were diagnostic of different aspects of text processing. If this condition were met, it would be possible in principle to map out the areas where the program could be streamlined or modified. Many of the programs attempt to achieve their goal by bringing about changes in several components of performance. An evaluation "profile" would help streamline a program by indicating which processes have in fact been influenced and which have not been modified through the intervention. If the gains in performance are significant, the program might then be reduced in scope by eliminating those aspects associated with unmodified components; alternatively, if the program might achieve larger gains, revisions would be aimed at the processes not appropriately affected in the earlier version.

A nice example of the diagnostic value of appropriately selected multiple dependent measures comes from Weinstein, Underwood, Reed, Conlon, Wild, and Kennedy (1981). In a series of experiments investigating the effects of teaching imagery, elaboration, and grouping strategies, they included posttraining assessments of free-recall and paired-associates learning, as well as a variety of tests of reading comprehension. As they noted:

Performance differences were found in all but one instance on the free recall and paired-associates tasks in these two studies, as well as on the [atypical] numbers reading comprehension tests in the second study . . . thus, it may be that the absence of differences on the reading tasks is not related to the length or complexity of the readings, but rather to some aspect of the training which limits its usefulness for improving reading comprehension but generally not for paired-associate and free recall tasks [pp. 15–16].

The use of multiple outcome measures in these studies highlighted areas in which the program was effective and where it was not, indicating ways in which modifications needed to be introduced. This information then feeds into the next step of the process and provides valuable information that Weinstein and her colleagues can use in the design of larger scale intervention programs (see Weinstein & Underwood, this volume).

Dansereau is also a strong proponent of the use of multiple dependent measures. He uses many kinds of test probes: immediate, delayed, open-ended, multiple-choice, main idea versus detail questions, etc. Although we are in full sympathy with this approach, we would like to see it supplemented in a number of ways. First, the conclusions derived from the different dependent variables tend to be highly inferential; they are not direct indicators of specific components of comprehension. Given different patterns of performance across the dependent variables produced by alternative programs, or different learners, we are not in a position to conclude as much as we would like about the reasons. We still need a theory to explain why dependent measures X and Y indicate operation of Z, whereas A and B reflect process C. This is not a criticism of Dansereau, but a comment about the current state of theory.

We do believe, however, that Dansereau could include more direct assessments of processing components. Consider his work on networking. There is little emphasis on individual differences in either overall performance or the more directly relevant quality of the networks produced. There are indeed occasional comments that all students appeared to take appropriate notes, but no attempt to evaluate their quality was reported. For other sets of activities we have reviewed (e.g., underlining and note-taking), there is a strong relation between strategy quality and performance; carrying out some rote version of the activity is not sufficient for good performance (Brown & Smiley, 1978). Further, the ways in which inefficient users perform may provide hints about the nature of the additional instruction needed. It is essential to have direct measures of the quality of execution of instructed strategies, as well as the relation between strategy use and performance, if an instructional program is to be evaluated adequately (Belmont & Butterfield, 1977; Brown & Campione, 1978). Without such data, it is impossible to distinguish failures of a program due to inefficient strategy use from those due to choice of a strategy inappropriate to the task at hand.

What is needed for evaluations and assessments is direct measures of process change, supplemented by information on product change, rather than a preponderance of productlike dependent variables from which inferences about processes are made. With regard to Dansereau's work, for instance, it would be valuable to have measures of the quality of student networks, and of the relation between these quality measures and other indices of performance. Assume that students required to generate networks do outperform an uninstructed control group on some index of comprehension. Suppose further that networking quality and performance were significantly related; that would suggest, though not prove, that some components of the specific activity were important. Differences between good and poor users would presumably indicate which aspects were of particular importance, allowing a refinement of both the instructional procedure and of extant theory. Alternatively, quality of strategy use and performance could be unrelated. One suggestion would then be that it is not any specific aspect of the strategy that is important, but some other process stimulated by the strategy. For example, requiring students to generate a network may lead them to monitor their comprehension more fully than they usually do and/or induce them to engage in more frequent or deeper self-questioning, and this, rather than any specific networking component, is responsible for the beneficial outcomes. Such a finding, if obtained, would allow modifications in instruction and inform theories of comprehension.

From this perspective, the ideal experiment would begin with a theoretical analysis of comprehension activities. Instruction could then be designed within the framework of that theory, and the theory would also be used to predict the expected changes, thus dictating the form of the evaluation probes. Throughout the course of the experiment, detailed analyses of the use, and quality of use, of the instructed activities could be undertaken, and their relation to other aspects of performance monitored. We believe that small-N or single-subject type designs would represent an efficient way to proceed initially with this type of research. The lack of generality resulting from the use of few subjects would be more than compensated for by the increased amount of data obtained on each subject (cf. Palincsar & Brown, 1981).

Group Dynamics

In this final section, we highlight one research topic that we see as central to issues regarding the instruction of comprehension skills. Although reading instruction frequently occurs in group settings, there has been little work of which we are aware concerned with assessing the effects of different types of group composition and interaction on the development of individual thinking skills. This discussion is stimulated by Herber's emphasis on small-group instruction involving children of heterogeneous abilities. Herber suggests that in such settings, poor learners get to recite more and thus get more encouragement and feedback about their ideas. As there are good students in the groups, the poorer students are also more directly involved in discussions in which appropriate reasoning activities are being modeled.

This suggestion is an attractive one. We have already noted some of the research that indicates that students assigned to lower reading groups get little practice in the kinds of comprehension-fostering skills emphasized by the developers of the programs we have reviewed. Mixing ability groups would seem to be one way of dealing with this problem. We believe that there are two issues involved in this approach, and that we do not have the data available to evaluate either of them. One is whether the different-ability children would be treated comparably by teachers, or whether they would continue to be treated differently. The second is whether that matters.

Answers to the first question would simply require ethnographic analyses of mixed ability groups. Assume that these analyses indicate that the poorer students are still being treated differently from the more capable ones. It may still be the case that they benefit from such a placement. The instruction they would be receiving might be regarded as representing something of a middle ground— they still do not receive "direct" instruction in the use of critical comprehension skills, but nonetheless do have those processes modeled for them by both the better students and the teacher. There are some data (e.g., Botvin & Murray, 1975) indicating that exposure to some critical interaction can be as beneficial as actual participation in that interaction, but this remains to be tested in the context of reading groups.

We can conclude by emphasizing that studies of the ways teachers interact with high- and low-ability groups of students, and with children of varying ability within groups, are a fertile ground for future learning research. If the descriptive work is supplemented by more detailed analyses of the effects of various group patterns on individuals, we would be in a much better position to make suggestions about the ways instruction should be structured and individual differences accommodated. We would also be in a position to advance our views about the nature of learning.

ACKNOWLEDGMENTS

This chapter was commissioned for the NIE–LRDC Conference on Thinking and Learning Skills through National Institute of Education grant #0E–NIE–G–78–0215 and was also supported in part by PHS Grant HD05951.

REFERENCES

Allington, R. Teacher interruption behavior during primary-grade oral reading. *Journal of Educational Psychology,* 1980, *73* (3), 371–377.

Anderson, T. H., & Armbruster, B. B. Reader and text-studying strategies. In W. Otto & S. White (Eds.), *Reading expository material.* New York: Academic Press, 1982.

Armbruster, B. B., & Anderson, T. H. *The effect of mapping on the free recall of expository text* (Tech. Rp. No. 160). Champaign: University of Illinois, Center for the Study of Reading, February 1980.

Au, K. *A test of the social organizational hypothesis: Relationships between participation structures and learning to read.* Unpublished doctoral dissertation, University of Illinois, 1980.

Baker, L., & Brown, A. L. Cognitive monitoring in reading and studying. In J. Flood (Ed.), *Understanding reading comprehension.* Newark, Del.: International Reading Association, in press. (a)

Baker, L., & Brown, A. L. Metacognitive skills of reading. In D. Pearson (Ed.), *Handbook of reading research.* New York: Longman, in press. (b)

Belmont, J. M., & Butterfield, E. C. The instructional approach to developmental cognitive research. In R. V. Kail, Jr., & J. W. Hagen (Eds.), *Perspectives on the development of memory and cognition.* Hillsdale, N.J.: Lawrence Erlbaum Associates, 1977.

Binet, A. *Les idées modernes sur les infants.* Paris: Ernest Flammarion, 1909.

Block, J. H. *Mastery learning—theory and practice*. New York: Holt, Rinehart, & Winston, 1971.

Block, J. H., & Burns, R. Mastery learning. In L. J. Shulman (Ed.), *Review of research in education* (Vol. 4). Itasca, Ill.: F. E. Peacock, 1977.

Bloom, B. S. Learning for mastery. *Evaluation Comment*, 1968, *1* (2). Los Angeles: University of California, Center for the Study of Evaluation.

Bloom, B. S. *Human characteristics and school learning*. New York: McGraw–Hill, 1976.

Bloom, B., & Broder, J. L. Problem-solving processes of college students. *Supplementary Educational Monographs*. Published in conjunction with the *School Review* and *The Elementary School Journal*, Number 73, July 1950, University of Chicago Press.

Botvin, G. J., & Murray, F. B. The efficacy of peer modeling and social conflict in the acquisition of conservation. *Child Development*, 1975, *46*, 796–799.

Bransford, J. D. *Human cognition: Learning, understanding, and remembering*. Belmont, Calif.: Wadsworth, 1979.

Bransford, J. D., Nitsch, K. E., & Franks, J. J. Schooling and the facilitation of knowing. In R. C. Anderson, R. J. Spiro, & W. E. Montague (Eds.), *Schooling and the acquisition of knowledge*. Hillsdale, N.J.: Lawrence Erlbaum Associates, 1977.

Bransford, J. D., Stein, B. S., Shelton, T. S., & Owings, R. A. Cognition and adaptation: The importance of learning to learn. In J. Harvey (Ed.), *Cognition, social behavior, and the environment*. Hillsdale, N.J.: Lawrence Erlbaum Associates, 1980.

Brewer, W. F., & Lichtenstein, E. H. Event schemas, story schemas, and story grammars. In J. D. Long & A. D. Baddeley (Eds.), *Attention and performance* (Vol. 9). Hillsdale, N.J.: Lawrence Erlbaum Associates, 1981.

Brown, A. L. The role of strategic behavior in retardate memory. In N. R. Ellis (Ed.), *International review of research in mental retardation* (Vol. 7). New York: Academic Press, 1974.

Brown, A. L. Knowing when, where, and how to remember: A problem of metacognition. In R. Glaser (Ed.), *Advances in instructional psychology* (Vol. 1). Hillsdale, N.J.: Lawrence Erlbaum Associates, 1978.

Brown, A. L. Metacognition and reading and writing: The development and facilitation of selective attention strategies for learning from texts. In M. L. Kamil (Ed.), *Directions in reading: Research and instruction*. Washington, D.C.: The National Reading Conference, 1981.

Brown, A. L. Learning and development: The problem of compatibility, access and induction. *Human Development*, 1982, *25*, 89–115. (a)

Brown, A. L. Learning how to learn from reading. In J. Langer & T. Smith-Burke (Eds.), *Reader meets author, bridging the gap: A psycho-linguistic and social linguistic perspective*. Newark, Del.: International Reading Association, Dell Publishing, 1982. (b)

Brown, A. L., Bransford, J. D., Ferrara, R. A., & Campione, J. C. Learning, remembering, and understanding. In J. H. Flavell & E. M. Markman (Eds.), *Handbook of child psychology* (4th ed.). *Cognitive development* (Vol. 3). New York: Wiley, 1983.

Brown, A. L., & Campione, J. C. Permissible inferences from cognitive training studies in developmental research. In W. S. Hall & M. Cole (Eds.), *Quarterly Newsletter of the Institute for Comparative Human Behavior*, 1978, *2* (3), 46–53.

Brown, A. L., & Campione, J. C. The effects of knowledge and experience on the formation of retrieval plans for studying from texts. In M. M. Gruneberg, P. E. Morris, & R. N. Sykes (Eds.), *Practical aspects of memory*. London; Academic Press, 1979.

Brown, A. L., & Campione, J. C. *Research with retarded and learning disabled children: Parallel or interactivity paths*. Paper presented at the meeting of the American Educational Research Association, Boston, April 1980.

Brown, A. L., & Campione, J. C. Modifying intelligence or modifying cognitive skills: More than a semantic quibble? In D. K. Detterman & R. J. Sternberg (Eds.), *How and how much can intelligence be increased*. Norwood, N.J.: Ablex, 1982.

Brown, A. L., Campione, J. C., & Day, J. D. Learning to learn: On training students to learn from texts. *Educational Researcher*, 1981, *10*, 14–21.

Brown, A. L., & Day, J. D. Macrorules for summarizing texts: The development of expertise. *Journal of Verbal Learning and Verbal Behavior*, 1983, *22*(1), 1–14.

Brown, A. L., & DeLoache, J. S. Skills, plans, and self-regulation. In R. Siegler (Ed.), *Children's thinking: What develops?* Hillsdale, N.J.: Lawrence Erlbaum Associates, 1978.

Brown, A. L., & French, L. A. The zone of potential development: Implications for intelligence testing in the year 2000. *Intelligence*, 1979, *3*, 255–277.

Brown, A. L., & Smiley, S. S. Rating the importance of structural units of prose passages: A problem of metacognitive development. *Child Development*, 1977, *48*, 1454–1466.

Brown, A. L., & Smiley, S. S. The development of strategies for studying texts. *Child Development*, 1978, *49*, 1076–1088.

Bruce, B. C., & Newman, D. Interacting plans. *Cognitive Science*, 1978, *2*, 195–233.

Campione, J. C., & Brown, A. L. Toward a theory of intelligence: Contributions from research with retarded children. *Intelligence*, 1978, *2*, 279–304.

Campione, J. C., & Brown, A. L. Learning ability and transfer propensity as sources of individual differences in intelligence. In P. H. Brooks, R. Sperber, & C. McCauley (Eds.), *Learning and cognition in the mentally retarded*. Hillsdale, N.J.: Lawrence Erlbaum Associates, 1984.

Campione, J. C., Brown, A. L., & Ferrara, R. A. Mental retardation and intelligence. In R. Sternberg (Ed.), *Handbook of human intelligence*. Cambridge: Cambridge University Press, in press.

Collins, A., Brown, A. L., Morgan, J. L., & Brewer, W. F. *The analysis of reading tasks and texts* (Tech. Rep. No. 43). Champaign: University of Illinois, Center for the Study of Reading, April 1977. (ERIC Document Reproduction Service No. ED 145 404).

Collins, A., & Smith, E. E. Teaching the process of reading comprehension. In D. K. Detterman & R. J. Sternberg (Eds.), *How and how much can intelligence be increased*. Norwood, N.J.: Ablex, 1982.

Collins, A., & Stevens, A. Goals and strategies of inquiry teachers. In R. Glaser (Ed.), *Advances in instructional psychology* (Vol. 2). Hillsdale, N.J.: Lawrence Erlbaum Associates, 1982.

Collins, J. Differential treatment in reading groups. In J. Cook-Gumperz (Ed.), *Educational discourse*. London: Heinemann, 1980.

Ericsson, K. A., & Simon, H. A. Verbal reports as data. *Psychological Review*, 1980, *87*, 215–251.

Ferguson, G. A. On learning and human ability. *Canadian Journal of Psychology*, 1954, *8*, 95–112.

Ferguson, G. A. On transfer and the abilities of man. *Canadian Journal of Psychology*, 1956, *10*, 121–131.

Feuerstein, R. *Instrumental enrichment: An intervention program for cognitive modifiability*. Baltimore: University Park Press, 1980.

Flavell, J. H. Cognitive monitoring. In W. P. Dickson (Ed.), *Children's oral communication skills*. New York: Academic Press, 1981.

Flower, L., & Hayes, J. Plans that guide the composing process. In C. Frederiksen, M. Whiteman, & J. Dominic (Eds.), *Writing: The nature, development, and teaching of written communication*. Hillsdale, N.J.: Lawrence Erlbaum Associates, 1980.

Frase, L. T. Paragraph organization of written materials: The influence of conceptual clustering upon the level and organization of recall. *Journal of Educational Psychology*, 1969, *60*, 394–401.

Gagné, R. H., & Smith, E. C. A study of the effects of verbalization and problem solving. *Journal of Experimental Psychology*, 1962, *63*, 12–18.

Garrett, H. E. A developmental theory of intelligence. *American Psychologist*, 1946, *1*, 372–378.

Hayes, J. R., & Flower, L. S. *Identifying the organization of writing processes*. Paper presented at the meeting of the American Educational Research Association, Toronto, March 1978.

Jenkins, J. J. Four points to remember: A tetrahedral model of memory experiments. In L. S. Cermak & F. I. M. Craik (Eds.), *Levels of processing in human memory.* Hillsdale, N.J.: Lawrence Erlbaum Associates, 1979.

Jones, B. F. *Individual differences in the use of diverse learning strategies on recall and achievement in high school.* Unpublished doctoral dissertation, Northwestern University, Evanston, 1976.

Jones, B. F., & Hall, J. W. *Effects of cross-classification strategies for recalling prose and for writing compare-and-contrast essays.* Paper presented at the meeting of the American Educational Research Association, San Francisco, April 1979.

Mandler, J. M., & Johnson, N. S. Remembrance of things parsed: Story structure and recall. *Cognitive Psychology,* 1977, *9,* 111–151.

Masur, E. F., McIntyre, C. W., & Flavell, J. H. Developmental changes in apportionment of study time among items in a multitrial free-recall task. *Journal of Experimental Child Psychology,* 1973, *15,* 237–246.

McDermott, R. *Kids make sense: Ethnographic account of the interactional management of success and failure in one first-grade classroom.* Unpublished doctoral dissertation, Stanford University, 1976.

Newell, A. Production systems and human cognition. In R. A. Cole (Ed.), *Perception and production of fluent speech.* Hillsdale, N.J.: Lawrence Erlbaum Associates, 1980.

Palincsar, A. S., & Brown, A. L. *The comparative effects of corrective feedback and strategy training on the comprehension skills of junior high students.* Unpublished manuscript, University of Illinois, 1981.

Resnick, L. B., & Glaser, R. Problem solving and intelligence. In L. B. Resnick (Ed.), *The nature of intelligence.* Hillsdale, N.J.: Lawrence Erlbaum Associates, 1976.

Rosner, J. Teaching hard-to-teach children to read: A rationale for compensatory education. In L. B. Resnick & P. A. Weaver (Eds.), *Theory and practice of early reading* (Vol. 2). Hillsdale, N.J.: Lawrence Erlbaum Associates, 1979.

Smiley, S. S., Oakley, D. D., Worthen, D., Campione, J. C., & Brown, A. L. Recall of thematically relevant material by adolescent good and poor readers as a function of written versus oral presentation. *Journal of Educational Psychology,* 1977, *69*(4), 381–387.

Spearman, C. "General intelligence," objectively determined and measured. *American Journal of Psychology,* 1904, *15,* 206–219.

Spearman, C. *The nature of "intelligence" and principles of cognition.* London: Macmillan, 1923.

Spearman, C. *The abilities of man.* New York: Macmillan, 1927.

Vygotsky, L. S. *Mind in society: The development of higher psychological processes.* Cambridge, Mass.: Harvard University Press, 1978.

Weinstein, C. E. Elaboration skills as a learning strategy. In H. F. O'Neil, Jr. (Ed.), *Learning strategies.* New York: Academic Press, 1978.

Weinstein, C. E., Underwood, V. L., Reed, M. M., Conlon, C. M. T., Wild, M., & Kennedy, T. J. *The effects of selected instructional variables on the acquisition of cognitive learning strategies.* Army Research Institute Technical Report, 1981.

Wertsch, J. V. *The social interactional origins of metacognition.* Paper presented at the meeting of the Society for Research in Child Development, San Francisco, March 1979.

Program Presentations and Analyses:
Problem Solving

10 The CoRT Thinking Program

Edward de Bono
University of Cambridge

Venezuela has become the first country in the world, and in history, to include the teaching of thinking skills in the school curriculum as a subject in its own right. One program being used is the CoRT (Cognitive Research Trust) Thinking Program developed by the author of this chapter and adapted for local use by Dr. Margaretta Sanchez. So successful was the local pilot test of this program that the Venezuelan Minister of Education decided to introduce the program into all the elementary schools throughout the country. Thus, plans are now underway to train 42,000 teachers to teach thinking skills to 1.2 million Venezuelan school children in grades 4, 5, and 6.

The Venezuelan project is important because it shows that direct instruction in thinking skills is no longer a dream, or a matter of research discussion, but a practicality. Elsewhere in the world, the CoRT Program has been in use for over 8 years and is now used by more than 5000 schools in England, Scotland, Wales, Eire, Australia, New Zealand, Canada, Spain, Malta, and Nigeria. A report from Canada (Maier, 1980) indicates that there is a growing interest among superintendents and directors of school boards in this program. This is not surprising because Canadian studies (Maier, 1980; McGill University, 1978) have suggested that, even at the college and graduate school levels, students do not consider themselves to be competent thinkers and learners and would like to have received formal instruction in these skills prior to entering college.

Professor George Gallup (1980) has also reported an interest among Americans in instruction in thinking skills:

> In the annual surveys of the public's attitudes toward the schools in the United States, conducted by the Gallup Poll, we find that of all the goals of education, teaching students to think is always rated as the very most important by the public.

And yet, in the United States and elsewhere, one finds little or nothing being done on a systematic basis to teach students to think.

It was a consciousness of this need and this deficiency that led to the development of the CoRT Thinking Program 10 years ago. Since then, we have collected a huge amount of experience with the direct teaching of thinking across all ages and abilities. The program has also been used in corrective institutions and detention centers (Copley & Copley, 1978). It has been our experience that the actual teaching of thinking skills is quite different from the theorized teaching of thinking skills. In the initial stages, many schools and educational psychologists would have long theoretical discussions about likely problems. In practice, these problems never occurred in the classroom. More importantly, effects that could not easily have been predicted in theory became very obvious in the classroom. For example, younger pupils who had been academically regarded as less able suddenly turned out to be very effective thinkers—to the surprise of their peers and their teachers. Similarly, many high-IQ students, who had been regarded by their peers and teachers as gifted, also became more competent thinkers as a result of participation in this program (Maier, 1980). All this is important because the classroom is the best educational laboratory, and years of experience in a variety of conditions, the best way to use that laboratory.

In the sections that follow, we describe our attempts to develop a practical program of instruction in thinking skills. First, we describe the various constraints that have influenced the design of the CoRT Program. Next, we briefly review several popular approaches to instruction in thinking skills that have been used by others and discuss their limitations. Having thus given the reader some background information about our objectives and the methods used by others, we describe the major features of the CoRT approach, the individual skills in which instruction is offered, how lessons are typically structured, and our findings from field testing the program in diverse settings.

DESIGN OBJECTIVES

Our objectives in designing the CoRT Program were as described in the following sections.

1. The Program Should be Simple and Practical.   This is the most important objective and takes precedence over all others. The history of curriculum development shows that many theoretically advanced programs are never used because they are impractical and complicated. To be practical, a program needs to be simple enough for the teacher to grasp what is intended and for the pupils to understand. There should not be a need for expensive materials or special audio-visual aids. It is this priority emphasis on simplicity and practicality that has led to the widespread use of the CoRT Program and its adoption in Venezuela. Teacher training does improve the quality of delivery of the CoRT Program, but many thousands of teachers have successfully taught the program without any prior training at all.

2. The Program Should have Utility Across a Wide Range of Ages, Abilities, and Cultures.   This is an unusual requirement in the educational world where programs are usually targeted quite specifically at students of a given age or ability level. The break with this tradition came about with an appreciation that fundamental thinking processes really are fundamental. In practice, the CoRT Program has been used by children as young as 4½ years and also by senior executives in such major corporations as IBM and ITT. In a field test in New York, for instance, the same program is being used by elementary schoolchildren and also by lay adults (Gleeson, 1980). The ability spread ranges from pupils with IQs of over 140 to educationally subnormal students in the IQ range of 75 to 80. Use across cultures includes rural Venezuela, metropolitan England, Australia, and Canada, and also countries like Nigeria and Malta. With the very youngest, or the least able, lessons have to be slower and somewhat simplified.

3. The Thinking Skills Trained Should be the Thinking Skills Required in Real Life.   This is an important consideration. Education is not an end in itself, but a preparation for life outside school and after school. We were not interested in devising a program that would make children perform better on IQ tests and school examinations. There is evidence that grades and school learning skills do improve, but this was not the prime objective. Thinking is and must be treated as a life skill. Along with reading and writing, it may be the most important life skill that a youngster can take with him or her from school. We therefore regard with great interest the reports we get about children using the skills outside school. We regard with even greater interest the many reports, from all quarters, of the children taking the skills home and making their own parents use them in decisions involving changing a job, moving to a new house, or purchasing a new car. As a matter of interest, the chief executive of the Ford motor company in the United Kingdom makes use of the CoRT skills in solving the industrial problems involved in running a large and very successful company.

Because of this objective, the CoRT Program keeps away from puzzles, games, and other abstract teaching aids, which have no relation to real-life thinking. For the same reason, the program puts a heavy emphasis on projective as contrasted with reactive thinking. Throughout school, the emphasis is on reactive thinking—sorting out the information given, and putting the pieces of the puzzle together in the right way. In real-life situations, in business as well as outside it, very little information is given. The thinker has to collect information, assess it, and supplement it—that is, to think projectively, rather than reactively. One of the features picked up in the McMaster survey of university students mentioned earlier (Maier, 1980) was the feeling that problem solving consisted of "playing around with the given symbols and data until a solution is found that uses up all the given information."

4. Training in Thinking Skills Should Not be Dependent on the Prior Acquisition of a Knowledge Base.   The practice items used in the CoRT Program are very simple and consist of a sentence or two. They make use of a youngster's actual or imagined experience. Only the minimum information required for defining the task is given. This means that all pupils begin at an equal level in the CoRT thinking lessons. This is very important because certain youngsters, due to their backgrounds, interests, or opportunities, acquire a better knowledge base than others. This then controls their performance in almost every other school subject. The CoRT approach of using practice items that do not involve specialized knowledge also means that the material is useful across the wide range of ages, abilities, and cultures mentioned earlier. Information-rich material cannot be used in this way.

5. Students Should be Able to Transfer the Thinking Skills They Have Learned to a Variety of Real-Life Situations.   The problem of transfer is the most important problem facing any program that sets out to teach thinking skills. Thinking is of little use if it remains a game played only during that class period. It is not enough that it should transfer to tests or examinations in that subject or in others. To be of any use, a thinking-skills program must provide skills that are transferred right from the classroom, and from the school itself, into life outside and after school. Transfer is notoriously difficult. Youngsters can be heavily involved in and apply effective thinking to one particular situation but be quite unable to transfer the skill to another. An excellent chess player may be unable to transfer that skill to a new game.

The CoRT Program tackles the transfer problem in two ways. As indicated previously, the thinking that takes place in the CoRT lessons is directly about the sorts of things that real-life situations involve, for example, choosing a hairstyle, a career, or a plan for one's holidays. The practice items are not all of immediate relevance to the children. For example, one practice item asks, "If you were interviewing someone to be a teacher, what factors would you consider?" Through a very careful selection and mixture of practise items, the children come to realize that the thinking skills can be applied to a wide range of thinking situations. The evidence mentioned earlier of children taking the skills home and applying them to their parents' problems supports this approach (Buhagiar, 1980; Copley, 1980; Tripp, 1978).

The second part of the strategy to assure transfer is to create, quite deliberately, specific attention-directing tools that give unfamiliar labels to familiar processes in order to help students use them in a more deliberate manner. These artificial tools keep the students' attention focused on the thinking processes taught in the CoRT lessons, so that they can remember to use these processes in new situations.

6. Instruction Should be Based on an Understanding of the Information Handling Characteristics of the Mind. The CoRT Program is based directly on a model of information handling called the *self-organizing, self-stabilizing, active information net.* That is, a central assumption underlying the program is that the mind is pattern making and pattern using. This model and the evidence supporting it are described in my book, *The Mechanisms of Mind* (de Bono, 1969). The model has been translated into a full computer simulation by Lee and Madurajan (1982) with results that support the behavioral predictions made from it. Consistent with the view of mental processes assumed by the model, the CoRT Program places a great emphasis on the importance of perception in thinking, as becomes evident in our subsequent description of the program.

DIFFERENT APPROACHES TO THE TEACHING OF THINKING SKILLS

In this section, we describe a variety of approaches to teaching thinking skills that have enjoyed popularity in recent years and we discuss some of the problems associated with them.

Teaching the Rules of Logic

From time to time, the teaching of logic, as such, has been part of the curriculum in various schools. I refer here to logic in its operative sense as the rules of deduction, induction, implication, and contradiction, rather than in the lay sense that everything sensible is logical. There is no question that bad logic makes for bad thinking. But unfortunately, the opposite does not hold true—good logic does not necessarily make for good thinking. At one time it did, but not any longer. In the heyday of Scholastic logic (Aquinas based), there was a set of accepted premises arising from a uniform world view and a constructed theology. Arguing logically within these accepted premises was a valid exercise much used to attack heresies and so preserve the constructed theology. Today we accept that logic is only a servicing tool and can do no more than process the perceptions we have. If the perceptions are inadequate, they cannot be put right by an excellence of logic. Indeed, there is a real danger that we accept an error-free argument as correct when the logic may be correct, but the perceptions on which it is based are grossly faulty.

Computer logic and mathematical logic will always retain their validity as subsets of mathematical processing. We do need to pay attention to the logic of thinking, but we must be aware of the danger of assuming that logic is more than a small part of the thinking process. In real life, outside of puzzles and closed problems, logic may actually play a much smaller part than does perception in ordinary, day-to-day thinking.

Helping Students Create Knowledge Files

God cannot think. Complete information makes thinking unnecessary and impossible, because thinking is moving from a state of imperfect information to a state of more useful information. Education has always worked on the assumption that it should make pupils as god-like as possible with regard to the completeness of information they acquire. As knowledge has expanded, we now see that this ambition is receding rather rapidly—hence, the attention to thinking skills. If we do have complete information in a small field, we can trace the knowledge routes and find answers without too much thinking other than knowledge sorting. Unfortunately, in real-life situations, as in business, we rarely have more than a small portion of the information we need. We have to generate the rest through the active operation of perception, by broadening the field and changing the way we look at things. Our own experience, which is supported by others, suggests that toward the end of education pupils are so heavily knowledge dependent that they expect the information to do their thinking for them. They believe that thinking consists of juggling the information given until a solution is recognizable. Older children often refuse to think about problems that require projective rather than reactive thinking, although such problems are tackled fluently by much younger children. This difficulty can be exacerbated with gifted children in what we call "the Everest effect," because gifted children are stretched by being given ever more daunting tasks in which they are asked to puzzle out some information-rich problem. As a result, they become unable to tackle simple problems in which the context and perceptions have to be generated by the thinker.

Using Case Studies

This is possibly the most popular approach today. Elaborate, information-rich case studies are constructed. The pupils are asked to perform the thinking required by the case study—either singly or in groups. In its pure application, pupils derive their own thinking lessons from applying their thinking skills to the information in the case studies. In other cases, the teacher or the text highlights aspects of thinking that the pupil should become aware of, as he or she studies the case. In theory, the method should work. Certainly, motivation and interest levels can be very high; that is the chief advantage of the method. The pupils are interested in the subject, they see themselves applying thinking, and they see themselves reaching an objective. The weakness, however, is in transfer.

The more interesting the case itself, the more difficult it is for any attention to be paid directly to the thinking process. It is like asking a person fascinated by a horror film to look, in an abstract way, at the techniques of suspense being used by the director. We have had a large number of reports from teachers employing various social studies kits, who found that their pupils tackled with interest and fluency one particular topic but were unable to apply those same skills to another topic a week later.

Another weakness of the method is that the range of thinking skills that can be acquired in this way is rather limited: use of evidence, argument skills, handling of prejudice, and reaching conclusions. It is still largely reactive thinking, concerned with information sorting. The method does increase fluency and articulation, but not a wide variety of thinking skills. The very nature of the method also means that the material has to be designed specifically for different ages, abilities, and cultures and this is a practical limitation. It is also important to note that with the case study method, the brighter pupils benefit far more than the weaker ones, who struggle to absorb the given information. It is worth noting also that, in many ways, the case study method is almost the exact opposite of the CoRT method.

Using Abstract Tasks to Simulate Real-Life Thinking Situations

We know that it is possible to improve children's performance on IQ tests by analyzing the separate elements involved in successful performance and training children on each. This simply makes IQ tests inappropriate for such children. The more important question is whether training of this sort is helpful in improving the general thinking skills required in real-life situations. This question can be extended to all methods that use abstract items like puzzles and games to simulate real-life thinking situations. In contrast to the case study method, the skills are practiced in an abstract manner, so that the content of the task does not distract the learner. The approach is somewhat similar to that of mathematics—learning the abstract processes as abstract processes and then applying them later.

The problem with this kind of training is that transfer is difficult to achieve, especially transfer to real-life situations (for academic situations can often resemble the abstract practice items). If these fundamental skills were useful in everyday life, we might expect that those who already had them—and hence had performed well on IQ tests—would be effective thinkers in a variety of real-life situations. This does not seem to be the case. The jump from abstract thinking skills to skills applied in day-to-day living is enormous. Brilliant chess players tend to remain brilliant chess players, not brilliant general-purpose thinkers. They have learned the operating tricks and patterns of a particular situation.

Analyzing and Classifying the Component Skills
Involved in Thinking

From a psychological standpoint, we can analyze what we perceive to be the various operations involved in successful performance on some set of thinking tasks and proceed to train students in each. For example, we might use artificial intelligence models or observations of expert learners to identify the knowledge and skills involved in coping with some set of clearly delineated thinking tasks. Having thus identified the processes involved, we would then group them into trainable segments and use the resulting classification as the basis for instruction.

The weakness of this method is that, whereas it is important to base instruction on a view of how the mind operates, it is also important to take pedagogical factors into consideration. In many instances, the classification of skills that works best in describing successful performance may be quite different from the one that works best in helping students become successful performers. For example, in analyzing successful performance, one's goal is to arrive at a set of distinct operations. However, in teaching students to become successful performers, one may in fact find it more effective to work with a set of overlapping operations.

The CoRT method is based on considerations such as these. The thinking tools in which instruction is offered are derived in part from a view of how the mind operates and in part from pragmatic instructional considerations. Thus, there is a great deal of overlap among the individual skills that are taught. For example, there is a lesson on "Consider all factors" and then another lesson on "Consequences." Logically, consequences are part of the factors that should be considered,but from an operational point of view, it is worth emphasizing this set of skills separately, in order to allow them the special attention they require. Similarly, many CoRT skills are taught indirectly. For example, to help students become more careful observers, we sometimes ask them to form preferences about different kinds of events—that is, to comment on what they like and dislike about these events. Through using indirect methods like these, we find that we can strengthen some of the skills emphasized in our program more effectively than by teaching them in a direct way.

THE CoRT METHOD

The particular approach used in the CoRT Program was derived partly from observing the limitations of and dissatisfactions with the preceding approaches (particularly the transfer problem), partly from consideraton of the perceptual behavior of the mind and its pattern-making habits, and partly from many years of experience in teaching thinking directly as a skill to students and adults at all levels. The design objectives listed earlier in this chapter also exerted a considerable influence on the shape and style of the method

The approach used in the CoRT Thinking Program is more fully described in my book *Teaching Thinking* (de Bono, 1976), but the outline following indicates the basic features.

Role of Perception in Thinking. Imagine a person (male) sitting reading in a room. The telephone rings. He gets up and crosses the room to reach the telephone. All very simple. He can see where the phone is. He can see the furniture and avoid it. Imagine the same scene at night. The person cannot see the furniture; he cannot exactly see where the phone is. As he crosses the room, he has to do a great deal of working out: "There should be an arm chair somewhere here. Let me feel for it and then step around it. Now the phone is not on top of the row of books, but then there's the sculpture and it is not that far—so it must be just to the right of the lamp." In other words, a lot of logical deduction is required, because the perceptual map is not clear. The same thing might happen, to a lesser extent, if it was not night, but the person was nearsighted and had misplaced his glasses.

The purpose of the CoRT Program is to provide a sort of perceptual spectacles, so that the person can see a broader and clearer view and thus have a better perceptual map with which to work. Once the perceptions are right, the amount of logical processing required may be small and the logic of the simplest sort. Traditionally, most of the emphasis in thinking has been on the logical processing aspects, and we have developed various techniques for handling this processing. But in most situations, perception is even more important, because it provides the premises for our subsequent logic or action. In many situations, a clear view of the circumstances can lead directly to action.

If we look at the type of information-processing system described in *The Mechanism of Mind* (de Bono, 1969), we can see that the main purpose of the brain is to be brilliantly uncreative. The system allows incoming information to organize itself, as quickly as possible, into patterns. Once a pattern is established, it serves to organize perception on future occasions. The behavior of patterns in such a system has a dynamic geometry of its own. The system is marvelously effective.

In the typical "point to point" thinking of a child, one pattern is followed and then another. For example, 23 out of 24 groups of children aged 10 years old disagreed with the suggestion that bread, fish, and milk should be free on grounds of thinking such as these (from Cognitive Research Trust & Inner London Education Authority, 1975):

If they were free the shops would be crowded.
The buses going to the shops would be crowded.

The drivers would ask for more money.
They would not get it.
They would go on strike.
Others would join the strike.
So there would be chaos.

In point to point thinking, instead of a general scan of the terrain around the thinking focus, there is a scurrying down one track after another. These tracks include emotions, prejudices, anecdotes, short-term attractions, ego-centered considerations, and so on. In the end, there is no comprehensive perceptual map.

Exhortation and pointing out the fault are of little value in curbing point to point thinking that is, after all, the most natural way to think. What we have to do is to create other patterns, superpatterns, that will allow attention to move in other directions. The superpatterns are deliberately designed to be scanning patterns that allow the terrain to be surveyed and a perceptual map to emerge.

CoRT Attention Tools.   The superpatterns just mentioned are really attention tools or frames. They are designed to lead attention in a different direction from the one that would have otherwise been the case. Let us take the first CoRT lesson, which is labeled the PMI. One of the major faults in thinking that we have noticed in both youngsters and adults, even at the most elite level (Cognitive Research Trust, 1976a), is the habit of taking an initial stand on a subject and then using thinking simply to support that stand. The PMI is an attention director designed to overcome this problem. Attention is first directed at the "Plus" aspects, then at the "Minus" aspects, and then at the "Interesting" aspects. The thinker who follows this superpattern is thus forced to explore the subject, rather than just support a prejudice.

Of course, everyone would claim to follow this simple strategy, but our experience suggests that they do not. On one recent occasion, we divided 140 senior executives into two random groups. One group was asked to consider the suggestion that currency should be dated (1980 dollar, 1981 dollar, etc.), and the other group was asked to consider whether marriage should be a 5-year contract. At the end of a 5-minute period, the problems were switched around and this time each group was asked to carry out a formal PMI. If they had done this on the first occasion, there should have been no difference in the results. Before the PMI, 44% were in favor of a dated currency; after the PMI, only 11½% were in favor. Before the PMI, 23% were in favor of the 5-year marriage contract, after the PMI, 38% were in favor. So asking sophisticated thinkers to do something obvious had a marked effect. This is characteristic of all thinking training. The obvious things are worth doing but do not get done. The obvious things are also the most difficult to teach.

Some of the attention-directing tools have code labels like PMI, CAF, OPV, AGO. These labels are a deliberate attempt to make a familiar process seem strange, so that it can get the attention it deserves. Exhorting someone to look at something called the consequences of his or her actions is less effective than asking for a C & S from time to time. The appellation creates a more tangible pattern for that process. When first introduced to our code labels, teachers were against this apparently unnecessary jargon. After teaching our lessons, however, they saw the point and actually asked that other lessons be given codes.

The kind of process we are trying to encourage through use of code labels is illustrated in the following example. Imagine the different approaches that one might take to teaching art appreciation. One approach is to ask pupils to look at a series of pictures and comment on them. A different approach is to direct their attention by asking them to look at the brushwork, the composition, the color balance, the lighting, the perspective, and so on—that is, to give them attention frames or superpatterns to guide them in studying the pictures. These attention frames enable them to engage in a scanning process that enriches perception and provides detail on the perceptual map. At first, pupils might go through these attention frames one after another. With practice, however, the process would become quicker and more automatic. In the end, pupils would become capable of scanning pictures without even being conscious that they were doing so. Our approach is similar to the one just described. We are attempting to give pupils tools for scanning more broadly, and to encourage them to practice using these tools so that they can be applied in an automatic and effortless way.

CoRT Practice Items. How are the attention tools to be practiced? Practice in the CoRT Program is very much like the practice in a sport. Attention has to stay on the process being practiced, not on the content. The method is almost exactly the opposite of the case study method. The practice items are very short and consist of a line or two of text. The pupils practice that item with the attention tool that is the subject of the lesson. The teacher keeps attention firmly on this tool and prevents it wandering off into a general discussion of the item, no matter how interesting or tempting such a discussion might be. The time allowed for thinking about or discussing each item varies from 2 to 4 minutes.

At first, this thinking time seems much too short, and both teachers and pupils resent the tight discipline. The pupils want to get their teeth into a discussion and to get excited by the content. They want to focus their thinking toward some conclusion, not have it abruptly terminated after a few minutes. Teachers find the idiom very different from the idiom used in other subjects. They too want finite answers. In the sports analogy, they want to play a game, not practice strokes.

After a while, the resistance ceases and both teachers and pupils recognize the special idiom of the CoRT thinking lessons. They become interested in the processes, in their deliberate focused use, and no longer want to be bound by the content. The pupils take pride in being able to aim their thinking and use it as a tool, instead of being carried along in the excitement of a discussion. In teacher training, this aspect is the most difficult to get across, yet it is absolutely fundamental to the CoRT method. Here are some further examples of the practice items used:

What makes a TV or radio program interesting? Do a CAF (CAF stands for Consider All Factors) and then a FIP. (FIP stands for First Important Priorities).

Mail services usually lose a lot of money. If you were running these services, what alternatives might you suggest? (from the APC lesson on Alternatives, Possibilities, Choices)

A father forbids his 13 year old daughter to smoke. What is his point of view and what is hers? (from the OPV lesson on Other Points of View)

The reports from the teachers about the value of the different practice items tend to be contradictory. Some teachers prefer the backyard problems that immediately concern the pupils. Others say the more remote problems provide the best thinking practice (for example, what would be the objectives of an alien space ship captain approaching earth?). It seems likely that the teachers' own prejudices and expectations determine which items work best. It is part of the CoRT method to have a wide variety of practice items all mixed in together. This keeps attention on the process, rather than on the content, prevents stereotyped replies, and encourages pride in a thinking skill that can be directed to any situation.

Strategy for Encouraging Transfer. As I mentioned earlier, the transfer strategy is based on two principles. The first principle is to maintain attention on the thinking process itself, not on the content. Thus, attention is attached to a specific tool. That tool can be talked about and practiced. The tool itself can be transferred to other situations as, for example, when a child goes home and makes her parents do a C & S on moving to a new town. Underlying all this is a consciousness that the thinking lessons are actually about thinking as such— not about any other subject. Children soon develop pride in their thinking ability, much as they might in their swimming ability.

The second principle is to have a mixture of practice items that involves a wide variety of situations typical of those pupils encounter in their everyday experience. Thus, in this sense, no transfer is required, because children are learning to think about the very situations to which they would otherwise have had to transfer their thinking skills.

Identification of Skills in Which to Offer Instruction. Each lesson in the CoRT Program centers around a different thinking skill. As indicated previously, the major criterion in selecting skills was their usefulness in enabling individuals to function effectively in a wide range of practical thinking situations. In this respect, I was in the fortunate position of being able to draw on many years' experience in discussing the thinking needs and habits of architects, designers, scientists, computer scientists, engineers, lawyers, administrators, armed forces, and business executives at all levels. I was also in a position to discuss thinking in a wide range of cultures: North and South American, European, Southeast Asian, Japanese, Australian, New Zealand, and African. This breadth became possible as a result of interest generated by the concept of lateral thinking that I originated in 1967 (de Bono, 1970).

THE CoRT PROGRAM

The CoRT Program is divided into six sections of 10 lessons each. Each section covers one particular aspect of thinking. The sections are designed as coherent wholes, with one lesson adding to or qualifying the effects of another. Thus, when teachers use individual CoRT sections, they should include all the lessons involved. The sections may be used in any order. However, it is usually advisable to begin with CoRT I. CoRT I has been used as an abbreviated program of instruction in thinking skills with a wide range of students. CoRT VI has also been used in this way, and CoRT I, IV, and V have been used, in combination, in this way.

CoRT I: Breadth

This section is concerned with helping students develop tools and habits for scanning widely around a thinking situation. The following tools are emphasized:

TREATMENT OF IDEAS (PMI): Deliberately examining ideas for good, bad, or interesting points, instead of immediately accepting or rejecting them.

FACTORS INVOLVED (CAF): Looking as widely as possible at all the factors involved in a situation, instead of only the immediate ones.

RULES: Draws together the first two lessons.

CONSEQUENCES (C & S): Considering the immediate, short, medium, and long-term consequences of alternative strategies.

OBJECTIVES (AGO): Selecting and defining objectives; being clear about one's aims and understanding those of others.

PLANNING: Draws together the preceding two lessons.

PRIORITIES (FIP): Choosing from a number of different possibilities and alternatives; putting one's priorities in order.

ALTERNATIVES (APC): Generating new alternatives and choices, instead of feeling confined to the obvious ones.

DECISIONS: Draws together the preceding two lessons.

VIEWPOINT (OPV): Considering all the viewpoints involved in a situation.

CoRT II: Organization

This section is concerned with teaching students how to be organized and systematic in coping with a thinking situation. The following tools are emphasized:

RECOGNIZE: Deliberately labeling a situation in order to make it easier to understand and deal with.

ANALYZE: Deliberately dividing up a situation in order to think about it more effectively.

COMPARE: Using comparison to understand a situation; learning to make systematic comparisons.

SELECT: Deliberately selecting from among different alternatives those that fit one's requirements.

FIND OTHER WAYS: Deliberately finding alternative ways of looking at a situation.

START: Determining the first steps in thinking about a situation.

ORGANIZE: Organizing all the steps in thinking about a situation.

FOCUS: Knowing which aspect of a situation is under consideration at the moment.

CONSOLIDATE: Knowing what one has accomplished in thinking about a situation and what still remains to be accomplished.

CONCLUDE: Arriving at a definite conclusion, including determining that no definite conclusion is possible.

CoRT III: Interaction

This section is concerned with situations involving debate and discussion. The following tools are emphasized:

EXAMINE BOTH SIDES (EBS): Deliberately examining both sides of an argument instead of blindly supporting one side.

TYPE OF EVIDENCE: Knowing the types of evidence that can be put forward in an argument; distinguishing between fact and opinion.

VALUE OF EVIDENCE: Knowing that not all evidence is of equal value; being able to assess the value of evidence.

STRUCTURE OF EVIDENCE: Examining evidence to determine whether it stands on its own, or whether it is dependent on other evidence.

AGREEMENT, DISAGREEMENT, IRRELEVANCE (ADI): Determining how evidence can be pieced together to increase areas of agreement and reduce areas of disagreement.

BEING RIGHT 1: Knowing two ways of being right: (1) examining the idea itself, its implications, and effects, and (2) referring to facts, authority, and feelings.

BEING RIGHT 2: Knowing two other ways of being right: (1) using names, labels, and classifications, and (2) making judgments.

BEING WRONG 1: Knowing two ways of being wrong: (1) exaggerating, that is, making unwarranted generalizations, and (2) basing conclusions on only part of the situation.

BEING WRONG 2: Knowing two other ways of being wrong.

OUTCOME: Knowing what has been achieved at the end of an argument—that is, distinguishing seven possible levels of achievement short of complete agreement.

CoRT IV: Creativity

This section is concerned with creative thinking, including elements of lateral thinking. The following tools are emphasized:

YES, NO, AND PO: Using ideas creatively while suspending judgment on their worth.

STEPPING STONE: Using ideas, not for their own sake, but because they can lead to other ideas.

RANDOM INPUT: Entering random, unrelated ideas into a situation as a stimulus for new lines of thought.

CONCEPT CHALLENGE: Testing the uniqueness of concepts to identify other ways of doing things.

DOMINANT IDEA: Identifying the dominant ideas in a situation, so that they can be pushed aside for purposes of considering other ideas.

DEFINE THE PROBLEM: Defining a problem exactly to make it easier to solve.

REMOVE THE FAULTS: Assessing the faults associated with an idea in order to remove them.

COMBINATION: Examining the attributes of seemingly unrelated ideas as an aid in creating new combinations of ideas.

REQUIREMENTS: Using the requirements of a situation as a way of identifying new ways of coping with that situation.

EVALUATION: Determining whether an idea fits the requirements of a situation and knowing its advantages and disadvantages.

CoRT V: Information and Feeling

This section is concerned with the place of information and feeling in thinking. The following tools are emphasized:

INFORMATION (FI–FO): Knowing what information is available in thinking about a situation and what additional information is needed.

QUESTIONS (FQ & SQ): Being able to use questions in a skillful way; understanding the difference between shooting questions and fishing questions.

CLUES: Using clues to make deductions and identify implications; examining clues separately and in combination.

CONTRADICTION: Avoiding false jumps and false conclusions; distinguishing contradictions from false conclusions.

GUESSING: Guessing when confronted with incomplete information; estimating the likelihood that one's guesses are correct; differentiating small guesses from larger ones.

BELIEF: Differentiating the various kinds of evidence that can support one's beliefs; distinguishing among credibility, proof, certainty, consensus, and authority.

READY-MADES: Using prepackaged ideas, either as a help to thinking, or as a substitute for thinking. Understanding stereotypes, cliches, prejudices, standard opinions, etc.

EMOTIONS AND EGO: Knowing the ways in which emotions can enter into thinking; recognizing ego emotions such as having to be right, face saving, and power playing.

VALUES: Knowing the ways in which values can enter into thinking and influence the acceptability of an outcome. Accepting the values involved in a situation rather than trying to impose new ones.

SIMPLIFICATION AND CLARIFICATION: Knowing how to simplify a situation; being able to capture the essence of a situation in a succinct way.

CoRT VI: Action

This section constitutes an action plan or framework that can be used to draw all the previous lessons together into a set of steps for effective thinking. The framework is explained to students both verbally and through use of diagrams. It consists of the steps described in the following:

TARGET: Directing attention to the specific matter that is to be the subject of thinking; being able to pick out the thinking target in as definite and focused a manner as possible.

EXPAND: Expanding on the thinking target in depth, in breadth, and in seeking alternatives.

CONTRACT: Narrowing the expanded thinking to something more tangible and usable: the main points, a summary, a conclusion, or a choice.

TARGET-EXPAND-CONTRACT: Using the three preceding tools in a coordinated fashion.

PURPOSE: Being clear about one's exact purposes in thinking about a situation; knowing whether one is trying to arrive at a set of decisions, a solution to a problem, an action plan, or an opinion; knowing one's general purposes and one's specific objectives.

INPUT: Knowing the various factors that need to be considered in thinking about a situation—the scene, the setting, the information available, and the people involved.

SOLUTIONS: Identifying alternative solutions, including the most obvious ones, traditional ones, and new ones; knowing methods for generating solutions and filling in gaps.

CHOICE: Choosing among generated alternatives, taking into consideration priorities and constraints; reviewing decisions in terms of their consequences.

OPERATION: Implementing one's decisions; identifying steps to put the chosen course of action into effect.

THE FIVE STAGES (TEC–PISCO): Using the thinking steps listed previously in a coordinated way. Treating the last five steps—purpose, input, solutions, choice, and operations—as the five major stages involved in thinking about any situation. Treating the first three steps—target, expand, and contract—as activities that can help one define and elaborate the objects of thought within each stage.

CONDUCT OF A CoRT THINKING LESSON

In this section, I provide an overview of how individual CoRT lessons are conducted. The detailed conduct of each lesson varies from one section to another. There is a teachers' handbook for each of the six sections that gives background information for the section as a whole and pedagogical notes for each lesson. There is also a pupil leaflet for each lesson that briefly explains the lesson and contains practice items.

Focus.   It is very important that the teacher remains clearly focused on the theme of the lesson being given. This may need re-emphasizing from time to time. One of the worst teaching faults is the general waffle in which the purpose of the lesson is lost, and each lesson seems the same to the pupils.

Explanation.   The lesson starts with the teacher explaining very simply and briefly its theme or purpose. This is often done through use of an example taken from the lesson notes. The explanation for the lesson theme arises directly from the example and can be further emphasized with additional examples. The explanation should not be philosophical in any way. The main thing to avoid is confusion. Thus, philosophical grey areas are acknowledged and then ignored, in the interest of practicality. The main purpose of the lesson is to offer students practice in using thinking skills, not to have them engage in philosophical analysis. Thus, the explanations for the lessons should be brief—just long enough for the pupils to know what they are about.

Illustration.   The purpose of the lesson is made clear by illustration rather than explanation. Example after example can be given by way of illustration. This involves the process of "teaching from the center" as distinct from "teaching from the periphery." This means that instead of spending time trying to distinguish one peripheral case from another, the examples used are clearly in the center.

Practice.   This is the most important aspect of the lesson. As mentioned previously, only a short time is allowed for each practice item (2 to 4 minutes). The practice items are given in the lesson notes but may be supplemented by the teacher. The teacher should not be too eager to devise other practice items because there are many aspects of these items that have been carefully worked out. The occasional substitution of a new item for an obviously inappropriate one, or the insertion of an item of local interest, are to be encouraged—but not wholesale alteration according to the whim of the teacher.

Groups.   The pupils work on the practice items in small groups. In many schools, the CoRT thinking lessons are the only occasion for group work of this sort. Depending on the size of the class, there should be four to five pupils per group. The overall number of groups in the class should not be greater than six; otherwise, feedback takes too long. Groups may be of mixed ability.

Feedback.   At the end of the allotted time, the teacher asks for feedback from the group. This may be provided by a group spokesperson or by members speaking as individuals. There are various techniques for feedback: Each group gives one idea, one group gives its output, and the others add new points, and so on. At times, the teacher may want to list the ideas on a board. The feedback aspect is very important and very difficult. It can take up too much of the lesson time, yet the youngsters want to have their ideas listened to. The teacher needs to develop a repertoire of responses to give value to each contribution without suggesting that there is one right answer. Some teachers find this open-ended style of teaching easy. Others are uncomfortable without the authority of a book of right answers. The teacher can comment upon, build up, relate, and link together the ideas offered, but only as a fellow thinker, not with the implication that his or her thinking is better just because of teacher status. A good teacher will introduce a lot of variety into the feedback section. Above all, it must be brisk.

Discussion. At some stage in the lesson, the teacher discusses with the pupils the tool or theme of the lesson, its advantages and disadvantages, and its place in thinking. The purpose of this discussion is simply to give even more attention to the process being taught. This should be a relatively minor part of the lesson, for the practice sessions have more teaching value. Understanding how to play tennis is not the same as playing it. Philosophical discussion of a thinking process can lead to confusion rather than fluency in its use.

Projects. Pupils may be given individual writing assignments that require use of one or more of the tools taught in the CoRT lessons. This is not essential to the success of the program, but it has been found on occasion to be a useful technique (Buhagiar, 1980; Copley, 1980).

Variations. Imaginative teachers have introduced many variations into the conduct of the lessons. These include having younger children illustrate their thinking through drawings. Dramatization and role playing seem obvious choices in certain lessons; for example, they can be useful in helping children understand other points of view. This is to be recommended, so long as these methods remain adjuncts to the main purpose of the lesson and do not become ends in themselves.

Review. Teachers should stick closely to the purpose of a particular lesson. It is not possible to teach too much at once without confusion. Occasionally, the processes from a previous lesson may be allowed in, or referred to, but no lesson should become a general stew of CoRT processes. The teacher must remain single minded concerning the lesson under his or her nose. From time to time, special review lessons can attempt to put together and integrate the various CoRT processes.

FIELD TESTING THE CoRT PROGRAM

Over the last few years, there has been a great increase in knowledge regarding the detailed neurochemistry of the brain. This subject is an interest of the medical department at Cambridge University, with which I am associated. It is just conceivable that sheer practice in thinking may have a chemical effect on the brain, altering the subtle balance of neuroenzymes and memory proteins. At the moment, this is speculation and so we must concern ourselves with the more usual effects of training. Following, we discuss what we have learned from several years of field testing the CoRT Program. We discuss methodological issues involved in evaluating the program, what happens to students as a result of participation in the program, and what we have learned about the practical conditions under which the program works most effectively.

Methodological Issues

The data we have collected to assess the effects of the CoRT Program are basically of two kinds: systematic observations of student performance on tasks similar to those used during instruction, and informal teacher anecdotes about student performance both during instruction and in subsequent learning situations. In evaluating the effects of instruction in a new curriculum area like thinking skills, it is important to take into consideration both data collected under carefully controlled conditions and more informal observations. The informal observations are helpful in two ways. First, because we have not had a great deal of experience offering direct instruction in thinking skills, some of the outcomes of instruction may be ones that were not expected in advance. Informal observations can be helpful in identifying these unexpected outcomes. Secondly, there are many aspects of proficiency in thinking that we cannot now measure in a precise way. Informal observations can be helpful in calling our attention to these kinds of outcomes.

In selecting instruments for use in making formal observations, the temptation is to use standardized tests of intelligence and verbal reasoning because these are available and, in a lay sense, have to do with thinking. The problem in using such instruments is that they are not sensitive to the range of thinking skills in which the CoRT Program offers instruction. We would not predict that performance on these tests would be affected by CoRT training—although it might be. For example, on one occasion, in a carefully controlled trial with 300 pupils (Cognitive Research Trust, 1976a), a large shift was reported in performance on a test measuring intelligence (the Alice Heim number 4). In general, however, the CoRT lessons train the thinking required in real-life situations; therefore, the most appropriate tests are performance tests.

In a performance test, pupils are asked to apply their thinking to a typical real-life situation, similar to the ones that are used as practice examples in the CoRT Program. When this is done on an individual basis, the output is either written or tape recorded. When it is done on a group basis, the output is recorded. This output constitutes an individual's performance and is then analyzed.

In working with CoRT performance data, Dr. David Tripp (1979) has developed an elaborate system of matrix analysis that tabulates and classifies the different points an individual makes in responding to each item. This system has the advantage of analyzing the content of each response. However, it has the disadvantage of yielding a total score that can easily become biased in that misinterpretation of any one of the respondent's points can have a disproportionate influence on the overall score assigned to that response. Given current difficulties inherent in conducting complex analyses of verbal discourse, I prefer a simple scoring system.

Because the CoRT lessons set out to broaden and clarify the perceptual map, students who have participated in the program should show a larger and more detailed map. In other words, a simple point count can indicate the exposure of the terrain around the thinking situation. This simple point count can, with experience, be subdivided into broad categories such as concern for consequences, realization of other points of view, balance of argument, consideration of alternatives, and sense of objective. In theory, there are still problems with the method because a trivial point may seem to count as much as a major point (as happens in tests of creativity), but in practice this has not become a serious problem.

Student Outcomes

We have a considerable amount of unpublished data confirming that CoRT-trained pupils show wider consideration of thinking situations than do control groups. For example, when 13-year-old girls were asked to consider the suggestion that everyone should do a year's work on leaving school, the CoRT-trained group came up with the following number of points in contrast to the control group: (1) egocentric points, CoRT 224, Control 174; (2) points in favor, CoRT 149, Control 90; (3) points against, CoRT 188, Control 98; (4) points relating to society, CoRT 41, Control 16; (5) exploratory points, CoRT 250, Control 82; (6) administrative points, CoRT 209, Control 46; (7) points relating to others, CoRT 91, Control 28 (Cognitive Research Trust, Unpublished).

As might be expected, the difference increases as one moves away from egocentric points, which even untrained students tend to consider, toward more practical points. With younger children, the differences are even more striking (Shallcrass, 1977; Tripp, 1979). We have a considerable amount of data of this sort, including a large backlog of material, some of which has not yet been analyzed, and some of which has only been analyzed in a preliminary way. In addition to data suggesting that participation in the CoRT Program helps to broaden the pupil's perceptual map, we have received a preliminary report from S. Tyler (1980) based on her work in a United States Department of Defense Elementary School, suggesting that participation in the program may result in improvements in performance on tests of academic achievement in several different school subject-matter areas.

Over the years, we have also accumulated a large number of anecdotal reports from teachers (Cognitive Research Trust, unpublished). Single anecdotal instances of improvement are not important, but the cumulative data, from a variety of sources and countries, adds up to a clear picture of the observed effects of CoRT training. We can summarize this anecdotal evidence under the following points:

1. With even a small amount of instruction, pupils begin considering themselves as thinkers and begin considering thinking as a familiar skill. This leads to more confidence, more rapid responses, a greater breadth of view, a greaer willingness to consider alternatives and other points of view, and more respect

for the thinking of others. That is, many pupils achieve what we have described as level-one CoRT thinking; they become more at ease with the idea of thinking and become capable of concentrating on specific thinking tasks for longer periods of time. Still others achieve what we have described as level-two CoRT thinking; they adopt many of the thinking tools taught in the CoRT Program even though they are not always aware that they are using these tools, and even though they do not always apply them systematically to all the situations for which they might be appropriate.

2. With more intensive instruction, pupils make more extensive and sophisticated use of the CoRT tools. Some pupils achieve what we have described as level-three CoRT Thinking. They spontaneously refer to the CoRT processes by name and use them deliberately and systematically in coping with a wide range of thinking situations. Still others achieve what we have described as level-four CoRT thinking. They begin to use CoRT processes automatically, rather than self-consciously, and use them in a structured and coordinated fashion so that these tools become, for the student, a system of interrelated thinking processes, rather than a set of independent skills. Our experience in field testing the CoRT Program to date suggests that attainment of levels three and four are unusual. Pupils attain these levels only with intensive instruction, over a long period of time.

3. Instruction in CoRT processes often results in transfer to other school subject-matter areas. Most typically, improvements have been reported in English language proficiency and essay-writing skills. Improvements have also been reported in performance in social studies, geography, and history.

4. Pupils who have received instruction in CoRT processes are often described as more motivated and more disciplined in their attempt to cope with school work.

5. Instruction in CoRT processes often results in increased use of these processes and improved thinking at home and in other nonschool situations.

The various effects just described are produced by the total impact of the CoRT approach, including instruction in CoRT thinking processes, exposure to the CoRT teaching style, use of CoRT practice items, and work in small group settings. CoRT provides the concrete framework within which youngsters can focus their attention directly upon thinking as a skill. That is the ultimate purpose and value of the program.

Considerations in Implementing the Program

Over the 8 years during which CoRT has been in use, many things have been learned about the conditions under which the program works most effectively and about practical problems requiring special attention. These are now summarized.

Conditions under Which the CoRT Lessons can be Effectively Used. The CoRT lessons have been successfully used with a wide range of different student populations including high-ability, low-ability, and mixed-ability groups (de Bono, 1976; Tripp), children having behavior problems (Shallcrass, 1977), children who are underachievers (Copley) and children who are learning English as a second language (Shallcrass 1977). As discussed earlier, the lessons have been used across a huge age range that includes 4½-year olds at one extreme and adults at the other. To avoid confusion, only one CoRT lesson should be presented to the students each week. This lesson may be taught in a single class period, a double class period, or two separate periods. Concerning the amount of time required for instruction, 35 minutes per week is a minimum, 45 minutes to an hour is ideal, and 1½ hours is leisurely. Finding special time for instruction is a practical problem and is often solved by including the program under a variety of different curriculum areas like social studies, humanities, general studies, and English language.

The lessons are highly sensitive to teacher expectations and prejudices. It is possible to tell from a teacher's initial attitude how the lessons will go. As noted earlier, the style and idiom of the lessons are rather different from those obtaining in other subject areas. Some teachers are uncomfortable without the authority of a right answer style, or when process rather than product is demanded. The status of the lessons in the eyes of the pupils is also very important. When the teacher is seen to be dabbling, or when the thinking lessons are the only nonexaminable subject in a curriculum full of examination status subjects, pupils may come to resent the lessons. Conversely, an enthusiastic teacher with an open-ended teaching style can be very successful without any need for philosophical subtlety.

Problems. Problems encountered in teaching the CoRT Program have been mentioned at different points in this chapter. Getting used to the CoRT idiom and the emphasis on process rather than content, keeping the focus of the lessons very clear, sticking to the short time for each practice item, changing teachers' expectations, finding time for instruction, devising adequate measuring instruments, and avoiding philosophical digressions and alterations that ignore the coherence of the program are the principle difficulties that may be faced in using the CoRT Program.

CONCLUSIONS

I was once teaching a demonstration class of 10-year-old children in Sydney, Australia. I asked them whether they would like to be given $5 a week for attending school. All 30 of them liked the idea and gave their reasons for doing so (buy sweets, chewing gum, comics, etc.). I then introduced the idea of the

PMI and asked them to apply this to the suggestion, working in groups of five. After 4 minutes, I asked for their output. They raised the following kinds of issues: Parents would stop pocket money, schools would increase charges, bigger boys would beat up smaller ones—and where would the money come from? Twenty-nine out of the 30 had now completely reversed their opinion. This was without any suggestion from me as to which considerations they should bring to mind. This example illustrates the purpose of CoRT thinking: the use of a simple perceptual framework to bring about a conclusion through exploring the experience in a more thorough manner.

The justification for a program designed to teach thinking skills is well illustrated in the following excerpt from an interview between Mrs. Copley, Deputy Director of the Cognitive Research Trust, and Susan Young, a teacher at an American elementary school:

Mrs. Copley: Do you believe thinking should have a place in the curriculum like any other subject?

S. Young: I think a certain amount of time should be spent on thinking. I think it is the kind of thing such as spelling, reading, or whatever, that carries over into many content areas. It is not something that you only do for twenty minutes on Thursdays and that's it. So often it can help people in their personal lives, and this in turn helps them with their entire school.

Mrs. Copley: If I were the principal, how would you persuade me to give up a period of, say math, to thinking?

S. Young: I feel that math is based on an organized structure, and in the same way, if your thinking is not organized, too much of your time is wasted and nonproductive in doing any subject. People who teach math especially should see the futility of trying to teach someone formulas and theorems, and things like this and rules, when the children's thinking is so unstructured that they cannot attend to tasks and find priorities, plan their time and be responsible for their materials. So basically, I think we need that before we teach anything else.

In Venezuela, there is a suggestion that in the outlying areas the teaching of thinking skills should be given equal priority with the teaching of reading and writing, because thinking, and confidence in one's thinking, is so basic to progress.

The ultimate purpose of the CoRT Program is to get children and adults to regard thinking as a skill and to regard themselves as thinkers able to use that skill, at will, and in any direction. This rescues them from reflex response, prejudice, cliche, stereotypes, slogans, and all the other substitutes for thinking. How well the thinking is carried out is actually of less importance than the willingness to use thinking as a deliberate skill.

Traditionally in education, we have put all the emphasis on cleverness—the acquisition of knowledge and complex concepts, the passing of examinations, the achievement of a high IQ rating. Cleverness is a sharp focus lens that is very useful for closed fields and detailed work. But for open fields we need a wide-angle lens. The wide-angle lens is wisdom as distinct from cleverness. Wisdom is a breadth of perception, a comprehensive perceptual map. This is precisely what the CoRT program sets out to teach.

How would one define thinking? Most definitions end up by being circular through including such words as reason, logic, and effectiveness. We do not need to include such value-laden words. I would define thinking as, "The operating skill with which intelligence acts upon experience for a purpose." The purpose may also be pleasure.

Perhaps the most important aspect of the deliberate teaching of thinking is the realization that there may be many effective thinkers who are wasted by the current education system, because thinking ability is not disclosed by the usual academic idiom. Our experience certainly suggests this. Given an opportunity, children who are considered backward academically may emerge as effective thinkers. Conversely, children who are intelligent and who do well academically may not be very effective thinkers. So there are strong grounds for giving the first group an opportunity to show their thinking talent and giving the second group some direct training in thinking skills. Otherwise, we waste the resources of society. It is ironic that Venezuela, which is so well endowed with natural resources, should be the first country to make a formal effort to develop its human resources through the training of thinking skills.

ACKNOWLEDGMENTS

I would like to acknowledge the many people whose work and cooperation have developed and sustained the CoRT Program over the many years of its practical operation. Clare Connel, Brian Oliver, and Audrey Davies were of great help in the development stage. David Tripp carried the main burden of teacher liaison and research in the middle period. Today, my Deputy Director, Edna Copley, is invaluable in sustaining the practical operation of the program and its various projects including teacher training. William Copley was responsible for the continued training of the teachers throughout the pilot stage of the Venezuela project, and the success of that project is largely due to him. Previously he had done a great deal of work in special areas, some of which were noted earlier in this chapter. The seed money for the project came from the Leverhulme Foundation.

REFERENCES

Buhagiar, C. *Malta Report*. Unpublished manuscript, 1980.
Cognitive Research Trust and Inner London Education Authority. *Teaching of thinking in primary schools*. Unpublished report, 1975.

Cognitive Research Trust. *Examination of the CoRT Program for teaching thinking.* Unpublished report, 1976. (a)

Cognitive Research Trust. *Study at Atlantic College.* Unpublished manuscript, 1976. (b)

Cognitive Research Trust. *Development of measuring techniques.* Unpublished manuscript.

Copley, E. *Practical aspects of CoRT teaching.* Publication in preparation, 1982.

Copley, W. *Venezuela Report.* Unpublished manuscript, 1980.

Copley, W., & Copley, E. *Internal Report.* Cognitive Research Trust, 1978.

de Bono, E. *The mechanism of mind.* New York: Simon & Schuster, 1969.

de Bono, E. *Lateral thinking.* New York: Harper & Row, 1970.

de Bono, E. *Teaching thinking.* London: Temple Smith, 1976.

Gallup, G. Projective thinking. In *Serious Fun.* Copenhagen: Lego, 1980.

Gleeson, M. *New York Report.* Unpublished manuscript, 1980.

Lane, D. Cognitive strategies. In D. Tripp (Ed.), *Teachers teaching thinking.* Cambridge: Cognitive Research Trust, 1977.

Lee, M., & Madurajan, A. *A computer simulation of the de Bono memory surface model.* Manuscript submitted for publication, 1982.

Maier, N. *McMaster University Study.* Unpublished manuscript, 1980.

McGill University. *Centennial College Study.* Unpublished manuscript, 1978.

Shallcrass, J. The use of CoRT in elementary schools. In D. Tripp (Ed.), *Teachers teaching thinking.* Cambridge: Cognitive Research Trust, 1977.

Tripp, D. *Internal Report.* Cognitive Research Trust, 1978.

Tripp, D. *Changes in children's corporate thinking.* Paper presented at the symposium on Language, Communication, and Thinking at the 49th Congress of the Australian and New Zealand Association for the Advancement of Science, Auckland, 1979.

Tripp, D. *The CoRT thinking project in special education.* Paper presented at the meeting of the West Australian Association of Special Education, Perth, 1979.

Tyler, S. *Preliminary Report.* Unpublished manuscript, 1980.

11

Strategic Thinking and the Fear of Failure

Martin V. Covington
University of California, Berkeley

The purpose of this chapter is to explore the various causes of student anxiety, indifference to learning and motivational deficits that characterize much school life today, and to consider how schools can combat these self-defeating achievement patterns. This involves an exploration of a variety of cognitive and affective factors that influence school achievement and of how cognitive skills instruction can be combined with attempts to create an appropriate affective climate for classroom learning. Much of our present knowledge about the nature of learning and thinking comes from laboratory evidence; yet, in actuality, most classroom learning occurs in a context far removed from the laboratory and involves personal stress, anxiety, and the threat of academic failure. For this reason, we attempt to build a bridge between the kinds of cognitive variables that are typically studied in laboratory research and the kinds of affective variables that enter into actual school learning. Thus, the overall intent of the chapter is integrative in nature, embracing such topics as social cognition and attribution, achievement motivation, fear-of-failure dynamics, and current views of information processing and problem solving as they apply to actual classroom learning.

The chapter is divided into three main sections. The first is an account of the largely negative motivational basis for learning in the institutional context of schools. In this section, we examine how classroom reward structures influence many students to be motivated more by a desire to avoid failure than by a desire to pursue success. This limits the amount of constructive effort such students are willing to invest in academic activities, thereby producing the very failures they are seeking to avoid. In the second section, we suggest two different approaches to creating a more positive motivational basis for academic achievement. One is to modify classroom reward systems so that more students have the opportunity to achieve success. The other is to help students develop more effective thinking skills so that they can take advantage of these newly created opportunities for classroom achievement. In the third section, we discuss more fully the approach of helping students develop effective thinking skills. This approach centers around the concept of strategic thinking, which is defined as the capacity to identify and analyze problems and to create and monitor plans for their solution. In this section, we consider the component skills thought to be involved in strategic thinking, discuss recent research indicating that many students lack these skills, and consider efforts to train students in strategic thinking.

FEAR OF FAILURE

The Threat to Self-Worth

We begin with an acknowledgment of an achievement crisis in the classroom. This need not detain us long. Ample and depressing documentation is available from a number of sources (e.g., Silberman, 1970). Suffice it to say that the dimensions of this problem are captured by several chilling statistics: that, for example, 15% of our ghetto students never complete the eigth grade; and that among those students who do graduate from high school the mean reading proficiency is below the ninth-grade level.

The recently proposed *self-worth* theory of achievement motivation (Beery, 1975; Covington, 1983; Covington & Beery, 1976; Covington & Omelich, 1984) asserts that the negativism, apathy, and lack of motivation implied by such statistics are largely reactions to a threat to the student's sense of worth. Basically, individuals believe that their personal value depends on their ability to achieve, and that if they cannot succeed they will be unworthy of the approval of others. Given the tendency in our society to tie one's worth to personal accomplishment (Gardner, 1961), it is understandable that the ability to achieve competitively becomes so important to students, and explains why so many of them come to view competitive achievement as a test of their personal value. Naturally, however, anchoring one's sense of worth in ability is a risky step. Such a belief is too easily threatened by failure, and schools intensify the individual's predicament. This occurs because many classrooms are failure oriented; that is, they provide insufficient rewards for students of *all* ability levels to experience success. Far too many students must struggle simply to avoid failure, with its negative implications for ability. Insufficiency of rewards occurs largely because of the competitive nature of classrooms.

An analysis by Alschuler (1973) suggests that in a majority of American classrooms students are forced repeatedly to compete with one another for a fixed number of rewards (grades and other forms of adult approval) that are distributed unevenly. Typically, this process is set in motion and abetted by grading "on the curve," a practice in which a few students succeed at the expense of the many. In such an atmosphere, we find that grades become valued not because of any intrinsic merit associated with a task well done, but rather because of their scarcity. In this way, successes in school appear to follow the dictates of commodity theory (Brock, 1968), which assumes that all other things being equal, the less frequent an event, the more valued and sought after it becomes. Translated into the school achievement context, the value of a grade resides in its potential as evidence of high ability. For example, Johnny's reputation as a brilliant student would be enhanced if he were the only child singled out for special praise. If the performances of a number of his classmates were also acknowledged as outstanding, then the task would likely be perceived as a relatively easy one, certainly not requiring extraordinary ability.

The available evidence regarding competitiveness is not particularly comforting. In the main, it suggests that children become more competitive as they grow older and that success can easily corrupt, especially if it is attained at the expense of others. The research of Nelson and Kagan (1972) is particularly illuminating on this point. They found that children freely cooperated in solving problems as long as all children received a reward for their efforts. However, once fewer rewards than participants were available, a conflict of interest arose, and children became antagonistic and competitive toward one another. Here, illustrated in the laboratory microcosm, are all the elements of a vicious cycle: Insufficient rewards breed competition, and in turn, such competitive pressure further increases the scarcity of rewards, and with scarcity comes a sense of exaggerated importance of these rewards. As a consequence of such exaggeration, success and failure become psychologically remote from one another and there remains no middle ground for the subtle qualifications of the kind suggested by John Holt (1964), when he urged a semantic distinction be established between success and nonsuccess rather than between success and failure.

Eventually a restricted supply of rewards pushes student aspirations for grades (and other forms of recognition) beyond the capabilities of many children, with the result that they are unable to keep pace with these inappropriate goals. Such circumstances tend to force a fateful decision for countless youngsters. The child may reason, unwittingly and without recognition of the consequences, that if he cannot be sure of succeeding, then at least he can try to protect a sense of dignity by avoiding failure. Thus there emerges a widespread and ultimately self-defeating pattern of achievement motivation: the avoidance of failure, akin to the basic socially conditioned drive described originally by Atkinson (1964), by Atkinson & Raynor (1977), and by McClelland (1965), and more recently articulated by Covington and Omelich (1979a, 1979b).

Failure-Avoiding Tactics

Failure-avoiding students tend to harbor doubts about their ability; yet, because ability is linked to their sense of worth, they have little choice but to manuever to avoid failure. A number of failure-avoiding and success-insuring tactics have been documented by Birney, Burdick, and Teevan (1969), and by others (e.g., Berglas & Jones, 1978; Sigall & Gould, 1977), ranging from academic cheating to setting goals that are so easily attained that virtually no risk is involved. Naturally, such tactics do little, if anything, to enhance a sense of positive self-regard; indeed, they are likely to hamper the development of self-esteem. Cheaters come to fear their ill-gotten successes because they know they cannot repeat them (Shelton & Hill, 1969), and successes gained without some risk of failure become cheapened and lose their intrinsic value. But, what of those situations where failure is inevitable? Here at least, the student can attempt to avoid the implications of failure. For examle, students may strive for unattainable goals that literally invite failure, but "failure with honor." Because so few students are expected to succeed against such long odds, failure does not necessarily imply low ability. Naturally, such self-serving tactics actually set up the very failures these students seek to avoid and, as a consequence, they are neither protected for long, nor can they perform up to their actual levels of ability. By adopting such failure-avoiding techniques, students progressively cut themselves off from an already scarce supply of classroom rewards, thereby exacerbating an already difficult situation. An example of this process is found in the work of Pauline Sears (1940), who found that many failing students set their achievement aspirations without realistic regard for their current performance levels, often wildly overestimating how well they would do; this behavior, in Sears' view, reflected an unfulfilled desire for teacher approval in which the mere statement of a worthy goal, whether or not it was attained, became a source of satisfaction.

Student effort is the linchpin of this self-serving drama to preserve a sense of competency and worth. Not only does effort represent a potential threat to the individual because a combination of high effort accompanied by failure is compelling evidence of low ability (Covington & Omelich, 1979b; Kun, 1977; Kun & Weiner, 1973), but also, conversely, not trying is likely to be an effective strategy for minimizing information about one's abilities in the event of failure. Here, not trying can be viewed in attributional terms as a special example of Kelley's (1973) "discounting principle." A given cause of failure (in this case, low ability) is discounted and left vague and uncertain if other more plausible reasons (low effort) are available. Thus, by this analysis, students have available a variety of defensive options. For example, they can invest little study effort; they can also feign indifference to learning, as in the case of the "closet" achiever who studies secretly and therefore can appear brilliant without really trying; or they can work hard but be forearmed with plausible explanations for why their effort did not pay off.

The survival value of low effort and excuses is illustrated in a study by Covington and Omelich (1979b). College students introspected about their affective reactions to each of a combination of four hypothetical test failures: little effort without excuse; little effort with excuse; high effort without excuse, and high effort with excuse. The high-effort excuse was that the instructor emphasized material on the test different from that studied by the student; little effort in failure was justified by reason of illness. Students experienced the greatest loss of esteem under conditions of high effort with failure and least shame under conditions of low effort with failure. Moreover, shame was sharply reduced when an excuse was present to explain why high effort did not help.

The role of excuses in this coping process has been highlighted in yet another way (Covington & Omelich, 1978). It was found that individuals egotistically overestimated their own ability compared to that of others only when plausible excuses were available for why their effort did not work. When these same individuals were known to have studied hard in the absence of extenuating circumstances, egotism tendencies were markedly reduced. Indeed, confidence in one's ability to achieve deteriorates rapidly whenever excuses lose their credibility. In a related study, Covington and Omelich (1981a) studied this process in the naturally occurring context of repeated test taking in the college classroom. As study time (effort) accumulated over repeated but futile attempts to succeed, self-ascriptions to low ability dramatically increased. This occurred because inability alone now became the unavoidable explanation for failure, as low effort was no longer a plausible cause.

A Conflict of Values

Students are not entirely free to pursue self-aggrandizing strategies of the kinds documented in the preceding section because effort is highly valued in the school context. The central importance of a teacher work ethic has been demonstrated in a series of studies by Weiner and his colleagues (Rest, Nierenberg, Weiner, Heckhausen, 1973; Weiner 1972; Weiner & Kukla, 1970). In the typical procedure, teachers (or college students role playing teachers) dispensed rewards and punishments to hypothetical students who were characterized by varying levels of effort, ability, and test outcome. Students who were perceived as having expended effort were rewarded more in success and punished less in failure than those who did not try. Moreover, these evaluative reactions appeared largely independent of student ability level. Further evidence on this point comes from the Covington and Omelich study cited previously (1979b) concerning affective reactions to failure given different effort levels. In addition to estimating their own reactions to failure, our college subjects also adopted the role of teachers and punished hypothetical students under the same four achievement conditions. It was found that the classroom failure that elicited the least student shame, and that was most preferred by students (low effort/failure), led to the greatest teacher punishment; and conversely, that the most shameful failure (high effort/failure) was least punished by teachers.

Thus, overall, the evidence regarding ability and effort valuation suggests the existence of a teacher–student conflict of values: Teachers encourage achievement through effort, yet many students attempt to avoid the implication that they lack ability by not trying. Moreover, the excuse dimension provides further insights into the kinds of accommodations available to students in avoiding teacher punishment. Teachers make considerable allowances for low effort if the student has a plausible explanation for why he or she did not study. Perversely, this data pattern suggests a "winning" strategy for students when risking failure: Try, or at least appear to try, but not too energetically, and with excuses always handy!

It is important to note that students pay a considerable price for such subterfuge in the form of an intense intrapsychic conflict, as illustrated in a study by Covington, Spratt, and Omelich (1980). Whereas low effort in failure led predictably to reduced inability ascriptions and to less frustration and anxiety at having failed, insufficient study also triggered traitlike, self-referent labels such as lazy and procrastinating, judgments which have a highly negative social value. The tendency of students not only to set up their own failures but to do so in socially demeaning ways suggests that they are driven to avoid the low ability implications of failure at almost any price.

This student–teacher conflict intensifies as students grow older. Developmental data (Harari & Covington, 1981; Covington, in press) suggest that although all students—from first grade through college—value ability highly, youngsters in the earliest grades also value effort and are therefore compatible in their views with the dominant teacher effort–value schema. Interestingly, such early-grade effort valuation occurred largely because these youngsters equated effort expenditure with high ability. They reasoned—not without some logic—that study actually increases ability; and moreover, that effort is preemptive evidence of ability (First grader: "Smart people study, dumb ones don't"). In time, however, starting around the end of the elementary years, students began to perceive effort and ability as independent dimensions. Ability emerged as a stable, immutable entity that was seen as a necessary, even sufficient, condition for success (Eleventh grader: "When people who are not smart study, they usually do badly"; College level: "Well, if someone is not too smart, they can only do so well"). Also, by the high school years, the reciprocal relationship between effort and ability attributions documented earlier was firmly in place for most students. High effort in failure led to a clear suspicion of low ability. Not surprisingly, the self-serving advantages of low effort also became clearly apparent. Low effort in success enhanced a reputation for brilliance while obscuring the causes of failure, should it occur (Eleventh grader: "If he does not try, you don't know how smart he is").

Summing Up

This misalignment of teacher–student values in the event of failure illustrates the inherent difficulties to be overcome in improving current educational practice. Such a conflict is another aspect of the largely incompatible role of schools as places for students to learn and, simultaneously, as places for students to be sorted out according to their ability to learn. The fact that teachers function as mentors and as screening agents is reflected both in their tendency to reward student effort whenever learning is the objective, and to value student ability when selection for occupational success is the criterion (Kaplan & Swant, 1973). As formidable and intransient as this conflict may be from the point of view of educational reform, at least it provides us with a clearer understanding of the true causes of failure avoidance and of student indifference to learning. First, let us note what is *not* the cause. The cause is not a lack of motivation on the part of the student, although disapproving of low effort as they do, teachers are likely to pronounce the student lazy and unmotivated. Indeed, calling the student "unmotivated" does not explain the problem, but only identifies one result of it. If academic failure becomes a chronic way of life for a student, he or she will naturally come to regard himself or herself as a poor student, perhaps even worthless. But these attitudes and feelings are not the root cause of the problem, although they will eventually become *part* of the problem. Rather, these self-protective behaviors are the outcome of whatever conditions led to the student's lack of success originally. Thus it is argued that negative self-attitudes and feelings of failure are largely due to improper learning conditions and to the relative absence of self-management skills necessary for independent achievement.

ELEMENTS OF A SOLUTION

We now turn to the various elements of a solution for dealing with these self-defeating achievement patterns. Basically it is suggested that any successful countervailing strategies must contain at least two elements: (1) a provision for sufficient classroom rewards so that individuals are no longer forced to avoid failure, but can also pursue the rewards of success; and (2) a fostering of the skills and attitudes that allow for personal acceptance of these newly abundant rewards as caused by the student's own efforts. Achievement of these objectives depends on changing the typical classroom reward structure from competitive to individual striving, and simultaneously, on strengthening the capacity among students to identify and analyze school-achievement tasks, to set realistic goals, and to develop and monitor their own strategic plans of action toward a solution.

We first review briefly the evidence on modifying classroom reward systems and then devote the remainder of this chapter to a consideration of strategic thinking. But before proceeding, we need to broaden our focus of concern beyond the original reference group of decidedly failure-oriented students, and prepare to argue for the advantages of skill training in self-management for all students at all ability levels, irrespective of their particular achievement orientation. Such inclusiveness is defensible because the struggle for self-esteem appears so universal. As stated elsewhere (Covington & Beery, 1976): "Neither this [self-serving] process nor its end result is uniform for all. Different kinds and combinations of defensive strategies can lead to an almost endless variety of maladaption. Moreover, there are different degrees of impairment. Some individuals become thoroughly convinced of their incapacity, whereas others are left uncertain due to the fact that failure in one academic area is offset by success in another [p. 61]." Moreover, even the most capable students are not immune to these self-defeating dynamics. By holding themselves to unrealistically high self-expectations, brilliant students often experience the humiliation of failure, whereas, in reality, their academic record is outstanding (Martire, 1956). Furthermore, it is only the brighter student who has the capabilities for making one of the most dangerous failure-avoiding gambles of all: attempting to avoid failure by insuring success through inordinate preparation (Covington & Beery, 1976). However, no one can avoid failure indefinitely, for with each new success comes the need to accomplish more in order to experience continued feelings of worthiness (Diggory, 1966). And, when failure finally occurs, these superstrivers are in the most threatening position of all, having tried hard and failed anyway.

Restructuring Classroom Reward Systems

The vital role of rewards in the achievement process is reflected in the shared benefits that accumulate for teachers and students when success, not failure, is the outcome. In a companion study to their research on failure and effort level cited earlier, Covington and Omelich (1979c) asked college students to introspect about their affective reactions to test successes involving varying amounts of effort. Then, in the role of teachers, these subjects also administered rewards to hypothetical students under identical conditions of success. Not only was it found that these surrogate teachers rewarded most those successes achieved through high effort, but equally important was the fact that as students, they too most preferred success accompanied by high effort. This student preference occurred because success at a difficult task is preemptive evidence of ability, irrespective of amount of effort expenditure, and also because effort mediates pride (Brickman & Hendricks, 1975; Covington & Omelich, 1981b; Weaver & Brickman, 1974). In short, success accompanied by high effort allows students to share the best of two possible worlds—they can appear *virtuous* by reason of effort and *able* as well. But the key to the positive benefits of this form of success is the compatability of teacher–student values it achieves regarding effort.

Investigators have recently begun to explore classroom reward systems that allow sufficient opportunity for individual, student-defined successes so that each pupil can strive for success rather than simply attempt to avoid failure. These alternative reward systems feature individual student goal setting and absolute performance standards such that any number of students can achieve a given grade so long as their accomplishments reach or surpass preannounced criteria (for reviews of this literature, see Covington & Berry, 1976; Covington &

Omelich, 1982; Thomas, 1980). Combining absolute standards with individual student goal setting creates a powerful structure for fostering a positive achievement orientation. Basically, this procedure has the effect of redefining success in terms of exceeding one's own standards rather than surpassing the accomplishments of others. With an adequate supply of self-rewards thereby possible, students can, in principle, act in a more success-oriented manner, with a consequent reduction in defensive maneuvering. Available evidence suggests that such restructuring facilitates both individual and group achievement (Alschuler, 1973; Rubin, 1975) and promotes gains in student self-confidence (Woodson, 1975). Restructuring also acts to redefine the teacher's role as a facilitator of learning rather than a dispenser of external rewards and punishments (Coopersmith & Feldman, 1974). It is in this way that the potential conflict of teacher–student values may also be bridged.

Naturally, it is critical that these opportunities for defining one's own successes do not result in self-reinforcers of diminished value due to their increased frequency. Meaningless successes cannot long sustain a sense of positive self-regard nor increase achievement. Fortunately, as we have seen, the value of scarcity appears to be largely a phenomenon of peer-group competition. Once the focus shifts toward individual striving, the value of a success depends more on task difficulty and on the work required to achieve it, and less on its scarcity. Success can be devalued in this context only when one's goals are set so low that success is assured, and the available research suggests that this is unlikely to happen. When individuals are not competing directly with one another, they usually tend to set moderate learning goals slightly beyond their current performance level (Diggory, 1966).

The role of hard work in creating self-reinforcing accomplishments is illustrated in a series of studies by Covington and his colleagues (Covington & Jacoby, 1973; Covington & Polsky, 1974; Schnur, 1975). In one study, several hundred college students took part in an introductory psychology course that required completion of various projects calling for solutions to a number of issues and problems confronting the field of psychology (Covington & Jacoby, 1972). One group of students was given full credit for their projects as long as the work met minimal standards of quality that were well within the capabilities of most students. A second group was required to strive against standards of excellence commensurate with the grade they desired; that is, the standards were quite stringent for a grade of A, somewhat less demanding for a B, and so on. Hence, success at the higher grade levels required a combination of both high effort and ability, and, as a consequence, students desiring such success had to work much harder than those who were evaluated against a minimal standard. Even so, those students exposed to the more stringent standard were more satisfied with their performance, believed they measured up more favorably to the instructor's expectations, and felt more deserving of their grades. Thus, working hard to achieve one's goals at some risk of failure not only increased the quality of performance, but also increased satisfaction and a sense of accomplishment, self-judgments that were independent of the grading distribution.

Clearly, too, realistic goal setting also plays a vital part in this positive motivational process as illustrated by the research of Woodson (1975). This investigator created various degrees of mismatch between student ability level and the difficulty of various school achievement tasks. The amount learned by students and their willingness to continue learning depended largely on the degree to which ability matched task difficulty. Those students who enjoyed a close match learned the most, and this was true at all ability levels. In contrast, a mismatch disrupted learning, and at all ability levels. This occurred because the less able students who were saddled with high expectations became demoralized and gave up, whereas highly able students who competed against easy standards became bored. As a consequence, both groups became underachievers, but for different reasons.

Realistic goal setting also strengthens the proper attributional alignment regarding the causes of success and failure. When students work on a task within their reach, degree and quality of effort become the overriding factors in achieving success; and, conversely, in the event of failure to attain a goal, blame falls more naturally to insufficient or improper effort, because the task *was* manageable. These are precisely the attributional lessons that teachers attempt to impart through rewarding successful effort. In effect, realistic goal setting and proper task analysis reinforce the vital, causal linkage between personal effort and successful outcome. Moreover, absolute standards also tend to foster a positive interpretation of failure. After reviewing the accumulated research, Kennedy and Willcutt (1964) concluded that when a well-defined standard of performance is expected of students, failure to achieve that standard tends to motivate them to try harder.

Providing Instruction in Strategic Thinking

The benefits to the learner of individual goal setting are not automatically assured merely by altering classroom reward systems. Such restructuring demands considerable expertise in self-management skills to take proper advantage of the resulting freedom, yet it is precisely failure-prone students who do not exercise effective control over their learning. To them success is an unexpected event that they may be unable to accept, let alone plan for; they unwittingly misjudge their capabilities and pursue irrational goals for self-serving purposes, and are crippled in their problem-solving efforts by anxiety and self-doubt. How can such dispositions and attitudes be overturned? Among the few investigators who have directly addressed this question, perhaps the best advice comes from Mettee (1971). He suggests that eventually individuals might be persuaded to assume personal responsibility for their successes if they begin by first accepting only some of the credit—just enough to raise their confidence without arousing threat. Another somewhat different but not incompatible approach is suggested by the nature of the threat as we have outlined it. Existing evidence suggests that most failure-oriented individuals want to accept credit but dare not because they believe themselves incapable of reproducing future successes (Sigall & Gould, 1977). But if students can bring school achievement demands under their control through a combination of realistic goal setting, task analysis, and proper effort, then success *is* replicable. Under these circumstances, we can hope that students will not only accept credit for their accomplishments, but will also come to express optimism about the chances for future success as well.

The remainder of this chapter focuses on the managerial aspects of controlling one's learning. The concept that provides us with the most comprehensive yet manageable context within which to couch this discussion is the notion of meta-cognitive skills or, as I have previously referred to it, a capacity for *strategic thinking* (Covington, 1966; 1984). By strategic thinking, we mean that aspect of thinking concerned with the effective management of information and resources to achieve a desired goal. It is required for success in virtually all sustained problem-solving activities, both group and individual—everything from developing a national program for future energy production, to balancing the demands of homework against the requirements of an after-school paper route, to creating and carrying out a winning game plan in professional football. Such thinking involves being able to formulate a problem in workable terms, to establish priorities, and to develop and alter tactics as work proceeds. It also involves being able to recognize and deal with the strategic implications of new, unexpected events—unforseen obstacles or changes in the value of a tactic—because plans that are effective at one point in time can quickly become inappropriate or even counterproductive as circumstances change. Thus strategic thinking involves not only formulating and organizing, but also constantly re-evaluating and monitoring plans and possibilities for action.

In the present context of classroom achievement, strategic thinking involves the self-conscious planning, organizing, and management of one's personal resources, including *ability* (with a realistic recognition of one's strengths and limitations), *time,* and *energy level,* in an effective study effort in response both to course demands and to one's own grade goal aspirations. Evidence generated by Covington and his students (Covington & Jacoby, 1973) indicates that successful students perceive school basically as a problem-solving event in which they must analyze assignments, in terms of their own momentary and long-term resources, to maximize the likelihood of attaining the desired grade with a minimum expenditure of effort. One of the more obvious examples of such calculating behavior is the student who studies only briefly, if at all, for a course where a satisfactory grade is already assured, and instead spends the time preparing for another course where the grade is in doubt. Such flexibility and a continuing vigilance to revise one's study plans is necessitated by a vast array of obstacles and unforeseen events that besiege students, including extracurricular sources of stress such as financial difficulties, interpersonal problems, and health-related concerns (Covington, 1974).

To my knowledge, no problem-solving taxonomy has adequately treated the dimensions of the task that typically confronts students in preparing for classroom achievement tests. Perhaps Getzels (1976) comes closest when he characterizes one of the most difficult of problem modes as: problem unknown, with the solution thereby free to vary (as in "Prose a problem and solve it") and with the means or method to attain a solution unclear. Typically speaking, the situation in achievement testing is not quite as indeterminate as this, yet, on balance, this description is not a bad approximation. The better student does, of course, possess a formidable arsenal of study methods—including knowledge-acquisition strategies, mnemonic devices, and study habits. But as to problem formulation, most students can, at best, only dimly anticipate potential test items and the levels of performance expected for a given grade; at worst, problem formulation goes little beyond an expression of a desired state of affairs: "The problem is not to fail." The main struggle is to bring the task into focus and under manageable control in the face of incomplete information. Little wonder that under the circumstances failure-avoiding strategies can come to dominate this problem-formulation process.

INSTRUCTION IN STRATEGIC THINKING

In the previous section, we argued that two of the factors contributing to a lack of student effort in school are inappropriate classroom reward structures and student failure to develop effective strategic thinking skills. In this section, we explore ways of helping students improve their capacity for strategic thinking. First, we elaborate the concept of strategic thinking by describing the component skills that are involved. Then, we consider some recent research on student proficiency in these various aspects of strategic thinking. Finally, we discuss both our experiences with the *Productive Thinking Program* and some research now in progress on the feasibility of improving strategic thinking.

Components of Strategic Thinking

What are the basic components of strategic thinking as they relate to problem solving in the classroom? There are at least three discernable elements: (1) formulating a problem or learning task; (2) selecting appropriate strategies for solving it; and (3) monitoring one's progress in achieving a solution. The latter two components are reminiscent of Flavell's distinction between "knowing about knowing" and "knowing *how* to know" (Flavell & Wellman, 1977). Let us briefly consider each component in turn.

Problem Formulation. First, any successful planning and orchestration of a sustained problem-solving effort involves a well-developed sense of the problem; in effect, an understanding of what makes it a problem in the first place, and how it might be reformulated to reduce its difficulty. This point is manifestly self-evident, yet students are notorious for commencing study without a clear idea of future retrieval and performance demands (Karplus, 1977). The difference between the knowledgable problem solver and the novice in this regard is forcefully delineated by Bransford, Nitsch, and Franks (1977): "Experts would ask questions like, 'what must I remember?', 'how many times?' 'how much time will there be?' 'what's the nature of the test?' They would know what they needed to know in order to perform optimally—and would settle for nothing less [p. 38]."

For effective test performance there must be a close correspondence between how the student learns the material originally and how it will be used later. This assertion embraces the concept of *encoding specificity* (Postman, 1975; Tulving & Thompson, 1973). As applied to the present context, effective recall occurs when learners correctly anticipate the form in which information will later be needed, and then organize, rehearse, and store it accordingly. Thus, if information is rehearsed originally as a collection of isolated events, recall may be adequate for answering rote-type test questions, but insufficient for the demands of productive thinking. For example, Covington (1980) found that poor learners tended to master conceptually oriented material (where the transformation of facts was required) by rote overlearning. As a consequence, their retention was far less than that of good learners, who initially assimilated the material as an exercise in concept formation.

Proper problem formulation and, when necessary, reformulation, stands at the heart of strategic functioning. In essence, it involves knowing how to represent a problem or a distant goal in the form of a conceptual schema consisting of an initial or present state and a desired end state as well as a sense for what broad steps or moves are needed to transform one state into the other. Such a knowledge system is reminiscent of what Newell and Simon (1972) have called a means–ends problem space. Strategic problem formulation also requires a constant vigilance regarding changing priorities and unexpected events. An earlier problem statement may no longer serve to represent circumstances realistically, as when, for example, the teacher decides without warning to advance the date of a test. This problem-formulating function is so critical that, as Perkins (*Thinking and Learning Skills,* Volume 2) points out, the payoff of skill training in this area may well provide far greater leverage for the effective use of the individual's resources than interventions at any other stage in the problem-solving process.

Strategy Selection. Having defined a problem in terms of an initial state and an end state and having identified possible strategies for solving that problem, one must then select the strategy that is likely to be most effective. Research on how effective learners and problem solvers cope with different kinds of tasks has helped pinpoint some of the factors that need to be considered in strategy selection. We conclude from the literature on study habits and techniques (Dansereau, Collins, McDonald, Holley, Garland, Diekhoff, & Evans, 1979) that informed selection of study methods depends on such factors as the nature of the to-be-learned material; the conditions under which the material must be recalled or subsequently used; and the degree of familiarity of the material. Concerning the matter of prior familiarity, for example, the novice would be well advised to attempt first to make the unfamiliar familiar by creating everyday analogs or metaphorical equivalents to the new concepts. In this manner, learners can transform the task so that new information may be fitted meaningfully into their preexisting conceptual world, and thus allow them to engage in reproductive thinking of the kind emphasized by Greeno (1973) and Crutchfield (1966).

Self-Monitoring.   Third, and finally, strategic thinking requires knowledge of one's own capacities, limitations, and idiosyncracies regarding the learning of different kinds of material. A person has such knowledge if, for example, he or she knows that some things are harder to learn than others, and how to compensate. Another aspect of such self-knowledge concerns monitoring one's progress toward a goal, as when, for instance, the learner must decide in the course of study whether or not he or she now knows something sufficiently well for an upcoming test. Naturally, this question can be answered only by knowing how important the test is to the student and his or her achievement aspirations; whether or not there is sufficient time remaining to rehearse the material again, and how much of the grade will depend on knowing different aspects of the material. By mentioning all these considerations, we again can appreciate something of the circumlocutive quality of strategic decision making, embracing as it does simultaneously social–personal factors, time constraints, and the anticipation of teacher standards.

Comprehension monitoring also appears to form an important aspect of this process. As Markman (*Thinking and Learning Skills,* Volume 2) argues, there are many degrees of understanding, which complicates the problem of deciding whether or not one has understood something. Regarding the matter of "knowing when one knows something," a reasonable working hypothesis, in light of recent research on memory monitoring (e.g., Brown, 1978; Flavell & Wellman, 1977; Shaughnessy, in press), is that poor learners are inaccurate in their estimates of when they have learned something sufficient to the task at hand. Such a deficiency may lead to counterproductive distributions of study time so that some material may be overlearned at the expense of other material. A related aspect of such monitoring is knowing how well a given strategy is working, and then understanding what to do if the strategy is no longer appropriate (Brown & DeLoache, 1978; Flavell, 1976).

Of course, students who lack some of the self-management skills I have just described may adopt a position of not trying in order to have a ready excuse available for their failures. However, precisely how much strategic mismanagement of study reflects cognitive deficiencies as distinct from the self-handicapping and protective tendencies described earlier is an intriguing question for which there is at present no adequate answer.

This brief overview of the major characteristics of strategic thinking would be incomplete if I failed to comment on the intimate and vital relationship between memory and strategic thinking. Strategic planning implies the ability to retrieve a plethora of material from semantic memory, including, as Greeno (1973) suggests, both content knowledge and knowledge of procedures for transforming existing content knowledge, such as making inferences and creating generalizations. All of this implies the existence of a working memory (Feigenbaum, 1970) for the purpose of holding in mind temporarily the facts of the problem until its resolution. Critical too, as we have seen, is an accurate self-appraisal of one's own idiosyncrasies and limitations regarding memory. In such strategic matters as being able to judge one's memory capacity (Flavell, Friedrichs, & Hoyt, 1970; Yussen & Levy, 1975); estimating the amount of time needed to learn something (Neimark, Slotnick, & Ulrich, 1971), and judging the difficulty of a memory task (Moynahan, 1973; Salatas & Flavell, 1976), there is a wide range of individual differences in accuracy, marked developmental trends, and on occasion disquieting evidence that even adults are far from perfect in making realistic judgments (Denhiere, 1974).

Student Competency in Strategic Thinking

The concept of strategic thinking firmly locates cognitive attributions as antecedent determinants of behavior. This treatment represents a decided shift in emphasis from the role accorded them earlier in this chapter as postdictive explanations (excuses) for success and failure. The classic internal dimensions of ability and effort (or energy level) have now become personal resources to be managed, whereas the external dimension of task difficulty and a newcomer, time, are constraints on successful academic problem solving. Given this conceptualization, we can now ask what students know about the role of these resources and constraints in effective thinking. Direct evidence on this point comes from my laboratory and confirms our suspicions of considerable strategic deficiencies (Schnur, 1981). Junior high school students and teachers were asked to estimate the degree of success they believed hypothetical pupils would enjoy on a social studies test, given various combinations of factors: student aptitude for the topic (high/low), amount of time available for study (sufficient/insufficient), intensity of study effort (high/low), and test difficulty (easy/hard). Information was also available as to whether each hypothetical pupil had succeeded or failed previously on a similar test. Teachers were included as a standard against which to judge the accuracy of student predictions on the grounds that teachers, above all other adult occupational groups, should have a well-articulated picture of school achievement dynamics.

Although these young students could readily distinguish between the single condition in which all factors were loaded against achievement success and the one in which all were positive, their estimates were otherwise generally insensitive to combinations of positive and negative factors. Moreover, the only consistently dominant cue for degree of success was amount of effort and ability. Hypothetical achievers who tried hard or were highly able were seen as more likely to succeed than those who did not study or were less able, irrespective of the remaining factors. Knowing that a test was easy or difficult or that the hypothetical pupil had little or much time to prepare made little difference in student predictions. Such findings reveal a grossly inadequate appreciation of the achievement factors, and of their interactions, which influence subsequent test performance. The teacher group proved more sensitive to both internal (ability and effort) and external (time and task difficulty) factors in making their judgments. However, here too, few significant interactions occurred, suggesting that adults, like adolescents, are generally unresponsive to the more subtle nuances one is apt to associate with metacognitively sophisticated individuals. For example, it is reasonable to expect that the knowledgeable person would appreciate the fact that a combination of, say, high effort and easy task presents a greater likelihood of success than either high effort or easy task alone. It is possible, however, that some attributional theorists are correct in assuming that most individuals, including adults, perceive the action of causal variables as largely independent of one another. Although we know that adults are able to entertain interactive-type attribution hypotheses when directed to do so, their spontaneous, real-life calculations may omit such subtleties. At a time (junior high school) when children stand on the threshold of truly independent learning in the form of increasingly complex homework assignments, long-range term projects, and take-home examinations, they appear altogether naive regarding the rudiments of achievement management.

In a second phase of this research, these same students offered advice as to how the hypothetical achiever might improve his or her chances of doing better on the test. Given the high saliency of effort, we were not surprised to find that most suggestions involved the admonition simply to work harder (e.g., "Study more, longer"; "Try *really* hard."). As such, these responses reveal little strategic understanding of *how best* to work harder as in the case of reviewing material periodically, taking notes, or asking the teacher questions, to name only a few obvious possibilities. Yet, the reluctance of students to ask for help or to change their learning tactics is understandable when we recognize that, from the student perspective, "not knowing something" is often considered wrong, and seeking assistance casts doubt on one's capabilities (Covington & Berry, 1976). In effect, these students have confused ignorance with stupidity, and by remaining ignorant, they are acting contrary to their own interests. We found the same poverty of strategic imagination when elementary school children were asked to advise a fellow student about what to do when the due date of a school report was unexpectedly advanced by the teacher. Hard work was again the dominant response. Only occasionally did the replies indicate that some few students had access to strategic possibilities as reflected in such suggestions as "don't make the report so fancy"; "turn in an outline now, and the rest of it later"; "put together several unfinished reports [in a group effort]."

Improving Strategic Thinking

Research in Progress.   Efforts are now underway in our laboratory to identify more fully the kinds of strategic planning deficiencies revealed by the series of experiments just described, and to initiate steps to remediate them. This research is being conducted in parallel studies at both the junior high school and college levels. Our working assumptions are that: (1) students differ markedly in their ability to analyze an achievement task in a strategic manner; and (2) the quality of their planfulness is related to subsequent achievement performance. Although this view seems reasonable, perhaps even somewhat obvious, little previous research has taken into account such a strategic overview of school achievement. The basic paradigm involves a series of learning/retention tasks. Students are administered to-be-learned textual material in a simulated study hall context; then, on a second subsequent occasion, they are tested for recall and applications of the information learned earlier. Our intention is to simulate the kinds of study scenarios and strategic planning choices typically required of students in the course of actual classroom work. For example, one obvious circumstance, commonplace among procrastinating students, is the existence of too much material to be fully assimilated in the time available. The study task conditions vary along several dimensions including amount of study time available, amount and type of material to be learned, and type of achievement test. By varying these circumstances programmatically, as well as manipulating the amount of information available to the learner about the task, we address various questions alluded to earlier. Basically, we ask: "Do students take advantage of strategic information in order to alter their study approaches?" If they do, then knowledge of the kinds of test to be used, either essay or objective, should influence choice of knowledge-acquisition strategies. Moreover, the presence of information about those aspects of the text that will receive the greatest emphasis should, if the student is but sensitive to it, lead to a more efficient distribution of study time. Such a strategic study decision may involve the need to change or reduce the scope of the learning task to make it easier or to fit existing time constraints. In the parlance of the expert problem solver, the task is divided into more manageable subparts. Indeed, the weight of evidence (Frase, 1968, 1970) suggests that when the information load of prose material is heavy, individuals tend to focus on the text in selected ways, and that it is specifically during this process of spontaneous reorganization that deficiencies appear among poor learners (Cromer & Wiener, 1966; Lefevre, 1964; Steiner, Wiener, & Cromer, 1971).

Of special interest to us is the availability of strategies for facilitating the productive use of previously learned facts. The acquisition of facts and their subsequent manipulation in productive ways are not unrelated processes, as we have seen from the literature on encoding specificity, and from the evidence of horizontal transfer as well as from findings on the effects of advanced organizers (Mayer, 1979). It seems reasonable to conclude that if students are aware of the future uses to which the to-be-learned material must be put, they will not only remember it better, but will be better able to manipulate and transform it. For example, degree of transfer to unexpected, novel situations may depend on the breadth of situations emphasized during initial learning. As robust as the influence of advanced organizers has proven to be in the acquisition and recall of factual material (see Mayer, 1979), little is yet known about their impact on subsequent productive thinking.

After learning about the relative saliency of various task cues for prompting changes in student study patterns, we intend to provide instruction in areas where students are insensitive to task demands and approach studying in a stereotypic manner. The more these sensitivities depend on task and individual difference factors, the more the instruction must become situation specific. In this second main phase of research, we envision the development of systematic practice materials, using study scenarios similar to those developed in the exploratory phase of research. We will concentrate on those scenarios most frequently occurring in real life and/or on those found to present the greatest challenge to proper study management. This latter category will doubtless include high-risk situations such as "too much material to learn, too late." Because this and similar situations invariably cause heightened personal stress, we anticipate the need to provide didactic commentary on such topics as fear-of-failure dynamics, test-taking anxiety, and stress management (Covington & Beery, 1976).

There is reason to believe that remedial efforts of the kind just described will prove beneficial given the growing body of evidence on the successful training of various component aspects of strategic thinking. For example, a spate of studies indicates that the direct retraining of negative attributional patterns through strengthening the proper effort/outcome covariation is not only feasible, but results in increased task persistence and better performance especially among failure-oriented students (Andrews, 1977; Andrews & Debus, 1978; Chapin & Dyck, 1976; Dweck, 1975, 1977). Training in realistic goal setting in which students learn to reduce discrepancies between their aspirations and previous levels of performance also leads to the same positive achievement outcomes (deCharms, 1972; Litwin & Ciarlo, 1961). Again, such training appears particularly effective for failure-oriented students who initially hold unreasonable self-expectations (Shea, 1969). Moreover, improvement in task analysis skills has also been demonstrated among underachieving students with the result of increased achievement level (Kolb, 1965).

The Productive Thinking Program.   Other investigators have focused on teaching more generalized thinking skills relevant to problem formulation and to the self-monitoring of one's level of understanding and comprehension. Evidence on this point comes from research over the past decade on the *Productive Thinking Program,* a course in learning to think for students in the upper elementary grades (Covington, Crutchfield, Davies, & Olton, 1972, 1974; a brief overview is available in Olton & Crutchfield, 1969). The program consists of a series of complex problems that students attempt to solve. In the process, they receive practice and feedback on a variety of broad-gauged strategies including techniques for generating new ideas; techniques for discovering and formulating problems; and techniques for restructuring one's problem-solving approach when previous strategies no longer prove effective. From a contemporary information-processing framework, the program represents a dual and simultaneous focus on diverse idea production and on the basic skills involved in means–ends analysis (Polson & Jeffries, this volume). In this latter respect, emphasis is placed on initial problem finding and problem formulation with constant monitoring and, when necessary, modification of goals as work on the problem proceeds.

A number of evaluation studies of the *Productive Thinking Program* have been conducted in which the problem-solving performances of instructed students are compared to those of untrained, control students (Covington & Crutchfield, 1965; Mansfield, Busse & Krepelka, 1978; Olton & Crutchfield, 1969; Ripple & Darcey, 1967). Typically, multiple-output criteria have been employed for assessment purposes including ideational fluency, rated quality of ideas generated, the actual number of 'best' solutions attained, as well as other related indices of efficient functioning such as the ability to look at problems in new ways, and the propensity to ask questions and to seek answers. Overall, the results indicated that students using the *Productive Thinking Program* made substantial improvements on all performance indices sampled, and that these students profited irrespective of their intellectual ability or initial levels of thinking proficiency. The schema in Fig. 11.1 presents the typical findings of several aggregated studies. It illustrates the general pattern of performance gains for instructed students across a wide range of ability. The productive thinking index represents a composite of the various cognitive measures indicated previously.

In addition to gains in ideational fluency and actual solutions attained, other aspects of problem-solving behavior more closely allied to our present concern for strategic thinking have also been shown to improve as a result of training. For example, in one study (Covington, 1965), students participating in the program showed improved comprehension monitoring. They were better able than their control counterparts to detect inconsistencies and discrepancies in text

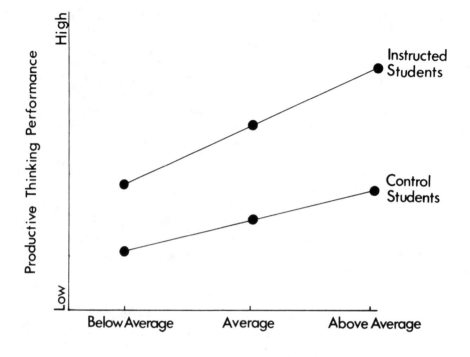

FIG. 11.1   Schematic of the effect of productive thinking training and intellectual level on performance gains.

passages, and were also better able to make use of such ambiguities to solve problems. Trained students were also better able to outline a plan of action for dealing with ill-defined problem situations.

Further research on the *Productive Thinking Program* also suggests that skill training and subsequent performance gains can enhance the student's self-confidence in a number of important ways. For example, training increased the likelihood that students would tackle complex problems where success was uncertain (Olton & Crutchfield, 1969). Another index of self-confidence used was the degree of independence shown in judging the worth of one's ideas. Here, trained students were less likely than untrained students to abandon their beliefs simply because these differed from peer-group opinion (Allen & Levine, 1967). Also, the student's own subjective evaluations of themselves as thinkers improved as a consequence of skill training. Instructed students came to hold more positive beliefs about thinking and saw themselves as more able to make productive use of their minds (Olton, 1975; Treffinger & Ripple, 1970).

Ability Management as an Acquired Skill.   Much of the focus of this chapter has been on identifying ways to help students make more effective use of their abilities in coping with school learning tasks. The assumption underlying this chapter as a whole, and the training research just described in particular, is that students can be taught to become better thinkers by improving the management of personal resources such as ability and effort. In concluding, we need pause to consider the assumption that ability management is a learnable skill, as, in some ways, this seems to contradict the lay person's notion of ability as an attribute that is stable and immutable. We must clarify in what sense ability can be managed and consider whether in fact there is evidence that this aspect of intelligence can be modified as a result of instruction.

Although it goes beyond our purposes here to review the enormous and frequently controversial literature on the nature of intelligence, suffice it to say that there is broad agreement among contemporary cognitive psychologists that to understand intelligence, it is important to make a distinction between basic abilities and the mechanisms by which abilities are translated into intelligent thought and action (e.g., Reitman, 1970; Sternberg, *Thinking and Learning Skills,* Volume 2). The linkage between native abilities and effective thinking behavior depends on intervening strategies. In the case of problem solving, these strategies take the form of plans, heuristics, and rules for operating in problem-solving situations: for example, Scandura's (1977) higher-order rules; Brown's (1978) explication of the role of "Bundy-type rules" in learning to solve algebra problems; and the "executive function" postulated by Butterfield and Belmont (1975) that initiates strategic adaptations to suit new task conditions. Presumably, the individual moves from an initial problem state to a final, desired solution state, by means of a sequence of thinking steps that in turn depend on and uniquely reflect the individual's particular constellation of abilities. This mobilization of abilities lies at the heart of our definition of strategic thinking. Indeed, I have argued elsewhere (Covington, 1966) that intelligence, in its nuclear, definitional sense, is the capacity to think strategically, that is, the ability to plan for and to make the most of one's resources. These plans, heuristics, and rules typically operate at an unconscious level during the problem-solving act, but can be made explicit and hence are modifiable through direct skill training, as we have seen.

Rather than investigate the question of the *nature* of intelligence as was the preoccupation a generation ago, largely through factor analytic studies of IQ tests, today's researchers are more likely to pursue the different question of what information-processing and assembly strategies are important components of *intelligent behavior.* Although the fundamental nature of intelligence will likely remain as elusive as ever, this newer approach should lead us to a more complete and sophisticated understanding, largely through the recognition that intelligence can be defined only in terms of the context in which it is required. In effect, what counts as intelligent behavior depends in part on the task at hand and on the prevailing criteria for excellence in performance.

By this reasoning, we are led back to those matters that engaged our attention earlier, but with a more useful perspective on ability, its relationship to behavior, and possibilities for improvement. Intelligent behavior in school means acting to make a difficult assignment easier, redefining a problem space in light of new contingencies, and recognizing when one does not understand a concept. All these actions are governable by rules, and it is in this sense that intelligence can be modified and improved. These notions are scarcely new and, interestingly enough, have as their most eloquent spokesperson Alfred Binet, the pioneer developer of the intelligence test, who wrote in 1909: "Some recent philosophers appear to have given their moral support to the deplorable verdict that the intelligence of an individual is a fixed quantity. . . . We must protest and act against this brutal pessimism. . . . A child's mind is like a field for which an expert farmer has advised a change in the method of cultivating, with the result that in place of desert land, we now have a harvest. It is in this particular sense, the one which is significant, that we say that the intelligence of children may be increased. One increases that which constitutes the intelligence of a school child, namely, the capacity to learn, to improve with instruction [pp. 54–55]."

Some additional research from our laboratory, using the *Productive Thinking Program,* illustrates how cognitive skill training can moderate the relationship between ability and problem-solving performance, and thus bears on the question of whether and how the capacity to manage one's mental resources can be altered through instruction. One experimental approach is to establish the "baseline" importance of various abilities, such as verbal IQ, in contributing to successful problem solving when no instruction is provided, and then to determine if the relative importance of these same factors changes as a result of training. To the extent that instruction reduces the dependency of performance on ability and increases the saliency of various trainable plans and rules, it can be said that individuals can now exercise more personal control over their mental resources.

Using the standard evaluation paradigm described earlier, the *Productive Thinking Program* was administered to a group of upper elementary school students while a comparable group served as a control (Covington & Fedan, 1978). The posttest performance data were subjected to two separate regression analyses, one for the instructed students and one for the controls. The criterion variables were the respective problem-solving performances of each group. Several predictor variables were used for both groups, including verbal IQ and measures of ideational fluency. We knew from previous experience that these latter measures were highly sensitive to training effects. For many problem-solving tasks, cognitive instruction had the effect of reducing the importance of ability factors in achieving solutions and, conversely, increased the role of trainable skills such as ideational fluency. Because these skills took on a greater causal importance in effective thinking, and because the level of skill proficiency increased dramatically as a result of instruction, a 'compensatory' dynamic occurred. Many of the less bright instructed students, who formerly were unable to do well owing to the heavy dependency of performance on ability, now outperformed the less bright control students, who possessed neither the trainable heuristics nor the native capacity to generate them spontaneously. Here, then, we see ability being managed more effectively, through the introduction of organizing rules and strategies, and deficiencies in ability compensated. It is in this sense that ability is a resource to be orchestrated.

A final observation leads to my closing remarks. Inspection of Fig. 11.1 indicates that individual differences in productive thinking depend heavily on variations in ability: the higher the ability level, the more likely an individual or a group is to perform well. This fact has been documented so frequently that it scarcely deserves mention here except that it bears on a second fact also illustrated by Fig. 11.1. Cognitive instruction can lead to substantial changes in the absolute level of problem solving among most students, irrespective of their initial ability level. Taken together these two observations tell us that: (1) thinking processes are trainable over a broad range of intelligence, even though initial level of functioning depends heavily on ability; and yet (2) cognitive instruction is unlikely to reduce significantly the range of individual differences in thinking proficiency nor to alter the relative standing of groups within a given school population. With this latter observation in mind, we come full circle to our earlier concerns about self-worth. Increasing one's academic performance alone will not abolish the threat to self-worth so long as the individual's sense of worth is tied to competitive achievement; the individual may improve, but then so will others. Ultimately, it is the meaning of what is learned—satisfaction in self-improvement or in a job well done—rather than relative achievement standing per se that holds the key to sustained personal motivation. The challenge and the difficulties inherent in altering the prevailing reward system in our schools was brilliantly captured by John Gardner (1961) when he inquired, "How can we provide opportunities and rewards for individuals of every degree of ability so that individuals at every level will realize their full potentialities, perform at their best and harbor no other resentment toward any other level? [p. 115]"

REFERENCES

Allen, V. L., & Levine, J. M. *Creativity and conformity* (Tech. Rep. No. 33). Madison: University of Wisconsin Research and Development Center for Cognitive Learning, 1967.

Alschuler, A. S. *Developing achievement motivation in adolescents.* Englewood Cliffs, N.J.: Educational Technology Publications, 1973.

Andrews, G. R. *Persistence and the causal perception of failure: Modifying cognitive attributions.* Unpublished bachelor's thesis, University of Sydney, 1974. (Reported by B. Weiner, An attributional model for educational psychology.) In L. Schulman (Ed.), *Review of research in education* (Vol. 4). Itasca, Ill.: Peacock, 1977.

Andrews, G. R., & Debus, R. L. Persistence and the causal perception of failure. Modifying cognitive attribution. *Journal of Educational Psychology,* 1978, *70,* 154–166.

Atkinson, J. W. *An introduction to motivation.* Princeton, N.J.: D. Van Nostrand Co., Inc., 1964.

Atkinson, J. W., & Raynor, J. D. *Personality, motivation and achievement.* New York: Hemisphere, 1977.

Beery, R. G. Fear of failure in the student experience. *Personnel and Guidance Journal,* 1975, *54,* 190–203.

Berglas, S., & Jones, E. Drug choice as a self-handicapping strategy in response to noncontingent success. *Journal of Personality and Social Psychology,* 1978, *36,* 405–417.

Binet, A. *Les idées modernes sur les enfants.* Paris: Ernest Flamarion, 1909.

Birney, R. C., Burdick, H., & Teevan, R. *Fear of failure.* New York: Van Nostrand–Reinhold Co., 1969.

Bransford, J. D., Nitsch, K. E., & Franks, J. J. The facilitation of knowing. In R. C. Anderson, R. J. Spiro, & W. E. Montague (Eds.), *Schooling and the acquisition of knowledge.* Hillsdale, N.J.: Lawrence Erlbaum Associates, 1977.

Brickman, P., & Hendricks, M. Expectancy for gradual or sudden improvement and reaction to success and failure. *Journal of Personality and Social Psychology,* 1975, *32,* 893–900.

Brock, T. C. Implications of commodity theory for value change. In A. G. Greenwald, T. C. Brock, & T. M. Ostrom (Eds.), *Psychological foundations of attitudes.* New York: Academic Press, 1968.

Brown, A. L. Knowing when, where, and how to remember: A problem of metacognition. In R. Glaser (Ed.), *Advances in instructional psychology* (Vol. 1). Hillsdale, N.J.: Lawrence Erlbaum Associates, 1978.

Brown, A. L., & DeLoache, J. S. Skills, plans and self-regulation. In R. Siegler (Ed.), *Children's thinking: What develops?* Hillsdale, N.J.: Lawrence Erlbaum Associates, 1978.

Butterfield, E. C., & Belmont, J. M. Assessing and improving the executive cognitive functions of mentally retarded people. In I. Bialer & M. Sternlicht (Eds.), *Psychological issues in mentally retarded people.* Chicago: Aldine, 1975.

Chapin, M., & Dyck, D. G. Persistence in children's reading behavior as a function of N length and attribution retraining. *Journal of Abnormal Psychology,* 1976, *85,* 511–515.

Coopersmith, S., & Feldman, R. Fostering a positive self-concept and high self-esteem in the classroom. In R. H. Coop & K. White (Eds.), *Psychological concepts in the classroom.* New York: Harper & Row, 1974.

Covington, M. V. *The effectiveness of training for problem-solving efficiency and creative thinking as a function of differing ability levels among children.* Paper presented at the meeting of the Western Psychological Association, Honolulu, June 1965.

Covington, M. V. Programmed instruction and the intellectually gifted: Experiments in productive thinking. *Programmed instruction and the gifted.* Symposium presented at the International Convention of the Council for Exceptional Children. Toronto, April 1966.

Covington, M. V. An empirical test of Maslow's need hierarchy theory in an educational setting. *Fostering student motivation and satisfaction in the college classroom.* Symposium presented at the meeting of the Western Psychological Association Convention, San Francisco, April 1974.

Covington, M. V. *Do slow learners deserve high grades? An analysis of individual differences in mastery learning.* Unpublished manuscript, Department of Psychology, University of California, Berkeley, 1980.

Covington, M. V. Motivated cognitions. In S. G. Paris, G. M. Olson, & H. W. Stevenson (Eds.), *Learning and motivation in the classroom.* Hillsdale, N.J.: Lawrence Erlbaum Associates, 1983.

Covington, M. V. The motive for self-worth. In R. Ames & C. Ames (Eds.), *Motivation and education: Student motivation,* Volume I. New York: Academic Press, 1984.

Covington, M. V. The self-worth theory of achievement motivation: Findings and educational implications. *The Elementary School Journal,* in press.

Covington, M. V., & Beery, R. *Self-worth and school learning.* New York: Holt, Rinehart, & Winston, 1976.

Covington, M. V., & Crutchfield, R. S. Experiments in the use of programmed instruction for the facilitation of creative problem solving. *Programmed Instruction,* 1965, *4,* 3–5; 10.

Covington, M. V., Crutchfield, R. S., Davies, L. B., & Olton, R. M. *The productive thinking program: A course in learning to think.* Columbus, Ohio: Merrill, 1972, 1974.

Covington, M. V., & Fedan, N. *Metastrategies in productive thinking.* Unpublished manuscript, Department of Psychology, University of California, Berkeley, 1978.

Covington, M. V., & Jacoby, K. E. *Thinking psychology: Student projects, Sets I and II:* Berkeley: Institute of Personality Assessment and Research, University of California, 1972.

Covington, M. V., & Jacoby, K. E. *Productive thinking and course satisfaction as a function of an independence-conformity dimension.* Paper presented at the meeting of the American Psychological Association, Montreal, April 1973.

Covington, M. V., & Omelich, C. L. *Sex differences in self-serving perceptions of ability.* Unpublished manuscript, Department of Psychology, University of California, Berkeley, 1978.

Covington, M. V., & Omelich, C. L. Are causal attributions causal? A path analysis of the cognitive model of achievement motivation. *Journal of Personality and Social Psychology,* 1979, *37,* 1487–1504. (a)

Covington, M. V., & Omelich, C. L. Effort: The double-edged sword in school achievement. *Journal of Educational Psychology,* 1979, *71,* 169–182. (b)

Covington, M. V., & Omelich, C. L. It's best to be able and virtuous too: Student and teacher evaluative responses to successful effort. *Journal of Educational Psychology,* 1979, *71,* 688–700. (c)

Covington, M. V., & Omelich, C. L. As failures mount: Affective and cognitive consequences of ability demotion in the classroom. *Journal of Educational Psychology,* 1981, *73,* 796–808. (a)

Covington, M. V., & Omelich, C. L. *A psychological and behavioral cost/benefits analysis of mastery learning.* Unpublished manuscript, Department of Psychology, University of California, Berkeley, 1981. (b)

Covington, M. V., & Omelich, C. L. Achievement anxiety, performance and behavioral instruction: A cost/benefits analysis. In R. Schwarzer, H. van der Ploeg, & C. Spielberger (Eds.), *Test anxiety research* (Vol. 1). Amsterdam: Swets & Zeitlinger, 1982.

Covington, M. V., & Omelich, C. L. Controversies or consistencies? A reply to Brown and Weiner. *Journal of Educational Psychology,* 1984, *76,* 159–168.

Covington, M. V., & Polsky, S. Introduction to the program of research: The Berkeley Teaching–Learning Project. *Fostering student motivation.* Symposium presented at the meeting of the Western Psychological Association, San Francisco, April 1974.

Covington, M. V., Spratt, M. F., & Omelich, C. L. Is effort enough or does diligence count too? Student and teacher reactions to effort stability in failure. *Journal of Educational Psychology,* 1980, *72,* 717–729.

Cromer, W., & Wiener, M. Idiosyncratic response patterns among good and poor readers. *Journal of Consulting Psychology,* 1966, *30,* 1–10.

Crutchfield, R. S. Creative thinking in children: Its teaching and testing. In O. Brim, R. S. Crutchfield, & W. Holtzman (Eds.), *Intelligence: Perspectives 1965.* New York: Harcourt, Brace, 1966.

Dansereau, D. F., Collins, K. W., McDonald, B. A., Holley, C. D., Garland, J. C., Diekhoff, G., & Evans, S. H. Development and evaluation of an effective learning strategy program. *Journal of Educational Psychology,* 1979, *71,* 64–73.

deCharms, R. Personal causation training in the schools. *Journal of Applied Social Psychology,* 1972, *2,* 95–113.

Denhiere, G. Apprentissages intentionnels à allure libre: Etude comparative d'enfants normaux et debiles mentaux. *Enfance,* 1974, September–December (3–5), 149–174.

Diggory, J. C. *Self-evaluation: Concepts and studies.* New York: Wiley, 1966.

Dweck, C. S. The role of expectations and attributions in the alleviation of learned helplessness. *Journal of Personality and Social Psychology,* 1975, *31,* 674–685.

Dweck, C. S. Learned helplessness and negative evaluation. *UCLA Educator,* 1977, *12,* 44–49.

Feigenbaum, E. A. Information processing and memory. In D. A. Norman (Ed.), *Models of human memory.* New York: Academic Press, 1970.

Flavell, J. A. Metacognitive aspects of problem solving. In L. B. Resnick (Ed.), *The nature of intelligence.* Hillsdale, N.J.: Lawrence Erlbaum Associates, 1976.

Flavell, J. H., Friedrichs, A. G., & Hoyt, J. D. Developmental changes in memorization processes. *Cognitive Psychology,* 1970, *1,* 324–340.

Flavell, J. H., & Wellman, H. M. Metamemory. In R. V. Kail & J. W. Hagen (Eds.), *Perspectives on the development of memory and cognition.* Hillsdale, N.J.: Lawrence Erlbaum Associates, 1977.

Frase, L. T. Effect of question location, pacing and mode upon retention of prose material. *Journal of Educational Psychology,* 1968, *59,* 244–249.

Frase, L. T. Boundary condition for mathemagenic behaviors. *Review of Educational Research,* 1970, *40,* 337–347.

Gardner, J. *Excellence: Can we be equal and excellent too?* New York: Harper & Row, 1961.

Getzels, J. W. Problem-finding and the inventiveness of solutions. *Journal of Creative Behavior,* 1976, *9,* 12–18.

Greeno, J. G. The structure of memory and the process of solving problems. In R. L. Solso (Ed.), *Contemporary issues in cognitive psychology.* Washington, D.C.: Winston, 1973.

Harari, O., & Covington, M. V. Reactions to achievement behavior from a teacher and student perspective: A developmental analysis. *American Educational Research Journal,* 1981, *19,* 15–28.

Holt, J., *How children fail.* Dell, 1964.

Kaplan, R. M., & Swant, S. G. Reward characteristics in appraisal of achievement behavior. *Representative Research in Social Psychology,* 1973, *4,* 11–17.

Karplus, R. Personal communication, 1977.

Kelley, H. H. The processes of causal attribution. *American Psychologist,* 1973, *28,* 107–128.

Kennedy, W. A., & Willcutt, H. C. Praise and blame as incentives. *Psychological Bulletin,* 1964, *62,* 323–32.

Kolb, D. A. Achievement motivation training for underachieving high school boys. *Journal of Personality and Social Psychology,* 1965, *2,* 783–92.

Kun, A. Development of the magnitude-covariation and compensation schemata in ability and effort attributions of performance. *Child Development,* 1977, *48,* 862–873.

Kun, A., & Weiner, B. Necessary versus sufficient causal schemata for success and failure. *Journal of Research in Personality,* 1973, *7,* 197–207.

Lefevre, C. A. *Linguistics and the teaching of reading.* New York: McGraw–Hill, 1964.

Litwin, G. H., & Ciarlo, J. A. *Achievement motivation and risk-taking in a business setting* (Tech. Rep.). New York: General Electric Company, Behavioral Research Service, 1961.

Mansfield, R. S., Busse, T. V., & Krepelka, E. J. The effectiveness of creativity training. *Review of Educational Research,* 1978, *48,* 517–536.

Martire, J. G. Relationships between the self-concept and differences in the strength and generality of achievement motivation. *Journal of Personality,* 1956, *24,* 364–75.

Mayer, R. E. Can advanced organizer influence meaningful learning? *Review of Educational Research,* 1979, *49,* 371–383.

McClelland, D. C. Toward a theory of motive acquisition. *American Psychologist,* 1965, *20,* 321–333.

Mettee, D. R. Rejection of unexpected success as a function of the negative consequences of accepting success. *Journal of Personality and Social Psychology,* 1971, *17,* 332–341.

Moynahan, E. D. The development of knowledge concerning the effect of categorizing upon free recall. *Child Development,* 1973, *44,* 238–246.

Neimark, E., Slotnick, N. S., & Ulrich, T. The development of memorization strategies. *Developmental Psychology,* 1971, *5,* 427–432.

Nelson, L. L., & Kagan, S. Competition: The star-spangled scramble. *Psychology Today,* 1972, 53–56; 90–91.

Newell, A., & Simon, H. A. *Human problem solving.* Englewood Cliffs, N.J.: Prentice–Hall, 1972.

Olton, R. S. Personal communication, 1975.

Olton, R. M., & Crutchfield, R. S. Developing the skills of productive thinking. In P. Mussen, J. Langer, & M. V. Covington (Eds.), *Trends and issues in developmental psychology.* New York: Holt, Rinehart & Winston, 1969.

Postman, L. Test of the generality of the principle of encoding specificity. *Memory & Cognition,* 1975, *6,* 663–672.

Reitman, W. What does it take to remember? In D. A. Norman (Ed.), *Models of human memory.* New York: Academic Press, 1970.

Rest, S., Nierenberg, R., Weiner, B., & Heckhausen, H. Further evidence concerning the effects of perceptions of effort and ability on achievement evaluation. *Journal of Personality and Social Psychology,* 1973, *28,* 187–91.

Ripple, R. E., & Darcey, J. The facilitation of problem solving and verbal creativity by exposure to programmed instruction. *Psychology in the Schools,* 1967, *4,* 240–45.

Rubin, S. E. Personal communication, 1975. Also *Newsweek,* Feb. 10, 1975.

Salatas, H., & Flavell, J. H. Behavioral and metamnemonic indicators of strategic behaviors under remember instructions in first grade. *Child Development,* 1976, *47,* 81–89.

Scandura, J. M. *Problem solving.* New York: Academic Press, 1977.

Schnur, A. E. *Fear of failure, effort motive, and student satisfaction in the college classroom.* Paper presented at the meeting of the Western Psychological Association, Sacramento, April 1975.

Schnur, A. E. *The assessment of academic self-management skills in adolescents.* Unpublished doctoral dissertation, University of California, Berkeley, 1981.

Sears, P. S. Levels of aspiration in academically successful and unsuccessful children. *Journal of Abnormal and Social Psychology,* 1940, *35,* 498–536.

Shaughnessy, J. J. Confidence–judgement accuracy as a predictor of test performance. *Journal of Educational Psychology,* in press.

Shea, D. J. *The effects of achievement motivation training on motivational and behavior variables.* Unpublished doctoral dissertation, Washington University, 1969.

Shelton, J., & Hill, J. Effects on cheating of achievement anxiety and knowledge of peer performance. *Developmental Psychology,* 1969, *1,* 449–55.

Sigall, H., & Gould, R. The effects of self-esteem and evaluator demandingness on effort expenditure. *Journal of Personality and Social Psychology,* 1977, *35,* 12–20.

Silberman, C. E. *Crisis in the classroom: The remaking of American education.* New York: Vintage Books, 1970.

Steiner, R., Wiener, M., & Cromer, W. Comprehension training and identification for poor and good readers. *Journal of Educational Psychology,* 1971, *62,* 506–513.

Thomas, J. W. Agency and achievement: Self-management and self-regard. *Review of Educational Research,* 1980, *50,* 213–240.

Treffinger, D. J., & Ripple, R. E. *Programmed instruction in creative problem solving: An interpretation of recent research findings.* Lafayette, Ind.: Purdue University, 1970.

Tulving, E., & Thomson, D. M. Encoding specificity and retrieval processes in episodic memory. *Psychological Review,* 1973, *80,* 352–373.

Weaver, D., & Brickman, P. Expectancy, feedback and disconfirmation as independent factors in outcome satisfaction. *Journal of Personality and Social Psychology,* 1974, *30,* 420–428.

Weiner, B. *Theories of motivation: From mechanism to cognition.* Chicago: Markham Publishing Co., 1972.

Weiner, B., & Kukla, A. An attributional analysis of achievement motivation. *Journal of Personality and Social Psychology,* 1970, *15*, 1–20.

Woodson, C. E. *Motivational effects of two-stage testing.* Unpublished manuscript, Institute of Human Learning, University of California, Berkeley, 1975.

Yussen, S. R., & Levy, V. M., Jr. Development changes in predicting one's own span of short-term memory. *Journal of Experimental Child Psychology,* 1975, *19*, 502–508.

12

Instruction in General Problem-Solving Skills: An Analysis of Four Approaches

Peter G. Polson
University of Colorado

Robin Jeffries
Carnegie-Mellon University

This chapter analyzes two textbooks on problem-solving techniques and two programs that teach general problem-solving and thinking skills. Our goal is to determine the relationship of the material presented in the programs and textbooks to modern work on problem solving. One consequence of our analysis will be to demonstrate that there are limitations to current theories of problem-solving processes and of the processes involved in the learning of cognitive skills.

There is reasonably general agreement that the educational system as currently constituted does not successfully teach general problem-solving skills to a majority of its graduates. Many high school graduates cannot solve elementary problems involving installment purchases, simple interest, or taxes, which require application of basic computational and algebraic skills. Students have difficulty with elementary college courses in science and mathematics. Graduates from engineering programs are unable to apply the theoretical knowledge acquired during their years in school to actual engineering problems. Many observers have concluded that these separate deficiencies are all due in part to the failure to teach successfully general problem-solving skills. Thus, development of courses of instruction in problem solving would represent a significant contribution to the educational system.

On the other hand, basic research on problem solving has focused almost exclusively on models of skill in particular task domains. There has been little work on what the common processes across domains are and even less on how these processes might be taught. Development of a theory of general problem-solving skills, to a level of specificity such that courses of instruction could be derived from it, would represent a real advance in our understanding of how the human mind functions.

THEORETICAL BACKGROUND

Any armchair analysis of specific programs and textbooks must originate from some theoretical perspective. As cognitive psychologists, our viewpoint comes out of the *information-processing framework*, currently the dominant theoretical paradigm in the area of cognition. Before beginning the description and analysis of the four programs, we present a fairly detailed overview of what information-processing psychology has to say about learning and problem-solving skills and how they might be taught. In contrast, many of those who advocate the teaching of general problem-solving skills come from a quite different theoretical tradition, one we will refer to as the *divergent-production paradigm*. We briefly describe the main tenets of this framework also and compare them to the assumptions of the information-processing perspective.

Problem Solving and Skill Acquisition from the Information-Processing Perspective

The current state of theoretical knowledge of problem solving from the information-processing perspective can best be characterized as a global framework, plus a collection of process models for individual problem-solving tasks. The framework provides a rationale and support for models of particular tasks. However, the models are not derived from a combination of general theory and the specifics of an experimental task. The information-processing framework was initially developed by Newell and Simon (1972); a summary and revision of it has been described by Simon (1978). The core elements of this framework provide the conceptual structure that underlies much of the work on information-processing models of cognition (Bower, 1975). Two assumptions underlie this paradigm. The first is that the human problem solver can be characterized as an information-processing system. The second is that problem solving can be characterized as both a search process and a process of understanding.

Simon (1978) describes the human information-processing system, apart from its perceptual mechanisms, as a serial system whose elementary processes are executed in from tens to hundreds of milliseconds. The inputs and outputs of these elementary processes are held in a short-term working memory with a capacity of from four to seven chunks, or symbols. The system incorporates in long-term memory an almost unlimited amount of information, with an access time of tens of milliseconds to several seconds. It takes several seconds to write a new chunk into long-term memory. This memory system contains declarative information (factual knowledge) and procedural knowledge (knowledge of how to do things). The declarative information is represented as a network of concepts with labeled links describing the relationships between them. The procedural information is represented as sets of condition–action pairs, which specify the actions one can take and the conditions under which they are appropriate.

The information-processing paradigm characterizes problem solving as the interaction between the problem solver and the task environment, i.e., the experimenter's representation of the task presented to the subject. There are two separable sets of processes involved in this interaction. The first is a collection of understanding processes that generate a problem space. A problem space is the solver's representation of the task, including his or her understanding of the givens, the goal, the underlying structure of possible solutions, and any problem-solving strategies that can be used to solve this task. Each node in a problem space represents a possible state of knowledge on the part of the solver. The second set of processes, the search processes, can be characterized as transitions between knowledge states in the problem space.

In the discussion that follows, we distinguish between understanding mechanisms and search mechanisms. This is a convenient, but potentially misleading, division. Search and understanding processes interact intimately. The nature of the solver's search is completely determined by his or her understanding of the task and the resulting representation in the form of a problem space. Search processes can lead to the discovery of important new information about a problem, which in turn changes the solver's understanding of the task and leads to restructuring of the problem space.

To review, the information-processing framework assumes that the solution to a problem involves search through a problem space. The problem space is the solver's representation of the task, and this representation is contructed by understanding processes that make use of both general comprehension mechanisms and the problem solver's knowledge of the specific domain. Once a problem space is constructed, efforts to solve the problem may lead to an increase in the solver's understanding, which leads to the generation of a new problem space, and so on, with search and understanding processes alternating in complex ways.

Problem Solving and Search.   Early work in artificial intelligence and on information-processing models of problem solving focused on various kinds of search strategies (Newell, 1969, 1972; Newell & Simon, 1972; Nilsson, 1971). In fact, the terms search and problem solving were, and in some cases still are, used interchangeably by many authors. Pioneering work in artificial intelligence showed that almost any problem could be recast as a search task. This led to the development of a large number of search algorithms and an understanding of their properties (e.g., Nilsson, 1971). Subsequent psychological research has contributed to the understanding of the kinds of search processes that are used by human problem solvers (Atwood & Polson, 1976; Newell & Simon, 1972;

Polson & Jeffries, 1982; Restle, 1970). In particular, the serial character of the human information-processing system and its limited short-term memory impose severe constraints on the kinds of search processes used by humans (Atwood, Masson, & Polson, 1980; Simon, 1978).

The ubiquity of search mechanisms in artificial intelligence programs and in human problem-solving behavior has led Simon (1980) and Newell (1969, 1972, 1980) to assert that search mechanisms are a central component of general problem-solving skills, and that instruction in the use of these search mechanisms would be effective technique for enhancing general problem-solving skills. Newell (1980) calls these general search strategies "weak methods," because they trade power for generality. Two of these methods are so general in their scope and so common in both human and artificial problem solvers that we discuss them briefly. They are *Generate and Test* and *Means–Ends Analysis*.

Generate and Test is the least structured of the weak methods and can vary in its sophistication depending on the capabilities of the generator. Possible solutions are generated one at a time by a process that proposes candidate solutions. Each solution is then evaluated to see if it is acceptable. Unacceptable solutions are rejected, and the generation process continues. The power of the generate-and-test method is completely dependent on the sophistication of the generator. At one end of the continuum, a generator can simply produce solutions in a trial-and-error fashion (Restle, 1970). At the other end, the generator may be a complex process that enumerates all possible solutions in the order of their likelihood of being successful in the particular task.

Means–Ends Analysis is a problem-solving method that guides search by having the solver isolate certain goals to be achieved (ends) and then select the best methods to achieve the specified goal (means). In the classical version of means–ends analysis, as used by a program called the General Problem Solver (GPS)(Ernst & Newell, 1969), the problem solver compares his or her current state with the goal state and generates a list describing the differences between the two states. These differences are then rank ordered by their importance. The most important difference is selected, and the solver retrieves an operator that will reduce this difference, while at the same time producing minimal side effects due to increasing other differences. If possible, the operator is applied. If the operator cannot be applied in this situation, a goal of applying this operator is created, and the means–ends process is applied to the new goal. Means–ends analysis is a powerful and general strategy that has been used in a variety of artificial intelligence programs and has been shown to be used by human problem solvers. It can be used profitably to solve problems ranging from simple puzzlelike tasks (Ernst & Newell, 1969) to extremely complex tasks like writing programs (Simon, 1972) and solving design problems (Simon, 1973).

Research on human problem solving and on artificial intelligence has shown that search processes are used in a variety of task environments by both human and artificial problem solvers. Simon (1980) argues that these search strategies are true general problem-solving mechanisms, that they can be taught, and that extensive instruction in them, especially means–ends analysis, should be the core of any instructional program that attempts to teach general problem-solving skills.

In recent work (Heller & Greeno, 1979; Simon, 1978) the notion of search has been extended to include the concept of search for information as well as direct search to reach a well-specified goal. Pattern completion and pattern recognition processes become a central part of such problem-solving mechanisms. They are important in specifying when necessary information is available and in detecting when enough information has been derived for the orginal goal to be achieved. Solution plans and solvers' ability to exploit partial match information are also important in such situations.

In spite of its many success, serious limitations to the use of search have been uncovered. It is true that almost any task can be recast as a search problem; however, it is also the case that most tasks of any real interest can only be solved in huge search spaces. Work in artificial intelligence has shown that a correct representation of a problem is a critical component in a program to perform the task. Programs that perform tasks like medical diagnosis and the identification of chemical structures at expert levels must incorporate a large amount of knowledge about their specific domain. This suggests that complex problems cannot be solved solely by the use of general search processes. The problem solver must have both powerful search strategies and knowledge about the specific task environment in order to limit the search to fruitful lines of attack.

The Understanding Process.   The analysis and study of understanding processes in problem solving have been related to and influenced by research in understanding of texts. Computer programs that have contributed to our knowledge of language understanding have also often influenced our understanding of problem solving. Examples are programs by Winograd (1972) and Novak (1976), which demonstrated the sophistication of their language comprehension processes by solving problems in a limited domain: a blocks world (Winograd, 1972); elementary physics problems (Novak, 1976). Current theories of the psychological processes involved in language comprehension provide a useful framework from which to examine similar processes used in problem solving.

We use the general theoretical structure proposed by Kintsch and van Dijk (1979), with extensions of this framework by Miller and Kintsch (1980). Alternative analyses of the comprehension process have been presented by Anderson (1976), Norman and Rumelhart (1975), and Schank (1972). Although there are variations in emphasis and detail in these treatments of comprehension, there is agreement as to the major processes.

The Kintsch and van Dijk framework assumes that there are three main elements of the comprehension process. The top level, or executive process, which Kintsch and Van Dijk call the control schema, is a collection of high-level, domain-specific knowledge structures that coordinate problem-solving mechanisms. An example of a control schema for a problem-solving task is the design schema described by Jeffries, Turner, Polson, and Atwood (1981) for the task of software design.

The second component of the Kintsch and van Dijk framework is a generalized set of comprehension processes that are employed in understanding any text. This component controls the parsing of the input into a low-level semantic representation and the subsequent integration of this information into an organized, coherent memory structure representing the comprehender's understanding of the input. This component includes knowledge structures stored in long-term memory that represent the meaning of individual words and more complex concepts, such as frames (Minsky, 1975) or scripts (Schank & Abelson, 1977). Much of this knowledge is both domain and task specific.

There are two functions involved in this domain-independent comprehension process. The first involved the parsing of the text into some sort of semantic representation. The second function is the construction of a coherent representation of the information contained in the text. This second process involves organizing the atomic elements of the semantic repesentation into higher level units on one of two bases. The comprehender first tries to incorporate these elements into some kind of higher level knowledge structure. It such a knowledge structure does not exist, semantic units can be organized on the basis of their internal structure. Text comprehension involves the interaction of the text structure, the reading strategies used by the reader, and the knowledge structures possessed by the reader. The comprehensibility of a piece of text is not simply a property of the text itself.

Recent work on understanding and problem solving can be characterized by the framework provided by the work of Kintsch and his colleagues. Hayes and Simon (1974) present an analysis of the processes used to understand written problem instructions for puzzle tasks like the Tower of Hanoi, water jug problems, and river crossing problems. The Hayes and Simon model is not a general theory of the comprehension process. It contains a specialized control schema and the minimal framelike knowledge structures necessary to generate representations of information required by a GPS-like means–ends problem solver. On the basis of a superficial analysis of the text, UNDERSTAND is able to generate descriptions of initial, intermediate, and goal states for the problem and descriptions of legal moves, using framelike knowledge. For example, UNDERSTAND can deduce that the species of moves required for one particular problem come from the class of *transfer* moves, which involve two agents and an object. The program can then use additional knowledge about transferring that is not explicit in the problem—e.g., that the giver no longer has the object, but the receiver does—to execute correctly the moves needed to solve the problem. UNDERSTAND can also generate predictions of subjects' ratings of the relevance of various components of texts describing such problems. The model is able to account for variations in the difficulty of various isomorphs of the Tower of Hanoi based on differences in the representations that it generates for those isomorphs.

Greeno (1977) presents three criteria that a solver's understanding of a problem must meet to permit its effcient solution. First, the representation of the problem must be coherent; the elements of the solver's understanding of the task must be interrelated in a logical and well-organized fashion. Second, the representation must correctly describe the actual underlying structure of the task. Third, the representation should be well integrated with the remainder of the solver's world knowledge. Observe that the Kintsch and van Dijk theoretical framework specifies the conditions under which a solver can derive from a text a representation of a problem that will satify Greeno's three criteria. Such a structure will result from a knowledge-based comprehension process that makes use of framelike structures and possibly a specialized control schema. The analyses of expert of problem-solving behavior on tasks such as the solution of algebra word problems (Hinsley, Hayes, & Simon, 1977; Paige & Simon, 1966), physics problems (Larkin, 1977), and engineering thermodynamics problems (Bhaskar & Simon, 1977) all demonstrate that expert behavior is mediated by specialized control schemata and domain-specific, framelike knowledge structures.

General Techniques Involving Both Understanding and Search.   Some problem-solving methods employ search in the construction of an adequate understanding of the problem to be solved. They can be conceived as forms of planning, where the search is through a space of possible solution plans. The resulting plan represents the solver's understanding of the task, and its implementation can be carried out by a variety of search strategies. Planning by abstraction and the solution of a problem by decomposing it into a collection of simpler subproblems are two such techniques that have been discussed in the literature (Heller & Greeno, 1979; Polya, 1957; Simon, 1973). Successful employment of either of these general problem-solving strategies requires both knowledge of the general strategy and task-specific information.

Planning by abstraction requires the solver to generate and solve a simplified version of the problem. A simplification is defined by generating an abstract representation, omitting certain details in the problem description. One solves the simplified version by suitable specialized techniques or by a general technique such as means–ends analysis. Then, the solution to the abstract version of the problem is used as a plan for solving the original problem. Planning by abstraction is a powerful general strategy; the most detailed analysis of this strategy has been given by Sacerdoti (1975). Sacerdoti's system, NOAH (*N*ets *o*f *A*ction *H*ierarchies), solves robot planning problems by generating a succession of more detailed abstractions of the problem. NOAH uses the following iterative cycle. First, a representation of the problem at the current level of abstraction is generated. Then, *critics* order the sequence of actions in the abstract plan into a self-consistent, efficient plan for the solution of the problem. This plan is then expanded to the next level of detail, creating a new plan to be criticized.

We claim that although planning by abstraction can be described as a general problem-solving process, its implementation in any particular domain requires that the problem solver have a rich understanding of that domain, including the ability to generate alternative representations of the problem. Although the process of planning by abstraction can be described in a domain-independent manner, and heuristics for constructing abstract representations, deleting irrelevant elements, and then solving the simplified problem can be proposed that are independent of the specific task, the clear examples of planning by abstraction are employed by individuals who have had extensive experience in the domain in question.

Decomposition is a problem-solving strategy in which the problem is reduced to a collection of subproblems. Decomposition can be characterized as a search process, the problem-reduction method (Nilsson, 1971). It is a technique that is extensively used in design tasks (Jeffries et al., 1981; Simon, 1973). Miller and Goldstein (1976) present an analysis of the decomposition process and propose planning grammars to describe the resulting structures. However, their analysis lacks any discussion of how the decomposition method could be applied in an actual problem-solving situation. Schoenfeld (1979) and others have commented that decomposition as described by Polya (1957) is difficult to apply in concrete cases, because although the heuristic itself is clear enough, there is no adequate description of the conditions under which it could apply or of how it is to be applied in a specific case.

We argue that planning by abstraction, decomposition, and other general problem-solving strategies all have one requirement in common—that the solver have complete knowledge of the technique and the domain of application. The qualifications "complete" is the difficulty. Most, if not all, of these strategies are easy to describe and can be easily illustrated. However, they are difficult to apply unless one has sufficient knowledge of the relevant domain to know what constitutes an abstract representation of the problem in question, or how to divide that problem into an appropriate set of subproblems. Although planning by abstraction and decomposition can be described in a domain-independent manner for a given problem solver, a technique may not be separable from the specific domain in which it is used. That is, each of the separate instances that the theorist sees as exemplars of a general technique, such as planning by abstraction, may actually be distinct methods for an individual problem solver, because the general technique and the solver's domain-specific knowledge may be so tightly linked.

Acquisition of Problem-Solving Skill.   At this point in time, we have little knowledge of how the skills represented by the processes and strategies in various models of problem solving are acquired. Information-processing theories of learning and skill acquisition have not progressed to the point where one could make definitive statements on how to construct an instructional program to teach thinking and problem-solving skills. What follows are speculations derived from various researchers' intuitions concerning how modern work in cognition can contribute to education, and conjectures derived from the limited amount of work that has been done on learning to date.

There is broad agreement that any educational program must have specific objectives to maximize its chances of being successful. There has been much emphasis in education on the specification of behavioral objectives. Greeno (1976) and others have generalized these criteria to include cognitive objectives. Cognitive objectives are the knowledge structures and the processes to operate on those structures that must be acquired by the student in order to perform a task successfully. The information-processing framework gives us the tools to develop explicit models of an individual's performance on a variety of tasks. These models specify the knowledge and processes required to solve problems in some narrowly specified domain. They specify at least partially the cognitive objectives in terms of the processes and knowledge structures that must be learned to become effective at that task.

In information-processing research, metacognitive knowledge—that is, conscious awareness of oneself as a problem solver—plays an important role in problem-solving success. It has been suggested that the importance of this kind of knowledge be communicated to students to enable them more effectively to monitor their learning and problem-solving behavior (Nickerson, Perkins, & Smith, 1980; Norman, 1980; Simon, 1980). Simon (1980) suggests that students should be taught that much of their knowledge needs to be organized procedurally, as condition–action pairs, or productions. A completely understood concept in the form of a production contains both the applicability conditions and the relevant procedural steps; the student must understand that both are necessary to acquiring a useful piece of knowledge.

Any course attempting to teach problem-solving skills must ensure that students understand both the conditions under which the components of their knowledge are applicable and relationships among various pieces of knowledge, so that they can coordinate the use of several techniques to attack a complicated problem. In short, a large collection of problem-solving information requires some kind of higher order control schema or executive process for its effective management and utilization.

Simon (1980) argues that much of our procedural knowledge is communicated through worked-out and annotated examples in textbooks. The process of learning by examples has been studied in the area of artificial intelligence. Two programs that learn from examples are one that acquires concepts, written by Winston (1970), and another that learns generalized algebraic operations from worked-out examples (Neves, 1978). In both programs, the structure of the examples and the relationship between successive examples is critical for the learning process. No skill can be learned without practice on the operations involved. Because examples form the basis of much practice on problem-solving skills, learning can best take place if there are both a sufficient number of examples and practice problems, and if these problems are structured to give the most useful amount of information.

Thus, although we are far from a theory of how to teach problem-solving skills, we can point to several attributes that any such theory should have. It should have explicit cognitive objectives, explicitly teach metacognitive skills and executive processes, and convey information via an appropriately constructed set of examples.

The Divergent-Production Paradigm

There is a large literature outside the information-processing framework that deals with instruction in general problem-solving and other cognitive skills (Davis, 1973; Feldhusen, Speedie, & Treffinger, 1971; Nickerson et al., 1980). This second theoretical tradition, which we refer to as the divergent-thinking framework, dominates work on general problem solving and creativity in educational and other applied settings. The primary objectives of writers in this tradition are to develop programs to enhance creativity in many areas of instruction (e.g., science, language arts), and to improve thinking and problem-solving skills, especially those necessary to deal with ill-structured problems (e.g., eliminating air pollution, selecting a career). Well-known programs founded on this theoretical framework include the CoRT and the Productive Thinking Programs reviewed here, brain storming (Osborne, 1963), lateral thinking (de Bono, 1970), and synectics (Gordon, 1961).

We perceive the majority of the writers and specific instructional programs that have been developed in the context of the divergent-production framework to share the following set of assumptions:

1. Thinking is viewed as a skill.
2. Motivation of students and development of positive self-image are stressed.
3. The importance of perception and pattern recognition in problem solving, including both positive and negative effects, is stressed.
4. Many programs incorporate some or all of the problem-solving heuristics discussed by Polya (1957).
5. Divergent thinking is emphasized; great emphasis is placed on the skills required to generate a large number of alternatives in the process of formulating a problem, considering alternative solutions, etc.

Comparison of the Two Approaches

The information-processing and divergent-production frameworks have both important commonalities and differences. Research in the information-processing tradition has focused on the development of a theoretical understanding of thinking and problem solving in a wide variety of task environments ranging from puzzlelike tasks to physics, geometry, and algebra word problem solving to developing an understanding of problem solving in ill-structured domains like musical composition and design. Writers in the divergent production tradition have focused on issues of creativity in the arts and sciences and dealing with ill-structured problems like choice of career. There has been little emphasis in the information-processing tradition on the development of programs to enhance general problem-solving skills (but see Tuma & Reif, 1980). Little systematic work on motivation has been done within the information-processing tradition, although Simon (1967) has presented an information-processing analysis of motivational processes. Both paradigms share the view that thinking is a skill (Anderson, 1981). In addition, both agree on the central importance of perception and pattern recognition in problem solving. Finally, both view general problem-solving skills in a fashion that is not dissimilar to that of Polya (1957), in that both claim there are a large number of understanding and search techniques and that the solver must have efficient management strategies to coordinate this large body of strategic knowledge.

On a superficial level, the two paradigms seem to make little contact with each other in that they do not subscribe to a shared body of theoretical ideas, there is little overlap in the literature that each group of writers cite, and treatments of common tasks can be very different. However, the two paradigms share an important body of historical ideas about problem-solving processes. Working through the writings of workers in the divergent production paradigm is an interesting experience for individuals like ourselves, whose intuitions have been shaped by the information-processing framework. Much of what researchers in the divergent-thinking paradigm say about problem solving is consistent with current theoretical thinking in the information-processing framework.

The core ideas underlying the divergent-production paradigm seem to be derived from a combination of Duncker (1945), Katona (1940), and Wertheimer (1959), and Polya's work on problem solving in mathematics. Polya and the Gestalt work on the problem solving also had a central role in the development of the current information-processing framework. The two frameworks also share the view that understanding processes and the construction of the representation of the problem are critical for successful performance in any task environment and that a large part of the solution of any ill-structured problem is dominated by understanding processes. Current work in the information-processing tradition on comprehension, perception, and pattern recognition could be used as a theoretical basis for the exploration of many of the issues raised and phenomena described by workers in the divergent-production framework.

There is complete agreement on the importance of a correct conceptualization or representation of a problem. Writers in both traditions emphasize the importance of perceptual and comprehension mechanisms in generating a representation that will mediate successful solution of a problem. Much of the current work in the information-processing framework attempts to explicate the detailed structure of representations underlying problem solving in various domains. There is also substantial effort being devoted to theoretical analysis of basic perceptual and comprehension processes. Many of the problem-solving techniques proposed by adherents to the divergent-production framework generate a large number of alternative representations of a given problem through the training of appropriate perceptual and comprehension processes.

However, the two frameworks have different views about the functions of domain-specific knowledge in perception and comprehension. All information-processing analyses of these processes conclude that both require extensive domain-specific information. Characterizations of perception (Marr, 1982), masters' level performance in chess (Chase & Simon, 1973), skilled memory (Chase & Ericsson, 1981), and story comprehension (Schank & Abelson, 1977) all assume that building the representations necessary to mediate skilled performance in these areas involved extensive domain-specific knowledge. Similar conclusions come from studies of a wide variety of problem-solving tasks, ranging from the solution of elementary physics problems (Larkin, McDermott, Simon, & Simon, 1980) to software design (Jeffries et al., 1981).

As we understand it, writers in the divergent-production paradigm implicitly or explicitly assume that domain-independent perceptual and comprehension processes can be taught, and it is possible to teach students general, domain-independent, problem-solving skills. Thus, the most central disagreement between the two paradigms concerns the role of domain-specific knowledge in problem solving.

In spite of the important similarities between the two frameworks, we have two strong reservations about programs that have been developed within the divergent-production framework. The first is that few of these programs seem to be based on a well-formalized set of notions about thinking and problem solving. A majority of the concepts incorporated into these programs are not unreasonable, but they are abstract and at times surprisingly difficult to grasp. There is no characterization of the detailed descriptions of process that dominate much of the work in the information-processing paradigm. We feel that lack of an explicit characterization of problem-solving processes can compromise attempts to construct instructional programs. Explicit notions about process define behavioral and cognitive objectives for an instructional program. Without well-defined objectives it seems to us to be difficult to generate reasonable lecture material, well thought through, worked-out examples, and as effective set of grades problems for drill and practice.

Our second reservation about the divergent-production framework has to do with its focus on sheer fluency in the generation of ideas, alternative solutions, and alternative courses of action. A large number of the techniques described in these programs are simply ways of generating alternative representations or courses of action. There is little discussion of the kinds of knowledge involved in the generation process and of the constraints necessary to generate candidate solutions that have some reasonable probability of being useful or successful. From the point of view of the information-processing perspective, the emphasis on sheer fluency leads to a primitive variant of a generate-and-test method as an individual's sole general problem-solving method. Students are not provided with specialized techniques or detailed background that would enable them to control the generation process so that the potentially most useful hypotheses are generated, nor is there much emphasis on the careful evaluation of the ideas produced.

We have strong reservations about problem-solving techniques dominated by notions of ideational fluency in many problem-solving situations (e.g., physics problems). However, even restricting consideration to open-ended, ill-structured problems that are the focus of work in the divergent-production tradition, it is unclear whether skill at generating unevaluated ideas improves thinking or creativity. Summaries of results presented in Nickerson et al. (1980) and in Mansfeld, Bussey, and Krepelka (1978) suggest that they do not.

OVERVIEW OF THE FOUR PROGRAMS

The following are short descriptions of each of the four programs analyzed. For each we give the goals and objectives of the program, its intended audience, a description of its contents, its theoretical basis, and a review of research done to evaluate it. Our analysis of the programs is postponed until we discuss the criteria we use for conducting such an analysis.

Productive Thinking Program

The Productive Thinking Program of Covington, Crutchfield, Davies, and Olton (1974) is a set of commercially marketed materials that attempts to teach fifth and sixth graders to use their minds "in an effective, intelligent, and creative way directed at the solution of the problem." It purports to teach generalized problem-solving skills, such as generating hypotheses and determining what is relevant to a solution. It consists of a set of 15 lessons to be used over approximately one semester by children in the upper elementary grades. The lessons can easily be used either individually or in groups.

The materials consist of 15 student booklets, each containing a basic lesson plus a set of supplementary problems, a teacher's guide, and some auxiliary materials (duplicating masters, visual aids). The basic lessons introduce Lila and Jim, two children who embark on a series of adventures under the tutelage of their Uncle John. In each escapade they are called upon to solve a mystery, where they learn to make use of one or more "thinking guides," which form the basis of the program. For example, in one lesson they discover how some seemingly supernatural "tricks" are performed. The lessons are presented in a "cartoon" format. After each basic lesson there are a set of supplemental problems designed to give additional practice in the newly learned skills. These problems are taken from a variety of domains—puzzles, social studies, science, etc.

The program also contains a teacher's guide. It delineates the points to be emphasized in each lesson, provides answers to the supplemental problems, and gives ideas for areas of additional discussion. A large wall chart is also provided so that the thinking guides can be made constantly available to students.

The core of the program is the set of 16 thinking guides presented as Fig.12.1. They attempt to develop thinking skills in several areas. First the student is encouraged to solve a problem in an organized, hierarchical fashion (e.g., think planfully; check the facts; start with general possibilities and expand them into particular ideas). Second, the importance of generating many ideas is stressed, and ways to accomplish this are given (e.g., think of unusual ideas; pick out the important concepts in the problem and generate ideas from each one). Third, the ideas generated must be evaluated (e.g., check ideas against the facts). Finally, the student is encouraged to have positive attitudes toward the thinking process and his or her thinking skills (e.g, don't give up, keep an open mind).

The program appears to have as its foundation three basic concepts. First, to solve problems effectively students must go about it in a systematic fashion

1. Take time to reflect on a problem before you begin work. Decide exactly what the problem is that you are trying to solve.

2. Get all the facts of the problem clearly in mind.

3. Work on the problem in a planful way.

4. Keep an open mind. Don't jump to conclusions about the answer to a problem.

5. Think of many ideas for solving a problem. Don't stop with just a few.

6. Try to think of unusual ideas.

7. As a way of getting ideas, pick out all the important objects and persons in the problem and think carefully about each one.

8. Think of several general possibilities for a solution and then figure out many particular ideas for each possibility.

9. As you search for ideas, let your mind freely explore things around you. Almost anything can suggest ideas for a solution.

10. Always check each idea with the facts to decide how likely the idea is.

11. If you get stuck on a problem, keep thinking. Don't be discouraged or give up.

12. When you run out of ideas, try looking at the problem in a new and different way.

13. Go back and review all the facts of the problem to make sure you have not missed something important.

14. Start with an unlikely idea. Just suppose that it is possible, and then figure out how it could be.

15. Be on the lookout for odd or puzzling facts in a problem. Explaining them can lead you to new ideas for a solution.

16. When there are several different puzzling things in a problem, try to explain them with a single idea that will connect them all together.

FIG. 12.1. The 16 thinking guides from the Productive Thinking Program.

with explicit awareness of what they are trying to accomplish at each step. Second, thinking skills need to be encouraged, and students must be convinced that it is possible to improve their thinking. Third, there is a specific set of cognitive skills whose development will lead to more effective thinking. The ideas about the nature of those skills appear to come from the Gestalt tradition. They focus particularly on ideational fluency, the ability to generate large numbers of preferably unusual ideas, and on ways of restructuring or redefining the problem.

As of this writing, an impressive amount of research has been conducted in order to evaluate the effectiveness of the Productive Thinking Program, and additional research is now in progress (see Covington's chapter, this volume). The results have been uniformly positive. We discuss one such study by Olton and Crutchfield (1969). The study assesses the effects of the program on fifth and sixth graders when presented over an 8 week period, in comparison to a control group. A split-class technique was used, and the two groups were equated for both IQ and achievement test level. Pretests, posttests and follow-up tests six months later were given. Although the groups did not differ on pretest measures, the instructed group was significantly better than the control both immediately after the program and six months later. This superiority existed both for measures of thinking skill and for improved attitudes toward thinking. The improvement occurred for students at all intelligence levels, not just for selected subgroups.

The major difficulty in interpreting the results of this study lies in the dependent measures and how they were scored. A variety of "productive thinking" tests were administered. These range from a puzzle in which the student had to discover which of 10 suspects is buried in an ancient tomb and justify his or her choice, to an essay on poverty in the United States. They were scored for such things as number of acceptable ideas generated, number of puzzling facts explained, number of causes listed. The scores for each variable measured were ranked, and the subject was rescored as being above or below the median for that variable. The sum of these latter scores over all variables constitutes the main dependent measure. The justification for such a measure is not clear, nor is its effect on the outcome of the study, if any, apparent.

The variables scored for are problematic,. The test items were quite open-ended, and clearly could not be scored as simply right or wrong. The selection of appropriate dimensions in such a case is a difficult decision. In this study, the focus seems to have been on measures of number of ideas generated. Fluency in generating ideas is one of the explicit goals that the program trains for; however, for these items it is hard to determine the relationship between number of ideas mentioned and a "good" or "correct" solution to the problem. Moreover, some of the scoring dimensions may have been biased against the controls. For instance, on one problem subjects were scored on the "number of relevant information-seeking question asked." Although the Productive Thinking Program encourages students to seek out additional facts, it is not apparent whether the control subjects were aware that asking for information was even permitted.

Another area of concern is how the scoring was carried out. With such subjective scoring criteria it is important to remove any sources of potential bias from the scores. Not only should the scoring be carried out blind, but the scorers should not be highly familiar with the program itself. The Productive Thinking Program would appear to engender in students a particular style of problem solving that an experienced observer might be able to pick out from cursory examination of a subject's response to an item. Unfortunately no information is given in the article about how the scoring was conducted.

This study points out the difficulties of conducting an evaluation of such programs. It is by far the most rigorous of the studies we encountered. Careful attention has been paid to subject selection procedures and other methodological issues. The remaining matters of concern—dependent variables and scoring methods—are particularly difficult issues to resolve in these studies.

CoRT Thinking Materials

The CoRT (*Co*gnitive *R*esearch *T*rust) Thinking Lessons are a 2-year course for improving general thinking skills by de Bono (1973). They attempt to teach thinking skills in a range of areas—problem solving, interpersonal discussions and creative thinking. The lessons are intended to be used in groups and are claimed to be useful for children of all ages.

The materials are divided into six units, each intended to be used over a 10-week period. In addition, there is a separate "Thinking Course for Juniors" for children ages 5 to 12, who may not have sufficient verbal skills to make productive use of the regular course. There is also a collection of games called "Think Links," intended to provide practice in developing creative thinking skills. The materials in the basic course consist of a teacher's manual for each unit and a set of leaflets to be handed out to students (the final unit does contain a textbook). The teacher's manual is quite detailed. It contains a discussion of the goals of the lessons, specific suggestions on how to teach them to different age and ability groups, reports of research studies, potential exam questions to test the thinking skills, and suggestions on how to cope with problems. The individual lesson descriptions include an overview of the points to cover, practice items with suggested answers, and guidelines as to the amount of time to be spent on each item.

The four-page student leaflet contains a discussion of the principle being taught, examples of its use, practice items, discussion of points to keep in mind, and ideas for a longer project to practice the concept. Each lesson focuses on a single concept or thinking mechanism. The practice items and projects are questions for group discussions or essays. They allow students to develop fluency with the principle being taught. For example, in the first lesson, PMI (consider the good (plus), bad (minus), and interesting points of an idea), students are asked to practice this concept by examining the idea that all cars should be required to be painted yellow.

The organization of the six units and the principles taught in each are shown in Fig. 12.2. The first unit covers basic thinking skills, the ability to examine an idea in detail, evaluate it from different perspectives, and generate alternative solutions. The second unit focuses on basic operations of thinking—comparison, analysis, drawing of conclusions, etc. The third unit deals with thinking in adversarial situations. It discusses the use of evidence, ways of making a point, and mistakes in thinking. Creative thinking is the goal of the fourth unit—restructuring problems, brainstorming techniques, combining ideas. The fifth unit covers the role of information and feelings in thinking. It distinguishes among types of information gathering and discusses beliefs, values, and emotions. The final unit teaches a concrete procedure for employing thinking skills. It gives an ordered list of activities to be carried out when solving a problem. This unit can be used as the final summing up of the course, or separately as a "short course" in thinking.

The Thinking Course for Juniors is intended for elementary school age children. It makes use of visual items to compensate for the lesser verbal skills of this age group. The course centers around designs, or inventions. Students are asked to draw designs (e.g., a chocolate-making machine), complete partial drawings, criticize completed drawings, or illustrate a situation in a cartoon. No specific instruction in thinking is given; these are simply a set of exercises to practice thinking.

Think Links is a collection of games that facilitate thinking practice. The basic apparatus is a set of cards with drawings of objects or words on them. In a typical game, cards are selected and a player must describe the relationship between them. There are several dozen variations on the game for different age groups and different numbers of players.

De Bono, who is perhaps best known for his ideas on creativity, which he calls lateral thinking, distinguishes between two types of thinking processes—perceptual and logical. He feels the logical thinking process is currently well taught by the school system, but that most people are notoriously poor at the perceptual aspects of thinking. In this category he includes generating ideas, defining the problem, and restructuring the problem. Again, notice the similarity to the Gestalt tradition. De Bono particularly stresses the role of patterns and the need for an effective thinker to break loose from these patterns. Many of his thinking principles are means of dealing with explicit patterns in people's thinking. For example, one principle forces a student to look at a problem from someone else's viewpoint (e.g., the issue of exams from a teacher's point of view), as a means of gathering information relevant to its solution. He also emphasizes creating new patterns, as in using a random word or object as a stimulus to generate new ideas about a topic.

CoRT I: Breadth
　　Treatment of Ideas　　　　　　　Planning
　　Factors Involved　　　　　　　　Priorities
　　Rules　　　　　　　　　　　　　Alternatives
　　Consequences　　　　　　　　　Decisions
　　Objectives　　　　　　　　　　Viewpoint

CoRT II: Organization
　　Recognize　　　　　　　　　　Start
　　Analyze　　　　　　　　　　　Organize
　　Compare　　　　　　　　　　　Focus
　　Select　　　　　　　　　　　　Consolidate
　　Find Other Ways　　　　　　　Conclude

CoRT III: Interaction
　　Examine Both Sides　　　　　　Being Right 1
　　Evidence: Type　　　　　　　　Being Right 2
　　Evidence: Value　　　　　　　　Being Wrong 1
　　Evidence: Structure　　　　　　Being Wrong 2
　　Agreement, Disagreement, Irrelevance　　　Outcome

CoRT IV: Creativity
　　Yes, No, and Po　　　　　　　Define the Problem
　　Stepping Stone　　　　　　　　Remove Faults
　　Random Input　　　　　　　　Combination
　　Concept Challenge　　　　　　Requirements
　　Dominant Idea　　　　　　　　Evaluation

CoRT V: Information and Feeling
　　Information　　　　　　　　　Belief
　　Questions　　　　　　　　　　Ready-mades
　　Clues　　　　　　　　　　　　Emotions and Ego
　　Contradiction　　　　　　　　Values
　　Guessing　　　　　　　　　　Simplication and Clarification

CoRT VI: Action
　　Target　　　　　　　　　　　Input
　　Expand　　　　　　　　　　　Solutions
　　Contract　　　　　　　　　　Choice
　　Target–Expand–Contract　　　　Operation
　　Purpose　　　　　　　　　　　The Five Stages

FIG. 12.2.　The Six CoRT thinking units and the ten lessons in each unit.

The teaching of thinking is best done by giving practice in thinking, according to de Bono. The lessons spend a few minutes explaining the new principle, and the rest of the time is spent practicing that principle. De Bono emphasizes that the focus of the practice should be on the skill of thinking, not on the content of the problems being solved. To assist students in remembering the devices and aids to effective thinking that he teaches, he makes extensive use of mnemonics and visual aids.

De Bono relates a great deal of "research" done with CoRT thinking materials. Each of the teacher's guides contains a section describing some experiments that have shown the superiority of CoRT-trained students. Much of this research is quite informal: testimonials from teachers and students who have used the materials, summaries of discussions by CoRT-trained groups versus an untrained group on the same topic. He does give the results of several group studies. In none of the studies does he report any statistical analyses, however; he leaves one to draw conclusions from the tabulated data. The point of some of the studies is less than obvious. For example, he describes an experiment that compares a group who were given a choice of two responses to a statement: agree or disagree, to another group given three choices: agree, po (meaning—more or less—abstain), or disagree. Not surprisingly, for the group given three choices, a large fraction (about one-third over several groups) selected "po." For most of the other experiments, the dependent variable is the number of ideas generated. The CoRT-trained groups consistently generate more ideas than the untrained groups. In some experiments the ideas are classified by types. In these, the CoRT-trained groups show a larger relative increase in ideas that de Bono categorizes as "nonegocentric." None of the research described was done with students who had taken the full CoRT sequence. Some had done only one lesson, and the most experienced group had done only 14 of the 60 lessons.

Patterns of Problem Solving

Rubinstein's (1975) *Patterns of Problem Solving* is intended to be used as a textbook in a one-term college-level course in general problem solving. It is the basis of one such course, taught in the Engineering School at UCLA for over 10 years, and it has been used at several other universities. The course has been taken by college students at all levels and from a wide variety of disciplines. The author attempts to impart a set of guidelines for use when solving problems, as well as to teach a range of techniques that can be usefully applied in many problem-solving situations.

A selected table of contents for the book appears as Fig.12.3. The first chapter gives some general advice that should be applicable to solving many types of problems. This included such precepts as (1) get the total picture; (2) keep an open mind; (3) work backwards; (4) use analogies; (5) discuss the problem with someone as a means of getting unstuck.

The next three chapters cover some basic entities whose concepts may be applicable to solving problems. These are: language systems, computers, and probability theory. A general overview of each of these topics is given, concentrating on terminology and basic background information. The language chapter discusses formal and informal languages, metalanguages, set theory, communication systems, and redundancy. The computer chapter covers the basic

Chapter 1: Problem Solving
  1–3 Models of problem-solving process
  1–4 Kinds of problems
  1–5 Guides to problem solving
  1–6 Failure to use known information—Difficulty 1
  1–7 Introduction of unnecessary constraints—Difficulty 2
  1–9 Paths to a solution
  1–10 Discussing your problem

Chapter 2: Language and Communication
  2–2 The structure of language
  2–4 Knowledge of the language and
      knowledge of the world
  2–6 The numbers
  2–8 Language of statements—Symbolic logic
  2–9 Truth tables
  2–12 Algebra of logic and switching circuits
  2–14 Language of sets—Sets, subsets, and operations on sets
  2–16 Modern communication systems
  2–18 Computer language

Chapter 3: Computers: Fundamental Concepts
  3–3 Basic components of a digital computer
  3–5 Flow chart
  3–10 How a computer computes

Chapter 4: Probability and the Will to Doubt
  4–2 Probability and doubt
  4–4 Laws of probability
  4–5 Bayes' equation and relevance of information
  4–9 Probability and credibility

Chapter 5: Models and Modeling
  5–2 The purpose of models
  5–3 The nature of models
  5–4 Validation of models
  5–5 Classification of models

Chapter 6: Probabilistic Models
  6–2 Populations and samples
  6–3 Probability distribution models
  6–4 Normal distribution model
  6–6 Central limit theorem and its application
  6–8 From sample to population—Estimation of parameters
  6–9 Testing hypotheses—Errors of omission and commission
  6–10 Simulation of probabilistic models—Monte Carlo method

Chapter 7: Decision-making Models
  7–2 Decision models
  7–4 Decision making under risk
  7–5 Decision making under certainty
  7–6 Utility theory
  7–8 Decision making under conflict—Game theory

Chapter 8: Optimization Models
  8–3 Linear Programming—Exposure
  8–6 Nonlinear programming
  8–7 Dynamic programming
  8–8 Sequential decisions with random outcomes

Chapter 9: Dynamic System Models
  9–2 Building blocks in dynamic system models
  9–4 Homeostasis—Control of feedback systems
  9–7 Characteristics of feedback systems
  9–8 Simulation of dynamic systems

Chapter 10: Values and Models of Behavior
  10–2 Role of values in problem solving
  10–6 A model of ethical behavior
  10–10 Cost–benefit assessment of values
  10–13 Metrization of preferences
  10–14 The Delphi Method

FIG. 12.3.   Selected Table of Contents for Rubinstein (1975).

constructs of computer hardware and software, machine language, and the operation of the computer. The section on probability discusses basic probability concepts, Bayes' theorem, objective and subjective probabilities, and information theory.

The topics covered in these three chapters seem to be constrained by the author's ideas about what is interesting and useful about these domains. No attempt is made to give comprehensive coverage of an area or to cover any concept in depth. Rubinstein appears to be trying to select topics that will be useful as analogies to problems encountered in other domains. Some of the subjects are quite idiosyncratic. For example, the computer chapter devotes much time to a description of a hypothetical machine language, but gives only cursory treatment to higher level languages, which college students are more likely to have been exposed to and would find more useful in their problem-solving activities. Moreover, it contains an extended explanation of the workings of a half adder, which would seem to be little more than an intriguing diversion to anyone outside the field of engineering.

The next chapter examines the role of models in problem solving. Rubinstein defines models as abstractions of the real word and claims that their use is, or should be, pervasive in problem solving. He discusses the uses of models, their validation and falsification, and the need to be aware of the simplifying assumptions made. He then describes models from a variety of domains, but concentrates on mathematical and physical models. Rubinstein's claim is that all complex problem solving is at least implicitly model driven, and that performance can be improved both by making students more aware of how to use models and by giving them a larger collection of models to build upon.

The rest of the book focuses on particular types of models: probabilistic models, decision models, optimization models, dynamic models, and models of ethical behavior. Each chapter included the material that would be covered in approximately the initial few weeks of a course devoted to the same topic. Some idea of the items covered can be gained from examining Fig.12.3. The material is quite technical. There does not appear to be any attempt to water it down for the mathematically disinclined student.

The final chapter, on models of ethical behavior, discusses the roles of personal and cultural values in problem solving. It does not teach any aids to problem solving, but tries to make the student more aware of how and when values enter into the solution process. The chapter seems oriented more toward setting up topics for lively discussion than anything else.

Each chapter of the book contains a large number of exercises ranging from puzzles to open-ended discussion questions. One set of exercises recurs throughout the book. In Chapter 1 students are asked to select a problem of interest to them, perhaps a problem in the area of their major, or the problem of how to choose an apartment. After each chapter, the student is asked to apply the concepts taught in that chapter to the solution of the selected problem.

Rubinstein's book is an eclectic mixture of techniques that might be useful in solving problems, ranging from the most general (e.g., work backwards) to the very specific (e.g., linear programming). The approach is primarily pragmatic—material is presented, examples of its use are given, and the student is left to find ways to apply it (if possible) to the problem he or she wishes to solve. When Rubinstein does cover some general aspects of problem solving (e.g., the role of memory), an information-processing approach is taken. The human mind is described as an information-processing system, analogous to a computer, and the use of the general guidelines is covered within this framework.

Pervasive throughout the book is Rubinstein's emphasis on models. The model used to solve a particular problem may be as simple as the translation of an algebra word problem into an equation or as complex as the abstractions and simplifications that underlie Newtonian mechanics. Although pains are taken to show that models can be used in any discipline, the models explored in detail are often drawn from the engineering physical, and mathematical sciences.

Some attempt has been made to evaluate the course on which the book is based (Rubinstein, 1980). The course employs additional teaching techniques; for example, the use of peer tutors—students who have recently taken the course—to work with students in a one-to-one basis on the exercises. In the 10 years the course has been used, Rubinstein has generated a large number of testimonials from students in many disciplines about its use. Perhaps the best testimony to the popularity of the course is the fact that it currently has an enrollment of 1200 students each quarter.

Popularity is not the same as effectiveness, however. The only study we discovered on the effectiveness of the course came from S. Barlett, who taught a course from the same book at St. Louis University. He gave students pre- and posttests using the California Test of Mental Maturity. Gains were found in the posttest. This is surprising, particularly as nothing that the course teaches would seem to be particularly relevant to the types of items usually found on such tests (e.g., analogies). However, not enough information is given to determine what alternative explanations might be possible. The most likely one, since no control group was used, is that the improvement is due to practice on the test used.

How to Solve Problems

Wickelgren's (1973) *How to Solve Problems: Elements of a Theory of Problems and Problem Solving* combines a theoretical treatment of an information-processing theory of problem solving with practical instruction in how to solve problems. The book is intended to be a textbook for a problem-solving course or for individual use at the college or possibly advanced high school level. Wickelgren explicity limits the focus of the book to "formal" problems, primarily in the sciences and mathematics. By formal he means problems that are at the well-structured end of the well/ill-structured continuum; that is, having well-specified given information, clearly delineated allowable operations, and an easily recognizable "correct" solution. Thus, solving a mathematical theorem and solving a chess puzzle are formal problems, but composing a fugue and designing a building are not.

The book covers a variety a problem-solving strategies. First, the concept of a problem space is explicitly covered. Students are taught to parse a problem into the givens, goal, and allowable operations. From this framework several strategies are covered: inference (making implicit properties of the problem explicit), generate-and-test strategies, state evaluation, subgoaling, solution by contradiction, working backwards, solving by analogy to a similar problem (e.g., special cases). All these topics are covered, using puzzles or simple algebra and geometry problems. The final two chapters of the book teach some specific techniques needed for solving mathematics and science problems—issues of representation and techniques for particular domains.

The strategies are illustrated by numerous examples. For each example, the student is given guidance in solving the problem, by means of a series of more and more detailed hints, and admonitions to attempt a solution after each, until one is finally given. However, there are no practice exercises in the book. Wickelgren makes an effort to point out the relationships between problems and techniques. He frequently begins the discussion of an example by describing several techniques that do not work, but might be reasonably tried, as well as explaining those methods that should not be attempted.

The information on how to apply the various strategies suffers from the same lack of specificity that all these programs share to a greater or lesser degree. For example, in his discussion of solving a problem by generalizing from a special case, Wickelgren has an extended explanation of the criticality of choosing the right special case. He gives several examples of how the wrong special case can lead one seriously astray. However, no advice is given about how to choose cases or how to tell if a selected special case is the wrong one (other than that it does not lead to discovering the solution). Of course, to the best of our knowledge, no such procedure exists, but that is of little consolation to the student trying to solve a difficult problem.

The book is strongly based on an information-processing view of problem solving. It is also intended to be used as a textbook on the theory of problem solving. In fact, in some places more attention has been paid to describing the theory underlying a given technique than to presenting a viable procedure for its use. Wickelgren cites Newell and Simon and Polya as the originators of most of the principles taught in the book. To the best of our knowledge, there has been no research done evaluating their effectiveness.

ANALYSES OF THE FOUR PROGRAMS

Analysis Procedures and Dimensions

On the following pages we analyze the instructional programs by asking whether their assumptions, objectives, and techniques are consistent with modern research on problem solving. In analyzing the programs, we take two approaches. First, we have derived from the basic research literature on problem solving in content domains some ideas about criteria that successful programs of instruction in general problem-solving skills should meet. As indicated earlier, our present knowledge of general problem-solving skills is limited. Thus, although we can spell out criteria that we would like successful programs to meet, we cannot always describe how a program might go about meeting these criteria, nor should we expect existing programs to meet fully all these criteria, as that would pre-suppose a more detailed understanding of general problem-solving skills than presently exists. Our goal in using these criteria is to give the reader some insight into desirable features that are completely or partially missing from existing programs and to help the reader understand ways in which our knowledge about general problem-solving skills needs to be further developed so that it can serve as a better foundation for instruction. We have listed the criteria and questions that will guide this part of the analysis as follows:

1. Explicit cognitive objectives.
   Is the program based on an explicit model of thinking and problem solving?
   Earlier, we discussed the need for a clear statement of cognitive objectives as well as behavioral objectives. We feel that well-structured lessons that have explicit goals, worked-out examples, and problem sets that provide for useful feedback and effective self-monitoring, all depend on a fully articulated model of the cognitive skills to be taught.
2. A wide variety of explicit problem-solving techniques.
   Does the program introduce the variety of comprehension and search techniques appropriate to a wide range of problem-solving tasks? Futhermore, are the various techniques described in a clear, detailed manner, so the processes involved and the applicability conditions of each are effectively communicated to the student?
   Polya (1957), de Bono (1970), and writers in the information-processing framework all agree that effective problem solving involves a large collection of techniques. These programs should include instruction in a rich variety of techniques that have been identified as being effectively used by humans, e.g., means-ends analysis.
3. Development of a control schema.
   Are the various problem-solving techniques presented to the student in

a structure that makes clear the relationships among them and provides for the development of management strategies or a control schema?

Artificial intelligence programs (e.g., Ernst & Newell, 1969; Stefik, 1981) that employ a number of problem-solving techniques all incorporate a complex executive that is capable of making decisions about when to employ a particular technique. Many writers (e.g., Simon, 1973) argue that effective problem solving on the part of humans also requires that there be some kind of executive process that enables solvers to select appropriate techniques for application in specific situations.

4. Useful examples and problems.

Does each lesson include worked-out examples and problems of graded difficulty that provide relevant drill and practice?

The purpose of instruction in the programs we are discussing is the acquisition of various cognitive skills. Both the information-processing and divergent-production frameworks assume that part of the acquisition process will involve drill and practice on exercises that instruct in the cognitive skill of interest. A clear description of the skill to be taught is a useful aid in instruction. However, well-designed opportunities for drill and practice are the necessary ingredient for the development of any cognitive skill.

As the reader can see by examining the foregoing criteria and reviewing our earlier characterizations of the research literature, these are criteria for the future—ones that we hope that programs of instruction in general problem-solving skills will eventually be able to meet, as our understanding of these skills advances. Even though existing programs of instruction have limitations when appraised according to these criteria—that is, even though none possesses all the features that we consider characteristic of a completely successful program—the existing programs do contain some interesting ideas about the nature of problem solving that are consistent with current knowledge, and in some ways they go as far in teaching general problem-solving skills as current knowledge permits. Thus, as an additional part of our analysis of each program, we examine the various techniques in which the programs are offering instruction and ask whether these seem to be sensible ones to ask students to learn in view of our present limited knowledge about the nature and acquisition of general problem-solving skills.

Observe that our approach to analyzing the instructional programs omits many topics and issues that are clearly relevant in conducting a more comprehensive evaluation of them. For example, our analysis does not deal with the formats of the actual instructional material, instructors' manuals and the requirements for teacher training, the resources required to implement the program, the amount of time required by the program, and the host of similar issues. We do not claim that such issues are irrelevant. However, we feel that the issues we have focused on are central to the utility of any program that attempts to teach basic skills.

Discussion of issues involved in the actual implementation of the program or its effectiveness in the classroom should follow the kind of analysis undertaken here.

Productive Thinking Program

Explicit Cognitive Objectives.   The Productive Thinking Program is designed for use in fifth- and sixth-grade classrooms. It is not based on one particular model of problem solving, but the various principles taught in this program are drawn from a variety of traditions—the divergent-production framework, Gestalt psychology, Polya's work, and motivational concerns. The authors have clearly taken an eclectic approach in selecting techniques that they feel can be taught to their target age group during a 6-week course. The cognitive objectives of the course are summarized in the 16 thinking guides presented in Fig. 12.1. The guides are stated at a level similar to that of Polya's heuristics for mathematical problem solving. They are taught using a fairly extensive collection of concrete examples presented in the training material.

Wide Variety of Explicit Problem-Solving Techniques.   As we said in our description of the Productive Thinking Program. It focuses on three basic sets of issues: metacognitive skills, improvement of the student's self-image concerning his or her thinking abilities, and specific problem-solving skills. Of the 16 techniques taught by the Productive Thinking Program, eight are methods for idea generation and constructing alternative representations of a problem, six train metacognitive skills such as planning, goal formulation, and persistence, and two describe the processes for evaluating proposed solutions in light of the givens in a problem. The program also provides students with instruction in the generate-and-test strategy using several simple generators and evaluators. This is certainly not a wide range of problem-solving techniques, although for the targeted age group and time span, it is probably as many as can profitably be dealt with. The techniques it does cover are described in a clear, detailed fashion.

Development of a Control Schema.   The control schema taught by this program is an extremely elementary one: Whenever a student is working on a problem, he or she should examine the list of thinking guides for ideas about how to proceed. The techniques taught are applicable in all conditions. This is because for their generality. For example, "check ideas against the facts" is invariably a useful exhortation, but it is not specific enough to provide strong control of an individual's problem-solving activity. With a small number of principles dealt with in the program, this simple control schema is not unreasonable, but it is unclear how students would go about generalizing this control schema when they acquire more powerful program-solving techniques later in their education.

Useful Examples and Problems.   Each lesson contains many examples, both in the lesson itself and in the supplemental problems. Each lesson is focused on the solution of one extended problem, which is typically broken down into a half-dozen subproblems. Thus, together with the supplemental exercises, the student is taken through 100 to 150 problems. This is a large number for the scope of the course. The format of the lessons is to have students work through the problems themselves, with guidance given along the way, until finally (presumably after the student has found the answer), the solution is given.

Although it is hard to evaluate difficulty for the type of informal, ill-structured problems used in the text, we saw no evidence that the exercises were graded as to difficulty. At least, it does not seem that the problems given in the last lesson are any more "difficult" than those in the first. The rationale for problem selection seems to be to generate as wide a range of problems from as many different content areas as possible.

Conclusions.   The Productive Thinking Program, in our opinion, is by far the most thoroughly developed of the four programs described in this chapter or the other programs that we examined in reviewing the literature on instruction and general problem-solving skills. Futhermore, there is an impressive body of evaluation research that supports claims for the effectiveness of this program. Although in our earlier remarks describing the Productive Thinking Program we express some reservations about the interpretation of these results, we don't mean to ignore their significance. We feel that these evaluations are models for the type of research that needs to be done on other programs claiming to teach cognitive skills. We think it would be profitable to develop more advanced versions of the Productive Thinking Program for students in higher grade levels, and to cover more complex problem-solving techniques including means–ends analysis and the problem-solving heuristics described by Polya.

CoRT Thinking Materials

Explicit Cognitive Objectives.   The CoRT program is based on a theory of thinking processes developed by de Bono (1979, 1976). We find many aspects of it difficult to specify precisely. De Bono develops his model of mental processes through a series of detailed examples and analogies. He sees the human mind as a pattern receiver, and claims that the fundamental role of many of his problem-solving techniques is to break away from preexisting patterns and to reformulate representations of the problem. The theory is not described in terms of an explicit series of process assumptions although de Bono (this volume) refers to a recently developed computer simulation model of his basic theoretical paradigm.

The other aspect of de Bono's writing that makes it difficult to gain a better understanding of his theoretical thinking is that he provides very few, if any, clues as to the historical antecedents of his theory. In our opinion, his view seems related to that of the Gestalt psychologists in its emphasis on perception, and to those of other writers in the divergent-production framework in its emphasis on idea generation.

Wide Variety of Explicit Problem-Solving Techniques.   De Bono does present a large number of thinking techniques—60 in all. One section containing 10 principles deals with situations involving arguments and discussions. The remaining five sections deal with thinking and problem-solving skills. Using the same classification scheme that was employed to characterize the Productive Thinking Program, there are 14 divergent-production techniques, 15 evaluation techniques, and 21 metacognitive techniques. One major difficulty was attempting to gain some understanding of what the differences among techniques actually were. For example, the lessons labeled "Define the Problem," "Target," and "Purpose" all seem to deal with goal formation. There are other examples that clearly demonstrate that the principles explicated in separate lessons overlap. De Bono acknowledges this, but gives no guidance as to their interrelationships or the conditions under which to use one of several related techniques. In fact, he discourages teachers from "worrying" about such details. The overlap is intentional, he claims.

The closest he comes to explaining how the techniques interrelate is in the final section, "Action," where a series of principles along with an ordering of their application is presented. The sequence of steps includes goal-formation techniques and an elementary version of the generate-and-test method. Other divergent-production and evaluation techniques described in earlier lessons can be characterized as different kinds of generation and evaluation heuristics that could be incorporated into a sophisticated set of generate-and-test heuristics.

Development of a Control Schema.   The only attempt at conveying a global management strategy occurs in the aforementioned final set of lessons, where an explicit sequence of principles for solving a problem is given. Each lesson is intended to be used in a particular type of problem-solving situation (e.g., debates, "creative" problem solving), and to that extent a very high-level control process is taught. No further efforts are made to compare techniques and to teach individuals under what particular circumstances each special case should be employed; in the teacher's manual, de Bono explicitly discourages such efforts. As in the Productive Thinking Program, presumably all techniques are applicable in all situations.

We feel that the lack of an explicit set of management strategies to organize the large number of problem-solving techniques presented in the CoRT program, the large amount of overlap among individual principles, and the failure to teach explicit applicability conditions for each principle makes the CoRT material difficult for a student to integrate and employ effectively in novel situations.

Useful Examples and Problems.   Each lesson begins with a brief statement of the principle to be taught. The principle is not explained in detail but is communicated using an illustration. The recommended time for each lesson is 35 minutes with about two-thirds of this time allocated for solving practice problems. Practice items are included in the lesson notes and the materials given to students; 2 to 4 minutes are allocated for each practice item. Each is closely linked to the current principle being studied; there is no practice in choosing the relevant technique. Practice items are not graded in difficulty. In fact, the instructor is encouraged to invent additional items, if the ones given in the lesson notes do not make contact with the interests and abilities of the students.

Conclusions.   The central focus of the de Bono program is the development of a useful problem representation. Thus, the principles taught deal with a mixture of metacognitive skills such as planning and memory retrieval, a wide variety of evaluation techniques, and an extensive collection of idea and solution-generation techniques (divergent-production techniques).

The most disturbing aspect of the de Bono program is the lack of well-designed evaluation studies such as the excellent research on the Productive Thinking Program. De Bono does deal with the evaluation issue in his presentation for this volume, in the teacher's manual for the CoRT program, and in his other writings on the CoRT program. None of the evaluation studies have been published either in journals or in books; the references are to unpublished notes. Experiments that are described are informal studies incorporated into an instructional program. We find the lack of adequate evaluation studies on the CoRT program to be both surprising and disturbing. The program has been in existence for over 10 years and is claimed to be in wide use both in the British Isles and in Venezuela. Futhermore, de Bono makes strong claims concerning the effectiveness of the CoRT program. Yet after 10 years of widespread use, we have no adequate evidence concerning those claims and thus no support for the effectiveness of the program or the theoretical assumptions from which it was derived.

Patterns of Problem Solving

Explicit Cognitive Objectives.   This text incorporates a wide variety of problem-solving techniques geared to the author's conceptions of what skills are useful in solving problems in engineering and related disciplines. The information-processing paradigm is discussed in the introduction, but the techniques included don't seem to have an overall theoretical rationale, beyond the strong emphasis on formal models that pervades the book. There are explicit cognitive objectives to the extent that most of the problem-solving techniques have a mathematical basis.

Wide Variety of Explicit Problem-Solving Techniques. The book provides instruction in about a half dozen classes of techniques, with several submethods in each category. Because each class of techniques is quite complex (e.g., optimization methods), only a rough overview of the basic topics and various subtechniques are described. In a one-semester course, we think it unlikely that a student would become proficient in any one of these techniques, much less in all of them.

The techniques are specific methods, which may be applicable to a wide variety of problem-solving situations—at least within engineering and related disciplines—and which are more restricted (and more powerful) than general methods like generate-and-test or means–ends analysis. The major difficulty that the student would have in employing these techniques is mapping the components of a novel problem onto the concepts and operators required by a given method.

Development of a Control Schema. No attempt is made to teach a management strategy for the use of these techniques. In other words, no explicit applicability conditions are described for any of them, nor is there any discussion about how to select among competing methods. In fact, the emphasis is on using techniques in areas where they may not have been applied before, rather than clearly delineating situations in which a given technique is or is not useful.

Useful Examples and Problems. A large number of exercises are given at the end of each chapter, and the book is filled with examples. If this book does anything, it gives the student copious opportunities for practice at solving problems. The exercises vary widely in difficulty from drill on basic concepts to problems that would make a challenging term project. The exercises do not seem to be graded, but vary randomly in diffculty throughout a set. Little attention is given to exercises that contrast techniques or focus on applicability conditions.

Conclusions. This book attempts to teach problem-solving methods used in engineering and related disciplines and to provide students with novel applications of these techniques in a wide variety of problem environments. Except for the popularity of the course at UCLA from which the book was developed, and other testimonials, we have no adequate evidence about the effectiveness of an instructional program based on the book.

How to Solve Problems

Explicit Cognitive Objectives. The Wickelgren book is based on what was known about problem solving from the information-processing perspective in 1972. It teaches the concept of problem space and introduces means–ends analysis as a basic technique for all types of problem solving. The focus of the book, though, is almost entirely on search techniques. The book is also limited to problems in mathematics and puzzles with well-defined solutions. Except for a section on mathematical representation, including the usefulness of diagrams, little attention is given to comprehension and representation issues, although their importance is stressed.

Wide Variety of Explicit Problem-Solving Techniques. This text introduces a relatively complete selection of search techniques. More emphasis could be placed on problem representation and generation techniques, or combined search and comprehension processes, especially as the author has limited himself to a small number of domains, and students would be expected to have already some of the necessary background knowledge required to build powerful representations. The methods are described as explicitly as current understanding (circa 1972) allowed (which, in some cases, means not very explicitly), and Wickelgren attempts to demonstrate when a particular technique might or might not be useful.

Development of a Control Schema. Beyond the comparison of the relative usefulness of specific techniques on particular problems, no explicit control structure or set of applicability conditions for each technique is taught. As in other programs, there seems to be an implicit "if one doesn't work, try another" assumption.

Useful Examples and Problems. The text contains a large number of well thought-out, effective examples. They are used to demonstrate techniques, delimit their applicability conditions, and compare alternative methods. However, excepting that the student is given several chances to solve example problems before answers are given, there are no practice exercises in the entire book.

Conclusions. *How to Solve Problems* represents a prototype for a course in general problem-solving skills from an information-processing perspective, circa 1972. It covers a wide variety of problem-solving techniques in a manner that makes their procedural nature very clear, under the assumption that problem solving is primarily a matter of search through a problem space, although the importance of an appropriate representation as the basis of that problem space is made clear. Although Wickelgren's basic approach meets our criteria for the properties that such a course should have, there are several important flaws in its implementation. These flaws are a direct reflection of the limitations of our knowledge concerning problem solving in the early 70s.

Nickerson et al. (1980) describe basic operations to the problem-solving techniques presented in this text. First, Wickelgren does not include an explicit problem-solving executive. The student is presented with a large collection of techniques, but with no clear picture of their relationships or exact applicability conditions. Second, although Wickelgren describes the procedures required to use techniques like evaluation functions and hill climbing quite lucidly, successful application of these strategies represents a rather nasty set of insight problems. An evaluation function requires subtle insight into the structure of the problem as well as the search heuristic that is going to employ that function. Thus, the appropriate application of the various techniques described is in itself a difficult problem. The problem solver still requires a nontrivial understanding of the specifics of a particular task and the relationships amongst a complex set of problem-solving techniques. Understanding of a technique per se is clearly not enough.

CONCLUSIONS AND RECOMMENDATIONS FOR FURTHER RESEARCH

The programs that we have reviewed present an almost bewildering array of viewpoints on issues concerning instruction in general problem-solving skills. The summary we present in the following paragraphs is derived from the information-processing paradigm of the early 1980s; we feel that many of our criticisms are in part due to the programs being as much as 10 years old. Thus, their now apparent shared weaknesses are evidence of the advances in our knowledge of problem solving.

All four programs share the assumption that a correct representation is fundamental to the solution of a problem. They differ widely in the techniques that they attempt to teach for constructing representations and on the amount of emphasis placed on such techniques in the context of an individual program. There is also agreement that perceptual and comprehension processes are the fundamental mechanisms involved in the construction of both effective and ineffective problem representations. In short, all programs have a common intellectual legacy derived from the Gestalt work on problem solving.

All programs share a common set of weaknesses in that they do not provide an adequate set of management strategies that would enable students to coordinate successfully the activities of a diverse set of comprehension and problem-solving techniques, and they do not provide adequate treatment of the applicability conditions of individual techniques. Questions concerning management strategies and applicability conditions are relatively new concerns in the study of problem solving. Thus, we conclude that such criticisms are in fact due to the superiority of hindsight rather than to failures of the authors to consider such issues at the time the programs were developed.

All programs also share the view that general problem-solving skills involve a large number of comprehension and problem-solving techniques. Those programs that teach a subset of the potential techniques had specific motivations to limit their coverage. For example, the Productive Thinking Program is a fairly brief intervention, 6 weeks, and is targeted for fifth and sixth graders. The Wickelgren book explicitly deals with problem solving in science and mathematics. There is still the question of what techniques should be included in a comprehensive course on general problem-solving skills. We feel that this is one of the most important unsolved problems in this area. We have no taxonomy of problem-solving techniques, comprehension techniques, and metacognitive skills relevant to the broad domain of general problem solving. We have no clear understanding of how seemingly closely related techniques are in fact interrelated. The lack of such a taxonomy makes it difficult to evaluate programs for completeness and to construct successful management strategies that are based on assumptions about the interrelationships and specific applicability conditions of individual techniques.

Our most serious reservations concern the techniques proposed for constructing representations. In an earlier section, we discussed our concerns about the divergent-production framework's emphasis on ideational fluency and related techniques. We pointed out that current work in the information-processing paradigm suggests that constructing useful representations involves the utilization of large amounts of domain-specific knowledge. One might conclude from this that useful representation-building heuristics that are independent of domain-specific knowledge may not exist.

The recommendations presented here are motivated by our perception that current thinking about general problem-solving techniques has several deficiencies. None of the programs reviewed are based on an understanding of the processes by which cognitive skills are acquired. The problem-solving techniques that these programs attempt to teach are not well enough understood that one can formulate clear instructional objectives and effective worked-out examples and practice exercises. A detailed understanding of the processes underlying some problem-solving technique should provide us with a description of a set of cognitive objectives to be achieved by a program instructed in that technique. In this section we propose a set of research programs involving both theoretical investigations of basic cognition mechanisms and attempts to apply to the classroom what we already know about problem solving. Our recommendations are grounded in analysis of the strengths and weaknesses of the programs and in three plausible theoretical models of general problems-solving skills described herein. The diversity of these models makes clear the weakness of our current understanding of the processes underlying instruction in basic skills, and therefore the imprecision of any claims about educational practice.

There are three defensible models of the nature of general problem-solving skills and how they might best be taught that are consistent with the information-processing framework. Each of these models establishes a theoretical paradigm that dictates which research questions would be of primary importance. The authors of the programs we have analyzed clearly differ in the models they subscribe to. Our claim is that as yet there is insufficient evidence to warrant our preferring one model to another. A high research priority would be to gather data relevant to making such a choice.

Model I assumes that there are general problem-solving skills and that they can be taught independently of content area. A Model I program would provide instruction in a range of search techniques, specialized understanding heuristics, and a general control scheme that would integrate these techniques into a coherent body of problem-solving knowledge and permit their application in particular problem-solving situations. The heuristics and techniques included in the program would be motivated by information-processing models of problem solving in particular paradigms. A focus of such a program would be generalized search heuristics and specialized instruction in dealing with problem descriptions and the effective use of worked-out examples. Such a program would also include instruction in metacognitive skills involving the monitoring of understanding, search behavior, and resource allocation. On the surface, a Model I program would seem quite similar to Polya (1957).

Model II likewise assumes that there are general problem-solving skills, but claims they are too abstract to be taught directly. In addition, Model II postulates that successful application of general techniques often requires specific information about the particular task domain. The designers of a Model II program would argue that the most effective way to teach general problem-solving skills would be to combine instruction on general problem-solving techniques with instruction on specific topics. Initial courses in this sequence would consist of traditional content with an emphasis on problem-solving methods appropriate to the particular discipline. In later courses in the sequence, instruction about both particular and general problem-solving skills would be incorporated into the course content. The Model II program assumes that the most efficient way to instruct students in a general skill is to first get them to master a particular instance of that skill, then master a second exemplar, and finally have them abstract the problem-solving techniques from the content of the disciplines.

Model III argues that direct instruction in general problem-solving skills is a waste of time. The designers of such a program would claim that information-processing models of problem solving in particular disciplines can provide a base for effective instructional programs on problem solving only in that specific discipline. the general problem-solving methods that have been abstracted from various models of the problem-solving process are the abstractions of the cognitive theorists and have no reality for an individual who is a practitioner of these skills. An individual arguing fo a Model III approach would point out that problem-solving techniques and the specific knowledge required to achieve expertise are so completely intertwined that it is not an effective instructional technique to teach the two separately. The Model III approach does not assume that the insights that have been developed in the information-processing framework are invalid. Rather, its claim is that it is not an effective instructional tactic to separate the problem-solving skills appropriate to a domain from the knowledge of that domain. Newell (1980) has called variations of the Model III position the *big-switch* and the *big-memory* views of problem solving. The big-switch view claims that effective problem solving involves a large collection of domain-specific methods. An expert is one who has mastered the specific problem-solving techniques appropriate to a particular domain of expertise. Such a person might show some generalizable problem-solving skills to the extent that the specific techniques mastered are useful in novel situations. The big-memory view claims that successful problem solving is in large part due to detailed knowledge about the particular area and that generalized problem-solving skills play little role in expert performance.

The primary goal of the research program that we outline presently is to discover which of the three Models is correct. This is a nontrivial task, because it requires that we be able to answer fundamental questions about the cognitive processes involved in learning and transfer. However, we feel that even partial achievement of the goal would be a contribution to our understanding of cognitive processes and basic educational practice.

We do not think that it is possible to select among these three Models by a program of applied research that develops and compares three instructional programs that claim to incorporate the primary features of each of the Models. Successful development of such programs must be based on a far deeper understanding of basic cognitive processes. Furthermore, the direct approach would commit large resources to a single experiment that could be easily in invalidated by mundane methodological problems. The program of research we propose attempts to acquire knowledge of basic processes, while at the same time applying our current understanding in demonstration projects.

The differences among Models I, II, and III are due to differing assumptions concerning cognitive mechanisms of learning and transfer; all three programs are consistent with current theoretical thinking about program-solving processes. Thus, we set as the first research priority the development of a stronger theoretical understanding of learning and transfer processes. Serious efforts to improve our capabilities to teach basic cognitive skills must be based on a more complete understanding of the processes underlying the acquisition and transfer of such skills.

Our second recommendation is that research on problem solving in the information-processing paradigm be expanded to include more of the processes that are discussed in Polya (1957). We do not have a theoretical understanding of planning by abstraction, decomposition, or problem solving by analogy, among others. We feel that the information-processing framework has provided us with an understanding of search processes. However, our theoretical descriptions of understanding processes (e.g., problem solving by analogy) and mechanisms involving complex mixtures of understanding and search are much less well developed.

Our third recommendation is that more definitive research be done on the basic assumptions underlying the divergent-thinking paradigm. We have argued that much of the research evaluating particular applied programs has been flawed. Many of the difficulties have been due to the complexities introduced by the attempts to develop and evaluate an actual program. We suggest that a program of laboratory research be started using appropriate tasks, e.g., insight problems, to develop explicit descriptions of problem-solving processes in which divergent production plays a central role.

Our fourth recommendation is an ambitious program of applied research that has two distinct phases. The first is the development of a program like the Productive Thinking Program based on the information-processing framework. The second is the development of courses in science and mathematics that would incorporate explicit instruction in problem-solving processes. One valuable aspect of the divergent-thinking paradigm is that there have been efforts made to develop practical applications of these ideas. Proponents of the information-processing paradigm have for the most part remained in an "ivory tower." Exceptions are the Wickelgren and Rubinstein book reviewed here, and Hayes (1981). We suggest that efforts to develop instructional programs at the college and university level on general problem-solving skills should continue. We view Wickelgren's and Hayes' texts as initial efforts to teach general problem-solving skills in the classroom based on the information-processing framework. However, like Glaser (1976), we realize that there is no direct mapping of what is known in the laboratory to successful practice in the classroom. Thus, successful application of information-processing concepts in the classroom may involve a good deal of trial and error.

We suggest that resources be allocated to support both the development and the evaluation of such programs. We feel that the evaluation component is particularly important. Many of the attempts to evaluate programs derived from the divergent-thinking approach were worthless. Many of the flaws involved violations of the most elementary principles of experimental design. However, even well-designed experiments were compromised by a lack of clear specification of the objectives of the programs. Attempts to evaluate any program that claims to teach basic skills must be based on specific descriptions of those skills and of their generality. Simply showing that students can perform the tasks that were incorporated into the training program will not do. The developer of a program must show that the specified skills are generalized to novel tasks.

In short, we argue that clear specifications of the behavioral and cognitive objectives of a program are required for the successful formulation of both instructional and evaluation programs. In fact, it could be argued that basic skills are theoretical constructs. Thus, development of instructional and evaluation programs is a test of a theory that claims such skills exist.

ACKNOWLEDGMENTS

Preparation of this review was supported primarily by the National Institute of Education Grant OE–NIE–G–78–0215 and also by National Science Foundation Grant BNS 77–06779 to the University of Colorado.

During the final phases of the writing and editing, use was made of the computer facilities of SUMEX–AIM, which is supported by grant RR–00785 from the Biotechnology Resources Program, Division of Research Resources, National Institutes of Health, and of the computer facilities of Carnegie–Mellon University.

REFERENCES

Anderson, J. R. *Language, memory, and thought.* Hillsdale, N.J.: Lawrence Erlbaum Associates, 1976.

Anderson, J. R. *Cognitive skills and their acquisition.* Hillsdale, N.J.: Lawrence Erlbaum Associates, 1981.

Atwood, M. E., Masson, M. E. J., & Polson, P. G. Further explorations with a process model for water jug problems. *Memory & Cognition,* 1980, *8,* 182–192.

Atwood, M. E., & Polson, P. G. A process model for water jug problems. *Cognitive Psychology,* 1976, *8,* 191–216.

Bhaskar, R., & Simon, H. A. Problem solving in semantically rich domains: An example from engineering thermodynamics. *Cognitive Science,* 1977, *1,* 193–215.

Bower, G. H. Cognitive psychology: An introduction. In W. K. Estes (Ed.), *Handbook of learning and cognitive processes* (Vol. 1). Hillsdale, N.J.: Lawrence Erlbaum Associates, 1975.

Chase, W. G., & Ericsson, K. A. Skilled memory. In J. R. Anderson (Ed.), *Cognitive skills and their acquisition.* Hillsdale, N.J.: Lawrence Erlbaum Associates, 1981.

Chase, W. G., & Simon, H. A. Perception in chess. *Cognitive Psychology,* 1973, *4,* 55–81.

Covington, M. C., Crutchfield, R. S., Davies, L. B., & Olton, R. M. *The productive thinking program: A course in learning to think.* Columbus, Ohio: Charles E. Merrill, 1974.

Davis, G. A. *Psychology of problem solving.* New York: Basic Books, 1973.

de Bono, E. *Lateral thinking: Creativity step by step.* New York: Harper & Row, 1970.

de Bono, E. *CoRT thinking materials.* London: Direct Education Services, 1973.

de Bono, E. *Teaching thinking.* London: Temple Smith, 1976.

Duncker, K. On problem solving. *Psychological Monographs,* 1945, *58* (Whole no. 270).

Ernst, G. W. & Newell, A. *GPS: A case study in generality and problem solving.* New York: Academic Press, 1969.

Feldhusen, J. F., Speedie, S. M., & Treffinger, D. J. The Purdue creative thinking program: Research and evaluation. *NPSI Jurnal,* 1971, *10,* 5–9.

Glaser, R. Cognitive psychology and instructional design. In D. Klahr (Ed.), *Cognition and instruction.* Hillsdale, N.J.: Lawrence Erlbaum Associates, 1976.

Gordon, W. J. *Synectics: The development of creative capacity.* New York: Harper & Row, 1961.

Greeno, J. G. Cognitive objectives of instruction: Theory of knowledge for solving problems and answering questions. In D. Klahr (Ed.), *Cognition and instruction.* Hillsdale, N.J.: Lawrence Erlbaum Associates, 1976.

Greeno, J. G. Process of understanding. In N. J. Castellan, D. B. Pisoni, & G. R. Potts (Eds.), *Cognitive theory* (Vol. 2). Hillsdale, N.J.: Lawrence Erlbaum Associates, 1977.

Hayes, J. R. *The complete problem solver.* Philadelphia: The Franklin Institute Press, 1981.

Hayes, J. R., & Simon, H. A. Understanding written problem instructions. In L. W. Gregg (Ed.), *Knowledge and cognition.* Hillsdale, N.J.: Lawrence Erlbaum Associates, 1974.

Heller, J. I., & Greeno, J. G. Information-processing analyses of mathematical problem solving. In *Testing, teaching, and learning.* Washington, D.C.: The National Institute of Education, 1979.

Hinsley, D. A., Hayes, J. R., & Simon, H. A. From words to equations: Meaning and representation in algebra word problems. In M. A. Just & P. A. Carpenter (Eds.), *Cognitive processes in comprehension.* Hillsdale, N.J.: Lawrence Erlbaum Associates, 1977.

Jeffries, R., Turner, A., Polson, P. G., & Atwood, M. E. The processes involved in designing software. In J. R. Anderson (Ed.), *Cognitive skills and their acquisition.* Hillsdale, N.J.: Lawrence Erlbaum Associates, 1981.

Katona, G. *Organizing and memorizing.* New York: Columbia University Press, 1940.

Kintsch, W., & van Dijk, T. A. Toward a model of text comprehension and production. *Psychological Review,* 1979, *4,* 407–413.

Larkin, J. H. *Skilled problem solving in physics: A hierarchical planning model.* Unpublished manuscript, Group in Science and Mathematics Education, University of California, Berkeley, 1977.

Larkin, J. H., McDermott, J., Simon, D. P., & Simon, H. A. Expert and novice performance in solving physics problems. *Science,* 1980, *208,* 1335–1342.

Mansfeld, R. S., Busse, T. V., & Krepelka, E. J. The effectiveness of creativity training. *Review of Educational Research,* 1978, *48,* 517–536.

Marr, D. *Vision.* San Francisco: W. H. Freeman, 1982.

Miller, J. R., & Kintsch, W. Readability and recall of short prose passages: A theoretical analysis. *Journal of Experimental Psychology: Human Learning and Memory,* 1980, *6,* 335–354.

Miller, M. A., & Goldstein, I. P. *Overview of a linguistic theory of design* (Memo 383). Cambridge: Artificial Intelligence Laboratory, 1976.

Minsky, M. A framework for representing knowledge. In P. Winston (Ed.), *The psychology of computer vision.* Hillsdale, N.J.: Lawrence Erlbaum Associates, 1975.

Neves, D. M. A computer program that learns algebraic procedures by examining examples and by working problems in a text book. *Proceedings of the Second National Conference of the Canadian Society for Computational Studies of Intelligence,* 1978.

Newell, A. Heuristic programming: Ill-structured problems. In Aronofsky (Ed.), *Progress in operations research* (Vol. 3). New York: Wiley, 1969.

Newell, A. Artificial intelligence and the concept of mind. In R. Schank & K. M. Colby (Eds.), *Computer models of thought and language.* San Francisco: Freeman, 1972.

Newell, A. One final word. In D. T. Tuma & F. Reif (Eds.), *Problem solving and education.* Hillsdale, N.J.: Lawrence Erlbaum Associates, 1980.

Newell, A., & Simon, H. A. *Human problem solving.* Englewood Cliffs, N.J.: Prentice-Hall, 1975.

Nickerson, R. S., Perkins, D. N., & Smith, E. E. *Teaching thinking.* Unpublished manuscript, Bolt, Beranek, & Newman, 1980.

Nilsson, N. J. *Problem-solving methods in artificial intelligence.* New York: McGraw–Hill, 1971.

Norman, D. A. Cognitive engineering and education. In D. T. Tuma & F. Reif (Eds.), *Problem solving and education.* Hillsdale, N.J.: Lawrence Erlbaum Associates, 1980.

Norman, D. A., & Rumelhart, D. *Explorations in cognition.* San Francisco: Freeman, 1975.

Novak, G. S. Computer understanding of physics problems stated in natural language. *American Journal of Computational Linguistics*, 1976, Microfiche 53.

Olton, R. M., & Crutchfield, R. S. Developing the skills of productive thinking. In P. Mussen, J. Langer, & M. Covington (Eds.), *Trends and issues in developmental psychology*. New York: Holt, Rinehart & Winston, 1969.

Osborne, A. F. *Applied imagination*. New York: Scribner's, 1963.

Paige, J. M., & Simon, H. A. Cognitive processes in solving algebra word problems. In B. Kleinmuntz (Ed.), *Problem solving: Research, method, and theory*. New York: Wiley, 1966.

Polson, P. G., & Jeffries. R. Problem solving as search and understanding. In R. Sternberg (Ed.), *Advances in the psychology of human intelligence* (Vol. 1). Hillsdale, N.J.: Lawrence Erlbaum Associates, 1982.

Polya, G. *How to solve it* (2nd ed.). Garden City, N.Y.: Doubleday, 1957.

Restle, F. Theory of serial pattern learning. *Psychological Review*, 1970, *77*, 481–95.

Rubinstein, M. *Patterns of problem solving*. Englewood Cliffs, N.J.: Prentice-Hall, 1975.

Rubinstein, M. A decade of experience in teaching an interdisciplinary problem-solving course. In D. T. Tuma & F. Reif (Eds.), *Problem solving and education*. Hillsdale, N.J.: Lawrence Erlbaum Associates, 1980.

Sacerdoti, E. D. *A structure for plans and behavior* (Tech. Note 109). Menlo Park, Calif.: Stanford Research Institute, Artificial Intelligence Center, 1975.

Schank, R. C. Conceptual dependency; A theory of natural language understanding. *Cognitive Psychology*, 1972, *3*, 552–631.

Schank, R. C., & Abelson, R. P. *Scripts, plans, goals, and understanding*. Hillsdale, N.J.: Lawrence Erlbaum Associates, 1977.

Schoenfeld, A. H. Can heuristics be taught? In J. Lochhead & J. Clement (Eds.), *Cognitive process instruction*. Philadelphia: Franklin Institute Press, 1979.

Simon, H. A. Motivational and emotional controls of cognition. *Psychological Review*, 1967, *74*, 29–39.

Simon, H. A. The heuristic compiler. In H. A. Simon & L. Siklossy (Eds.), *Representation and meaning*. Englewood Cliffs, N.J.: Prentice-Hall, 1972.

Simon, H. A. The structure of ill-structured problems. *Artificial intelligence*, 1973, *4*, 181–202.

Simon, H. A. Information-processing theory of human problem solving. In W. K. Estes (Ed.), *Handbook of learning and cognitive processes* (Vol. 5): *Human information processing*. Hillsdale, N.J.: Lawrence Erlbaum Associates, 1978.

Simon, H. A. Problem solving and education. In D. T. Tuma & F. Reif (Eds.), *Problem solving and education*. Hillsdale, N.J.: Lawrence Erlbaum Associates, 1980.

Stefik, M. J. Planning with constraints. *Artificial Intelligence*, 1981, *16*, 111–140.

Tuma, D. T., & Reif, F. *Problem solving and education: Issues in teaching and research*. Hillsdale, N.J.: Lawrence Erlbaum Associates, 1980.

Wertheimer, M. *Productive thinking*. New York: Harper & Row (Enlarged ed.), 1959.

Wickelgren, W. A. *How to solve problems: Elements of a theory of problems and problem solving*. San Francisco: W. H. Freeman, 1973.

Winograd, T. Understanding natural language. *Cognitive Psychology*, 1972, *3*, 1–191.

Winston, P. H. *Learning structural descriptions from examples* (AI–TR–231). Cambridge: Artificial Intelligence Laboratory, 1970.

Educators' Experience

13

A Practitioner's Perspective on The Chicago Mastery Learning Reading Program with Learning Strategies

Walter E. Thompson
Chicago Public Schools

The problem of low reading achievement in large urban schools is chronic and pervasive; it seems resistant to a variety of remedies. The use of basal reading systems has been inadequate in diminishing this problem. Some might suggest that the situation persists because of the very exigencies of urban education in general. If the problem is to be abated, special reading instructional materials must be designed that can be used instead of or in conjunction with basal reading systems to permit poor readers to acquire basic reading comprehension skills.

As a means of addressing this problem, the Chicago public school system is in the process of developing a K–8 package of instructional materials in reading: the Chicago Mastery Learning Program (CMLR). The upper levels of these materials contain explicit instructions in learning strategies and therefore are referred to as the Chicago Mastery Learning Reading Materials with Learning Strategies (CMLR/LS). Additionally, the Chicago Public Schools sponsor a staff development program called the Intensive Reading Improvement Program (IRIP), which allows eligible schools to assign a key teacher to serve as a reading coordinator within the school. The function of the IRIP teacher is to assist the other teachers and the principal in improving the program of reading instruction. The purpose of this chapter is to describe the implementation of CMLR/LS materials in a particular school, the May Elementary School, from the perspective of the IRIP teacher.

This chapter: (1) discusses some of the cognitive needs of low-achieving urban students; (2) considers reasons why basal reading systems have been inadequate in meeting the needs of such students; (3) discusses how CMLR/LS was designed specifically to address the problems of urban education; (4) examines implementation problems and procedures for CMLR/LS; and (5) describes the cognitive and affective changes resulting from the successful implementation of CMLR/LS in a typical, large urban elementary school.

COGNITIVE NEEDS OF LOW-ACHIEVING URBAN STUDENTS

There is strong evidence that low-achieving students in the middle and upper levels of elementary school fail to process effectively the materials they read and have limited retrieval skills. They rely heavily on rote memory, are not able to consider word meanings in terms of their abstract referents, and are unable to use the syntactic cues implicit in texts. Hence, these students are limited in their recall of specific information and concepts, and in their ability to comprehend and use what they do comprehend. A possible explanation for these deficiencies lies in the emphasis in the primary grades on establishing readiness and decoding skills, often at the neglect of establishing comprehension skills. There is uncertainty as to how these readiness and decoding skills come together to produce the complex cognitive skills of reading with understanding. Moreover, there is a definite change in the nature of the instructional materials used in the middle and upper levels of elementary school in contrast to those used in the primary grades. The materials for the upper grades are expository in nature, require the use of inference, and are more complex and abstract.

With this change in the nature of the instructional materials comes a change in the kinds of reading demands placed on students. Instruction in reading comprehension skills is now essential because the comprehension tasks with which students are confronted are much more difficult. Two aspects of comprehension instruction, often overlooked in helping students learn to read more difficult materials, are vocabulary development and concept development. Students' proficiency in both areas is influenced by the nature of their daily life experience. Because the objects in the environment, the people, and the language experience of many urban students are often different from the objects, people, and language described in the basals, these students fail to bring the appropriate background, vocabulary, and grammar to bear in comprehending the basals. Students who do not have an appropriate experiential base in reading and who have difficulty thinking in terms of abstract concepts and making inferences require special help. This should be done within a framework that teaches students how to represent concrete experiences in more abstract ways. At the same time, such students should be deliberately instructed in effective memory and comprehension strategies. Failure to offer instruction in these strategies will produce the kind of student who often is mistakenly identified as a "good reader," but is actually limited to engaging in decoding and word calling. Such students can readily be found in most urban classrooms; they are the readers who can pick up a textbook and read all the words orally, yet fail to understand their meaning.

In addition to more complex forms of literature, the curriculum in the middle and upper elementary school grades for the first time begins to include content area textbooks. Teachers of low-achieving students often either avoid teaching content-area materials or provide only a cursory exposure without reliance upon textbooks. Their excuse is that content-area textbooks are too difficult for their students. Teachers offer this excuse without understanding that different reading tasks require different thinking and learning strategies. Low-achieving students do not seem to "discover" these strategies themselves; therefore, they must be systematically taught them.

This need for explicit instruction in thinking and learning strategies is most evident when one witnesses how low-achieving students approach content-area materials. Classroom observations reveal that, besides the need for vocabulary and concept development, these students are completely unaware of the differences between structurally important and unimportant information; they seem to have neither an idea of the theme or key points in an argument, nor of key words in a sentence. Additionally, they tend to make little or no effort to analyze or visualize what they read. Characteristically, these students read word by word without attempting to associate word meanings, to use context clues, or to use the structural emphasis devices that are present in the text. In short, they either have no reservoir of thinking and learning strategies to apply or are confused in applying them. These obstacles to comprehension can be overcome by providing explicit instruction in appropriate thinking and learning strategies.

Low-achieving students without explicit instruction in thinking and learning strategies experience repeated failures in comprehending content-area materials. These failures cause the students to develop a disinterest in and a poor attitude toward reading in general. This in turn leads to low expectations on the part of both students and teachers, which further inhibit learning and achievement. Yet, these problems are not insurmountable. The solution lies in deliberately providing these students with thinking and learning strategies instruction within a framework in which they can experience success.

PROBLEMS WITH BASAL READING SYSTEMS

In no other academic subject-matter area are there so many materials of so many types, and from so many sources as in reading. Most of the basal reading systems provide the teacher not only with basic stories, instructional activities, and workbooks, but also with numerous optional instructional activities. In addition, there is an endless array of commercially published specialty kits, instructional games, and multimedia materials available to teachers. Teachers use these commercially published materials year after year in addition to an abundance of teacher-made materials. Yet, the general decline in reading achievement levels of far too many students in urban schools continues because of the almost exclusive reliance upon basal systems for reading instruction.

Perhaps the inadequacy of basal reading systems may be attributed to the following factors. First, there is a *lack of organization* to these systems. Within many basal systems, activities relating to a given objective or skill are often scattered over different sections of a given text or over different texts within the same system. Teacher decision making and planning are made more difficult because of this lack of organization. To plan a lesson on any given objective, the teacher must search for activities relating to the objective in a number of different places, thus having to reorganize the basal to suit his or her individual needs. Second, most basal reading systems require *an unnecessary amount of complex information processing* in conjunction with learning new skills. This increases the difficulty of the learning task and builds in failure as students struggle to learn new skills in contexts requiring that they simultaneously bring several other partially learned skills to bear. Third, overall *sequencing of objectives and skills* varies from one basal system to another. In most urban schools, there are high mobility rates. Different schools use different basal systems. As students move from school to school and fluctuate from one basal system to another, confusion rather than progress occurs. Fourth, *teachers are inadequately prepared* to teach basal systems. Basal systems presume multiple reading groups within a classroom. Working with multiple reading groups is a skill possessed more readily by primary school teachers than by teachers trained to teach middle and upper elementary school students. Also, with multiple reading groups, the question of time on task becomes a problem in that a single teacher may find it difficult to supervise several reading groups simultaneously. Thus, the lack of organization of the materials and the presumption of multiple reading groups combine with the constraints of time to make basal systems inappropriate for low-achieving students.

One standard by which one can evaluate the effectiveness of reading instruction is the level of reading comprehension achieved by the students who undergo that instruction. Reading comprehension is an application of thought process. Yet, perhaps of greater significance than any of the foregoing list of basal inadequacies, is a fifth one: the *lack of effort to teach students how to work out by thinking the meaning of what they read.* Basal systems are saturated with the tools for assessing comprehension, yet they provide no explicit methods for teaching comprehension. For example, using the basal reader, teachers frequently ask students the "5W" questions (Who, What, Where, When, and Why) without helping the students use these questions to understand the instruction in the text. Oftentimes, students can respond correctly to such questions on the basis of the syntactic order of the sentences without any understanding whatsoever of the ideas expressed by the author. It is also common that during a single reading period, teachers using basal systems will switch rapidly from one activity to another, for example, from identifying the main ideas of paragraphs to identifying possessive nouns. Teachers who use basal systems do not notice this as a deficiency and are ill equipped to bridge these transitions.

This is not intended as an unqualified criticism of basal reading systems. With exceptional teachers who know how to use them, basals have produced some good readers. These same teachers most probably could accomplish the same results using a chalkboard and chalk. But, the large number of low-achieving students in urban schools is evidence of the failure of the basals to meet these needs.

DESCRIPTION OF CMLR/LS

The Chicago Mastery Learning Reading Program with Learning Strategies offers instruction in reading comprehension skills emphasizing the mental operations involved in executing these skills. The major features of this program have been described in the paper by Jones, Amiran, and Katims in this volume and are briefly summarized in the following paragraphs.

The program is divided into learning units based on Bloom's (1976) mastery learning philosophy. A four-phase cycle of instruction is followed for each unit. The cycle involves teaching, testing, reteaching, and retesting. That is, unlike traditional instructional programs, CMLR/LS materials include regular and systematic attempts to diagnose and correct student errors.

The program offers instruction in five broad types of strategies for acquiring information from text: (1) organizational strategies—that is, noticing how a text is organized and how the ideas it contains are related to one another; (2) imagery strategies—that is, forming mental pictures and making drawings for purposes of more adequately encoding the meaning of words and ideas; (3) contextual strategies—that is, using context clues to define unfamiliar words and to make inferences from text; (4) critical thinking strategies—that is, using inductive and deductive reasoning strategies to make inferences from text; and (5) reflective thinking strategies—that is, approaching reading comprehension tasks in a systematic way. The instructional materials include scripts for teachers to use in describing skills to students, thinking-aloud models for students to use in learning how to execute various skills, prompted and unprompted practice exercises, formative achievement tests to assess student learning, additional learning activities for those who fail to pass the formative tests, and enrichment and transfer activities for those who succeed in passing these tests.

All the learning units begin at level zero—that is, they assume that the student knows absolutely nothing about the skill to be learned. Systematically, all definitions, concepts, and thought processes necessary to master the skill are presented along a continuum ranging from concrete to abstract. This organization of each unit enables students to begin the CMLR/LS materials at different points depending on previous knowledge. Skill instruction is sequenced *within* the learning units, not across units as in basal reading systems. Hence, CMLR/LS materials are specifically designed to eliminate the confusion experienced by many low-achieving students as they move from school to school and from one basal system to another.

IMPLEMENTATION OF CMLR/LS

The Role of the IRIP Teacher

In the Chicago Public Schools, 192 elementary schools have been designated on the basis of need to have Intensive Reading Improvement Program (IRIP) teachers. The IRIP teacher is responsible to the building principal. His or her role is that of resource person, advisor, inservice training leader, diagnostician, instructor, and coordinator of all elements of the instructional program, with an emphasis on implementing the reading program within his or her school. The range of activities with which the IRIP teacher is concerned includes: (1) inservice training to teachers; (2) involvement in classrooms; (3) service to learners with special needs; (4) service to staff; and (5) involvement with the community. A question of primary and constant concern to the IRIP teacher in a large urban school is: In a class of 30 or more students who are below level in reading achievement, how does one ensure that *every* student eventually learns to read at least at his or her grade level? Because the basal readers had not been effective at May Elementary School, a major task of the IRIP teacher was to work with the principal to select and implement other instructional materials, namely CMLR/ LS.

The Role of the Principal

Implementation of CMLR/LS would not have been successful if it were not for the leadership role assumed by the principal. Essential to this success was the fact that, through the principal's leadership, the new instructional program was considered to be top priority in the school. Subscribing to a firm belief *that all children can learn* and *that teachers can change,* the principal was willing to implement a special program specifically designed to achieve our instructional goals. Once the decision was reached to implement CMLR/LS, a firm commitment was made to the program. As affective and cognitive changes began to reveal themselves in the school, this commitment became even stronger.

Throughout the implementation period, the principal had several major tasks. With the financial problems experienced by the school during 1979–80, cuts in personnel were a major problem. As the role of the IRIP teacher was considered essential to successful implementation of the program, the principal redirected funds, including ESEA funds, to ensure that sufficient resource personnel and materials were made available to provide the necessary services to teachers and students. Additionally, the principal provided two other important functions. First, he was actively involved in weekly conferences with the resource teacher and the classroom teachers. In these conferences, the principal continuously assessed students' progress, provided general support to teachers, set specific goals for teachers and students, and resolved other problems that arose. Secondly, as students progressed from one reading level to another, the principal called them into his office and personally presented each one with a certificate of achievement and a paperback book selected by the student for his or her personal library. This served as a highly effective encouragement to student success.

Implementation Context

CMLR/LS materials provide an alternative method of instruction to basal reading systems. Whether these materials succeed or fail depends on how they are implemented. To help the reader understand the kinds of challenges with which we were confronted in successfully implementing these materials in our school, we need to pause briefly to describe the overall context within which implementation occurred. We list here several characteristics of large urban schools, as well as some local Chicago events that created the context for our implementation efforts.

1. Urban students vary greatly in background and ability. Any given classroom in Chicago might, for example, have as many as five different reading levels and two to three different age groups. This creates a need to accommodate to cultural diversity and, at the same time, provide reading instruction for pupils of different ages who are at the same reading level.

2. Usually there are 30 to 40 students in a classroom who are reading 1 to 3 or more years below grade level, with a single teacher and no auxiliary classroom resources. High levels of absenteeism and mobility are prevalent. Students have become so accustomed to failure and their self-concept is so low that they have come to believe that they will always fail. Many students present behavioral problems because they accept this "reality" and school loses all meaning for them.

3. Teachers with varying degrees of experience and expertise in teaching reading are compelled to use basal reading systems because it is the only approach to teaching reading that they know. Teachers who use the basal systems and continue to witness a decline in reading achievement levels experience such frustration that their absenteeism increases as they try to escape teacher "burnout." They seek scapegoats to explain their lack of success. The attitudes of these teachers toward themselves and their students lead them to: (1) label students with any number of misnomers, ranging from "learning disabled" to "dumb"; (2) make complaints about basal materials, for example, that these materials are not of interest to the students or that certain components are missing; or (3) make complaints about the possibility of individualizing instruction, for example, that they cannot cope with the large number of reading groups that would be necessary to create a truly individualized program.

4. As part of the Board's efforts to implement the concepts of continuous progress and mastery learning, the Chicago Public Schools developed a mastery-based system of criterion-referenced tests along with plans to monitor pupil progress through a matrix of key objectives. To implement these plans, the Board developed a complex record-keeping system that caused considerable controversy. Teachers began to object both to the need to keep complex records and the general concept of mastery learning.

Given this overall context, we developed the following guidelines for use in directing implementation efforts at May Elementary School.

1. Do not attempt implementation on a schoolwide basis initially. Teachers resist abrupt change. They need to be convinced of the worth of the materials, a process that should be undertaken gradually.

2. Do not discard the basal program entirely. Teachers are accustomed to it and will not willingly abandon it for something new. Therefore, it is strongly suggested that CMLR/LS be used in conjunction with the basal reading system. In the last analysis, it is the teacher who must implement the materials. Teachers' enthusiasm and attitude toward the materials must always be kept in mind. Without this consideration, the process of implementation will not be successful.

Implementation Model

There are perhaps any number of implementation models that might have proved successful at May Elementary School. However, given our general strategy, as just described, of initiating change on a gradual basis, we preferred a bottom-up model. Using this model, a small number of teachers were carefully selected to begin initial work with the materials. As they began to experience success and as their techniques were refined through close monitoring, the number of teachers was increased until implementation was accomplished throughout the entire school.

Implementation Procedures

During the first year of implementation, two teachers were encouraged to use CMLR/LS materials. Both used these materials along with the basal system. One teacher used the basal system 3 days per week and the CMLR/LS materials 2 days per week; the other teacher used the basal system 2 days per week and CMLR/LS materials 3 days. They were able to combine these two instructional programs successfully by selecting basal stories that emphasized the same skills covered in the CMLR/LS units. In keeping with CMLR/LS procedures, the entire class received instruction on each unit at the same time, thus freeing the teacher from having to work with a class that was organized into several different groups.

After a unit was taught, the entire class was tested for mastery of its objectives. Individual deficiencies were identified and students who failed to reach a predetermined level of mastery were given additional instruction. Students who achieved the mastery level were given three choices: (1) they could participate in Enrichment Activities (EAs); (2) they could engage in SQUIRT (Sustained Quiet Uninterrupted Reading Time); or (3) they could tutor their peers who had not attained mastery. In this way, almost all students eventually mastered the content of the units that they were taught.

Close observation of these two classrooms revealed that, as students began to have successful learning experiences and as both students and teachers became aware that learning was taking place, a remarkable change occurred; namely, the students' thwarted hunger for success evidenced itself by their pushing the teachers for more material. This resulted in their mastering units far faster than expected. Classroom disruptions decreased; and teachers began to indicate an acceptance of the program.

Perhaps of equal importance was the fact that the teachers using the materials began to discuss their successful experiences with their colleagues. Other teachers began to inquire as to when they were going to be able to use the materials. With the interest stimulated, the use of CMLR/LS was expanded to include additional classrooms. With expanded use, positive learning effects and attitudinal changes began to occur in these classrooms as well.

During the second year of implementation, as the positive effects of use of the materials became quite evident, the decision to implement the CMLR/LS program on a schoolwide basis was made, principally because of teacher demand for it. It must be pointed out that, in the classrooms that had used the materials up to this point, very little inservice or follow-up assistance had been provided. Schoolwide implementation necessitated a thorough schoolwide program of inservice training that addressed the following topics: rationale for CMLR/LS, mastery learning teaching model, day-to-day scheduling, important dos and don'ts, and important teacher concerns. This inservice training program was the only formal staff development training that was provided.

An important concern in testing the CMLR/LS materials in the classroom was to monitor their use carefully. Three monitoring tools were found helpful. One was conferences in which the resource and classroom teacher jointly attempted to work out appropriate learning goals both for the class as a whole and for individual students. The springboard for these conferences was a wall chart, which was present in every classroom. The column headings of this chart listed the skills students were required to master at each reading level. The row headings listed the students' names. As students mastered skills, their success was noted on the chart. Thus, anyone examining the chart could both assess the progress of each individual student and the progress of the class as a whole. In conferences this chart was useful in identifying students who were not progressing at the pace of the group and in determining whether the goals for both the individual and the group were realistic. Initially, frequent conferences between the resource and classroom teachers were needed to set and/or refine learning goals. After the program had been operating for some time in an individual classroom, however, these conferences became less frequent.

Classroom visitations constituted a second important monitoring tool. These visits served two main purposes, namely, to gather information for teacher conferences and to observe the affective reactions of students as they became involved in using the materials.

Weekly conferences involving the principal, resource teacher, and classroom teacher constituted a third important monitoring tool. The purpose of these conferences was to discuss the affective and cognitive changes that were occurring in the students.

When schoolwide implementation was instituted, resource teacher–classroom teacher conferences, classroom visitations, and the weekly conferences with the principal continued to be the primary monitoring tools. These devices were employed as the need for them was indicated, with teachers evidencing the greatest need for assistance being given priority. Interestingly, monitoring was often requested by classroom teachers. These frequent requests constituted evidence of their desire for successful implementation of the program.

An important classroom management issue that teachers and administrators raised in using CMLR/LS materials was the problem of what to do with the faster students who would typically complete their seatwork first and pass the formative test without requiring additional corrective activities. Their success raised two questions: (1) what could be done to keep them from being bored and/or disruptive while waiting for others to finish; and (2) what could be done to keep them challenged so that they would continue to learn at an appropriate rate for their ability level. As noted previously, the CMLR/LS manual provides three solutions. Such students may tutor peers, engage in sustained silent reading (SQUIRT), or complete the Enrichment Activity provided in the manual. At May Elementary School, each of these solutions involved special implementation concerns that are mentioned in the following paragraphs.

SQUIRT. In the CMLR/LS manual, it is suggested that interested teachers work with the librarian or principal to select multiple copies of high-interest paperback novels so that each classroom has a small library. With such a library, each student can have a paperback within reach at all times when work has been completed. The rationale for having multiple copies of a small number of novels was to encourage both informal and formal discussion of the books. It was assumed that students who had read a book and liked it would recommend it to others and would enjoy discussing it with them. To facilitate discussion, the CMLR/LS manual included SQUIRT discussion questions that students could work on in small group settings. These questions required that the students analyze novels they were reading in terms of concepts that had been emphasized in the CMLR/LS instructional materials. Implementing SQUIRT involved informing teachers of the possibility of creating SQUIRT discussion groups and helping them organize classroom libraries.

Peer Tutoring. Peer tutoring is offered as an educational option to the faster students because, as the old adage goes, there is no better way to learn something than to teach it. Peer tutoring often fails because the student tutors are not taught how to teach or what to teach. CMLR/LS solves this problem to a large extent by providing the instructional materials that are to be used during peer tutoring. One approach to peer tutoring is to have students tutor others of their own age. Another approach is to have older students tutor younger ones in other classrooms. All the tutor must do, in either situation, in working with the CMLR/ LS materials, is to monitor the progress of the tutee and use the materials as a springboard for answering any questions the tutee may have. Implementing peer tutoring involved informing teachers about the usefulness of this option and, where necessary, helping to organize the temporary transfer of older students to the classrooms of younger ones.

Enrichment Activities. According to the CMLR/LS manual, Enrichment Activities are a third option for faster students. Having three options for one set of students and a required corrective activity for the other means that a teacher may have as many as four different activities going on simultaneously. Some teachers find this diversity of activities difficult to manage and would like to eliminate the special options for faster students. This problem can often be solved by helping teachers come to understand why it is important to maintain these options and how to implement them.

COGNITIVE OUTCOMES OF CMLR/LS

One source of evidence of the success of the CMLR/LS materials, as implemented at May Elementary School, was an increase in student reading achievement scores on the Iowa Test of Basic Skills (ITBS). During the 1978–79 school year, two eighth-grade classrooms used the materials for the first time. During the previous school year (1977–78), Room A had achieved a median ITBS grade level score in reading of 5.8; Room B a median ITBS grade level score of 5.9. After using CMLR/LS for an entire academic year, the median grade level scores for these classrooms for the 1978–79 school year were: Room A, 7.3 and Room B, 7.1. That is, there was an increase in median score of 1.5 grade levels for Room A and 1.2 for Room B. These kinds of gains contributed to an increased interest on the part of teachers throughout the school in using CMLR/LS.

During the 1979–80 school year, CMLR/LS materials were implemented in all 39 classrooms in the school. This was a year in which the Chicago Public

Schools experienced considerable turmoil caused by financial problems, high teacher turnover, and a teacher strike. Of the 39 classrooms using the experimental materials, about 10 had more than one teacher during this year. In many cases, the reassigned teacher was not only new to the school but was also inexperienced in teaching the age groups and reading levels to which he or she had been assigned. Frequent teacher reassignments caused a double-edged problem: (1) low morale on the part of teachers who were being forced to leave the school; and (2) feelings of frustration on the part of new teachers who had to adapt to working with students of different ages and reading levels. Additionally, there were gaps in instruction caused by a 2-week closure of the schools and discontinuities created by teacher reassignments. In spite of this turmoil, students of all ages in the school registered gains on the ITBS Test of Reading Comprehension that ranged from respectable to outstanding for an inner-city school.

For students in the 10- to 13-year-old group (those students who received the level of CMLR/LS materials that included explicit instruction in learning strategies), dramatic gains were observed after an initial 7-month period of instruction. The median gains in ITBS reading achievement scores for students in each of these three age groups were as follows: age 10, 1.5 years median gain; age 11, 1.2 years median gain; age 12, 1.1 years median gain. Although grade equivalent scores for these students were still below the national norms, it should be kept in mind that these gains occurred after only a year of full implementation of the program and during a year characterized by much loss of instructional time due to closures and transfers as just described. We hope that during the second year of full implementation, all students will score at or above national norms for their grade levels.

As important as the rise in achievement test scores was the fact that textbooks in the content areas that, it was said, could not be used before, because they were at too advanced a reading level, were now being taken off the shelves. With the foundation provided by the CMLR/LS units, students were able to move from a knowledge level, as evidenced by mastery scores on CMLR/LS formative tests, to a habit level, as evidenced by the successful application of sophisticated reading comprehension skills in deriving meaning from content area textbooks. Students began to perceive structural emphasis devices such as center and side headings, pictures, graphs, and charts as offering useful information about the organization of text. They also began to discover relationships among ideas, discover the principles underlying organization of information in text, and engage in appropriate processes to derive meaning from and think critically about the information contained in text. In other words, for the first time, low-achieving students were able to use content-area materials and experience success.

In Chicago, there are certain schools that have minimum standards of achievement for students desiring admission. Two such schools are Lane Technical High School and Westinghouse Vocational High School. During the 1978–79 school year, much letter writing and personal contact were required to enable three May School students to be accepted at Lane and seven at Westinghouse. As a result of the achievement levels attained by students after using CMLR/LS during the 1979–80 school year, 11 eighth-graders immediately qualified for admission to Lane, and 35 to Westinghouse. For the first time, May School students had an opportunity to turn down admission to these prestigious schools because of other attractive options.

AFFECTIVE OUTCOMES OF CMLR/LS

Along with the cognitive changes, there were also changes in attitude on the part of both teachers and students as they began to experience actual learning in the classroom. Teachers displayed a rekindled joy and excitement about teaching their students. Instead of discussing what students couldn't do, they excitedly began to relate their positive achievements. Teachers who had displayed a pattern of high absenteeism became regular in attendance.

Experiencing success produced a new excitement about school and learning in the students. They showed a new sense of confidence in themselves and became actively and intimately involved in learning. Discipline problems and truancy from school virtually disappeared. Prior to the 1977–78 school year, May Elementary School had the highest student suspension rate in the entire school system. In contrast, during the first year of full implementation of CMLR/ LS, only five suspensions occurred. It was not uncommon for students who moved to a new attendance area to ask to remain at May School. Some students traveled from the far south side of the city to the west side of the city, using public transportation, just to remain at May School. They came daily and on time.

The positive effects of CMLR/LS permeated the entire school. These included: (1) a calm atmosphere conducive to learning throughout the school; (2) more student time devoted to learning and less student time devoted to getting into mischief—for example, students who used to go to the cafeteria and throw food around, frequently now carried a paperback book to lunch and read as they ate; (3) greater enthusiasm and effectiveness on the part of teachers; and (4) greater involvement on the part of parents in their children's academic activities, a deep sense of appreciation for the changes that have occurred in their children, and increased willingness to cooperate with the school.

The affective changes brought about by use of the CMLR/LS materials might best be summarized by a statement from a teacher of students, ages 12–14, some of whom are reading as much as 4 years below grade level—that is, students who would usually be written off as complete failures in the typical inner-city school.

The single most important factor for the successful use of the Mastery Approach (CMLR/LS) as it relates to Room 317 pupils is that the units presuppose success.

This, and this alone, has given the pupils a positive image of self. It has in a sense killed off the failure idea and almost overnight I've seen the emergence of an "I can and will attitude." Now, these same pupils are eager to attempt anything I throw at them.

SUMMARY

CMLR/LS is no panacea for the ills of large urban schools. Yet, at May Elementary School, where it has been implemented in all grades from kindergarten through eighth, the positive changes in attitudes and behavior on the part of both teachers and students, as they experienced successful teaching and learning, are desired goals for any school. Teachers who teach reading year after year and do not witness achievement in their students actually do desire to produce competent readers; students who experience failure year after year, are truant from school, present behavior problems, and are "turned off" by school, actually do desire to experience success in school. Success can be achieved by a program of mastery learning with learning strategies. Its very organization, including formative tests, corrective instruction, and embedded learning strategies are built-in success factors. Because most elementary school teachers of reading came from a background of experience with basals and because many are hesitant to try completely different approaches, CMLR/LS has been designed either for use as a stand-alone system or as a complement to the basals. As the latter, it succeeds in compensating for their failure to offer adequate instruction in reading comprehension skills.

Whatever approach to teaching reading is used, the long-range objective is to help students learn to apply the skills being taught to the materials they read both in school and out of school. CMLR/LS materials have been of interest to teachers primarily because they help students develop general learning strategies, because they help students develop the higher order cognitive skills involved in reading comprehension, and because they provide tremendous affective benefits as both students and teachers begin to experience genuine learning and teaching in the classroom. Because the materials are specifically designed to develop the thought processes involved in executing important reading comprehension skills, transfer can be expected to a wide variety of situations. For example, transfer has been observed among May School students as they apply these skills on their own to the reading of content-area textbooks and find that they can now comprehend the information in these books. Success with one teacher spreads to other teachers; success with one student spreads to other students. It is this phenomenon that led May Elementary School to use a "bottom-up" model for implementation.

REFERENCES

Bloom, B. S. *Human characteristics and school learning.* New York: McGraw-Hill, 1976.

14 Making Choices: It Ought to be Carefully Taught

Curtis Miles
Piedmont Technical College

This chapter addresses the question of why colleges should foster choice-making skills in their students. The term "choice making" is used in an effort to find a phrase that is as inclusive yet as semantically neutral as possible. Problem solving, decision making, cognition, critical thinking, logic, creativity, and the like all capture overlapping segments of applied thought. Yet each also seems to exclude, or at least deemphasize, some conscious or unconscious processes involved in making choices. Choice making may encompass all of them.

Choosing is the context for much of our learning and application of learning. Facing an open-ended or right-answer choice stimulates a quest for new knowledge, a scanning of existing knowledge for relevance, a speculation on possibilities, and a rallying of whatever choosing skills we might possess. This may not occur systematically, but it does occur. We know far too little about the individual pieces of choice making, or about their interconnections, to state with any confidence that this or that aspect of applied thought can be safely deleted from education's framework. Inclusiveness, not exclusiveness, needs to be the guideline at this stage.

Three types of resources support the general conclusion in this chapter that colleges should foster the development of choice-making skills. The first is selected portions of the research literature on thinking and learning. The second is several years of experimentation with diverse ways of helping students learn to think, choose, and learn more functionally at a technical college. The third resource is the shared experiences and knowledge of some two dozen practitioners in 2-year colleges, 4-year colleges, and universities across the country. These individuals have actively sought to improve student learning and thinking skills in a variety of ways and under a variety of circumstances. Their views mirror what many practitioners have to say to the research community about helping

473

students learn to choose more functionally. They were asked to reflect on and share their experiences with the author as grist for the deliberations in this chapter. They have generously done so in published writings, in letters, and in person. In the pages that follow, we report on many of their ideas and experiences. The reader should note, however, that the conclusions the author draws from these ideas and experiences were arrived at independently and may not be shared by these individuals.

A final preparatory note concerns the organization of the chapter. The first section depicts the universe of students who can benefit from instruction in choice-making skills. The second section addresses the question of why instruction in these skills is needed, from both an academic and a personal/social perspective. The third section depicts the kinds of choice-making skills that should be taught. These skills are grouped into four categories: basic tools, techniques, strategies, and attitudes. The final section raises some implementation and research issues, especially from the point of view of practitioners who must select and implement whatever is done to enhance choice-making competence in postsecondary education.

WHO NEEDS INSTRUCTION IN CHOICE MAKING?

There can be little serious argument about the value of fostering the development of choice-making skills during students' years of formal education. The prime questions revolve around the types of skills that should be fostered, the types of students who can benefit from special instruction in these skills, and the degree of attention that should be devoted to such instruction. One way to begin to address these issues is to investigate the attributes of those identified as competent at making choices. Suydam (1980, p. 36) lists a composite of 10 key characteristics of a good choice maker:

1. Able to understand mathematical concepts and terms.
2. Able to note likenesses, differences, and analogies.
3. Able to identify critical elements and to select correct procedures and data.
4. Able to note irrelevant detail.
5. Able to estimate and analyze.
6. Able to visualize and interpret quantitative or spatial facts and relationships.
7. Able to generalize on the basis of a few examples.
8. Able to switch methods readily.
9. Higher scores for self-esteem, confidence, and good relationships with others.
10. Lower scores for test anxiety.

Fuller, Karplus, and Lawson (1977, p. 28) portray a somewhat different individual. They suggest that someone operating at the level of Piagetian formal reasoning:

1. Can reason with concepts, relationships, abstract properties, axioms, and theories.
2. Uses symbols to express ideas.
3. Applies combinatorial, classification, conservation, serial ordering; proportional reasoning in these abstract modes of thought.
4. Can plan a lengthy procedure to attain given overall goals, and resources.
5. Is aware of and critical of his own reasoning, and actively checks on the validity of his conclusions by appealing to other information.

These and other such characterizations are obviously of similar type, yet reflect peculiar differences. They can be recognized when encountered, but it is difficult to know how to go about deliberately trying to develop one in the classroom.

Another way to pinpoint the target audience might be to seek the negative, the characteristics of students who do not function well when forced to make unguided choices. Bloom and Broder (1950) have described the "one-shot thinkers" who, if they choose at all, grasp almost randomly at the first conclusion that floats into view. Blum and Spangehl (1978, p. 1) have given examples of such thinking in several of its natural environments, situations every college teacher has encountered:

In an introductory geology class, a student can't identify rocks by type (igneous, sedimentary, etc.) because he doesn't understand the principles used in setting up classification schemes.

In reading a research summary, students are unable to separate the facts reported from the conclusions and opinions of the researcher.

Students in a political science class won't participate in a discussion of specific effects of pollution because they've already reached the general conclusion that pollution is bad.

The student selects from the library a book published in 1916 for documentation in a report on current directions in molecular biology.

While reading Dreiser's *Sister Carrie,* students can't infer what social conditions existed in turn-of-the-century Chicago.

These are extremes, yet suggest that virtually all students are imperfect at making systematic, informed, and functional choices. Carol McCombs of Tri-County Technical College, South Carolina, when queried as to the types of students needing choice-making education, expressed the opinion of many practitioners: "All students can benefit from this type of instruction: students in mathematics, sciences, humanities, social sciences, and all technical, industrial, business, and human services curricula. Students who are potential consumers, jurors, and voters or who are presently consumers, jurors, and voters. Students who are or will be exposed to one-sided, opinionated, mass media, or political campaigns, or advertising blitzes."

WHY IS INSTRUCTION
IN CHOICE-MAKING SKILLS NEEDED?

Choice Making and Academic Life

Strong or weak choice-making skills can obviously influence academic performance and prospects, though the full interplay between such skills and academic success is murky at best. Any comprehensive analysis, however, would surely include the following dimensions of academic choice making, which create difficulty for far too many students.

Handling Complex Types and Levels of Thought.   Fuller (1977, p. 27), Whimbey (1978, p. 26) and others report variously that from 33% to 60% of American adolescents and adults do not consistently use what Jean Piaget calls formal operational reasoning. Percentages may differ somewhat, but the educational implications do not. Much postelementary instruction is predicated on student capacity to manipulate generalizations, concepts, and similar forms of symbolic thought. Students lacking such functional capability are crippled in their ability to grasp and then wield the intellectual materials that are being presented to them. D. Martin (1979) suggests that this phenomenon goes beyond entering students, and that a noticeable proportion of those entering professional law and medical schools exhibit similar "arrested developmental functioning [p. 3]."

The impact of such a mismatch between student readiness to learn and teacher expectations is noticeable in many spheres. James Langford of Kansas State University comments that: "students need to be able to analyze a problem by taking it apart or identifying variables. Piagetians (I am one) talk about the control of variables being a formal operation, but it seems that the identification of these variables is a prerequisite to their control. In administering the 'Mealworm Puzzle' it is amazing how few students even realize that more than one variable is involved in the problem." Such students, who must often struggle to deal with phenomena and relationships that are primarily mental rather than purely physical, will have equivalent difficulties in making the sophisticated choices posed to them both inside and beyond the classroom.

Performing Basic Academic Skills (Reading, Writing, and Mathematics).   There is increasing evidence that difficulties with the 3R's are linked in meaningful ways to cognitive limitations. Richard Upchurch of Piedmont Technical College, South Carolina, after years of experimentation with placing developmental mathematics on a problem-solving basis, is struck by the implications of things which his students can, and usually cannot, do:

They Can	*Yet Cannot*
Add $\frac{1}{2} + \frac{2}{3}$	Add $-\frac{1}{2} + -\frac{2}{3}$
Add $\frac{1}{2} + \frac{1}{3}$	Add $\frac{1}{x} + \frac{1}{x+1}$
Solve $2x + 4 = 6$, for x	Solve $EF + G = H$, for F
Solve a problem using an algorithm or given procedure	Select the proper algorithm or procedure to fit a given problem
Read a graph	Interpret a graph
Perform basic calculations	Judge the reasonableness of the result
Perform algebraic manipulations	Recognize different forms of the result
Use a calculator	Attend to the limitations imposed

Such contrasts evoke images of students who have failed to grasp the fundamental concept of what they are doing, who tote formulas and actions across the landscape upon command yet who never understand the larger design and flow of which their efforts are supposed to be a part. Such a conclusion is supported by research reported by Mary Wilber of Pasco Hernando Community College, Florida, who correlated the performance of 70 students on the mathematical reasoning and mathematical fundamentals segments of the Test of Adult Basic Education before and after completion of a developmental mathematics course. (See Table 14.1.)

Such data suggest that these may be linkages between reasoning skills and mathematics proficiency. Similar patterns may be found in reading and writing skills. Elaine Greenwood of Valencia Community College, Florida, posits that sentence combining and other techniques often fail because the students lack a fundamental awareness of "connectiveness." She observes that their sentences

TABLE 14.1
Results of Tests on Mathematical Reasoning

Pretest Reasoning: Range/Grade Level	*Posttest Gain: Reasoning*	*Posttest Gain: Fundamentals*
6.75– 7.95	1.27	.77
8.00– 8.95	1.09	1.37
9.00– 9.95	.99	1.34
10.00–11.75	.95	2.18

often consist of a half-dozen terminal units strung together with endless "and"s. Connectives such as "therefore," "yet," "thus," "because," and the like are seldom encountered, because they imply causal connections between events, data, or ideas that many students simply do not comprehend.

Eva Kerr of New York reports research on writing skills among students in advanced studies who have already graduated from 2-year college programs. Evaluation of many students' writing samples reveals that: 75.2% failed to support answers (theses) with clear, well-developed arguments or appropriate evidence; 81.5% failed to make logical, smooth transitions between ideas; 70.4% failed to state clearly the problem (thesis) being addressed—and/or clearly describe it; and 62.8% failed to construct sentences that correctly communicated logical relationships between ideas.

Reg St. Clair of Mountain Empire Community College, Virginia, adds that: "people can't say what they mean because they don't *know* what they mean, not because of a grammatical sentence-structure/English class problem."

Blanc and Martin (1979) report on research that indicates that "reading comprehension is a subset of thinking, and that the individual's ability to comprehend through reading is limited by his capacity to reason." Beryl Brown, of the University of California, San Diego, holds that: "when teachers and parents and administrators cry 'Johnny can't write' (or whatever), I believe they are really describing the fact that he can't think of *what* to say or *how* to say it."

Adopting Knowledge and Skills to Meet Situational Demands.   A third set of choosing capabilities relates to doing more than blindly plugging in formulas for solving standardized problems. Lochhead, Clement, Whimbey, Herron, Flower, and many others have observed and reported on the phenomenon of "algorithmic thinking" among students. Schoenfeld (1980) characterizes algorithmic thinkers as follows: "they either saw what to do immediately or they gave up entirely. They were unable to, or at least unaware that they should, think, analyze, and explore—activities that are at the heart of problem solving [p. 226]."

The student who blindly imitates grammatical mechanics without purpose or grace, the psychology student who explains all human actions by recourse to Maslow's hierarchy of needs, and the electronics student who designs a single type of circuit for all occasions may well be unable to see beyond the technique to its meaning and purpose. Beetle Bailey's character Zero is the military equivalent of an algorithmic thinker: capable of learning to do something, but not why or when to do it.

For example, our basic reasoning course exerts substantial effort equipping the students to dissect and summarize real-world choices by using simple matrices. Relevant alternatives appear on the vertical left side and major factors, categories of data, and the like across the top. The concluding practice exercise analyzes the choice between three different jobs. The final exam uses a situation relating to marital problems, and more than one apparently well-prepared student has responded with a chart like that shown in Fig. 14.1.

As Mary Wilber of Pasco Hernando Community College, Florida, notes: "it seems that too many students have never heard the question 'Does your answer look reasonable?'"

Bringing Relevant Knowledge and Skills to Bear in Coping with Novel Problems.   Beyond the problem of selecting proper algorithms to use in relatively familiar types of problems lies the difficulty of dealing with open-ended or highly complex right-answer choices. Most of the truly significant choices, both within and outside academic life, demand an amalgamation of at least rudimentary techniques and facts from several disciplinary worlds. Such transferability is as important as it is difficult.

Butler (1977) states that: "the most important, the most instrumental knowledge and skills are those that are generalizable. The ultimate goal of education is not only to provide students with a particular body of knowledge and skills but also to insure that students can adapt, transfer, and use that knowledge and skill beyond the confines of the classroom in which they were learned. It is not enough to provide students with generalizable concepts, principles, and processes; students must also learn how to transfer that generalizable knowledge to new tasks, in new contexts [p. 11]."

The context to which Butler refers will in most cases be choices that the individual must face and make. A useful analogy is the stereotypical country doctor, armed with a black bag of medications and devices. The bag's contents have been carefully chosen to cover the widest possible range of expected needs. The doctor is skilled at diagnosing a complex set of symptoms and problems, and then pulling from the bag the exact combination of elements that will meet the need. Students need similar capabilities.

Engaging in Critical Thinking in Academic Disciplines.   Each discipline views and studies important questions somewhat differently, yet with a common concern for the principles and perspectives of disciplined thought. House (1980,

| | FACTORS TO CONSIDER | | | | |
ALTERNATIVES	Hourly Wages	Fringe Benefits	Promotions	Education Required	Location of Job
Separate					
Divorce					
Stay Together					

FIG. 14.1. An example of misapplied information.

p. 168), Sadler (1979, p. 17), and many others agree with Bloom's (1978) belief that disciplinary materials should be taught "as much for the ways of thinking they represent as for their traditional content [p. 573]." Klemp (1977), studying career success, states that: "perhaps the most consistent—yet counterintuitive—finding that we have discovered is that the amount of knowledge of a content area is generally *unrelated* to superior performance in an occupation and is often unrelated *even to marginally acceptable performance* . . . it is not the acquisition of knowledge or even the use of knowledge that distinguishes the outstanding performer, but rather the cognitive skills that are exercised and developed in the process of knowledge acquisition and use that constitutes our first factor of occupational success [p. 2]."

The evidence suggests that too few students are able to view their disciplines in this way, as much more than unconnected techniques, theories, or facts. Bloom (1978) concludes that: "Our textbooks emphasize specific content to be remembered and give students little opportunity to discover underlying concepts and principles and even less opportunity to attack real problems in the environments in which they live. . . . After the sale of over one million copies of the *Cognitive Taxonomy of Educational Objectives,* our instructional material, our classroom teaching methods rarely rise above the lowest category of the taxonomy—knowledge [p. 573]."

Schlesinger (1975) comments that: "All our academic disciplines *exhibit* man's higher order competencies in the sense that they display the products of their operation, but the disciplines are inarticulate—even unconcerned—about how those competencies can be best ignited and matured within the learner [p. 19]."

Krulik and Rudnick (1980) conclude that: "In many mathematics classes, students do not see any connections among the various ideas taught during the semester's course of study. Most regard each topic as a separate entity [p. 5]."

Blum and Spangehl (1980), studying students enrolled in the University of Louisville's basic social science research courses, find almost 40% performing poorly in thoroughness, almost 80% performing poorly in originality, over 50% performing poorly in logic, indicating "a large population of students needing basic remediation in these complex variables which underline critical thought and research in college life [p. 14]."

Mastery of a particular discipline may well lead to what Philip Phenix (1964) described as a "way of knowing" reality, and to pursuing questions and choices of substance with orderly and effective cognitive tools and knowledge. Such mastery, however, clearly requires conscious and persistent efforts to help students reach beyond the daily dose of facts to the underlying patterns of choice-making techniques and perspectives.

Viewing Choice Making as an Important Component of Academic Competence. Many of the things we accept as "necessary evils" of the teaching/learning process may, in fact, be rooted in student unpreparedness or unwillingness to become choice makers. These include:

Teachers' acceptance of the need to reteach anything covered in an earlier course (or, often, in an earlier segment of the current course) before using it to move further.

Students' views that all content is equally relevant (i.e., liable to appear on a test) or irrelevant (i.e., does not matter in the real world).

Students' demand for certainty, and their marked discomfort when course materials imply that there may be no certain right answers to something.

Student difficulty in breaking down and assaulting problems composed of several different techniques or elements.

Students' beliefs that their teachers have all the information and answers, and that the purpose of the course is for the student to pry it loose, and then keep it for a few weeks.

Each of these constraints hampers the teaching/learning process, and each relates in some way to students' perceptions of themselves as learners within an educational process. Viewing learning from the perspective of preparing the students to make informed and effective choices rather than simply learn facts conjures up the opposite set of conditions: students able to judge some content as more important than other content, students prepared at least to try to recall and apply earlier learnings, students comfortable with ambiguity, etc. Such conditions would not make the teaching/learning process more simple; it would probably become more complex and demanding. But there is evidence that it would also become more vital and stimulating.

Hobbs (1980) observed Feuerstein's Instrumental Enrichment program and noted that "at the outset, what impressed me most was the high level of motivation of the students. Hands waved for recognition, and the performance of others was eagerly attended to [p. 568]." Tomlinson-Keasey and Eisert's (1977) evaluation of the University of Nebraska's Piagetian-based ADAPT program concluded that it: "seems to create a climate for exploration that positively influences student development along intellectual dimensions. These students, by being responsible for their learning, have acquired new thinking skills and have learned to savor the accomplishments that accompany the use of these skills [p. 19]." Schoenfeld (1980) concludes that: "a class in which the students are helping the teacher work out problems and (at least apparently) contributing actively to their solutions is more likely to be dynamic and motivating than one that follows the classical 'show and drill' mode. Explaining to students where arguments come from—or better yet, working the arguments out with them when possible—can help to demystify mathematics and allow the students to approach it with less fear and trepidation [p. 15]."

Conclusion.   Absence of a choice-making emphasis has a pervasive effect on what does and does not occur in the classroom. The evidence suggests that far too little is being done, in far too many areas, to prepare most students to be effective choice makers. As Schlesinger (1975) puts it: "The crucial question involves what the student *does* with the bits of information he or she picks up in a course or text, or from personal experience. If all we ask is that the student remember it, we do a disservice; if we ask that he or she wield it, we acknowledge our claims for the liberal arts and general education [p. 42]." And for all other disciplines.

Choice Making and Personal/Social Life

The second major sphere in which students are confronted with choices involves their personal lives and their contributions to our society. Recent research by Piedmont Technical College suggests substantial underpreparedness on the part of students to make these choices.

Some 110 faculty and staff from over a dozen colleges rated 12 traditional academic and 9 open-ended personal choices on a scale of 1 (low) to 9 (high). One-half rated them in terms of how *well prepared* their graduates were to make each type of choice; the other half rated the same choices in terms of how *important for success* (undefined) was the ability to make these choices. The teachers were asked to assess their students' ability to make academic choices by answering questions like the following: "What are the similiarities and differences between Stokely Carmichael's and Martin Luther King's views of race relations?"; "What voltage will cause 5 amps to flow through a 20-ohm resistor?"; and "What is John Steinbeck's most enduring contribution to American literature?" The educators judged that on the average their students were prepared to answer such questions at the 4.32 level, but that the questions themselves were only important at the 3.90 level: The students were seen as somewhat overprepared for these only moderately important choices. The teachers were then asked to assess their students' ability to make personal/social choices by indicating the likelihood that the students could handle such questions as the following:

You have just observed John McKay, your co-worker, good friend, and nephew of the third shift supervisor, stealing company equipment. What do you do?

An insurance agent urges you to buy whole life, because despite its expense it is a 'better buy' in the long run. What do you do?

Your retired parents ask you to tell them the best way to spend $450 in order to reduce their fuel bills in the long run. What do you tell them?

The educators judged that on the average their students were prepared for such choices at the 4.53 level, but that the choices were important at the 6.99 level: The students were seen as drastically unprepared for these very important choices.

The need for greater personal/social choice-making preparation is clear. In the following sections we discuss several dimensions of personal and social choice making that are difficult for many students.

Being in Control.   Far too many students, and citizens, do not feel themselves in control of their lives or their institutions. Deb Rozeboom of Rock Valley College, Illinois, points out that: "many students do not hold themselves in high regard. Contributing to this low self-esteem is the feeling that they do not control much of what happens in their lives. They tend to believe that luck, 'the government,' school, or some other factor outside themselves determines much of their existence. They don't view their actions as choices they have made." The newspapers, journals, prisons, and psychiatric wards are full of written and human evidence of a lack of what Mark Blum of the University of Louisville calls "a sense of potency, and the skills to be potent," both personally and in interaction with corporations, government, technologies, and other institutions of our mass society.

Deciphering and Accepting Reality.   Poor choice-making skills, and a sense that one is not in control of one's choices, contribute mightily to an inability or unwillingness to deal with situations as they actually are. Students who have difficulty adding two-digit whole numbers will cheerfully enroll in electronics programs; viewing the world as mainly beyond their comprehension or control, they consider everything equally possible or impossible. Such tendencies are exacerbated by the fact that so often the realities are unpleasant, and a very human desire to ignore them can easily leap to life. Yet it is axiomatic that effective choices occur only if we wrestle with things as they are rather than as we would like them to be.

One particular aspect of the reality/unreality issue is propaganda, both political and commercial. Fleming and Weber (1980) report that only 32% of a group of 1012 high school juniors and seniors were able even to identify the (rather blatant) point of view of the writer of various materials. Their data suggested that "assuming it is agreed that the skill of detecting and resisting propaganda is an important part of social studies, it is apparent, based on this survey, that critical reading skills are either not being taught or not being taught well [p. 156]." Far too many people actually believe that they will spend less money on gas if they buy a Buick with a 510-mile range and a 30-gallon tank than if they buy a Datsun with "only" a 390-mile range and a 13-gallon tank.

Making Value Choices.   The role of values in choice making merits an entire chapter devoted just to this topic. Students are unequipped to deal with value choices. They see facts and values as polar opposites, instead of interconnecting them in what Scheffler (1977) calls the "cognitive emotions," or allowing the *fact* of values to play a legitimate part in choosing. Grace Rhodes, of Olympia College, Washington, points out that: "most of the values and beliefs . . . [most people] hold are the result not of their own thinking and searching for meaning and value, but rather of their accepting what others have told them is right." Unexamined values, hidden from overt roles in making choices that often have substantial moral, ethical, and/or personal dimensions, will too often lead to terrible decisions, with terrible consequences.

Locating and Using Information.   Some 15 students in Piedmont's basic reasoning courses recently indicated that they had purchased at least one expensive car in the past 3 years, that this was a major choice, and that they had been significantly concerned with getting "the most for their money." Yet *not one* of the 15 had consulted *Consumer Reports* or comparable sources before or after the choice; only three knew of the magazine's existence as a rater of cars. Experienced in seeking and using information within the academic world, they are somehow unmotivated to do the same in their personal lives even when the stakes (money, health, etc.) are far higher than "good grades."

This is irony indeed when our educational practices are so heavily information based. Choice-based education could scarcely do a poorer job of preparing students to use information after graduation. In fact, as Kurfman (1977) points out: "as students become more aware of how knowledge operates in making decisions, they should become more conscious of its usefulness. Thus, a decision-making focus does not diminish the importance of knowledge; instead, it should heighten the value students place on the kind of knowing which serves their purposes in resolving personal and social problems [p. 17]."

Coping with Job Demands.   There is unquestionable evidence that various types of choice-making skills, and the propensity to use them, are among the most important determinants of long-term career success. Lusterman (1977), in a nationwide survey of relationships between industry and education, summarizes the opinion of many with a business executive's quote that: "It's impossible to know what our manpower needs will be in 5 or 10 years, and therefore the basic need is for flexible people who have been trained in reading, writing, basic computational skills, and thinking. We can teach them the rest [p. 62]." *The Chicago Tribune,* in June 1980, cited the growing desire of companies that had previously hired specialized technicians to employ liberally educated workers who could reason, solve problems, understand a variety of points of view, and have a wider perspective of themselves and their roles as employees. The benefits of better choice-making capabilities to both employer and employee are many and need no enumeration.

Coping with Interrelatedness.   Our technological and economic worlds have become intertwined almost beyond comprehension. As James Langford of Kansas State University points out: "There was a time . . . when a decision as to where to build the tiger pit was about as complex a problem as man faced. Today's students will enter a world where each problem they face is made up of many variables, a large body of distorted facts are presented to them, jobs at even the 'lowest' level require complex mental and physical operations, and man's very existence can be determined by solutions to these problems. Schools have been teaching cognitive skills designed to solve the problem of the tiger pit, but not those designed to solve the problems of the modern, complex, technological society."

Bronson (1975) concurs, and adds that: "the world is smaller, and the interrelatedness of people is more pressing; the degree of orthodoxy of a sheik's advisor may determine whether or not we are warm this winter! The schools must train people to handle information, and information comes in patterns and can be dealt with only by patterns. And patterns are for thinking [p. 353]."

Coping with Social Problems.   The social and political consequences of affluence, technology, economic interdependence, militarism, and other attributes of our civilization will undoubtedly not vanish from among us, no matter what golden age of education might be peeking over the horizon. Yet few of us can be content with the effectiveness with which we, as individuals and as a society, are addressing our social ills and political dilemmas. Few could argue with Sam Kintzer, of Lansing Community College, Michigan, in his comment that: "It seems self-evident that a more perceptive, reflective citizenry is critical for the survival of a democracy in these difficult times."

Conclusion.   A final validation of the value of solid choice-making skills in personal and societal life comes from a seven-county survey conducted by Piedmont Technical College (M. Martin, 1976). Some 1,000 persons, including community leaders, those associated with the college, and randomly selected heads of households, were asked the question "Which three items (of 26 choices) do you think are the most important for people to know or be able to do to be successful?" "Success" was deliberately not defined. The responses of the three populations were almost identical; the following 12 items were in each group's top 10 choices:

1. Get a job and keep it.
2. Make decisions.
3. Get along with fellow employees and supervisors.
4. Feel good about themselves.
5. Get along with family members.
6. Know how to think things through.
7. Know how to read well.
8. Take directions.
9. Know how to solve problems.
10. Know about handling money.
11. Use good English in talking.
12. Know how to learn new things.

Eleven of these twelve personal-success prerequisites involve choice making.

Evidence of Practitioner Concern About Instruction in Choice-Making Skills

Our education system needs to deliberately foster choice makers among its students. Perhaps the most convincing evidence, beyond the specific instances already offered, lies in the breadth of attention that choice-making instruction is already receiving. Respected and cautious professional associations such as the National Council of Teachers of Mathematics, the National Council of Supervisors of Mathematics, the National Council for the Social Studies, and the National Education Association have emphasized the criticalness of choice-making skills. At least two problem-solving newsletters have been launched within the past 18 months. Regular columns on choice making are appearing in professional journals (e.g., the *Journal of Developmental and Remedial Education*). Recent publications have devoted entire issues to choice making. Single articles on basic reasoning skills can elicit letters and calls of interest from colleagues in more than 35 states. One of the most frequent topics of proposals submitted for federal funding to programs like the Fund for the Improvement of Post-Secondary Education is some form of choice-making endeavor. The 1980 NIE–LRDC Conference on Thinking and Learning Skills, which served as an impetus for the present volume, was itself a response to a surge of interest among both practitioners and researchers.

The need for choice-making education is far clearer than the target. The aspects of choice making explored in the foregoing paragraphs are diverse; some perhaps conflict, and some are perhaps impossible to educe. No single student could ever possess all these attributes in full, and all students now possess some of them at least in part. The task seems to be not to decide *if* something should be done, but to determine *what* should be done. What skills are crucial? The section that follows summarizes some of the attributes that seem to contribute to choice-making competence in and beyond the classroom.

WHICH SKILLS SHOULD BE TAUGHT?

William Martin of George Mason University, in Virginia, suggests the range of needed choice-making skills with his statement that: "problem solving encompasses the entire set of processes by which needs are felt, goals are set, tasks defined, options searched for, decisions made, and solutions evaluated. It incorporates the areas of decision making and inquiry training."

It is difficult to pinpoint the exact skills on which programs of instruction in choice making should focus, in part because of our general paucity of knowledge about the nature of successful choice making and in part because of our lack of a conceptual framework for organizing skills into larger groupings. One way of viewing the scene would be the following conceptualization of choice making as involving four categories of skills:

1. Basic reasoning tools: the individual reasoning operations that constitute the building blocks out of which more complex choice-making techniques are constructed.
2. Choice-making techniques: complex choice-making skills that incorporate basic reasoning tools.
3. Choice-making heuristics: rules for mixing and matching tools and techniques to meet particular needs.
4. Choice-making attitudes: awarenesses and propensities that are required for successful choice making.

Generally, these four categories might constitute different levels of choice-making proficiency, with skills at lower levels embedded within skills at higher levels. The pages that follow attempt to describe further the nature of each category.

Basic Reasoning Tools

Fraenkel (1973) identifies 11 important intellectual operations: "observing, describing, developing concepts, differentiating, defining, hypothesizing, comparing and contrasting, generalizing, predicting, explaining, and offering alternatives [p. 189]." Other writers on cognition have their own lists, similar yet distinct. Most would agree with Fraenkel that such lists are not final, absolute, or mutually exclusive.

The diversity of terms on lists like these, and the uncertainty about relationships among terms, tend to leave us at some loss to decide exactly how many basic reasoning tools exist and how to elicit them. Nevertheless, there does seem to be a set of basic reasoning tools that, if missing or imperfectly developed, undercut the student's ability to learn to choose. Six such tools that are worthy of attention in instructional programs on choice making are:

1. The ability and propensity to see relationships.
2. Skill in classifying and ordering, as a flexible tool adaptable to the needs of the moment.
3. Skill in forming analogies as an aid both in understanding and in communicating what one has understood.
4. Specificity in thinking and in expressing one's thoughts.
5. A grasp of the distinction between the products of thought and the processes by which these products were achieved.

6. Skill in "coming close," estimating, approximating, and judging reasonableness.

This list of basic reasoning tools is by no means exhaustive; it merely offers some concrete examples that are of particular importance to practitioners. In fact, some of these tools may actually be more complex than basic; given our present state of knowledge, it is difficult to separate the two categories in precise ways.

Choice-Making Techniques

These are combinations of basic tools that have been supplemented in complex ways. There seems to be more agreement as to the items to be included in this category, although none of these techniques is very well understood in the sense that one can specify the chain of cognitive operations that are involved in its successful execution.

We list here eight choice-making techniques that should receive attention in instructional programs. Again, the listing is not to attempt to spell out the universe of such techniques, but rather to offer some concrete and important exemplars, distilled again mainly from practitioners' published writings and personal communications:

1. Identifying the real problem: going beyond the apparent issue to a more comprehensive and adequate definition of the underlying problem.

2. Analyzing the interrelated components of a choice into their separate factors.

3. Synthesizing complex bodies of facts: recognizing the patterns and consistencies embedded in data.

4. Identifying and manipulating alternative solutions to a problem.

5. Blending values with information in making decisions.

6. Communicating (to oneself and others) ideas about and solutions to problems.

7. Engaging in questioning techniques (of self and others), as described by Payne (1951), Hunkins (1976), and others.

8. Analyzing information and circumstances both inductively and deductively.

Choice-Making Heuristics

The third level of choice-making skills consists of broad and highly flexible strategies, or heuristics, that the individual uses to guide his or her selection of tools and techniques for use in meeting particular needs. This level of choice making is by far the most slippery of all. It is difficult to know exactly what a choice-making heuristic is, how it works, when it changes, what affects it, and how individuals apply it.

Krulik and Rudnick (1980) describe heuristics as: "a general strategy, independent of a particular topic: suggestions that individuals can follow to help them approach a problem, understand the problem, and arrive at a solution to that problem. Techniques for solving specific problems should not be considered heuristics [p. 19]." Engineering students at McMaster University (1979) reported a list of problem-solving heuristics that they had devised over a period of many months as ways to tackle complex engineering problems; their list included heuristics with such titles as "overcoming the initial panic," "attribute listing," "personal analogy," "juxtaposition or the use of chance," "estimating orders-of-magnitude," and " 'what if?' in the extremes." The lack of heuristics is often more evident than its presence. Kantowski (1980) notes that "We have all heard students say, 'I see what you did, but how did you think of doing that?', or 'I can always follow your solutions, but I would never think of doing some of those things myself.' Something else—a skill different from computational skill— is a necessary component of successful problem solving [p. 198]."

The nature of that skill (or those skills) seems shrouded in controversy. Apparently it is not a lockstep set of problem-solving processes (though such may be useful). As Lochhead (1979) points out, there is no one best approach, yet as Ewing (1977) suggests, each person tends to have a scheme that is "best" for him or her. Davis (1973), Kantor and Perron (1977), and many others hold that overall strategies involve use of both lateral and linear thinking. Despite such gaps in understanding, it is clear that a third major ingredient in choice-making success is the series of overarching strategies that the individual tailors to meet a particular situation.

Attitudes Toward Choice Making

A final major attribute of effective choice making is attitudinal; the individual must *want* to choose, must be *aware* that he or she is capable of effective choice, and should be interested in making a *good,* rather than merely acceptable, choice. As with the other dimensions, attitudes towards choice making have many components.

Elizabeth Steltenpohl of New York City remarks on the number of adult learners who, though possessing many experiences that build the foundation for mature judgment and critical thinking, remain unaware of their proficiency, or of themselves as individuals already capable of critical thought. Restak (1979) believes that: "as things now stand, the typical graduate of most major universities knows next to nothing about the workings of his own brain. This is particularly ludicrous when you consider that all mental life is directly dependent on the integrity and optimal functioning of the brain [p. 383]." Those unaware that they think, or ignorant of the mechanics of thinking, may have difficulty with the process, regardless of their other skills.

John Craig of Trident Technical College, South Carolina, believes that far too many students lack a "realization that thinking patterns can be modified"; he holds such insights to be one of the four most important types of cognitive skills that need to be elicited in all students. Klemp (1977) identifies a variable, "*cognitive initiative,* which is related to whether a person habitually thinks in terms of causes and outcomes or whether a person sees the self as an ineffective victim of events which have an unknown cause [p. 6–7]." Awareness that one can grow in choice-making skills and that one is the prime determiner of what happens seems to be a prerequisite attitude.

A final contributor is the matter of the quality of choice. Many students are content merely to choose the first alternative that comes along, either because they know no better one or merely want "to get it over with." Rubinstein and Pfeiffer (1980, p. 7) call for "an attitude of wanting to create a *good* solution," and a "will to doubt" an initial choice until it has been carefully inspected. Mathematicians often call for solutions that are "elegant" rather than merely good. Given that most choices are open-ended, a desire to seek quality undoubtedly contributes to choice-making competence.

Implications for Restructuring the Curriculum

Taken separately, many of these choice-making tools, techniques, strategies, and attitudes could be accommodated without major disruption to the course structure typically found in institutions of higher education. Taken together, however, they suggest a broader, certainly different, vision of what education should be about. It is a vision that is consistent with that portrayed by Botkin, Elmandjra, and Malitza's recent Club of Rome report on worldwide education (1979), which concluded that:

> Innovative learning must not be misconstrued as merely a new technique, simply to be added to the existing curricula. It involves the total human being. Anticipatory and participatory learning requires holistic approaches. Learning must again affect the intellect, the emotions, and the willpower of humans. Today, education is intellect biased. Old ideas of education are often neglected in daily practice. Fantasy, creativity—on which both science and the arts are based—solidarity, tolerance, and empathy are affective qualities which must be developed and exercised as well as willpower, decision making, and participation. Students must experience to participate, must learn to integrate work and life, to develop critical facilities, to apply new knowledge and implement new ideas, and to change their way of life [p. 137].

HOW CAN THE CURRENT INTEREST IN INSTRUCTION IN CHOICE-MAKING SKILLS BE APPROPRIATELY FOSTERED AND GUIDED?

This section discusses issues associated with implementing practical programs of instruction in choice-making skills. It also offers a practitioner's view of questions that should guide future research on choice-making skills—an agenda of questions to which practitioners engaged in cognitive skills instruction are seeking answers.

The perspective in this section is a skeptical one. The constraints on schools, researchers, and funding sources make very improbable a major, permanent shift toward instruction in choice-making skills, no matter what the next decade's research and development activities. Much of the change that does occur will be short-lived and/or limited in its impact. Much that occurs, of whatever scale, will occur aside from, rather than because of, deliberate research and development efforts. These outcomes are not inevitable, but seem likely, given patterns of innovation during the past two decades.

Barriers to the Spread of Instruction in Choice-Making Skills

Difficulties arise on all sides: human nature, funding, teaching practices, curriculum, ignorance, attitudes, teacher preparation, and so forth. There are two particular sets of difficulties: (1) conflicting attitudes, beliefs and practices prevalent among practitioners; and (2) conflicting role pressures experienced by those sympathetic to instruction in choice-making skills.

Conflicting Attitudes, Beliefs, and Practices.   The reasons offered by researchers and practitioners for the failure of colleges to offer more instruction in choice-making skills speak for themselves and need to be heard clearly:

Bloom: We tend to believe that some students have the ability to learn while others lack it, and we do not regard it as a major goal of the schools to develop learning ability.

Gomez: We have a widespread belief that English and mathematics can perform by themselves the whole role of a reasoning–training course . . . and the belief that a mere elementary course in Symbolic Logic can play that role.

Glenn: Studying about a problem does not mean that students are learning or practicing problem-solving skills . . . [and] studying a problem that is primarily of interest to adults does not necessarily involve students in problem solving.

McCombs: Fostering these skills is much more demanding on a teacher's time and ability than providing instruction at the knowledge level. More intense preparation of teaching strategies is essential; evaluation requires more time because evaluation must be somewhat subjective.

Upchurch: We who teach mathematics claim to be teaching quantitative thinking skills, yet we continue to impose the refinements of thousands of years of mathematical development on our students over the course of one or two terms— and then we are surprised when they seem reluctant to accept this highly distilled knowledge. We fail to consider that mathematical learning involves understanding.

Kerr: Educators are not very secure with the ambiguous and invisible, and like to teach what they can control.

Banton: A surprising 75 percent of the questions [in 70 elementary school texts] were found to be narrow, requiring low-level thinking, short and factual answers, or predictable yes/no responses.

Rozeboom: Most people assume that the ability to reason is acquired through the natural developmental process . . . that people learn to think at home . . . [or] that the ability to reason is more a state of being equated with IQ than a skill.

Greenfield: The step-by-step procedures instructors present to students, such as blackboard problem solutions, may not be ordered in the way that the problem was solved by the instructor initially, but rather may be edited to be more elegant. Further, the strategy used by the instructor for problem solution may not be identified.

Meyer: The reasons for this state of affairs are legion, and each one might suggest at least one book, for example, alienation of youth, the nonparticipatory nature of educational institutions, competition of subject areas, lack of competency or mastery training or orientation, and the uncontrollability of established structures and procedures.

Brown: If done properly, the result of teaching is a subversive activity. You end up with students who question authority. Many people are fearful of that possibility.

Overcoming these and other impediments will be difficult under the best of circumstances. Most of the forces that have created or maintained the current situation will continue to operate as forces resisting change. Unfortunately, it is probable that the forces *promoting* change will be in a minority, and will be in disarray. Major shifts toward instruction in choice-making skills will occur only if the researchers, the curriculum developers and publishers, the funding agencies, and the practitioners can cooperate with a degree of harmony and creativity seldom, if ever, witnessed on a major scale in American education.

Conflicting Role Pressures.   Even among those most sympathetic to instruction in choice-making skills, there are conflicting role pressures and natural temptations that must be considered.

There will be tendencies among *researchers:* (1) to seek basic truths more for their own sake than for their practical importance; (2) to demand the time (often many years) to understand concepts, relationships, and outcomes fully before seeking to apply them to the classroom; (3) to conduct research mainly in areas where grant support is easily available; (4) to carry on research under carefully controlled conditions that substantially differ from actual classroom learning situations; (5) to eschew responsibility for practical implementation of theories; (6) to pursue more and more esoteric language and sophisticated issues as knowledge accumulates; and (7) to interact with novices and practitioners as "the expert," if at all. Not all researchers will fall prey to these sorts of pressures, but the temptations will surely influence the pace and direction of research activities.

There will be tendencies among *practitioners:* (1) to settle for things that "seem to work" at first glance; (2) to undertake only limited investigation, training, and evaluation before adopting a new approach and materials; (3) to tinker with programs and materials before, during, and after installation; (4) to reinvent; (5) to expect simple answers to complex issues; (6) to implement yesterday, out of desperation or by imitation; (7) to lose interest when problems appear; and (8) to demand proof of effectiveness before, or as a safeguard against, implementation. Again, not all will succumb, but many will be influenced.

Others interested in instruction in choice-making skills will also experience conflicting pressures. *Curriculum developers* will tend to: focus on creating more sophisticated materials; follow grant funds; reduce everything to "complete packages"; apply only one approach; and create special courses in choice-making skills that are taught apart from the rest of the curriculum. *Publishers* will tend to: focus on what is profitable; emphasize consumable student-oriented materials; overlook the cognitive demands being made on students in coping with these materials; and issue materials that are incompletely proven, lack comprehensiveness, etc. *Funding agencies* will continue to be beset by conflicting and changing priorities, by limits on grant durations that make long-term investigations difficult, by demands that success be guaranteed in advance, and by a lack of centralized networks and clearinghouses to disseminate information to those who are interested.

The point is not to disparage any or all of these groups. Their tendencies are natural and in many cases beneficial. The point is to better understand and blend the diversity of viewpoints and interests concerned with instruction in choice-making skills. Maintaining control of what is clearly becoming one of the "hot" instructional topics of the 1980s will demand new and creative approaches to partnership among researchers, practitioners, and others forged not in isolation but in the midst of attempts by practitioners to implement new programs.

A Practitioner's Research Agenda

The field of cognition supplies endless numbers of researchable questions: momentous, trivial, and in-between. For most practitioners, the more important questions are those representing a collision between what we would like to know, and what we must do in the classroom. The following are some examples of these questions, and suggestions as to ways of approaching them that practitioners would find fruitful. The questions themselves cannot be fully answered within a decade, much less a year or two. Interim answers, or even suggestions, hints, and clues, may already exist, however, or could be derived if these questions received sufficient attention. Many classroom teachers, curriculum designers, and the like would welcome even such partial answers to questions like these.

How can we accommodate diverse rates and stages of cognitive development in the same classroom?

How do degree and type of cognitive development correlate with chronological age, academic tracks, socioeconomic groups, sex, and academic achievement?

What do the major strands of cognitive research imply in terms of what teachers should be and do?

What methods are useful in inducing an educational institution to become concerned about and committed to instruction in cognitive skills?

What would effective communications bridges between researchers and practitioners look like, and how could they be developed?

How do cognitive strategies useful in academic environments compare to the cognitive strategies useful in personal/societal environments?

Do cognitive-based teaching and learning events that are focused on academic success show signs of transferring to nonacademic choices and actions? Which ones?

How can we assess the explicit and implicit cognitive requirements of instructional materials, including both commercial and locally developed materials?

How can cognitive-based teaching and learning approaches be systematized for maximum efficiency and adoption without becoming mechanized?

Does cognitive-based teaching and learning require substantially different types of teachers in terms of attitudes, personality, preparations, etc? If so, what are the implications?

What is generalizable about problem-solving skills?

What are the relative merits, both theoretical and pragmatic, of instruction in cognitive skills administered as part of content-area courses versus administered as a separate course?

What cognitive skills did postsecondary developmental students miss during their earlier education, when did they miss these skills, and why?

To what degree, and in what ways, do difficulties with basic skills reflect difficulties with cognitive skills?

What are the similarities and differences in cognitive structures and functioning between adults and children with similar types of basic skills performances?

What benefits would accrue if substantial numbers of cognitive researchers and practitioners focused on a single population, such as postsecondary developmental students?

What instruments can diagnose the cognitive functioning of students with sufficient precision and ease of implementation that they are useful to practitioners?

How do cognitive skills and attitudes toward cognition interrelate?

What framework of understandings, language, values, and attitudes do cognitive reseachers and practitioners have in common?

What attitudes, habits, and reference points do practitioners reflect that hamper their ability to be informed by cognitive research?

What attitudes, habits, and reference points do researchers reflect that hamper their ability to be informed by cognitive skills practitioners?

How can cognitive research be disseminated effectively?

How can cognitive-based teaching and learning be effectively introduced into existing classrooms and schools?

Are open admissions students and adult learners different from traditional students in terms of cognitive orientation and/or capabilities? If so, in what ways, and why? If not, why not?

What useful mechanisms can be established to allow cognitive practice to profoundly influence the direction and pace of cognitive research?

What are the effects of instructor role models on the problem-solving skills of students?

What expectations and models concerning cognition have we implicitly institutionalized in our educational settings? What are the implications?

Each question seems entangled in several others, leading to considerable ambiguity and frustration. A first need is thus to provide a framework that will organize such questions so that we can simultaneously *learn about* teaching thinking *while implementing* our findings or clues. This, in turn, calls for far more creative, effective, and responsive forms of partnership between researchers and practitioners. This cannot be overemphasized, lest we emerge at the end of a decade with some major insights, methodically published in obscure (to the practitioner) journals, only to find the classroom instructor having long ago adopted someone's superficial "package deal," found it wanting, and moved on to the "buzzword of the nineties." Two brief examples suggest the types of creative approaches that merit exploration.

Each research and development effort in cognitive skills instruction has tended to focus on a particular, very limited population of its own: third graders, freshmen engineering students at 4-year colleges, developmental mathematics students at 2-year colleges, etc. The generalizability of the resulting insights is quite limited. An alternative would be to select some clearly delineated, broad population for concentrated research and development attention. A very good choice might be postsecondary developmental students—students who are enrolled in postsecondary education but who are academically underprepared to cope with work at this level. Such students require instruction in basic academic skill areas; they constitute a growing body of students; they tend to have few choice-making skills appropriate to their age level; they are taught by instructors who have shown themselves to be open to innovation and free from most traditional disciplinary constraints; and they can be relatively easily identified, isolated, and comparatively studied. This group offers many advantages. The suggestion, however, is to find *some* coherent group on whom both researchers and practitioners can focus their work to maximize coordination of effort and generalizability of results.

Secondly, it can be argued that much of the linkage between researchers and practitioners imitates the lecture model of instruction. The researcher (teacher) finds out things and passes them on to the practitioner (students). The entire concept of choice-making instruction calls for a different model, one in which the researcher (teacher) acts as skilled guide/mentor/resource person for the practitioners (students) as they explore, and eventually act upon, a problem of concern to them. Would such an analogy provide a useful perspective for creating more functional relationships among the various allies in the choice-making endeavor?

The questions and possibilities are legion, stubborn, confused, and urgent. From a practitioner's point of view, the most important need is to erect a creative, realistic framework within which to pursue them while continually remaining concerned with what happens to the individual student, in the individual classroom, as a result of efforts to foster choice-making education.

REFERENCES

Banton, L. Broadening the scope of classroom questions. *Virginia Journal of Education*, 1977, *71*, 34–38.

Blanc, R., & Martin, D. *A case study of the effect of an experimental teaching methodology in American History on cognitive development and reading achievement of inner-city high school students.* Unpublished manuscript, University of Missouri, Kansas City, 1979.

Bloom, B. New view of the learning: Implications for instruction and curriculum. *Educational Leadership*, 1978, *35*, 562–568.

Bloom, B., & Broder, L. L. *Problem-solving process of college students.* Chicago: University of Chicago Press, 1950.

Blum, M. E., & Spangehl, S. D. *College instruction in critical thinking.* Unpublished manuscript, University of Louisville, 1978.

Blum, M. E., & Spangehl, S. D. *Testing entry and exit level research competencies in general education courses.* Unpublished manuscript, University of Louisville, 1980.

Botkin, J., Elmandjra, M., & Malitza, M. *No limits to learning: Bridging the human gap.* A report to the Club of Rome. Oxford: Pergamon Press, 1979.

Bronson, D. B. Thinking and teaching. *The Educational Forum*, 1975, *39*, pp. 347–353.

Butler, C. The major factors that affect learning: A cognitive process model. *Educational Technology*, 1977, *17*, 5–12.

Davis, G. *Psychology of problem solving.* New York: Basic Books, Inc., 1973.

Ewing, D. W. Discovering your problem-solving style. *Psychology Today*, 1977, *11*, 68–70.

Fleming, D., & Weber, L. Recognizing point of view: A critical reading skill in the social studies. *Social Education*, 1980, *44*, 153–156.

Fraenkel, J. R. *Helping students think and value: Strategies for teaching the social studies.* Englewood Cliffs, N.J.: Prentice–Hall, 1973.

Fuller, R., Karplus, R., & Lawson, A. Can physics develop reasoning? *Physics Today,* 1977, *30,* 23–28.

Glenn, A. Problem solving in social studies: Two examples from the classroom. *Social Education,* May 1977, 416–418.

Greenfield, L. Student problem solving. *Engineering Education,* April 1979, 709–712.

Hobbs, N. Feuerstein's instrumental enrichment: Teaching intelligence to adolescents. *Educational Leadership,* 1980, *37,* 566–568.

House, P. Risking the journey into problem solving. In S. Krulik (Ed.), *Problem solving in school mathematics.* Reston, Va.: NCTM, 1980.

Hunkins, F. P. *Involving students in questioning.* Newton, Mass.: Allyn & Bacon, 1976.

Kantor, K., & Perron, J. Thinking and writing: Creativity in the modes of discourse. *Language Arts,* 1977, *54,* 742–749.

Kantowski, M. G. Some thoughts on teaching for problem solving. In S. Krulik (Ed.), *Problem solving in school mathematics.* Reston, Va.: NCTM, 1980.

Klemp, G. O. *Three factors of success in the world: Implications for curriculum in higher education.* Boston: McBer and Co., 1977.

Krulik, S., & Rudnick, J. *Problem solving: A handbook for teachers.* Newton, Mass.: Allyn & Bacon, 1980.

Kurfman, D. G. (Ed.). *Developing decision-making skills* (47th Yearbook). Arlington, Va.: National Council for the Social Studies, 1977.

Lochhead, J. *An anarchistic approach to teaching problem-solving methods.* Paper presented at the meeting of the American Educational Research Association, San Francisco, April 1979.

Lusterman, S. *Education in industry.* New York: The Conference Board, 1977.

Martin, D. *Learning assistance centers in professional schools: Challenging the traditional assumptions.* Unpublished manuscript, University of Missouri, Kansas City, 1979.

Martin, M. *Community survey report.* Unpublished manuscript, Piedmont Technical College, 1976.

Meyer, John R. The status of the education of judgment. *Educational Leadership,* 1978, *35,* 449–452.

Payne, S. L. *The art of asking questions.* Princeton: Princeton University Press, 1951.

Phenix, P. H. *Realms of meaning: A philosophy of the curriculum for general education.* New York: McGraw–Hill, 1964.

Restak, R M. *The brain: The last frontier.* Garden City, N.Y.: Doubleday, 1979.

Rubinstein, M., & Pfeiffer, K. *Concepts in problem solving.* Englewood Cliffs, N.J.: Prentice–Hall, 1980.

Sadler, W. Tapping the potentials of interdisciplinary studies in a freshman core program. *Interdisciplinary Perspective,* 1979, *4,* 20.

Scheffler, I. In praise of the cognitive emotions. *Teachers College Record,* 1977, *79,* 171–186.

Schlesinger, M. A. *Implementing competency-based education: Critical thinking isn't a competency?* Paper presented at the meeting of the AAHE, Toledo, Ohio, April 1975.

Schoenfeld, A. Heuristics in the classroom. In S. Krulik (Ed.), *Problem solving in school mathematics.* Reston, Va.: NCTM, 1980.

Suydam, M. Untangling clues from research on problem solving. *Problem solving in school mathematics.* Reston, Va.: NCTM, 1980.

Tomlinson-Keasey, C. A., & Eisert, D. Second year evaluation of the ADAPT program. *Multidisciplinary Piagetian-based programs for college freshman,* University of Nebraska, Lincoln, 1977.

Whimbey, A. *A cognitive skills approach to the disciplines* (CUE Project Publication). Bowling Green State University, 1978.

15 Teaching Problem Solving to Developmental Adults: A Pilot Project

Richard T. Hutchinson
Manhattan Community College
CUNY

In this chapter we describe some impressions we have derived from our attempts to teach problem-solving skills to academically underprepared adults ("developmental" students) seeking to participate in higher education. In the spring semester of 1980, we began work on the Cognitive Studies Project, a pilot project at Manhattan Community College concerned with helping such students become more effective thinkers and learners. In the sections that follow, we describe our rationale for offering these students instruction in thinking and learning skills. We then present a brief overview of the pilot project, describing both the kinds of students who were involved and the instructional approaches that were used. Next we discuss some insights we derived from engaging in this project. These include insights with respect to the intellectual competencies of developmental students, with respect to the special difficulties that are entailed in offering cognitive skills instruction to this population, and with respect to barriers that exist in higher education settings to attempts to introduce cognitive skills instruction.

RATIONALE FOR THE COGNITIVE STUDIES PROJECT

The open admissions policy of the City University of New York (CUNY) constitutes a commitment to develop the vital human resources of the city. As Lavin, Alba, and Silberstein (1979) point out, CUNY's open admissions policy obligates its colleges to effectively teach all students and views the student's failure as the institution's failure. However, little has been done in a systematic way to equip faculty with the skills necessary to teach effectively increasing numbers of academically underprepared students entering the University. As a result, the critical nexus of student learning ability and faculty instructional ability has become a point of disjunction rather than one of continuity and complementarity.

For the students, this disjunction is the result of deficiencies that exceed those in basic academic skills, such as reading, writing, and arithmetic, although serious deficiencies do exist in those areas. In addition, students frequently have not developed the ability to process information, as Moore (1976) notes: "to reason and conceptualize . . . to organize, analyze, and synthesize, . . to make use of available resources, . . . to interpret data, . . . to attack the problems of the specific subject matter, . . . to abstract, paraphrase, characterize, compare, contrast, and conclude" (p. 67). Confronted with demands to exercise these abilities, but not receiving any help in developing them, such students often find college an inhospitable environment and leave in distressingly large numbers.

Among faculty, this disjunction is experienced as frustration—frustration both with the students' deficiencies and with not knowing, as instructors, how to cope with these deficiencies. The faculty's lack of knowledge is understandable, however, when one considers that institutions of higher education seldom aid faculty in upgrading their teaching skills or in understanding and managing the special learning needs of developmental students. Unfortunately, those faculty who do make the effort to improve their skills or to understand their students are largely unrewarded on these bases alone. Schalock (1976) contends that, generally, college administrators tend to reward activities other than teaching. Faculty frustration is further abetted by the fact that most faculty have little if any pedagogical training and often unwittingly rely heavily on the academic abilities of their students rather than on their own teaching abilities for whatever success they manage to achieve in the classroom.

In a succinct article, Arons (1979) identifies 16 reasoning capacities implicitly expected of college students. They are all higher order cognitive abilities reflective of Piagetian formal operational thought. Arons argues that instructors tend to take their presence for granted, and to structure their courses to tap these presumed abilities. To quote Arons (1979):

> In recent years the administration of Piagetian tasks in logical reasoning has revealed that a very large proportion of college students tend to use predominantly concrete as opposed to formal patterns of reasoning. This observation points to a profound discrepancy between most secondary school and college-level course content on the one hand, and the actual student reasoning patterns on the other: most course presentation assumes that students are generally prepared to utilize formal reasoning processes. (p. 209)

Arons, Bauman (1976), and others estimate that the number of college freshmen actually achieving formal operational thought on different tasks ranges between 25 and 75%. This suggests that many faculty may be teaching over the heads of many of their students. However, when these reasoning deficiencies are overlaid by basic skills deficiencies such as we mentioned earlier, the problems associated with providing instruction are compounded, and faculty are often overwhelmed. Reflecting this dilemma, one of our colleagues expressed the sentiment of a small group attending a faculty symposium when she candidly said, amid affirming nods, "I don't know how to teach them." We believe this note would be echoed in many other institutions that serve academically under-prepared students.

The feeling of not knowing "how to teach them" is bad enough, but not getting any help is worse. For the most part faculty are on their own. This condition has an extremely negative impact on faculty self-esteem and on the faculty's regard for their students. The result is a demoralized faculty, and among developmental students, extremely high academic mortality.

The Cognitive Studies Project addresses itself to this issue—the discontinuity between student learning ability and faculty instructional ability. Our objectives are to achieve clearer understandings of students' learning processes, to identify and develop effective methods for stimulating the intellectual development of students, and to provide faculty with assistance in adapting these methods for use in their classrooms. The method we employ can be subsumed under the label *cognitive processes instruction.*

Lochhead and Clements (1979) and Lin (1979) define cognitive processes instruction as an instructional approach that emphasizes the development of mental abilities essential for understanding and thinking rather than simply mastering the content covered in specific courses. Cognitive processes instruction aims more at teaching students how to think, than what to think. Consequently, we believe that cognitive processes instruction can complement a variety of other instructional methods typically used in higher education because these methods assume the cognitive abilities that cognitive processes instruction seeks to foster.

We do not, however, view cognitive process instruction as a panacea for all instructional and learning problems. Other factors impinge on these problems, from both within the institution and without. However, we do consider it a means of contributing to the attainment of the university's goal of providing effective instruction to all students.

Our objective of stimulating intellectual development raises questions about the issue of whether intelligence can be learned. We do not recast that debate here but rather simply summarize our position. We believe that the cognitive deficiencies exhibited by developmental students can largely be remediated. Our view is that the failure of these students to employ the mental processing skills required for college work is due to the fact that they have not had adequate opportunities to learn these skills, rather than to some more fundamental lack of capacity. This view is supported by a large number of cross-cultural studies indicating that cultural experiences play an important role in influencing the contexts in which individuals exhibit various thinking and learning skills (Good-now, 1979; Karplus, 1979; Karplus, Karplus, Formisano, & Paulsen, 1979; Neisser, 1976). These studies suggest that individuals who fail to exhibit sophis-ticated thinking and learning skills in one context often succeed in producing these skills in other contexts. Thus, the fact that developmental students do not produce appropriate thinking and learning skills in academic situations does not necessarily imply that they are incapable of using these skills. Rather, we think they may be capable of using them in other contexts and with appropriate instruc-tion can also be taught to extend their use to academic situations.

OVERVIEW OF THE COGNITIVE STUDIES PROJECT

The Cognitive Studies Project is in its formative stages and our activities are exploratory. Although this project is being conducted at Manhattan Community College, a unit of the City University of New York, the population currently being served is veterans returning to school for either high school equivalency preparation or for college preparatory courses. The program was first offered in the spring semester of 1980. It consisted of semester-long high school level courses in reading, mathematics, science, social science, and English, along with a course in problem solving. The problem-solving course was the only one that focused on instruction in cognitive skills; all the other courses were taught in standard ways.

The problem-solving course had three functions. Firstly, it provided students with instruction in those problem-solving skills that we believed would contribute to their ability to learn more effectively. Secondly, it provided us with information about their cognitive deficiencies for use in further developing special instruc-tional programs for this population. Thirdly, it offered an opportunity to pilot test instructional materials that we were hoping to subsequently use on a more widespread basis.

Student Population

The population for this program consisted of 34 black, white, and Hispanic males ranging from 18 to 45 years of age. The Test of Adult Basic Education (TABE) was used to determine their levels of academic attainment. The TABE assesses language skills (mechanics and spelling), mathematics skills, and reading skills. Total Battery Scores yielded the distribution shown in Table 15.1:

Although we do not have TABE scores for Manhattan Community College population as a whole, we consider the students in the pilot project to be quite similar in their previous achievement levels to entering freshmen at the college. Ninety-five percent of the entering freshmen at the college are assigned to at least one remedial basic skills course and more than 40% of these are required

TABLE 15.1
Results of Test of Adult Basic Education

Total Battery (TABE) N = 34	
Grade	Percentage
3	.05
4	.15
5	.21
6	.18
7	.21
8	.15
9	.05
	1.00

TABLE 15.2
Instructional Groupings

TABE Grade Level	Group	Percentage of Experimental Students
8 and 9	C	20
5, 6 and 7	B	60
3 and 4	A	20

to take at least three remedial courses. Remedial courses are offered in basic mathematics, reading, English composition, and English as a second language. Because of poor performance, large proportions of the students must repeat these courses. The performance of these students on various assessment instruments (the Stanford Test of Academic Skills and tests constructed by the College's Mathematics Department) are consistently and substantially below the means for typical college students. The director of the College's Office of Instructional Testing and Research (Lachica) commented in his 1975 report: "The results of the placement examinations, as in the previous semesters, underscored the widespread unpreparedness of the majority of the incoming students for regular college work and the need to continually reinforce our remediation programs" (p. 10).

Further, with the exception of the fact that there are no females in the population for the experimental program, the two groups share other important characteristics. The groups are similar in demographic characteristics such as income level, ethnic composition, and age range. They are also similar in terms of attitudes and experiences affecting academic performance, such as attitudes toward school, quality of previous instructional experiences, and interest in pursuing further education.

For instructional purposes, the students were organized into three groups based on their performance on the TABE (see Table 15.2).

Course Description

The problem-solving course lasted one semester and had as its objectives: (1) to assist students to become aware of and intervene in their own thinking processes, (2) to assist students to become more active learners, and (3) to familiarize students with systematic and deliberate methods of thought that would enhance their problem-solving and thinking abilities.

The course was based on a method and set of instructional materials originally developed by Arthur Whimbey and Jack Lochhead (1979) with modifications as described following. The major features of this method are briefly summarized in the succeeding paragraphs. They are also further discussed in chapters by both Lochhead (this volume) and Bransford, Stein, Arbitman–Smith, and Vye (this volume).

The Whimbey–Lochhead method attempts to raise to an overt level mental activities that are usually covert and automatic, if not unconscious. The content of the program includes four different types of problems: verbal reasoning and reading comprehension problems, analogical reasoning problems, analysis of trend and pattern problems, and mathematical word problems. In solving these problems, students are asked to work in pairs and to alternate in the role of listener and problem solver. In carrying out their respective roles, they are asked to adhere to the following procedures: (1) the problem solver is asked to think aloud as he or she attempts to solve the problem; (2) the listener is asked to determine whether the problem solver is vocalizing all the major steps being taken to solve the problem, to probe continually the problem solver's thought processes, and to point out errors in thinking. Students are given examples of the thinking procedures used by experts in solving these problems and are also taught specific strategies for analyzing each of the four different types of problems. Throughout the program, great importance is placed on the role of accuracy in problem solving. Students are continually encouraged to monitor their own and each other's thinking processes to make sure that the problem solver has accurately understood the problem being addressed and is attempting to solve it in a careful and systematic fashion.

In determining the role the instructor should play in our course, we were guided by the following assumptions:

1. As noted previously, like Feuerstein, Rand, and Hoffman (1979), and Feuerstein et al. (this volume), we believe that, in slow learners, specific cognitive functions are more likely to be underdeveloped than nonexistent.

2. Cognitive development can be facilitated by the intervention of an agent who functions to point out the aspects of phenomena that are significant and who helps the student interpret experiences. This function is expressed in Bruner's (1978) idea of a tutor and is incorporated in Feuerstein's theory of Mediated Learning Experience (Feuerstein, Rand, Hoffman, & Miller, 1980).

3. Students ultimately teach themselves by actively engaging in the examination, manipulation, and reconstruction of experiences presented to them.

From this perspective, the role of the instructor was designed to complement the activity of the students. Lectures were generally limited to an explanation of exercises followed by responses to questions. During the exercises, the instructor circulated and listened to students' responses that were analyzed to identify the probable ways problems were being processed; thinking processes were emphasized rather than simply arriving at an answer; students were encouraged to view incorrect responses as valuable opportunities for learning how thinking went awry; students were encouraged to slow down and to take their time; guessing was discouraged and students were asked to supply thorough explanations of their answers as a check against guessing.

The Whimbey–Lochhead method was not entirely appropriate for our groups, because the reading, computational, verbal, and reasoning skills required by many of the exercises were beyond the ability of many of our students. This necessitated careful selection of the items to be used and the incorporation of material from other sources. For example, we used the Ravens Progressive Matrices to provide tasks in nonverbal analogical reasoning.

Students in group A (the group that scored the lowest on the TABE) required special treatment. Their level of skill was such that additional time had to be spent explaining exercises, and the assigned exercises had to contain only elementary words or none at all. Also, computational problems had to be held to a minimum for these students.

Additionally, for all three groups, the roles of the listener and problem solver had to be altered to that of discussants. This was necessary because the role of the listener in particular requires many of the thinking skills we were attempting to develop. Another factor that contributed to the alteration of these roles was the interpersonal tension they generated. We comment further on this point in the following section.

Finally, the Whimbey–Lochhead method does not provide adequate guidance for the instructor when students encounter blocks in the process of solving a problem. It is true that Whimbey and Lochhead identify behaviors that interfere with effective problem solving, and the instructor must be alert to these behaviors and to assisting the student to recognize and correct them. However, the difficulties some students experience during problem solving may be a result of more fundamental problems than those addressed by Whimbey and Lochhead. Unless instructors recognize this, they will not be in a position to offer effective interventions. For assistance in this area we turned to Feuerstein et al. (1979, 1980). They have developed a comprehensive theory for the diagnosis and treatment of deficient cognitive functions. Their conceptualization of the components of deficient cognitive functions is highly specific and offers instructors an extensive guide in attempting to understand the probable nature of students' problems.

FINDINGS FROM THE COGNITIVE STUDIES PROJECT

Intellectual Competencies of Developmental Students

As just noted, the cognitive deficits of most of our students required us to take greater cognizance of the demand requirements of the tasks in the Whimbey–Lochhead workbook and to simplify them sufficiently so that students could gain access fairly easily. As the course progressed, most students in all groups addressed the workbook problems with increasing tenacity. After halting starts, their attitudes toward their abilities became more positive and they began to believe that they could successfully solve the problems they were assigned. In their interactions they began to develop the ability to identify inconsistencies and gaps in each others' reasoning and to challenge and stimulate one another effectively.

Not all students experienced these achievements; a few simply did not believe they could manage activity of this sort. Even when working closely with the instructor and arriving at a solution, the process by which they got to the solution was still totally obscure to them. However, these students would episodically exhibit impressive analytical ability—a flash of brilliance. Then just as quickly, the light would go out and the insight would be gone; they could not remember how they knew or understood that particular thing. At such times, the instructor would probe more deeply for the companion mental events that might have led to the conclusion. Frequently, this helped the student retrieve the constituent thoughts and reconstruct the process. At other times, the attempt was not effective. But even when the effort was effective, these students often could not accept their own success. We are, however, encouraged by such flashes of insight, because it suggests to us the availability of cognitive capabilities that are waiting to be stimulated and developed. Nonetheless, the students' profound disbelief in their own mental ability, buttressed by a history of academic failure, greatly militated against their willingness to give themselves a chance. They seemed to believe firmly that they were born with a fixed amount of mental ability and that they were not going to develop any more.

Special Difficulties Implementing the Whimbey–Lochhead Method with Developmental Students

Bloom and Broder (1950), Bereiter and Engelmann (1966), Whimbey and Whimbey (1975), Feuerstein et al. (1980), and others offer exhaustive descriptions of the cognitive deficiencies poor learners are likely to manifest. The students in all three of our groups exhibited many of these deficiencies. Across groups, however, two behaviors were particularly problematical because they affected the nature and quality of the interaction within pairs of students. Not all students in all groups exhibited these behaviors, but a sufficient number did to justify identifying these behaviors as ones that may require significant modifications in the Whimbey–Lochhead method to increase its usefulness with developmental students.

The first behavior that was problematical was the inability of many students to treat the roles of problem solver or listener objectively. They tended to personalize these roles and to defend themselves when the other member of the pair challenged their intellectual behavior. As a result, exchanges within pairs were often reduced to arguments because one or the other member perceived the challenge on an issue or an explanatory response as an attack. This development led us to modify these roles to those of discussants, an approach that seemed to us more cooperative and less confrontational. This new arrangement produced some confrontational problems, but over time, with the instructor intervening and distinguishing between the issue and the person, most students developed the ability to sustain the interaction with little if any tension. However, a few continued to exhibit antagonistic behavior.

Learning tasks place demands on a student's affective as well as cognitive capacities, demands that can have significant effects on performance. For example, we just mentioned the interpersonal tensions that occurred among our students as a by-product of our instructional methods. The overt level of activity and participation required in a course of this nature immediately confronts low-ability students with the full register of their past academic inadequacies, as well as with their feelings about these inadequacies. These feelings can induce students to attempt to protect themselves from what they may consider to be threats to maintaining a positive self-image. Frequently, these responses are inappropriate and can interfere with the learning the instructor is attempting to encourage.

To moderate the negative effect of such feelings, we attempted to make the classroom a place in which it was safe to make a mistake. We did this by modeling the behaviors we were encouraging. For example, when the instructor would make a mistake in the process of solving a problem, he would encourage discussion and analysis of it. If the mistake was made while he was preparing the lesson in his office, he would subsequently report it to the class and compare it to the mistakes students were likely to make. When students made mistakes, the instructor would identify them as learning opportunities and proceed to consider just how the student arrived at the wrong answer.

Additionally, we encouraged an attitude of acceptance among class members. We not only wanted students to be comfortable with their own mistakes, but also with their peers' mistakes. Consequently, we emphasized that differences in rates of performance could be expected, should be accepted, and should not become the basis of ridicule. We believe we were successful in creating an atmosphere of security as evidenced by a reduction in inappropriate behaviors and interpersonal tensions.

The second behavior that proved problematical in successfully implementing the Whimbey–Lochhead method was our students' lack of verbal skills. Whimbey and Lochhead's method requires adequate communication skill on the part of both the problem solver and the listener. Students must be able to communicate to one another labels, categories, definitions, concepts, etc. For many of our students, communication ability was poorly developed. As a result, overt problem-solving activity often was reduced to silent musings by a member of the working pair. For those who could communicate, the degree of verbal precision required by the Whimbey–Lochhead materials often posed too large a challenge. Developmental students are often content to provide approximate answers to questions they are asked. However, to solve the problems they were assigned, these students had to be specific and clear.

To aid the students in coping with these challenges, we encouraged them to use dictionaries to look up words with which they were unfamiliar, to use language with which they were comfortable, and to attempt to get their ideas firmly in mind before expressing them. These suggestions helped students to work more efficiently but did not completely eliminate communication problems. Facility with language takes time and practice to develop, and our students were at a beginning point.

From our perspective, the verbal limitations of our students highlight two issues. One is the need for instructors to diagnose carefully the nature of difficulties that underlie observed errors in thinking; that is, one must determine if such errors reflect failure to engage in appropriate thinking processes or an inability to accurately communicate the nature and results of one's thinking. A mistaken assessment of the nature of the student's difficulty can lead to an inappropriate or inadequate intervention.

Feuerstein et al. (1979) offer a useful model for conceptualizing the different sources of difficulty that can contribute to errors in thinking. He proposes that information processing be conceptualized as occurring in three separate phases— Input, Elaboration, and Output—each of which involves a wide range of cognitive functions. If one can identify the phase in which a problem occurs and the cognitive behaviors that are implicated, then one is in a better position to attempt to remediate the problem.

The other issue with which the verbal deficiencies of our students confronted us is a refinement of the first; it concerns the extent to which language can obscure cognitive processes. For example, we were continuously impressed by the performance of two students in the lowest ability group. These students could often identify correct answers but could not offer an appropriate rationale for their responses. There was a quality to their struggle to verbalize their thoughts that suggested to us both that solid thinking was in progress, and that inadequate language ability was interfering with its adequate expression. This experience served to alert us that our perception of students' abilities may be skewed by our predisposition, despite our intentions, to accept the traditional standard of verbal ability as the measure of mental ability. Huttenlocher (1976) among others has pointed out the need to distinguish between thought and its representation in language. Our experience with developmental students convinces us that it is important to look for ways other than verbal facility alone by which we can recognize the representation of knowledge.

General Conclusions from the Pilot Project

Did we achieve our objectives of assisting students to intervene in their own thinking processes, to become more active in their learning experience, and to become familiar with methods for improving their thinking abilities? We think modestly at least. By what criteria do we measure our results? One is students' reports. Many students informed us that they had begun to use the problem-solving skills we were emphasizing in other courses and felt they were becoming more effective as students. Additionally, teachers reported an improvement in students' performance in the classroom and attributed this development to our course.

We realize that these comments by no means validate the method we used or constitute an adequate scientific evaluation. Our goals in this pilot test with developmental students were modest and evaluation was not systematically undertaken in this initial work. Thus, although we did have the opportunity to observe our method at work and to assess student reactions, we have no way of knowing to what extent the practices we encouraged became a part of students' cognitive repertoire, whether they will continue to engage in them, and to what extent they can or will transfer them to new learning situations. Certainly, these are issues that must be addressed in future research.

A prerequisite for future work with this course is the substantial revision of its content and structure. This requires the development and/or acquisition of material that is more appropriate to the cognitive levels of the students. We do not mean material that is elementary and unchallenging, but material that, although challenging, is accessible to the students. From our observations, there is little material prepared especially for developmental adults. We must begin the process of constructing it.

In concluding this chapter, we have some general comments to share, based on our experiences field testing our pilot program. The first set of comments pertains to the special needs with which instructors and academic institutions are confronted in attempting to educate developmental students.

1. With developmental students, the instructor must be prepared to facilitate learning, not simply direct it.

2. Developmental students should be encouraged to accept more responsibility for their learning and be assisted in acquiring academic skills necessary for the assumption of this responsibility.

3. Instruction should be structured and paced with the students' needs in mind, not the instructor's.

4. Open door policies obligate institutions to more adequately prepare their instructional staff to meet the demands imposed on them by developmental students.

The second set of comments pertains to the kinds of changes in developmental students that can occur as a result of participation in cognitive process instruction:

1. Such instruction tends to demystify the learning process. It helps the student to understand that learning is not a smooth, automatic process determined simply by innate capacities. Rather, it is a process with identifiable, definable, and comprehensible parts that can be mastered.

2. Instruction makes the students' thinking processes accessible to them, so that they can be more active in their learning and develop confidence in their ability as thinkers.

3. It confirms the student as a capable person. As noted earlier, cognitive instructional methods assume that developmental students have the potential to become competent thinkers and learners. This assumption is based, in part, on evidence that individuals who function poorly in academic settings may engage in sophisticated mental operations in other settings. Neisser (1976) has helped us to better understand the difference between general intelligence and academic intelligence. Considering general intelligence, he takes an ethnological view. He defines general intelligence as "intelligent performance in natural situations," that is, as "responding appropriately in terms of one's long-range and short-range goals, given the actual facts of the situation as one discovers them" (p. 137).

In contrast he defines academic intelligence as the ability to master tasks constructed by academicians. This form of intelligence is much more narrowly focused; it requires one to be disciplined and to sustain a particular attitude toward academic tasks. Further, it necessitates the use of specific cognitive skills. To quote Neisser (1976):

> in school, a problem should be tackled the same way no matter which teacher assigns it to you [teachers keep changing]; numerical problems are worked out similarly, regardless of whether apples or bombs are to be added [or without any specific numbers at all, as in algebra]; geography is to be mastered whether or not one has any interest in traveling. The school child learns to use one particular skill or heuristic to solve many different puzzles, even if they differ in any details, simply because they share an abstract structure. He also learns to work on problems as they are presented, whether he cares about the solutions or not. (p. 136)

Generally, it is this lack of focus, discipline, and experience that characterizes low-ability students. Hence, they are unintelligent, but only academically so. When cognitive abilities are refocused and sharpened, such students become capable of bringing to bear on academic matters those mental abilities they regularly employ in the daily course of living.

Our third set of comments pertains to other teachers' reactions to our course. The course we taught was not concerned with the transmission of specific content: Instead it was concerned with the learning process itself. Nonetheless, as we discussed the mental behaviors that students exhibited in our course with other teachers in the program, they immediately recognized them as ones that confounded or abetted their instructional efforts and they gained a better understanding of the mental processes that were at work. They indicated that these insights would make them more effective with subsequent students.

PROBLEMS AND PROSPECTS

Thus far we have presented several findings suggesting that cognitive process instruction may play a useful role in educating developmental students. In closing, we want to briefly summarize some barriers that exist in higher education settings to the introduction of this form of instruction.

Lack of Incentive Supporting Innovations in Instruction. As noted earlier, Schalock (1976) comments that administrators pay lip service to excellence in teaching but, in fact, reward virtually every other activity but that. Consequently, innovations in teaching methods go largely unexplored. With regard to developmental students, the indisposition of faculty to "tool up" is more severe. Teaching developmental students enjoys every low status among most faculty, and it is something they would rather not do. So, it is doubtful that they will extend themselves to acquire skills relevant to the instruction of developmental students without powerful institutional incentives.

Faculty Ignorance About the Cognitive Abilities of Developmental Students. Many faculty still believe that intelligence is a single characteristic, a product almost solely of the genes (and a minimum of environmental factors): if a student does not have it, there is no instructional method that will help him or her get it. Hence, his teachers invest their time in other clearly rewarding pursuits. To the extent that this view represents ignorance rather than prejudice, it may be susceptible to the influence of evidence. Whatever the source of this view, it is held tenaciously.

Lack of Adequate Instructional Time. Bloom (1976) comments that whatever can be learned by one person can probably be learned by any other normal person, given time. Cognitive instruction takes time. The development of one mental ability that contributes to the development of more complex mental abilities cannot be rushed. However, we have only a limited amount of time in an academic year in which to cover a set amount of material. These set limits on the time that can be made available for cognitive process instruction. Bloom suggests that increasing time on the learning task—the actual time the student is actively engaged in learning experience—must become the focus of attention, in the absence of any major revision in the way institutions construct their academic calendars.

The future is no more promising for the cognitive processes instructional method than it is for other instructional innovations. There is considerable inertia in academia that is difficult to overcome. However high academic attrition will probably induce administrators and faculty working with developmental students and concerned with the survival of their institutions to seek vigorously more effective instructional methods. In such a context, cognitive processes instructional methods may constitute a significant bridge between developmental students' ability to learn and traditional faculty members' ability to teach them.

REFERENCES

Arons, A. B. Some thoughts on reasoning capacities implicitly expected of college students. In J. Lochhead & J. Clement (Eds.), *Cognitive process instruction*. Philadelphia: The Franklin Institute Press, 1979.

Bauman, R. P. *Teaching for cognitive development: A status report*. Unpublished manuscript, University of Alabama at Birmingham, Department of Physics and Project on Teaching in University College, 1976.

Bereiter, C., & Engelmann, S. *Teaching disadvantaged children in the preschool*. Englewood Cliffs, NJ: Prentice–Hall, 1966.

Bloom, B. S. *Human characteristics and school learning*. New York: McGraw–Hill, 1976.

Bloom, B. S., & Broder, L. *Problem-solving processes of college students*. Chicago: University of Chicago Press, 1950.

Bruner, J. S. *Toward a theory of instruction*. Cambridge, MA: Belknap Press, 1978.

Feuerstein, R., Rand, Y., & Hoffman, M. B. *Instrumental enrichment*. Baltimore: University Park Press, 1979.

Feuerstein, R., Rand, Y., Hoffman, M. B., & Miller, R. *The dynamic assessment of retarded performers*. Baltimore: University Park Press, 1980.

Goodnow, J. J. The nature of intelligent behavior: Questions raised by cross-cultural studies in cognitive process instruction. In J. Lochhead & J. Clement (Eds.), *Cognitive process instruction*. Philadelphia: The Franklin Institute Press, 1979.

Huttenlocher, J. Language and intelligence. In L. B. Resnick (Ed.), *The nature of intelligence*. Hillsdale, NJ: Lawrence Erlbaum Associates, 1976.

Karplus, R. Proportional reasoning in the Peoples Republic of China. In J. Lochhead & J. Clement (Eds.), *Cognitive process instruction*. Philadelphia: The Franklin Institute Press, 1979.

Karplus, R., Karplus, E., Formisano, M., & Paulsen, A. Proportional reasoning and control of variables in seven countries. In J. Lochhead & J. Clement (Eds.), *Cognitive process instruction*. Philadelphia: The Franklin Institute Press, 1979.

Lachica, G. M. *Report on placement examinations: Spring 1975*. Unpublished manuscript, Borough of Manhattan Community College, 1975.

Lavin, D. E., Alba, R. D., & Silberstein, R. A. Open admissions and equal access: A study of ethnic groups in the City University of New York. *Harvard Educational Review,* 1979, *49,* 53–92.

Lin, H. Approaches to clinical research. In J. Lochhead & J. Clement (Eds.), *Cognitive process instruction.* Philadelphia: The Franklin Institute Press, 1979.

Lochhead, J., & Clement, J. Preface. In J. Lochhead & J. Clement (Eds.), *Cognitive process instruction.* Philadelphia: The Franklin Institute Press, 1979.

Moore, W., Jr. Increasing learning among developmental education students. In O. T. Lenning (Ed.), *Improving educational outcomes.* San Francisco: Jossey–Bass, 1976.

Neisser, U. General, academic, and artifical intelligence. In L. B. Resnick (Ed.), *The nature of intelligence.* Hillsdale, NJ: Lawrence Erlbaum Associates, 1976.

Schalock, A. D Structuring process to improve student outcomes. In O. T. Lenning (Ed.), *Improving educational outcomes.* San Francisco: Jossey–Bass, 1976.

Whimbey, A., & Lochhead, J. *Problem solving and comprehension: A short course in analytic reasoning.* Philadelphia: The Franklin Institute Press, 1979.

Whimbey, A., & Whimbey, L. S. *Intelligence can be taught.* New York: E. P. Dutton, 1975.

16 Thinking Skills: The Effort of One Public School System

Herbert W. Ware
Arlington, Virginia, Public Schools

In this chapter, the Arlington, Virginia, public schools provide a setting for examining the realities of developing and implementing an instructional program in thinking skills for all pupils. Arlington Schools is an urban system of 15,000 pupils (grades K–12) in 30 schools. This particular system has wrestled directly with the issues surrounding the teaching and assessment of thinking skills since 1974. That wrestling has been characterized by varying degrees of intensity in the intervening years. A description of aspects of Arlington's experiences can be helpful to those who are interested in the difficulties of converting theoretical approaches to instruction in thinking skills into practical school programs. It can be useful in distinguishing responsibilities that can be assigned to the schools from those that must be assumed by the research and teacher-training communities outside the schools.

The origins of Arlington's attention to instruction in thinking skills illustrate how a school system can be brought to focus on a particular goal. A description of the current status of the effort gives some indication of the achievement possible through modest effort and of the accomplishments yet to be realized. The reaction of staff members—teachers, principals, program specialists, and other instructional personnel—to the expectation that they offer instruction in thinking skills illuminates the realities of program development, implementation, and assessment. The contrast with a highly successful program in expository writing provides some clues as to matters deserving further attention, if programs of instruction in thinking skills are to become more widespread.

In the sections that follow, I address these issues, organizing my discussion as follows: First, I explore the history and success of Arlington's attempts to implement a new program of instruction in thinking skills. Next, I explore the history and success of Arlington's attempts to implement a new program of instruction in expository writing skills. Finally, with these case studies as background, I draw some conclusions as to: (1) why the program of instruction in writing skills was more successful than the program of instruction in thinking skills; and (2) what kinds of additional knowledge are needed to permit future attempts at instruction in thinking skills to yield more positive outcomes.

IMPLEMENTING INSTRUCTION IN THINKING SKILLS

Major Initiating Events

By 1974, the Arlington School Board had adopted instructional goals in four areas: reading, computation, humanities, and human relations. During 1975–76, the board added a fifth goal: to improve thinking skills, that is, to insure that each child develop and strengthen problem-solving, logical-reasoning, and decision-making skills.

During the years 1975 to 1977, Arlington's effort to improve thinking skills was reasonably intense. However, after 1977, attention to this goal waned until 1979, when it again increased through a request from the superintendent that procedures be developed for assessing student proficiency in thinking in three academic areas: mathematics, social studies, and science. The students were to be measured at three points in their academic careers—once during the elementary grades, once during the intermediate grades, and once during high school. A taxonomy of thinking skills, which had been developed in conjunction with the board's initial adoption of thinking skills as an instructional goal, was offered as the framework for defining the kinds of skills that students were expected to acquire.

The District's Response to the Board's Adoption of Thinking Skills as an Instructional Goal.   The Arlington School District requires that each school have an annual plan that describes the instructional objectives, the strategies for accomplishing those objectives, and the assessment procedures for determining whether the objectives have been achieved. Each plan must include objectives in the goal areas established as priorities by the board.

After the school board had adopted its four initial goals, in 1974, both the professional and lay communities realized that: (1) adoption of subject-area goals could have substantial impact on the inclusion or exclusion of an area in the annual plans of individual schools and in the establishment of budget priorities; and (2) significant, worthy subject areas (e.g., science and social studies) had been omitted, at least symbolically, from the board's initial choice of goals.

The board subsequently appointed a Task Force on Critical Thinking to consider the feasibility of adopting a goal in this area. Simultaneously, the program specialists—those charged with developing curriculum and providing the related staff training activities—began to think through the issues associated with implementing a district-wide program of instruction in critical thinking. By the end of the 1976 school year, the school board had adopted thinking skills as a goal area, and the program specialists, with the aid of external consultants, had identified a five-level hierarchy of objectives for instruction. They defined proficiency in critical thinking as involving the following five sets of skills: inquiry, application, analysis, synthesis, and evaluation. These skills were assumed to form a hierarchy, with each successive level involving more complex skills. The last four levels are the familiar higher levels of the taxonomy of Bloom, Engelhart, Furst, Hill, and Krathwohl (1956).

As noted earlier, the board's identification of thinking skills as a goal area meant that each school was expected to include thinking-skills objectives in its annual plan. Each objective was to be accompanied by a statement of both the school's strategies for accomplishing that objective and its procedures for assessing success. There was considerable evidence of solid staff development activities related to instruction in thinking skills in various academic content areas during the years 1976–1977. A high-water mark was a county-wide staff development day in October 1976 on which the entire afternoon was devoted to over 15 different presentations on instruction of thinking skills.

Afterwards, however, there was only limited evidence that thinking skills were a focal point of the instructional program. The primary evidence existed in the individual school annual plans. In the fall of 1979, all 22 elementary schools had included a total of 69 objectives relating to thinking-skills instruction. Many of the objectives employed items from standardized or criterion-referenced tests of minimal and basic skills as measures of pupil achievement in thinking skills. Generally, these items were drawn from tests assessing reading and writing skills. Only four of the 69 objectives related directly to science, four to mathematics, and three to social studies. This set the stage for the superintendent's fall 1979 request for renewed and increased attention to the school board's thinking-skills goal, a request that met with less than an enthusiastic response from the central office personnel responsible.

It is instructive to look at elements of that response to what was essentially a second request—in fact, an admonition—in order to understand better the difficulties involved in implementing a program of instruction in thinking skills.

The District's Response to the Superintendent's Request for Additional Attention to Instruction in Thinking Skills. The superintendent's request for additional attention to instruction in thinking skills identified three curriculum areas for substantial effort, mathematics, science, and social studies. A request for updated summaries of information about instruction in thinking skills in those areas elicited comprehensive memoranda from the program specialists for each area. The contents of these memoranda help to clarify what activities the schools labeled "thinking-skills instruction."

In two of the three areas, mathematics and social studies, eight of the 30 schools in the district reported special activities. One school offered "calculator activities," without further elaboration, as evidence of its attempts to provide thinking-skills instruction in mathematics. Another school indicated that their students were receiving thinking-skills instruction in social studies, citing as evidence the fact that the school's social studies texts asked students to engage in operations like "comparing," "contrasting," "showing likenesses and differences," "evaluating," and "being aware of other points of view." In all three curriculum areas, the fact that students routinely received special instruction in learning to read content-area textbooks was offered as one element of a total program of instruction in thinking skills.

Subsequent discussions revealed that the teachers had several reservations about the board's goal of improving thinking skills. They questioned the justification for devoting special attention to this kind of instruction. They questioned the appropriateness of the five-level hierarchy the program specialists had suggested. They questioned their own ability to develop and implement a special program of instruction in thinking skills, especially given the fact that no additional financial resources were being made available to support staff training or the purchase of special curriculum materials. They questioned the fairness of being asked to add this task to all the others for which they were responsible. In the paragraphs that follow, I look more closely at the grounds for their reservations.

Teaching is isolated. There is little exchange of ideas inside or outside the classroom. Consequently, each teacher's perception of the adequacy of his or her own instruction is probably a very personal one. Thus, one could anticipate that a request for teachers to focus on thinking-skills instruction would be met with challenges and requests for justification. "After all," the teacher would respond, "I am already teaching thinking skills." Where there is ignorance about the nature of instruction in thinking skills, that is a legitimate response. That response was among those made to the superintendent's request. A legitimate rejoinder is, "Then let's show that pupils are learning the skills we are teaching." Such a rejoinder would be likely to produce an invitation from the teacher to "Observe my teaching." Although observing instruction is a very legitimate way of determining that thinking skills are being taught, it is unrealistically expensive and is a dubious way of measuring what pupils are learning. Anticipation of such difficulties (and of their ultimately unsatisfactory resolution) creates high levels of anxiety for those who must oversee curriculum development and implementation.

When the fall 1979 request was formulated, teachers were expected to use the five-step hierarchy referred to earlier (inquiry, application, analysis, synthesis, and evaluation) in designing instruction in thinking skills. Although the hierarchy had evolved through group discussions, only one of the program specialists involved in those 1975–76 discussions was part of the new group responsible in 1979 for overseeing and advising the schools on instruction. The hierarchy posed two problems. First, it was not clear why those five categories had been chosen. Even the remaining program specialist did not understand how inquiry reached the list. Secondly, the categories provided a more adequate description of proficiency in thinking in some academic content areas than in others. In mathematics, for example, the program specialists preferred the following set of categories proposed by Avital and Shettleworth (1968, p. 7): (1) recognition and recall; (2) algorithmic thinking and generalization; and (3) open search.

The development of an instructional program requires an ability to perceive a need and to specify means of answering it. The successful implementation of a new instructional program requires a substantial amount of self-confidence. This self-confidence is needed to counter these skeptical recipients of staff development activities who insist that a given program objective cannot be accomplished either because "No one has ever done it before," or because "We don't know enough about doing it." It is difficult to deal confidently with such confrontations without knowing the substantive issues surrounding a program. Confidence rests on being able to articulate the skills required to teach successfully.

With respect to thinking-skills instruction, program specialists found themselves expected to provide training to teachers who had no explicit preparation in this area. Teachers found themselves in the same position with respect to their students. In 1974, when the district first became interested, educators across the country did not share this interest. This meant that the program specialists could not readily find examples of effective staff-training programs, of effective student materials, or even discussions, in professional journals, of issues related to thinking-skills instruction. Even today such examples and discussions are scarce.

In addition, program specialists are confronted annually with so many requests to conduct program and staff development activities that they have to limit their attempts to collect information about new instructional approaches in each area to superficial searches. Declining enrollments in our district have forced reductions in the size of support staffs over the last several years, with the result that the human resources currently available for pursuing program development activities are quite limited. In such times, the extensive pursuit of knowledge in the work setting becomes a luxury. If adequate time is not available to staff leaders, it is even less available to regular classroom teachers who are responsible for the actual instruction in thinking skills that eventually occurs in the classroom.

Alternatively, money can buy the opportunities for staff training and reflection. Lots of money can buy lots of opportunities. Unfortunately, "lots of money" is not available in most public school jurisdictions. Of the three subject areas involved in addressing thinking skills, only in mathematics was there money for staff development, though the specialists for the three areas had been allocated $100 *each* in travel money for the *year*. For the ensuing school year, both the staff development money and the travel money were eliminated to fund salary increases for all staff members.

In summary, although community interest in and school board commitment to the importance of thinking skills is needed for the pursuit of instruction in this area, there have been factors that militated against enthusiastic acceptance of the board's goal of improving thinking. These factors are an important part of the reality that must be considered in developing useful programs for school application.

Nonetheless, it is important to realize that a great deal can be accomplished even in the face of such odds. Some examples of what program specialists and teachers accomplished shed light on the progress made.

Specific Examples of Work

Program specialists, working with teachers in their respective subject areas, have made progress toward assessing pupil mastery of thinking skills. For example, they have developed word lists for use in constructing objectives and test items, and they have provided examples of appropriate test items. The word lists and examples of test items have been useful in clarifying for teachers the kinds of skills students are expected to learn as evidence that they are proficient thinkers in various academic content areas.

In both mathematics and science, lists of verbs and phrases correlated with each of the five levels of the hierarchy were offered to teachers for their use in constructing daily classroom questions and tests. For example, the lists that follow were offered to teachers for constructing items to measure analysis skills in mathematics and science.

Mathematics
Analyze the elements, identifying the parts.
Analyze the relationships, identifying each one.
Analyze the organizational principles, identifying the way the parts are organized.
Categorize.
Classify.
Diagram.
Differentiate.
Distinguish between useful and nonuseful information.
Estimate.
Find differences.
Find similarities.
Infer from statistical data.
Point out.
Recognize patterns.

Science
Analyze.
Classify and state the basis for the classification.
Distinguish cause and effect relationships.
Distinguish between fact and hypothesis.
Distinguish between relevant and irrelevant.
Extrapolate.
Give examples.
Hypothesize.
Infer.
Identify motive.
Recognize assumptions.
Recognize and state the difference between _____ and _____.
Recognize which facts are essential.

Recognize shortcuts.

Recognize when additional information is needed.

Recognize obvious answers.

Select the appropriate operation.

Separate.

Subdivide.

Survey.

Recognize and state the similarities.

State differences.

State which method.

State difficulties that _____had in doing _____.

State what further information is needed.

State your interpretations.

State how this event in this country is related to this other event.

For the past several years the district has been using locally constructed tests to determine whether students were mastering the basic objectives of various secondary school mathematics courses. In conjunction with the superintendent's request for increased attention to thinking-skills instruction, items on these tests were correlated with the thinking-skills hierarchy. Two items from a geometry test, along with the levels of the thinking-skills hierarchy to which they were assigned and the percentage of students responding correctly to each are provided as examples:

1. For synthesis:
   The greatest area which a parallelogram having sides of 10 inches and 6 inches can have is:
   A. 16 sq. in.   D. 100 sq. in.
   B. 30 sq. in.   E. 120 sq. in.
   C. 60 sq. in.
   Percentage answering correctly: 88
2. For analysis:
   A rectangular field is 40 meters by 90 meters. The amount of wire fencing needed to fence a square field of the same area is:
   A. 100 meters   D. 240 meters
   B. 120 meters   E. 260 meters
   C. 200 meters
   Percentage answering correctly: 35

These items and their results prompt questions regarding the assignment of items to levels in the thinking-skills hierarchy. As might be expected, the process of assigning items to levels generated considerable long discussions and controversy. Because such discussions were not always productive, an attempt was made to subordinate them to the more fundamental issues of identifying and offering instruction in thinking skills.

In social studies, the staff of program specialists and selected teachers who were responsible for advising the schools took several actions to clarify further the nature of the skills students were expected to acquire. They decided that the lowest level of the thinking-skills hierarchy—the level called "inquiry"—was equivalent to the category called "comprehension" in the Bloom et al. (1956) taxonomy. That is, they defined "inquiry" or "comprehension" as "the remembering of previously learned material." They also provided teachers with the following paraphrases of definitions from Bloom et al. for the other four terms of the hierarchy:

Application is using previously learned material in a new situation.
Analysis is breaking down material into its component parts in order to understand its organizational structure.
Synthesis is putting the parts together to create a new whole.
Evaluation is judging the outcome according to a set of standards.

Thirdly, they identified a set of criteria that social studies teachers could use in determining whether 11th graders had achieved proficiency in social studies thinking skills. They advised teachers that 11th graders should be able to:

1. Distinguish the difference between statements of fact and statements of opinion.
2. Determine the appropriate source of information.
3. Distinguish between relevant and irrelevant information.
4. Evaluate the relative importance of various types of reference sources.
5. Read and evaluate a graph, a table, and an editorial cartoon.
6. Infer meaning from a specific passage.
7. Distinguish between primary and secondary sources.
8. Apply previously known principles to new situations.
9. Identify the relationship of ideas in a given series of statements.
10. Synthesize facts from a body of data.

The following question, which appears on an 11th-grade social studies test as an analysis question, is offered as an illustration of how the definitions given earlier for each level of the hierarchy were applied in assigning questions to levels.

Congressman Rosnee has been campaigning throughout the state in an effort to get votes from all possible groups of people. He has advocated high prices for farm produce to the farmers. He has told various patriotic groups that he favors 100% Americanism and is opposed to un-American activities. He has told the laborers that he is in favor of high wages and low prices on the necessities of life. He has promised the businessmen that he will reduce taxes and has championed the increasing of the national defense forces and the continuation of the national public works program.

Directions: Which of the following questions would Congressman Rosnee have difficulty in answering directly and to the point? Mark all such items with a D. Mark those which he would not have difficulty in answering directly with N. All questions should be marked with one of these two symbols.

1. Would you permit communists to have police protection in their meetings?
2. Do you favor a high tariff on all imports?
3. Do you believe that labor unions have the right to call a strike?
4. Would you favor loyalty tests for public office holders?
5. How would you secure low prices on the necessities of life?
6. Do you believe that the United States should share the atomic bomb with other countries?
7. Do you favor any new form of taxation?
8. Do you favor the repeal of the tax on oleomargarine?
9. Should the federal government have the right to censor radio and television speeches?
10. Do you favor strong government control over industry and business?

These attempts to further define thinking skills and to identify test items provide useful insights into the perception of thinking skills at the school level and into how the school district went about developing and implementing aspects of an instructional program in higher cognitive skills. Now that I have described the difficulties associated with identifying strategies for thinking-skills instruction, it is instructive for purposes of comparison to examine the evolution of the Arlington public schools' highly successful program of instruction in expository writing.

IMPLEMENTING A PROGRAM OF INSTRUCTION IN WRITING SKILLS

During the same period of time, that is, since approximately 1974, our school system has focused substantial attention on the improvement of student skills in expository writing. This attention arose in a manner similar to that given thinking skills; community concern was expressed through a committee of laymen to the school board. The school board became interested, and staff were instructed to follow up with a new instructional program. On this occasion, however, the English curriculum specialist met the request for a new program by successfully applying for a Title IV–C grant. The grant permitted the employment of two teacher consultants—one at the elementary level and one at the secondary level. These teachers were to develop the curriculum and provide staff training for classroom teachers and school principals who, in turn, were expected to implement the new program. The result has been a highly successful and exportable program. The program has been judged successful because large gains have been achieved in student proficiency in writing expository paragraphs. There are aspects of this effort that may be useful in identifying the components required for the successful implementation of an instructional program in thinking skills.

The grant made possible careful program design and planning. Objectives were linked to a composing process of five steps—prewriting (brainstorming), outlining, writing, proofreading, and rewriting. Simultaneously, two devices for evaluating the pupils' skills were developed—an objective test and a procedure for scoring writing samples. As part of the overall evaluation students were expected to write a paragraph each week to be scored by the teacher using this procedure.

Once the curricular and evaluation aspects of the writing program were developed, the two staff members combined the procedures and materials in a staff development package that they then circulated to teachers through an extensive training program. As a first step in the training program, the staff members visited each school to distribute the package in person, to offer their help in using it, and to train the teachers and the principal in the paragraph-scoring procedure. For teachers, this initial training was followed by three opportunities for further training. First, afterschool sessions were available to further elaborate each of the five steps of the writing process. Second, college equivalency credit courses geared to this program were established so teachers could obtain more extensive training. Third, the two teacher consultants were available to provide classroom demonstrations of teaching techniques.

Other characteristics of the program also contributed to its success. First, the timing was significant. The program was initiated just as national interest in the improvement of writing was emerging. As already noted, the stimulus for the program was a need expressed by the lay community. This meant that there was public support for the program. The expectation emerged that everyone in Grades 1–12 would participate. Thus, although initial training was provided only to elementary teachers and secondary school teachers of English, subsequent training was provided to those in other fields. All students were expected to improve their competence in writing. In short, there was substantial support from many different sources, as evidenced by the fact that the Arlington school board ultimately adopted the improvement of writing as a sixth goal.

Secondly, the early preparation of a set of staff training materials, including a description of the writing process and related instructional and assessment strategies, had some advantages. The trainers were able to have these materials in front of them when they worked with teachers. This created an air of completeness about the program. Additionally, this facilitated consistency of presentation from school to school and from department to department. Such consistency enhanced the probability of uniform implementation of the program.

Finally, as noted earlier, assessment took two forms. Students were expected to complete a writing sample every week. Ultimately, teachers were trained to teach students to do a substantial portion of the grading of these samples as part of the proofreading step. But the practice was expected *every* week. At key grades—5, 8, and 12—there was the expectation that every pupil would take a pretest, using an objective test, in the fall and a follow-up posttest in the spring. Each spring those same pupils would produce paragraphs from which samples would be drawn for scoring as part of the evaluation of the Title IV–C project. Even without Title IV–C support, the annual administration of an objective test of writing has remained in the testing schedule for the school system. This assessment has enabled teachers to see the gains of their pupils and may well have reinforced the commitment to writing.

The writing project has been successful because of the clarity of its objectives (both programmatic and instructional), because of its replicability, which facilitated staff development, because of expectations about practice, and because it generated assessment. This clarity, replicability, expectations of scheduled practice, and assessment were possible given the nature of the teaching of writing. There is an accepted, basic technology for teaching writing. Accepted techniques for teaching thinking skills do not exist. There are well-established ways of assessing writing proficiency. Thinking proficiency is more difficult to assess. Finally, most professionals in education have had formal training in writing skills. That is not true for thinking skills. Factors like these made it possible for the writing project to provide the school system with an asset that the expiration of funding cannot diminish—the increased skills of the teachers trained in the program. The art, or science, of teaching thinking skills has not reached a level where even the same kinds of supporting events would produce results similar to those for writing.

SUMMARY AND CONSIDERATIONS FOR THE FUTURE

The current status of the efforts of the Arlington County public schools to include thinking skills among its goals has been described. The resistances to instruction that have been encountered have also been outlined. Impediments to more extensive attempts at instruction have included: the lack of staff knowledge and preparation for teaching higher cognitive skills; the need for a clear, generalizable hierarchy or taxonomy of skills for use in formulating instructional objectives; and the lack of adequate time and financial resources to permit staff to acquire the knowledge and strategies required for creating an adequate program of instruction.

The contrasts between the work involving thinking skills and the work of the writing project provide insight into the obligations of researchers. To be more explicit: It would be a mistake to conclude that Arlington's thinking-skills program was an innovation of questionable quality simply because of inadequate resources, insufficient staff development activities, or from-the-top-down mandates. The more fundamental issue is that the factors that impeded progress transcend the particulars of the experience in this school system. They devolve from a lack of information that can be supplied by the research and teacher-training communities. It is important to list what is required, so that these communities can better understand how they can meet the needs of practitioners:

1. No established hierarchy of thinking skills exists. Without that hierarchy, it is not possible to construct a sequence of objectives.

2. There is no established, accepted set of verbs for formulating instructional objectives for thinking skills as there are for the lower levels, say, of the taxonomy of Bloom et al. (1956).

3. In the absence of instructional objectives, there is a void in the procedures appropriate for measuring pupil progress in acquiring thinking skills. This was illustrated in the mathematics test questions given earlier where a higher percentage of pupils answered the synthesis question correctly than answered the analysis question.

4. The two special teacher consultants for the writing program created a staff development package for conveying instructional techniques to teachers. What techniques and materials would be included in such a package for higher cognitive skills instruction?

5. If one were to train principals to observe the behaviors of classroom teachers in thinking-skills instruction, what behaviors would the principal be instructed to look for? Similarly, if program specialists performed demonstration teaching, what skills would they demonstrate?

6. How would students be expected to "practice" thinking skills each week?

The approach used in the thinking-skills work reported here has assumed that higher cognitive skill instruction has an intradisciplinary, content orientation rather than an interdisciplinary, process orientation. This was assumed for very practical reasons. If an interdisciplinary model had been assumed, the *expectation* of instruction would be present for teachers in all disciplines, but the responsibility would be assumed by no one. With the use of an intradisciplinary model, both expectations *and* responsibility are more easily identified.

If the suggestions for development of programs in thinking-skills instruction described here seem blurred, it is for good reason. They have been sketched without definitions of thinking skills, without knowledge of the methodology of thinking-skill instruction, without knowledge of the appropriate hierarchies for sequencing thinking-skill instruction, without knowledge of strategies for sound teaching in higher cognitive skills, and without knowledge of standard procedures for assessing proficiency in higher skills. In short, they are evidence of our lack of a theory of higher cognitive skill instruction. (If such a theory exists, the practitioners in this school setting are not aware of it. And that, too, would have a message.) Thus, there *is* a need for the formulation, clarification, and communication of a theory of instruction in higher cognitive skills and for the presentation of examples of that instruction.

In summary, the description provided here of the district's attempts to offer instruction in higher cognitive skills can be useful in determining the issues to be addressed in the formulation of programs of instruction in this area. These issues should be examined carefully for their implications for the assignment of responsibilities to local school districts versus the research and teacher-training communities.

ACKNOWLEDGMENTS

The comments and suggestions of the following individuals have been very helpful in the preparation of this chapter: Michele Bajek, Donald Brandewie, Larry Cuban, Catherine Eckbreth, Margaret McCourt-Dirner, Carolyn Smith, Seymour Stiss, Walter Taylor, and Judith Segal. Their help is greatly appreciated.

REFERENCES

Avital, S. M., & Shettleworth, S. J. *Objectives for mathematics learning: Some ideas for the teacher*. Toronto: The Ontario Institute for Studies in Education, 1968.

Bloom, B. S., Engelhart, M. D., Furst, E. J., Hill, W. H., & Krathwohl, D. R. *Taxonomy of educational objectives: The classification of educational goals: Handbook I: Cognitive domain*. New York: McKay, 1956.

17 The Development of Human Intelligence: The Venezuelan Case

José Dominguez
Venezuelan Ministry for the Development of Human Intelligence

In this chapter I consider an issue that in my opinion is the most important one of our time—the issue of improving thinking and learning skills. In essence, what we are discussing here is intelligence and its development and the heightening of mental functioning and its implications for the future of mankind. We have been able to put man on the moon, but we have not been able to fully develop human potentiality on earth. Human beings have been able to dominate their external environment but know little about and have too little control over their own mental life.

I am not a psychologist nor a physiologist; I am an educator and a university professor who has studied sociological, philosophical, and political issues, and who has attempted to apply social science research findings to work of social benefit. In the pages that follow, I describe an ambitious research program presently being carried out in my country, Venezuela, which is aimed at raising the intelligence of the entire population. This program is being carried out under the general direction of the Minister of State for the Development of Human Intelligence, Dr. Luis Alberto Machado. In the section that follows, I briefly describe the philosophy and rationale underlying this effort. In the subsequent section, I briefly describe the various projects that are underway in this program.

PHILOSOPHY AND RATIONALE

A major belief underlying the Venezuelan project is that, just as there is no such thing as aristocratic or "blue" blood, there is also no such thing as an aristocratic or "blue" brain (Dominguez, 1980). With the exception of subnormal people, nature does not determine human potentials. It does not impose aristocracies,

529

does not determine social classes, does not precondition destinies, does not prefabricate history, does not establish leadership based on pedigree. Nature establishes a base from which human potentialities can develop; then, life, society, and opportunities take over. Nature introduces us to the world as individuals who are free and equal, but not identical, and as individuals who share a similar natural potential to learn, acquire, and develop. In this sense, mankind is in essence an "intelligent possibility." Intelligence is what makes people different from other living things. If intelligence were to be predetermined—completely dependent on heredity—freedom would make no sense. Equality would be possible only in utopia, and democracy just demagogy. If this were the case, we would have to say: Underdeveloped countries, obey those nature imposed as your natural masters.

Fortunately, we are continually accumulating better scientific evidence that sociocultural factors play an important role in the development of intelligence. In other words, intelligence is in large part made up of skills that can be greatly influenced by appropriate experiences. This idea has been expressed by Bronowski (1973) as the ascent of man—that is, as the ascent of human intellectual capability.

I share with Minister Machado (1980) the view that intelligence can be taught. He has described intelligence as a "teachable and learnable faculty"—a position that is supported by evidence from an increasing number of scientific publications and research projects. Traditionally, educators have held that knowledge and rules of behavior can be taught, but not intelligence. And yet now there exists a considerable amount of scientific research that shows that intelligence too can be encouraged. This is important not only from a scientific point of view, but also from a political one.

As Minister Machado (1981) has said:

> In the same way that investment of resources and political strategy are planned, so should the different nations by means of a common effort, plan the attainment of a higher degree of intelligence in the least time possible and by all mankind. . . . And those political leaders who do not realize the magnitude of this possibility, will be unable to avoid having their countries, no matter how important now, be inevitably left behind. . . . .When the necessary means are organized to systematically improve the intelligence of all people, mankind will have taken the most important step toward progress. Then, the greatest revolution in history will be achieved. (pp. 3–4)

The idea that intelligence can be taught is not simply the fruit of intellectual speculation practiced without any end other than self-satisfaction; to the contrary, as the views of Minister Machado suggest, this idea has profound social implications. This is an idea for action that is supported by researchers of various nationalities including several whose chapters appear in this volume and its companion.

For example, consider the following statements from a variety of different researchers about the nature of intelligence, about aspects of intelligence that may be modifiable, and about the possibility of improving intelligence through instruction. Reuven Feuerstein (1980) offers: "Intelligence is considered a dynamic, self-regulated process that is responsive to external environmental intervention" (p. 2). Robert Sternberg (1980) has written that: "intelligence, broadly defined, must take into account a wide variety of cognitive processes and their interactions, as well as the motivational processes that drive the conitive ones" (p. 5). Edward de Bono (1976) has also written: "Thinking is the operational skill through which intelligence acts upon experience. Knowledge or information is the basic material handled by thinking" (pp. 32–33). Jack Lochhead (Lochhead & Clement, 1979) confirms that: "We should be teaching students how to think; instead we are primarily teaching them what to think. In brief, we are more concerned with what answers are given than with how they are produced" (p. 1). Arthur Whimbey (1975) has written: "Intelligence is a complex skill. As such, it cannot be defined as a unidimensional characteristic" (p. 104). Finally, Jose Delgado (1979), the well-known neuropsychologist, tells us:

Newborn brains are similar in all healthy human babies, in black, white, and yellow races, in poor and rich families, and in every corner of the world, regardless of geographical or political climate. All human beings are born with immature brains, ready to receive from the environment but unable at first to understand, choose, or reject incoming information. . . . The functional–structural development of the brain is implemented by the quality and quantity of sensory stimuli received. It is the social environment and not personal preference that determines the ideological framework of the individual mind. (p. 2).

In Venezuela, we are attempting to put these ideas about the modifiability of human intelligence to work in the service of mankind. To achieve this goal, the President of Venezuela, Dr. Luis Herrera, appointed on December 12, 1979, a Minister of State for the Development of Human Intelligence, Dr. Luis A. Machado. This political decision, unique in history, is of such a transcendental character that its importance cannot as yet be measured. By creating this new ministry, President Herrera (1980) gave evidence of his special qualifications as chief of state and set an example that is likely to be followed by other states in the near future. He described his decision as follows:

When I took office, one of the most difficult decisions I had to make, and also one of the most highly criticized at the beginning, was the creation of the Ministry of State for the Development of Human Intelligence. . . . After an initial period of criticism, however, support soon followed, and as a result many programs have now been implemented with the cooperation of outstanding universities, famous scholars, artists and social scientists from all over the world. (pp. 7–8).

Although Venezuela's work on the development of human intelligence is being carried out under the direction of its newly created Ministry of State for the Development of Human Intelligence, this work has received complete cooperation from the Ministry of Education, which shares with the Ministry of Intelligence an interest in renewing, transforming, and revolutionizing the Venezuelan educational system. The joint goal of these two ministries is to address an unfortunate reality in Venezuela—that in the recent past the educational system has been destroying the creativity and curiosity of Venezuelan children. It is the shared goal of both ministries to build a new educational system that will help students become critical, creative, and analytic thinkers.

In Venezuela, programs to foster the development of intelligence are based on the following fundamental principles:

1. *Scientific Endorsement:* All programs promoted by the Ministry for Intelligence will have a scientific basis.

2. *Nonpoliticization:* The programs will not, in any case, serve the ends of any political party or ideology.

3. *Popularization:* Programs will be designed not only to serve Venezuela's needs, but also with a view toward maximizing Venezuela's resources for purposes of promoting intelligence on a world-wide scale.

4. *Universality:* The impact of the effort is intended to go beyond national limits, with a view to making maximum use of the resources available on a world-wide scale.

The activities of the Ministry for the Development of Human Intelligence are aimed at achieving the democratization of science, that is, at helping people enjoy the benefits of scientific knowledge. This is seen as an important prerequisite for creating a more participatory democracy in Venezuela.

PROJECTS IN PROGRESS

We now briefly describe the projects that are currently underway as part of Venezuela's overall program to improve the intellectual functioning of its population.

Family Project

This project is attempting to impart to mothers and other adults who work closely with young children the motivation and scientific knowledge necessary to optimal child development from the prenatal period up to the age of six. With this end in mind, all mothers admitted to any of the maternity hospitals in the country will be attended by trained teams of professionals knowledgeable about the physical, social, and intellectual development of young children. The mothers will receive instruction in early childhood stimulation techniques both through face-to-face encounters with these professionals and through use of audiovisual and printed materials. In addition, an attempt will be made to train the entire Venezuelan population in early childhood stimulation techniques through use of the mass media. The family project will begin with a pilot test in which maternity hospitals offer expecting mothers different training methods and materials. These women will be followed on a longitudinal basis to determine whether they use the different techniques they are taught. Training methods and materials that are found to be effective will be introduced into other maternity hospitals and will serve as the basis for mass media presentation.

Learning to Think Project

This project is based on Edward de Bono's ideas, adapted for use in school and work settings throughout the country of Venezuela. The program is directed at improving such aspects of thinking as the ability to analyze problems, to identify alternative solutions, and to think creatively (see de Bono's chapter in this volume for a detailed description of his method). The project began with a controlled field test of the CoRT method in several Venezuelan elementary schools. Current plans involve extending instruction to 42,000 teachers who will use this method with 1,2000,000 schoolchildren. Future plans also include offering instruction to Venezuelan workers and members of the armed forces.

Instrumental Enrichment Project

This project involves the experimental use of the Instrumental Enrichment Program designed by Dr. Reuven Feuerstein to improve cognitive development. Its aim is to increase learning capacity and improve school performance among children from socially and culturally underprivileged groups. The Instrumental Enrichment Program consists of 500 exercises divided into 20 instruments, each one of which is aimed at developing specific cognitive skills and creating the mental prerequisites for further learning. The program attempts to develop proficiency in the following cognitive areas: analytical perception, spatial–temporal orientation, categorization, transitive relations, syllogisms, analogies, and convergent and divergent thinking. The exercises included in the program build on one another and lead to a progressive systematization of thought and to applications of thinking skills in a variety of different content areas (see Feuerstein's chapter in this volume for a detailed description of his method). A field test of the Instrumental Enrichment Program is now underway in schools in two Venezuelan cities. If the results are successful, the program will eventually be used throughout the country.

Visual Education Project

The aim of this project is to design a visual education program that will help young children learn to derive meaning from visual symbols as a complement to verbal language; that is, children are being taught to analyze visual stimuli into component parts for purposes of improving comprehension and memory. Direct consultation on this project is provided by Yaacov Agam, a kinetic artist. He has emphasized the importance of perceptual analysis skills and has argued that the play of colors, lines, and volumes in a perceptual array constitutes a vocabulary that is useful in understanding and remembering visual information (Agam, 1979).

Chess Project

This project involves research on the effects of systematic instruction in chess on the intellectual development of children ages 7 to 11. Successful chess playing involves attaining a mental solution to highly complex problems. Thus, it is possible that systematic chess playing may raise children's overall level of intellectual functioning. The purpose of this project is to ascertain whether substantial and significant differences in intellectual functioning will be observed in children who receive such instruction for a 3-year period. As a first step in implementing the project, 200 second graders, ages 7 to 9, will receive systematic instruction in chess for a period of 6 months. They will then be tested for transfer of thinking skills to problem-solving tasks encountered in everyday life. If the project is successful, chess instruction will be incorporated into all levels of education.

Project Intelligence

The Ministry for the Development of Human Intelligence has formalized an agreement with Harvard University and Bolt, Beranek, and Newman to develop a special program of instruction in thinking skills that will be appropriate for use in Venezuela. This project includes three stages: (1) a design stage in which the contractor will engage in a major review of the literature on instruction in thinking skills and will design an experimental program for use in Venezuela; (2) a formative evaluation stage in which the experimental materials will be pilot tested and revised; and (3) an application stage in which a formal evaluation of the program will be undertaken.

Creativity for Higher Education Project

The Ministry for the Development of Human Intelligence has sponsored experimental projects in various institutions of higher education to enable university students to acquire the cognitive skills necessary for creative thinking. A course on stimulating operational areas of the mind has been designed and is in the process of being validated by an interdisciplinary commission.

Creativity for Public Administration Project

Jointly with the Central Personnel Office, the Ministry for the Development of Human Intelligence is designing a program of instruction in creativity skills for public officials. The goals are to motivate public officials to consider their work in new ways and to improve communication channels in government. The program is expected to produce greater efficiency in state agencies, thereby contributing to the provision of better service to the Venezuelan people.

Project for Showrooms on Creativity and Inventiveness

Preparatory work is underway to establish a showroom on creativity and inventiveness. This showroom will be open to all citizens and will provide an opportunity to bring together individuals who, with imagination and creative capacity, have discovered new techniques, produced inventions, or formulated projects and ideas that are likely to contribute to Venezuela's development.

International Labor Organization Project

The International Labor Organization (ILO) is currently formulating a program in the field of adult education with the help of the Institute of Labor Studies in Geneva. The program will be aimed at developing the thinking skills of workers throughout the world. A pilot test of the program will be carried out in Venezuela. If the results are successful, steps will be taken through the ILO to disseminate the program to other member countries.

UNESCO Project

To make the results obtained through the projects just described available to the international community, the Ministry for the Development of Human Intelligence has established a permanent liaison with UNESCO. UNESCO has agreed to cooperate with Venezuela's efforts to improve human intelligence by systematically supplying information on relevant instructional programs throughout the world, especially programs involving prenatal education and the intellectual stimulation of young children. As part of its efforts in this area, UNESCO has sent a special mission to France, the United Kingdom, Germany, Switzerland, Belgium, and Russia to draw up as complete an inventory as possible of all research relating to the development of human intelligence. UNESCO has also been asked to design and prepare a set of instructional materials for use in Venezuela to teach creative, critical, and dialectic thinking skills. In keeping with Venezuela's policy of working closely with UNESCO, Minister Machado has been instrumental in having the subject of the development of human intelligence included on the agenda for the general assembly of UNESCO.

The repercussions nationally and internationally of Venezuela's activities with respect to the development of human intelligence have been extraordinary. Thousands of letters, telegrams, and articles in the press and scientific journals from all over the world have been received. One very gratifying event was the recent creation in Uruguay of the Latin American Center for the Development of Human Intelligence (Celadi, 1980). This is a nongovernmental organization that in its declaration of principle stated that: (1) "The right to the development of intelligence is the basis for the full and integral development of all human beings," and (2) "We are obligated to promote the cultivation of intelligence. Our time demands the democratization of intelligence so that this will no longer be a privilege of elites" (p. 1).

REFERENCES

Bronowski, J. *The ascent of man*. Boston: Little, Brown, 1973.

Celadi. *Declaration of principles*. Uruguay: Latin American Center for the Development of Human Intelligence, 1980.

de Bono, E. *Teaching thinking*. London: Temple Smith, 1976.

Delgado, J. *Basis for future learning*. Spain: Ramon y Cajal Center, unpublished material, 1979.

Dominguez, J. *El Cerebro Azul*. Revista Resumen, 1980.

Feuerstein, R. *Instrumental enrichment*. Baltimore: University Park Press, 1980.

Herrera, L. *The development of human intelligence*. President's address to the Congress, 1980.

Lochhead, J., & Clement, J. *Cognitive process instruction*. Philadelphia: The Franklin Institute Press, 1979.

Machado, L. A. *The right to be intelligent*. Oxford, England: Pergamon Press, 1980.

Machado, L. A. The development of intelligence: A political outlook. *Intelligence*, 1981, *5*, 2–4.

Sternberg, R. J. A componential approach to the intellectual development. In R. Sternberg (Ed.), *Advances in the psychology of human intelligence*. Hillsdale, NJ: Lawrence Erlbaum Associates, 1980.

Whimbey, A. *Intelligence can be taught*. New York: E. P. Dutton, 1975.

Author Index

A

Abelson, R.P., 8, *18*, 422, *455*
Abrams, J.D., 276, *285*
Actkinson, T.R., 2, *17*, 214, 220, *237*, *238*, 245, *257*
Adams, J.L., 150, 152, *204*
Adelman, L., 272, 275, *288*
Agam, 534
Alba, R.D., 499, *513*
Algaze, B., 251, *258*
Allen, V.L., 408, *411*
Allington, R., 277, *285*, 352, *356*
Alschuler, A.S., 390, 397, *411*
Alvermann, D.E., 311, *314*
Amiran, M., 259, 264, 268, 279, 280, 281, *285*
Ammon, M.S., 243,*257*
Anastasi, A., 244, *256*
Anderson, J.R., 421, 427, *453*
Anderson, L.W., 274, 275, 276, *285*, *286*
Anderson, R.C., 8, *16*, 227, 233, *236*, 243, *256*, 277, *285*
Anderson, T.H., 9, 10, *16*, 244, *256*, 269, 276, 277, 281, *285*, *286*, 330, 333, 337, *356*
Andre, M.D.A., 277, *286*
Andre, T., 228, *236*
Andrews, G.R., 406, *411*
Anton, W.D., 251, *258*
Arbitman-Smith, R., 144, *204*
Arlin, P., 13, *16*

Armbruster, B.B., 221, *237*, 269, 277, *286*, 330, 333, 337, *356*
Arons, A., 126, *130*, 500, *512*
Arthur, G.A., *81*
Atkinson, J.W., 391, *412*
Atkinson, R.C., 277, *289*
Atwood, M.E., 419, 420, 422, 424, 428, *453*
Au, K., 352, *356*
Auchenbach, T.M., 277, 281, *286*, *289*
August, G.J., 277, *289*
Austin, H., 123, *130*
Ausubel, D.P., 307, *314*
Avital, S.M., 519, *527*

B

Bailey, G.W., 275, *286*
Baker, L., 153, 179, 197, *204*, 332, *356*
Banton, L., 496
Barber, C., 275, *286*
Barclay, C.R., 13, *16*
Baron, J., 13, *16*
Barowy, W., 129, *130*
Barron, R.F., 307, 308, 311, *314*, *315*
Bartlett, F.C., 8, *16*, 137, *204*
Barton, W.A., Jr., 9, *16*
Bauman, R.P., 500, *512*
Beck, I.L., 1, *16*

Beery, R., 390, 395, 396, 404, 406, *412*
Belmont, J.M., 354, *356*, 409, *412*
Bennett, C.E., 135, *204*
Bereiter, C., 269, 270, *286*, 506, *512*
Berglas, S., 392, *412*
Berliner, D.C. 201, *204*
Betts, E.A., 307, *315*
Bhaskar, R., 423, *453*
Biddle, W.B., 227, *236*
Binet, A., 4, *16*, 334, *356*, 410, *412*
Birney, R.C., 392, *412*
Bisanz, J., 147, 148, *205*
Blanc, R., 478, *496*
Block, J.H., 276 *285*, *286*, 321, *357*
Bloom, B., 110, *130*, 137, *204*, 272, *286*, 307, *315*, 321, 338, *357*, 475, 479, 480, *496*, 506, 511, *512*, 517, 526, *527*
Bloom, L., 146, *204*
Blum, M.E., 475, 480, *496*
Bluth, G.S., 277, *288*
Botkin, J., *496*
Botvin, G.J., 356, *357*
Bower, G.H., 418, *453*
Bracewell, R., 270, *286*
Brandt, D.M., 277, *288*
Brainerd, C.J., 13, *16*
Bransford, J.D., 144, 150, 153, 174, 175, 193, *204, 206*, 330, 331, 331f, 332, 346, *357*, 401, *412*
Brewer, W.F., 167, *204*, 332, 336, *357*, *358*
Brickman, P., 396, *412, 416*
Bridge, C., 277, *289*
Briggs, R.D., 217, *237*
Bristol, G.P., 135, *204*
Brock, T.C., 391, *412*
Broder, J.L., 338, *357*
Broder, L., 137, *204*, 506, *512*
Broder, L.J., 110, *130*
Broder, L.L., 475, *496*
Bronowski, J., 530, *536*
Bronson, D.B., 485, *496*
Brooks, L.W., 210, 214, 221, 227, 230, 234, *237, 239*
Brophy, J.E., 277, *286*
Brown, A.L., 5, 7, 9, 13, *16*, 146, 147, 150, 153, 167, 174, 175, 179, 192, 202, *204, 206*, 277, 279, 281, *286*, 330, 332, 334, 335, 336, 337, 339, 340, 344, 349, 351, 352, 354, 355, *356*, *357*, *358*, *359*, 402, 409, *412*
Brown, J.I., 251, *256*
Brown, J.S., 8, *17*, 124, *130, 204*

Brown, P.J., 221, *238*
Brown, W.F., 218, 226, *237*, 251, *256*, *257*
Bruce, B.C., 332, *358*
Bruner, J.S., 5, *17*, 307, 308, *315*, 512
Bugliosi, V., 150, *205*
Buhagiar, C., 366, 381, *387*
Burdick, H., 392, *412*
Burnes, B., 105, *106*
Burns, R., 276, *286, 321, 357*
Burton, R.R., 124, *130*
Busse, T.V., 211, *238*, 407, *414*, 429, *454*
Butler, C., 479, *496*
Butterfield, E.C., 354, *356*, 409, *412*

C

Campione, J.C., 147, 150, 174, 175, 197, *204*, 277, 281, *286*, 330, 332, 334, 335, 336, 337, 344, 349, 351, *357, 358, 359*
Carmichael, J.W., Jr., 128, *130*
Carroll, J.B., 215, *237*
Carter, H.D., 244, *257*
Case, R., 145, 146, *205*, 277, *286*
Celadi, 536, *536*
Cera, D.J., 277, *289*
Chall, J., 3, *17*
Chapin, M., 406, *412*
Chase, W.G., 138, 179, *205, 428, 453*
Chatham, K.M., 1, *17*
Christensen, F.A., 245, *257*
Ciarlo, J.A., 406, *414*
Cinquino, D., 105, *106*
Clarke, A.D.B., 184, *205*
Clarke, A.M., 184, *205*
Clement, J., 501, *513*, 531, *536*
Cohen, J., 261, *288*
Cole, M., 2, *18*, 84, *107*
Collins, A., 8, *17*, 202, *204*, *286*, 332, 336, 338, 340, 348, *358*
Collins, J., 352, *358*
Collins, K.W., 209, 211, 214, 215, 216, 217, 218, 220, 221, 224, 225, 227, 228, 229, 230, 234, *237, 238, 239*, 244, *257*, 269, *286*, 402, *413*
Commons, M.L., 13, *17*
Conlon, C.M.T., 353, *359*
Coopersmith, S., 397, *412*
Copley, E., 364, *388*
Copley, W., 364, 366, 381, *388*

Coulson, D., 261, *288*
Covington, M.V., 390, 391, 392, 393, 394, 395, 396, 397, 399, 400, 401, 404, 406, 407, 409, 410, *412, 413, 414*, 429, *453*
Craik, F.I.M., 211, 228, *237*
Cromer, W., 277, *286*, 406, *413, 415*
Cronbach, L.J., 216, *237*
Cross, K.P., 243, *257*
Crutchfield, R.S., 402, 407, 408, *413, 415*, 429, 431, *453*
Cubberly, W.E., 243, 244, 246, *258*, 277, *290*
Cummings, N., 105, *107*

D

Dangel, T.R., 261, 277, *287*
Dansereau, D.F., 2, *17*, 209, 210, 211, 213, 214, 215, 216, 217, 218, 220, 221, 224, 225, 227, 228, 229, 230, 234, 235, *237, 238, 239*, 244, 246, *257*, 269, 277, *286*, 402, *413*
Darcey, J., 407, *415*
Darlington, R., 23, *40*
Davies, L.B., 407, *413*, 429, *453*
Davis, G., 389, *496*
David, G.A., 426, *453*
Davis, G.E., 263, *286*
Day, J.D., 5, *16, 17*, 150, 197, *204*, 227, 279, *286*, 336, 337, 344, 349, 351, *358*
Dean, R.S., 277, *287*
de Bono, E., 150, 173, 175, *205*, 367, 371, 375, 385, *388*, 426, 432, 440, 443, *453*, 531, *536*
Debus, R.L., 406, *411*
de Charms, R., 406, *413*
Deffenbacher, J.L., 229, *238*
Deffenbacher, K.A., 277, *287*
DeGood, H., 277, *288*
Deignan, G.M., 216, 228, 233, *238*
Delgado, J., 531, *536*
DeLoache, J.S., 146, 192, *204*, 335, *358*, 402, *412*
Denhiere, G., 403, *413*
Denny, E.C., 251, *256*
Dewey, J., 122, *130*, 193, *205*
Diekhoff, G.M., 209, 218, 220, 221, 225, 234, *237, 238*, 244, *257*, 269, *286*, 402, *413*
Diggory, J.C., 396, *413*
DiVesta, F.J., 227, *239*, 261, 277, 279, *287, 289*
Doctorow, M., 277, *287*

Dominguez, J., 529, *536*
Dubin, R., 215, *238*
Duffy, S.A., 9, *18*
Duncker, K., 427, *453*
Durkin, D., 1, *17*, 278, *287*
Durrell, D.D., 307, *315*
Dweck, C.S., 406, *414*
Dyck, D.G., 406, *412*

E

Earle, R., 307, 311, *315*
Eisert, D., 481, *497*
Ellis, A.M., 220, 224, *237, 238*
Elmandjra, M., *496*
Engelhart, M.D., 517, 526, *527*
Engelmann, S., 506, *512*
Ennis, R.H., 307, *315*
Ericsson, K.A., 124, *130*, 337, *358*, 428, *453*
Ernst, G.W., 420, 441, *453*
Evans, E.D., 23, *40*
Evans, S.H., 209, 214, 217, 218, 220, 221, 225, 234, *237, 238*, 244, *257*, 269, *286*, 402, *413*
Ewing, D.W., 489, *496*
Ezergaile, L., 270, *286*

F

Fedan, N., 410, *413*
Fegan, M., 244, *257*
Feigenbaum, E.A., 403, *414*
Feldhusen, J.F., 426, *453*
Feldman, R., 397, *412*
Ferguson, G.A., 335, *358*
Ferrara, R.A., 150, 175, *204*, 330, 332, 334, 335, 336, 340, *357, 358*
Feuerstein, R., 45, 64, 65, 76, 78, *81, 82*, 179, 180, 181, 182, 183, 184, 185f, 189, 190f, 194, 195, 197, 199, *205*, 340, *358*, 504, 505, 506, 508, *512*, 531, *536*
Fine, J., 270, *286*
Finkel, D., 111, *130*
Fischer, G., 124, *130*
Fischer, K.W., 13, *17*
Fitts, P.M., 137, *205*
Flavell, J.H., 13, *17*, 146, 153, 192, *205*, 335, 344, *358, 359*, 400, 402, 403, *414, 415*
Fleming, D., 483, *496*

Flower, L.S., 270, 287, 319, *358, 359*
Ford, G.W., 307, *315*
Formisano, M., 502, *512*
Fraenkel, J.R., 487, *496*
Franks, J.J., 174, 193, *204*, 332, *357*, 401, *412*
Frase, L.T., 261, 277, 287, 319, *358*, 405, *414*
French, L.A., 339, *358*
Fridell, R., 259, 264, *285*
Friedrichs, A.G., 403, *414*
Fuller, R., 475, 476, *497*
Furby, L., 216, *237*
Furst, E.J., 517, 526, *527*
Furukawa, J.W., 277, *287*

G

Gagné, R.M., 211, 214, *238*, 298, 307, *315*, 337, *359*
Gallup, G., 363, *388*
Gardner, J., 390, 411, *414*
Garland, J.C., 209, 211, 215, 216, 217, 218, 220, 221, 224, 225, 228, 229, 230, *237, 238*, 244, *257*, 269, *286*, 402, *413*
Garrett, H.E., 335, *359*
Getzels, J.W., 400, *414*
Glaser, R., 4, *18*, 340, *359*, 452, *453*
Glasman, L.D., 3, *17*
Gleeson, M., 354, *388*
Glenn, A., *497*
Glock, M.D., 277, 281, *288, 289*
Goetz, E.T., 281, *287*
Goldman, R., 245, *257*
Goldman, S.R., 146, 147, 148, *205*
Goldstein, I.P., 424, *454*
Golinkoff, R.A., 243, *257*
Gonzalez, H.P., 251, *258*
Good, T.L., 277, *286*
Goodman, J., 224, *239*
Goodnow, J.J., 502, *512*
Gordon, C., 277, 281, *288*
Gordon, W.J., 426, *453*
Gorsuch, R.L., 251, *258*
Gould, R., 392, 399, *415*
Graham, K., 126, *130*
Gray, R.L., 129, *131*
Gray, W.S., 307, *315*
Greenfield, L., *497*
Greeno, J.G., 11, *17*, 402, 403, *414*, 421, 423, 425, *454*

Grove, E., 245, *257*
Guilford, J.P., 307, 315
Guzak, F.J., 308, 315

H

Haas, H.J., 102, *107*
Hall, J.W., 263, 277, 281, *287*, 319, *359*
Hamid-Buglione, V., 2, *18*
Hansen, J., 277, 281, *288*
Harari, O., 394, *414*
Harris, G., 8, *17*, 202, *204*
Hayes, J.R., 147, *205, 206*, 270, *287*, 319, *358, 359*, 422, 423, 452, *454*
Haywood, H.C., 198, 199, *205*
Heckhausen, H., 393, *415*
Heller, J.I., 421, 423, *454*
Henderson, A., 105, *107*
Hendricks, M., 396, *412*
Herber, H.L., 297, 302, 303, 308, 309, 311, 314, *315*
Herrera, L., 531, *536*
Hidde, J.L., 277, *285*
Hidi, S., 270, *287*
Higa, W.R., 105, *107*
Hill, J., 392, *415*
Hill, W.H., 517, 526, *527*
Hilyard, A., 270, *287*
Hinsley, D.A., 423, *454*
Hobbs, N., 481, *497*
Hoffman, M., 197, 200, *205*
Hoffman, M.B., 179, 180, 181, 182, 183, 184, 185f, 189, 190f, 194, 195, 197, 199, 200, *205*, 504, 505, 506, 508, *512*
Holley, C.D., 209, 211, 214, 215, 216, 218, 220, 221, 224, 225, 227, 228, 229, 230, 234, *237, 238, 239*, 244, *257*, 269, *286*, 402, *413*
Holmes, J.A., 307, *315*
Holt, J., 149, *205*, 391, *414*
Holtsman, W. H., 218, 226, *237*, 245, 251, *257*
Honeycutt, C.D., 311, *315*
Hood, L., 146, *204*
House, P., 479, *497*
Hoyt, J.D., 403, *414*
Huey, E.B., 139, *205*
Hunkins, F.P., 488, *497*
Hunt, E., 4, *17*
Huttenlocher, J., 508, *512*

I

Inhelder, B., *131*

J

Jacobsen, E., 224, *238*
Jacoby, K.E., 397, 399, *413*
Jarombeck, J., 277, *287*
Jeffries, R., 420, 422, 424, 428, *454, 455*
Jencks, C., 3, *17*
Jenkins, J., 277, *287*, 331, 331f, *359*
Jensen, A., 3, *17*, 62, *82*
John-Steiner, V., 84, *107*
Johnson, D.D., 311, *315*
Johnson, D.M., *205*
Johnson, N.S., 332, *359*
Johnson-Laird, P.N., 147, *205*
Jones, B.F., 259, 262, 263, 264, 272, 274, 275, 276, 277, 279, 280, 281, 282, 283, 284, *285, 287, 288*, 319, *359*, 392, *412*

K

Kagan, S., 391, *415*
Kantor, K., 489, *497*
Kantowski, M.G., 489, *497*
Kaplan, R.M., 395, *414*
Karplus, R., 401, *414*, 475, *497*, 502, *512*
Karrus, R.W., 104, *107*
Katims, M., 272, 275, 283, 284, 287, *288*
Katona, G., 427, *454*
Kelley, H.H., 392, *414*
Kendall, J.R., 277, *288*
Kennedy, T.J., 353, *359*
Kennedy, W.A., 398, *414*
Kintsch, W., 227, 232, *238*, 277, *288*, 421, *454*
Klemp, G.O., 479, 490, *497*
Kohler, W., 11, *17*
Kolb, D.A., 407, *414*
Kotovsky, K., 147, 148, *205*
Kozminski, E., 277, *288*
Krathwohl, D.R., 517, 526, *527*
Krepelka, E.J., 211, *238, 407, *414*, 429, *454*
Krulik, S., 480, 489, *497*
Kuhn, D., 13, *17*
Kukla, A., 393, *416*
Kulhavy, R.W., 277, *287*

Kun, A., 392, *414*
Kurfman, D.G., 484, *497*
Kurth, R.J., 277, *288*

L

LaBerge, D., 139, *205*, 300, *315*
Lachica, G.M., *512*
Lane, D., *388*
Larkin, J.H., 423, 428, *454*
Larson, C., 230, *239*
Larson, D., 214, 227, *237*
Lavin, D.A., *513*
Lawson, A., 475, *497*
Lawton, S.C., 277, *286*
Lazar, I., 23, *40*
Lee, M., 367, *388*
Lefevre, C.A., 406, *414*
Lesgold, A.M., 277, *288*
Levin, J.R., 277, *288*
Levine, D.U., 284, *288*
Levine, J.M., 408, *411*
Levy, V.M., Jr., 403, *416*
Lichtenstein, E.H., 167, *204*, 332, *357*
Lightbrown, P., 146, *204*
Lin, H., 501, *513*
Lipman, A.H., 154, 155, 156, 157, 158, 159, 160, 162, 163, 169, 170, 177, 179, *205*
Lipman, M., 101, *107*, 154, 168, *205*
Litwin, G.H., 406, *414*
Lochhead, J., 111, 117, 121, 129, *130, 131, 206*, 489, *497*, 501, 504, *513*, 531, *536*
Lockhart, R.S., 211, 228, *237*
Long, G.L., 1, *17*, 214, 217, 220, *237, 238*, 246, *257*
Luchins, A.S., 11, *17*
Luschene, R.E., 251, *258*
Lusterman, S., 484, *497*

M

MacGinitie, W.H., 1, *17*
Machado, L.A., 530, *536*
Mack, R.L., 9, *18*
Madsen, S.C., 277, *287*
Madjurajan, A., 367, *388*
Maeroff, G.I., 5, *17*
Maier, N., 363, 364, 366, *388*

Maier, N.R.F., 11, *17*
Malitza, M., *496*
Mandel, T.S., 277, *288*
Mandler, J.M., *359*
Mann, L., 4, *17*, 133, 134, 135, 136, *205*
Mansfield, R.S., 211, *238*, 407, *414*, 429, *454*
Maratsos, M.P., 175, *205*
Markman, E.M., 2, 14, *17*, 146, 152, 153, 179, 197, *205, 206*
Marks, C., 277, *287*
Marr, D., 428, *454*
Marshall, N., 277, 281, *288*
Martin, D., 476, 478, *496, 497*
Martin, J.F., 105, *107*
Martin, M., 485, *497*
Martire, J.G., 396, *414*
Mason, J.M., 277, *288*
Masson, M.E.J., 420, *453*
Masur, E.F., 344, *359*
Maultsby, M., 224, *239*
Maxon, G., 311, *315*
Mayer, R.E., 9, *18*, 277, 279, *288*, 406, *414*
McClelland, D.C., 129, *131*, 391, *414*
McCombs, B.L., 244, *257*
McDermott, J., 428, *454*
McDermott, R., 3, *18*, 352, *359*
McDonald, B.A., 2, *17*, 209, 211, 215, 216, 217, 218, 220, 221, 224, 225, 234, *237, 238*, 244, 246, *257*, 269, *286*, 402, *413*
McIntyre, G.W., 344, *359*
Meichenbaum, D.H., 13, *18*, 224, 229, *239*
Mettee, D.R., 398, *414*
Meyer, B.J.F., 243, *257*, 277, 281, *288*
Meyer, J.R., *497*
Miller, G.A., 242, *257*
Miller, J.R., 421, *454*
Miller, M.A., 424, *454*
Miller, P.H., 13, *18*
Miller, R., 179, 181, 182, 183, 184, 185f, 189, 190f, 194, 195, 197, 199, 200, *205*, 504, 505, 506, *512*
Minsky, M., 422, *454*
Miscik, J.G., 277, *287*
Monk S., 111, *130*
Monroe, A., 244, *257*
Montague, *W.E.*, 243, *256*
Moore, W., Jr., 500, *513*
Morgan, J.L., 332, 336, *358*
Morison, A., 3, *18*
Morley, R.M., 217, *237*
Morris, C.D., 174, 193, *204*

Moseley, P.A., 277, *288*
Moynahan, E.D., 403, *415*
Murray, F.B., 356, *357*
Musgrave, B.S., 261, *288*
Myers, J.L., 281, *288*

N

Navon, D., 242, *257*
Neimark, E., 403, *415*
Neisser, U., 502, 510, *513*
Nelson, J., 302, 308, 311, 314, *315*
Nelson, K., 167, *206*
Nelson, L.L., 391, *415*
Nelson, M.J., 251, *256*
Neves, D.M., 425, *454*
Newell, A., 11, 12, *18*, 139, 144, 150, *206*, 335, *359*, 401, *415*, 418, 419, 420, 441, *453, 454*
Newman, D., 332, *358*
Nezworski, T., 277, 288, *289*
Nickerson, R.S., 425, 426, 429, 448, *454*
Nierenberg, R., 393, *415*
Niles, O.S., 307, *315*
Nilsson, N.J., 419, 424, *454*
Nitsch, K.E., 174, 193, *204, 206*, 332, *357*, 401, *412*
Norman, D.A., 10, *18*, 138, 167, *206*, 421, 425, *454*
Novack, G.S., 421, *455*

O

Oakley, D.D., 344, *359*
Ogbu, J.V., 4, *18*
Olson, D.R., 168, *206*
Olson, G.M., 9, *18*
Olton, R., 407, 408, *413, 415*, 429, 431, *453, 455*
Omelich, C.L., 390, 391, 392, 393, 394, 396, 397, *413*
Ortony, A., 211, *239*, 265, *289*
Osborne, A.F., 426, *455*
Oscanyan, F.S., *107*, 154, 155, 156, 157, 158, 159, 160, 162, 163, 169, 170, 177, 179, *205*
Overall, J.E., *239*
Owings, R., 153, 154, 203, *204*, 332, 346, *357*

P

Paige, J.M., 423, *455*
Paivio, A., 211, *239*, 242, *257*
Palincsar, A.S., 340, 352, 355, *238, 359*
Papert, S., 109, *131*
Paulsen, A., 502, *512*
Payne, S.L., 488, *497*
Pearson, P.D., 277, 281, *288*, 311, 312, *315*
Pellegrino, J.W., 4, *18*
Peper, R.J., 277, 279, *288*
Perkins, D.N., 425, 426, 429, 448, *454*
Perlmutter, J., 261, *288*
Perron, J., 489, *497*
Perry, W.G., Jr., 127, *131*
Pezdek,K., 261, *288*
Pfeiffer, K., 490, *497*
Phenix, P.H., 480, *497*
Piaget, J., 123, 125, *131*
Pichert, J.W., 233, *236*
Polsky, S., 397, *413*
Polson, P.G., 419, 420, 422, 424, 428, *453, 454, 455*
Polya, G., 13, *18*, 423, 424, 426, 427, 440, 450, 451, *455*
Posner, M.I., 137, *205*
Postman, L., 401, *415*
Pressley, M., 277, *288*
Pugano, L., 307, *315*
Purcell, L., 340, 352, *358*

R

Rabinovitch, M.S., 277, *290*
Ramanaiah, N., 245, *257*
Rand, Y., 179, 180, 181, 182, 183, 184, 185f, 189, 190f, 194, 195, 197, 199, 200, *205*, 504, 505, 506, 508, *512*
Raugh, M.R., 277, *289*
Raynor, J.D., *412*
Reder, L.M., 242, *257*
Reed, M.M., 353, *359*
Reed, R., 105, *107*
Reif, F., 427, *455*
Reitman, W., 409, *415*
Resnick, L.B., 269, *289*, 340, *359*
Rest, S., 393, *415*
Restaino, L.C.R., 277, *289*
Restak, R.M., 489, *497*
Restle, F., 420, *455*

Ribich, F.D., 245, *257*
Richards, D.D., 3, 13, *18*
Richards, F.A., 13, *17*
Richelle, M., 76, *82*
Rickards, J.P., 277, *289*
Ripple, R.E., 407, 408, *415*
Robinson, F.P., 210, *239*
Rohwer, W.D., Jr., 24, *40*, 242, 243, *257*, 277, 278, *289*
Roney, L.K., 243, 246, *258*
Rosenshine, B., 201, *204*, 277, *289*
Rosner, J., 351, 352, *359*
Rosnick, P., 124, *131*
Ross, S.M., 227, *239*
Royer, J.M., 261, *288*
Rubin, S.E., 397, *415*
Rubinstein, M., 152, *206*, 435, 438, *455*, 490, *497*
Rudnick, J., 480, 489, *497*
Rumelhart, D.E., 211, *239*, 265, *239*, 300, *315*, 421, *454*
Russell, D.H., 307, *315*
Ryan, E.B., 243, *257*

S

Sacerdoti, E.D., 423, *455*
Sadler, W., 479, *497*
Salatas, H., 403, *415*
Salomon, M., 277, *289*
Samuels, S.J., 139, *205*, 300, 314, *315*
Sanders, P.L., 311, *315*
Sarason, I.G., 218, 226, *239*
Scandura, J.M., 409, *415*
Scardamalia, M., 269, 270, *286*
Schalock, A.D., 500, 511, *513*
Schank, R., 8, *18*, 421, 422, *455*
Schechler, J., 277, *289*
Scheffler, I., 483, *497*
Schlesinger, M.A., 480, 481, *497*
Schmeck, R.R., 245, *257*
Schnur, A.E., 397, 403, *415*
Schoenfeld, A.H., *455*, 478, 481, *497*
Schulte, A.C., 244, *257, 258*
Schultz, C.B., 261, 277, 279, *287, 289*
Schwartz, B.J., 277, *287*
Scott, R., 244, *257*
Scribner, S., 3, *18*, 84, *107*, 171, *206*
Sears, P.S., 392, *415*

Shallcrass, J., 383, 385, *388*

Sharan, S., 229, *239*

Sharp, A.M., *107*, 154, 155, 156, 157, 158, 159, 160, 162, 163, 169, 170, 177, 179, *205*

Shaughnessy, J.J., 402, *415*

Shaw, J.C., 11, *18*

Shea, D.J., 406, *415*

Shelton, J., 392, *415*

Shelton, T.S., 153, 154, 203, *204*, 332, 346, *357*

Shettleworth, S.J., 519, *527*

Shifrin, Z., 281, *285*

Shimmerlik, S.M., 211, 228, *239*

Shipman, V.C., 103, 105, *107*

Siegler, R.S., 2, 13, *18*, 145, 146, *206*

Sigall, H., 392, 399, *415*

Silberman, C.E., 390, *415*

Silberstein, R.A., 499, *513*

Simon, A., 12, *18*

Simon, C., 104, *107*

Simon, D.P., 11, *18*, 428, *454*

Simon, H.A., 11, *18*, 124, *130*, 138, 139, 144, 147, 148, 179, 202, *205*, *206*, 337, *358*, 401, *415*, 418, 419, 420, 421, 422, 423, 424, 426, 428, 441, *453*, *454*, *455*

Sindell, L., 277, *289*

Slavin, R.E., 229, *239*

Slotnick, N.S., 403, *415*

Smiley, S.S., 5, *16*, 277, *286*, 337, 344, *358*, *359*

Smith, E.C., 337, *359*

Smith, E.E., 338, *358*, 425, 426, 429, 448, *454*

Smith, H.K., 2, *18*

Smith, N.B., 307, *315*

Smith, R.A., 198, 199, *205*

Snow, C., 3, *17*

Sochor, E.E., 307, *316*

Souberman, E., 84, *107*

Spangehl, S.D., 475, 480, *496*

Spearman, C., 334, *359*

Speedie, S.M., 426, *453*

Spielberger, C.D., 251, *258*

Spiro, R.J., 243, *256*

Spratt, M.F., 394, *413*

Spurlin, J.E., 221, 227, 230, 234, *237*, *239*

Stefik, M.J., 441, *455*

Stein, B.S., 153, 154, 174, 193, 203, *204*, *206*, 332, 346, *357*

Stein, N.L., 277, 281, *288*, *289*

Steiner, R., 406, *415*

Steingart, S.K., 277, *289*

Sternberg, R.J., 4, *18*, 147, 148, 150, *206*, 281, *289*, 531, *536*, *415*

Stevens, A., 338, 340, 348, *358*

Sticht, T.G., 244, *258*, 276, 277, *289*

Stoll, L.J., 274, 278, *289*

Suydam, M., 474, *497*

Svensson, L., 244, 245, *258*

Swant, S.G., 395, *414*

T

Taveggia, T.C., 215, *238*

Taylor, C.J., 251, *258*

Teevan, R., 392, *412*

Thomas, J.W., 397, *415*

Thompson, D.M., 401, *415*

Thorndike, E.L., 136, 200, 201, 203, *206*

Thorndyke, P.W., 232, *239*

Tierney, R.J., 277, *289*

Tighe, L.S., 277, *289*

Tighe, T.J., 277, *289*

Tobias, S., 149, *206*

Tomlinson-Keasey, C.A., 481, *497*

Tosi, D.J., 217, *237*

Trabasso, T.R., 277, *288*

Treffinger, D.J., 408, *415*, 426, *453*

Tripp, D., 366, 382, 383, 385, *388*

Tulving, E., 167, *206*, 277, *289*, 401, *415*

Tuma, D.T., 427, *455*

Turk, D., 244, *239*

Turner, A., 422, 424, 428, *454*

Tyler, L.E., 4, *18*

Tyler, R.W., 179, *206*

Tyler, S., 383, *388*

U

Ulrich, T., 403, *415*

Underwood, V.L., 243, 244, 246, 250, *258*, 277, *290*, 353, *359*

V

Vacca, R., 311, *316*

Van Dijk, T.A., 227, *238*, 421, *454*

Varenne, H., 3, *18*
Von Glaserfeld, E., 125, *131*
Vygotsky, L.S., 84, *107*, 146, 159, 167, *206*, 338, 339, *359*

W

Wagner, M., 277, 281, *289*
Walker, N., 311, *316*
Warren, R., 245, *257*
Weaver, D., 396, *416*
Weaver, P.A., 277, *289*
Weber, L., 483, *496*
Weiner, B., 392, 393, *414, 415, 416*
Weinstein, C.E., 2, *19*, 153, *206*, 242, 243, 244, 246, 249, *257, 258*, 277, *290*, 346, 353, *359*
Weinstein, M.L., 105, *107*
Weinstein, P., 277, *290*
Weiss, M.G., 13, *18*
Wellman, H.M., 146, 153, 192, *205*, 400, 402, *414*
Wertheimer, M., 427, *455*
Wertime, R., 117, *131*
Wertsch, J.V., 3, *19*, 181, *206*, 339, *359*
Whimbey, A., 111, 117, 121, *131*, 137, 152, *206*, 476, *497*, 504, 506, *513*, 531, *536*

Whimbey, L.S., 506, *513*
White, R.T., 211, *238*
White, S.H., 179, *206*
Whitehall, R.P., 217, *239*
Whiting, L., 270, *290*
Wickelgren, W.A., 147, 152, *206*, 438, 447, *455*
Wicker, F.W., 243, 244, 245, *258*, 277, *290*
Wiener, M., 277, *286*, 406, *413, 415*
Wild, M., 353, *359*
Willcutt, H.C., 398, *414*
Williams, S., 220, *237, 238*
Winograd, T., 8, *19*, 421, *455*
Winston, P.H., 425, *455*
Wittrock, M.C., 242, 243, *258*, 277, *287, 290*
Wolpe, J., 224, *239*
Womack, S., 228, *236*
Woodson, C.E., 397, 398, *416*
Woodward, J.W., 216, *239*
Woody, T., 135, *206*
Worthen, D., 344, *359*

Y

Yeazell, M.I., 105, *107*
Yussen, S.R., 403, *416*

Subject Index

A

Abstraction and skill instruction, 369–370
Advanced organizers, 9, 406
Affect and cognition, 36
Affect and instruction, 38, 74, 97–98, 471,
    506–507, *see also* Fear of Failure
Analogical thinking, 144–145, 147–152, 171–
    173
    role in everyday life, 150–151
Arlington School District skills programs, 38,
    see also Ch. 16 (Ware)
Assimilation and accommodation, 60, 125–126
Attention and instruction, 372–373
Automatic cognition, 124, 336–337, *see also*
    Practice and instruction

B

Basal reading programs
    problems with, 461–463
    teacher attitudes, 465

C

Case studies, as instructional tools, 368–369
Categorization skills, 70–71
Cheating, to avoid failure, 392
Chicago Mastery Learning Reading Program
    with Learning Strategies (CMLR/LS), 32,
    37, 270–284, 320–323, 463–472, *see also*

Ch. 7 (Jones et al.), Ch. 13 (Thompson)
    analyzer commentary, 320–323, 341–352
    evaluations, 275–276, 281–284, 469–472
    goals and targeted skills, 271–272, 320–
        321, 463
    implementation methods and materials,
        272–275, 464–469
    theoretical basis, 259–260, 276–281, 321–
        323
Choice making skills, 37, *see also* Ch. 14
    (Miles)
    future research suggestions, 493–495
    goals and targeted skills, 486–490
    populations targeted, 474–476, 495–496
    public perceptions and, 491–493
    theoretical basis, 473–486
Coding, in short term memory, 242–243
Cognitive development
    of general learning skills, 152–154
    individual differences in, 15, 43–45, *see*
        also MLE
        and instructional compensation, 34, 53–
            58, 215–216, 339–340, 350–351, 460–
            461, 499–512
        determinants of, 56
    intellectual maturity, 344–345
Cognitive Learning Strategies Project, *see also*
    Ch. 6 (Weinstein & Underwood)
    analyzer commentary, 325–326, 341–352
    evaluations, 249–250, 325–326

Cognitive Learning Strategies Project (*cont.*)
  goals and targeted skills, 246–248, 325–
  326
  implementation methods and materials,
  248–250, 252–254
  theoretical basis, 242–244
Cognitive modifiability, theory of, 43–53
Cognitive processes instruction, *see* Thinking
  skills instruction, Learning skills
  instruction, Problem solving
Cognitive Research Trust (CoRT) Thinking
  Program, 35, 39, *see also* Ch. 10 (de
  Bono)
  analyzer commentary, 432–435, 443–445
  evaluations, 381–385, 435, 443–445
  goals and targeted skills, 36, 375–381,
  386–387, 432–433
  implementation methods, 379–381, 384–
  385
  populations studied, 363–365, 385
  theoretical basis, 433–435, 363–375
Cognitive Studies Project, *see also* Ch. 15
  (Hutchinson), Pair Problem Solving
  evaluation, 506–512
  implementation methods and materials,
  504–505
  populations addressed, 502–503
  theoretical basis, 499–502
Competitiveness in the classroom, 391
Comprehension, *see* Reading
Content-dependent instruction, 254–255, 278,
  344, 461, *see also* Teaching Reading in
  Content Areas
  difficulties with, 75–77
  examples of, 211, 231–235
  future research directions, 235
Content-free instruction
  description and rationale, 75–77, 189,
  219–225, 323–325
  difficulties with, 343–344
  evaluations, 225–230
  future directions, 230–231, 366
Coordinating thinking skills, 97, *see also*
  Metacognition, self-management skills
Creativity, instructing, 173, 175–176, 179
Critical thinking, 479–480
Culture and thinking skill instruction, 50, *see
  also* Cognitive modifiability

D

Decision-making instruction, 372–373

Developmental psychology and instruction, 13,
  127–128
Developmental students, *see* Learning-disabled
  students
Dialogue and learning, 85–87, 168–169, *see
  also* Metacognition, dialogue and
Direct exposure learning, 46, *see also* MLE

E

Educable mentally retarded students, *see*
  Learning-disabled students
Efficiency and learning, 109
Elaboration, *see also* Cognitive Learning
  Strategies Program
  incorporating into instructional programs,
  32
  as learning technique, 32, 242–243, 346
  types of, 32
Emotionally handicapped children and
  Philosophy for Children Program, 104–
  105
Encoding specificity, 401
Ethics instruction, 176, 437
Exercise difficulty and learning, 117, *see also*
  Sequencing instruction
Expert-novice research, 10, 423
Expert learners, 332
Evaluating programs, 7, 21, 128–130, 224–
  225, 243–244, 268–270, 313–314, 431–
  432
  classroom observation, 309–313, 467–468,
  518
  comparison of programs, 275–276, 329–
  352, 440–448
  criteria for comparing, 440–442
  evaluation plans, 353–355
Evaluating student abilities
  assessment techniques, 216–218, 244–246,
  525
  shortcomings of current techniques, 247–
  248, 369
  test item examples, 521–523
Evaluation of specific programs
  CMLR/LS (Jones et al.), 275–276, 281–
  284, 469–472
  Cognitive Learning Strategies Project
  (Weinstein & Underwood), 249–250,
  325–326
  CoRT (de Bono), 381–385, 435, 443–445

Cognitive Studies Project (Whimbey & Lochhead), 506–512

Instrumental Enrichment Program (Feuerstein et al.), 77–81, 189–194, 197–200

MOAN (Jones et al.), 268–270

Learning Strategies Instruction System (Dansereau), 225–231, 323–325

Pair Problem Solving (Whimbey & Lochhead), 128–130, 144–154, *see also* Cognitive Studies Project

Philosophy for Children Program (Lipman), 101–106, 166–179

Productive Thinking Program (Covington), 407–411, 431–432, 442–443

F

Family Relations Instrument, 70

Fear of Failure, 77, 149, *see also* Ch. 11 (Covington), Strategic thinking, instruction of

failure-avoiding tactics, 391–393

general considerations, 395–396

restructuring classroom rewards, 396–398

threat to self-worth, 390–391

Formal logic instruction, *see* Logic rules instruction

Formal operational reasoning, 476–477, 334–335, 500–501

G

General problem solver (GPS), 420, 422

General versus specific skills, 14, 25, 34, 36, 200–203, 211, 278–279, 334–335, 343–345, 449–451

Gestalt psychology, *see* Problem solving, divergent approach to

Goal setting, by students, 398

Group dynamics and instruction, 84–85, 307, 355–356, 492–493

H

Habit formation and instruction, 59–60

Heuristics, 488–489, *see also* Problem solving, search and

Higher-order cognitive skills, *see* Learning, Problem solving, Intelligence, Metacognition, Reasoning, Comprehension

I

Identity conservation, 70

Imagery, 9, 220–221, 242, 273

Individual differences, *see* Cognitive development, individual differences in

Insight, 11, 60–61

Instrumental Enrichment Program, 28–29, 39, 533, *see also* Ch. 1 (Feuerstein et al.)

analyzer commentary, 179–200

evaluations, 77–81, 189–194, 197–200

goals and targeted skills, 58–62, 75–77, 194–197

implementation methods and materials, 62–75, 185–189

populations studied, 28

theoretical basis, 28–29, 58, 180–185

Intelligence, conceptions of, 4–5, 109–110, 307, 409–411

effect on instructional policy, 44, 410

nurture view, 529–532

social implications, 529–530

Intelligence instruction, *see* Venezuelan intelligence instruction

Intelligence tests

and CoRT, 382

as tests of knowledge, 4

Intentionality during learning, 48, *see also* Metacognition

K

Knowledge

acquisition, 8–10, *see also* Learning strategies, Cognitive Learning Strategies, MOAN, CMLR/LS, Teaching Reading in Content Areas

and general thinking skills, 154

need of a theory of, 10

management skills, 368

mapping techniques, *see* Organization of information

schema, for scientific theory instruction, 231–235

states, characterizing, 10

utilizing, 153–154

L

Learning

approaches to, 331–341, 347–350

copy theory, 127–128

internalization model, 338–339

Learning (*cont.*)
approaches to (*cont.*)
SQ3R, 210, 220
from text, 331–352, *see also* CMLR/LS,
Learning strategies, Teaching Reading in
Content Areas
passive, 109–111
Learning-disabled students
and MLE, 182–183
and reading ability, 276–278, 460–461, *see
also* CMLR/LS
and urban education, 37
definition, 43–45, 180, 499
potential for improvement in thinking
skills, 510
skill unpreparedness, 340, 480–482, 499–
502
special instructional needs, 509–510
teacher competencies, 38
temporal abilities, 68
traditional measures, problems with, 44
transfer of strategies by, 34
verbal limitations, 508–509
Learning strategies
characteristics and definition, 210–211, 241
designing learning strategy instruction,
212–216, 333
examples of, 251–252, 273, 323
identifying for instruction, 210–212
primary versus support strategies, 209–212,
219–224, 323–324
theoretical issues, 210–218
verbalization and, 13
Learning strategies instruction
and language arts, 32
approaches to, 212–213, *see also* Ch. 5
(Dansereau), Ch. 6 (Weinstein &
Underwood), Ch. 7 (Jones et al.), Ch. 8
(Herber)
cognitive research and, 31
methods, 274
results of, 31–32
Learning Strategies Instruction Program
(Dansereau), *see also* Ch. 5 (Dansereau)
analyzer commentary, 323–325, 341–353
evaluation, 225–231
goals and targeted skills, 219–224
theoretical basis, 210–216
Logic rules instruction, 72–74, 160–162, 367–
368, *see also* Philsophy for Children
Program

M

Mastery learning, 272–273, 321, 350, *see also*
CMLR/LS
and academic promotion, 271–272
Mathematical thinking, 477
Mathematics instruction
and Philosophy for Children Program, 177–
178
program objectives, 520
Mathematical word problems, *see* Ch. 3
(Lochhead)
Matrices as learning and problem-solving aids,
32, 478, *see also* MOAN
Matrix Outlining and Analysis Program
(MOAN), 32, *see also* Ch. 7 (Jones et
al.)
analyzer commentary, 318–320, 341–352
evaluations, 268–270
goals and targeted skills, 318–320
implementation methods and materials,
264–268
theoretical basis, 261–264
Measurement, *see* Evaluation
Mediated Learning Experience (MLE), 45–57,
180–185, 190, 202, *see also* Cognitive
modifiability
Metacognition, 12–14, 334, *see also* Choice
making skills, Knowledge, management
skills, Learning strategies, MOAN,
Productive Thinking Program, Strategic
thinking
awareness, 336–338
checking answers, 111–112
coordinating thought, 97
definition, 7, 13, 425
dialogue and, 158–159, 162–164
during comprehension, 241, 336–338
and learning from text, 333
reflection, 99, 122–123, 158, 273
self-management skills, 36, 196, 219, 224,
228–230, 395–396, 398–400, 402–403,
448–449
skill transfer and, 338
thinking aloud, 148, 274
Memory ánd instruction, 367
Mnemonics, 31, 153–154, 220–221
Motivation, 61, 110–111, *see also* Fear of
Failure
Motor skills, related to symbolic skills, 137–
138

N

Novelty during instruction, 193
Number progression instruction, 70

O

Open admission policy
  effects of, 499–500
  instructional compensation, 29, 38
Organization of information
  as a basic learning ability, 4, 51, 261–262,
    307
  instruction of organizational skills, 74–75,
    262–264, 273, 376, *see also* MOAN, Learn-
    ing Strategies Instruction System

P

Pair Problem Solving, *see also* Ch. 3
    (Lochhead)
  analyzer commentary, 137–154
  evaluations, 128–130, 144–154, *see also*
    Cognitive Studies Project
  goals and targeted skills, 30, 149–154
  implementation methods and materials,
    111–120, 142–143
  theoretical basis, 120–128, 137–147
Parental influence on study skills, 3–4, 48–56,
    see also MLE
Peer tutoring, in CMLR/LS, 469, *see also*
    Ch. 3 (Lochhead)
Perception
  importance of, in problem solving, 35, 371
  and learning, 52, 66, 70, 74
Philosophy instruction, 83–106, 155–158, *see*
    also Philosophy for Children Program
  views towards, 98–99
Philosophy for Children Program, *see also*
    Ch. 2 (Lipman)
  analyzer commentary, 154–179
  evaluations, 101–106, 166–179
  goals and targeted skills, 87–101, 174
  implementation methods and materials,
    160–164
  theoretical basis, 84–87, 155–169
Planning skills, 219, 423–424
Populations in instructional programs
  adolescent, 197–200, 249
  college, 225–226, 502–503

elementary, 101–106, 270, 282–283, 363
high school, 268
junior high school, 103, 383, 469–470
other adult, 58, 364
Practice and instruction, 26, 97, 164, 169–
    170, 186–187, 252–253, 373–374, *see*
    also Repetition
Problem solutions as instructional devices,
    194–200
Problem solving, *see also* Pair Problem
    Solving, Productive Thinking Program,
    CoRT Program, Reasoning skills
  acquisition of problem solving skill, 424–
    426
  advice during, 147–148
  components of, 7, 35, 400, 418–424
    basic arithmetic operations, 139–140
    decoding, 139
    search, 419–421, 423–424
    vocabulary, 139
  functions of problem solving instruction,
    502
  functional fixedness, 11
  ill-structured problems, 36
  imprecise thinking during, 140–42
  insight, 11, 60–61
  instructional implications, 11, 12
  instructional textbook reviews, 435–439,
    445–446, 447–448
  of novel problems, 479
  problem definition and instruction, 149–
    150, 186, 192
  reasons for failure, 140–141
  representation and, 35, 401, 448–449
  search and, 66, 335, 375–376, 420–421
  simulation of, 11–12, 367
  theoretical approaches to, 10–12
    information processing, 36, 418–426
    divergent-production paradigm, 426,
      452
    comparison of, 426–429
  transfer of skill and, 35
  understanding and, 419, 421–424
  weak and strong methods and education,
    335–336
Production systems, 12
Productive Thinking Program, *see also* Ch. 11
    (Covington)
  analyzer commentary, 429–432, 442–443
  evaluations, 407–411, 431–432, 442–443
  goals, 429

Productive Thinking Program (*cont.*)
implementation methods and materials,
429–431
theoretical basis, 398–407, *see also* Fear of
Failure

R

Readiness for skill instruction, 138–139
Reading, *see also* CMLR/LS, Teaching
Reading in Content Areas, Ch. 5
(Dansereau), Ch. 6 (Weinstein &
Underwood)
complex skills in, 8–9, 219–224, 299–300,
460
comprehension, 152–154, 522, *see also*
Problem solving, understanding and
importance in reading skill, 2
subskills of, 308–309, 327
demands placed on students, 460–461
elaboration during, 9, 220–224
evaluating reading strategy instruction,
227–230
expertise, 332
headings as aids during, 234–235
and general knowledge, 8
goal-directed, 2
group instruction, 300–301, 304–305
inference instruction, 300–301
Intensive Reading Improvement Program,
464
low achievement in urban schools, 271,
459
Philosophy for Children Program and, 168,
177
plans during, 8–9
and problem solving, 421–423, 449
readiness and decoding skill instruction
effects, 460
strategies, techniques, & mnemonics, 9–
10, 220–224, 402–403
text structure and, 9, 164, 332, *see also*
Text structure and instructional materials
topic finding, 349
vocabulary and, 308
Reality, grasp of as a learning necessity, 53,
66, 483
Reasoning skills instruction, 109–131, 137–
154, *see also* Syllogistic reasoning
instruction
and Philosophy for Children Program, 174–
175, 178–179

Repetition and learning, 59
Representational skill instruction, 68, 72–74,
see also Problem solving, representation
and
Rewards and instruction, *see also*
Competitiveness
and self-image, 390–391
systems in classrooms, 395–398
Role models during instruction, 29, 99, 160–
162, 215, 324–325, 393–395

S

Schema theory, 243, 265, 421–422, *see also*
Knowledge, schema
Science instruction, program objectives, 520
Search, *see* Problem solving, search and
Self-image, effect on learning, 51, 61, 390–
391, 481, 483
Semantic memory, 403, 418
Short-term working memory, 403, 418
Sequencing instruction, 63, 68, 213–214, 274–
275, 277–278, 347–348, 462
Social influences and instruction, *see* Affect
and instruction, Fear of Failure, Pair
Problem Solving, Peer tutoring, Mediated
Learning Experience, Philosophy for
Children Program
Social studies instruction, 261, 522–523
Spatial ability, 66–68
and Instrumental Enrichment Program, 185
Strategic thinking
competency in, 403–405
components of, 400–403
general strategies, 13
improving
ability management, 409–411
research in progress, 405–407
instruction of strategic thinking, 1–2, 398–
400
problem formulation, 400–401
student views of, 403–405
Student as instructional designer, 9, 397–398,
see also Self-image, effect on learning,
Fear of Failure
Study skills, *see also* Productive Thinking
Program
assessing instruction effects, 226, 244–248
identifying deficiencies, 405
rarity of instruction, 3, 403–405
as skill area, 2, 9
underlining and outlining, 9, 337

Summarization, 168–169, 188, 227–228, 344
Sustained Quiet Uninterrupted Reading Time (SQUIRT), 467–469
Syllogistic reasoning instruction, 72, 170–172

T

Taxonomies of thinking skills, 87–97, 299, 487, 517, 519
  problems with, 519
Teacher roles in thinking skills programs, 33, 59, 61, 64–65, 99–100, 112, 145–146, 163, 252–255, 297–306, 347–350, 379–381, 403–405, 464, 504–505, 518–519, 524, *see also* MLE, Teaching Reading in Content Areas, implementation methods and materials
Teaching, returned emphasis on, 301–302
Teaching Reading in Content Areas, *see also* Ch. 8 (Herber)
  analyzer commentary, 326–329, 341–352
  evaluation, 309–14
  goals and targeted skills, 326–327
  implementation methods and materials, 297–306
  theoretical basis, 307–309
Temporal relationship instruction, 68–70, 303–306
Text comprehension strategies, *see* Reading strategies, Comprehension, Mnemonics
Text structure and instructional materials, 227–228, 273–274, 277, 280
Thinking aloud, as an instructional technique, 144–147, *see also* Pair Problem Solving
Thinking skills, *see also* Strategic thinking
  and academic excellence, 5
  affect and, 25
  algorithmic, 478
  attitudes about, 97–98, 491–492
  complexity increases with age, 24
  conceptual frameworks, 7, 137–138
  decline of, in schools, 2
  definition as an issue, 6–8, 83, 387
  interaction between research and instruction, 6
  need for thinking skill instruction, 1–3
  poor performance at post-secondary levels, 37
  as real life skills, 1, 365–366
  related to motor skills, 137–138
  role pressures of various groups, 492–493
  teachability of, 3–4, 14, 83–84, 138

Thinking skills instruction
  and personal growth, 176
  approaches to, 25–26, 158–159, 345–350, 367–370, 450–451, 501–502, *see also* Generality versus specificity
    direct approach, 25, 38–39, 77–78, 349–350
    indirect approach, 25, 33, 158–159
    separate versus integrated, 25–26, 349–350
    subskills versus complex skills, 26, 214
  as a subject area, 100–101
  criteria for selection, 22–24
  district-wide implementation, 516–520
  goal variability among programs, 342–347
  history of advocation, 4–5, 133–137
  nationwide implementation, 529–536
  objectives during program development, 517
  post-secondary students, 30
  process versus strategic instruction, 24
  proficiency desired, 26
  public support for, 38
  student attitudes during, 481
  specific programs, *see* CMLR/LS, Cognitive Learning Strategies, Cognitive Studies Project, CoRT, Instrumental Enrichment, MOAN, Pair Problem Solving, Philosophy for Children, Productive Thinking, Teaching Reading in Content Areas, Venezuelan intelligence instruction
Transitive relations instruction, 72
Transfer
  CoRT Program and, 366–369, 374
  failure during learning, 60, 277, 338
  of generalized knowledge, 479
  instructing transfer skills, 187–188, 196–197

U

Understanding, *see* Reading, comprehension
Urban education, *see* Reading, low achievement in urban schools, CMLR/LS Program

V

Venezuelan intelligence instruction, *see also* Ch. 17 (Dominguez)
  fundamental principles, 532

Venezuelan intelligence instruction (*cont.*)
  philosophy and rationale, 529–532
  specific programs in progress, 532–536
Verbal skills, *see also* Pair Problem Solving,
    Philosophy for Children
  effects of deficiency on learning, 507–509
  instruction of verbal skills, 72, 122–126,
      173–174, 179

W

Writing skills instruction, 319, 523–525
  objectives, 524